Origins, Traditions, and Trends of Organizational Communication

The second edition of *Origins, Traditions, and Trends of Organizational Communication* provides an updated overview of organizational communication, assessing the field to date and demonstrating a communicational approach to the study of organization.

Tracing the field's history and development to the present, this edition is framed by the recent anti-racist decolonial turn in the field, offering a set of conceptual structures and vocabularies to facilitate appreciation of the field's literature grounded in an understanding of its biases. It again provides students with background knowledge of foundational management theories in order to understand their influence on our thinking and our organizational world. Literature reviews on focused topics, written by experts, link organizational communication theory and research to practice.

This edition is an ideal text for graduate courses in organizational communication and communication history.

Online support materials for instructors include an instructor's manual with key discussion questions and suggested activities. Access the support materials at www.routledge.com/9781032775388.

Anne M. Nicotera (PhD, Ohio University) is Professor of Communication at George Mason University, USA. Her research, grounded in a constitutive perspective, focuses on intractable conflict, race and gender, and aggressive communication, with particular interest in healthcare organizations, postcolonial approaches, and anti-racism. Her research has been published in numerous communication and health-related journals, as well as in six books and numerous chapters. Her applied work focuses on designing and delivering organizational communication-based management and leadership training. She is the organizer for the biennial D.C. Health Communication (DCHC) Conference.

Origins, Traditions, and Trends of Organizational Communication

A Comprehensive Introduction to the Field

Second Edition

Edited by Anne M. Nicotera

Routledge
Taylor & Francis Group
NEW YORK AND LONDON

Designed cover image: Jian Fan/Getty

Second edition published 2026
by Routledge
605 Third Avenue, New York, NY 10158

and by Routledge
4 Park Square, Milton Park, Abingdon, Oxon, OX14 4RN

Routledge is an imprint of the Taylor & Francis Group, an informa business

First edition published by Routledge 2020

ISBN: 9781032777696 (hbk)
ISBN: 9781032775388 (pbk)
ISBN: 9781003484639 (ebk)

DOI: 10.4324/9781003484639

Typeset in Sabon
by KnowledgeWorks Global Ltd.

Access the Support Materials: www.routledge.com/9781032775388.

For my students – past, present, and future

Contents

Preface

This book is a culmination of over 30 years of studying organizational communication. Over the many years of being responsible for the instruction of organizational communication at the introductory graduate level, and with my own development as a theorist, I had developed a deep dissatisfaction with accessible texts available to help my students understand and become excited by the field. The first edition was a decade in the making, engaging with students to generate and pilot explanations and material we had confidence would work beyond our own classroom. The first edition went to press in the summer of 2019 and appeared at the beginning of 2020 – just in time to be too late to account for the revolution in anti-racism and decolonization in the field, the COVID-19 pandemic, the historic global attention to racism in public life, the rise of struggle over DEI and identity politics, and other developments that have had dramatic impact on organizational life. I felt the book was outdated almost as soon as it hit the shelves. Yet, this is the nature of our organizational world – always fluid and dynamic, a constantly shifting landscape.

My original vision was to provide a single volume that explains organizational communication both as a set of human social phenomena and a field of study, to educate students about a communicational approach to studying organization and get them excited about its insights, and to do so at an accessible level for early-graduate-career students without sacrificing the requisite sophistication needed for advanced graduate students. The impetus for the second edition was to enrich the book with a postcolonial and anti-racist framework that accounts for some ongoing sea changes in our professional contexts. I remain humbled by the caliber of scholars who worked with me on this project and am eternally grateful to all of them for their support of a second edition, dedication to the project, and careful attention to the details of its mission.

I hope instructors find this volume, and the ancillary materials available online, helpful in making our fascinating and rich field accessible to students. I hope the updates in the early chapters provide frameworks to discuss race, colonialism, and decolonization in fruitful ways. I hope students use it as a foundation to pursue further academic study and to carry on with a communicational approach to understanding the fascinating everyday of organizational life.

Introduction

The goals of this volume are to provide knowledge of the history of theorizing about communication and about organizations that led to the establishment of the field of Organizational Communication, an understanding of advancements in that field, awareness of the field's place among other organizational studies disciplines, and surveys of the literature on a variety of specific organizational communication phenomena. The book provides a framework by which to understand the literatures on various topics according to the fundamental tension in all organizational communication theory between action and structure; seeks to educate the reader on the disciplinary definition and history of Organizational Communication as a field; critiques foundational organizational theory from a contemporary framework; provides a set of literature reviews on focused topics written by experts in each area following a common template for explanation and critique; and links organizational communication theory and research to practice.

Each chapter includes an annotated list of recommended supplementary readings, a set of key concepts and questions for discussion, and a "practitioner's corner" with concrete implications for application and practice. These pedagogical materials are compiled in a single document downloadable from the Routledge website.

Organization of the Book

Part I summarizes the origins and history of the field of Communication, providing a comprehensive overview of the field from its inception to the present. Chapter 1 defines the field and its fundamental concepts and biases, frames the book in an anti-racist stance, and explains the emergence of the field. A conceptual model applied throughout the book highlights the reciprocally enabling and constraining relationship between organization and communication as they are generated and regenerated in one another. Chapters 2 and 3 present the theoretical and conceptual developments in the 20th and 21st centuries. Chapter 4 explains postcolonial approaches to organizational communication that contextualize our field and its work in historical-cultural systems of power and privilege.

Part II reviews the traditional/historical organizational theories treated in previous generations as foundations of organizational communication – not just as conceptual foundations for the field but also as societal forces that shaped (and continue to shape) organizational forms, practices, and management. One cannot adequately understand contemporary organizations as communicatively constructed and constituted without appreciation of the constitutive power of these foundational bodies of theory. As prescriptions, these theories quite literally wrote the scripts that contemporary organizations follow.

Part III provides comprehensive literature reviews authored by established scholars with specialized expertise of 14 areas of theory and research. While it is not possible to cover every possible topic in the field, literatures that comprise the core knowledge base in the field are provided here. These chapters can be read in any order.

Acknowledgments

As with any project of this magnitude, the list of people I couldn't have done without cannot be generated. The number of people in my life who support what I do and help me do it is humbling. Heartfelt thanks to Felisa Salvago-Keyes for supporting my vision for a second edition. Thank you to my graduate students who engage with this material. Many of the discussion questions generated by students are repeated from the first edition. And to my family, my constant source of joy amid the storms – especially Theo who made his entrance in the middle of it all.

Part I

Organizational Communication History

In this part, the origins and history of the field of Organizational Communication are summarized, providing a comprehensive overview of the field from its inception to the present. Chapter 1 defines the field and its fundamental concepts and explains the emergence of the field in the context of the emergence of communication studies in general, accompanied by a discussion of recent turbulence surrounding institutional racism. A set of conceptual models (applied throughout the book) are presented that frame an understanding of conceptual approaches to organization and the reciprocally enabling and constraining relationship between organization and communication. Chapters 2 and 3 present the theoretical and conceptual developments in the 20th and 21st centuries, respectively. Finally, Chapter 4 provides an overview of postcolonial approaches and the decolonial turn in the field occurring in the 2020s.

DOI: 10.4324/9781003484639-1

1 Organizing the Study of Organizational Communication

Anne M. Nicotera and Xavier D. Clark

Organizational Communication and Organizational Studies

The meaning of *organizational communication* is twofold. First, it is a complex set of processes and structures through which people interact to coordinate action and accomplish goals. Second, *Organizational Communication* is a subfield of the discipline of Communication. It is also an important contributor to the multidisciplinary arena of *Organizational Studies*, which includes Management, Business, Organizational/Industrial Psychology, Human Relations, and other disciplines interested in understanding organizational life (usually defined as workplace). Sometimes, scholars from other disciplines do not recognize Organizational Communication as a distinct scholarly discipline; sometimes they use the term *organizational communication* differently than we would prefer. These issues are diminishing as multidisciplinarity increases and we connect across boundaries.

Disciplinary boundaries mark unique conceptual and political histories that bias their members' understanding of their work and the subjects they study. When studying a topic, it is crucial to examine literatures across disciplines to gather all available knowledge. It is also vital to contextualize that knowledge with an understanding of disciplinary biases, values, vocabularies, and theoretic foundations. Understanding your own discipline allows you to be a critical consumer of existing knowledge, actively address biases in your own work, and work more effectively in multidisciplinary arenas.

Organizing Is Communicating Is Organizing

Organizing is older than society. Organizing is defined most simply as the coordination of individual activities to accomplish collective tasks – whether the task at hand is warding off predators, cultivating crops, building a pyramid, marching in an army to battle, managing a corporate budget, trading and selling goods, implementing grand-scale emergency response to a natural disaster, or planning a family gathering. Organizing is natural to human beings and accomplished through communication. Organizing can form a social collective, which can become a formal organization. *Organizational communication* refers to interaction that occurs in three contexts: human activity coordination; structures that emerge and guide that coordination; and entities that institutionalize it. Organization and communication continually enable and constrain one another.

Communication is the essence of organization. Our organizing communication creates organizations – entities to whose authority we then surrender. Organizations permeate all aspects of human life. Postindustrial society is defined by them – the manufacturers

DOI: 10.4324/9781003484639-2

of clothing and distributors of food; the companies that build homes, roads, and cities; the corporations that collect rent; the banks that hold mortgages; the businesses and institutions that employ people; the agencies that control marketplaces; the service companies and agencies that provide necessities and luxuries; and the governments that regulate all of these. Organizational communication theory seeks to untangle these fundamental processes of human social life. How do humans (and nonhumans) coordinate their activities, often in the context of communicatively structured social collectives, to get things done, to be who we are, and to create new realities and structured collectives? This book will help you understand the field of Organizational Communication and provide a disciplinary base for your study of organizational communication phenomena. A disciplinary base is important because every discipline has biases, and we are better prepared to think critically when we understand the disciplinary roots of theory and research.

Organizational Communication as Hybrid

It is incorrect to define organizational communication as interaction inside an organization and/or between an organization and its environment. Organization is inseparable from communication. Organization is achieved through communication, and communication is achieved through organization. Organizational communication occurs among humans and nonhumans (e.g., documents, rules, traditions, technology, hierarchies, and organizations themselves). Material and nonmaterial *things* participate in organizational communication. Humans and nonhumans communicate with, through, and for one another. Organizational communication is a *symbolic process* that creates meaning. It is also a *material process* that creates things, which then become communicators themselves. For example, a corporate spokesperson materializes the organization by identifying as its agent. When they speak on its behalf, it communicates through them. The spokesperson communicates through a press release and communicates for the organization. A press release communicates for the spokesperson, in like fashion.

Organizational communication is a *connective process*, tying humans and nonhumans together in networks of meaning and activity coordination. Further, organizational communication is an *affective process* that transmits feeling (Kuhn et al., 2019) – not personal feelings, but *feeling* as transpersonal "pre- or extralinguistic intensities of encounter, which register in the body alongside, in excess of, or even apart from" linguistic meaning (p. 107). Organization is *felt* both emotionally and biologically. In short, communication brings things into being, connects them, and renders them sensible and felt (Kuhn et al., 2019).

Hybrid Agency

Agency is crucial to the study of organizing (Brummans, 2018). Humanity has traditionally been defined by capacity for action. "To be an agent means to be capable of exerting some degree of control over the social relations in which one is enmeshed, which in turn implies the ability to transform those social relations" (Sewell, 1992, p. 20). Agency depends on being connected to social meaning structures (Sewell, 1992). For humans, this is *knowledge*, which enables us to choose our actions. Actions create new structures and transform old structures, and activity (inherently communicative) becomes increasingly self-reflexive through structure.

Nonhumans also have agency and are organizational participants. For example, procedural structures exert significant power over daily human activities. Organizations can be seen as a plenum of agencies (Cooren, 2006; Chapter 3). Nonhumans do not have motivations or consciousness but are routinely viewed as the source of action. For example, in the sentence, "the sign told me to use the other door," *the sign* is understood to be acting on me, ascribing it agency.

Organizational communication is *contextual* and *transactional*, the participants simultaneously and continually influencing one another as their interaction constitutes meaning. All agents are defined by their actions in a network of interaction. Human and nonhuman agents are defined by one another and by their connectedness – in a perpetual state of *becoming*. In this view, communicatively constructed social, organizational, and institutional structures are considered *nonhuman agents*. They don't just structure and organize social behavior; they are full participants in organizational communication (Kuhn et al., 2019). For example, in a business setting, meetings are governed by *agendas*; decisions are structured by *policies*; resources are allocated by *budgets*. None of these are humans; yet, they function as agents.

Organizational Communication as both Transmissive and Constitutive

Organizational communication is both *transmissive* and *constitutive*. Early communication theory focused on transmission of messages through channels, later incorporating *feedback*. This *transmissive* view of communication also carried a notion of interpretation, the conceptual basis for meaning-centered approaches. By the 1970s, communication scholars focused on communication as *constitutive*. From the start, Organizational Communication scholars have presumed communication is constitutive – it creates things (agreements/disagreements, markets, organizations and their parts, documents, policies, procedures, events, relationships, etc.). But that does not necessitate a conceptual abandonment of sources and receivers, information, messages, channels, meaning-creation, and relationships. In fact, the transmissive and relational properties of organizational communication are among key contemporary conceptual advancements in organizational communication theory (Kuhn et al., 2019). As we organize, all players – human and nonhuman – become channels of information and instruments of coordination.

Defining "Organizational"

The word *organizational* in the label *organizational communication* may refer to one of three basic types of enduring social constructions. First, O_1, organizing (v.), is a *process* of coordinating/ordering among persons and things. In this sense, theory and research might examine interaction processes by which people arrange themselves and manage their joint activities (e.g., decision-making, group formation, negotiation). Alternatively, we could mean O_2, organizational (adj.), the *state* of coordination or order, or the extent to which a social collective's activities indicate *organizationality* (Schoeneborn et al., 2019) – this might be seen as the structuring of organizing (O_1). Theory and research might explicate the emergence and/or function of rules, policies, or procedures or the formation of relational structures (e.g., networks, organizational formation). Yet a third possibility is O_3, organizations (n.), coordinated/ordered *entities* arising from O_1 and O_2. Theory and research that examines formalization, institutions, boundaries, organizations as social actors (e.g., corporate social responsibility, branding),

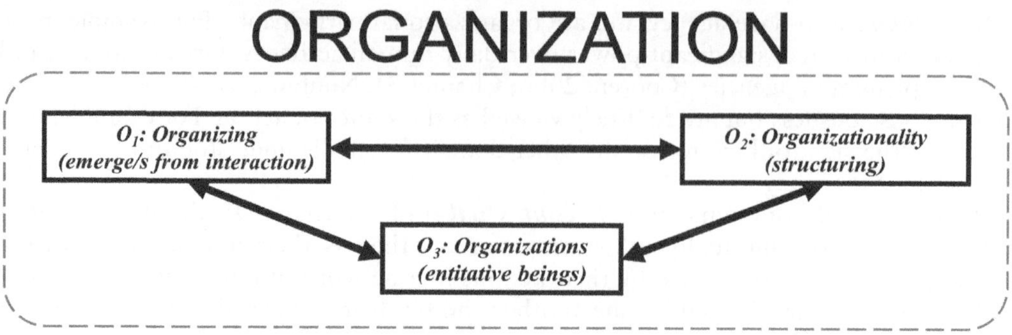

Figure 1.1 Three Types of Social Construction for "Organizational"

and the like is focused here. Figure 1.1 depicts the conceptual relationship among these three constructs.

What Is an Organization?

An *organization* has often been erroneously equated with *formalization* or *boundary recognition*, but while both are properties of an organization, neither defines it. An organization (O_3), as it is implicitly understood in Organizational Communication, has three fundamental characteristics. First, there must be a socially signified collective – named and referred to as a recognizable entity, but this alone does not make the collective an organization. For example, these are socially signified collectives: that family, the neighbors, American voters, this committee, that department. Clearly, these are not organizations, no matter how highly organized (O_2) they may be. Second, the authority ascribed to the collective in its social signification must allow it to authorize individuals to represent its interests and act on its behalf. "An organization does not act primarily on behalf of and in the name of another entity (collective or not) but is attributed the authority to compel others (individual and collective actors and actants) to act on its behalf" (Nicotera, 2013, p. 68). The organization is a nonhuman agent who has the authority to bestow that agency on others – human and nonhuman. Finally, to be an organization, the collective must also have *entitative being*. "A socially signified entity can be said to have entitative being (or to be an entitative being) when, by virtue of authority attributed to it, its identity *transcends and eclipses any human individual or human collective*" (Nicotera, 2013, p. 68, emphasis in original). [The concept of *organizationality* (Dobusch & Schoeneborn, 2015; Smith, 2022) is another way of theorizing the transformation of a social collective to an organization.]

The *organization* presumed in the label *organizational communication* is a particular form of socially signified social collective that, first, is granted authority to give individuals and groups permission to act on its behalf and, second, has an identity that transcends its human membership as an entity unto itself. An *organization* (O_3) has three defining characteristics: social signification of a social collective as an authority; authorization of representative agents; and entitative being.

The Communication-Organization Cycle

The action-structure (communication-organization) pair has long been considered a central tension in organizational communication inquiry (Kuhn et al., 2019). Yet, the distinction between communication (action) and organization (structure) is blurry. Rather than tensioned,

Figure 1.2 The Communication-Organization Interplay in Organizational Communication Theorizing

it is more accurate and productive to see them simultaneously and mutually constitutive. Action constitutes structure while structure constitutes action; each generates the other. By reconciling the tension between action and structure, we relieve the pressure to privilege one over the other. Communication reflects, creates, and perpetuates organization, which then reflects, creates, and perpetuates communication. In perpetual cycling fashion, communication and organization enable and constrain each other. Rather than seeing organization as underneath communication, it is more accurate to conceive of them as *generating and regenerating within one another*. Organization (re)generates in communication; communication (re)generates in organization. The action-structure (communication-organization) pair permeates the organizational literature, often implicitly. This model, used throughout the book to examine organizational communication theory and research, removes the tension between them, seeing them as co-creating one another and driven by agency (see Figure 1.2).

For easy reference, this text will refer to this model as the C–O cycle. When applying it, keep in mind the characteristics of *organizational communication* as symbolic, material, transmissive, constitutive, connective, and affective. Also, remember that *organization* can be any or all of O_1, O_2, or O_3.

Disciplinary Biases

Like any discipline, Organizational Communication is biased in many ways. As you will see in Chapters 2–7, academic, cultural, and social histories have created enduring implicit assumptions that unintentionally bias our work. We treat organizations as containing communication and presume a container is always there. We see people as organizational members inside organizational boundaries. We equate organization with corporations, conceptually ignore everyone except college-educated professionals, and privilege the viewpoint of management. Furthermore, like all social disciplines, the field is steeped in racial bias.

The conceptual and topic area reviews in this book reflect the biases of the literature. Understanding implicit biases that have shaped knowledge is crucial. Translation to practice is enhanced through understanding the boundaries of knowledge, as is our capacity to expand and deepen knowledge. One objective of this chapter is to bring these biases to your attention, making you a more critical consumer of theory and research in the field as you learn about it. Established scholars and practitioners must *unlearn* these patterns, but you can frame your understanding as you enter the field with a conscious awareness of these implicit biases and their implications.

The Container Bias

Organizational Communication scholars are sensitive to *container metaphors*, the implicit treatment of organizations as containing communication, usually with the phrase *communication in organizations* (Smith, 1993). Neither communication nor organization can be adequately understood this way because both organization and communication are dynamic and socially constructed – neither simply contains the other. Yet, our literature continues to implicitly treat organizational boundaries as fixed, ignoring their constructed nature. To resist this tendency, we often consciously use phrasing such as *in organizational contexts* or *in organizational life*, but this still carries the O_3 *bias*.

The O_3 *Bias*

The implicit assumption that *an organization* (O_3) must be present as the context of organizational processes (O_1) and structures (O_2) is deeply embedded and seldom considered (for an exception, see Frankel, 2022). Historically, organizational theory has addressed formal organizations – almost exclusively Western corporations. Even when O_1 or O_2 is the focus, O_3 is presumed to be the setting in which processes and structuring occur. The result is missed opportunities to study complex sophisticated organizing that occurs without an organization (O_3). Cruz and Sodeke (2021) illustrate the conceptual inadequacy of organizational theory to capture and explain the fluid organizing processes of market sellers in Nigeria and Liberia. Their analysis reveals sophisticated organizing (O_1) and structuring (O_2) processes with no O_3 in sight except among external threats to market sellers. Market seller communities are social collectives but cannot be defined, and do not function, as organizations (see Chapter 4 for a fuller description of this study). Because organizational scholars implicitly assume some formal entity must exist as a context for organizational communication, work that transcends this conceptual limitation has been marginalized or considered "exotic" (Broadfoot et al., 2008, p. 332). Such work is often called *groundbreaking* – which marginalizes it by placing it outside the boundaries of the field as it is normally conceived (Hanchey, 2020).

THE MEMBER BIAS

The O_3 bias creates a *member bias*. Discussions of organizational communication invariably address interaction among *organizational members*. First, labeling humans as *members* of an organization hides nonhuman agency. Second, it creates a hidden implication of humans being *possessed by* an organization. Third, it creates an erroneous view of the organization as being *populated* or *constituted* by human members, which obfuscates the communication-organization connection. Even contemporary work seeking to reconceptualize foundational definitions of organizational communication discusses organizational "members" without examining that concept (e.g., Kuhn et al., 2019). Yet, recent research, such as that cited previously (Cruz & Sodeke, 2021), reveals a great deal of organizing and structuring in the absence of an O_3 with "members."

The Corporate Managerial Professional Bias

Only certain formal organizational types have traditionally been studied. *Organization* is used synonymously with *workplace*; workplaces studied are mostly business, corporate, or bureaucratic institutional settings in the US with White, college-educated, upper-middleclass employees. The result is a rich knowledge base about the communication of white-collar American office workers – who are mostly, often exclusively, White. Even research on non-corporate or non-business organizational forms, like nonprofits (e.g., Jensen & Meisenbach, 2015) or religious organizations (McNamee, 2011), is marginalized. Moreover, methodological biases camouflage important communication variations among social classes (Gist-Mackey & Kingsford, 2020). Further, we focus on managerially prioritized outcomes, treating effectiveness as the most valuable organizational goal and viewing it as performance/productivity – as defined by managers. The full range of organizational processes and phenomena are eclipsed by this bias.

The Racial Bias

The 21st century has brought attention to uncomfortable truths about systemic and institutional racism. The anti-DEI political movement in the US unfolding as this book is in production is a rejection of this awakening. Yet, systemic and institutionalized racism are persistent in academia and in the organizational processes and contexts we study. This can only be changed if it is addressed. After clarifying basic terminology, we focus here on three important moments in our disciplinary history – two across the field of Communication and one in Organizational Communication – before turning to a more general discussion of race in organizational theory. The incidents related here are important to note because they starkly illustrate how the institutionalized racism saturating academia is resistant to change, as it is reflexively enacted and reproduced in our disciplinary practices, perpetuating its impact (the C–O cycle in action).

DEFINING BASIC TERMS: RACE, WHITENESS, WHITE SUPREMACY, AND SYSTEMIC RACISM

Race, whiteness, white supremacy, and systemic racism can only be understood in relation to each other, and all must be considered a function of colonialism (see Chapter 4). *Race* is a socially constructed taxonomic system dividing humanity into groups based on phenotypical differences, but race does not categorize humans genetically (Keita et al., 2004; Lewontin, 1972). In 17th-century Europe, contemporary racial categories were created and ranked for the political purpose of justifying and prolonging the slave trade and colonial rule. The very idea of *race* is racist, steeped in cultural structures of colonialism and white supremacy (Hirschman, 2004).

Despite public controversy, the terms *whiteness* and *white supremacy* are simply descriptive of the dominant viewpoint from which the world is viewed. *Whiteness*, the lens through which *race* has been historically understood, is the process by which White racial identity is deemed neutral, marginalizing other identities. What is white (customs, cultures, beliefs) or seen from the viewpoint of White persons (history, law, policy, news) is presumed to be standard or normal (see Chapters 4 and 14). Whiteness breeds *white supremacy*, ideology that centers and prioritizes the white viewpoint, assuming its superiority. White supremacy underlies the false equivalency between race and competence that permeates the anti-DEI political movement in the US (see Chapters 2, 4, and 14). The presumption that nonwhite identities and viewpoints are abnormal and inferior often happens beneath the level of awareness. White supremacy is, quite simply, the set of ideological structures that position White people as superior to other racial groups and privilege whiteness as the neutral and thus preferred perspective, consequently creating and maintaining the social, economic, and political systems that collectively enable White people to maintain dominance.

These deep-seated biases rooted in colonial histories manifest as *systemic racism*, embedded meaning structures stemming from white supremacy that position race as a fundamental determinant of human traits and capacities, positioning White people as inherently superior. Systemic racism becomes institutionalized by driving repeated practices. A simple application of the C–O cycle reveals colonial and white supremacist presumptions lurking in all Western organizational structures – including those of academic disciplines – and manifesting daily in social practice. Through institutionalization in social practices, systemic racism is reflexively and unintentionally enacted, often by those who value diversity, equity, and inclusion.

SYSTEMIC RACISM IN OUR SYSTEMS OF MERIT AND RECOGNITION

Among other anti-racism initiatives, the National Communication Association (NCA) Executive Committee (EC) convened a 2007 task force to examine bias in the selection of Distinguished Scholars (DSs), nominated and chosen by sitting DSs. Of 62 DSs named between 1992 and 2007, all were White and only 8 were women, despite ample evidence of a more diverse set of association members meeting selection criteria. Initially, the bias was addressed by informing DSs (after voting) of nominees' gender and ethnicity. For 2008–2014, the proportion of women selected had improved to 25%, but only 1 of the 28 selected was a person of color, largely because qualified association members of color were still absent from the nominee pool. Starting in 2015, instead of only current DSs nominating candidates, all NCA members were invited to nominate candidates for DS status. This shift still did not yield a diverse pool, likely because those who might nominate qualified scholars of color did not participate due to distrust in the selection process. Here, systemic racism can be revealed by a simple application of the C–O cycle. Repeated exclusionary practices denying opportunities to marginalized groups have a chilling effect on their efforts to participate in those exclusionary systems. Potential nominators who believe it will be a futile effort thus decline to participate. When systemic bias is ignored by dominant group members, their presumption that we all perceive equity in the system creates the appearance that an *absence* of qualified group members in a pool (like the nomination pool for DS) means none *exist* who are qualified for inclusion. Efforts to create inclusion are often met with resistance stemming from the institutionalized presumption that qualifications are the driving factor for visibility to the dominant class, creating false equivalencies between visibility and existence and thus between exclusion and inferiority. The C–O cycle is clear: Institutionalized racism erects barriers to participation that cultivate exclusion, which entrenches those barriers.

To remove those barriers for 2019, the EC implemented a process modeled after other NCA awards: a selection committee of NCA members appointed and approved by NCA-elected officers. The backlash was immediate and dramatic. In editorial essays in journals and social media commentary, several DSs decried the EC's persistence to create inclusiveness as an attack on rigor, falling prey to that false equivalency between exclusion and inferiority. This false equivalency is, of course, rooted in systemic racism and white supremacist structures – assuming that *diverse others* are inherently underqualified by virtue of the fact that they hadn't been selected previously. Yet, the transformative impact of the new selection process on systemic bias was soon evident: The 27 DSs selected from 2019 to 2023 included 14 women and 12 scholars of color, without weakening the qualification standards (for a detailed history of the controversy and its impact, see Dutta, 2019; Flaherty, 2019; Rodriguez et al., 2019).

#COMMUNICATIONSOWHITE

At the peak of the DS controversy, a wave of protest crested, identifying systemic racism in Communication. An article entitled, "#CommunicationSoWhite," analyzes patterns of authorship, citation, and editorial membership, revealing the severity of nonwhite scholars' underrepresentation in the Communication field (Chakravartty et al., 2018). This article vitalized a social movement across the field, including a petition sent to NCA leadership in 2018 (referred to as #NCASoWhite) and a #CommunicationSoWhite preconference at the 2019 International Communication Association (ICA) Conference addressing racial hierarchies in the discipline. That preconference generated a special issue of *Communication, Culture, and Critique* (Ng et al., 2020) offering numerous analyses of the field's embedded racism and racial bias. #CommunicationSoWhite engendered subfield efforts, including in Organizational Communication. One example is the crowdsourced *#OrgCommSoWhite Reading List* of work in organizational studies authored by BIPOC (Black, Indigenous, and People of Color) scholars or directly addressing racism (#OrgCommSoWhite, n.d.).

NCA ORGANIZATIONAL COMMUNICATION DIVISION TURNING POINT

Systemic bias in academia is difficult to change, as it is invisible to most people who enact it in disciplinary practices – even those who value equity and inclusion. An incident at the 2019 NCA conference proved to be a critical turning point for the Organizational Communication Division (OCD), and thus for the field generally. The respondent at the OCD top paper panel reproduced structures of white supremacy in a critique of a paper about that very thing. In the paper presentation, the author quoted Ahmed (2012, p. 149): "Even exercising the critical vocabulary of racism can generate a set of defenses, such that an exchange ends up being about the defenses rather than about racism (which is how such defenses are successful)." *This is precisely what transpired after the presentation.* The paper author identified organizational communication as a field constituted through communication that organizes whiteness, pulling several examples from our disciplinary literature where critiques of the field's underlying white supremacy were met with responses denying that whiteness and reifying the claim of our raceless discipline. The panel respondent's commentary was a dramatization of the point – they immediately did exactly as Ahmed (2012) and the paper author described. The response reproduced racist and white supremacist ideologies of our disciplinary structures, equating *white supremacist ideology* with *neo-Nazism*, reducing it to a descriptor of extremist groups rather than the paper's theoretical framework. Further, they admonished the author to *tone down* their *fiery language*. Such tone policing and civility-demand typify systemic racism in academia (Patton, 2004, see Chapter 4). By labeling the paper author's language as divisive, the response attempted to silence scholarly observations of white supremacist structures and suppress considerations of intersectionality (see Chapter 14). Half of the panelists and many audience members walked out while the respondent was still speaking (for fuller accounts, see Ganesh, 2019; Hanchey, 2020).

We can see the C–O cycle clearly. The respondent applied disciplinary rules for acceptable academic discourse, characterizing racial critique as radical and inflammatory. Their self-image and their image of NCA as non-racist became their evidence that writing about underlying white supremacist structures is divisive. The backlash was swift and passionate, and after issuing an apology, the panel respondent stepped down from their elected position in the OCD. An important element of this illustration of systemic bias is that the respondent had been actively contributing to the diversity, equity, and inclusion literature, yet didn't see how their comments reproduced white supremacy and structural racism – *until they saw their impact* – making this a deeply instructive opportunity. Had the analysis under critique been out-facing instead of aimed inside our borders, the presentation would have likely been uneventful. As it happened, the incident was a wake-up call, bringing awareness to many who had not clearly seen our own disciplinary racial biases (or saw them as inconsequential). This dramatic painful event is a cautionary tale about the depth and saturation of racial bias in our disciplinary structures. None of us is immune to implicit bias. All of us are vulnerable to enacting unintentional reproductions of structural biases. Consequently, the incident created broader interest in postcolonial approaches, hastening the field's decolonial turn (see Chapter 4).

#TONEUPORGCOMM

Several panelists and audience members published a set of essays entitled "No Time for Intersectionality Like the Present: A Response to the 2019 National Communication Association Organizational Communication Division's Top Paper Panel." The authors describe the incident as they experienced it, analyze those experiences, discuss the ongoing pain caused by it, scrutinize the field's racism, and perform resistance in the form of prose and poetry (Cruz, 2020; Gist-Mackey, 2020; Hanchey, 2020; Harris, 2020; Jensen, 2020; Kenney, 2020; Leslie, 2020). They conclude with a group-authored "manifestx" declaring "an intersectional present and future for organizational communication, one that embraces fiery language, is undisciplined, arises in relation, destabilizes White righteousness, and will not be silent" (#ToneUpOrgComm Collective, 2020, p. 152). The panel incident also prompted a series of OCD town hall meetings, the creation of a standing committee to address the underlying issues, and other ongoing efforts to achieve self-assessment and create an equitable environment (Statement from Organizational Communication Division Leadership, 2019).

THE DECOLONIAL TURN

The field of Communication, not unlike our broader society, sits at a crossroads. Through social media and in our journals, a growing community of scholars is voicing the racism and white supremacy embedded in our institutional structures.

> A disgraceful white boys' club persists in the field of Communication. Those admitted to its felicitous circle find themselves sitting on the boards of scholarly associations, plucked for plum editorships of top-ranked journals in the field. Their work, more often than not, finds its way into the proverbial canon, appearing at conferences and in field-shaping anthologies, and tracking feedback loops that, in turn, position them as experts, the leading thinkers in the field.
>
> (Mukherjee, 2020, p. 152)

Ballard et al. (2020) point out that

> systemic racism harms everyone. For example, even those who most benefit from privilege cannot help but become stunted by partial knowledge and narrow exposure, their human development hampered by the very inequities that seem to profit them. Particularly for higher ed, such harm should be a central concern for all of its stakeholders.
>
> (p. 601)

An increasing number of Organizational Communication scholars are beginning to see that our scholarship and disciplinary practices are steeped in structural racism, culturally biased knowledge structures, and presumptions stemming from Western colonization and conquest. Chapter 4 provides a summary of this *decolonial turn* in Organizational Communication.

Race and Organizational Theory

There is a long history of racial critique in Organizational Communication (e.g., Allen, 1995, 2004, 2007, 2011, 2023; Allen et al., 1999; Ashcraft & Allen, 2003; Ballard et al., 2020; Flores & Moon, 2002; Grimes, 2002; Grimes & Glenn, 2024; Haulani et al., 2006; Orbe & Allen, 2008; Orbe et al., 2022; Parker, 2001, 2003). In Chapters 2 and 3, this work is reviewed in overviews of the 20th and 21st centuries. The brief overview here provides the background you need to understand the racial foundations (Ashcraft & Allen, 2003) of organizational studies broadly, so that you can more critically consume the material reviewed in this book.

The Timeless Racial Script of Organizational Studies

Race remains a source of domination rooted in colonial histories that privilege and disenfranchise select bodies (Nkomo, 1992). Across organizational disciplines, "the poverty of our racial attention span" (Ashcraft & Allen, 2003, p. 32) is insidious. Yet, "race merits theoretical and practical attention because it is an enduring, contested phenomenon with important implications for communication studies, and for transforming society" (Allen, 2007, p. 259). Race is "one of the most powerful ideological and institutional factors for deciding how identities are categorized and power, material privileges, and resources distributed" (Giroux, 2003, p. 200). In short, just as we have accepted that organizations are gendered (see Chapter 13), we must also accept that organizations are raced (Ashcraft & Allen, 2003). Because the concept of *race* is a white supremacist structure, organizational scholars attempting to dismantle racism and promote anti-racism unintentionally reproduce the white supremacist structures they seek to eradicate (Nkomo, 1992, 2021). When we treat race as a neutral descriptor, demographic, or objective fact, we reproduce the white supremacist structures of its formation. *Race* is a construct created for the very purposes of racism and colonial rule. Examining racism in our own structures requires remembering that.

The Emperor Is Still Naked because Nobody Cared

In 1992, Stella Nkomo published an article in the *Academy of Management Review* (AMR) entitled, "The Emperor Has No Clothes: Rewriting 'Race in Organizations'," in which she examined how we might make "race a necessary and productive analytical category for theorizing about organizations" (p. 489). Her work was praised as *groundbreaking*. Yet, nothing changed, in evidence of that label's marginalizing effect (Hanchey, 2020). *Race* is still rarely an analytical concept or the subject of organizational theorizing. In a subsequent analysis of the concept of *race* in AMR 1993–2020, Nkomo (2021) found that of 1329 articles, 4 reference race and 2 reference racism. In these few, race is merely a category used to explain outcomes for racial minorities. Racism is oversimplified as discrimination and greater attention to racism is recommended without analysis (Nkomo, 2021). Race and racism are passing subjects with little conceptual attention. Editors and reviewers occasionally include it in our literature, but no one finds it vital to transform our own structures – or even to see the workings of race in our own disciplines (Nkomo, 1992, 2021).

Race in Organizational Communication Literature

Although many have called attention to persistent false race-neutrality in Organizational Communication (e.g., Ashcraft & Allen, 2003; Flores & Moon, 2002; Grimes, 2002;

Haulani et al., 2006; Nicotera & Clinkscales, 2003; Parker, 2001, 2003), few have addressed organizations as fundamentally raced (Parker, 2004). White scholars often feel a sense of exemption from the responsibility of dealing with race through surface-level nods under the guise of anti-racist action (Ramasubramanian & Martinez, 2017). Further, because racial categories are activated subconsciously (Dovidio et al., 2011; Ramasubramanian & Martinez, 2017), White and BIPOC scholars alike continuously (re)produce academic hierarchies that dictate who should and should not critique, explore, and unpack the impact of race (see Chapters 2–4 and 14).

Omitting race from theorizing reinforces racial hierarchies (Nkomo, 1992). Presumptions of race-neutrality lead to race- and gender-based exclusion (Kent & Logan, 2020) and lead to *racial paralysis*, "the tendency for people to opt out of situations that require choices seemingly made on the basis of race" (Norton et al., 2013, p. 387). Race-neutral ideology requires appearance of impartiality; racial paralysis occurs when "people's concern with appearing unbiased can inhibit both what they say and what they do – all in the direction of saying and doing nothing, but rather opting out of such situations altogether" (Conyers & Wright Fields, 2020, p. 3). As a result, disciplinary gatekeepers continue to mute race-related research by scholars of color (Afifi & Cornejo, 2020). This idleness from those in power develops into institutional racial paralysis (Conyers & Wright Fields, 2020).

Communication's attention to race has been inadequate (Valiavska & Gist-Mackey, 2023), despite recognition of the problem from the start. In 1968, the Speech Association of America's (now NCA) social relevance committee "wrote a 'Manifesto to the Speech Profession,' that started with a question: 'Are we a field aimed only at the perpetuation of white, middle-class standards and concepts?'" (Afifi & Cornejo, 2020, p. 239). Circumstances may be changing as of 2024, with the publication of *The Routledge Handbook of Ethnicity and Race in Communication* (Calafell & Eguchi, 2024) and the inauguration of a new NCA journal, *Communication and Race*.

Ashcraft and Allen's (2003) analysis of Organizational Communication textbooks illustrates the "intellectual hegemony" (p. 10) of the field, identifying five inaccurate messages that continue to characterize *race* in our textbooks. First, if discussed at all, race is separated into a chapter and treated as a unique interest of people of color. Second, race is relevant only as identifiable differences that need to be managed to improve performance. Third, international variations are assumed to be the only relevant cultural differences. Fourth, racial discrimination is defined as individual and interpersonal, happening when diversity is not well-managed. Finally, White people in white-collar workplaces are assumed to typify a universal experience.

Whiteness creates a research literature that ignores nonwhite persons, assuming white organizational settings populated by White people (Hendrix & Wilson, 2014). Orbe and Allen (2008) analyze *Journal of Applied Communication Research* (JACR) articles over a 30-year timeframe (1973–2005). Research in the journal is "best described as White scholarship" (p. 205) ignoring race altogether. Whiteness is the unquestioned norm; White people are treated as raceless (Roediger, 1998), as are organizational contexts, implying universal generalizability of findings. "Race matters only when the research explicitly contrasts people of color with Whites, or focuses on people of color in particular contexts, such as gangs or prisons" (Orbe & Allen, 2008, p. 206). As you will see in Chapters 2–4, this may change as the field begins to decolonize. We now turn to an overview of the origins of the field of Organizational Communication.

Origins of Organizational Communication

This section provides a brief history of the origins of Organizational Communication. While traditional academic histories privilege people, dates, and ideas, every moment occurs in a socio-political environment of organizational activities and academic cultures embedded in Western thinking. In documenting academic history, little attention is paid to the history of the phenomena under study. This review strives to provide that socio-historical context to the extent allowed by existing documentation.

Communication's fundamental roots are speech and media, both heavily influenced by persuasion theory. By the 1930s these areas had matured to become the foundation of communication theorizing, conjoining in the 1960s into the discipline that became Communication. See Eadie (2022) for a well-documented history of this disciplinary emergence. Communication is a 20th-century American discipline, emerging from previously existing fields (e.g., English, Psychology, Sociology, Social Psychology, and Political Science) and developing independence in the early 1960s. Early commentary about "borrowing" from other disciplines or being "fragmented" created a self-image of fighting for legitimacy that still flavors our multidisciplinary efforts, even though the field has matured and our theoretic base has a strong disciplinary identity, distinct from that of other fields. Communication is a highly diverse discipline that studies everything from cognitive processes to texts and broad societal phenomena. Communication is centered on the study of interaction among humans – from dyadic relationships to mass messaging – remaining tightly connected to literatures of other disciplines. While all social disciplines examine communication, our central focus is to explicate the communication process itself.

Organizational Communication scholars and students who understand the intellectual history of the field are more critical consumers and producers of knowledge. The history written here contextualizes developments in the emergence of Organizational Communication (Redding, 1985; Redding & Tompkins, 1988) with developments in the emergence of Communication (Delia, 1987; Eadie, 2022). Redding's observations (Redding, 1985; Redding & Tompkins, 1988) about the history of Organizational Communication are based on cataloguing publications in the field, examining labels applied to the study of communication and organization, and tracking graduate degree conferrals.

Communication's Origins

Speech (public speaking and rhetoric) originated in departments of English. In 1914, public speaking teachers in the National Council of Teachers of English (NCTE) voted to create the National Association of Academic Teachers of Public Speaking (NAATPS). NAATPS eventually became NCA with a far broader mission and membership. The first media research examined WWI propaganda, and in the 1920s, a focus on human interaction emerged in Sociology, which shifted to Social Psychology in the 1930s as the study of speech began to employ a scientific approach to persuasion, attitude change, decision-making, and sending/receiving messages. Public opinion research became an important area of study in the 1920s and a distinct field in the 1930s. Concerns about the impact of cinema on youth spurred the first "new media" research activities in the 1930s (Delia, 1987).

Origins of the Field of Organizational Communication

Organizational Communication is rooted in the European industrialization of the 1750s, which brought large organizational systems that forever changed business and society.

Business scholarship began a century later, emphasizing the importance of communication as a management tool, with the first business school established at Harvard in 1908. By 1940, the groundwork was laid for Organizational Communication (Redding & Tompkins, 1988), as scholars of speech and media pursued an interest in business/industrial communication.

Early management theory (covered in Part II) had a profound effect on organizational theory and practice. Because they were overtly prescriptive, early management theories powerfully shaped (and continue to shape) organizational forms and practices. The communicative construction of contemporary organizations remains driven by the constitutive power of these foundational theories. Contemporary workplace organizations are constituted by early management theory prescriptions (e.g., arrangement of authority hierarchies, conventions and sanctions for communication channels). Early management theories also propagated Organizational Communication's business, corporate, and management biases.

Principles of public address were increasingly applied to business education in the early 20th century, as were business writing, managerial communication, and persuasion. By 1930, academics and practitioners recognized the importance of effective speaking and writing for business executives. This emphasis on effective message construction/delivery, including examinations of channels/media, is central to Organizational Communication's origins. With business/industrial managerial foundations, the focus remained on downward communication and the separation of management and labor. Its grounding in business and industry is a chief explanation for Organizational Communication's continuing orientation to the corporate workplace.

WWII Era through the 1950s

WWII is an important historical context for Communication generally and Organizational Communication specifically. The US war effort brought applied research on communication problems, granting professional legitimacy and attracting prominent researchers. Communication-focused research became acceptable to American academia and created a community that would later become the field of Communication (Delia, 1987). In pursuit of this applied research, a "triple alliance" (Redding, 1985, p. 24) formed among the military, academia, and training-within-industry to shape the field of Business/Industrial Communication – which evolved later into Organizational Communication. In the 1940s, business/industrial communication theory and research expanded beyond information dissemination and managerial messaging to include communication networks and informal communication.

After WWII, *communication research* and *mass communication research* absorbed specialized labels (e.g., propaganda, persuasion, radio, print), creating a disciplinary focus for Communication. Communication was viewed as central to democracy and public good, best understood through scientific analysis (Delia, 1987). Speech professors began extending doctoral-level mentoring, resulting in the first industrial communication doctoral degrees awarded by Speech departments in the early 1950s (Redding & Tompkins, 1988). Speech departments also began hosting industrial communication conferences, with multidisciplinary research literature proliferating.

In 1950, the National Society for the Study of Communication (NSSC) was founded, now ICA. Two disciplinary divisions took shape: mass communication vs. interpersonal communication, theory/research vs. practice (Delia, 1987; Eadie, 2022). Mass communication practical work became Journalism. Business/industrial communication was similarly split:

internal vs. external communication, theory/research vs. practice. Internal/theory/research efforts became Organizational Communication. External/practice work evolved into Public Relations (Redding & Tompkins, 1988), maturing in the 21st century to reintegrate theory/research and practice as Strategic Communication. Note the *container presumption*. Organizational boundary was a defining mechanism for organizing the field into subspecialties.

Arrival: The 1960s

By 1960, Communication existed in Speech departments with faculty in speech and rhetoric, interpersonal interaction, and mass communication. The study of organizational communication expanded to incorporate more relationally oriented research. Concentrated attention in the field shifted from persuasion to information receiver. This change from sender- to receiver orientation in organizational communication research led to the presumption in Organizational Communication that *the message received is the only one that matters* (Putnam & Cheney, 1985). The study of relationships in organizational contexts increased, with particular attention to superior-subordinate communication and communication climate. As Mass Communication and Interpersonal Communication split into separate disciplinary arenas, it is easy to see how the reification of organizational boundary was perpetuated, and why Public Relations – with its focus on effective messaging to broad external audiences – remains associated with Mass Communication, whereas Organizational Communication became united with Interpersonal.

Organizational Communication materialized as a discipline in 1968 (Redding & Tompkins, 1988). First, two publications documented a discrete corpus of knowledge (Thayer, 1967, 1968). Second, the 1967 *Conference on Organizational Communication* at NASA's Marshall Space Flight Center (MSFC) convened academics and MSFC contractors and managers to discuss theory and research. The conference and the main speech by Phillip K. Tompkins, with its accompanying paper, represent the earliest work summarizing research under the label *organizational communication*. Finally, in 1968, ICA (then NSSC) established its first four interest groups, with the Organizational Communication Division designated as Division IV. This served to institute Organizational Communication as a distinct field.

Organization of This Text

Part I provides an overview of advancements in Organizational Communication. Chapter 1 offers a set of foundational concepts and a socio-historical context from which to understand organizational communication theory and research. Chapters 2 and 3 provide overviews of the development of the field from its formation in the late 1960s to the present, including both theoretical shifts and trends in research topics. Chapter 4 explains postcolonial theory and the field's decolonial turn in the 2020s.

Part II comprises chapters explaining early 20th-century management theory, taking us to the same point (late 1960s) as the historical context in Chapter 1. Simultaneous with the socio-historical circumstances that framed the emergence of Organizational Communication, management theorists were developing foundational organizational theories that have profoundly influenced organizational studies disciplines. Three foundational schools of thought in management theory are classical management, focusing on formal communication processes and prescriptions to improve productivity (Chapter 5); human relations (HR), focusing on informal communication processes and prescriptions to improve worker satisfaction as a path to productivity (Chapter 6); and human resources management (HRM), focusing on participative management processes and prescriptions to maximize the potential of workers' intelligence for organizational gain (Chapter 7).

Early management theory is important to organizational communication for two fundamental reasons. First, this work represents the first systematic thinking about communication and organization, continuing to influence how we identify, define, and prioritize basic concepts. Second, as prescriptive formulations, early management theory profoundly shaped practice, creating many of the organizational communication phenomena we study today (e.g., authority, hierarchy, and organizational form).

Finally, Part III offers reviews of specialized areas of research and theory written by subject matter experts. Every chapter will apply a template of understanding to help you synthesize what you are learning about the field and its literature by considering two central questions:

- What is the approach taken to organization (as process, as structured, as entity)?
- How can we see the C–O cycle in this body of literature (Figure 1.2)?

Several chapters also consider the postcolonial implications of their body of literature.

Recommended Supplementary Readings

Ashcraft, K. L., & Allen, B. J. (2003). The racial foundation of organizational communication. *Communication Theory*, *13*(1), 5–38.

Analysis of organizational communication textbooks' approach to race, revealing five implicit messages about our approach. Still relevant, as little has changed since then.

Brummans, B. H. J. M. (Ed.). (2018). *The agency of organizing: Perspectives and case studies*. Routledge.

Chapters from this book might be read by more advanced students to engage in study of the conceptual operation of agency as an important concept in organizational communication theory.

Buzzanell, P. M., & Stohl, C. (1999). The Redding tradition of organizational communication scholarship: W. Charles Redding and his legacy. *Communication Studies*, *50* (4), 324–336.

Provides a critical appreciation of the influential work of Charles Redding, widely regarded as the "founding father" of organizational communication.

Eadie, W. (2022). *When communication became a discipline*. Lexington Books.

Provides a well-documented account of the emergence of Communication as a discipline.

Grimes, D. S., & Glenn, C. L. (2024). Race and organizational communication: Tired of saying it. In B. M. Calafell & S. Eguchi (Eds.), *The Routledge handbook of ethnicity and race in communication* (pp. 508–520). Routledge.

A thorough review and critique of organizational-communication-relevant work on race.

Putnam, L. L., & Cheney, G. (1985). Organizational communication: Historical development and future directions. In T. Benson (Ed.), *Speech communication in the 20th century* (pp. 130–156). Southern Illinois University Press.

Provides a comprehensive history of the field of Organizational Communication up to the early 1980s.

Redding, W. C. (1985). Stumbling toward identity: The emergence of organizational communication as a field of study. In R. D. McPhee & P. K. Tompkins (Eds.), *Organizational communication: Traditional themes and new directions* (pp. 15–54). Sage.
Redding, W. C., & Tompkins, P. K. (1988). Organizational communication: Past and present tenses. In G. Goldhaber & G. Burnett (Eds.), *Handbook of organizational communication* (pp. 5–34). Ablex.

These two chapters can be read as companion pieces. In the 1980s, these essays were regarded as the official history of the field.

Tompkins, P. K. (1993). *Organizational communication imperatives: Lessons of the space program*. Roxbury.

This book is an excellent historical accounts of Tompkins' work with NASA, how he came to develop theories of effective organizing based on NASA's Apollo-era organizational practices and principles, and how this applied work contributed to the birth of the field of Organizational Communication.

Tompkins, P. K. (2005). *Apollo, Challenger, Columbia: The decline of the space program*. Roxbury.

Tompkins' second NASA book chronicles the changes in organizational communication practices at NASA in the shuttle era, providing an organizational communication analysis of the US space program's decline. These are excellent books to demonstrate the practical applications of organizational communication theory and are highly recommended reading for practitioners.

Important Concepts: Define and Discuss

Agency
Biases of organizational communication
Business/industrial roots of organizational communication
Organizational in its three forms
Race as a racist social construction
Redding's triple alliance
Reflexivity
Social collective
Social construction
Whiteness and white supremacy

Discussion Questions

1 Using concrete examples, explain how organization and communication are related.
2 Using an organization with which you are very familiar, illustrate O_1, O_2, and O_3. Explain how this organization possesses all three of the fundamental characteristics of entitative being. Then trace how the three expressions (organizing, organized, and organization) are interrelated in actual occurrences.
3 Can you think of examples of O_1 and O_2 in the absence of O_3? Think more broadly than *workplaces*.
4 How might the conceptualization presented here of organization and organizational communication be applied to social networks? Are social networks examples of organizational communication in action? Why or why not?
5 Can you identify each of the biases about organizational communication in your own experience?

Practitioners' Corner

Communication practitioners and their work vary considerably. Communication practitioners may serve any combination of functions: information dissemination, education, training, development, promotion, marketing, customer relations, and so on. These various functions are served across a variety of contexts, including corporate, government, nonprofit, and educational settings. Each chapter of this book will include a "Practitioner's Corner." Some of these will be suggestions for application of the material; some will be case studies illustrating application. Some chapters will provide more concrete applications than others. This first chapter is necessarily abstract, but it provides a uniquely insightful vocabulary for communication practitioners to think through important issues.

All communication professionals have at least two fundamental things in common: They must act as agents of someone/something other than themselves and they must bridge the socially constructed organizational boundary that divides their audiences into internal and external publics. The abstract definitional material in this chapter can be helpful to the practitioner in several ways across these two commonalities. Underlying these implications are important questions of agency.

- *First, the communication practitioner is an agent who is professionally obligated to represent the interests of some entity.* Conceptualizing who/what constitutes that entity brings an important set of ethical considerations. Every communication professional must wrestle with the question of whose interests are primary to the task at hand. The practitioner must ask herself: Whose interests do I represent? The organization (O_3)? The stockholders? The public? Which public? What are the limits on that representation? What are the equity concerns? The theoretic constructions of O_1, O_2, and O_3 provide a language to assist the practitioner in thinking through these questions to both devise strategy and create a code of ethics.
    - Representing the organization to a set of "external" publics is a very different task than representing one "internal" group to another or representing the organization to its internal audiences. Who is accountable for actions attributed to O_3? Should that information be revealed to message recipients? How? How can messaging be constructed equitably for a diverse audience? When representing the entitative being, it is crucial to remember that the organization has no conscience of its own. Moreover,

when the corporate body is the entity represented, the identities of those humans who are actually responsible and accountable for organizational actions are obfuscated. These implications of the construct O_3 have profound impact on considerations for ethical communication.

- Good strategic messaging is nuanced. When is it best to attribute a message to an organizational entity (O_3) rather than to the individual persons in charge of the project or announcement at hand? How can messaging be tailored equitably to multiple audiences? Thinking through the meaning and persuasive power of attributions using the theoretic considerations offered here can be helpful in the design of effective messages that accomplish ethical purposes.

- *Second, the line that divides "external" and "internal" publics is fluid and socially constructed.* In practice, organizational boundary is enforced, with audiences (or publics) divided into internal and external groups. Construction of strategic messaging is enhanced when the practitioner remembers that these boundaries are a human construction.
  - "Outsiders" can become "insiders" – carrying with them the memory of previous messaging. Are there inconsistencies between internal and external messaging? How might these inconsistencies be best addressed to successfully transition newcomers into "insider" roles? How might these inconsistencies be interpreted through an equity lens?
  - "Insiders" simultaneously occupy "outsider" roles. Corporate employees are members of the public with families. Military members are consumers of goods. Public health officers drink from municipal water sources and breathe air from the same atmosphere as everyone else. Any construction of messages designed for internal audiences must be mindful of these blurs in the organizational boundary. Is it important for internal messaging to remain internal? How is "internal" defined, and how is this best communicated to the recipients? Given the ubiquity of social media, are leaks possible? How damaging might such leaks be? To whom? Is any training necessary to prevent them? Harkening back to the first point – whose interests does the practitioner serve in these matters?

While these questions can be thoughtfully considered without the theoretical frameworks presented in this chapter, these frameworks do provide useful language for the practitioner to think through these issues. The frameworks provide both the genesis of important questions and a language with which to formulate answers. Who am I? Where do I sit in the organizational construction? Whose interests do I represent? How can we best organize (O_1) to create organized structures (O_2) to achieve the goals of the organization (O_3)? A communication professional in any context will be better prepared to strategize and implement communication plans having thought through these kinds of questions.

References

#OrgCommSoWhite. (n.d.). Reading list. https://docs.google.com/document/d/1EDXx2BJoCVSZFPYpHOV9FcRWON8oDKm1jyMQVR45CPE/edit#heading=h.j345x3xsfh6c

#ToneUpOrgComm Collective. (2020). #ToneUpOrgComm: A manifesto. *Critical Departures in Qualitative Research*, *20*(9), 152–154. https://online.ucpress.edu/dcqr/article-abstract/9/2/152/110317/ToneUpOrgCommA-Manifestx?redirectedFrom=fulltext

Afifi, W. A., & Cornejo, M. (2020). #CommSoWEIRD: The question of sample representativeness in interpersonal communication research. In M. L. Doerfel & J. L. Gibbs (Eds.), *Organizing inclusion: Moving diversity from demographics to communication processes*. Routledge.

Ahmed, S. (Ed.). (2012). *On being included: Racism and diversity in institutional life*. Duke University Press. https://doi.org/10.1215/9780822395324
Allen, B. J. (1995). "Diversity" and organizational communication. *Journal of Applied Communication Research*, *23*(2), 143–155. https://doi.org/10.1080/00909889509365420
Allen, B. J. (2007). Theorizing communication and race. *Communication Monographs*, *74*(2), 259–264.
Allen, B. J. (2004). *Difference matters* (1st ed.). Waveland Press.
Allen, B. J. (2011). *Difference matters* (2nd ed.). Waveland Press.
Allen, B. J. (2023). *Difference matters* (3rd ed.). Waveland Press.
Allen, B. J., Orbe, M. P., & Olivas, M. R. (1999). The complexity of our tears: Dis/enchantment and (in)difference in the academy. *Communication Theory*, *9*(4). 402–429. https://doi.org/10.1111/j.1468-2885.1999.tb00206.x
Ashcraft, K. L., & Allen, B. J. (2003). The racial foundation of organizational communication. *Communication Theory*, *13*(1), 5–38. https://doi.org/10.1111/j.1468-2885.2003.tb00280.x
Ballard, D., Allen, B., Ashcraft, K., Ganesh, S., McLeod, P., & Zoller, H. (2020). When words do not matter: Identifying actions to effect diversity, equity, and inclusion in the academy. *Management Communication Quarterly*, *34*(4), 590–616. https://doi.org/10.1177/0893318920951643
Broadfoot, K. J., Carlone, D., Medved, C. E., Aakhus, M., Gabor, E., & Taylor, K. (2008). Meaning/ful work and organizational communication. *Management Communication Quarterly*, *22*(1), 152–161. https://doi.org/10.1177/0893318908318267
Brummans, B. H. J. M. (Ed.). (2018). *The agency of organizing: Perspectives and case studies.* Routledge.
Calafell, B. M., & Eguchi, S. (Eds.). (2024). *The Routledge handbook of ethnicity and race in communication.* Routledge.
Chakravartty, P., Kuo, R., Grubbs, V., & McIlwain, I. (2018). #CommunicationSoWhite. *Journal of Communication*, *68*(2), 254–266. https://doi.org/10.1093/joc/jqy003
Conyers, A., & Wright Fields, C. (2020). A critical race theory analysis of institutional racial paralysis in organizational culture. *Public Integrity*, *23*(2), 1–12. http://dx.doi.org/10.1080/10999922.2020.1832365
Cooren, F. (2006). The organizational world as a plenum of agencies. In F. Cooren & J. R. Taylor (Eds.), *Communication as organizing: Empirical and theoretical explorations in the dynamic of text and conversation* (pp. 81–100). Erlbaum.
Cruz, J. M. (2020). Object: Letter of disapplication. *Critical Departures in Qualitative Research*, *20*(9), 126–132. https://doi.org/10.1525/dcqr.2020.9.2.126
Cruz, J. M., & Sodeke, C. U. (2021). Debunking Eurocentrism in organizational communication theory: Marginality and liquidities in postcolonial contexts. *Communication Theory*, *31*, 528–548. https://doi.org/10.1093/ct/qtz038
Delia, J. G. (1987). Communication research: A history. In C. R. Berger & S. H. Chaffee (Eds.), *Handbook of communication science* (pp. 20–98). Sage.
Dovidio, J. F., Gaertner, S. L., Saguy, T., & Hehman, E. (2011). Obama's potential to transform the attitudes of White Americans. In G. S. Parks & M. Hughey (Eds.), *The Obamas and a (post) racial America* (pp. 245–262). Oxford University Press.
Dobusch, L., & Schoeneborn, D. (2015). Fluidity, identity, and organizationality: The communicative constitution of *Anonymous*. *Journal of Management Studies*, *52*(8), 1005–1035. https://doi.org/10.1111/joms.12139
Dutta, M. J. (2019, June 10). Whiteness, NCA, and distinguished scholars. *Mohan Dutta: Culture-centered approach* (blog). https://culture-centered.blogspot.com/2019/06/in-post-made-in-response-to-changes-to.html
Eadie, W. (2022). *When communication became a discipline*. Lexington Books.
Flaherty, C. (2019, June 12). When White scholars pick White scholars. *Inside Higher Ed*. https://www.insidehighered.com/news/2019/06/13/communication-scholars-debate-how-fields-distinguished-scholars-should-be-picked
Flores, L., & Moon, D. (2002). Rethinking race, revealing dilemmas: Imagining a new racial subject in *Race Traitor*. *Western Journal of Communication*, *66*(2), 181–207. http://dx.doi.org/10.1080/10570310209374732
Frankel, C. (2022). The object of inquiry and organization studies. *Organization Studies*, *43*(12), 2013–2025. https://doi.org/10.1177/01708406211053201

Ganesh, S. (2019, November 17). I am posting the following collaboratively produced account... *Communication Scholars for Transformation* (Public Facebook Group). https://www.facebook.com/groups/457629181722810/posts/563189687833425/ Also available at https://docs.google.com/document/d/1SmrkYHByhyiyLZlg8kY1gCOrFGtnyE795pY89fLkcHw/edit

Giroux, H. A. (2003). Spectacles of race and pedagogies of denial: Anti-black racist pedagogy under the reign of neoliberalism. *Communication Education*, *52*(3–4), 191–211. https://doi.org/10.1080/0363452032000156190

Gist-Mackey, A. (2020). The pain of performative professionalism: Emotionally embodying business as usual. *Critical Departures in Qualitative Research*, *20*(9), 140–143. https://doi.org/10.1525/dcqr.2020.9.2.140

Gist-Mackey, A., & Kingsford, A. N. (2020). Linguistic inclusion: Challenging implicit classed communication bias in interview methods. *Management Communication Quarterly*, *34*(3), 402–425. https://doi.org/10.1177/0893318920934128

Grimes, D. S. (2002). Challenging the status quo? Whiteness in the diversity management literature. *Management Communication Quarterly*, *15*(3), 381–409. https://doi.org/10.1177/0893318902153003

Grimes, D. S., & Glenn, C. L. (2024). Race and organizational communication: Tired of saying it. In B. M. Calafell & S. Eguchi (Eds.), *The Routledge handbook of ethnicity and race in communication* (pp. 508–520). Routledge.

Hanchey, J. N. (2020). Beyond race scholarship as groundbreaking/irrelevant. *Departures in Critical Qualitative Research*, *9*(2), 122–125. https://doi.org/10.1525/dcqr.2020.9.2.122

Harris, K. L. (2020). Time to #ToneUpOrgComm. *Critical Departures in Qualitative Research*, *20*(9), 147–151. https://doi.org/10.1525/dcqr.2020.9.2.147

Haulani, R. T., Fassett, D. L., Morrison, J. H. T. A., & Dodge, P. S. (2006). Between the structural and the personal: Situated sense-makings of "race. *Communication and Critical/Cultural Studies*, *3*(1), 70–93. https://doi.org/10.1080/14791420500505700

Hendrix, K. G., & Wilson, C. (2014). Virtual invisibility: Race and communication education. *Communication Education*, *63*(4), 405–428. https://doi.org/10.1080/03634523.2014.934852

Hirschman, C. (2004). The origins and demise of the concept of race. *Population and Development Review*, *30*(3), 385–415. https://www.jstor.org/stable/3401408

Jensen, P. R. (2020). Reflections on complacency and inadequacy in the face of violence. *Critical Departures in Qualitative Research*, *20*(9), 137–139. https://doi.org/10.1525/dcqr.2020.9.2.137

Jensen, P. R., & Meisenbach, R. J. (2015). Alternative organizing and (in)visibility: Managing tensions of transparency and autonomy in a nonprofit organization. *Management Communication Quarterly*, *29*(4), 503–643. https://doi.org/10.1177/0893318915600577

Keita, S., Kittles, R., Royal, C., Bonney, G., Furbert-Harris, P., Dunston, G., & Rotimi, C. (2004). Conceptualizing human variation. *Nature Genetics*, *36*(11 Suppl), S17– S 20. https://doi.org/10.1038/ng1455

Kenney, S. C. (2020). (Un)disciplining the graduate student, and a queer otherwise. *Critical Departures in Qualitative Research*, *20*(9), 144–146. https://doi.org/10.1525/dcqr.2020.9.2.144

Kent, M., & Logan, N. (2020). Rhizomatous dialogue, organizational engagement, and inclusion. In M. L. Doerfel & J. L. Gibbs (Eds.), *Organizing inclusion: Moving diversity from demographics to communication processes*. Routledge.

Kuhn, T., Ashcraft, K. L., & Cooren, F. (2019). Introductory essay: What work can organizational communication do? *Management Communication Quarterly*, *33*(1), 101–111. https://doi.org/10.1177/0893318918809421

Leslie, K. J. (2020). Scenes from the margins: One queer's response to navigating professionalism at NCA. *Critical Departures in Qualitative Research*, *20*(9), 133–136. https://doi.org/10.1525/dcqr.2020.9.2.133

Lewontin, R.C. (1972). The apportionment of human diversity. In T. Dobzhansky, M. K. Hecht, & W. C. Steere (Eds.). *Evolutionary biology* (pp. 381–398). Springer. https://doi.org/10.1007/978-1-4684-9063-3_14

McNamee, L. G. (2011). Faith-based organizational communication and its implications for member identity. *Journal of Applied Communication Research*, *39*(4), 422–440. http://dx.doi.org/10.1080/00909882.2011.608697

Mukherjee, R. (2020). Of experts and tokens: Mapping a critical race archaeology of communication. *Communication, Culture and Critique*, *13*(2), 152–167. http://dx.doi.org/10.1093/ccc/tcaa009

Ng, E., White, K. C., & Saha, A. (2020). #CommunicationSoWhite: Race and power in the academy and beyond. *Communication, Culture & Critique*, *13*(2), 143–151. https://doi.org/10.1093/ccc/tcaa011
Nicotera, A. M. (2013). Organizations as entitative beings: Some ontological implications of communicative constitution. In F. Cooren & D. Robichaud (Eds.), *Organization and organizing: Materiality, agency, and discourse* (pp. 66–89). Routledge.
Nicotera, A. M., & Clinkscales, M. J. (2003). *Understanding organization through culture and structure: Relational and other lessons from the African-American organization*. Erlbaum.
Nkomo, S. M. (1992). The emperor has no clothes: Rewriting "race in organizations. *Academy of Management Review*, *17*(3), 487–513. https://doi.org/10.2307/258720
Nkomo, S. M. (2021). Reflections on the continuing denial of the centrality of "race" in management and organization studies. *Equality, Diversity and Inclusion: An International Journal*, *40*(2), 212–224. https://doi.org/10.1108/edi-01-2021-0011
Norton, M. I., Mason, M. F., Vandello, J. A., Biga, A., & Dyer, R. (2013). An fMRI investigation of racial paralysis. *Social Cognitive and Affective Neuroscience*, *8*(4), 387–393. https://psycnet.apa.org/doi/10.1093/scan/nss010
Orbe, M. P., & Allen, B. J. (2008). "Race matters" in the Journal of Applied Communication Research. *The Howard Journal of Communications*, *19*(3), 201–220. https://psycnet.apa.org/doi/10.1080/10646170802218115
Orbe, M. P., Austin, J. T., & Allen, B. J. (Eds.). (2022). 'Race matters' in applied communication research: Past, present, and future [Special issue]. *Journal of Applied Communication Research*, *50*(3), 229–235. https://doi.org/10.1080/00909882.2022.2083407
Parker, P. S. (2001). African American women executives' leadership communication within dominant-culture organizations: (Re)conceptualizing notions of collaboration and instrumentality. *Management Communication Quarterly*, *15*(1), 42–82. https://doi.org/10.1177/0893318901151002
Parker, P. S. (2003). Control, resistance, and empowerment in raced, gendered, and classed work contexts: The case of African American women. *Annals of the International Communication Association*, *27*(1), 257–291. https://doi.org/10.1080/23808985.2003.11679028
Parker, P. S. (2004). *Race, gender, and leadership: Re-envisioning organizational leadership from the perspectives of African American women executives*. Psychology Press.
Patton, T. O. (2004). In the guise of civility: The complicitous maintenance of inferential forms of sexism and racism in higher education. *Women's Studies in Communication*, *27*(1), 60–87. https://doi.org/10.1080/07491409.2004.10162466
Putnam, L. L., & Cheney, G. (1985). Organizational communication: Historical development and future directions. In T. Benson (Ed.), *Speech communication in the 20th century* (pp. 130–156). Southern Illinois University Press.
Ramasubramanian, S., & Martinez, A. R. (2017). News framing of Obama, racialized scrutiny, and symbolic racism. *Howard Journal of Communications*, *28*(1), 36–54. https://psycnet.apa.org/doi/10.1080/10646175.2016.1235519
Redding, W. C. (1985). Stumbling toward identity: The emergence of organizational communication as a field of study. In R. D. McPhee & P. K. Tompkins (Eds.), *Organizational communication: Traditional themes and new directions* (pp. 15–54). Sage.
Redding, W. C., & Tompkins, P. K. (1988). Organizational communication: Past and present tenses. In G. Goldhaber & G. Burnett (Eds.), *Handbook of organizational communication* (pp. 5–34). Ablex.
Rodriguez, A., Dutta, M. J., & Desnoyers-Colas, E. F. (2019). Introduction to the special issue on merit, whiteness, and privilege. *Departures in Critical Qualitative Research*, *8*(4), 3–9. https://doi.org/10.1525/dcqr.2019.8.4.3
Roediger, D. (1998). Introduction. In D. Roediger (Ed.), *Black on white: Black writers on what it means to be white* (pp. 1–28). Schoken Books.
Schoeneborn, D., Kuhn, T. R., & Kärreman, D. (2019). The communicative constitution of organization, organizing, and organizationality. *Organization Studies*, *40*(4), 475–496. https://doi.org/10.1177/0170840618782284.
Sewell, W. H. (1992). A theory of structure: Duality, agency, and transformation. *The American Journal of Sociology*, *98*(*1*), 1–29. https://doi.org/10.1086/229967
Smith, R. C. (1993). *Images of organizational communication: Root-metaphors of the organization-communication relation*. Paper presented to the Organizational Communication Division at the International Communication Association Convention, Washington, D.C.

Smith, W. R. (2022). On relationality and organizationality: Degrees of durability, materiality, and communicative constituting a fluid social collective. *Organization Studies*, *43*(11), 1815–1837. https://doi.org/10.1177/01708406211035497

Statement from Organizational Communication Division Leadership on Top Paper Panel. (2019, November 29). https://www.natcom.org/wp-content/uploads/2021/02/OCD-Statement-on-Top-Paper-Panel-to-post.pdf

Thayer, L. (1967). Communication and organizational theory. In F. Dance (Ed.), *Human communication theory* (pp. 70–115). Holt, Rinehart and Winston.

Thayer, L. (1968). *Communication and communication systems*. Irwin.

Valiavska, A., & Gist-Mackey, A. N. (2023). Decade of race publications: Meta content analysis of race in communication scholarship from 2010–2020. *Howard Journal of Communications*, *34*(4), 337–352. https://doi.org/10.1080/10646175.2023.2178267

2 Developments in the 20th Century

Anne M. Nicotera

Traditional Paradigms

This chapter provides an overview of trends from the field's formation in the late 1960s to the turn of the century. During this period, three major paradigms developed, which co-exist today in a pluralistic field. A *paradigm* is a way of knowing, a complex, internally consistent set of assumptions that constitute a conceptual stance. Through its *metatheory*, each paradigm creates a distinct approach to theorizing the relation between communication and organization. Metatheory has four basic sets of assumptions: *ontology*, reality; *epistemology*, knowledge; *axiology*, values; and *praxeology*, practice/action.

Functionalism

Post-positivism, labeled *functionalism* in Organizational Communication, relies on objectivity and deductive reasoning, using quantitative methods to formulate predictions. Functionalist *ontology* assumes external reality drives human action. Functionalist *epistemology* is objective, assuming knowledge is discovered through empiricism. Because functionalism is objective, the knower (researcher) must be separated from the known (phenomenon). To separate themselves, functionalists refer to the people observed as *subjects* or *respondents*. Functionalists use scientific methods, emulating physical sciences. Functionalist *axiology* assumes values contaminate the research process and should be used only to guide topic selection and ethical conduct. Functionalist *praxeology* limits practice to empirically tested principles for effective communication. In the 1970s, organizational communication theory and research were focused on understanding organizational communication processes scientifically, with variable-analytic research examining links between outcomes and such things as communication networks, superior–subordinate communication, and communication climate.

Interpretivism

The 1980s brought an interpretive turn, accompanied by attention to culture and the mutual influence between self and society. *Interpretivism* uses disciplined subjectivity as an important source of understanding, relies heavily on inductive reasoning, and uses qualitative methods allowing rich description of lived experience. Interpretivist *ontology* assumes that our social reality lives in us, often referred to as *the social constructionist view*, and that human action is internally driven. Interpretivists seek to investigate situationally embedded unique phenomena to understand meaning-creation.

DOI: 10.4324/9781003484639-3

Interpretivist *epistemology* is subjectivist, assuming that knowledge is internal, created, embedded in persons and contexts, and created through the disciplined use of subjectivity. The knower *cannot* be separated from the known. To unite themselves with people observed, interpretivists refer to them as *participants* or *co-researchers*, whose points of view and interpretations are a crucial part of creating scholarly knowledge. Interpretivists often engage in *participant-observation*, immersing themselves in the experience under observation. The *member-check* is a key technique, asking participants to review research conclusions. Interpretivism uses humanistic methods following humanities traditions (e.g., history, literature, art), in addition to anthropological methods of cultural ethnography.

Axiologically, interpretivism dictates that values are an important tool that drives research design and data interpretation. A disciplined process of *bracketing* examines values so they become tools for research rather than biases. Interpretivists seek to understand the social world as it is situated in context; interpretivist *praxeology* applies theory by sensitizing actors to context and teaching them to examine communication patterns in ways the research has shown to be insightful.

Critical Approaches

The 1990s saw a critical turn, growing out of interpretivism. Organizational Communication critical theory takes an interpretivist approach with a focus on deconstructing systems of societal power, domination, and oppression (see Chapter 12). *Praxeology* is the metatheoretical distinction between interpretivism and critical-interpretivism. Critical theory, by definition, must work toward the eradication of dominance/oppression. *Critical praxis* is shedding false consciousness, ideologies that serve ruling group interests, to promote individual and social change. Critical-interpretivist theory is committed to dismantling structures of oppression by helping group members perceive the embedded oppression of dominated groups and understand their own complicity in it.

Implications for Research

Functionalism uses causal reasoning and explanations of prediction or influence among variables. Theory-building is deductive, generating hypotheses or predictions from existing knowledge and using observation to test theory. Communication and organization are conceptually reduced to measurable *variables*. Organizational variables influence communication, and manipulation of communication variables can result in organizational changes. For example, a functionalist might hypothesize that managers using employee-development strategies have more productive departments than managers using reward/punishment strategies. To test that hypothesis, an empirical study would measure managerial strategy, productivity, and other differences between the groups. The communication–organization relationship is accounted for with reductionist conceptualizations of both. Quantifiable observations are necessary to achieve the precision demanded by functionalist research. Functionalists do not deny social constructionist functions of communication but do not examine meaning-creating processes; such research questions are not driven by functionalist ontology. Functionalist research accounts for meaning by examining quantified, self-reported perceptions.

Interpretivists build theory inductively, privileging observation as the discovery point from which theory is derived. For example, an interpretivist may divide managers into groups based on the productivity of their units and observe them to discern patterns among high- and low-performing units. Applying inductive logic, the researcher may conclude that the observable and consistent patterns for high- and low-performing groups explain their different outcomes, possibly turning to existing theory of leadership or management to conceptualize an abstract transferable explanation. If no existing theory fits, the conclusions are used to generate new theory. Social-constructivist ontology and epistemology provide a processual approach in which meaning-creation can be foregrounded and directly theorized.

Late 1960s and 1970s: Structural-Functionalism and Systems

Organizational Communication began with a business-focused managerial orientation seeking principles for effective communication to improve employee performance and other outcomes, such as job satisfaction (see Chapter 1). Research followed a linear and deductive variable-analytic tradition in a structural-functionalist approach. Later, systems theory emerged as a more dominant perspective. Popular topics included message contents, channels, flows, barriers, and interpretations; rumors/grapevine; communication networks (formal and informal); nonverbal communication; communication load; methodologies for auditing communication effectiveness; symbolism and shared meaning systems; superior–subordinate communication and leadership; socialization; climate; productivity; participative decision-making; effectiveness and efficiency; rationality; control and coordination; innovation; and gender (mainly understood as sex differences).

The International Communication Association (ICA) Communication Audit was developed by the ICA Organizational Communication Division in the 1970s to integrate theory and practice by providing access to a normed data bank for comparisons across organizations and for testing theories. This comprehensive set of instruments measures organizational communication using a variety of respondents (supervisors, subordinates, and peers) and data collection methods (open- and closed-ended surveys, network measures, and interviews) to assess numerous communication variables, including need, load, network, and effectiveness. (For the history and impact of the ICA Audit, see Goldhaber, 2002.)

Structural-Functionalism

Structural-functionalism, a positivist form of systems theory, was dominant across the social sciences at the time (see Katz & Kahn, 1978). *Functionalism* assumes reality is external, simply received by humans. Functionalists assume organizations are unified by the pursuit of common goals through a cooperative system (Conrad & Sollitto, 2017). This linear, reductionist, variable-analytic tradition prevailed until it was challenged by interpretive and qualitative approaches in the early 1980s.

Systems Theory

By the 1980s, structural-functionalism had given way to interpretive applications of systems theory. Organizations were seen as less mechanical and more fluid as conceptions of both *communication* and *organization* evolved. As meaning-centered approaches took hold, a social constructivist view of communicators as *interpreters* supplanted conceptualizations of communicators as *receivers*. Systems theory allowed exploration of human interpretation as a social process.

The most fundamental systems theory assumption is the *organismic principle.* Organizations are seen as living organisms, rather than mechanical constructions. A *system* is a set of interconnected components with three defining characteristics. First, *hierarchical ordering*: systems are nested, existing inside and around other systems. A system contains subsystems, each of which contains sub-sub-systems. Likewise, a system exists within a larger supra-system, which is one component of an even larger supra-supra-system, and so on. Second, the system components are *interdependent*, the function of each relying upon the functions of others. Finally, systems differ in *permeability* or openness to their environment. Organizations are open systems, dependent on context and intersecting with multiple other systems, with varying degrees of permeability.

Systems are analyzed according to their environmental exchanges: *input-throughput-output*. *Input* is information introduced to a system. *Throughput* consists of actions taken on that input. *Output* places the result into the environment, creating input for another system. For example, a patient enters a U.S. hospital emergency department (ED) with chest pain. He and his symptoms are inputs. The ED's complex system acts on these inputs, accomplishing throughput by its established rules. A clerk records the patient's information and places the patient in queue. Triage nurses assess the patient's condition and assign the patient to a care priority, system rules dictating that his waiting period be determined relative to other patients' needs. He is then moved to a treatment room where care is provided. In each stage, input-throughput-output occurs in the sub-systems (registration, triage, care), the output of each becoming input for the next. Once placed into care, the system's standard procedures for monitoring and treatment are performed. When it is determined that he has not suffered a heart attack, he is transformed into *output* as he is discharged with a referral for follow-up care. He and his records become input to that other system.

Feedback is crucial to successful system operation. Negative feedback is corrective, reducing deviance from rules. If the referral doctor sees something the hospital missed, she can provide feedback resulting in an investigation that identifies faulty procedures. Positive feedback is progressive, amplifying deviation from rules to create new ones, allowing innovation and improvements. In this way, the quality of outputs reflects on, reinforces, and alters throughput processes.

Systems operate by four important principles. First, *nonsummativity* (holism): the system is not simply the sum of its component parts. The essence of the system emerges from interaction among those parts. Imagine that two people who yearn to eat chocolate cake assemble identical ingredients. One mixes the ingredients in a bowl, pours the batter into a pan, sets the pan in a hot oven for 30 minutes, allows it to cool, and enjoys a perfect slice. The other eats each ingredient separately, choking down flour, cocoa powder, baking powder, sugar, and salt, then washing it down with vegetable oil, eggs, and milk. While each consumed precisely the same ingredients, only one ate cake. The other consumed the parts of a cake. What makes a cake a cake? Not the ingredients themselves; a cake is a cake because of the way the ingredients interact with one another and are transformed by environmental factors (bowl, mixer, pan, and heat). The cake is a system; the sum of its ingredients is not.

Second, *equifinality* is defined as the achievement of similar outputs from varied processes. For example, organizations with different manufacturing processes can yield nearly identical competitive products. Third, *negative entropy* describes how openness/permeability maintains equilibrium. Closed systems decay; open systems counteract decay through exchanges with the environment. For example, the human body's inputs (nutrients, water, oxygen) and outputs (excretions of various sorts) sustain life by interaction with the environment.

Finally, *requisite variety* is the evolution of a system's internal complexities to match environmental complexity. As environments grow more complex, internal complexities evolve to process those inputs. For example, a store in a sparsely populated area with a culturally homogenous customer base maintains a narrower variety of products and services than a store with a dense and culturally diverse population. A successful system matches the variety demanded by its environment.

Organizational Communication Systems Theories

Systems theory is a perspective or approach to theorizing. Organizational communication systems theories include cybernetic systems theory and self-organizing systems theory.

CYBERNETIC SYSTEMS THEORY

Cybernetic systems theory examines how communication controls a system's processes to achieve its goals. In organizational studies, cybernetics applies to improving human performance at the individual and group level through information/feedback (provided by managers, customers, etc.). At the micro-level, communicating information about the outcomes of past activity leads to individual performance improvement, amplifying group performance. At the macro-level, feedback from the environment about the success or failure of strategies compels intensifying or changing them. The system is forced to adjust to maintain equilibrium (Lai & Lin, 2017).

SELF-ORGANIZING SYSTEMS THEORY

Self-organizing systems theory examines the emergence of system functions to meet equilibrium. Through *autopoiesis* (self-production), system components interact to recursively regenerate the processes that produced them (Contractor, 1994; Contractor & Seibold, 1993). We simply repeat what works. Norms evolve in response to changes in inputs or components, bringing system equilibrium manifesting in habits and expectations – for example, meetings on Wednesdays in Room 6. We even have routines (systems) for recurring personal tasks (e.g., laundry, showering, cooking, cleaning), but few people consciously design these task systems. Social systems theory (Luhmann, 1995; see Chapter 3) examines communication as the self-organizing mechanism. Communication processes are mutually influential and recursive, creating and maintaining system boundaries.

The 1980s and the Interpretive Turn

The 1980s saw great theoretical advancement in organizational communication. Systems theory flourished, especially in textbooks, due in part to Karl Weick, a social psychologist working in the field of management; his second edition of *The Social Psychology of Organizing* (1979) revolutionized Organizational Communication. Weick argued that *organization* was more verb than noun. His systems theory, *organizational information theory*, focuses on information management and complexity, addressing how organizations reduce uncertainty through information collection, use, and management. Weick proposed that organizing is accomplished collectively through communication. For scholars seeking to explicate organizational communication processes, these ideas were electrifying.

Second, with the introduction of interpretivism, scholars began to question structural-functionalist presumptions, such as the primacy of top-down communication and authority hierarchies. For example, organizational communication scholars and practitioners assumed clarity in communication was desired and practiced by effective organizational leaders and members. Eisenberg (1984), however, pointed out that ambiguity is often deliberate and used strategically to accomplish organizational and individual goals—only some of which are noble or for the common good. He advocated intensive study of *strategic ambiguity* employing naturalistic and critical methods to examine its purposes and effects, such as promoting unified diversity, facilitating change, and preserving positions of power. This revolutionary idea would not have been possible without the interpretive turn.

The paradigm shift rejected the objectivity of functionalism, advocating disciplined subjectivity as a source of knowledge and understanding. Systems theory set the tone for the paradigm shift to interpretivism in the early 1980s because while systems theory supports functionalist/positivist research, its social-constructivist assumptions also invite interpretive and qualitative analyses explicating meaning-creation.

At the 1981 *Summer Conference on Interpretive Approaches to the Study of Organizational Communication*, scholars debated the utility of interpretive approaches. Work from this conference launched *the interpretive turn* in Organizational Communication and was published in a special issue of the *Western Journal of Speech Communication* (Pacanowsky & Putnam, 1982), including an essay on the critical-interpretive approach (Deetz, 1982) and a taxonomy of paradigms (Putnam, 1982). Subsequently, an edited volume (Putnam & Pacanowsky, 1983), documented the interpretive turn with interpretive critiques of the mechanistic approach of functionalism and its inability to account for social process, meaning, and other nonlinear phenomena (Putnam, 1983).

Historical Roots of Interpretivism

Interpretivism is rooted in German Idealism, hermeneutics, phenomenology, and symbolic interactionism. 1600s Enlightenment philosophers favored rationality and empirical data. Later, *German Idealists* (particularly Immanuel Kant in the 1700s) reacted by privileging subjectivity, rejecting René Descartes' focus on rationality that underlies positivism/functionalism. Kantian philosophy re-emerged in the mid-19th century, with a renewed emphasis on understanding the subjective, the life world.

Hermeneutics emerged with humanism in the 15th century. Originally focused on sacred texts, modern hermeneutics embraced the study of literal and cultural texts. Human action, product, and expression are texts that can be understood only through consideration of that text's author, context, and situation, and through the researcher's theoretical knowledge. The goal of hermeneutic analysis is *embedded understanding* or subjective significance. Through the *hermeneutic circle*, interpretivists reject any distinction between the knower and the known. The hermeneutic circle develops understanding through a constant interchange among frames of reference (of both the observer and the observed): theory and scholarly knowledge, tacit knowledge (the taken-for-granted), actual textual data, and contextual/situational features.

Phenomenology, developed in the early 20th century, assumes knowledge exists in individual consciousness. Any meaning ascribed to an object or experience depends on the individual's consciousness of his/her background and current life. Phenomenologists assume experience of the world and development of meaning are accomplished through language. In a method referred to as *époche*, Husserl's classical phenomenology posits that subjective understanding is gained by transcendence—bracketing out attitudes (personal biases, histories, values, and interests) of the taken-for-granted life world. Later, Schutz's *social phenomenology* emphasized examination of *typifications* (similar to social rules) in social interaction. We organize typifications into complex bodies of cultural knowledge that social researchers can describe and understand.

Finally, *symbolic interactionism* underlies interpretivism. *Mind, Self, and Society* (Mead & Morris, 1934) delineates three central concepts. *Mind*, developed in interaction, is the ability to use symbols with common social meanings. Without social interaction, we cannot think; thought allows role-taking (seeing others' perspectives), from which *self* develops. We change selves based on feedback received from others (reflected appraisal or looking-glass self); we change to match expectations of others (Pygmalion self). The self is the *I* and the *me*. *I* is spontaneous and impulsive, whereas *me* is reflective, evaluative, and socially aware. *Society* is our web of social relationships: *particular others* (people we know personally) and *generalized others* (composite mental image of the community and its expectations). Symbolic interactionism assumes humans are active agents who respond to one another based on meanings created in interaction and modified through interpretive processes. Self-concept develops through interaction and provides motives for behavior. Individuals and groups are influenced by cultural and social processes created by social interaction.

Impact on Organizational Communication

The interpretivist perspective introduced qualitative and ethnographic research methods, inviting organizational communication scholars to explore meaning-creation and phenomena emerging from interaction. Interpretivism increased attention to social construction, expanding the field beyond its managerial, production, and business biases. Organizations began to be seen *as* cultures rather than *having* cultures (Pacanowsky & O'Donnell-Trujillo, 1982, 1983) and as communicative constructions rather than communication containers (Smith, 1993). Applications of structuration theory (see Chapter 3) entered the literature, initially in the study of group interaction. Ideas about organizations as social collectives (e.g., Hawes, 1974) were expanded. Though corporate settings remained the dominant research site, alternative kinds of organizations began to be studied (e.g., religious, social, and community organizations). Interest in supervisor–subordinate communication (see Chapter 17) and networks (see Chapter 9) continued, with more emphasis on relational aspects. Interest developed in examining intercultural communication and diversity. Studies of power took on a social-constructionist nature, while interest in nonverbal communication and structure declined (Allen et al., 1993). Examinations of gender increased, as did studies of organizational culture, organizing processes, systems, conflict, strategic ambiguity, technology, satisfaction, organizational rhetoric, and identification.

Weickian Theory

Weickian theory focuses on the intersection of organizing and communicating through *collective sensemaking*. *Sensemaking* is equivocality reduction and reality construction. The application of socially shared cognitive structures transforms the incomprehensible into the comprehensible. Together, active agents communicate to structure the unknown, making events *sensable* (able to be sensed/perceived) and *sensible* (able to be understood). Sensemaking is the social construction of cognitive frameworks and the application of those frameworks to equivocal stimuli. Sensemaking is driven by discrepancies between what we expect (assumptions/anticipations driven by cognitive frameworks) and what we encounter. "To engage in sensemaking is to construct, filter, frame, create facticity, and render the subjective into something more tangible" (Weick, 1995, p. 14). *Reality* is "an ongoing accomplishment" (p. 15) of sensemaking.

Properties of Sensemaking

Sensemaking has seven properties (Weick, 1995). First, *sensemaking is grounded in identity construction.* Identities are constituted in interaction (see Chapter 11). We discover ourselves by observing ourselves in interaction, shifting among self-definitions as we shift among interactants. We have multiple selves, with self and situation mutually defining. Three self needs impact sensemaking: self-enhancement (positive self-affect), self-efficacy (self-perception of competence), and self-consistency (coherence/continuity). We know which self to enact by observing others' behavior. The self that feels appropriate tells us what the situation means.

Second, *sensemaking is retrospective.* We attend to a stimulus after its occurrence, act then reflect. Unclear meaning of past events impedes current decision-making; we make judgments based on outcomes. Third, *sensemaking is enactive of sensible environments.* Literally, we *make* that which is *sensed.* Individual and social actions create material environments that become constraints and opportunities. This organizational environment created from interaction gets bracketed and punctuated, thus animated (made sensible). This socially created world constrains actions and orientations. Sensemaking leads to institutionalization (see Chapter 3).

Fourth, *sensemaking is social,* occurring through intersubjectivity and interaction. Even solitary actions are contingent upon others' actions. The meaning-making that is important is shared, not individual; the cognition we must attend to is *social cognition.* Collective coordinated action is key. Fifth, *sensemaking is ongoing.* It is an ontological presumption with no beginning or end. Intuition, the *feel* of things, guides constructions of ongoing flows (see Chapter 1).

Sixth, *sensemaking is focused on and by extracted cues.* Sense made is easier to see than sensemaking in action. Cues are extracted: noticed, attended to, and embellished (interpreted). Extracted cues are simple, familiar structures intertwined with context from which we develop a larger sense of what is happening. Context drives what is noticed and how it is interpreted/embellished; interpretation, in turn, becomes context. These are joined cognitively and become substantial (acted upon as real). Weick calls this *bracketing.* Extracted cues evoke action, which creates a material order in place of a presumed order. For example, a military unit lost in a snowstorm in the Alps maneuvered their way back using a map of the Pyrenees, mistakenly believed to be of the Alps. "Once people begin to act (enactment), they generate tangible outcomes (cues) in some context (social), and this helps them discover (retrospect) what is occurring (ongoing), what needs to be explained (plausibility), and what should be done next (identity enhancement)" (Weick, 1995, p. 55). Finally, *sensemaking is driven by plausibility rather than accuracy.* Once order, clarity, or rationality is felt, retrospective sensemaking stops. Cues continue to be extracted to enact a sensible/sensable environment and create the material reality allowing coordinated collective action. Sensemaking is about coherence and reasonableness, accounts that are socially acceptable and credible.

Weick's Organizational Information Theory

Weick (1979) explains organizing as a self-reflexive sequence of enactment, selection, and retention. In *enactment*, organizational members constitute their social environment through bracketing (acting on interpretations). In *selection*, they make sense of this enacted environment. In unequivocal information environments, sensemaking is accomplished through the application of assembly rules/recipes (pre-existing interpretive schemes). For equivocal information environments, communication cycles discover plausible understandings of the environment. In *retention*, successful interpretive schemes are stored for future use: *causal maps* that provide a link back to enactment and selection in earlier phases of the model.

Organizing (O_1) is an ongoing process reducing the equivocality perceived in important enactments. *Organizationality* (O_2) results from selection—what works is retained. Change is constant; *organizations* (O_3) are never permanently organized ($O_{1\&2}$). Organizations are characterized by *loose coupling*: segmented sub-units (sub-assemblies or sub-systems) provide stability. Though linked, each has its own identity and autonomy and maintains its own adaptations. Organizing is accomplished by *social cognition*. Complex tasks are achieved by *heedful interrelating*. Rather than merely repeating previous behaviors, individuals link their actions together heedfully (carefully, critically, consistently, purposefully, attentively, studiously, vigilantly, conscientiously, pertinaciously) (Weick & Roberts, 1993). *Organizational intelligence* is a set of complex patterns encoded by patterns of activation and inhibition among richly interpretively connected simple units, a process of collective mind. "This pattern of distributed representation explains the transindividual quality of collective mind. Portions of the envisaged system are known to all, but all of it is known to none" (Weick & Roberts, 1993, p. 365). For example, Weick and Roberts (1993) examined the complex set of organizational tasks that operate a military aircraft carrier.

> The men in the tower (Air Department) monitor and give instructions to incoming and departing aircraft. Simultaneously, the men on the landing signal officers' platform do the same thing. They are backed up by the men in Air Operations who monitor and instruct aircraft at some distance from the ship. From the aviator's viewpoint, he receives integrated information about his current status and future behavior from an integrated source when, in reality, the several sources are relatively independent of one another and located in different parts of the ship.
>
> (p. 362)

Weick's theories of organizing and sensemaking enable exploration of connections among individual-, group-, and organizational-level processes.

Organizational Communication as Cultural Performance

Pacanowsky and O'Donnell-Trujillo (1982, 1983) united micro- and macro-processes. Earlier approaches to organizational culture were prescriptive, teaching executives and managers how to impose effective cultures. For example, Deal and Kennedy's (1982) theory of cultural types, Peters and Waterman's (1982) treatise on excellence, and Schein's (1985) onion model examined cultural features of financially successful organizations with high morale, advising how to impose such cultures to foster the development of organizationally desirable values and norms. They were not embraced by communication scholars because of their values-engineering orientation.

Pacanowsky and O'Donnell-Trujillo (1982, 1983) focused on the ways organizational culture *is performed* in communication, reflecting and generating organizational culture, defining culture as an emergent, communication-centered, and naturally occurring interaction process. Cultural performances have four important features: *interactional* dialogues with multiple participants; *contextual*—situationally embedded in the very reality they bring to completion; *episodic*—nameable as distinct events (e.g., a budget meeting); and *improvisational*—loosely scripted. Through field observations in a variety of organizational contexts, Pacanowsky and O'Donnell-Trujillo (1982, 1983) illustrated five categories of cultural performance, each with numerous types, that display the culture's regularity and uniqueness: ritual, passion, sociality, politics, and enculturation.

The Late 1980s to 1990s: Critical, Naturalistic, and Postmodern Turns

During the critical turn, feminist (see Chapter 13) and race and difference theorizing flourished (see Chapter 14). Communicative constitution of organization (CCO) theories (see Chapter 3) began to appear. Other trends included teamwork, globalization, leadership, self-organizing systems, organizational democracy, stories, metaphors, gender, conflict, technology, identity, work–life balance, and ethics.

The interpretive turn ushered in *postmodernity* and a rejection of the received view. Postmodern theory rejects universal explanations, focusing on organizational realities as constituted by interaction, multiple truths "competing for legitimacy" (Mease, 2017, p. 5). Derrida, Lyotard, and Foucault had profound influence on organizational communication postmodern theory (see Mease, 2017).

Derrida's *deconstruction* is a method of analyzing text by examining meaning as it emerges *between* words and signs rather than *in* them. The meaning of a word or sign is neither static nor fully apprehended; it is found only in an infinite chain of reference to other words and signs. Words gain meaning through *différance*, or juxtaposition. No pair of words is free of a dominance hierarchy. Inverting the hierarchy of a pair (e.g., rationality/emotion to emotion/rationality) reveals the power structure. Lyotard's *master narratives* are broad social structures of meaning driving sensemaking in local communities. Mutual understanding of local communities according to their own, and not a foreign, narrative is the foundation of ethical interpretation.

Foucault's *history of the present* explores the relations between the present and the past, examining *historical moments* for their potential to create alternative desirable futures. Organizational communication scholars apply his ideas about discourse and power. Discourse, inherently characterized by tension and contradiction, constrains and enables sensemaking in ways that perpetuate power structures. Power is defined as knowledge because a society's powerful create its knowledge (reinforcing their power). Power, a group phenomenon, functions when created knowledge is accepted as truth. Yet, that knowledge generally serves the interests of the powerful.

Critical theory in organizational communication is rooted in important historical influences: Karl Marx and the Frankfurt School. Marx saw the world as humanly created, reified, and objectified. Marx argued that the modes and means of production (economic substructure) profoundly influence culture and politics (superstructure). The *bourgeoisie* control the substructure; the *proletariat* engage in production for wages. Substructure and superstructure processes create alienation and require critique.

The *Frankfurt School*, a community of neo-Marxist social theorists associated with the Institute for Social Research at Goethe University Frankfurt in the 1920s and 1930s, critiqued oppressive political systems (capitalist, fascist, communist), developed theory to explain the proliferation of postindustrial capitalist societies, and criticized Soviet socialism. They rejected positivism and determinism, emphasizing dialectic and contradiction as endemic to social reality. To develop alternative systems, they emphasized a *revolutionary praxis* that included the central concepts of totality, consciousness, alienation, and critique.

Fundamentals of Critical Organizational Communication Theory

Power became increasingly important throughout the 1980s as interpretivist examinations of organizational culture and identification made clear the struggle over meaning-creation between dominant and nondominant groups. Rhetorical theory and critical-interpretivism were ongoing in Organizational Communication from its inception, building to another paradigmatic turn in the early 1990s. The term *critical approach* refers to an "interdisciplinary body of theory and research that conceives of organizations as dynamic sites of control and resistance" (Mumby, 2008, p. 1). Critical theorists focus on day-to-day interaction, language use, and micro-practices to examine power and resistance (see Chapter 12). Organizations are viewed as political sites—socially constructed and communicatively accomplished, with deep societal structures of dominance reproduced in daily interaction.

Critical-interpretivists assume reality is co-created and use methods of disciplined subjectivity. They examine the ways dominant societal groups create realities that subjugate the realities of others. The most influential early critical organizational communication scholars were Deetz (1982, 1988) and Mumby (1987, 1988; Deetz & Mumby, 1990). Feminist theory furthered the development of critical theory in Organizational Communication (see Buzzanell, 1994, and Chapter 13), as did theorizing the democratization of work. For example, Cheney (1999) analyzed worker cooperatives that construct cooperative economies by reifying ideologies of participation to accomplish democratic organizing and subvert the hegemony of traditional bureaucracy.

Critical theories of organizational communication center on four concepts: ideology, hegemony, naturalization, and praxis. First, *ideology* structures and controls interpretations of reality, so assumptions are controlled by a dominant class without question. Second, *hegemony* captures the processes by which dominated group members consent to their domination by their own complicit engagement in political, cultural, and economic ideologies that enforce the class structure. Third, examining processes of *naturalization* reveals how these hierarchical power relationships are reified—made concrete through action and social practices and then accepted as normal and natural. Finally, *praxis* requires some action be taken to resist or reverse the hegemonic system and emancipate the dominated class, or at least some members of it, from its hold.

> Organizations, bureaucratic or otherwise, are (arbitrary) sociohistorical creations made to *seem* natural and normal through discourse; are the products of political actions that privilege some interests and sacrifice others; are a key resource for perpetuating sociopolitical power inequalities; and are replete with tensions and contradictions that create a potential for transformation, democratization, and emancipation.
>
> (Conrad & Sollitto, 2017, pp. 11–12, emphasis in original)

Previous approaches to organizational communication sought to represent aspects of the social world; critical theorists sought to move beyond representation to be active agents of reform and change.

Narrative and Ideology

Narrative is a meaning formation carrying dominant ideology and reproducing organizational power structures in everyday practice through storytelling (Mumby, 1987).

A political treatment of narrative focuses on the complex relationships among narrative, power, and ideology. Attention to the relationship between narrative structure and processes of interpretation focuses on the process by which dominant meaning systems arise. Narratives create a fit with the individual's world-as-experienced (i.e., naturalization). Narratives can also delegitimize dominant meaning systems. Critical-interpretive theory focuses on the dialectic of dominance and resistance (see Chapter 12). In critical analysis, power is both a medium and a product of structuring—a means of control. "At the heart of both domination and power lies the transformative capacity of human action" (Mumby, 1987, p. 117). Some organizational members are privileged with access to resources necessary to produce and reproduce certain relations of power. Ideology constructs consciousness (subjectivity) to articulate and legitimate certain forms of social reality. Ideology is the legitimized dominant system of reality that directs our recognition of what exists (reality), what is good (values), and what is possible (agency). "Ideology is materially grounded in the organized practices of social actors" (p. 119).

Narrative is a material social practice that produces, maintains, and reproduces ideological meaning formations. Narrative is a signifying system that articulates a social reality acceptable to organizational groups regardless of their position in the hierarchy. Ideology functions to represent sectional interests as universal, deny contradictions, naturalize the present through reification, and exert control through hegemony. Through *hegemony*, one class articulates the interests of others to its own, producing a *collective will* of submissive self-identification. Through active consent, the dominated are complicit in their domination. Organizational narrative can be viewed politically because it both sustains and subverts the logic of the power structure. Narratives do not simply inform; they constitute the organizational consciousness (create organizational rationality). Organizational narratives are produced by and reproduce ideological meaning formations and power relations. They express and reproduce the material conditions of the socioeconomic context.

The Influence of the Naturalistic Paradigm

Organizational Communication scholars have been heavily influenced by the *naturalistic paradigm* (e.g., Lincoln & Guba, 1985) and grounded theory (Glaser & Strauss, 1967), which require the study of things in their natural settings, interpreting phenomena according to the meanings people bring to them. *Grounded theory* builds theory inductively from naturalistic data. For example, *concertive control theory* (Barker, 1993) explains how organizational members, especially in self-managed teams, internalize organizational values and norms to self-discipline in increasingly oppressive ways (see Chapters 7, 11, and 12).

The naturalistic paradigm's influence on Organizational Communication is apparent in the *bona fide groups* perspective (Putnam & Stohl, 1990). Recognizing the importance of contextual factors on group and organizational communication, *bona fide groups* (or *groups-in-context*) recommends the study of naturally occurring (naturalistic) groups over those assembled for the purposes of research. *Bona fide groups* have unique characteristics essential to communication: shifting memberships, permeable boundaries, multiple group memberships, and high interdependence with these and other contextual features (Putnam & Stohl, 1990). Barker (1993) is an exemplar of the shift to naturalistic research settings across Organizational Communication.

Organizational Communication as Raced

Critical theorizing on race in Organizational Communication is contextualized by disciplinary and societal developments. First is the critical/naturalistic turn. Second, *Workforce 2000* (Johnston & Packer, 1987), an influential government report, emphasized the urgency of attending to a rapidly diversifying workforce. Third, Cornel West's (1993) *Race Matters* (reissued in 2017 with an introduction addressing current events), a classic treatise on race in America, energized academic pursuits and brought social science theory and analysis to the broader public. Critical theorizing on organizational communication and race was also contextualized by the literature on diversity, particularly as practiced in the U.S. corporate setting. By the early 2000s, thinking had matured to an understanding that the core issue is *difference* (Allen, 2004, 2011, 2023). *Diversity* is an abstract characteristic of an aggregate or organizational entity (O_3), too vague to facilitate theorizing about interaction (O_1) or structuring (O_2). *Difference*, however, focuses on persons and the ways culturally embedded characteristics and experiences influence organizing and organizationality. (See Chapter 14.) The critical turn was essential here because it provides a disciplined way to focus on lived experiences of power, domination, and culture.

Diversity "Management"

Diversity, *multiculturalism*, and similar terms trended in 1980s–1990s managerial theory and practice. Although the goal of harmonious diversity was voiced, diversity was implicitly treated as a potentially damaging force that must be neutralized—revealing embedded whiteness in meaning (see Chapters 1 and 4). Corporations were urged to attend to the diversity forced upon them by politics and circumstance to avoid disaster, not because of documented potential for performance (Cox, 1994), but to survive. Corporate executives were warned that ignoring diversity would set them "on a disastrous course" (Thomas & Woodruff, 1999, p. 225). This anxiety is reflected in management article titles, such as "Diversity Dilemmas at Work" (Bond & Pyle, 1998) or "Diversity and Performance: A Shotgun Marriage?" (Carr, 1993). Regardless of the content, much of which actually documented the benefits of a diverse workforce, such titles perpetuated the fear that diversity is dangerous.

The problem is that adding diversity to a list of *things to be managed* is embedded in neoliberal assumptions that reproduce whiteness and coloniality (see Chapters 1 and 4). Failing to consider cultural underpinnings of nondominant group members' viewpoints reifies the organizational norm as the primary/only legitimate organizational reality, dehumanizing the experience of marginalized groups (Kirby & Harter, 2003). When *othered* ways of thinking get driven underground, their potential to enrich organizational processes is lost. For example, Stohl (1997) documents a multitude of disruptions in organizational functioning prompted by poorly implemented diversity.

From a managerial viewpoint steeped in whiteness, disruptive forces must be eliminated to protect the organization. This view prompted diversity initiatives in the form of assimilationist/accommodationist models. Nondominant group members were expected to find ways of functioning without disrupting the status quo, thereby reproducing and entrenching whiteness as the only appropriate frame of reference – casting nondominant group members as *outsiders-within* (Collins, 1990) who are left responsible for fitting into organizational reality by relinquishing their cultures.

See Chapter 14 for a discussion of contemporary resistance to diversity, driven once again by fearmongering. This newest rejection of diversity is deeply politicized and propagates a false equivalency between whiteness and competence.

The Call to Study Race in Organizational Communication

Echoing Nkomo's (1992) observations, Allen (1995) observed a dearth of attention to race-ethnicity in Organizational Communication. She attributed this to the managerial bias, a scarcity of persons of color in managerial positions, erroneous assumptions among dominant group members that legislation had solved racism, and discomfort discussing race. Inaccurate presumptions among academics and practitioners left little opportunity to pursue the topic. Moreover, theorizing race was considered of interest only to scholars of color (Nkomo, 1992), but studying one's own group was seen as a biased endeavor, so scholars of color were advised against it (Cox, 1990). The scarce work available on communication and race (e.g., stereotyping, cultural norms, interracial communication) had little acknowledgment in Organizational Communication. Allen (1995) provides a thorough analysis of conceptual and methodological implications, recommending a critical approach to race that addresses the power and control dynamics implicated in racism. Her foundational essay is a cornerstone for studies of race and difference in Organizational Communication.

Co-Cultural Theory

Orbe's (1998a, 1998b) grounded theory offers data-rich descriptions of nondominant group members' experience negotiating their way through dominant-culture organizations. The term *co-cultural* (rather than *subcultural*) centers the marginalized experience. Co-cultural theory identifies nine co-cultural orientations, each associated with specific communication strategies, arising from the intersection of three communication approaches (non-assertive, assertive, aggressive) with three preferred outcomes (separation, accommodation, and assimilation). The strategies in each orientation are grave personal choices made by individuals, with difficulty and uncertainty, at considerable personal and/or professional risk. Co-cultural theory posits that the common experience of marginalization drives the regularity of these patterns across groups.

Personal Narrative as Critical Autoethnography

By the mid-1990s, *autoethnography* (autobiographical ethnography) had become an accepted methodological approach (Ellis et al., 2011). In a foundational work for theorizing race and communication, Allen et al.'s (1999) critical autobiographical analysis of marginalization in Organizational Communication gave voice to a common experience among scholars studying socially constructed aspects of identity, such as race, ethnicity, sexual orientation, age, and class. "We are attracted to a profession and discipline that inherently promises an openness to studying and teaching difference, yet more often than not falls short of this promise" (p. 403). Grounded in feminist standpoint theory (see Chapter 13), they analyze their e-mail exchanges to investigate their lived experiences as *outsiders within* academia. Their multiply reflexive analysis includes the process of writing and revising the article itself, as well as exchanges with the journal editor and an unblinded reviewer. They accomplish incisive critique of the academy, document their own healing and transformation, and construct an ontological framework of dialogic complexity from which they invite conversations to expand the transformative potential of such critical analysis.

Approaches to Communication and Organization

The period from Organizational Communication's 1960s birth to the turn of the century saw tremendous shifts in paradigm, with concomitant changes in how scholars approach communication and organization. While messages and meanings continued to be important, a more consistent underlying presumption of communication as constitutive was well developed by 2000. Early structural-functionalist theorizing cast organizations (O_3) as containers in which communication occurred, without much attention to the interplay between those processes (O_1) and the structuring of organization (O_2, O_3). With the advent of Weickian and interpretivist theory in the early 1980s, a process orientation became dominant. Critical theory then brought an era that examined structures (O_2) of domination, as well as illustrating the ways communication practices perpetuate those structures—revealing the communication-organization cycle in mutually reflexive form. By 2000, the idea that communication and organization constitute one another was uncontroversial. These developments also cultivated a foundation for current critiques of the discipline's whiteness and coloniality. (See Chapters 1 and 4.)

Recommended Supplementary Readings

Allen, B. J. (1995). "Diversity" and organizational communication. *Journal of Applied Communication Research*, *23*(2), 143–155.

An insightful critique of organizational diversity research with recommendations for theorizing race and organizational communication.

Allen, B. J., Orbe, M. P., & Olivas, M. R. (1999). The complexity of our tears: Dis/enchantment and (in)difference in the academy. *Communication Theory*, *9*(4). 402–429.

A trailblazing analysis of marginalization in the academy that opened opportunities for theorizing race and organizational communication.

Barker, J. R. (1993). Tightening the iron cage: Concertive control in self-managing teams. *Administrative Science Quarterly*, *38*(3), 408–437.

Analysis of this case study evolved to create concertive control theory. The study is a good example of how critical-interpretive research can bring unique insight to organizational communication in situ.

Martin, J., Feldman, M. S., Hatch, M. J., & Sitkin, S. B. (1983). The uniqueness paradox in organizational stories. *Administrative Science Quarterly*, *28*(3), 438–453.
Mumby, D. K. (1987). The political function of narrative in organizations. *Communication Monographs*, *54*(2), 113–127.

These articles can be read as companion pieces. Martin et al. *is an interpretation of the IBM story, and Mumby re-examines the analysis with critical theory. Reading them together reveals the power of a critical lens.*

Orbe, M. (1998a). An outsider within perspective to organizational communication: Explicating communicative practices of co-cultural group members. *Management Communication Quarterly*, *12*, 230–279.

An exemplar of grounded theory, this analysis reveals that the experience of marginalization and communicative responses to it are driven by organizational structures rather than cultural or personal identities.

Pacanowsky, M. E., & O'Donnell-Trujillo, N. (1983). Organizational communication as cultural performance. *Communication Monographs*, *50*(1), 126–147.

Representing one of the earliest programs of interpretive research in organizational communication, this article is a perfect example of using data to derive theory. The excerpts of data provided are compelling and interesting.

Putnam, L. L. (1982). Paradigms for organizational communication research: An overview and synthesis. *Western Journal of Speech Communication*, *46*(2), 192–206.

In this early explanation of the distinctions among theoretical paradigms, Putnam clearly explains the underlying dimensions differentiating positivism/functionalism, interpretivism, and critical-interpretivism.

Putnam, L. L. (1983). The interpretive perspective: An alternative to functionalism. In L. L. Putnam & M. Pacanowsky (Eds.), *Communication and organizations: An interpretive approach* (pp. 31–54). Sage.

Traditionally used as a first reading on interpretivism, this chapter clearly lays out the problems posed by functionalism and the ways an interpretive approach provides conceptual advantages.

Weick, K. E. (1993). The collapse of sensemaking in organizations: The Mann Gulch disaster. *Administrative Science Quarterly*, *38*(4), 628–652.

One of many case studies written by Weick, this analyzes sensemaking and organizational decision-making during the Mann Gulch fire disaster, resulting in wide-scale loss of life among the firefighters. Weick examines the disintegration of role structure and sensemaking and discusses resilience that makes groups less vulnerable.

Important Concepts: Define and Discuss

Critical-interpretivism
Hegemony
Ideology
Interpretivism and its roots
Naturalistic paradigm
Naturalization
Organizational communication as cultural performance
Positivism
Postmodernism
Praxis
Racial foundations of organizational communication
Sensemaking

Structural functionalism
Systems theory principles
Variable-analytic research

Discussion Questions

1 Consider the paradigmatic shifts in the field from 1970 to 2000. Can you identify shifts in society and organizational phenomena that may be connected?
2 Identify an organizational system and give examples of its properties (nonsummativity, equifinality, openness, etc.).
3 Think of a time when you and coworkers were faced with a new or confusing situation. Apply Weick's theory of sensemaking to your subsequent interactions. Can you identify the enactment–selection–retention cycle?
4 How is critical theory in organizational communication an expansion of interpretivism?
5 Discuss the socio-political and disciplinary contexts that facilitated the advent of theorizing race and organizational communication.

Practitioners' Corner

It falls to a communication professional to figure out how to strategically communicate within and among groups, and how to guide that group in its communication strategy to external stakeholders. Perhaps the most important body of theory in this chapter for the communication practitioner is Weick's theory of organization. Communication professionals are often tasked with designing strategies that meet the need for stakeholders to act in concert in a context of equivocal environments and diverse views of the problems at hand.

All organizational action depends on processes of social sensemaking. Communication professionals are positioned to facilitate processes of problem analysis and solution-creation engaging Weickian concepts. Through a purposeful process explicitly guiding a group through dialogue that explicates the seven properties of sensemaking, a skilled facilitator can provide opportunities for mutual understanding. As you will learn in Chapter 15, thorough problem analysis is a crucial function for group problem-solving. Working relationships and organizational resilience improve when mutual understandings are achieved. A good understanding of Weickian theory and how to apply it is of great utility for a communication practitioner. Reading Weickian case studies (e.g., the 1993 Mann Gulch article in the Recommended Supplementary Readings list) is highly recommended. While sensemaking is retrospective, a purposeful sensemaking process that actively engages Weickian concepts provides organizational learning to prevent repetition of mistakes and improve organizational resilience.

For example, imagine you work as a communication director for a financial services organization. You are tasked with leading both internal and external communication. The company is about to launch a new online dashboard for its clients that will allow easier access to account information and more immediate customer-initiated changes to accounts. Just as the product is to be launched, a new federal regulation for data security is announced that will fundamentally alter the product and inevitably delay the rollout, as a redesign would be necessary to make the product compliant with the new law. No one expected the bill to be passed. The teaser advertising has already been made public, and customer service representatives have promised the opportunity to existing customers. The product is particularly attractive to high-balance accountholders, some of whom have previously expressed frustration about the existing online portal. Your management team fears they will lose their most valuable customers as a result of any delay. The team responsible for regulatory compliance is scratching their heads about how to provide the ease offered to the clients while maintaining compliance with the new regulation. You have been tasked with assigning people on your team to bring internal stakeholders to the table to discuss the problem and assign others to design an external communication strategy.

Let's examine the external communication problem first. Like all organizational crises, the stakes are high for the organization's PR team. Yet, from a Weickian perspective, the external communication demands are unequivocal. While the situation itself is fraught with ambiguity, how to communicate about it to clients is not. First, the communication problem is straightforward: customers will be disappointed in the delay and potential cancellation of the product. Potential customers may be scared away. Second, the consequences are clear: a good strategy will keep customers and attract new ones. Third, and most importantly, sound principles for such communication are standard in the field—this is not a new kind of problem. These principles, embedded in PR practice, exist as Weickian causal maps. Knowing this, you assign people from your team who are well versed in communicating unexpected and unwanted change to clients and who are well versed in marketing to attract new business. Employing assembly rules, you select individuals who have performed well on such tasks in the past. These individuals will follow proven principles, informing customers of a delay, communicating the situation as it evolves, and delivering advertising sensitive to this crisis. Depending on the outcome, your strategy will either perpetuate those causal maps or create new ones through naturally occurring processes of retrospective sensemaking.

The internal problem-solving here is another story. This is an equivocal information environment. Do the new requirements actually protect data security? Is it possible to alter the product to be compliant, or is there too much contradiction between customer freedom and data control? Will the new law be enforced or challenged? Should we just cancel the project? Should we delay to see how things play out? Should we work on alteration of the product?

The various internal stakeholder groups will naturally employ communication cycles to discover plausible understandings of the environment. Data security programmers are immobile—caught up in complaining to one another about the stupidity of the regulations enacted by "dinosaurs who don't know how the Internet actually works." The client relations team is divided—some want something to deliver to clients to keep them, while others point out that the company's competitors whose existing online portals are suddenly noncompliant have much larger problems and won't attract customers away. The legal team is convinced the law will be challenged successfully by competitors whose online portals were used as benchmarks in the design process. The web designers have jumped the gun and are already working on changing the dashboard's access protocols to get ahead of the competition—poorly, because they are not communicating with the data security programmers.

Your task is to get these groups communicating thoughtfully with one another in a purposeful process of sensemaking to arrive at the most plausible understanding of the current status and where to go from there. Let's examine the seven properties of sensemaking and how they are playing out here.

- *Sensemaking is grounded in identity construction.* Each of these groups is engaging in identity-based sensemaking, rooted in their self-preservation and revealing the cultures of their various professions.
- *Sensemaking is retrospective.* All are trying to get their heads around, in different ways, the unexpected turn of events.

- *Sensemaking is enactive of sensible environments.* All are trying to make sense of what comes next.
- *Sensemaking is social.* Everything is taking place through conversations within the groups. Your challenge is to create an opportunity for dialogue among the groups.
- *Sensemaking is ongoing.* No matter what you do, people will continue in their own sensemaking processes. A facilitated dialogue with a focus on mutual goals can provide far better decision-making capability.
- *Sensemaking is focused on and by extracted cues.* Each group is focusing on different cues unique to their interests and expertise. A dialogue among them brings information about cues they hadn't extracted, changing their overall understanding.
- *Sensemaking is driven by plausibility rather than accuracy.* In the end, the strategy enacted will be that which makes the most sense to the decision-makers at the executive level—regardless of what any individual stakeholder group feels is best. Your challenge is to unearth all the potentially plausible solutions from an open dialogue.

Processes of Weickian *enactment* fill information gaps, provide opportunities for learning, and improve organizational resilience. When a decision is made based on *selection* of the most plausible sense made, whatever happens is preserved in the organizational causal map (*retention*) to provide interpretive schemes and assembly rules evoked by similar occurrences in the future.

References

Allen, B. J. (1995). "Diversity" and organizational communication. *Journal of Applied Communication Research*, *23*(2), 143–155. https://doi.org/10.1080/00909889509365420

Allen, B. J. (2004). *Difference matters* (1st ed.). Waveland Press.

Allen, B. J. (2011). *Difference matters* (2nd ed.). Waveland Press.

Allen, B. J. (2023). *Difference matters* (3rd ed.). Waveland Press.

Allen, B. J., Orbe, M. P., & Olivas, M. R. (1999). The complexity of our tears: Dis/enchantment and (in)difference in the academy. *Communication Theory*, *9*(4), 402–429. https://doi.org/10.1111/j.1468-2885.1999.tb00206.x

Allen, M. W., Gotcher, J. M., & Seibert, J. H. (1993). A decade of organizational communication research: Journal articles 1980–1991. *Annals of the International Communication Association*, *16*(1), 252–330. https://doi.org/10.1080/23808985.1993.11678856

Barker, J. R. (1993). Tightening the iron cage: Concertive control in self-managing teams. *Administrative Science Quarterly*, *38*(3), 408–437. https://doi.org/10.2307/2393374

Bond, M. A., & Pyle, J. L. (1998). Diversity dilemmas at work. *Journal of Management Inquiry*, 7(3), 252–269. https://doi.org/10.1177/105649269873007

Buzzanell, P. M. (1994). Gaining a voice: Feminist organizational communication theorizing. *Management Communication Quarterly*, 7(4), 339–383. https://doi.org/10.1177/0893318994007004001

Carr, C. (1993). Diversity and performance: A shotgun marriage? *Performance Improvement Quarterly*, 6(4), 115–126. https://doi.org/10.1111/j.1937-8327.1993.tb00608.x

Cheney, G. (1999). *Values at work: Employee participation meets market pressure at Mondragón.* Cornell University Press.

Collins, P. (1990). *Black feminist thought: Knowledge, consciousness, and the politics of empowerment.* Unwin Hyman.

Conrad, C., & Sollitto, M. (2017). History of organizational communication. In C. R. Scott & L. Lewis (Eds.), *The international encyclopedia of organizational communication* (online edition). Wiley-Blackwell. https://doi.org/10.1002/9781118955567.wbieoc097

Contractor, N. S. (1994). Self-organizing systems perspective in the study of organizational communication. In B. Kovacic (Ed.), *New approaches to organizational communication* (pp. 39–66). State University of New York Press.

Contractor, N. S., & Seibold, D. R. (1993). Theoretical frameworks for the study of structuring processes in group decision support systems. *Human Communication Research*, *19*(4), 528–563. https://doi.org/10.1111/j.1468-2958.1993.tb00312.x

Cox, T. H. (1990). Problems with research by organizational scholars on issues of race and ethnicity. *The Journal of Applied Behavioral Science*, *26*(1), 5–23. https://doi.org/10.1177/002188639002600103

Cox, T. H. (1994). *Cultural diversity in organizations*. Barrett-Koehler.

Deal, T. E., & Kennedy, A. A. (1982). *Corporate cultures: The rites and rituals of corporate life*. Addison Wesley.

Deetz, S. (1982). Critical interpretive research in organizational communication. *Western Journal of Speech Communication*, *46*(2), 131–149. https://doi.org/10.1080/10570318209374073

Deetz, S. (1988). Cultural studies: Studying meaning and action in organizations. In J. Anderson (Ed.), *Communication yearbook 11* (pp. 335–345). Sage.

Deetz, S., & Mumby, D. K. (1990). Power, discourse, & the workplace: Reclaiming the critical tradition. In J. Anderson (Ed.), *Communication yearbook 13* (pp. 18–47). Sage.

Eisenberg, E. M. (1984). Ambiguity as strategy in organizational communication. *Communication Monographs*, *51*(3), 227–242. https://doi.org/10.1080/03637758409390197

Ellis, C., Adams, T. E., & Bochner, A. P. (2011). Autoethnography: An overview. *Historical Social Research*, *36*(4), 273–290. https://www.jstor.org/stable/23032294

Glaser, B. G., & Strauss, A. L. (1967). *The discovery of grounded theory: Strategies for qualitative research*. Aldine.

Goldhaber, G. M. (2002). Communication audits in the age of the internet. *Management Communication Quarterly*, *15*(3), 451–457. https://doi.org/10.1177/0893318902153007

Hawes, L. C. (1974). Social collectivities as communication: Perspective on organizational behavior. *Quarterly Journal of Speech*, *60*, 497–502. https://doi.org/10.1080/00335637409383259

Johnston, W. B., & Packer, A. H. (1987). *Workforce 2000: Work and workers in the 21st century*. Hudson Institute.

Katz, D., & Kahn, R. (1978). *The social psychology of organizations* (2nd ed.). John Wiley.

Kirby, E. L., & Harter, L. M. (2003). Speaking the language of the bottom-line: The metaphor of "managing diversity." *Journal of Business Communication*, *40*(1), 28–49. https://doi.org/10.1177/002194360304000103

Lai, C., & Lin, S. H. (2017). Systems theory. In C.R. Scott & L. Lewis (Eds.), *The international encyclopedia of organizational communication* (online edition). Wiley-Blackwell. https://doi.org/10.1002/9781118955567.wbieoc203

Lincoln, Y. S., & Guba, E. G. (1985). *Naturalistic inquiry*. Sage.

Luhmann, N. (1995). *Social systems*. Stanford University Press.

Mead, G. H., & Morris, C. W. (1934). *Mind, self & society from the standpoint of a social behaviorist*. University of Chicago Press.

Mease, J. J. (2017). Postmodern/poststructural approaches. In C.R. Scott & L. Lewis (Eds.), *The international encyclopedia of organizational communication* (online edition). Wiley-Blackwell. https://doi.org/10.1002/9781118955567.wbieoc167

Mumby, D. K. (1987). The political function of narrative in organizations. *Communication Monographs*, *54*(2), 113–127. https://doi.org/10.1080/03637758709390221

Mumby, D. K. (1988). *Communication and power in organizations: Discourse, ideology, and domination*. Ablex.

Mumby, D. K. (2008). Organizational communication: Critical approaches. In W. Donsbach (Ed.), *International encyclopedia of communication* (online edition). Wiley-Blackwell. https://doi.org/10.1002/9781405186407.wbieco019

Nkomo, S. M. (1992). The emperor has no clothes: Rewriting "race in organizations." *Academy of Management Review*, *17*(3), 487–513. https://doi.org/10.2307/258720

Orbe, M. (1998a). An outsider within perspective to organizational communication: Explicating communicative practices of co-cultural group members. *Management Communication Quarterly*, *12*, 230–279. https://doi.org/10.1177/0893318998122003

Orbe, M. (1998b). *Constructing co-cultural theory*. Sage.

Pacanowsky, M. E., & O'Donnell-Trujillo, N. (1982). Communication and organizational cultures. *Western Journal of Speech Communication*, *46*(1), 115–130. https://doi.org/10.1080/10570318209374072

Pacanowsky, M. E., & O'Donnell-Trujillo, N. (1983). Organizational communication as cultural performance. *Communication Monographs*, *50*(1), 126–147. https://doi.org/10.1080/03637758309390158
Pacanowsky, M. E., & Putnam, L. L. (Eds.) (1982). Interpretive approaches to the study of organizational communication. *Western Journal of Speech Communication*, *46*(2), 114–207. https://doi.org/10.1080/10570318209374071
Peters, T. J., & Waterman, R. H. (1982). *In search of excellence: Lessons from America's best-run companies*. Harper & Row.
Putnam, L. L. (1982). Paradigms for organizational communication research: An overview and synthesis. *Western Journal of Speech Communication*, *46*(2), 192–206. https://doi.org/10.1080/10570318209374077
Putnam, L. L. (1983). The interpretive perspective: An alternative to functionalism. In L. L. Putnam & M. E. Pacanowsky (Eds.), *Communication and organizations: An interpretive approach* (pp. 31–54). Sage.
Putnam, L. L., & Pacanowsky, M. E. (Eds.) (1983). *Communication and organizations: An interpretive approach*. Sage.
Putnam, L. L., & Stohl, C. (1990). Bona fide groups: A reconceptualization of groups in context. *Communication Studies*, *41*(3), 248–265. https://doi.org/10.1080/10510979009368307
Schein, E. H. (1985). *Organizational culture and leadership*. Jossey-Bass.
Smith, R. C. (1993). *Images of organizational communication: Root-metaphors of the organization-communication relation*. Paper presented to the Organizational Communication Division at the International Communication Association Convention, Washington, D.C.
Stohl, C. (1997). *Organizational communication: Connectedness in action*. Sage.
Thomas, R., & Woodruff, M. (1999). *Building a house for diversity: How a fable about a giraffe and an elephant offers new strategies for today's workforce*. American Management Association.
Weick, K. E. (1979). *The social psychology of organizing* (2nd ed.). Addison-Wesley.
Weick, K. E. (1995). *Sensemaking in organizations*. Sage.
Weick, K. E., & Roberts, K. H. (1993). Collective mind in organizations: Heedful interrelating on flight decks. *Administrative Science Quarterly*, *38*(3), 357–381. https://doi.org/10.2307/2393372
West, C. (1993). *Race matters*. Vintage Books.

3 Developments in the 21st Century

Anne M. Nicotera

This chapter provides an overview of developments in the field from the late 1990s to the present. The 21st century is marked by increasing interdisciplinarity; the discursive turn; the maturation of structurational and communicative constitution of organization (CCO) approaches; institutional theory; postcolonial theory; and a recent decolonial turn (see Chapter 4). In this contemporary period, all three conceptual expressions of organization (O_1, O_2, O_3) are explicitly present in organizational communication theorizing.

At the turn of the century, disciplinary self-reflection brought paradigmatic pluralism. Debates were put aside in favor of appreciating the relative advantages of the traditional paradigms (e.g., Corman & Poole, 2000). The literature became more integrated, as scholars increasingly relied on research generated by paradigms other than their own. Perspective became project-based, rather than a career choice. Scholars began to appropriate concepts and techniques from one perspective to another, as well as to combine the perspectives in their research programs and in multi-methodological projects.

Organizational Communication scholars have become increasingly involved with scholars from other disciplines, such as management, sociology, organizational behavior, organizational theory, and industrial psychology, through participation in conferences, professional associations (e.g., the European Group on Organizational Studies), and multidisciplinary journals (e.g., *Organization Studies*). Due to this interdisciplinary growth, structuration and CCO have flourished. (See below for details on these traditions.) This era has seen growing interest in research and theoretical development in the following topics and concepts: paradox, restructuring, institutions, terrorism, virtual organizing, framing, alternative organizations, difference, corporate social responsibility, wellness, work–life balance, spirituality, leadership, feminist organizing, ecological perspectives, participation, and democracy.

After 2010, in addition to theoretic advancements, important popular research topics include materiality, agency, bullying, knowledge management, health organizing (especially in the context of the COVID-19 crisis), relationship management, organizational justice, and race. Following anti-racism efforts (see Chapter 1), the racial foundations of the field have become apparent. Valiavska et al. (2023) review the study of race across communication journals from 2010 to 2020. A special issue of the *Journal of Applied Communication Research* (Orbe et al., 2022) theorizes communication as a raced practice across several contexts. In Organizational Communication, specifically, the racist National Communication Association (NCA) panel incident (see Chapter 1), in the context of broader societal racial crises, propelled organizational communication scholars in the 2020s to deeply examine the underpinnings of colonial legacies in our academic and scholarly pursuits (see Chapter 4). This stimulated our current decolonial turn. Organizational communication's discursive turn laid the groundwork for this contemporary theorizing.

DOI: 10.4324/9781003484639-4

The Discursive Turn

Perhaps the most important development of the early 2000s, the dawn of discourse studies parallels a linguistic turn across the social sciences. *Discourse* is difficult to define, but scholars are consistent in assumptions that discourse involves the production, use, processes, and consequences of language from the situated context of interaction to the broader enduring level of social thought and ideology. A discursive approach to organizational communication can examine *language itself*, examining meaning-making as a linguistic process with contradictions and hidden implications (O_1); *language-in-use*, studying language in everyday interactions to examine meaning-creation and reproduction of cultural structures (O_2); or the production of *texts* (O_3), with particular attention to research itself (Connaughton et al., 2017). Discourse is assumed to produce reality, social structures, and collectives (organizations).

Early organizational communication discourse theory had a distinct O_3 bias, explicating organizations as discursive constructions from three orientations: organizations as *objects* reflected in discourse; organizations in perpetual states of *becoming*; or organizations as grounded in *action*. Discourse, a medium for social interaction, maintains a language emphasis distinguishing it from *communication*. *Discourse* refers to talk and social texts and to enduring systems of thought. As a common shorthand, lower-case "d" *discourse* denotes activity, whereas upper-case "D" *Discourse(s)* is an enduring set of broad social structures and processes (Fairhurst & Putnam, 2004).

An *organization as object* (O_3) orientation casts the organization as stable and pre-existing, with discursive features or outcomes (artifacts). D/discourse is produced by and reflective of organization. This brings an implicit container metaphor, a focus on the product rather than the process of social construction, and a materialist reification of the organization as entity. The *organization as becoming* (O_1) orientation foregrounds agency, but loses a clear understanding of structure, explicitly focusing on discourse as constitutive of organizing. "The becoming perspective not only treats discourse as language in use but it also focuses on Discourses that reside in power/knowledge systems" (Fairhurst & Putnam, 2004, p. 14). Yet, this orientation fragments and obscures the whole. Enduring structures are underemphasized, a clear view of them lost.

An *organization as grounded in action* (O_2) orientation "treats action and structure as mutually constitutive" (Fairhurst & Putnam, 2004, p. 16). Language-in-use is privileged as the most powerful explanation of the relationship between discourse and Discourse(s). "The 'organization' emerges from associations among human actors and objects whose institutional origins carry the traces of past organizing" (p. 18). Human agency is conceived "from within … an active component of structure" (p. 19), with a focus on the emergence of structure, although many scholars privilege action over structure as they focus on social practice and language-in-use. This episodic view of social practice may obscure patterns across episodes (Fairhurst & Putnam, 2004). See Putnam and Fairhurst (2015) for a discussion of these three orientations' connections with CCO.

Paradox Theory

Traditionally, organizational communication researchers treated contradictions and tensions as anomalies needing correction. Critical and discursive approaches created a different approach. Rather than disruptive irregularities, contradictions and paradoxes are seen as normal conditions providing opportunities for growth and progress. For example, Stohl and Cheney's (2001) taxonomy of paradoxes generated by employee participation programs illustrates several hallmarks of 21st-century organizational communication theory. First, it relies on a discursive understanding of organization. Second, it derives theory inductively and critically (see Chapter 2). Third, it rests on a constitutive understanding of the mutually enabling and constraining relationship between communication and organization (see Figure 1.2, Chapter 1). Finally, it illustrates the field's evolution to a view of contradiction as normal and natural, even as it can also be troublesome.

Scholars have examined discursive processes through which contradictions are constructed and managed. Fairhurst and Putnam (2024) provide an organizational communication metatheory of paradox from a constitutive and discourse perspective, conceptualizing *paradox as communicatively performed*. They identify *dialectic* as the "generative motor" (p. 19) that, along with tensions and contradictions, constitutes paradox. A *dialectic* is a unity of opposites – seemingly contradictory forces (needs, goals, drives, etc.) that naturally and necessarily coexist (e.g., connection/autonomy; openness/closeness). Dialectic theory was introduced to communication studies through applications to personal relationships (Baxter, 1988; Montgomery, 1988). Dialectical theory has been applied in organizational communication to work–life balance; power and resistance; intercultural competence; identity negotiation; image management; conflict management; occupational tensions; and community development. (See Ballard-Reisch & Turner, 2017. See Chapter 20 for a discussion of dialectical tensions in globalization.) The broader concept *paradox* gained more traction among organizational communication scholars, spawning a large interdisciplinary literature. Fairhurst and Putnam's (2024) review of paradox scholarship across disciplines includes a discussion of their constitutive discursive approach.

Structuration Theory

Structuration theory is a sociological explanation for the ways daily social practices produce and reproduce deep structures of meaning (societal, institutional, organizational). Meaning structures provide knowledge so we know how to make sense of daily interaction and act appropriately. Social actions are constrained, to some extent dictated, by these structures but can also change structures and create new ones. Giddens (1979, 1984) introduced structuration theory in sociology to account for both human choice and social constraint. Communication scholars initially introduced structuration theory to group decision-making (Poole et al., 1985, 1986). Applications to organizational communication have continued to grow.

Structuration is the process by which social structures are produced and reproduced in social practice, structure being both the *medium* and *outcome* of interaction – the *duality of structure* (Giddens, 1984). Social structures are conceptualized as culturally based repositories of meaning, unobservable rules and resources that generate *systems*, which are defined as observable patterns of behavior (Giddens, 1979, 1984; Poole et al., 1985, 1986). Structuration theory posits that people act/interact coherently based on meaning provided by institutionalized structures and that those interactions, in turn, produce and reproduce structures. The communication-organization cycle guiding this text (see Figure 1.2, Chapter 1) is based on structuration theory.

Rules and Resources

Structure consists of "rules and resources, recursively implicated in the reproduction of social systems" (Giddens, 1984, p. 377). *Rules* tell us what things mean and how to act

(Sewell, 1992). *Resources*, which allow us to act, are authoritative and allocative (command over persons and objects); human (intelligence, strength, knowledge) and non-human (tools, documents); material (buildings, land, supplies, equipment) and non-material (regulations, tax codes, influential relationships) (Giddens, 1979). All humans have the capacity to act, but knowledge of rules and access to resources empower individuals differentially. *Agency* – the human capacity to act on the world – is a central concept. Rules tell us how to act, and resources allow us to do so. "To be an agent means to be capable of exerting some degree of control over the social relations in which one is enmeshed, which in turn implies the ability to transform those social relations" (Sewell, 1992, p. 20). *Doing* anything rests on agency provided by rules/resources. Agency is empowerment to act meaningfully. Power is the transformative capacity to change the social and material world (Giddens, 1987). Agency arises from knowledge of structure; recursively, structures arise from agency (ability to act and apply knowledge to new contexts) (Sewell, 1992).

Systems are recurrent interlocked social practices resulting from the application of rules and resources. This *duality of structure* means that structures shape the social practices that then recursively constitute those structures. The production and reproduction of structures in social practice is the heart of structuration. *Structure* also refers to "properties allowing the 'binding' of time-space in social systems, the properties which make it possible for discernibly similar social practices to exist across varying spans of time and space and which lend them 'systemic' form" (Giddens, 1984, p. 17). Rules, intertwined with resources, are "the modes whereby transformative relations are actually incorporated into the production and reproduction of social practices" (Giddens, 1984, p. 18). Rules constitute meaning and sanction modes of social conduct. Action produces, reproduces, and transforms structures in a continuous cycle. The interplay of O_1, O_2, and O_3 is clear in this set of constructs.

Modalities of Meaning

Giddens (1984) identifies three structural modalities, *signification, legitimation*, and *domination*, which allow us to act by assigning three kinds of meaning to every act/utterance. We assign denotative meaning to the act (signification), judge its appropriateness (legitimation), and ascertain our places in a hierarchy of power (dominance). In structuration theory, meaning is always plural; the three modalities function simultaneously. For example, raising a hand in a classroom means the student is asking permission to speak, reproducing a signification recognized by members of a particular culture. It also reproduces rules of legitimation, dictating for whom it is appropriate to speak and how they should do so. The reactions of others inform whether audience interaction is appropriate and whether permission to speak is granted. Finally, this action reproduces rules of dominance – who may speak without such permission.

If we invoke a structure that does not fit the rules of the context, we quickly learn our actions are inappropriate and must be adjusted to achieve meaningful interaction, for example in a cultural context where hand-raising has no common signification, where students do not speak in class, or where attempting to do so is considered insubordinate. Moreover, a group may create their own rules – such as in a small seminar where the instructor invites students to speak up in an egalitarian discussion, rather than wait to be called upon. New students joining the group quickly learn the structure by observing the social practice of speaking up as it reproduces the egalitarian rule for interaction. This example also illustrates the reproduction of dominance in the transformation of structure – the instructor retains the power to reinforce the existing structure or allow the new one. The dominance hierarchy remains undisturbed in this situation even as a structure for that specific setting is produced. Also, note that rules for legitimation remain in place in the form of politeness norms for discussion, such as turn-taking. Giddens' three modalities provide agency, as the group can smoothly interact to reproduce old structures, transform structures, and produce new ones, meeting their shared and individual goals. Structure is the socially shared or common meanings in these modalities that allow the exercise of agency to re/produce and transform structure. Structure is composed of common understandings of signification, legitimation, and dominance that provide coherence to interaction and power to produce, reproduce, and transform those very structures. The exercise of agency (and power) relies on knowledge of structure.

Structurational Organizational Communication Theories

Structuration theory is widely accepted in Organizational Communication. The idea that daily actions and interactions are enabled and constrained by social structures, and that those daily practices enable and constrain structures as they emerge and transform, is uncontroversial. Several scholars have developed organizational communication theories based on and extending structuration theory. The three most prominent are adaptive structuration theory (AST); structurating activity theory (SAT); and structurational divergence theory (SDT).

Adaptive Structuration Theory (AST)

AST explains the use of technology in small group decision-making, positing that group members intentionally adapt rules and resources as they interact through and with technology in ways that transform and create structures (DeSanctis & Poole, 1994; Poole & DeSanctis, 1990). AST challenged technological determinism – the presumption that technology itself causes organizational change. Technological systems have structures of their own and are embedded in institutional structures; AST explains that human interaction with and through technology drives organizational change through the process of social construction. Technological and institutional structures (rules and resources) provide capabilities, accompanied by an underlying intent, or *spirit*, for their use (DeSanctis & Poole, 1994). Advanced information technologies (AITs) provide structures with varying spirit and structural features, encouraging different forms of interaction. AIT use varies by task, environment, and other contingencies that offer alternative sources of social structures. New structures emerge as technology, task, and environmental structures are applied and an AIT's rules and resources are appropriated and reproduced. Group decision processes vary depending on these appropriations, the nature of which varies according to the group's internal system. Desired outcomes of AIT use result from appropriation and decision processes that fit the task at hand (DeSanctis & Poole, 1994). AST emphasizes the importance of social interaction in the application of technology, providing empirical evidence to challenge the techno-centric view of technology use. AST research illustrates that the impact of technology on group outcomes is heavily mediated by social practices and human interactions drawing from numerous other social and institutional structures.

Structurating Activity Theory (SAT)

SAT extends structuration theory to the construction of policy knowledge (Canary, 2010). SAT combines structuration theory with cultural-historical activity theory (CHAT).

CHAT is grounded in three fundamental ideas: action is collective; interaction uses tools, which it also creates and adapts; and meaning-making is community-based (Vygotsky, 1978). Activity systems constantly evolve through responses to structural contradictions (Foot, 2001). Elements of intersecting systems mediate situated actions and interactions. "CHAT focuses on the mediation of activity, connections between systems in the policy process, and the transformation of systems as knowledge is constructed" (Canary, 2010, p. 28). Structuration theory examines how system elements (i.e., rules and resources) reproduce and transform structures. CHAT examines ongoing activity occurring through mediation of system elements and how changes in these elements transform systems. SAT analyzes and explains policy knowledge construction through the application of four theoretic constructs: structuration through activity; mediation of social activity; contradictions; and intersections of systems. Social structure situated in social contexts enables and constrains knowledge construction. Ongoing systemic activity mediates situated action/interaction, shaping policy knowledge construction within and between activity systems. Mediated activity is driven by, reproduces, and transforms structure. Contradictions are generative mechanisms for the communicative construction of policy knowledge as individuals interact to resolve contradictions in the policy process. Policy knowledge is constructed between systems and mediated by systems' intersections. Construction of policy knowledge between intersecting activity systems is constrained and enabled by structural features, while at the same time constructed knowledge produces, reproduces, or transforms social structure (Canary, 2010). Policy knowledge and knowledge construction transcend interaction and organizational boundaries. SAT provides a communication-centered approach to organizational knowledge construction with adequate complexity to examine complicated processes.

Structurational Divergence Theory (SDT)

SDT extends structuration theory, addressing the paradox of intractable contradictions (Nicotera & Clinkscales, 2010). Giddens and others (e.g., Sewell, 1992) had discussed the interpenetration of multiple structures and potential contradictions, but previous applications of structuration theory assumed contradictions result in the transformation of structures or the evolution of new rules and resources for managing the contradictions. SDT extends structuration theory by considering those contradictory interpenetrations of multiple structures that remain unresolved, resulting in recurrent conflict cycles, revealing that in such conditions the structures produced and reproduced are unproductive or oppressive. SDT originated in the study of African-American organizations (Nicotera & Clinkscales, 2003) and was further developed in nursing communication (Nicotera & Clinkscales, 2010). Yet, like structuration, SDT is applicable to all human social systems.

There are two components of structurational divergence (SD) (Nicotera et al., 2010). First, the *SD-nexus* is an institutional positioning at the intersection of structures, characterized by simultaneous and equally compelling contradictory obligations. Second, the *SD-cycle* is a negative spiral of communication resulting from an SD-nexus: unresolvable conflict, immobilization, and the erosion of development (individual, group, organizational, and/or institutional) that exacerbates unresolved conflicts. The hallmark symptom of SD is immobilization – not lack of activity but a frustrating impasse, feeling stuck in the same place, repeatedly facing the same problems, marked by futility and hopelessness. SDT explicates the function and dysfunction of human interaction under conditions of intractable paradox. Rooted in structuration theory's fundamental assumptions about the recursive and mutually constitutive processes of everyday communication and enduring social structures,

SDT provides a framework to examine the intersection of incompatible social structures that simultaneously drive oppositional actions, resulting in recurrent negative spirals of conflict. SD is measured with a diagnostic self-report scale identifying the three components of the cycle and the cyclic connections among them (Nicotera et al., 2010). Training interventions can educate those in susceptible positions (e.g., at intersections of organizational, cultural, and institutional boundaries) to recognize SD and create dialogues to transcend the oppositional nature of SD communication (Nicotera et al., 2014).

SD is agency loss (Nicotera & Mahon, 2013). Because actions cannot reproduce a comprehensible structure, communication difficulties become entrenched. Numerous studies illustrate that those entrenched in SD-cycles lose ability to act meaningfully, illustrating inefficacy (e.g., Nicotera & Clinkscales, 2003, 2010). Those entrenched cannot make sense of interaction, cannot coherently use resources, and cannot apply rules smoothly. Because simultaneous oppositional structures are equally forceful and because the re/production of one violates another, the interaction system in the SD-cycle is incoherent. In a structurationally divergent interaction system, social practice does not coherently re/produce or transform structure because actors do not have adequate knowledge of resources. "An SD system is self-perpetuating; its contradictions re/produce contradictory actions. We always have action choices, but in SD none satisfy all structurational constraints in place.... Acting on one structure subverts another, negating agency for the whole" (Nicotera & Mahon, 2013, p. 94).

The interpenetration of equally compelling oppositional structures (SD-nexus) creates unknowable structures negating agency and giving rise to the self-perpetuating SD-cycle. Interaction cannot (re)produce comprehensible structures because actors cannot assign comprehensible socially sanctioned meaning. SDT provides a set of conceptual mechanisms to understand intractable conflict cycles at the intersection of incompatible and equally compelling structures.

Communicative Constitution of Organization

The recent publication of a handbook devoted to CCO theory (Basque et al., 2022) is an indication that CCO has matured into a core disciplinary area. Basque et al. (2022) provide comprehensive discussions of CCO's origins, current theoretic developments, methodologies, and practice applications across organizational disciplines. Given the breadth of CCO scholarship, only a brief overview is possible here. Students who desire to pursue a CCO approach in research or practice are encouraged to pursue more extensive reading, beginning with Basque et al. (2022).

CCO theory grew from two important ideas: the communicative co-construction of organizing and discourse/language as a performative enactment of organization (Putnam, 2022). CCO examines the mutually constitutive relationship between communication and organization. Communication is viewed as performative and recursive, involving humans and non-humans, as well as material and immaterial objects. Situationally embedded communicative recursivity constitutes organizational forms in C–O cycle relationships that become *distantiated* from their situated sites of construction to endure across time and space (Putnam, 2022). CCO approaches examine ongoing streams of discourse, focus on co-construction, and consider the communicative constitution of organizing (O_1), organizationality (O_2), and organizations (O_3). Regardless of ontological and epistemological differences among schools of thought, CCO scholarship explicitly studies communication events, rests on inclusive definitions of communication, acknowledges the co-constructed nature of communication; holds the identity of agent as an open question; maintains the centrality of communication as the primary organizationally constitutive force; and examines processes (O_1), organizationality and structures (O_2), and the creation of entities (O_3). CCO theory occupies three distinct branches: McPhee's four flows; the Montreal School; and Luhmann's social systems theory. (See Putnam, 2022, for detailed comparison.)

Four Flows Model

The term CCO was coined by McPhee and Zaug (2000) in a description of their four flows model of organizational communication, which carries an implicit O_3 assumption. The model identifies four distinct communicative flows through which interaction generates organization: organizational self-structuring, membership negotiation, activity coordination, and institutional positioning. Heavily influenced by structuration theory, McPhee and Zaug identify the ways these flows mutually influence one another through the structuring of the organization, both reproducing and resisting its rules/resources. Like other contemporary organizational communication theories, and all CCO theories, the four flows model integrates all three conceptual treatments of organization (O_1, O_2, O_3). See McPhee et al. (2025) for a thorough explanation of four flows theory and its conceptual development, as well as a comprehensive review of its associated literature.

Organizational Self-Structuring

Activities of deliberate organizing comprise this flow. Individuals and groups occupying organizational roles communicate dialogically and recursively to create and maintain organizational structures. Organizational practices, procedures, norms, and relations are designed, documented, and controlled by this flow, distinguishing an organization from other forms of social collective. The process is subjective, political, ambiguous, and never error-free. This communication flow constitutes the organization by explicitly defining it as a distinct entity and by imposing governance through self-reflexive internal mechanisms and rule-governed cycles of response (e.g., manuals, formal reporting structures, and organizational charts).

Membership Negotiation

Organizational membership is a communicatively negotiated process. These processes establish and maintain mutually agreed-upon relationships linking the organization to its members (through such practices as recruiting, orientations, socialization, and promotions). Membership negotiation takes place in the context of pre-existing structures (formal and informal) and expectations, to which members must adapt. Membership negotiation is ongoing, constantly renegotiating roles as the organization and its members develop.

Activity Coordination

Self-structuring and membership negotiation define workflows, policies, roles, and other structures that provide purpose to human activities. To meet organizational structuring demands, those activities need to be coordinated. That coordination restructures the organization as members adjust processes to accomplish tasks. Structuring is constant; activity coordination presumes interdependence of individual activities with each other, with social units, and with the organization. Even activities that resist organizational goals and structures are constantly coordinated as members pursue multiple, often contradictory, goals.

Institutional Positioning

This last flow links the organization to its environment (e.g., customers, suppliers, regulators, and competitors) through communication that spans the organizational boundary, whether cast as representing an individual, a group, or the organization itself. This communication must establish the organization's presence, inclusion, and image in its environment, as well as its relation to other organizations and social, cultural, or political structures.

Montreal School

So-called because of its association with the University of Montreal, this body of theory relies on a core set of ideas formulated by Taylor et al. (1996) and Taylor and Van Every (2000). Following European and American pragmatist traditions, Montreal CCO theory focuses on organizing properties of linguistic forms. Analysis centers on inherent organizing properties of communication as the basis for communication's constitutive force.

Coorientation

The foundation of Montreal theory is coorientational theory – the recursive interplay between *conversation* (interaction) and *text* (discourse). Text is both content and outcome of interaction. Conversation is interaction itself. Text is meaning and outcome and can be tangible; conversation is activity. Conversation is about text and produces/reproduces text. For example, a work group encountering a problem with tracking client orders has a meeting (conversation). In that meeting they collaborate (conversation) to create a set of standard procedures (text) for training salespeople (conversation), as well as a standard online tracking sheet (text) for processing orders. Later, the sales managers convene their employees in a training session (conversation), during which they provide the procedures and new tracking sheet (texts). After the training, salespeople discuss (conversation) the relative merits of the new procedures (text) among themselves and comment (conversation) on how boring they found the training session (text).

Based on Weick, conversations are interpreted through punctuation and bracketing (sensemaking), and bracketing depends on interpretive frames (see Chapter 2). Organization, then, emerges *in* (not through or from) communication. Organization is not seen through communication; rather it is in the communicational lens (Taylor & Van Every, 2000). Once emerged, organization becomes an object to which organizational actors coorient their activities as they engage in coordination, *coorientation* being the process by which organization is communicatively enacted (Taylor, 2009; Taylor & Van Every, 2000). *Closure* (Cooren & Fairhurst, 2004) is the punctuation of conversation to provide situated understanding. *Imbrication* refers to the layering of communicative practices that *scale up* to constitute the organization (Taylor, 2011). Communication is conceptualized as a mediating process, as conversations and texts are translated into one another. Communication is constitutive as a sensemaking process and through the creation of an organizational entity for which actors speak (Schoeneborn & Vasquez, 2017).

Materiality and Agency

Following actor-network theory (Latour, 1996), which posits that the social world is composed of a network of relationships among humans and non-humans, Montreal scholars point out that the organization also communicates through *non-human* agents (documents, technology, policies, organizational units). For example, individuals commonly act by following instructions given by a document, without any thought as to the human actions that resulted in that document. Agency, therefore, is attributed to the document; note the language here: the document (the "it," not any human) gave instructions. The organization itself is a non-human that speaks through humans and non-humans alike. *Incarnation* is the communicative process by which agency (or power) is transferred to material objects (Brummans, 2011).

Montreal CCO theory explores materiality and agency (Cooren, 2010) as texts and conversations are converted to material forms in which organization finds its expression. Yet, a conceptual gap arises between social construction and materialization, as early analyses commonly examined one or the other, but rarely the hybrid processes by which material and the discursive aspects of organizing are conjoined in CCO phenomena. Cooren (2006) defines organization as a *plenum of agencies*, positing that all action is hybrid – mobilizing participation of multiple entities in a wide variety of types (human, non-human, material, and discursive). *Presentification* is speaking and acting to make present in interaction things and beings not physically present in ways that influence the unfolding of a situation (Benoit-Barné & Cooren, 2009). *Ventriloquism* refers to the positioning of agents (both human and non-human) by their need to act as compelled by the structures that have been constituted – the organization speaks through its agents (Cooren et al., 2013). Actors, thus, do not need to be human, or even material, to be mobilized with and through. Moreover, the organization itself functions as a collective actor.

Luhmann's Social Systems Theory

Luhmann's (2003) sociology of organizations rests on the assumption that society is composed of a complex and dynamic interplay of numerous social systems. Similar to self-organizing systems theory (see Chapter 2), social systems theory draws on the concept of *autopoiesis*. Communication constitutes the social systems that produce the very elements of communication. Organizations are constituted by these self-recursive communication events. Luhmann distinguishes organizations from other forms of social systems as specifically constituted by *decisional communication*. Literally, organizations are made of decisions and, further, provide the capability to make the decisions that constitute them. Hence, this branch of theory is noted for its focus on self-referential CCO. Organizations are created and continue to exist through the continuous perpetuation of interconnected decisions. Moreover, decisions are nonpermanent events. The identification of an organizational entity provides the common reference point, or *social address*, that allows agents to make decisions on its behalf (Schoeneborn & Vasquez, 2017). In Luhmannian CCO theory, the system itself holds understanding, not the people. Human organizational actors are part of the system's environment, differentiated from the organization by its logic. Unlike Montreal theorists, however, Luhmannian theorists do not see the system as a discrete agent. Conceptual developments around organizationality (Dobusch & Schoeneborn, 2015; Schoeneborn et al., 2019; Smith, 2022) follow the Luhmannian tradition.

Institutional Theory

Rooted in 19th century theory, particularly in the works of Max Weber (see Chapter 5), institutional theory examines how large social structures influence daily life. In organizational studies, institutional theory gained great popularity in the 1970s as scholars sought to examine why organizations of the same type (e.g., hospitals, schools, public agencies) are so similar in form, function, and practice in isolation from one another. In the 2000s, organizational communication scholars began contributing to that literature (e.g., Cheney & Ashcraft, 2007; Green et al., 2008; Lammers, 2011; Lammers & Barbour, 2006; Lammers & Garcia, 2009; Taylor et al., 2001). Institutional theory is necessarily related to CCO, as it examines distanciation – how communication carries the social arrangements of institutions through generations across time and space (Lammers & Garcia, 2017). Organizational communication institutional theory remedies the neglect of *macrophenomena*: forms of social structure that are larger than interaction appear to be outside the direct control of organizational members and persist to constrain and manipulate interaction and perceptions of organizational members (Lammers & Garcia, 2017).

"Institutions are comprised of regulative, normative and cultural-cognitive elements that, together with associated activities and resources, provide stability and meaning to social life" (Scott, 2008, p. 48, considered the primary authority on institutional theory in organizational studies). There is no single agreed-upon definition of *institutions*, but persistence, reproduction, stability, and establishment are characteristic across definitions (Lammers & Garcia, 2017). Organizational communication institutional theorists examine the interplay between external institutional forces and internal organizational interaction. Organizations can be examined as actors in institutional environments, adapting to and influencing those environments. Institutional theorists have much in common with rhetorical, cultural, critical, structuration, and CCO theorists in examining symbolic interaction, belief systems, systems of domination, and other broad social structures. Institutional theorists do not attempt to explicate *microphenomena*, internal organizational behavior at the individual level (Lammers & Barbour, 2006). In institutional theory, individual-level analysis would examine internalization of social norms for conduct (similar to concertive control theory, see Chapters 7, 11, and 12) because the focus is on the organizational environment, its nature, and its force.

Rather than an interpersonal or cognitive approach, institutional theory looks to the institutional environment to contextualize and explain organizational communication behavior (e.g., decision-making, message formation, change strategies, management tactics, and conflict management strategies). By the 1980s,

> concerns with individual organizations becoming institutionalized, or particular institutions' fate or relevance, were replaced with recognition that organizing was persistently influenced by institutional ideas. Meyer and Rowan (1977) referred to these ideas as rational myths or untestable beliefs about what organizations should look like. DiMaggio and Powell (1983) contributed a way of thinking about institutional fields as continually structured by isomorphic forces that shaped organizations within a recognized area of institutional life, including the industry as well as regulating, supply, and market organizations. These concepts, the rational myth and field forces, laid the foundation for what has come to be known as *neo-institutionalism*, the study of external forces that influence organizational strategy, change, and behavior.
>
> (Lammers & Garcia, 2017, pp. 2–3)

Organizational communication neo-institutionalists study the mutual influence between organizational behavior and these field forces and how individuals' communication creates and alters institutions. Lammers and Barbour's (2006) institutional theory of organizational communication proposes that communication sustains institutions, aligns organizing with institutions, functions as the operational mechanism for institutions, can only achieve boundary-spanning in the presence of institutions, and manifests institutional hierarchy. Links between institutional theory and organizational communication are clear: communication-focused examinations of numerous processes: institutional logics that pattern organizational practices; deliberate attempts to create, maintain, or disrupt institutions; rhetoric that reveals institutionalization of activities, norms, beliefs, and rules; the logic and operation of professions as both an institutional and an organizational communication phenomenon; organizations themselves as actors in an institutional environment; and, finally, messages and message framing, where institutional messaging can be seen to manifest at institutional, organizational, and interactional levels (Lammers & Garcia, 2017).

Institutional theory's traditional approaches to communication were transmissive and linear. Cornelissen et al. (2015) articulate *communicative institutionalism*, a conceptual advancement adopting a meaning-centered view conceiving institutions and organizations as mutually constitutive, defining communication as a dynamic manipulation of symbols that create, maintain, transform, and destroy meaning. Moreover, that meaning process is considered central to all organizational processes. Interaction can be conceptualized at the institutional level as complex, rich, ambiguous, and diverse. Communicative institutionalism accounts for the communicative constitution of institution, the institutional constitution of organization, and the organizational constitution of institution. Like CCO, the perspective dismantles distinctions between structure and action and between micro- and macro-levels of analysis. It exceeds CCO in its ability to examine patterns that transcend organizations (Lammers & Garcia, 2017). Communicative institutionalism has been applied across organizational studies to topics such as institutional change (Krautzberger et al., 2020), corporate social responsibility (Lee, 2020; Vollero et al., 2022), entrepreneurship (Wurth & Mawson, 2024), and organizational agency in public relations (Buhmann & Schoeneborn, 2021).

COVID-19 Organizing

The COVID-19 pandemic had an unprecedented impact on organizing and organizations, reflected in a sizable literature that continues to grow. In addition to work in health communication, strategic communication, and other overlapping subdisciplines, we can identify a core organizational communication COVID-19 literature, though a full review is beyond our present scope.

Studies of emergent organizing (Burke et al., 2022; Sahay & Dwyer, 2021) and sensemaking (Stephens et al., 2020; van Zoonen et al., 2022) have flourished. An *International Journal of Business Communication* special issue (Mayfield & Mayfield, 2022) on organizational agility during the pandemic includes studies of crisis communication perceptions, employee trust, strategic silence, information adequacy, behavior change, social support, emotional exhaustion, and CDC strategic communication efforts. Other work focusing on stakeholder communication strategy examines communication between healthcare administrators and providers (McBeth et al., 2021); organizational transitions (Vukasovich & Kostic, 2022); resilience discourse (Anderson & Jones-Bodie, 2023); empathy (Sharma et al., 2023); employee identification (Sun et al., 2023); employee engagement (Lemon &

VanDyke, 2024; Tao et al., 2022); and the role of workplace communication in promoting public health (Tao et al., 2023). Work focusing on relationships with supervisors and co-workers includes studies of supervisor immediacy (Croucher et al., 2022; Rocker et al., 2021); family-supportive leadership (Lee & Kim, 2023); and the impact of social support on resilience (Kim et al., 2022). Technology and digital communication have received ample attention, including a comprehensive volume (Browning et al., 2022; see Chapter 19). With the crisis over and COVID-19 still present, scholars explore hybrid work (e.g., Wu et al., 2023).

Race, Difference, and the Decolonial Turn

The term *difference* is preferred to *diversity* (Allen, 2023; see Chapter 2), yet *diversity* remains in our vernacular. Halualani et al. (2006) examine how people living in the racially heterogeneous Silicon Valley make sense of *diversity* through the lens of *race*, concluding that race may be "a meaningful encoding and cultural resource that can be creatively resignified to speak to shifting needs, identity positions, and experiences" (p. 89). People use the idea of *race* to align with the dominant discourse of racelessness/color blindness (which reinforces racism as it nullifies racism claims) and to substantiate race as a marginalized position that resists the dominant discourse. Their participants engaged in *racial pivoting* – recurrently shifting between invoking and denying race as a social marker. Chapter 14 provides a review of difference and intersectionality research, including important theorizing on communication and race (e.g., Allen, 2007; Ferguson & Dougherty, 2022; Orbe & Allen, 2008; Parker, 2001, 2003).

Grimes and Glenn (2024) provide a review of underappreciated research in Organizational Communication with a useful framing of the issues to consider, specifically taking issue with disciplinary patterns that ignore race, imagine it as irrelevant, study it simplistically, and reinforce stereotypes. They recommend attention to method, theory, multiple disciplinary literatures, nonacademic writing, subtleties, and a skeptical approach to diversity, equity, and inclusion (DEI) work. They also advocate for consideration of academic workplaces as sites of organizational communication and recognition that the Organizational Communication discipline needs to change.

> Attend to who is speaking, who is in the room, who is empowered. Don't assume different means deficient. Don't ask those who are different to fix (what you consider to be) problems caused by their difference. Attend to the current anti–critical race theory environment playing out in multiple discussions, including in renewal, promotion and tenure meetings, classroom discussions, and funding processes. … Become a scholar-activist. Don't take progress for granted. Attend to backsliding and backlash.
> (p. 517)

In our scholarly field and on our academic campuses, we are long past the time when discussions of racial equity should have yielded progressive changes. Ballard et al. (2020) identify specific areas of action to effect tangible change, including faculty emotional labor, university structural change, and practices in student mentoring and scholarship to center marginalized viewpoints, integrate practice into research and theory, prioritize justice, and interrogate hidden colonial structures in our traditions (see Chapter 4). Jensen et al. (2020) provide an excellent example, critically considering the identity and positionality of qualitative ethnographic organizational communication researchers.

Contemporary organizational communication theory and research on race is grounded in a broader turn to postcolonial theory, a body of scholarship examining enduring structural features of colonialism and conquest in contemporary organizations and institutions. The *decolonial turn* of Organizational Communication is manifested in efforts to disrupt and alter those colonial structures. Chapter 4 focuses entirely on postcolonial theory and decolonizing.

Conceptual Frameworks for This Book: Structuration Theory and CCO

Based on structuration and CCO, this book grounds an understanding of the field and its contents as mutually constitutive with organizational practices. Though they are not communication theories, foundational management theories had significant constitutive power in the creation of both the field and the contemporary organizational landscape we study. These theories (Chapters 5–7) are both conceptual foundations for organizational communication theory and bodies of prescriptive principles that created the organizational structures and practices we study today (e.g., hierarchies, bureaucratic structures, and labor protections).

We study, live in, and act upon an organizational world that has been created and maintained, in significant part, by organizational theory. Contemporary organizational forms, structures, policies, procedures, practices, and so on are communicatively constituted. Structuration and CCO theories are prominent contemporary approaches to the study of organizational communication examining the ways social structures and social practices enable and constrain one another. As you study organizational communication theory, this text asks you to also consider the ways in which that theory creates cultural structures that become the thing that we study. To accomplish this, this text takes a structurational CCO perspective.

Recommended Supplementary Readings

Allen, B. J. (2023). *Difference matters*. Waveland Press.

This classic text theorizing "difference" is newly updated to incorporate multiple types of difference among persons across society, organizational, and personal contexts.

Canary, H. E., & Tarin, C. A. (2017). Structuration theory. In C. R. Scott & L. Lewis (Eds.), *The international encyclopedia of organizational communication* (online edition). Wiley-Blackwell.

An accessible overview of structuration theory in organizational communication.

Cooren, F., Matte, F., Benoit-Barné, C., & Brummans, B. H. J. M. (2013). Communication as ventriloquism: A grounded-in-action approach to the study of organizational tensions. *Communication Monographs*, *80*(3), 255–277.

Using fieldwork case studies from an extensive ethnographic study, this article examines how organizational tensions are communicatively constituted and can be managed.

Fairhurst, G. T., & Putnam, L. L. (2004). Organizations as discursive constructions. *Communication Theory*, *14*(1), 5–26.

Putnam, L. L., & Fairhurst, G. T. (2015). Revisiting "Organizations as discursive constructions": 10 years later. *Communication Theory*, *25*(4), 375–392.

The initial essay provides a deep analysis of the various discursive approaches in the field. The subsequent piece discusses the impact of the original and traces the ideas in CCO theory.

Fairhurst, G., & Putnam, L. L. (2024). *Performing organizational paradoxes*. Routledge.

A theoretical framework for paradox research grounded in constitutive and discursive approaches.

Grimes, D. S., & Glenn, C. L. (2024). Race and organizational communication: Tired of saying it. In B. M. Calafell & S. Eguchi (Eds.), *The Routledge handbook of ethnicity and race in communication* (pp. 508–520). Routledge.

Incisive critique of the neglect of attention to race in organizational communication that provides a review of race-related organizational communication research, noting that much of it falls outside the traditional boundaries of the field, and a framework for progress.

Haulani, R. T., Fassett, D. L., Morrison, J. H. T. A., & Dodge, P. S. (2006). Between the structural and the personal: Situated sensemakings of "race." *Communication and Critical/Cultural Studies*, *3*(1), 70–93.

Examines the ways that "diversity" is commonly understood through a racial lens, despite persistent beliefs that "race" is a non-issue in diverse communities.

Jackson, S. (2015). Toward an analytical and methodological understanding of actor-network theory. *Journal of Arts and Humanities*, 4(2), 29–44.

An excellent conceptual map for those encountering actor-network theory for the first time.

Lammers, J. C., & Garcia, M. A. (2017). Institutional theory approaches. In C. R. Scott & L. Lewis (Eds.), *The international encyclopedia of organizational communication* (online edition). Wiley-Blackwell.

An accessible overview of institutional theory as it has been developed in organizational communication.

Orbe, M. P., Austin, J. T., & Allen, B. J. (Eds.). (2022). 'Race matters' in applied communication research: Past, present, and future [Special issue]. Journal of Applied Communication Research, 50(3), 229–235.

A collection of articles examining concepts of race and their applications across communication studies. The introduction by Mohan Dutta is particularly recommended for its conceptualization of communication as raced practice.

Schoeneborn, D., & Blaschke, S. (2014). The three schools of CCO thinking: Interactive dialogue and systematic comparison. *Management Communication Quarterly*, *28*(2), 285–316.

A unique view of CCO theory, through a dialogue among the major theorists from each school of thought.

Important Concepts: Define and Discuss

Agency
Communicative constitution of organization
  McPhee's four flows
  Montreal school
  Luhmann's social systems theory

Discourse/discourse (big D, little d)
  Organization as becoming
  Organization as grounded in action
  Organization as object

Institutional theory
Structuration
  Duality of structure
  Rules and resources
  Modalities of meaning

Discussion Questions

1 What is discourse? Why is it important to contemporary organizational communication theory?
2 Choose a common organizational practice (e.g., budget requests, annual performance reviews) and trace its structuration. Identify the practice, its place in a system of practices, the underlying structure, rules, resources, and other structurational concepts. Can you trace the structurational C–O cycle through this practice?
3 How are the three theoretical traditions of CCO consistent with one another? How do they disagree?
4 What is the role of social construction in structuration theory and CCO?
5 What is the difference between CCO theory and institutional theory? How do they intersect?

Practitioners' Corner

At first glance, it may seem that developments in organizational communication in the 21st century have been more philosophical than practical. Yet, as always, organizational communication remains centered on daily experiences of organizational life. The structuration and CCO perspectives exemplify contemporary organizational communication theory as both abstract and immediately applicable. The central explanations of both emphasize the mutually enabling and constraining relationship between communicating and organizing. This basic understanding can empower organizational leaders and members to enact positive changes in daily activities to purposefully create repetitive structures that are more efficient and effective. Introducing new practices that can be communicatively linked to an existing structure (values, norms, goals, practices, etc.) can create new conventions for tomorrow. Working to eliminate ineffective practices can likewise open opportunities for positive permanent change as their underlying dysfunctional structures die away.

What we do every day, including how we communicate, is drawn from the conventions of yesterday and perpetuates those conventions. This understanding can create a fundamental self-awareness at the deepest level in how we frame, define, and approach our relationships with others. An understanding of the mutually enabling and constraining relationship between structures (or texts, for a Montreal approach) and communication helps us understand such things as applications of technology (AST), negative behavior cycles (SDT), and development of policy (SAT), and thus how to contribute to such things productively. As revealed by Cooren et al. (2013) and Nicotera et al. (2014), awareness of the underlying CCO processes that constitute our everyday realities improves individual and group organizational functioning.

References

Allen, B. J. (2007). Theorizing communication and race. *Communication Monographs*, *74*(2), 259–264.

Allen, B. J. (2023). *Difference matters*. Waveland Press.

Anderson, L. B., & Jones-Bodie, A. (2023). Facing adversity together: Toward a genre of organization-stakeholder resilience discourse. *Management Communication Quarterly*, *37*(1), 144–170. https://doi.org/10.1177/08933189221112045

Ballard, D., Allen, B., Ashcraft, K., Ganesh, S., McLeod, P., & Zoller, H. (2020). When words do not matter: Identifying actions to effect diversity, equity, and inclusion in the academy. *Management Communication Quarterly*, *34*(4), 590–616. https://doi.org/10.1177/0893318920951643

Ballard-Reisch, D., & Turner, P. K. (2017). Contradictions, tensions, paradoxes, and dialectics. In C. R. Scott & L. Lewis (Eds.), *The international encyclopedia of organizational communication* (online edition). Wiley-Blackwell. https://doi.org/10.1002/9781118955567.wbieoc043

Basque, J., Bencherki, N., & Kuhn, T. (2022). *The Routledge handbook of the communicative constitution of organization*. Routledge.

Baxter, L. A. (1988). A dialectical perspective of communication strategies in relationship development. In S. Duck (Ed.), *Handbook of personal relationships* (pp. 257–273). Wiley.

Benoit-Barné, C., & Cooren, F. (2009). The accomplishment of authority through presentification: How authority is distributed among and negotiated by organizational members. *Management Communication Quarterly*, *23*(1), 5–31. https://doi.org/10.1177/0893318909335414

Browning, L. D., Sørnes, J., & Svenkerud, P. J. (2022). *Organizational communication and technology in the time of coronavirus: Ethnographies from the first year of the pandemic*. Palgrave Macmillan.

Brummans, B. H. J. M. (2011). What goes down must come up: Communication as incarnation and transcension. *Communication and Critical/Cultural Studies*, *8*(2), 194–200. https://doi.org/10.1080/14791420.2011.567810

Buhmann, A., & Schoeneborn, D. (2021). Envisioning PR research without taking organizations as collective actors for granted. *Public Relations Inquiry*, *10*(1), 119–127. https://doi.org/10.1177/2046147X20987337

Burke, G. T., Omidvar, O., Spanellis, A., & Pyrko, I. (2022). Making space for garbage cans: How emergent groups organize social media spaces to orchestrate widescale helping in a crisis. *Organization Studies*, *44*(4), 569–592. https://doi.org/10.1177/01708406221103969

Canary, H. E. (2010). Structurating activity theory: An integrative approach to policy knowledge. *Communication Theory*, *20*(1), 21–49. https://doi.org/10.1111/j.1468-2885.2009.01354.x

Cheney, G., & Ashcraft, K. L. (2007). Considering "the professional" in communication studies: Implications for theory and research within and beyond the boundaries of organizational communication. *Communication Theory*, *17*(2), 146–175. https://doi.org/10.1111/j.1468-2885.2007.00290.x

Connaughton, S. L., Linabary, J. R., & Yakova, L. (2017). Discursive construction. In C. R. Scott & L. Lewis (Eds.), *The international encyclopedia of organizational communication* (online edition). Wiley-Blackwell. https://doi.org/10.1002/9781118955567.wbieoc063

Cooren, F. (2006). The organizational world as a plenum of agencies. In F. Cooren, J. R. Taylor, & E. J. Van Every (Eds.), *Communication as organizing: Practical approaches to research into the dynamic of text and conversation* (pp. 81–100). Erlbaum.

Cooren, F. (2010). Figures of communication and dialogue: Passion, ventriloquism and incarnation. *Intercultural Pragmatics*, *7*(1), 131–145. https://doi.org/10.1515/IPRG.2010.006

Cooren, F., & Fairhurst, G. (2004). Speech timing and spacing: The phenomenon of organizational closure. *Organization*, *11*(6), 793–824. https://doi.org/10.1177/1350508404047252

Cooren, F., Matte, F., Brummans, B., & Benoit-Barné, C. (2013). Communication as ventriloquism: A grounded-in-action approach to the study of organizational tensions. *Communication Monographs*, *80*(3), 255–277. https://doi.org/10.1080/03637751.2013.788255

Corman, S. R., & Poole, M. S. (2000). *Perspectives on organizational communication: Finding common ground*. Guilford Press.

Cornelissen, J. P., Durand, R., Fiss, P., Lammers, J. C., & Vaara, E. (2015). Putting communication front and center in institutional theory and analysis. *Academy of Management Review*, *40*(1), 10–27. https://doi.org/10.5465/amr.2014.0381

Croucher, S. M., Kelly, S., Green, M., Homsey, D. M., Cullinane, J., Rocker, K. T., Nguyen, T., Anderson, K., Chen, H., Ding, G. G., Ashwell, D., Wright, M., & Palakshappa, N. (2022). The link between supervisor-subordinate computer-mediated immediate behaviors and organizational identification in U.S., English, and Australian organizations. *Management Communication Quarterly*, *36*(4), 688–709. https://doi.org/10.1177/08933189221076859

DeSanctis, G., & Poole, M. S. (1994). Capturing the complexity in advanced technology use: Adaptive structuration theory. *Organization Science*, *5*(2), 121–147. https://doi.org/10.1287/orsc.5.2.121

DiMaggio, P. J., & Powell, W. W. (1983). The iron cage revisited: Institutional isomorphism and collective rationality in organization fields. *American Sociological Review*, *48*(2), 147–160. https://doi.org/10.2307/2095101

Dobusch, L., & Schoeneborn, D. (2015). Fluidity, identity, and organizationality: The communicative constitution of *Anonymous*. *Journal of Management Studies*, *52*(8), 1005–1035. https://doi.org/10.1111/joms.12139

Fairhurst, G., & Putnam, L. L. (2024). *Performing organizational paradoxes*. Routledge.

Fairhurst, G. T., & Putnam, L. L. (2004). Organizations as discursive constructions. *Communication Theory*, *14*(1), 5–26. https://doi.org/10.1111/j.1468-2885.2004.tb00301.x

Ferguson, M. W., & Dougherty, D. S. (2022). The paradox of the black professional: Whitewashing blackness through professionalism. *Management Communication Quarterly*, *36*(1), 3–29. https://doi.org/10.1177/08933189211019751

Foot, K. A. (2001). Cultural-historical activity theory as practice theory: Illuminating the development of a conflict-monitoring network. *Communication Theory*, *11*(1), 56–83. https://doi.org/10.1111/j.1468-2885.2001.tb00233.x

Giddens, A. (1979). *Central problems in social theory: Action, structure, and contradiction in social analysis*. University of California Press.

Giddens, A. (1984). *The constitution of society: Outline of the theory of structuration*. University of California Press.

Giddens, A. (1987). *The nation-state and violence*. University of California Press.

Green, S. E, Jr., Babb, M., & Alpaslan, C. M. (2008). Institutional field dynamics and the competition between institutional logics: The role of rhetoric in the evolving control of the modern corporation. *Management Communication Quarterly*, *22*(1), 40–73. https://doi.org/10.1177/0893318908318430

Grimes, D. S., & Glenn, C. L. (2024). Race and organizational communication: Tired of saying it. In B. M. Calafell & S. Eguchi (Eds.), *The Routledge handbook of ethnicity and race in communication* (pp. 508–520). Routledge.

Halualani, R. T., Fassett, D. L., Morrison, J. H. T. A., & Dodge, P. S. (2006). Between the structural and the personal: Situated sense-makings of "race. *Communication and Critical/Cultural Studies*, *3*(1), 70–93. https://doi.org/10.1080/14791420500505700

Jensen, P. R., Cruz, J., Eger, E. K., Hanchey, J. N., Gist-Mackey, A. N., Ruiz-Mesa, K., & Villamil, A. (2020). Pushing beyond positionalities and through "failures" in qualitative organizational communication: Experiences and lessons on identities in ethnographic praxis. *Management Communication Quarterly*, *34*(1), 121–151. https://doi.org/10.1177/0893318919885654

Kim, H., Mattson, L. D., Zhang, D., & Cho, H. J. (2022). The role of organizational and supervisor support in young adult workers' resilience, efficacy and burnout during the COVID-19 pandemic. *Journal of Applied Communication Research*, *50*(6), 691–710. https://doi.org/10.1080/00909882.2022.2141070

Krautzberger, M., Fohim, E., Cooren, F., & Schumacher, T. (2020). The communicative constitution of institutional change in expression games. *Strategic Organization*, *19*(4), 667–692. https://doi.org/10.1177/1476127020959253

Lammers, J. C. (2011). How institutions communicate: Institutional messages, institutional logics, and organizational communication. *Management Communication Quarterly*, *25*(1), 154–182. https://doi.org/10.1177/0893318910389280

Lammers, J. C., & Barbour, J. B. (2006). An institutional theory of organizational communication. *Communication Theory*, *16*(3), 356–377. https://doi.org/10.1111/j.1468-2885.2006.00274.x

Lammers, J. C., & Garcia, M. A. (2009). Exploring the concept of "profession" for organizational communication research: Institutional influences in a veterinary organization. *Management Communication Quarterly*, *22*(3), 357–384. https://doi.org/10.1177/0893318908327007

Lammers, J. C., & Garcia, M. A. (2017). Institutional theory approaches. In C. R. Scott & L. Lewis (Eds.), *The international encyclopedia of organizational communication* (online edition). Wiley-Blackwell. https://doi.org/10.1002/9781118955567.wbieoc113

Latour, B. (1996). On actor-network theory: A few clarifications. *Soziale Welt*, *47*, 369–381. https://www.jstor.org/stable/40878163

Lee, T. H. (2020). Communicative institutionalization of CSR: A content analysis of firms' motivations in social reports from three market economies. *Journal of Applied Communication Research*, *48*(3), 291–309. https://doi.org/10.1080/00909882.2020.1750668

Lee, Y., & Kim, J. (2023). How family-supportive leadership communication enhances the creativity of work-from-home employees during the COVID-19 pandemic. *Management Communication Quarterly*, *37*(3), 599–628. https://doi.org/10.1177/08933189221144997

Lemon, L. L., & VanDyke, M. S. (2024). Pandemic problems in the ivory tower: Exploring employee engagement during the COVID-19 crisis. *International Journal of Strategic Communication*, *18*(1), 38–55. https://doi.org/10.1080/1553118X.2023.2235333

Luhmann, N. (2003). Organization. In T. Bakken & T. Hernes (Eds.), *Autopoietic organization theory: Drawing on Niklas Luhmann's social systems perspective* (pp. 31–52). Copenhagen Business School Press.

Mayfield, J., & Mayfield, M. (Eds.). (2022). Special issue: COVID-19 pandemic. *International Journal of Business Communication*, *59*(2). https://journals.sagepub.com/toc/jobd/59/2

McBeth, B., Karanas, Y., Nguyen, P., Kurani, S., & Bhimani, M. (2021). Improving communication between hospital administrations and healthcare providers during COVID-19: Experience from a large public hospital system in Northern California. *Journal of Communication in Healthcare*, *14*(4), 274–282. https://doi.org/10.1080/17538068.2021.1975250

McPhee, R. D., Myers, K. K., & Iverson, J. O. (2025). *The communicative constitution of organizations: The four flows model*. Wiley.

McPhee, R. D., & Zaug, P. (2000). The communicative constitution of organizations: A framework for explanation. *Electronic Journal of Communication*, *10*(1–2). Retrieved from www.cios.org/EJCPUBLIC/010/1/01017.html

Meyer, J. W., & Rowan, B. (1977). Institutionalized organizations: Formal structure as myth and ceremony. *American Journal of Sociology*, *83*(2), 340–363. https://doi.org/10.1086/226550

Montgomery, B. (1988). A dialectical analysis of the tensions, functions and strategic challenges of communication in young adult friendships. In J. A. Anderson (Ed.), *Communication yearbook 12* (pp. 157–189). Sage.

Nicotera, A. M., & Clinkscales, M. J. (2003). *Understanding organization through culture and structure: Relational and other lessons from the African-American organization*. Erlbaum.

Nicotera, A. M., & Clinkscales, M. J. (2010). Nurses at the nexus: A case study in structurational divergence. *Health Communication*, *25*(1), 32–49. https://doi.org/10.1080/10410230903473516

Nicotera, A. M., & Mahon, M. M. (2013). Rocks and hard places: Exploring the impact of structurational divergence in nursing. *Management Communication Quarterly*, *27*(1), 90–120. https://doi.org/10.1177/0893318912458214
Nicotera, A. M., Mahon, M. M., & Wright, K. B. (2014). Communication that builds teams: Assessing a nursing conflict intervention. *Nursing Administration Quarterly*, *38*(3), 248–260. https://doi.org/10.1097/NAQ.0000000000000033
Nicotera, A. M., Mahon, M. M., & Zhao, X. (2010). Conceptualization and measurement of structurational divergence in the healthcare setting. *Journal of Applied Communication Research*, *38*(4), 362–385. https://doi.org/10.1080/00909882.2010.514001
Orbe, M. P., & Allen, B. J. (2008). "Race matters" in the Journal of Applied Communication Research. *The Howard Journal of Communications*, *19*(3), 201–220. https://psycnet.apa.org/doi/10.1080/10646170802218115
Orbe, M. P., Austin, J. T., & Allen, B. J. (Ed.). (2022). "Race matters" in applied communication research. *Journal of Applied Communication Research*, *50*(3). https://www.tandfonline.com/toc/rjac20/50/3
Parker, P. S. (2001). African American women executives' leadership communication within dominant-culture organizations: (Re)conceptualizing notions of collaboration and instrumentality. *Management Communication Quarterly*, *15*(1), 42–82. https://doi.org/10.1177/0893318901151002
Parker, P. S. (2003). Control, resistance, and empowerment in raced, gendered, and classed work contexts: The case of African American women. *Annals of the International Communication Association*, *27*(1), 257–291. http://dx.doi.org/10.1207/s15567419cy2701_9
Poole, M. S., & DeSanctis, G. (1990). Understanding the use of group decision support systems: The theory of adaptive structuration. In J. Fulk & C. W. Steinfield (Eds.), *Organizations and communication technology* (pp. 172–193). Sage.
Poole, M. S., Seibold, D., & McPhee, R. D. (1985). Group decision-making as a structurational process. *Quarterly Journal of Speech*, *71*(1), 74–102. https://doi.org/10.1080/00335638509383719
Poole, M. S., Seibold, D., & McPhee, R. D. (1986). A structurational approach to theory-building in group decision-making research. In R. Y. Hirokawa & M. S. Poole (Eds.), *Communication and group decision-making* (pp. 237–264). Sage.
Putnam, L. L. (2022). Foreword: The emerging paradigm of communication constitutes organization. In J. Basque, N. Bencherki, & T. Kuhn (Eds.), *The Routledge handbook of the communicative constitution of organization* (pp. xxvi–xliv). Routledge.
Putnam, L. L., & Fairhurst, G. T. (2015). Revisiting "organizations as discursive constructions": 10 years later. *Communication Theory*, *25*(4), 375–392. https://doi.org/10.1111/comt.12074
Rocker, K. T., Kelly, S., Cullinane, J., Croucher, S. M., & Anderson, K. (2021). Computer-mediated immediate behaviors and their impact on structural divergence in superior-subordinate relationships. *Communication Research Reports*, *38*(5), 315–324. https://doi.org/10.1080/08824096.2021.1974825
Sahay, S., & Dwyer, M. (2021). Emergent organizing in crisis: US nurses' sensemaking and job crafting during COVID-19. *Management Communication Quarterly*, *35*(4), 546–571. https://doi.org/10.1177/08933189211034170
Schoeneborn, D., Kuhn, T. R., & Kärreman, D. (2019). The communicative constitution of organization, organizing, and organizationality. *Organization Studies*, *40*(4), 475–496. https://doi.org/10.1177/0170840618782284
Schoeneborn, D., & Vasquez, C. (2017). Communicative constitution of organizations approaches. In C. R. Scott & L. Lewis (Eds.), *The international encyclopedia of organizational communication* (online edition). Wiley-Blackwell. https://doi.org/10.1002/9781118955567.wbieoc030
Scott, W. R. (2008). *Institutions and organizations* (3rd ed.). Sage.
Sewell, W. H. (1992). A theory of structure: Duality, agency, and transformation. *The American Journal of Sociology*, *98*(1), 1–29. https://doi.org/10.1086/229967
Sharma, H., Jain, V., Mogaji, E., & Babbili, A. (2023). Restorative power of empathetic communication for participatory governance and community well-being. *International Journal of Communication*, *17*, 7115–7138. https://ijoc.org/index.php/ijoc/article/view/20122
Smith, W. R. (2022). On relationality and organizationality: Degrees of durability, materiality, and communicatively constituting a fluid social collective. *Organization Studies*, *43*(11), 1815–1837. https://doi.org/10.1177/01708406211035497
Stephens, K. K., Jahn, J. L. S., Fox, S., Charoensap-Kelly, P., Mitra, R., Sutton, J., Waters, E. D., Xie, B., & Meisenbach, R. J. (2020). Collective sensemaking around COVID-19: Experiences, concerns, and agendas for our rapidly changing organizational lives. *Management Communication Quarterly*, *34*(3), 426–457. https://doi.org/10.1177/0893318920934890

Stohl, C., & Cheney, G. (2001). Participatory processes/paradoxical practices: Communication and the dilemmas of organizational democracy. *Management Communication Quarterly*, *14*(3), 349–407. https://doi.org/10.1177/0893318901143001

Sun, R., Li, J. Q., Lee, Y., & Tao, W. (2023). The role of symmetrical internal communication in improving employee experiences and organizational identification during COVID-19 pandemic-induced organizational change. *International Journal of Business Communication*, *60*(4), 1398–1426. https://doi.org/10.1177/23294884211050628

Tao, W., Lee, Y., Li, J., & He, M. (2023). How dialogic vaccine communication in the workplace facilitates employee advocacy for COVID-19 vaccine uptake. *Journal of Public Relations Research*, *35*(1), 17–36. https://doi.org/10.1080/1062726X.2022.2150624

Tao, W., Lee, Y., Sun, R., Li, J., & He, M. (2022). Enhancing employee engagement via leaders' motivational language in times of crisis: Perspectives from the COVID-19 outbreak. *Public Relations Review*, *48*(1), 102133. https://doi.org/10.1016/j.pubrev.2021.102133

Taylor, J. R. (2009). Organizing from the bottom up? Reflections on the constitution of organization in communication. In L. L. Putnam & A. M. Nicotera (Eds.), *Building theories of organization: The constitutive role of communication* (pp. 153–186). Routledge.

Taylor, J. R. (2011). Organization as an (imbricated) configuring of transactions. *Organization Studies*, *32*(9), 1273–1294. https://doi.org/10.1177/0170840611411396

Taylor, J. R., Cooren, F., Giroux, N., & Robichaud, D. (1996). The communicational basis of organization: Between the conversation and the text. *Communication Theory*, *6*(1), 1–39. https://doi.org/10.1111/j.1468-2885.1996.tb00118.x

Taylor, J. R., Flanagin, A. J., Cheney, G., & Seibold, D. R. (2001). Organizational communication research: Key moments, central concerns and future challenges. In W. B. Gudykunst (Ed.), *Communication yearbook 24* (pp. 99–137). Sage.

Taylor, J. R., & Van Every, E. J. (2000). *The emergent organization: Communication as its site and surface*. Erlbaum.

Valiavska, A., Gist-Mackey, A. N., & Holloway, M. (2023). Decade of race publications: Meta content analysis of race in communication scholarship from 2010–2020. *Howard Journal of Communications*, *34*(4), 337–352. https://doi.org/10.1080/10646175.2023.2178267

van Zoonen, W., Rice, R. E., & ter Hoeven, C. L. (2022). Sensemaking by employees in essential versus non-essential professions during the COVID-19 crisis: A comparison of effects of change communication and disruption cues on mental health, through interpretations of identity threats and work meaningfulness. *Management Communication Quarterly*, *36*(2), 318–349. https://doi.org/10.1177/08933189221087633

Vollero, A., Yin, J., & Siano, A. (2022). Convergence or divergence? A comparative analysis of CSR communication by leading firms in Asia, Europe, and North America. *Public Relations Review*, *48*(1), 102142. https://doi.org/10.1016/j.pubrev.2021.102142

Vukasovich, C. A., & Kostic, M. N. (2022). Communicating during COVID-19 and other acute-event scenarios: A practical approach. *Journal of Business and Technical Communication*, *36*(4), 524–534. https://doi.org/10.1177/10506519221105493

Vygotsky, L. S. (1978). *Mind in society: The development of higher psychological processes* (M. Cole, V. John-Steiner, S. Scribner, & E. Souberman, Trans.). Harvard University Press.

Wu, Y. J., Antone, B., DeChurch, L., & Contractor, N. (2023). Information sharing in a hybrid workplace: Understanding the role of ease-of-use perceptions of communication technologies in advice-seeking relationship maintenance. *Journal of Computer-Mediated Communication*, *28*(4), zmad025. https://doi.org/10.1093/jcmc/zmad025

Wurth, B., & Mawson, S. (2024). Beyond words: How visual imagery shapes collaborative sensemaking in entrepreneurial ecosystems. *Journal of Business Venturing Insights*, *21*, e00458. https://doi.org/10.1016/j.jbvi.2024.e00458

4 Postcolonial Approaches to Organizational Communication

Anne M. Nicotera and Angela N. Gist-Mackey

Defining Postcolonialism and Decolonization

Organizational communication scholars use the terms *postcolonial* and *decolonial* differently than the general postcolonial studies literature. In our literature, the distinction is made between theory and praxis. *Postcolonialism* refers to work identifying and critiquing the enduring legacy of colonialism; whereas, *decolonialism* actively pursues changes to deconstruct, acknowledge, mitigate, and replace colonial practices. Postcolonial approaches to organizational communication are rooted in ontological, epistemological, and axiological commitments of critical theory, pursuing deconstruction of tacit assumptions underlying social structures. Postcolonial theory seeks to reveal ways that processes, procedures, and practices conventionally treated as *neutral* are steeped in colonial histories and presumptions, resulting in dominance, marginalization, and loss of cultural sovereignty. Postcolonial theory opposes Western-centrism – ideologies presuming the universality of Western ways of knowing and being (Hegde & Shome, 2002; Shome, 1996), always connected to economic domination. Postcolonial approaches identify and confront the legacy of colonialism persisting in Western-centric logics, knowledges, and forms of representation to pursue alternative, ideally Indigenous, systems of logic and practice (Kalonaityte, 2010). For example, the cultural practice of *guanxi* is foundational for Chinese business but is interpreted as corruption in the Western colonial frame (Cheung, 2008). Rooted in Confucian philosophy, *guanxi* can be understood as the extension of self to the larger collective, an obligation to provide one another favors and services. Successful business practice depends on a relational network of *guanxi*. Since everyone is expected to serve the collective, the practice of *guanxi* should never be one-sided. However, because deep networks of connection and reciprocity run counter to the prevailing characteristics of individualistic Western cultures, *guanxi* is problematically interpreted through a colonial framework as "corruptive and disruptive" (Broadfoot & Munshi, 2014, p. 155). Such business dynamics result in muting Indigenous voices, suppressing Indigenous cultural values, ways of knowing, and norms while perpetuating ethnic prejudice/stereotyping, which foster practices that deepen economic disparity and colonialism.

Postcolonial Approaches

Born out of political resistance movements in the early-to-mid 20th century opposing colonial rule, postcolonial thought examines the societal impact of Western colonization that by the early 1900s controlled approximately 90% of the world (Prasad, 2003). Modern Western colonialism traces to the late 15th-century era of European seafarers/explorers financed by European monarchs in search of wealth (largely spices and gold). Unlike earlier

DOI: 10.4324/9781003484639-5

colonization, modern Western colonialism went beyond extractions of wealth to develop complex economic dependency structures imposing European capitalism around the globe. Moreover, modern Western colonization sought – and achieved – the conquest of culture, ideology, people, resources, and/or land. According to Prasad (2003, p. 5):

> The long history of Western colonialism, its global reach, and the uniqueness of many of its constitutive practices and structures imply that Western colonialism and non-Western resistance to such colonialism have played a significant role in shaping the contours of the world as we know it today. Indeed, the continuing imprint of colonialism and anticolonialism is discernible in a range of contemporary practices and institutions, whether economic, political, or cultural.

Postcolonial theory examines the continuing influence of this history on contemporary life, investigating the ways in which structures, processes, and practices are rooted in, and continue to reproduce, coloniality in contemporary times.

The concept of *subalternity* captures the loss of cultural autonomy associated with colonialism and imperialism suffered by Indigenous communities. The *subaltern* are Indigenous persons who have been culturally, economically, and often geographically marginalized, erased, removed, eviscerated, and/or displaced by imperial colonization. Indigenous ways of knowing have been silenced and denied, and in some cases completely eradicated. Subalternity has been called epistemological subjugation (Young, 2020), erasure from the dominant discourse (Spivak, 1988), or cultural genocide (Shaw, 2007) and is usually a precursor to literal genocide. "The destruction of the socio-cultural fabric has been often quoted as one of the harms of genocide, beyond the death of the group members" (Novic, 2016). Dutta and Pal (2010) advocate for an approach that employs subaltern studies dialogue theory to disrupt Western-centric epistemologies and transform communication studies.

Decolonizing

Decolonizing changes structures, processes, and practices – ideally to those of Indigenous cultures – to eliminate, reduce, or at least acknowledge the reproduction of colonialism and its harm. As critical praxis, decolonizing requires consciousness-raising and reflection and intentionally thoughtful change toward justice and equity. Decolonization brings awareness to, contests, and questions assumptions of research, theory, and practice that stem from colonial legacies to alter them and/or create alternative approaches. Decolonization tackles Western cultural presumptions that drive and are driven by colonial legacies: Eurocentrism, whiteness, white supremacy, and neoliberalism. *Eurocentrism*, the interpretation of the world from a European standpoint, implicitly or explicitly disregards other cultural views or relegates them to a stigmatized status. Eurocentrism constructs and is constructed by *whiteness*, societal structures that produce and perpetuate white privilege and produce *white supremacy culture* (Okun, 2021), which brings implicit assumptions of the inherent superiority of White people (see Chapter 1). *Neoliberalism* is a political/economic system that values and pursues unregulated free-market capitalism in the private sector, with economic interests taking top priority. Decolonization focuses on the intertwining of these legacies that undergird self-perpetuating biases in social and organizational life.

Decolonization requires attention to questions that challenge taken-for-granted assumptions in research and theory. *How do assumptions about power influence the study of organizational communication?; Who provides resources for research, and what explicit and implicit obligations are caused by this economic dependence?; How do disciplinary practices mute Indigenous and other underrepresented voices?; How might our discipline facilitate the involvement and inclusion of Indigenous researchers and scholars?;* and *How has their exclusion fostered distortion in methodologies and findings (Broadfoot et al., 2008)?* For example, Gist-Mackey and Kingsford (2020) identify cultural and class biases regarding silence, volume, and verbosity in common organizational communication interview methods. Interviewing norms taught as ideal for qualitative research implicitly privilege white-collar communication norms, muting working-class voices. A colonial legacy of class presumptions renders concerns and experiences of large communities invisible, precluding the ability to address those concerns or accurately observe the phenomena under study. They identify more inclusive techniques resting on *unlearning* class biases embedded in data collection methods. Decolonizing requires *unlearning* hegemonic norms and practices. Researchers' relationships with those being studied must establish accountability to Indigenous communities (Keane et al., 2017) or the obligation to provide participation in the research and benefit to those communities (Nelson-Marsh et al., 2008; Zavala, 2013).

Framing a Postcolonialist Approach for Organizational Communication

In the 1970s and 1980s, the current fields of postcolonial and subaltern studies emerged from several disciplines as scholars with subaltern identities critiqued Western constructions of Indigenous cultures, such as African (Chinweizu, 1975), Arab-Islamic (Said, 1978), Latin American (Cardoso, 1977), and Indian (Chatterjee, 1987). We must note that treating these works as foundational erases their own roots (e.g., Damas, 1937; DuBois, 1903; Fanon, 1952; James, 1938; as well as earlier and ancient texts) in a history of thought often overlooked by Western-centric accounts, which often ignore the fact that ideas always come from previous ideas.

Although some attempted to draw communication scholars' attention to postcolonial theory earlier (e.g., Fernandez, 1999; Shome, 1996), Shome and Hegde's (2002) special issue of *Communication Theory* was the first comprehensive introduction of postcolonial studies to communication scholars. Broadfoot and Munshi (2007b) offered the first challenge to organizational communication to apply postcolonial theory. During this same period, the multidisciplinary field of organizational studies devoted considerable effort to postcolonial theorizing. For example, special issues of *Critical Perspectives on International Business* (Banjeree & Prasad, 2008) and *Organization* (Jack et al., 2011) addressed such topics as the imposition of Western discourses of community engagement, bureaucracy, and governance on Australian Aboriginal communities; perceptions of corruption; linguistic imperialism; knowledge transfer; neo-patriarchy; discourses of diversity; African leadership; North American business discourse; and the colonizing function of development interventions.

Call to Action

In their foundational essay on postcolonial approaches in organizational communication Broadfoot and Munshi (2007b) observe that

> much organizational communication scholarship conducted within the global context is performed and interpreted from the dominant Euro-American intellectual tradition, privileging those concepts as well as particular voices and traditions and often ignoring inequality and exploitation within the scholarly community. This forgetting

> and the imagined scholarly community it creates continue to reify and legitimate a particular form of rationality and, in practice, lead to further colonization, subordination, and oppression of native/indigenous/other forms of understanding and organizing within our disciplinary field.
>
> (p. 249)

To illustrate, they critique Mumby and Stohl's (1996) essay in a special issue of *Management Communication Quarterly* (MCQ), where scholars from related disciplines (organizational communication, business communication, management communication, and corporate communication) discussed their fields' distinctions. Mumby and Stohl (1996) identify four central problematics that distinguish organizational communication: voice, rationality, organization, and the organization-society relationship.

To critique these problematics, Broadfoot and Munshi (2007b) draw on a Forum section (Barker, 2006) in MCQ (Ashcraft, 2006; Cooren, 2006; Prichard, 2006; Zoller, 2006) examining how well organizational communication scholars, especially in the US, leverage their marginal position in organizational studies to critique and expand disciplinary boundaries to include alternative and nontraditional forms of voice, knowledge, and being. Broadfoot and Munshi (2007b) address underlying colonial structures in Mumby and Stohl's (1996) assertions and the ways that global economic and political shifts had made those assertions untenable. "When we as scholars unthinkingly adopt the discourse and knowledge of mainstream Euro-American organizational communication scholarship, we potentially absorb, without reflection, a particular way of understanding the world" (p. 264).

The *problematic of rationality* demonstrates Shome's (1996) *discursive confinement*, with organizational communication scholars "confined to a narrow and marginalized discursive space constructed by dominant mainstream structures and ideologies. In other words, how research is articulated is closely regulated and monitored, that is, disciplined" (Broadfoot & Munshi, 2007b, p. 255). *Meta-ignorance* and *meta-insensitivity* are sources of persistent misrepresentation of subaltern groups in the organizational literature (Chowdhury, 2023). *Meta-ignorance* is epistemic positionality that leaves researchers ignorant of context, history, emotional, and political aspects of social issues – and incapable of seeing their illiteracy in interpreting such lived experiences. *Meta-insensitivity* arises from multiple missed opportunities to capture subaltern voices and experiences and renders scholars unable to understand how to cultivate the necessary sensitivity. These factors contribute to the production and dissemination of knowledge perpetuating misrepresentation of subaltern people and cultures, resulting in enduring harmful consequences that intensify subalternity, such as being rendered illegitimate, experiencing erasure, and being stigmatized.

The *problematic of voice* is disciplined to "the sanitized tone of the Master Narrative" (Broadfoot & Munshi, 2007b, p. 256). Only sanctioned colonized voices earn the legitimacy to be accepted, taken seriously, publish successfully, and gain the academic audience's attention. Rigid conceptual and methodological structures colonize lived experience in processes of knowledge creation, such as standard conventions for scholarly writing demanding conformity. Munshi metaphorically says, "the 'language of the heart' is choked. One major European journal declined to publish a paper of mine, even after it was officially accepted, because the publishers felt that the language in the paper 'needs toning down and needs to be less emotive and political'" (Broadfoot & Munshi, 2007b, p. 256). *Tone policing* pervades lived experiences of marginalized groups (Bray et al., 2018). The admonition, "tone down," is a common experience among those who challenge colonial structures of racism, white supremacy, and eurocentrism. "Dominant groups use tone policing to chastise the communication style of marginalized people who challenge their oppression.… (N)o matter the legitimacy of the content, tone policing prioritizes the comfort of the privileged" (Davis & Ernst, 2017). In organizational communication, the #ToneUpOrgComm Collective (2020) actively resisted tone policing in the discipline, arguing that it is time to directly address such hegemonic practices by embracing intersectionality. "Tone down" is a reprimand embedded in a discourse of silencing that also includes incivility accusations.

Civility is strategically leveraged to protect privilege (Kisselburgh & Dutta, 2009). "Hegemonic civility is an organized process which results in suppressing or silencing any opposition, in favor of the status quo" (Patton, 2004, p. 65). Incivility is marked, not by tone, but by "a message that challenges hegemonic frameworks" (Applebaum, 2020, p. 719). Mandates for civility and tone policing:

> ask those who argue for social justice to set aside their concerns to meet a standard of the common good that simply does not include them. Power has dropped out of the picture: civility is used not to have equal dialogue but to justify inequality and manage subordinate groups.
>
> (Tomlinson, 2010, p. 58)

Civility enforces organizational conformity. "The normative ideal of civility is a white, middle-class corporatized notion…the construction of civility marginalizes voices deemed uncivil, closes off the discursive space for such members, and minimizes opportunities for resistance" (Kisselburgh & Dutta, 2009, p. 124).

The *problematic of organization* enables "the discursive imperialism of Western scholarship" (Broadfoot & Munshi, 2007b, p. 258). Imperialism manifests in textbooks that attempt multiculturalism/inclusion by including work about non-Western and/or non-White populations but do so in separate chapters and sections, reifying their status as *others* and reinforcing the white American *mainstream* as central and neutral (Manning, 2020). Blind peer review, faculty hiring, promotion/tenure, and funding review practices also codify submission to these standards. *Border defensiveness* (Harris, 2019), the resistance to reorganizing and disorganizing against systemic racism, can be seen in academic and disciplinary standards that advocate for rigor but mask underlying colonial values pervading academia intensely, thereby stifling any consideration of alternative ways to achieve rigor. By nature, standards obstruct innovation (King & Frost, 2002). Discourse controlled from the organizational center marginalizes nontraditional voices and ways of knowing. Decolonizing would require explicit commitment to acknowledge multiple meanings of *standard* – both *a set of criteria for rigor* and *universality* – and appreciate the equal value of criteria for rigor from alternative cultural logics. We "need to question who determines such standards and practices and how these can act as gatekeeping and 'othering' practices designed to protect the walls of ivory towers" (Broadfoot et al., 2010, p. 807).

Broadfoot and Munshi (2007b) examine the potential for a postcolonial rationality, which might include multiple subjectivities, centering postcolonial voices, and the recognition that "difference can operate as an active force toward knowledge" (p. 262). They conclude by advocating for "writing back to the center" (p. 264), where epistemically marginalized scholars write about organizing practices from their own cultures, using their subjectivity to contextualize and reinterpret disciplinary constructs and theories. Though scholars have written back to the center, they often go unheard (e.g., Allen et al., 1999; D'Souza & Pal, 2018). Yet, such writing offers "multiple forms of cultural knowledge around organizing and communicating" (p. 264), thus deeply diversifying the knowledge produced and consumed in the field. "In engaging in such an enterprise, we begin to reimagine the scholarly community of organizational communication as a transdisciplinary and transgeographical entity capable of disrupting contemporary hierarchies of knowledge and making sense of our flattening world" (p. 264).

Mumby and Stohl's (2007) response asserted openness and dialogue, yet reproduced some of the very implicit bias being critiqued, leading Broadfoot and Munshi (2007a) to provide some clarifications. Grimes and Parker (2009) critiqued how both essays define boundaries. Mumby and Stohl (2007) engage in a way that reproduces the very coloniality and marginalization being critiqued. In response to the call to include voices on the margins, Mumby and Stohl label feminist, critical, and postmodern scholars as "on the margins," closing off consideration of voices outside *those* margins – communicatively constituting *border defensiveness* (Harris, 2019). They set disciplinary boundaries that exclude subaltern voices. Broadfoot and Munshi (2007b) focus on geography as they identify a Euro-American center for the discipline, conflating *Western* with *privileged* and rendering inequity and subaltern presence in the West invisible (see Gist-Mackey & Dougherty, 2021 for an exception). To solve such issues, Grimes and Parker (2009) advocate for a focus on visibility and voice rather than boundaries.

In response to Broadfoot and Munshi's (2007b) observations of tone policing in scholarly review, Mumby and Stohl (2007) counter that there is a robust organizational communication literature on emotion. Yet, the argument that

> organizational communication is already doing work that includes an emotional component obscures the fact that rejecting work as too emotional and political is a discursive move that downplays the colonizing practices. In addition, directing attention to research that includes emotion also directs attention away from Broadfoot and Munshi's critique of the review process.
>
> (Grimes & Parker, 2009, p. 508)

Mumby and Stohl (2007) trivialize the ways publication review functions to maintain colonial epistemological structures and control disciplinary boundaries – despite empirical evidence our practices do so (Grimes & Parker, 2009). Similarly, D'Souza and Pal's (2018) autoethnographic work illustrates how dominant approaches to diversity in academia perpetuate whiteness and obscure real difference – at great personal cost to those already marginalized.

Dutta (2006) proposed ten ways to decolonize academic peer review and demonstrate a kinder, gentler discipline: (1) approach reviewing as collaborative, (2) set one's ego aside, (3) engage reflexivity, (4) understand various paradigms, (5) work within the limitations of a project, (6) refrain from demonstrating how much you know, (7) offer actionable recommendations, (8) provide timely feedback, (9) be encouraging, and (10) treat others the way you'd like reviewers to treat you. These proposed peer review practices lean into Indigenous ways of being and knowing, which are often undergirded by values such as reciprocity, communal resources, and relational solidarity (Kimmerer, 2013).

A Framework for Postcolonial Theory in Organizational Communication

Broadfoot and Munshi's (2007b) essay motivated conversation (Broadfoot & Munshi, 2007a; Broadfoot et al., 2008, 2010; Grimes & Parker, 2009; Mumby & Stohl, 2007; Nelson-Marsh et al., 2008), but postcolonial approaches did not gain traction in organizational communication until a subsequent essay in *The Sage Handbook of Organizational Communication* provided scholars in the field with a set of guidelines. Here, Broadfoot and Munshi (2014) present the following commitments where postcolonial thought meets organizing practices.

Commitment 1: Disrupting and Reimagining Organizational Space(s)

Organizing practices and forms are deeply embedded in histories and geographies of conquest, imperialism, and colonialism (Broadfoot & Munshi, 2014). Eurocentric ideals permeate organizations and our study of them renders voices and rationalities from other contexts silent and invisible. An epistemological positioning *in-between* the marginalized and the dominant (Bhabha, 1996) examines how material aspects of organizing (and its study) perpetuate colonial structures. From *in-between* we can deconstruct "taken-for-granted configurations of space that privilege certain geographic-historical formations" (Broadfoot & Munshi, 2014, p. 157). Cheung's (2008) analysis of *guanxi* is an example of *in-between* theorizing. Nicotera and Clinkscales's (2010) *structurational divergence* (see Chapter 3), arising from observations of incongruities between structure and culture for African-American organizations, is conceptually similar to *in-between,* "where two sets of rules are in contest with one another, each requiring the suppression of the other" (Broadfoot & Munshi, 2014, p. 155).

Commitment 2: Resisting Colonialist Discourse and Rethinking Organizational Practices

Organizational discourse reproduces political dominance, for example, linguistic constructions reifying the West's positional superiority (Broadfoot & Munshi, 2014). National and global political tensions manifest in organizational communication and "normalize Euro-American political values as universal" (p. 158). For example, Hall's (2011) postcolonial theory discursive leadership study examines how Jamaican managers make sense of leadership in their colonial/neocolonial context and construct culturally Indigenous organizational practices. Hybridity, mimicry, and agency in practices and identity constitute cultural contexts, showing that control and agency are dialectical. "For postcolonial cultures like Jamaica, there may be no way to articulate an Indigenous concept of leadership outside of the scholarly constructs and the discursive practices and processes that constitute colonial and neocolonial practices of organizing" (p. 639). Privileging Indigenous voices reveals resistance, accommodation, transformation, and mimicry of colonial structures. The study documents the impact of colonial discourse by questioning how subaltern agents understand, negotiate, resist, and transform it into organizational practices that empower them. Centering subaltern voices provides insights into organizing processes that would otherwise have been missed.

Commitment 3: Decolonizing Thought and Reconfiguring Organizing Forms of Knowledge

Postcolonial thought interrogates transnational hegemonies, reclaiming cultural identities and forms of representation by inserting "subaltern histories into social thought and forms of knowledge through accounts of the lives, struggles, and aspirations of people at the grassroots rather than elitist versions of realities from above that silence *other* voices" (Broadfoot & Munshi, 2014, p. 160). Postcolonial theory's discursive space provides "ways to recover local epistemologies and reform global ethics to address the powerful inequality of organizing practices in global relations" (p. 161). Long and Mills's (2008) analysis of practices of "benign but latently colonialist supranational organizations," such as the United Nations (Broadfoot & Munshi, 2014, p. 162) provides compelling evidence that the 1994 genocide in Rwanda resulted from imperialist/colonial legacies manifested in the actions and inactions of these organizations.

These three commitments remain relevant in contemporary organizational communication. Gist-Mackey and Oliha-Donaldson (2023) argue that the #BlackLivesMatters movement is a form of postcolonial organizing, showing synergy between Broadfoot and Munshi's (2014) commitments and #BlackLivesMatters; concluding that in decolonization to achieve social justice, contemporary postcolonial organizing must address anti-Black racism.

Creating a Community Network

Broadfoot, Munshi, and their colleagues (Broadfoot et al., 2008, 2010; Nelson-Marsh et al., 2008) established *COMMUNEcation Network*, an international collaborative forum for postcolonial organizational communication scholars. Though short-lived, the group's activities fostered significant advancements contributing to today's fruitful decolonizing efforts (see Chapter 1). The community, and their 2008 conference, functioned as an *in-between space* (Bhabha, 1996) enabling a view of "our scholarly and academic diaspora as a perpetual state of flux and flow, a form of 'disorganization' that can help unearth the ways in which taken-for-granted practices lead to a silencing of diverse voices" (Nelson-Marsh et al., 2008). Broadfoot et al. (2010) demonstrate how participatory conferencing technologies prioritized collective interaction and collaborative knowledge-creation, deterritorializing scholarly activity and revealing the coloniality of traditional conferences as platforms for individual expertise.

To capture and disseminate the work accomplished, Broadfoot et al. (2008) provided a "mosaic" article – eight essays punctuated by editorial and summary commentary. Authored by 11 conference participants, the article addresses three themes emerging from discussions.

Theme 1: Resisting Silence

English is the language of academia, unifying insiders and dividing them from outsiders. The onus is on "outsiders" to become multilingual. Cultural particularities that cannot be expressed in English are lost, muting subaltern voices, eradicating culture, and fostering deficient theory. In Broadfoot et al (2008), Anuradha Malshe demonstrates how technology and media development in India resulted in loss of Indigenous culture; Mary Simpson illustrates that eldercare systems in Aotearoa New Zealand are modeled on Western market and commodification discourses, denying Indigenous ideas of aging, muting Māori voices as it renders local elders as nonparticipants in their own lives, and precluding discovery of organizing processes as they would naturally occur without Western interference.

Theme 2: Limits and Consequences of Linguistic and Theoretical Translations

Locally contextualized power and knowledge are rarely translated into academic literature (Broadfoot et al., 2008). Solving this requires deconstructing disciplinary boundaries and constructing borders between local realities, paying attention to their translation to academic texts. Research on organizational communication under different labels (e.g., public relations or human resources) is disregarded by US-based organizational communication scholars (do Carmo Reis, in Broadfoot et al., 2008). Distinctions in organizational theory may not be reflected in local practices and cultural constructions of organizing (Gautam, in Broadfoot et al., 2008). Moreover, knowledge is steeped in social relations. Hidden commercial practices of academic publishing obscure imbalances in knowledge-production. Monolingualism renders knowledge dissemination exclusionary. International business and development practices are "dominated by a technocratic vocabulary, overwhelmingly in English," (Srivinas, in Broadfoot et al., 2008, p. 340), while local-level implementation and organizing take place in local languages. Monolingualism obscures the mediation of culture and knowledge required by international management.

Theme 3: Communal Considerations of Research Politics and Participation

Assumptions about the ethics of participation with local actors and research participants must be challenged. Traditional participatory action research is "dominated by an interventionist 'expert' who 'collaborates' with participating others but retains the power to decide the 'intervention' and 'action'" (Broadfoot et al., 2008, p. 341). Research methodologies require investigators to cleanse collected data of emotion and values, sanitizing it of "the micro politics of everyday concerns and activities" (Cockburn-Wootten & Cockburn, in Broadfoot et al., 2008, p. 344), losing opportunities for insights. Similarly, Jenkeri Zakari Okwori (in Broadfoot et al., 2008) describes how theater in action research empowers local actors to construct narratives of issues and actions, deliberately examine the need for change, and generate solutions, resulting in sustainable action.

Postcolonial Organizational Communication Scholarship

A postcolonial perspective requires questioning the conceptualization of resistance (Hanchey, 2018; Kalonaityte, 2010; Pal & Dutta, 2008). Resistance from the margins of imperialistic and colonial structures may take subtle forms (Pal & Dutta, 2008). Postcolonial theory recognizes resistance as "both conscious and unconscious, and centering mimicry, ambivalence, and hybridity" (Hanchey, 2018, p. 280). Postcolonial theorists identify insights from subtleties, tensions, and dialectics. Early postcolonial scholars in Organizational Communication reached beyond our margins, providing inclusive approaches to studying experiences of Indigenous and subaltern communities. It soon became clear that these efforts require centering subaltern and Indigenous voices within the discipline. Scholarship that centers subaltern voices using postcolonial theory and methodology provides alternative theoretic constructions to overturn coloniality in organizational communication theorizing.

Identity, Power, and Agency

Early postcolonial organizational communication research examined how actors negotiate identity, power, and agency in postcolonial discursive contexts (e.g., Hall, 2011). Pal and Buzzanell (2008, 2013) examined lived experiences of Indian call center workers, revealing how they utilize and challenge discursive resources to form identity and reframe discourses of work, career, and family. A decentered self and a global-local dialectic pervade a working life of physically local transnational interaction, creating a site of struggle highlighted by fears of cultural loss and ambitions for economic progress (Pal & Buzzanell, 2008).

Power-resistance dialectics characterize workers' work-related transnational interactions (Pal & Buzzanell, 2013). Participants discussed how India's colonial history plays out as they conform to self-presentation demands mimicking the West while simultaneously resenting such practices. Rejecting neoliberal logics of benevolence, participants position India as a site of opportunity for the West. Asserting Indian workers' capability and American customers' inferior global understanding, participants reverse neoliberal discourses of Western-superiority/non-Western-inferiority. They recognize Western engulfment of their being but define dual life as temporary.

Engaged reflexivity achieves shared power. Norander and Harter (2012) examined collaboration and reflexivity in the transnational organizing of a Swedish NGO seeking to empower women in post-conflict areas. Postcolonial feminist critical interpretation of organizing practices that mobilize local culture and knowledge through reflexivity in relationships with partner organizations (in Bosnia-Herzegovina, Serbia, Montenegro, Kosovo, Abkhazia, and Lebanon) revealed three reflexivity practices at three sites of struggle (representation, space, and sustainability). First, local partnerships are purposefully crafted to reverse and prevent marginalization. Second, networks are built on inclusion of a diversity of voices. Finally, practices are sensitive to alternative subject positions and emergent alliances. Local groups "define their needs and own the process of fulfilling those needs" in partnerships "characterized by open dialogue, long-term relationships, and an emphasis on creating inclusive peace" (p. 87). Reflexivity in communicative practices results in the creation of environments in which diverse intelligences thrive, allowing the NGO and its partners to "build relationships and restore a sense of community among those who are devastated by violent conflict and then not included in official peace processes" (p. 98). This postcolonial feminist approach to communication research on resistance and transformation fosters understanding resistance at the macro level without sacrificing attention to subaltern local voices and knowledge.

The culture-centered approach (CCA), a framework for subaltern theories of health organizing (Dutta, 2008, 2018), has been applied to public relations (Dutta et al., 2012), global activism (Pal & Dutta, 2012), transnational management (Dutta & Dutta, 2013), and international development (Dutta, 2015). Intersections of *structure*, *culture*, and *agency* allow marginalized culture members to participate in community health interventions and create social change for their subaltern communities. Structural inequities are communication inequities. CCA seeks intersections between community communicative practices and dominant communicative structures to co-create processes and structures that facilitate community agency, organize effectively, and collectively solve local problems. Participation, partnerships, communication infrastructures, and reflexivity are centered to co-create local-national-global infrastructures for community-based knowledge production. (See Dutta, 2018, for CCA methodologies.)

Broadfoot and Munshi (2015) advocate critical assessment of *agency* as a process of *translation*. A Western definition of agency as individual action to achieve goals loses understanding of Others who are *acted upon*. *Translation* reflects on action *and* what it means to others, especially at discursive intersections. Postcolonial ethnography can define and study *agency as translation*, positioning participants and researchers as "collaborative co-constructors and interpreters of *accounts of agency*" (p. 471). Studying agency as locally understood and limited by others elicits multiple accounts embedded in multiple contexts, revealing "complex relationships between self, agency and culture" (p. 472). Reconceptualizing agency as translation through a postcolonial lens can uncover meanings and processes that remain invisible to Western conceptualizations.

Theorizing from the Global South

The *Global North/South* distinction is a geographic descriptor of economic inequity that corresponds to coloniality – evidence of the enduring and devastating effects of colonization. Communicatively the term *Global South* (which includes Central America, South America, the Caribbean, Africa, Mongolia, China, and Southeast Asia) names the persistent inequity in the worldwide distribution of power and situates present-day anticolonial liberation efforts (Dutta & Pal, 2020; Pal et al., 2023). Communication at large has problematically ignored perspectives from the Global South. A special issue of *Communication Theory* (Dutta & Pal, 2020) brings together what little media theory exists and provides frameworks for advancing theorizing from the positionality of the Global South. While organizational communication was not represented in the issue, Dutta and Pal (2020) point out that organizational structures, forms, and practices largely emerge from coloniality. Note that subalternity also exists in the Global North – for Indigenous, Black, Latinx, and immigrant peoples in the US, Canada, Aotearoa New Zealand, and Australia, for example.

A few organizational communication scholars have taken seriously the need to change traditional Western business approaches to globalization (Prichard, 2006) and to theorize resistance critically (Ganesh et al., 2005). Such scholars contend with the container metaphor falsely equating *organizational communication* with *communication inside organizations* – as well as the corporate and production biases discussed in Chapter 1. Tañongon's (2023) Montreal School approach (see Chapter 3) to agribusiness organizing in the Philippine South illustrates how *the market* functions as a nonhuman agent annexing the power of "background voices" ventriloquized in interaction (e.g., precolonial Indigenous beliefs, Spanish colonialism, village organizing, and agricultural technological developments). Analyzing text messages among three main actors of a community agribusiness organization, Tañongon (2023) demonstrates the extendibility of nonhuman agency in a hierarchy of agencies unique to this postcolonial context *in-between* traditional and modern agribusiness practices. Actors ventriloquize nonhuman agents (weather and market price) to imbue them with the power to mediate human activity with increasing influence. Background voices constitute collective organizational identity, allowing the market to drive human action in ways particular to this intertextual setting between Indigenous precolonial culture and modern technocratic business culture.

Pal et al.'s (2023) edited volume, *Organizing at the Margins: Theorizing Organizations of Struggle in the Global South*, engages in "democratizing knowledge building" (p. 5) by addressing ontological, epistemological, and methodological challenges, imaginations, and practices. The book identifies three modes of organizing (decolonizing dominant epistemologies; dismantling borders; and deconstructing structure), identifies key organizational processes Western-centric approaches would miss, and offers multiple critiques of neoliberal economy from the vantage point of communities resisting neoliberal policies. Locating research throughout the Global South, the collection examines research methodologies, analytical techniques, and numerous forms of engaged struggle while critically analyzing the cultural, class, and racial/ethnic constructions of our disciplinary knowledge bases.

African-Centered Organizing

Africa is home to thousands of ethnicities, cultures, and languages in dozens of countries, many with colonially imposed arbitrary national borders. Yet, Western-centric approaches conflate continent, nation, ethnicity, and culture when writing about or addressing Africa.

Focused on Western (usually Anglo-US) white-collar contexts with no attention to socio-cultural, material, and historical factors, traditional organizational literature provides little insight into African forms of organizing. A focus on African organizing can lift organizational communication theory out of its Eurocentrism to account for organizing as it occurs in the global context of economic, political, and social challenges (Cruz, 2015b) and to understand context and culture as constitutive features of communication and organizing (Maingi Ngwu, 2022).

Subaltern persons everywhere confront organizing suffused with the legacy of coloniality. Karikari and Brown's (2018) critical discourse analysis explores how leaders of US African student organizations navigate dominant discourses of Africa through strategies of resistance and accommodation. Although participants represent numerous African countries and cultures, their shared experience facing US campus ideologies about Africa manifests in common strategies for navigating postcolonial discourse about Africa. Participants identify coloniality as a primary driver of that discourse. They resist presumptions of inferiority, poverty, and homogeneity of Africa as they accommodate Western notions of leadership and organization. They construct their agency as leaders through a sensemaking process made possible by this dialectic of accommodation and resistance, creating a hybrid form of leadership.

Hanchey and Berkelaar's (2015) postcolonial approach reveals nuanced contextualized differences in discourse. They analyze discourses of career success in two Tanzanian youth magazines with different target audiences: urban in-school youth and rural out-of-school youth. Three interrelated dimensions – culture, materiality, and time – provide a discourse analysis framework. Four themes were common across the publications: encouraging self-reliance, working for the collective good, developing entrepreneurs, and emphasizing healthy relationships. Yet, their discursive frames differed by audience: career success as achievement vs. as survival. Detailed attention to context illustrates how Western nation-as-culture assumptions are inappropriate for postcolonial contexts. Intra-national contexts must be considered as "individual, local, and other regional contexts interplay with the material and temporal resources of everyday life to shape career discourses and corresponding actions" (p. 432).

Western-centric theorizing often misses cultural nuances regarding work and workplaces, for example in the foundational dirty work literature, which was US-centric for decades (e.g., Ashforth & Kreiner, 1999; Ashforth et al., 2007). *Dirty work* (Hughes, 1951) is physically, socially, or morally stigmatized labor. The literature on dirty work considers gender and social class but disregards broader cultural contexts, generally concluding that reframing negative discourse produces agency. More contemporary research addresses wider cultural experiences, such as immigrant labor (Alvarez, 2023). In addition, Cruz (2015a) applies an African feminist framework to consider cultural contexts alongside agency and discourse. Cruz's (2015a) use of African feminism transcends common Western binary logics, such as positive/negative meanings and discursive agent/subject. African feminism uses context to negotiate both with and around oppressive structures. "Context determines workers' choices to shift discourse or maintain the status quo" (p. 423); empowerment stems from this strategic compromise. By elevating context from the background to the foreground in post-war Liberia, Cruz (2015a) demonstrates that agency, discourse, and context intersect – overturning the assumption that discourse is an obstacle to agency, which is achieved only by rejecting stigmatizing meanings. Cruz's ethnographic observations reveal that Liberian market women *strategically employ* stigma to their advantage. Two discourses were examined: *civilized discourse* that emerged before the war, setting a standard for gender and class distinctions in stigmatized physical labor and Indigenous clothing; and *empowerment discourse* that emerged during the war and diversified acceptable labor for women. In the post-conflict environment, these oppositional discourses remain interlocked.

Cruz's (2015a) participants navigated discourse and agency in three ways. Through *appropriation of the stigma* of physicality, they exploited negative meetings to frame themselves as having superior capabilities needed in their environment. By *aligning with oppositional discourse*, they claimed empowerment from oppressive gendered discourses, such as market regulations and oversight, which collapsed during the war. Rather than reject civilized discourse, they took their place in its hierarchy. Finally, by *creating new meanings*, they fill discursive gaps left by societal shifts or crises (in this case, war) with alternative meanings of their own design. These women cast themselves as community keepers, embracing the roles they created in organizing food distribution and taking care of community members. The study illustrates the three foundational African feminist principles: holism, collectivity, and situationality (Cruz, 2015b).

Maingi Ngwu (2022) applies African Feminist Theory in a decolonizing historiography of women's organizing in Kenya documenting organizational communication in inter-regional exchange networks. Extending their role as community food providers, Kenyan women historically organized and conducted trade among communities, often traveling for weeks caravan style. Solidarity, gendered collaboration, and negotiation were key communicative principles. Maingi Ngwu (2022) shows how these communication structures remain in the organizing of traders in Nairobi's central business district.

Cruz's (2017) communicative situational model theorizes the ways in which Liberian market women negotiate *visibility* and *invisibility* on multiple dimensions. Susu groups are grassroots organizations regulated by the Liberian Market Association (LMA) that collect regular dues and distribute collected funds to members on a rotating basis. In a context of secret societies and invisible organizing, susu groups' covert nature is normative and valuable. Visibility and invisibility depend on three interrelated bivalent dimensions. On the *temporal* (everyday/exceptional) dimension, daily routine is invisible, but disruption to that routine creates visibility as the LMA is brought into leverage authority on transgressors. On the *relational* (secrecy/procedural) dimension, transgressions are managed relationally and invisibly unless the relationship is disrupted, in which case news of the issue spreads among members. Eventually, LMA procedures result in the ultimate visibility – the examination of the secret susu notebook. On the *structural* (group/market-office) dimension, their normative invisibility keeps susu groups accountable to themselves, coming to the attention of the LMA only if a problem drives them to access the regulatory structure. Cruz's (2017) analysis illustrates that communicative practices are embedded in culture, putting postcolonial cultures at high risk of being misread and misrepresented through a Western lens.

Cruz and Sodeke (2021) provide an insightful postcolonial analysis reconceptualizing *liquidity* as plural in African contexts. A sociological metaphor, *liquidity* captures social conditions of continual change and mobility characterizing global economics, identities, and relationships (Bauman, 2000). "Modern people are similar to liquid matter in their vulnerability and fluidity, unable to maintain the same identity for a long time, which reinforces this temporary state of social relations" (Eckhardt & Bardhi, 2020). Disenfranchised subjects in the Global South are often framed as unable to organize, but this Western framing is erroneous (Cruz & Sodeke, 2021). Rather, marginal organizing in postcolonial contexts is a continuous shape-shifting process of *liquidities* (social, political, and economic). Marginalized actors adapt and respond to involuntary conditions requiring them to "constantly develop strategies – rule bending, participative learning and solidarity, and shape-shifting – to evade neoliberal threats" (Cruz & Sodeke, 2021, p. 533). Case studies in Nigeria and Liberia illustrate the epistemological inadequacy of Western theory to capture the fluid processes of motion, solvency, and permeability characterizing these liquidities, evidence of profound organizational intelligences that appear chaotic and disorganized through a Western lens.

Motion describes the inherent mobility of liquid organizing unbound by location. Organizational activity (e.g., marketplace commerce) is "opportunistic, itinerant, and ebbs or flows in space depending on the latest threats or opportunities" (p. 536). For example, a traffic jam spawns a marketplace bound to that space temporarily, moving to other spaces according to opportunities and threats. The strategies themselves are liquid. *Where* cannot be planned, but *why* and *how* are deeply tactical. Traditional theory and methodology cannot account for such mobility in organizing.

Likewise, Western approaches cannot account for *solvency*. Marginal organizational actors have extraordinary capacity to disappear, dissolving into their surroundings to become imperceptible. Solvency "is tied to neoliberal policies and governmental measures – economic, political, and cultural – which specifically target the disenfranchised" (p. 538) under constant financial, spatial, physical, and existential threat. Deprived of spaces and resources that stabilize an organizing environment, marginal organizing maintains stability through its capacity to cease and resume activity spontaneously. Disassembly and assembly of organizing is spatial, social, and physical/material (e.g., market stalls).

Permeability captures the embeddedness of marginal organizing in its cultural contexts. Organizational boundaries cannot be delineated as Western theory expects. Organizing is simply the fabric of daily life. Worksites and homes converge. Parallel economies provide services to residents (e.g., barbershops and food shacks), with "blurred distinctions between work/friends, self/community, and public/private domains" (p. 540). Organizational theory presumes that organizations (O_3) exist and that organizing follows explicit decision-making, requires a hierarchy of authority, and depends on stable structures. None of these are true in the postcolonial context of liquid marginal organizing.

Decolonizing the Discipline

Many have argued that we must decolonize our own professional and academic practices if we are to broaden our perspectives on the external world. Two trends in communication studies contextualize work to decolonize organizational communication – our disciplinary history of racialization (see Chapter 1) and the decolonial turn across the social sciences and humanities. Despite decades of effort to motivate change, only a series of painful crises turned the discipline (see Chapter 1). Those collective experiences opened a space for genuine efforts to decolonize – by steeling the resolve of those wounded and by raising consciousness among complacent others to finally recognize that woundedness. In the 2020s, substantive decolonizing efforts are underway. We must remain vigilant so they do not function merely as performative virtue-signaling – an attempt to be remembered well on the right side of history (Jensen, in Pal et al., 2022).

A 2020 organizational communication preconference specifically addressing decolonization resulted in a published forum attempting "to decentralize the ways we think of the world in terms of its forms of organization and its social life in the neoliberal political order" and to turn "the analysis inward to dismantle the hegemony that has persisted within the discipline of organizational communication" (Pal et al., 2022, p. 549). In that forum, Kate Lockwood Harris grapples with the persistent false equivalency between *organizational* and *workplaces* that prevents attention to social unrest and its linguistic implications. Heewon Kim confronts neoliberalist human resource theories' appropriation of *organizational justice* as a set of corporate strategies for productivity. Ziyu Long, Jasmine Linabary, and Elizabeth Larson advocate for a relational approach to academic writing, publishing, and evaluation; "there is no 'individual accomplishment' in knowledge production" (p. 555). Peter Jensen seeks to recollect colonial violence erased by epistemic frameworks and the whiteness of organizing norms promoting "comfortable fictions" (p. 557) underlying organizational theory and practice. Angela Gist-Mackey identifies the ideology of *hierarchy* as a colonizing force. Cast as neutral, *hierarchy's* logics of ranking and exclusion prevail, resulting in power-hoarding – a key cultural characteristic of white supremacy. Jamie McDonald addresses the hegemonic function of monolingualism in the field, advocating for *linguistic plurality*. Beatriz Neito-Fernandez and Mahuya Pal explore decolonizing methodological interventions, including discourse analysis and fieldwork, to dismantle intellectual imperialism. Finally, Jing Jiang, Smita Misra, and Sarah Dempsey challenge us to dismantle colonizing logics and practices from within our universities, using our conceptual and methodological expertise to challenge the coloniality of the universities' material foundations – land, labor, and community relations.

Review of Communication published two consecutive special issues entitled "(Re) Theorizing Communication Studies from African Perspectives" (Asante & Hanchey, 2021; Hanchey & Asante, 2022) exploring the rich potential African knowledge systems offer for the study of communication. The issues address rhetoric, health communication, intercultural communication, cultural and media studies, and feminist organizational communication, providing comprehensive reviews of existing work, its decolonizing power, and the potential for further decolonial intervention. For example, Maingi Ngwu's (2022) African feminist historiography of Kenyan women's trade networks illustrates that organizational communication's disciplinary historiography is itself a colonial structure. Disciplinary identity constructs the boundaries around the forms and processes of organizing constructed as central or as marginal in our work. Maingi Ngwu (2022) disrupts the restrictive connection between how we view our field and what we study, backgrounding key institutionalized figures, programs, and scholarly work to foreground organizational actors themselves as central to understanding organizing. Terms like *alternative* both characterize and delegitimize the study of organizational forms and processes existing outside our biased margins for what counts as *organizational*, perpetuating these disciplinary biases (see Chapter 1). In a decolonized field, what we know as *Organizational Communication* (the discipline) would be driven by organizational forms and practices as they occur across all human experience. "Until then, what we have come to call organizational communication remains narrow, monolithic, and Western-centric" (p. 56).

Pal and Nieto-Fernandez (2024) suggest transnational feminism to confront assumptions of neoliberal hegemony and imperial legacy in feminist organizational communication theory (see Chapter 13). They recommend pursuing knowledge-making through epistemologies of disenfranchised women, disrupting the naturalization of neoliberal discourses, centering anticapitalist and antiimperialist critique, identifying pressing contemporary issues, and confronting the academy's neoliberal model. They call for constructing *insurgent knowledges* by cultivating collaborative relationships with activities and communities so our work generates knowledge *with* them rather than *about* them.

> Decolonization is not only about challenging dominant epistemologies and ontologies but is an active struggle for social justice at every level. A decolonial politics asks us to build a transnational solidarity across feminist movements connected by their critique of global capital, while interrogating imperial legacies and neoliberal landscape of corporate academy.
>
> (p. 78)

Decolonizing efforts can also be found in organizational rhetoric. Na'puti and Cruz (2022) offer a praxis-oriented theory-building model to the study of organizational rhetoric by mobilizing texture and depth to address whiteness and Indigenous erasure. Using their own fieldwork to illustrate the potential of Indigenous-centered work, they make three recommendations. *Decolonizing the self* is a process of interrogating our own whiteness and that which is embedded in the systems that define academic success. *An ethic of radical care* asks scholars to go beyond the basics of human subject protections to actively dismantle power structures of their interactions in colonial contexts, attuning to Indigenous communities by learning local language, seeking genuine non-instrumental relationships, and recognizing forms of invisible harm stemming from coloniality. Finally, *preparation for fieldwork* should include an authentic effort to understand local culture and history through immersion in local contexts and by mobilizing all available resources for understanding (historical accounts, creative literature, etc.).

Hanchey and Jensen (2022) argue that organizational rhetoric and ontological constructions are political. They assert that *subjectification* should be the foundation of understanding organizational rhetoric, rather than *identification. Identification* focuses on how individuals orient to the organization through recognition of some similarity; *subjectification* posits that "a subject is brought into being through shifting contexts, relations, and imbrication in forces of power" (p. 263). The organization shapes the being and becoming of organizational members, actors, and agents. *Identification* reifies the idea that individuals are whole and separate from organizations, normalizes colonial narratives and logics of inclusion and citizenship, and presumes both the possibility and desirability of achieving individual intentions (Hanchey & Jensen, 2022). A conceptual shift to *subjectification* builds on an inherent incompleteness of subject formation, unleashes potential for organizing beyond inclusion, and recognizes that organizational subjects are materially and affectively constituted by organization. This shift allows deeper conceptual analysis in at least three areas deep structural processes of persuasion rather than simple affinity; discursive imbrication of organizations and individuals; and fundamental processes of coloniality and racialization that create organizational membership and members. "By obscuring the politics inherent in subjectivity, other approaches renaturalize power relations and maintain the logics of colonial-modernity that universalize the modern liberal subject" (p. 279). *Subjectification* provides conceptual connections between organizational rhetoric and organizational communication to facilitate the decolonization of both fields.

Conclusion

In many respects, organizational communication scholarship has been intellectually colonized and disciplined. The hegemonic power of coloniality manifests in disciplinary borders and biases that have never served us well, rendering large swaths of organizational knowledge and experiences invisible and/or indecipherable. We must unlearn biases and border defensiveness so all types of organizational and communication ontologies and epistemologies are legitimated and included. Postcolonial theory, thinkers, and scholarship provide a metaphorical map for our journey to continually work toward decolonizing the field. Equity, inclusivity, and compassion are worthy goals, but the benefits of decolonization are more extensive. Decolonization can provide the ability to see organizational communication phenomena across contexts as they actually occur, expand methodologies and vocabularies to explore and analyze them, and appreciate the insight to cultivate practices that genuinely foster wellbeing in organizational lives.

Recommended Supplementary Readings

Ahmed, S. (2020). *On being included: Racism and diversity in institutional life*. Duke University Press.

This book offers an account of the diversity world based on interviews with diversity practitioners in higher education, as well as her own experience of doing diversity work despite the resistance of such work by institutional employers. This book explores the gap between symbolic commitments to diversity and the experience of those who embody diversity.

Asante, G. A., & Hanchey, J. N. (2021). African communication studies: A provocation and invitation. *Review of Communication*, *21*(4), 271–292.
Hanchey, J. N., & Asante, G. A. (2022). African communication studies: Applications and interventions. *Review of Communication*, *22*(1), 1–6.

These special issues explore the field of communication broadly as it might be expanded and deepened by employing African perspectives. In so doing, they demonstrate the Eurocentric biases of communication theory and research.

Broadfoot, K. J., & Munshi, D. (2014). Postcolonial approaches. In L. L. Putnam & D. K. Mumby (Eds.), *The Sage handbook of organizational communication* (3rd ed., pp. 151–171). Sage.

This chapter conceptually connects the fields of postcolonial studies with organizational communication using three central commitments.

Pal, M., Kim, H., Harris, K. L., Long, Z., Linabary, J., Wilhoit Larson, E., Jensen, P. R., Gist-Mackey, A. N., McDonald, J. Nieto-Fernandez, B., Jiang, J., Misra, S., & Depsey, S. E. (2022). Decolonizing organizational communication. *Management Communication Quarterly*, *36*(3), 391–577.

This forum manuscript was written by a group of scholar-teachers committed to addressing various critical social issues after a series of problematic incidents in the organizational communication division at a national conference. The forum challenges dominant ideas, paradigms, and structures within and beyond organizational communication. The collection of essays was written in the spirit of decolonization and social justice.

Pal, M., Cruz, J., & Munshi, D. (2024). *Organizing at the margins. Theorizing organizations of struggle in the Global South*. Palgrave Macmillan.

This is an edited collection of postcolonial scholarship by contemporary organizational communication scholars. This collection addresses organizing and organizations of struggle in the Global South. The essays collectively critique the neoliberal economy from the perspective of marginalized communities who resist neoliberalism.

Important Concepts: Define and Discuss

Coloniality
Critical theory
Decolonizing
Eurocentric
Global South
Hegemony
Marginalization
Meta-ignorance
Meta-insensitivity
Neocolonialism
Neoliberalism
Postcolonialism
Praxis
Subalternity
Unlearning
Western
White supremacy
Whiteness

Discussion Questions

1 How can coloniality be identified in epistemological biases in the methodologies used for data collection and analysis?
2 How are Indigenous and other marginalized ways of knowing excluded from traditional organizational communication conceptual frameworks and theoretical constructions?
3 Think of an organization or act of organizing you have been part of. How do you see the legacy of colonialism showing up in this organization? What are its effects on members of this organization? Does the manifestation of colonialism affect certain groups within the organization differently? How has communication been colonized at micro, meso, and macro levels ways? How can we decolonize our communication at the micro, meso, and macro levels?
4 Does the legacy of colonialism show up differently in different types of organizations or organizing (e.g., for-profit, non-profit, governmental organizations, and social organizations)?

Practitioners' Corner

At a glance colonialism seems like an antiquated history that has little to do with contemporary times. But that couldn't be further from the reality. The legacy of colonialism shows up in nuanced, implicit, and covert ways as well as in concrete, explicit, and overt ways. Practitioners working in contemporary organizational settings have a timely opportunity to learn more about colonialism and postcolonialism so that they can foster decolonial efforts. For instance, contemporary organizational members and community organizers can work on decolonizing policy. This would require a close examination of the legacy of colonialism embedded in existing policy and how such policies affect different groups disproportionately.

Decolonial effects could also include affirming and amplifying the dignity of people with a particular aim of re-centering those who have been and are being disenfranchised. In practice, this may look like listening sessions or cultural learning and unlearning hegemonic ways of organizing. Practitioners may also work on making more equitable conditions for people re-allocating resources to stigmatized members. Ultimately, decolonizing efforts would incorporate debunking white supremacy culture (Okun, 2021) by mitigating and eventually eliminating its following manifestations: (1) perfectionism, (2) sense of urgency, (3) defensiveness, (4) valuing quantity over quality, (5) privileging the written word, (6) belief in one superior way to do things, (7) paternalism, (8) binary either/or thinking, (9) power hoarding, (10) fear of open conflict, (11) individualism, (12) centering self, (13) belief that more is better, (14) value for objectivity, and (15) right to comfort. Practitioners who engage in initiatives to mitigate white supremacy culture (Okun, 2021) will have to adopt and adapt organizational practices, policies, structures, and procedures that are culturally competent, just, and equitable. This means that change is needed and may cause ambiguity, uncertainty, and discomfort. Finally, efforts at decolonizing may require decolonial relational development with marginalized communities uplifting and amplifying their ways of being and doing things in acts of humility.

References

#ToneUpOrgComm Collective (2020). #ToneUpOrgComm: A manifestx. *Departures in Critical Qualitative Research*, *9*(2), 152–154.

Allen, B. J., Orbe, M. P., & Olivas, M. R. (1999). The complexity of our tears: Dis/enchantment and (in)difference in the academy. *Communication Theory*, *9*(4), 402–429. https://doi.org/10.1111/j.1468-2885.1999.tb00206.x

Alvarez, W. (2023). *Everyday dirty work: Invisibility, communication, and immigrant labor*. Ohio State University Press.

Applebaum, R. (2020). When incivility is a form of civility: Challenging the comfort of willful ignorance. *Educational Theory*, *70*(6), 717–730. https://doi.org/10.1111/edth.12458

Asante, G. A., & Hanchey, J. N. (2021). African communication studies: A provocation and invitation. *Review of Communication*, *21*(4), 271–292. https://doi.org/10.1080/15358593.2021.2001844

Ashcraft, K. (2006). Falling from a humble perch? Rereading organizational communication studies with an attitude of alliance. *Management Communication Quarterly*, *19*(4), 645–652. https://doi.org/10.1177/0893318905285389

Ashforth, B. E., & Kreiner, G. E. (1999). "How can you do it?": Dirty work and the challenge of constructing a positive identity. *Academy of Management Review*, *24*(3), 413–434. https://doi.org/10.5465/AMR.1999.2202129

Ashforth, B. E., Kreiner, G. E., Clark, M. A., & Fugate, M. (2007). Normalizing dirty work: Managerial tactics for countering occupational taint. *Academy of Management Journal*, *50*(1), 149–174. http://dx.doi.org/10.5465/AMJ.2007.24162092

Banjeree, S. B., & Prasad, A. (2008). Introduction to the special issue on "critical reflections on management and organizations: A postcolonial perspective. *Critical Perspectives on International Business*, *4*(2/3), 90–98. https://doi.org/10.1108/17422040810869963
Barker, J. (2006). Forum: Whither management communication? Forum introduction. *Management Communication Quarterly*, *19*(4), 635–637. https://doi.org/10.1177/0893318905285387
Bauman, Z. (2000). *Liquid modernity*. Polity.
Bhabha, H. K. (1996). Culture's in-between. In S. Hall & P. duGay (Eds.), *Questions of cultural identity* (pp. 53–60). Sage.
Bray, S., Embrick, D. G., & Williams, J. E. (2018, November 15). Civility for whom? *Inside Higher Ed*. https://www.insidehighered.com/advice/2018/11/16/when-calls-civility-are-attempts-silence-messenger-opinion
Broadfoot, K., Cockburn, T., Cockburn-Wootten, C., Reis, M. Gautam, D., Malshe, A., Munshi, D., Nelson-Marsh, N., Okwori, J., Simpson, M., & Srinivas, N. (2008). A mosaic of visions, daydreams, and memories: Diverse inlays of organizing and communicating from around the globe. *Management Communication Quarterly*, *22*(2), 322–350. https://doi.org/10.1177/0893318908323574
Broadfoot, K. J., Munshi, B., & Nelson-Marsh, N. (2010). COMMUNEcation: A rhizomatic tale of participatory technology, postcoloniality and professional community. *New Media & Society*, *12*(5), 797–812. https://doi.org/10.1177/1461444809348880
Broadfoot, K. J., & Munshi, D. (2007a). Afterword: In search of a polyphony of voices. *Management Communication Quarterly*, *21*(2), 281–283. https://doi.org/10.1177/0893318907306039
Broadfoot, K. J., & Munshi, D. (2007b). Diverse voices and alternative rationalities: Imagining forms of postcolonial organizational communication. *Management Communication Quarterly*, *21*(2), 249–267. https://doi.org/10.1177/0893318907306037
Broadfoot, K. J., & Munshi, D. (2014). Postcolonial approaches. In L. L. Putnam & D. K. Mumby (Eds.), *The Sage handbook of organizational communication* (3rd ed., pp. pp. 151–171). Sage.
Broadfoot, K. J., & Munshi, D. (2015). Agency as a process of translation. *Management Communication Quarterly*, *29*(3), 469–474. https://doi.org/10.1177/0893318915585158
Cardoso, F. H. (1977). The consumption of dependency theory in the United States. *Latin American Research Review*, *12*(3), 7–24. https://www.jstor.org/stable/2502466
Chatterjee, N. (1987). *Nationalist thought and the colonial world: A derivative discourse*. University of Minnesota Press.
Cheung, I. I. (2008). Let the "other" speak for itself: Understanding Chinese employees from their own perspectives. *Critical Perspectives on International Business*, *4*(2/3), 277–306. http://dx.doi.org/10.1108/17422040810870024
Chinweizu. (1975). *The west and the rest of us: White predators, Black slavers, and the African elite*. Random House.
Chowdhury, R. (2023). Misrepresentation of marginalized groups: A critique of epistemic neocolonialism. *Journal of Business Ethics*, *186*, 553–570. http://dx.doi.org/10.1007/s10551-022-05229-4
Cooren, F. (2006). The organizational communication-discourse tilt: A refugee's perspective. *Management Communication Quarterly*, *19*(4), 653–660. https://doi.org/10.1177/0893318905285390
Cruz, J. M. (2015a). Dirty work at the intersections of gender, class, and nation: Liberian market women in post-conflict times. *Women's Studies in Communication*, *38*(4), 421–439. https://doi.org/10.1080/07491409.2015.1087439
Cruz, J. M. (2015b). Reimagining feminist organizing in global times: Lessons from African feminist communication. *Women & Language*, *38*(1), 23–41.
Cruz, J. M. (2017). Invisibility and visibility in alternative organizing: A communicative and cultural model. *Management Communication Quarterly*, *31*(4), 614–639. https://doi.org/10.1177/0893318917725202
Cruz, J. M., & Sodeke, C. U. (2021). Debunking Eurocentrism in organizational communication theory: Marginality and liquidities in postcolonial contexts. *Communication Theory*, *31*, 528–548. https://doi.org/10.1093/ct/qtz038
D'Souza, R. A., & Pal, M. (2018). Encountering the postcolonial in academia. *Journal of Organizational Ethnography*, *7*(3), 361–372. https://doi.org/10.1108/JOE-10-2017-0046
Damas, L. G. (1937). *Pigments*. Guy Lévis Mano.
Davis, A. M., & Ernst, R. (2017). Racial gaslighting. *Politics, Groups, and Identities*, *7*(4), 761–774. https://doi.org/10.1080/21565503.2017.1403934
DuBois, W. E. B. (1903). *The souls of Black folk*. A.C. McClurg & Company.

Dutta, M. J. (2006). The ten commandments of reviewing: The promise of a kinder, gentler discipline! *Health Communication*, *20*(2), 197–200. https://doi.org/10.1207/s15327027hc2002_11

Dutta, M. J. (2008). *Communicating health: A culture-centered approach*. Polity Press.

Dutta, M. J. (2015). Decolonizing communication for social change: A culture-centered approach. *Communication Theory*, *25*, 123–143. https://doi.org/10.1111/comt.12067

Dutta, M. J. (2018). Culture-centered approach in addressing health disparities: Communication infrastructures for subaltern voices. *Communication Methods and Measures*, *12*(4), 239–259. https://doi.org/10.1080/19312458.2018.1453057

Dutta, M. J., Ban, Z., & Pal, M. (2012). Engaging worldviews, cultures, and structures through dialogue: The culture-centered approach to public relations. *Prism*, *9*(2), 1–15. https://www.prismjournal.org/uploads/1/2/5/6/125661607/v9-no2-a2.pdf

Dutta, M. J., & Dutta, D. (2013). Multinational going cultural: A postcolonial deconstruction of cultural intelligence. *Journal of International and Intercultural Communication*, *6*(3), 241–258. https://doi.org/10.1080/17513057.2013.790989

Dutta, M. J., & Pal, M. (2010). Dialog theory in marginalized settings: A subaltern studies approach. *Communication Theory*, *20*, 363–386. https://doi.org/10.1111/j.1468-2885.2010.01367.x

Dutta, M. J., & Pal, M. (2020). Theorizing from the global south: Dismantling, resisting, and transforming communication theory. *Communication Theory*, *30*, 349–369. https://doi.org/10.1093/ct/qtaa010

Eckhardt, G. M., & Bardhi, F. (2020). The value in de-emphasizing structure in liquidity. *Marketing Theory*, *20*(4), 573–580. https://doi.org/10.1177/1470593120941038

Fanon, F. (1952). *Black skin, White masks*. Éditions du Seuil. (English language edition published in 1967 by Grove Press.)

Fernandez, M. (1999). Postcolonial media theory. *Third Text*, *13*(47), 11–17. https://doi.org/10.1080/09528829908576791

Ganesh, S., Zoller, H., & Cheney, G. (2005). Transforming resistance, broadening our boundaries: Critical organizational communication meets globalization from below. *Communication Monographs*, *72*(2), 169–191. https://doi.org/10.1080/03637750500111872

Gist-Mackey, A., & Kingsford, A. N. (2020). Linguistic inclusion: Challenging implicit classed communication bias in interview methods. *Management Communication Quarterly*, *34*(3), 402–425. https://doi.org/10.1177/0893318920934128

Gist-Mackey, A. N., & Dougherty, D. S. (2021). Sociomaterial struggle: An ethnographic analysis of power, discourse, and materiality in a working class unemployment support organization. *Communication Monographs*, *88*(3), 306–329. https://doi.org/10.1080/03637751.2020.1818801

Gist-Mackey, A. N., & Oliha-Donaldson, H. (2023). Black Lives Matter as postcolonial organizing. In M. Pal, J. Cruz, & D. Munshi (Eds.), *Organizing at the margins: Theorizing organizations of struggle in the Global South* (pp. 203–220). Palgrave Macmillan.

Grimes, D. S., & Parker, P. S. (2009). Imagining organizational communication as a decolonizing project: In conversation with Broadfoot, Munshi, Mumby, and Stohl. *Management Communication Quarterly*, *22*(3), 502–511. https://doi.org/10.1177/0893318908327010

Hall, M. L. (2011). Constructions of leadership at the intersection of discourse, power, and culture: Jamaican managers' narratives of leading in a postcolonial cultural context. *Management Communication Quarterly*, *25*(4), 612–643. https://doi.org/10.1177/0893318910389432

Hanchey, J. N. (2018). Reworking resistance: A postcolonial perspective on international NGOs. In P. Salem & E. Timmerman (Eds.), *Transformative practice and research in organizational communication* (pp. 274–291). IBI Global.

Hanchey, J. N., & Asante, G. A. (2022). African communication studies: Applications and interventions. *Review of Communication*, *22*(1), 1–6. https://doi.org/10.1080/15358593.2022.2027997

Hanchey, J. N., & Berkelaar, B. L. (2015). Context matters: Examining discourses of career success in Tanzania. *Management Communication Quarterly*, *29*(3), 411–439. https://doi.org/10.1177/0893318915584623

Hanchey, J. N., & Jensen, P. R. (2022). Organizational rhetoric as subjectification. *Management Communication Quarterly*, *36*(2), 261–287. https://doi.org/10.1177/08933189211043253

Harris, K. L. (2019, November). *Unlearning border defensiveness, undermining white supremacist violence: Renewing the case for interdisciplinary inquiry in organizational communication*. Paper presented on the Organizational Communication Division's Top Paper Panel at the 105th Annual Convention of the National Communication Association, Baltimore, MD.

Hegde, R. S., & Shome, R. (2002). Postcolonial scholarship—Productions and directions: An interview with Gayatri Chakravorty Spivak. *Communication Theory*, *12*, 271–286. https://doi.org/10.1111/j.1468-2885.2002.tb00270.x
Hughes, E. C. (1951). Work and the self. In J. H. Rohrer & M. Sherif (Eds.), *Social psychology at the crossroads* (pp. 313–323). Harper & Brothers.
Jack, G., Westwood, R., Srivinas, N., & Sardar, Z. (2011). Deepening, broadening and re-asserting a postcolonial interrogative space in organization studies. *Organization*, *18*(3), 275–302. http://dx.doi.org/10.1177/1350508411398996
James, C. L. R. (1938). *The Black Jacobins*. Secker & Warburg.
Kalonaityte, V. (2010). The case of vanishing borders: Theorizing diversity management as internal border control. *Organization*, *17*(1), 31–52. https://doi.org/10.1177/1350508409350238
Karikari, E., & Brown, C. (2018). Sensemaking in turbulent contexts: African student leadership in a postcolonial context. *Communication Studies*, *69*(4), 439–452. https://doi.org/10.1080/10510974.2018.1472126
Keane, M., Khupe, C., & Seehawer, M. (2017). Decolonising methodology: Who benefits from indigenous knowledge research? *Educational Research for Social Change*, *6*, 12–24. http://dx.doi.org/10.17159/2221-4070/2017/v6i1a2
Kimmerer, R. (2013). *Braiding sweetgrass: Indigenous wisdom, scientific knowledge and the teachings of plants*. Milkweed editions.
King, J. L., & Frost, R. L. (2002). Managing distance over time: The evolution of technologies of dis/ambiguation. In P. J. Hinds & S. Kiesler (Eds.), *Distributed work* (pp. 3–26). MIT Press.
Kisselburgh, L. G., & Dutta, M. J. (2009). The construction of civility in multicultural organizations. In P. Lutgen-Sandvik & B. D. Sypher (Eds.), *Destructive organizational communication: Processes, consequences, & constructive ways of organizing* (pp. 121–142). Routledge.
Long, B., & Mills, A. (2008). Globalization, postcolonial theory, and organizational analysis: Lessons from the Rwanda genocide. *Critical Perspectives on International Business*, *4*(4), 389–409. http://dx.doi.org/10.1108/17422040810915420
Maingi Ngwu, N. (2022). Toward a fluid, shape-shifting methodology in organizational communication inquiry: African feminist organizational communication historiography. *Review of Communication*, *22*(1), 42–59. https://doi.org/10.1080/15358593.2022.2027505
Manning, J. (2020). Examining whiteness in interpersonal communication textbooks. *Communication, Culture and Critique*, *13*(2), 254–258. https://doi.org/10.1093/ccc/tcaa010
Mumby, D., & Stohl, C. (1996). Disciplining organizational communication studies. *Management Communication Quarterly*, *1*, 50–72. https://doi.org/10.1177/0893318996010001004
Mumby, D. K., & Stohl, C. (2007). (Re)disciplining organizational communication studies: A response to Broadfoot and Munshi. *Management Communication Quarterly*, *21*(2), 268–280. https://doi.org/10.1177/0893318907306038
Na'puti, T. R., & Cruz, J. M. (2022). Mapping interventions: Toward a decolonial and indigenous praxis across communication subfields. *Communication, Culture and Critique*, *15*, 1–20. http://dx.doi.org/10.1093/ccc/tcab064
Nelson-Marsh, N., Broadfoot, K. J., & Munshi, D. (2008). COMMUNEcating in the spaces in-between: Creating new understandings of organizing and communicative practice around the globe. *Management Communication Quarterly*, *22*, 313–321. https://doi.org/10.1177/0893318908323573
Nicotera, A. M., & Clinkscales, M. C. (2010). Nurses at the nexus: A case study in structurational divergence. *Health Communication*, *25*(1), 32–49. https://doi.org/10.1080/10410230903473516
Norander, S., & Harter, L. M. (2012). Reflexivity in practice: Challenges and potentials of transnational organizing. *Management Communication Quarterly*, *26*(1), 74–105. https://doi.org/10.1177/0893318911415607
Novic, E. (2016). *The concept of cultural genocide: An international law perspective*. Oxford University Press.
Okun, T. (2021). *White supremacy culture. Dismantling racism: A workbook for social change groups*, 28-35. https://www.whitesupremacyculture.info/
Pal, M., & Buzzanell, P. (2008). The Indian call center experience: A case study in changing discourses of identity, identification, and career in a global context. *Journal of Business Communication*, *45*(1), 31–60. https://doi.org/10.1177/0021943607309348
Pal, M., & Buzzanell, P. (2013). Breaking the myth of Indian call centers: A postcolonial analysis of resistance. *Communication Monographs*, *80*(2), 199–219. https://doi.org/10.1080/03637751.2013.776172

Pal, M., Cruz, J., & Munshi, D. (Eds.). (2023). *Organizing at the margins: Theorizing organizations of struggle in the Global South*. Palgrave Macmillan.
Pal, M., & Dutta, M. J. (2008). Theorizing resistance in a global context: Processes, strategies, and tactics in communication scholarship. *Annals of the International Communication Association*, *32*(1), 41–87. https://doi.org/10.1080/23808985.2008.11679075
Pal, M., & Dutta, M. J. (2012). Organizing resistance on the internet: The case of the international campaign for justice in Bhopal. *Communication, Culture & Critique*, *5*, 230–251. https://doi.org/10.1111/j.1753-9137.2012.01129.x
Pal, M., Kim, H., Harris, K. L., Long, Z., Linabary, J., Larson, E. W., Jensen, P. R., Gist-Mackey, A. N., McDonald, J., Nieto-Fernandez, B., Jiang, J., Misra, S., & Dempsey, S. (2022). Decolonizing organizational communication. *Management Communication Quarterly*, *36*(3), 547–577. https://doi.org/10.1177/08933189221090255
Pal, M., & Nieto-Fernandez, B. (2024). Politics of transnational feminism to decolonize feminist organizational communication: A call to action. *Management Communication Quarterly*, *38*(1), 60–85. https://doi.org/10.1177/08933189231161620
Patton, T. O. (2004). In the guise of civility: The complicitous maintenance of inferential forms of sexism and racism in higher education. *Women's Studies in Communication*, *27*(1), 60–87. https://doi.org/10.1080/07491409.2004.10162466
Prasad, A. (2003). The gaze of the other: Postcolonial theory and organizational analysis. In A. Prasad (Ed.), *Postcolonial theory and organizational analysis: A critical engagement* (pp. 3–43). Palgrave Macmillan.
Prichard, C. (2006). Global politics, academic dispositions, and the tilting of organizational communication: A provocation to a debate. *Management Communication Quarterly*, *19*(4), 638–644. https://doi.org/10.1177/0893318905285388
Said, E. W. (1978). *Orientalism*. Pantheon.
Shaw, M. (20 March 2007). *What is genocide?* Polity.
Shome, R. (1996). Postcolonial interventions in the rhetorical canon: An "other" view. *Communication Theory*, 6, 40–59. https://doi.org/10.1111/j.1468-2885.1996.tb00119.x
Shome, R., & Hegde, R. S. (2002). Postcolonial approaches to communication: Charting the terrain, engaging the intersections. *Communication Theory*, *12*(3), 249–270. https://doi.org/10.1111/j.1468-2885.2002.tb00269.x
Spivak, G. C. (1988). Can the subaltern speak? In C. Nelson & L. Grossberg (Eds.), *Marxism and the interpretation of culture* (pp. 271–313). University of Illinois Press.
Tañongon, C. E. (2023). Agribusiness organizing in the Philippine South: The intertextual power play of weather and market agencies. *Management Communication Quarterly*, *37*(2), 396–419. https://doi.org/10.1177/08933189221111909
Tomlinson, B. (2010). *Feminism and affect at the scene of argument*. Temple University Press.
Young, R. J. C. (2020). *Postcolonialism: A very short introduction (2nd edition)*. Oxford University Press.
Zavala, M. (2013). What do we mean by decolonizing research strategies? Lessons from decolonizing, Indigenous research projects in New Zealand and Latin America. *Decolonization: Indigeneity, Education & Society*, 2, 55–71. https://jps.library.utoronto.ca/index.php/des/article/view/19113/16236
Zoller, H. (2006). Suitcases and swimsuits: On the future of organizational communication. *Management Communication Quarterly*, *19*(4), 661–666. https://doi.org/10.1177/0893318905285391

Part II

Foundational Organizational Theory

In this section, the traditional/historical organizational theories treated in previous generations as foundations of organizational communication are reviewed – not just as conceptual foundations for the field, but also as societal forces that shaped (and continue to shape) organizational forms, practices, and management. One cannot adequately understand contemporary organizations as communicatively constructed and constituted without appreciation of the constitutive power of these foundational bodies of theory. As prescriptions, these theories quite literally wrote the scripts that contemporary organizations follow.

DOI: 10.4324/9781003484639-6

5 Classical Management Theory

Anne M. Nicotera

Industrialization and the Advent of the Large Organization

Human organizing is, of course, as old as human social groups. Large organizations (e.g., governments, religious orders, militaries) have likewise existed for centuries but became the norm only with industrialization (Perrow, 1991). Industrialization was, of course, driven by commerce traced to the same 15th-century trade and exploration that facilitated colonialism and imperialism (see Chapter 4). In fact, the earliest large corporations predate industrialization, the most obvious of which are the Dutch East India Company and the British East India Company. Formed around 1600 and active into the 19th century, these massive corporations had quasi-governmental authority to assemble and deploy their own militaries, establish colonies, strike their own coins, negotiate treaties, and the like (Ames, 2008). The English East India Company eventually formed a monopoly that was larger than many countries with a thriving economy, which ruled much of India. It even had three armies that all together were double the size of the British Army (Sykes, 1847). The British East India Company illustrates the close relationship between capitalism and colonialism, as it ushered in a culture of consumerism in England that led to neoliberal capitalism (Erikson, 2014; see Chapter 4). This brand of capitalism (commerce by conquest and subjugation) became the template for the structuring of large organizations that became the norm as manufacturing grew under industrialization.

The shift in society to commonplace large organizations heralded the introduction of formal organizational theory to the mainstream. The postindustrial body of organizational theory (particularly management theory) was, of course, influenced by ancient texts – such as Kautilya's *Arthashastra* (Rangarajan, 1992, original circa 300 BCE, 1992), Sun Tzu's 6th Century *Art of War*, or Machiavelli's (2005, original 1515) *The Prince*. Such texts, however, were intended for the heads of nations, religions, and armies; whereas, postindustrial organizational and management theory was written for heads of commercial entities and their agents – and eventually for everyone, as employment by and membership in large organizations became increasingly more commonplace.

Industrialization brought *wage dependency* – surviving by "working for someone else (and their profit) and receiving compensation in the form of money" (Perrow, 1991, p. 729). Perrow notes that by 1820, 20% of the U.S. population was wage-dependent, surging to well over 80% by 1950 and continuing to rise thereafter. (Note here that Perrow's analysis does not consider the labor of those who were indentured or enslaved.) Other industrialized nations saw similar trends. As wage dependency became more widespread, the complexity and size of organizations increased, leading to the largely impersonal world of organizations we know today. Perrow's argument that contemporary society is an *organizational society*

DOI: 10.4324/9781003484639-7

is compelling, as is his theory that organizations have, in fact, *absorbed society* through wage dependency and two other ensuing developments. First, the social costs of large organizations (e.g., increased crime rates and decreased sanitary conditions) were externalized to the community. Second, factory bureaucracy accomplished unobtrusive control.

> Activities that once were performed by relatively autonomous and usually small informal groups (e.g. family, neighborhood) and small autonomous organizations (small businesses, local government, local church) are now performed by large bureaucracies. This is the "pure" case of absorption – the large organization with many employees. As a result, the organization that employs many people can shape their lives in many ways, most of which are quite unobtrusive and subtle, and alternative sources of shaping in the community decline.
>
> (Perrow, 1991, p. 726)

Prior to the Industrial Revolution (roughly 1760–1820), society was largely agrarian, and goods were produced by artisans working as individuals or in small groups. Individuals and families, in small communities, subsisted on their own production, consuming based on what they produced, trading surplus among themselves, and providing services to one another in exchange for goods. Then, technological advances created a workforce who, instead, sold their *labor* for *currency* that could be exchanged for goods and services. This shift disrupted the direct interdependency that had existed within communities, created dependency on organizations, and depersonalized the exchange of goods and services.

The European and American railroads, in particular, hastened the shift by allowing a wide distribution of products that created demand for increasing levels of mass production – resulting in even more large organizations to support that demand for distribution. As demand for mass-produced goods increased, the workforce to be managed became larger and less individualized, requiring more impersonal methods of controlling that production. Salaried managers, as an identifiable group, were fully in place by 1900 (Khurana, 2010). This group's need for management skills created a demand for management theory to teach them how to accomplish organizational tasks through managing a massive and depersonalized workforce. At the same time, the consequences of large-scale industrial production were externalized to the community (Perrow, 1991), creating more need for more large organizations to manage problems, such as unemployment, industrial accidents, pollution, and overcrowding in cities – further requiring assistance in the development of techniques to manage large workforces in the accomplishment of large-scale goals.

The classical management theory reviewed in this chapter is best described as postindustrial management theory and is the precursor to organizational communication theory. An appreciation of the prescriptive nature of classical management theory is exceedingly important for a full understanding of contemporary organizational communication phenomena and theory. Management theory generally, and early management theory in particular, is constructed with the express purpose of discovering and promoting practices that maximize effectiveness and efficiency for goal-attainment. Unlike social science theory (like that in the field of organizational communication), which seeks to describe and understand human social phenomena as they exist, management theory is intended to instruct managers on what to do to maximize their achievement of organizational objectives. The implications are profound: Classical management theory was a set of instructions for early managers. *Early classical management theory thus actually created and perpetuated practices that have fashioned the very phenomena studied by organizational theorists a century later.* Structures and systems for authority, formal and informal communication, power relationships, organizational form and design – all things organizational that are now the subject of our descriptive theorizing – were formed by the implementation of prescriptions from these early theories. Our social construction of organizing today is thus profoundly shaped by early management theory. As you will see, presumptions about such things as formalization, division of labor, chains of command, formal authority, and appropriate communication practices are rooted in the instructions given by classical management theory. As prominent writers told us (as a society), "*this is how it is done well,*" social constructions of organizing followed these directives to become entrenched and self-propagating.

Classical Economists, Industrial Innovators, and the Rise of the Salaried Manager

Classical management theory did not arise from a vacuum. Statesmen and scholars have been writing about society and its concerns for time immemorial – in earnest since The Enlightenment. Treatises on the human condition, moral living, and public success abound throughout history. For postindustrial management practices, classical economists Adam Smith and John Stuart Mill most influentially shaped how we think about organizing. Even if you have never heard of Adam Smith, you have probably heard reference to his treatise on economics, entitled *An Inquiry into the Nature and Causes of the Wealth of Nations* (Smith, 1776) but often shorthanded as *Wealth of Nations*. Because of this work, Smith is widely regarded as the father of modern economics. The work contains two central messages. First, marketplace competition improves economic prosperity. His other main point is more directly applicable to the management of workers (and thus to organizational communication): Each person, by working industriously for his own interests, promotes the economic interests of the group and of society. Productive labor at the individual level is the fundamental unit of production on a wide societal (or organizational) scale. ***In classical management theory, the very purpose of managerial effort is to increase and maintain individual-level worker productivity.***

John Stuart Mill's treatise, *On Liberty* (Mill, 1859), is a central foundation of the field of communication studies in its passion for the importance of free and ethical speech to individual and societal growth. However, his writings on economics, primarily *Principles of Political Economy* (Mill, 1848), set the ground for management theorists. Mill wrote extensively about the relationship between labor and production, remuneration to workers for their labor, the nature of productivity (material and immaterial products of labor), and capital as a stock produced by labor. These ideas, too, greatly influenced the way management theory later defined labor, laborers, and productivity.

At the same time these philosophies of economy were being produced, the actual work of industry progressed quickly. Prominent industrialists, such as Eli Whitney and James Watt, shaped industrial practices for production and efficiency (e.g., standardization, product quality control, cost-accounting, etc.) that management theorists examined in the search for the best way to manage labor. In these early days, worker productivity was the chief concern of management theorists. This often led to exploitation and inhumane treatment of workers, consistent with the classist system engendered by the colonial mindset accompanying capitalism.

Classical Management Theorists

Three theorists are commonly identified as comprising the classical era in management theory. *Max Weber*, a German sociologist, taught us how to understand authority and bureaucracy, their ties to sociological phenomena (such as religion and economics), and their social and political implications. The work of *Henri Fayol*, a French industrialist, is largely responsible for how we design organizational structures and forms to achieve managerial control and for identifying managerial imperatives. Finally, *Frederick Taylor*, an American mechanical engineer and management consultant, espoused the scientific study of labor to determine the most efficient means of productivity and the resolute separation of management from labor in both theory and practice.

Max Weber's Legal-Rational Model of Bureaucracy

Writing in the late 19th century, sociologist Max Weber was neither the first nor the last scholar to theorize bureaucracy. Weber did, however, provide the most well-known and widely influential scholarly treatise on the sociological functions of bureaucracy, *Economy and Society* (published posthumously in 1922), positing that bureaucracy was the most efficient and rational form of organizing, providing a form of authority "indispensable to the modern world" (Swedberg & Agevall, 2005, pp. 18–19). Because authority is a form of domination, it was of central concern for Weber as a sociologist. According to Weber (1978, translation of *Economy and Society*, p. 215), the legitimacy of domination may be validated in three ways. First, *legal authority* rests on rational grounds – "a belief in the legality of enacted rules and the right of those elevated to authority under such rules to issue commands." Second, *traditional authority* rests on "established belief in the sanctity of immemorial traditions and the legitimacy of those exercising authority under them." Finally, *charismatic authority* rests on "devotion to the exceptional sanctity, heroism and exemplary character of an individual person, and of the normative patterns of order revealed or ordained by him." Weber viewed the first of these, *legal-rational authority*, as superior in its function for modern society. Legal-rational authority constitutes the basis of modern bureaucracy.

Bureaucracy can be defined most simply as a system of legal-rational authority, accomplishing organizational administration of tasks through the implementation of departments with specialized functions. The bureaucratic form imbues each of these departments with legal-rational authority over the processes in its domain and arranges them so that work is processed sequentially by each – the output of one department becoming the input of another. Individual managers, then, hold the legal-rational authority afforded to them by the bureaucratic system over their own specialized territories.

Weber (1978) outlined six interrelated characteristics of the modern bureaucracy. First, there is the principle of official *jurisdictional areas* ordered by rules, laws, or administrative regulations. Within each area, three elements constitute a bureau (referred to as an *agency* in the public sector or an *enterprise* in the private sector):

1 Regular activities are assigned as official duties.
2 The authority to give commands is stably distributed and "strictly delimited by rules" (p. 956) governing the means that may be used to ensure compliance.
3 Individuals are hired based on general rules of qualification; the performance of duties and exercise of corresponding rights are ensured by methodical provisions.

The jurisdictional principle prescribes a division of labor dictating the creation of multiple bureaus, each with its own domain of specialization. Bureaus are traditionally categorized according to their functions as line and staff. *Line* departments are directly involved in the central purpose of the organization; whereas, *staff* departments perform functions that support the line departments. For example, in an automobile manufacturing corporation, we will have divisions and departments responsible for work products related to the organization's central function – the manufacturing of automobiles (e.g., engine parts fabrication and engine assembly, body parts and body assembly, and paint shop). The work products of these units are the inputs for other units so that all perform tasks in a sequential fashion (hence, the "line" function) to produce the final output or product. The line bureaus rely on the work of staff bureaus to provide support functions, such as an accounting office responsible for overseeing all things financial. Further, each bureau has sub-bureaus; for example, the accounting office may oversee a purchasing department to approve vendors and process purchases of goods and services and an accounts payable department responsible for receiving and paying invoices to those vendors. Each department employs people assigned to specifically defined positions that further divide the labor. Bureaucracy is thus a set of embedded systems and sub-systems of divided labor, arranged in rigid prescribed sequences-within-sequences that allow work to be completed efficiently through the routinization of tasks and chains of tasks.

Weber's (1978) second principle is *office hierarchy and channels of appeal* (chain-of-command). This principle reflects the operation of authority central to the rational-legal bureaucratic form. Hierarchy and command channels

> stipulate a clearly established system of super- and sub-ordination in which there is a supervision of the lower offices by the higher ones. Such a system offers the governed the possibility of appealing, in a precisely regulated manner, the decision of a lower office to the corresponding senior authority.
>
> (Weber, 1978, p. 957)

The work is administered by this hierarchy of supervisory authority according to Weber's third principle, that management is based upon *written documents*. It is with this standard that the modern bureaucracy achieved the separation of official business from private life.

> In principle, the modern organization of the civil service separates the bureau from the private domicile of the official and, in general, segregates official activity from the sphere of private life. Public monies and equipment are divorced from the private property of the official. ... In principle, the *Kontor* (office) is separated from the household, business from private correspondence, and business assets from private wealth.
>
> (Weber, 1978, p. 957)

The remaining three principles are far simpler and provide the means by which the first three are achieved. The fourth is that all managers are *thoroughly trained in their areas of specialization*. This is an important source of legitimate rational authority. Fifth, bureaucratic managers are expected to devote their *full working capacity* to official activity. The separation of private life from organizational life mutually necessitates and cultivates this expectation. Finally, Weber observes that modern bureaucracy stipulates management of the office according to *general rules*, "which are more or less stable, more or less exhaustive, and which can be learned. Knowledge of these rules represents a special technical

Table 5.1 Summary: Weber's principles of modern bureaucracy

The Principle of Jurisdictional Areas *Domains of specialization, each ordered by rules, laws, regulations. A* ***bureau*** *is constituted by* 1 *Regular activities assigned as official duties;* 2 *Stably distributed and strictly regulated authority to give commands and ensure compliance;* 3 *Hiring based on rules of qualification, with performance ensured by methodical provisions.*
The Principle of Office Hierarchy and Channels of Appeal *Chain-of-command is clear and implements rational-legal authority.*
The Principle of Written Documents *Documentation serves to separate official and personal business, correspondence, and assets.*
The Principle of Trained Specialization *All managers are thoroughly trained in their jurisdictional areas.*
The Principle of Full Working Capacity *All managers devote full capacity to official activity (cultivated by the separation of business life from private life).*
The Principle of Rules *Office management is stipulated by stable, exhaustive, and learnable general rules, knowledge of which represents the expertise of the bureau's officials.*

expertise which the officials possess" (Weber, 1978, p. 958). This last principle represents a dramatic departure from previous organizational norms of patrimonialism, which operated according to bestowals of favor. This last principle also provides the means by which the bureaucracy can achieve the degree of impersonalism necessary for the equal treatment of individuals. Weber's principles are summarized in Table 5.1.

Weber (1978) particularly noted that bureaucracy's ability to govern "without regard to persons" (p. 975) or *sine ira et studio* – "without hatred or passion and hence without affection or enthusiasm" (p. 225)– is both required by capitalism and a "threat to humanity" (Swedberg & Agevall, 2005, p. 19) that must be counterbalanced by business and government leaders. In *Economy and Society*, Weber argues that bureaucracy is the necessary form of organizing in a capitalist economy, but he also clearly advocates for the necessity of regulating and controlling bureaucracy's inherent domination. While Weber is usually depicted in summaries and textbooks as a cheerleader for bureaucracy, it is more accurate to describe his work as keenly observing the fit between the organizational needs of governance and commerce in capitalistic Western culture and the organizational form and control provided by bureaucracy. Weber predicted the increasing bureaucratization of society, noting both its organizational benefits and sociological dangers. "It is especially in his discussion of the future of bureaucracy that Weber was not simply an advocate of bureaucracy and its efficiency, but also fundamentally critical and fearful of it" (Swedberg & Agevall, 2005, p. 20). He coined the term *iron cage* as a metaphor for the system of rationality created and perpetuated by bureaucratic structures. Teleological, or means to end, reasoning produces efficiency because it affords control from the basis of rational logic, dispassionate to the individual and thus depersonalizing and dehumanizing. Weber warned that this threat to human freedom would create a "polar night of icy darkness and hardness" (Weber, 1994, p. 368). Contemporary organizational communication theory continues to explore these ideas. Because bureaucracy, as a rational system of organizing, is socially constructed, we are complicit in structuring our own iron cages.

Henri Fayol's Theory of Administration

Henri Fayol was a French industrialist and mining engineer who worked as managing director of *Compagnie de Commentry-Fourchambault-Decazeville* – a mining company with more than 10,000 employees that was one of the largest French producers of iron and steel by 1900 (Witzel, 2003). From his own experience, he developed a comprehensive theory of administration, which became widely known through a 1949 translation. Fayol identified six categories of activity necessary for industrial administration: Technical, commercial, financial, security, accounting, and managerial (Lamond, 1998), with management being his chief concern. Fayol contributed three fundamental management concepts: Elements of management, principles of management, and the organizational chart to display bureaucratic structure.

Fayol's five elements, or functions, of management endure as a standard in management education: Planning/forecasting, organizing, commanding, coordinating, and controlling. First, managers must forecast a direction and *plan* methods for the attainment of organizational goals. Second, managers must *organize* human resources in an arrangement designed to meet those goals and must formulate and implement methods for evaluating the work of those employees. This element is accomplished by the box-and-line organizational chart (displaying organizational units and vertical chains of authority) that remains a ubiquitous feature of organizational design. Third, managers *command* the execution of tasks that will meet organizational goals. The fourth managerial function is to *coordinate* those activities of multiple units into a coherent whole. Finally, the manager must enact some degree of *control* over organizational processes so that the planned activities and their outcomes can be evaluated against the goals to assess organizational functioning and success. It is important to note Fayol's underlying presumption of Weber's legal-rational bureaucratic form. While Fayol pioneered the organizational chart as a graphic depiction of the bureaucratic form, he did not invent the form itself.

Fayol's elements of management are supported by 14 principles through which the five functions should be carried out. First, reflecting the Weberian dictum, Fayol advocated work specialization in a strict *division of labor* as the most desirable application of worker activity. Second, also reflecting Weber, managers are granted *authority*, manifesting in the right to give orders. Fayol particularly noted that authority must be accompanied by responsibility. Third, Fayol identified employee *discipline* as a crucial principle. Respect and obedience of organizational rules must be enforced, and effective management accomplishes that. *Unity of command* dictates that every employee report to, and should receive orders from, only one manager or supervisor. This is accompanied by the principle of *unity of direction*, organizing activities with similar objectives under the direction of one manager who implements a single plan for the achievement of the common goal. A great deal has been written about span of control as a central concern. Fayol cautioned that managers must not be granted authority over more employees or functions than the limits of their abilities allow, with fewer direct reports at higher levels of the hierarchy.

Subordination dictates that the interests of the organizational whole should take precedence over the interests of any individual or group of individuals. Yet, the principles of *remuneration* and *equity* specify the necessity of fair wages and equitable treatment of employees. Decision-making should be *centralized* so that management has control, with the understanding that organizational size and the characteristics and skills of managers and employees should temper the degree of centralization to maximize the achievement of organizational goals. The principle of *initiative* dictates that employees' efforts will be improved when they are allowed to originate and carry out plans. The *scalar chain* principle requires a clear and enforced line of authority from the top to the bottom of the hierarchy, again reflecting Weber. Fayol specifically discussed prescriptions for communication, advocating limited horizontal interaction so as to minimize its interference with managerial control. Direct communication of employees among themselves was subject to prior managerial approval and formalization as a procedure. (This came to be known as *Fayol's bridge.*)

Order dictates that all people, machines, materials, and activities have an appointed place and a specified function in the organizational design. Correspondingly, orderly personnel planning should be used to ensure the principle of *tenure stability* – the avoidance of employee turnover – and the efficient filling of any vacancies that do occur. Finally, Fayol advocated the promotion of *esprit de corps* to build harmony and unity among employees. Table 5.2 summarizes Fayol's prescriptions.

Fayol also addressed interpersonal communication at the management level, specifying (in a departure from Weber's dictum) that verbal communication should be emphasized over written whenever possible to avoid the interdepartmental animosity engendered by

Table 5.2 Summary: Henri Fayol's theory of administration

Elements of Management				
Planning	*Organizing*	*Commanding*	*Coordinating*	*Controlling*
Principles of Management				
Division of labor *Work specialization is the most desirable application of worker activity.*	Authority *Managers have the right to give orders and are accountable for the outcomes.*	Discipline *Effective management enforces respect for and obedience to organizational rules.*	Unity of Command *Every employee reports to and receives orders from only one manager.*	Unity of Direction *Activities with similar objectives are under the direction of one manager.*
Subordination *Organizational interests take precedence over individual interests.*	Remuneration *Employees need fair wages.*	Equity *Employees should be treated equitably.*	Centralization *Decision-making is controlled by management.*	Initiative *Workers' efforts improve when they are allowed to originate and carry out plans.*
Scalar chain *A clear and enforced vertical line of authority with limited horizontal interaction, which is assumed to interfere with managerial control.*	Order *All resources, human and non-human, have an appointed place and specified function.*	Tenure stability *Employee turnover should be avoided, and vacancies should be filled efficiently.*	Esprit de corps *Managers should promote harmony and unity among employees.*	

the impersonal nature of the customary memorandum. He went so far as to recommend that corporations "forbid all communication in writing which could easily and advantageously be replaced by verbal ones" (Fayol, 1949, pp. 40–41, cited in Parker & Ritson, 2005, p. 184).

Fayol's theory is entirely prescriptive, based on his own experience. Fayol was not a social scientific scholar in the traditional sense, and his work has long been criticized as lacking the empirical basis to meet the rigorous standards of social science. However, recent analysis (Parker & Ritson, 2005) has pointed out that Fayol was trained as a research scientist in geology and metallurgy and that his naturalistic methods for deriving management theory closely resemble the grounded theory approach espoused by Glaser and Strauss (1967) decades later. Fayol's theory of administration, as it has been widely presented in secondary sources, is largely uncontroversial, and despite complaints about its lack of empirical evidence, it has been widely applied, although there has been some debate about whether the actual activities of practicing managers reflect Fayol's principles (as illustrated in Mintzberg's, 1973, classic study).

Parker and Ritson (2005) provide an interesting analysis of the primary sources, concluding that Fayol's writing actually advocated a far less authoritarian approach than is attributed by most scholars and textbooks. They contend that the Fayol who is taught in contemporary management schools is far more rigid than the original texts would suggest the real Fayol was in actuality. Rather than a strict adherence to authoritarian bureaucracy, Fayol advocated management practices that would later come to be known as *human relations* or *human resource management* (see Chapters 6 and 7). Fayol is, however, wholly depicted by secondary sources as a classical management theorist and an advocate of strictly formal vertical authority. Fayol's theory of administration, as presented in the literature, has had a profound effect on management and leadership education and training.

Frederick Taylor's Scientific Management

Frederick Taylor was an American businessman, a mechanical engineer, and one of the first management consultants. Taylor (1911) identified two pervasive problems in industrial workers' productivity: Uneven work quality and "soldiering" (deliberate "underworking") (p. 13). Piece-work – paying workers according to the number of pieces produced (e.g., the number of bricks laid or pounds of pig iron toted, or the number of shoes or shirt sleeves made) – had become standard practice to avoid soldiering, as paid-by-the-hour workers would naturally slow their pace to match the slowest among them. However, piece-work had not solved the problem. When fast workers produced more pieces, the economic dynamic created a system whereby the pay rate-per-piece was reduced (or *busted*). Workers put great pressure on one another to slow down – so as to avoid this *rate-busting* phenomenon. Taylor (1911) provides numerous anecdotes that illustrate both the problems and the ways his system solves them. Taylor's *scientific management* advocated a system of determining, through scientific study, the best and most efficient way to do every task, followed by the requirement that every worker strictly follow that procedure. Taylorism, as it came to be known, ushered in the industrial efficiency movement of the early 20th century.

Scientific management espoused four tenets. First, rigorous empirical investigation through time and motion studies can determine the most superior procedure (highest quality and efficiency) for every job. Second, workers should be matched to jobs through a scientific analysis of their skills and characteristics. Every worker assigned to the same job

Table 5.3 Summary: Tenets of Taylor's scientific management

Tenet 1: A superior procedure for every task can be discovered through scientific study of the task. Once discovered, one standard procedure for each task should be adopted.
Tenet 2: Scientific analysis of workers' skills and characteristic should be used to match them to tasks. Every worker should then be trained to the standard procedure and required to follow it.
Tenet 3: Management must closely supervise workers to ensure standard procedure is followed.
Tenet 4: Work should be strictly divided between management and labor. Management is responsible for planning and prescribing procedures; labor is responsible for carrying out procedures in the prescribed manner.

should be thoroughly trained on the standard procedure and required to follow it. Third, management should closely supervise and cooperate with workers to ensure that all work is done in accordance with the standard procedure that has been scientifically determined. Finally, the labor should be equally divided between laborer and manager so that the laborer is relieved of the responsibility of planning and is responsible only for carrying out the job in the prescribed way. Table 5.3 summarizes these tenets.

Taylor has been criticized as viewing workers as fundamentally lazy, motivated to provide quality work only by monetary reward. Even a cursory reading of the original source material reveals this bias, but it is equally clear that Taylor did not intend to mistreat workers – although others' applications of his methods often led to worker exploitation. Taylor stipulated that management's planning of workers' tasks should specify

> not only what is to be done but how it is to be done and the exact time allowed for doing it. And whenever the workman succeeds in doing his task right, and within the time limit specified, he receives an addition of from 30 per cent, to 100 per cent, to his ordinary wages. These tasks are carefully planned, so that both good and careful work are called for in their performance, but it should be distinctly understood that in no case is the workman called upon to work at a pace which would be injurious to his health. The task is always so regulated that the man who is well suited to his job will thrive while working at this rate during a long term of years and grow happier and more prosperous, instead of being overworked. Scientific management consists very largely in preparing for and carrying out these tasks.
>
> (Taylor, 1911, p. 39)

Taylor's viewpoint is both paternalistic and elitist. He saw his system as relieving workers of the burdensome responsibility for planning their work that had been "thrown upon" (p. 37) them, and for which they were naturally ill-suited, so as to allow them to more freely, efficiently, and effectively carry out that work.

> Even if the workman was well suited to the development and use of scientific data, it would be physically impossible for him to work at his machine and at a desk at the same time. It is also clear that in most cases one type of man is needed to plan ahead and an entirely different type to execute the work.
>
> (Taylor, 1911, p. 38)

The planning accomplished by managers was likewise designed scientifically. Henry Gantt (1910, 1916, 1919) provided such innovations as the Gantt chart for project management, prescriptions for scheduling, and remuneration (including that of managers, linking management bonuses to worker improvement).

Workers, however, did not respond positively, resisting Taylorism as unfriendly to them. Taylor experienced difficulties in implementation, complicated by the rapidly changing technological environment and others' faulty applications of his methods (Mullins, 2004). Alternatives to Taylorism were advocated by Taylor's contemporaries, who offered a more respectful view of the worker and highlighted the importance of taking human psychology into account in the management of employees. James Hartness (1912), a fellow mechanical engineer, wrote extensively about the importance of habit, employee relations, and human factors in mechanical design (George, 1968). Frank Bunker Gilbreth, Jr., an industrial efficiency consultant, with his business partner (and spouse), Dr. Lillian Moller Gilbreth, worked very closely with Taylor, devising implementations for scientific management. Like others at the time, however, they criticized Taylorism for its failure to seriously consider psychological factors.

Frank Gilbreth pioneered motion studies. Although Taylor focused more on time as a factor (producing quickly), F. Gilbreth emphasized motion (producing efficiently). His method broke a task into discrete motions, dubbed *therbligs* (Gilbreth backwards with the *th* transposed). Using a motion picture camera calibrated in fractions of seconds to capture the minute motions of workers, F. Gilbreth scientifically examined tasks to determine the *one best way* (George, 1968). Lillian Moller Gilbreth was one of the first women working engineers with a doctorate – reputed to be the first conferred in the field of industrial psychology. While her partner focused on motion studies, Lillian Gilbreth examined human factors – most notably fatigue. Together, the Gilbreths' work provided the foundations for the continuous quality improvement movement and the field of ergonomics.

Worker Exploitation as a Negative Consequence of Classical Management

The fundamental flaw in classical management theory is the depersonalization of work and thus the dehumanization of the worker. This is particularly true of Taylorism, which relied on replacing the craft knowledge of workers with management-controlled systematic methods of production (Lasch, 1987). The depersonalization of the industrial worker led to an implicit machine metaphor for the organization generally and its workers in particular, who were viewed as, and treated like, cogs in a machine (Morgan, 1986). Explicating the machine metaphor reveals three fundamental presumptions: Standardization, replaceability, and predictability. The standardization of process and the corresponding depersonalization of work often led to a callous treatment of workers as disposable – resulting in sweatshop conditions and the exploitation and mistreatment that led to the advent of labor unions. Worker abuse was common but only rarely subjected to public scrutiny, usually only in the face of tragedy, such as the Triangle Shirtwaist factory fire in 1911, which killed over 100 workers (most of them young immigrant women). The fire resulted in large-scale loss of life because exit doors had been locked to prevent unauthorized breaks and thefts (Hoenig, 2005). Public outcry led to legislation and oversight – and accelerated the formation of labor unions.

Yet, we must not presume to relegate these abuses to the archives of history. Contemporary industrial corporate cultures are equally as subject to the abuses of dehumanization, despite regulation and the protection of unions. In 1991, too recent for comfort, a fire at the Hamlet chicken processing plant in North Carolina killed more than 20 workers due to exits that were locked or blocked (Kilborn, 1992). More recently, a fire chillingly similar to the Triangle fire killed over 100 workers in Bangladesh at the Tazreen Fashion factory – likewise because of inadequate fire exits (Ahmed & Paul, 2012).

Classical Management's Contemporary Influence

Classical management theory continues to have profound influences on contemporary organizing. A cursory glance through the annual report of a corporation of any size will reveal the continued grip of Fayol's organizational chart that guides how we arrange organizational forms and conceive of authority as vertical. The inefficiencies we decry in government can be directly traced to the depersonalization inherent in bureaucracy (which ironically is designed to create efficiency) – for example, a social worker's inability to save a child because the immediate actions needed violate regulations and required standard processes. Taylor's strict division of management from labor created an elitist corporate class system that is even felt outside the industrial setting, in the office environment – for example, the cultural divide between *the suits* and *the cubicle dwellers.*

It is easy to see the negative aspects of classical management ideals, but we also enjoy benefits as well. Because of Fayol's emphasis on control in relation to his other four elements, large-scale projects run with accountability. Bureaucratic sequencing creates efficient processes for reporting hours worked and processing our pay – and the bureaucratic structure of the banking industry allows the funds to simply appear in our personal accounts through direct deposit. Finally, Taylor's insistence that managers scientifically standardize tasks has made possible great strides in efficiency that free capital for innovation and expansion – bringing new products to market and creating jobs for unskilled laborers. Bureaucracy is here to stay. Later developments in management theory, by mitigating its negative impact, have entrenched it.

Implications for Organizational Communication Theory

Before we turn to the next era in the management theory, however, we must take a moment to assess the implications of classical management theory to our thinking about communication, organization, authority, and culture. In so doing, we will create a basis for critical comparison of theoretical approaches, as well as an understanding of our implicit assumptions about organizing and organizational communication – both as scholars and as human organizers.

Approach to Communication

Classical management theory examines the formal aspects of communication, with control and standardization as primary concerns. Communication is treated mechanistically with a transmissive presumption of one-way and linear messaging from manager to laborer. In classical management theory, communication, with a focus on clear messaging, is cast as a management tool to accomplish worker productivity by establishing and maintaining organizational control vested in persons who hold authority. In so doing, the function of communication is nearly completely informational – its only acknowledged relational functions being to establish and maintain the authority chain and to offset the impersonal nature of written channels.

For example, Taylor's treatment of the worker is paternalistic, elitist, and dehumanized. By ignoring craft knowledge and thus eliminating it from organizational processes, Taylorism's one-way, transmissive, and mechanistic treatment of communication denies the human relationship as a function of the organization (and vice versa) and ignores meaning-creation and the constitutive properties of communication. The failure of pure Taylorism can be directly attributed to its denial that workers feel and think in equal capacity as do managers – and that the emotional and cognitive capacities of workers are essential forces in the organizational meaning created, and thus the outcomes achieved. Through his writing on the relational aspects of communication, Fayol actually delved into these meaning-centered and constitutive aspects of communication. This is so little known that it had a marginal effect on either theory or practice, but these principles are contributed later by human relations and human resources theories (see Chapters 6 and 7). Finally, Weber (as a sociologist) was well-versed in the constitutive power of communication and human relating. He warned us of the cold and harsh world that would be created by the dehumanizing nature of bureaucracy, but he left it to later thinkers to prescribe methods to ameliorate these phenomena.

Approach to Organization and Authority

Classical management theory treats the organization as a machine (Morgan, 1986), an external authoritative entity that is conceptually removed from the social collectivity that comprises its membership. The managerial class is ascribed with the authority to dictate the actions required of the labor class. Fayol's organizational chart, so powerfully ingrained in our conception of organizational structures, has reified our thinking – even to this day – of organizations as concrete, physical structures and of organizational authority as vertical. Certain positions in that vertical hierarchy, and thus the individuals who occupy those positions, have authority *over* those in *lower* positions. The vertical metaphor originates from religious texts, the first use of the word *hierarchy* (from the Ancient Greek) referring to systematic orders of angels and heavenly beings. Heaven being conceptualized as above Earth leads to a concomitant verticality in conceptions of authority.

Regardless of its origin, the vertical metaphor for authority is entrenched in Western bureaucracy. We speak of *moving up the ladder*, of executives occupying *high-up positions*, and of *low-level employees*. We even arrange the occupation of architectural structures accordingly so that those with greater authority have offices on higher floors in our buildings. The reification of verticality in our conception of authority is quite profound. This is one concrete way that the communication/organization cycle (Figure 1.2) can be seen in action. We actually arrange people physically to match the metaphor of vertical authority, and then that arrangement perpetuates verticality in our thinking. Every day, we enact organizing principles internalized from classical management theory. We create organizational charts, put all manner of things in writing to institutionalize them, standardize tasks into sequential routines, and generally follow the lessons of Fayol as they are currently taught in management degree programs everywhere. Even the most cursory glance at a fast-food establishment or manufacturing facility shows classical management principles in action. We choose to do things this way consciously as much as we do them by habit, and the more we put them into practice, the more habitual they become. We do so because they replicate patterns that have been successful before and are thus drawn upon for our current intentions. There are many sociological and social psychological theories that explain this human process of drawing on our collective societal knowledge base for organizing and structuring our collective actions, such as sensemaking (Weick, 1995) and structuration (Giddens, 1984), both of which were discussed in previous chapters.

Cultural Implications

The question of what this all means culturally is profound. First, classical management theory has enculturated a pattern of organizing that defines organizational authority concretely: As something one can *have* and *use* – a concrete tool that can be owned and operated tangibly. Further, classical management theory inculcated a colonial cultural presumption that centralizes power and authority with fewer individuals at the top of a hierarchy holding more power than the many individuals at the bottom. Contemporary culture also embraces class structures based on the division of the management classes into upper, middle, and lower levels, and the working classes as *white* or *blue collar* based on the nature of the work as the planning or implementing of labor. Finally, the absorption of contemporary society by large organizations (Perrow, 1991) is driven by the cultural internalization of classical management assumptions about the nature of work and its practices.

Recommended Supplementary Readings

Gotcher, J. M. (1992). Assisting the handicapped: The pioneering efforts of Frank and Lillian Gilbreth. *Journal of Management, 18*, 5–13.

This piece is highly recommended to link contemporary work in human factors, ergonomic design, and workplace accommodation to early management theory. The pioneering work of the Gilbreths and others (e.g., Gantt and Hartness) during the classical management period is usually glossed over in our field's textbook treatments of the era (if they are included at all). Yet, a great deal of current work traces its roots to those working in support of scientific task design.

Hough, J. R., & White, M. A. (2001). Using stories to create change: The object lesson of Frederick Taylor's "pig-tale." *Journal of Management, 27*, 585–601.

The criticism of Frederick Taylor as elitist and classist often obscures the brilliant insights of his work on scientific task design and worker assignment. This article focuses on one story told by Taylor to advocate for his methods, underscoring its continuing relevance for organizational science.

Parker, L. D., & Ritson, P. A. (2005). Revisiting Fayol: Anticipating contemporary management. *British Journal of Management, 16*, 175–194.

This article should be of interest, not just for its re-consideration of Fayol, but as a sobering reminder that reliance on secondary, tertiary, and subsequent generations of sources inevitably mis-represents the original. Much of what is "common knowledge" of Fayol is incomplete and misinterpreted.

Perrow, C. (1991). A society of organizations. *Theory and Society, 20*, 725–762.

This is a thought-provoking article for advanced readers to contemplate the nature of contemporary society as absorbed by organizations; highly recommended for students interested in organizations and democracy.

Taylor, F. (1911). *The principles of scientific management.* New York: Harper & Brothers. (digitized and in public domain, available from https://archive.org/details/principlesofscie00taylrich)

The original voice of Frederick Taylor provides a rich understanding of his scientific management as it was benignly intended; it also reveals the paternalistic and elitist distinction between management and labor that pervaded the time period.

Wren, D. A. (1972). In memoriam: Lillian Moller Gilbreth (1878–1972). *Academy of Management Journal, 15*, 7–8.

The contributions of women in early social science are obscured. This and other readings about pioneering women in organizational studies are highly recommended.

Important Concepts: Define and Discuss

Industrialization
Organizational society
Postindustrial management
Bureaucracy
Authority
Line vs. staff functions
Fayol's bridge
Scientific management
Control
Standardization

Discussion Questions

1 How (and where) can we see classical management principles operating in our contemporary organizational world? Name and discuss a few principles and give contemporary examples. What are the positive and negative consequences of these principles?
2 Weber was very concerned about the chilling effects of bureaucracy on the quality of human existence/society. If he were to appear today, a century later, to observe our 21st century organizational world, what would he say?
3 Given what we have learned about classical approaches to management and organizational design, how might we advise Taylor, Fayol, and their peers to do things differently? How might things have turned out if they did?
4 Scientific management was developed to counter the problems of uneven work quality and soldiering. How might we see these same problems among office workers, particularly those who telecommute? How might today's managers utilize Taylor's ideas for improving productivity in the face of a more skilled, specialized, and distant workforce conducting intellectual (rather than physical) labor?
5 Consider the principles and tenets of classical management theories from an ethical perspective. For example, how might an individual's decision based upon her own ethics violate or support the principle of subordination?
6 Is it possible to maintain order without using vertical authority? Can you find some contemporary organizational examples?

Practitioners' Corner

All contemporary work environments are rooted in formal organizational designs heavily influenced by classical management principles. Any person in a position of authority can enhance their unit's effectiveness by paying close attention to domains of responsibility for work groups. Better work products result from a clear shared understanding of the objectives for which the unit is responsible, careful analysis of what tasks are required to meet those objectives and how those tasks might best be done, and a clear shared understanding of who is responsible for each. Fayol's goal of a free flow of information and good relations between work groups is a worthy objective so that everyone is kept apprised of one another's efforts and can share knowledge and other resources. Positive outcomes can come from simple techniques such as a regular short Monday morning meeting, where each group updates one another on their efforts. Coworkers who are well-informed about each other's labor are more likely to support one another and to produce better and more consistent work products.

Communication professionals can uniquely benefit from a deep understanding of the roots of organizational design. Whether representing the organization to internal or external publics, the quality of that representation is enhanced by a deep understanding of the organization's design and function. Further, such understanding can inform an analysis of the organization's communication practices to create better, more effective policies and procedures. Communication practitioners are often well-trained in the principles of effective messaging, but few are knowledgeable about effective communication within organizational structures. There are obvious professional advantages, personally and organizationally, in being able to advise one's employer not only about effective formal messaging to audiences but also about effective communication in day-to-day operations that supports the organization's design and function.

References

Ahmed, A., & Paul, R. (2012). More than 100 die in garment factory fire, the deadliest in Bangladesh's history. *Christian Science Monitor*, November 25. https://www.csmonitor.com/World/Latest-News-Wires/2012/1125/More-than-100-die-in-garment-factory-fire-the-deadliest-in-Bangladesh-s-history

Ames, G. J. (2008). *The globe encompassed: The age of European discovery, 1500-1700*. Pearson Prentice Hall.

Erikson, E. (2014). *Between monopoly and free trade: The English East India company, 1600-1757*. Princeton University Press.

Fayol, H. (1949). *General and industrial management*. Trans. C. Storrs. Sir Isaac Pitman & Sons.

Gantt, H. L. (1910). *Work, wages, and profits: Their influence on the cost of living*. Engineering Magazine Company.

Gantt, H. L. (1916). *Industrial leadership*. Yale University Press.

Gantt, H. L. (1919). *Organizing for work*. Harcourt, Brace, and Howe.

George, C. S. Jr (1968). *The history of management thought*. Prentice Hall.

Giddens, A. (1984). *The constitution of society: Outline of the theory of structuration*. University of California Press.

Glaser, B. G., & Strauss, A. L. (1967). *The discovery of grounded theory*. Aldine Publishing.

Hartness, J. (1912). *The human factor in works management*. McGraw-Hill.

Hoenig, J. M. (2005). The Triangle fire of 1911. *History Magazine*, April/May.

Khurana, R. (2010). *From higher aims to hired hands: The social transformation of American business schools and the unfulfilled promise of management as a profession*. Princeton University Press.

Kilborn, P. T. (1992). North Carolina is told to improve safety role. *The New York Times,* January 9.

Lamond, D. (1998). Back to the future: Lessons from the past for a new management era. In G. Griffin (Ed.), *Management theory and practice: Moving to a new era* (pp. 3–14). Macmillan.

Lasch, C. (1987). Technology and its critics: The degradation of the practical arts. In S. E. Goldberg, & C. R. Strain (Eds.), *Technological change and the transformation of America* (pp. 79–90). Southern Illinois University Press.

Machiavelli, N. (2005). *The Prince with related documents*. Trans. & Ed. William J. Connell. St. Martins.
Mill, J. S. (1848). *The principles of political economy: With some of their applications to social philosophy*. John W. Parker & Son.
Mill, J. S. (1859). *On liberty* (2nd ed.). John W. Parker & Son.
Mintzberg, H. (1973). *The nature of managerial work*. Harper & Rowe.
Morgan, G. (1986). *Images of organization*. Sage.
Mullins, L. J. (2004). *Management and organisational behaviour* (7th ed.). FT Press Pearson.
Parker, L. D., & Ritson, P. A. (2005). Revisiting Fayol: Anticipating contemporary management. *British Journal of Management*, *16*(3), 175–194. https://doi.org/10.1111/j.1467-8551.2005.00453.x
Perrow, C. (1991). A society of organizations. *Theory and Society*, *20*(6), 725–762. https://www.jstor.org/stable/657602
Rangarajan, L. N. (trans.). (1992). *Kautilya: The Arthashastra*. Penguin Books.
Smith, A. (1776). *An inquiry into the nature and causes of the wealth of nations*. W. Strahan and T. Cadell.
Swedberg, R., & Agevall, O. (2005). *The Max Weber dictionary: Key words and central concepts*. Stanford University Press.
Sykes, W. H. (1847). Vital statistics of the East India Company's armies in India, European and Native. *Journal of the Statistical Society of London*, *10*(2), 100–131. https://doi.org/10.2307/2337686
Taylor, F. (1911). *The principles of scientific management*. Harper & Brothers.
Weber, M. (1978). *Economy and society: An outline of interpretive sociology*. Eds. G. Roth & C. Wittich. University of California Press.
Weber, M. (1994). *Weber: Political writings*. Ed. P. Lassman. Trans. Ronald Speirs. Cambridge University Press.
Weick, K. (1995). *Sensemaking in organizations*. Sage.
Witzel, M. (2003). *Fifty key figures in management*. Routledge.

6 Human Relations Theory

Anne M. Nicotera

Human relations (HR) theory and the HR movement in the U.S. are often misunderstood as a revolution against the dehumanizing nature of classical management theory Yet, the ideals of HR theory were discussed by theorists and practitioners far earlier than the onset of the HR movement (Bruce, 2006), and many businesses practiced this way. HR-like industrial practices stretch back well into the 19th century. HR theory supplemented and revised rather than replaced classical management, shifting the focus of management strategy from the *work* to the *worker* while the fundamental management goal remained maximizing productivity. Moreover, practices of classical management remain alive and well in 21st-century America, as anyone working in the fast-food industry (for example) can confirm. The advent of HR theory is evolutionary rather than revolutionary; the roots of the HR movement sit squarely in the center of scientific management. HR concepts and practices are paternalistic, keeping the worker/employee in a subservient role to the elite management class in an extension of capitalism and coloniality in which a ruling class benefits from the labor of a working class.

HR theory broadens the theoretic treatment of productivity to include motivation, satisfaction, and other humanizing elements in the design of management strategies. Worker satisfaction in HR theory is seen as a means to an end: a happy worker, it was presumed, is a productive worker. However, while the empirical connection between HR practices and satisfaction is well-evidenced, the link between satisfaction and productivity is tenuous. While HR theory's prescribed practices do indeed reduce worker turnover and create a more humane and ethical workplace, both of which improve the quality of the working environment, the HR movement's success in enhancing workers' quality of life did not result in the productivity gains anticipated. Significant advances in management strategies to improve productivity were not realized until the next generation of thinking, human resource management (HRM) theory, expanded management strategy to include workers' cognitive and intellectual contributions (see Chapter 7).

Distinguishing Classical Theory, HR, and HRM

We might simplify the differences between the three schools of thought (classical, HR, and HRM) by reducing the definition of a human being to three domains: working, feeling, and thinking. In classical management, emotion and other human psychological factors were acknowledged as an outcome of good management that served to ease worker acceptance of managerial control practices. For example, Frederick Taylor surmised that having managers think for them would make workers happy, but that was seen only as it enhanced workers' acquiescence to their prescribed role. Worker happiness was not seen as a tool to improve productivity.

DOI: 10.4324/9781003484639-8

Classical management restricted *thinking* to management and *working* to labor, with a focus solely on formal communication. *Feeling* was hardly considered at all, and certainly not as central to management strategy. In HR theory, however, human emotion and other psychological factors were seen as essential tools for management strategy, with motivation being the central concern. Workers and managers alike were seen as both working and feeling beings, with informal communication taking on increased significance as a strategy for enhancing productivity through enhancing human relationships. In HR theory, however, *thinking* is still the domain of management alone.

Later, applications of HRM theory (Chapter 7) emphasized worker intellect as a powerful resource for process improvement. Participatory management is thus a central tenet of HRM theories, but not HR theories. With HRM, both workers and managers are seen as equally multidimensional sources for management strategy: regardless of their place in the hierarchy, all human organizational members are seen as working, feeling, and thinking. HRM theory posits that it is this combination of human resources that improves processes and increases organizational value. Moreover, *working, feeling, and thinking* are essential elements of one another. HR theory, with its focus on human motivation and worker satisfaction, is an important step in the evolution of management theory, as a conceptual bridge between classical and contemporary management theory. It is important to keep this in mind while we review HR theory, to understand not only where it came from (classical management) but where it then led (HRM).

Birth of HR: The Hawthorne Studies

HR theory was born from the Hawthorne Studies, a series of scientific management experiments and observations conducted from 1924 to 1932 at the Hawthorne Works, a Western Electric factory near Chicago. The way this refrain is commonly repeated in most textbooks is, however, inaccurate (Bruce, 2006). First, most texts report that HR principles were an outcome of the studies, but the ideas about human motivation and human factors that underlie HR thinking were prevalent long before the Hawthorne Studies (as we saw from such theorists as Henri Fayol and Lillian Gilbreth in Chapter 5). Moreover, these ideas were a driving force for much of the *design* of the studies, not just a product of their results. Second, Elton Mayo and collaborators from Harvard are commonly credited as the studies' originators, yet did not join the project until 1928. The Harvard team is responsible for the design of later phases of research and for its impact on academia's subsequent development of management theory. The Hawthorne Studies were initiated by industry practitioners and industrial psychologists to establish a scientific basis for the claim, made by manufacturers in the electric light industry (including Thomas Edison), that their products would increase industrial output. Since this claim has an obvious bias, the studies were initiated by an organized group who sought to resolve any debate (Wrege, 1976). The illumination studies found that increases in electric lighting did not in fact increase productivity. So, in that sense the studies were a failure, but like most historic discoveries something unintended and unanticipated was revealed – something that revolutionized the industrial workplace.

The analyses and interpretations of Mayo and his associates (most notably Roethlisberger et al., 1939) launched the HR movement. The studies consisted of several phases, beginning with the Illumination Studies, a series of experiments that controlled physical conditions (such as temperature) in the factory while varying the level of lighting to find the ideal level of illumination for maximum productivity. Yet, changes in the lighting resulted in higher productivity regardless of the direction of change (brighter or dimmer).

These findings did not provide evidence that would sell more lighting, but they did raise many questions about the explanations for the change in productivity, leading to a set of studies involving direct observations, interviews, and the manipulation of other factors (e.g., length of shifts, length of breaks, and pay differentials) in addition to objective measurements of environmental conditions and productivity. (See Wrege, 1976, and Greenwood & Wrege, 1986, for detailed descriptions drawn directly from archival historical documents.) The Harvard team's conclusion that spurred the HR movement was that workers, due to the level of attention they were getting for the creation of ideal conditions, felt cared for by management and that this engagement increased their motivation to be more productive. (The term *Hawthorne Effect* was later coined to denote the idea that being observed is, in itself, an explanation for the behavior of research subjects.)

A large literature chronicles the history and interpretations of the Hawthorne Studies, including debates, reinterpretations, and re-analyses of the original data, such as gendered analysis (Acker & Van Houten, 1974). This literature largely agrees that the conclusion workers felt cared for was based in a faulty interpretation driven by classist/colonial presuppositions. It is more likely they felt fear upon being so closely watched. However, other branches of the studies, such as the Relay Room studies, documented the productivity benefits of interpersonal communication among workers. While a thorough review of this literature would be a worthwhile endeavor, it would distract from our central purpose to discuss HR theoretical advances and translation into practice, concentrating on the HR movement's fundamental tenets and its major theories, to examine implications for continuing influence on organizational communication theory.

Human Relations Theory and Theorists

The fundamental paradigm shift from the classical era to the HR era was from *mechanism* to *humanism*. Because the HR theory literature is far too broad and too large to fully review here, a small set of theories is presented, chosen for their historical prominence, influence on the field, and representativeness of HR principles. The fundamental assumption underlying HR theory is simple: human beings have emotional and social needs, and attention to those needs is a key factor in improving motivation and thus productivity. HR theories focus on motivation through recognition/appreciation, feelings/emotions, informal relations, job security and job satisfaction, effective communication, self-supervision, and participative decision-making (although neither self-management nor fully collaborative decision-making was widely practiced until the HRM era).

Mary Parker Follett: A Century Too Soon

Mary Parker Follett was a visionary. She was a social worker and the first person to implement the operation of community centers in impoverished neighborhoods. She was also a successful management consultant, a social and managerial philosopher who advocated for workplace democracy and self-governance through the power of the group. Her 1918 book, *The New State*, advocated a form of naturalistic democracy grounded in the emergence of organization from organic interaction among neighborhood residents. She theorized that group interaction and personal relations carry immense capacity to create power, authority, and freedom (Follett, 1919). This is remarkably similar in character to 21st-century organizational communication theory (see Chapter 3). In *Creative Experience* (1924), Follett applies her ideas to industrial management and labor relations. Her many papers and books, well-versed in scientific management, gained her a successful career in the 1920s as a lecturer to business scholars, practitioners, and government leaders in the U.S. and England. Her work continues to influence the field of public administration a century later.

While Follett is categorized as an HR theorist, her work is difficult to place because of its timing and character. In character, her work is more HRM theory than HR theory, with its application of human motivation and interpersonal communication to collaborative decision-making, organizational democracy, and self-governance. She gained attention among management theorists for her work on interpersonal relations and personnel management at the same time the Hawthorne Studies were being conducted. However, even though she has long been heralded as a pioneer of the HR movement, her work failed to gain enduring traction in the U.S. until the 1960s. It achieved far earlier and more enthusiastic attention among European scholars. Conceptually, Follett's work is a better fit for the late 20th and early 21st century, which may explain both its early marginalization and later resurgence.

As a member of the Taylor Society, Follett expressed support and appreciation for Taylorism's adherence to scientific objectivity and logic. However, "in contrast to Taylor's focus on engineering worker performance, Follett's focus is on the webs that connect workers to one another and to management and vice versa. Her work provided the groundwork for participatory management, total quality management, and teambuilding" (Newman & Guy, 1998, p. 294). Follett's chief focus was on *coordination,* using group and interpersonal relations as a primary source of managerial effectiveness. Follett's principles of organization are summarized as four degrees of coordination (Sethi, 1966, p. 13.):

1 Coordination by direct contact of the responsible people concerned,
2 Coordination in the early stages,
3 Coordination as the reciprocal relating of all the factors in a situation, and
4 Coordination as a continuing process.

The successful progression of coordination through this sequence depends on direct and timely communication, positive and creative thinking, a reciprocally shared vision across levels and roles, and the integration of the group and its accomplishments to continually perpetuate progressive organizational growth. Follett's ideas are quite contemporary, envisioning leadership as a function of the skills of all organizational members, the manager's job being to coordinate and integrate the contributions of the group members, accomplishing control from within group communication rather than imposed upon it.

Her sequential principles of coordination have important implications in Follett's body of theory, which reads more like a set of texts on teamwork and flattened organizing written in the 1990s than it does management theory discourse from the 1920s. The departure from classical management and Taylorism is quite profound. (The following summary is adapted from Sethi (1966).) First, coordination refers to unity rather than conformity, and unity presupposes organic and emergent groups (as opposed to a crowd or a collection of individuals). Second, collaborative conflict management is explicitly advocated, integrating opposing interests rather than compromising any. Such integration requires "dexterity and intelligence" (Sethi, 1966, p. 14). Moreover, coordination cannot be imposed, but must be driven from within the group, and coordinated values should assimilate one another. Of utmost importance is Follett's definition of coordination as an interpenetrating process of organizing (Sethi, 1962). The organizational environment is seen as dynamic, requiring progressive adjustment leading to increased coordination. Such adjustment, in turn, creates a new sense of interrelatedness, rather than mere capitulation. For Follett, then, every social process is threefold: interacting, unifying, and emerging. She also discusses *synthesis* as a natural process arising from coordination, emphasizing that all members, expert workers and executives alike, bring unique knowledge and experience. This equalizing notion allows authority to flow horizontally as well as vertically. Further, coordination does not subjugate any unit to another but rather integrates the integrity of the organization (seen by each unit from its own view). Perhaps the most radical departure from classical management theory is Follett's requirement that coordination start at the bottom rather than the top of the structure. Finally, coordination's growth sequence is reflected in direct contact, early awareness of the vision, reciprocal relationships, and the self-perpetuating mechanism of the process.

It is easy to understand both why Follett gained such early accolades and why her work was marginalized after her death in 1933. Management theory was just beginning to recognize the humanity of workers, and Follett's thinking was far more advanced than that. Her ideas were exciting and visionary, and that very visionary nature made them difficult to implement into a reality of practice that was just beginning to adjust to a humanistic rather than a mechanistic view of laborers and the nature of work. It was not until after Chester Barnard (1938) published *The Functions of the Executive* that Follett's role as an HR pioneer was established, and it was not until the full advent of collaborative practices under HRM that her teachings could effectively be implemented. The mainstream organizational world simply was not ready to allow workers to share authority with executives, although there are some examples of companies instituting Follett's recommended lateral processes very early (e.g., the matrix structuring of DuPont in the 1920s). Moreover, the state of theoretical advancement in the field was not ready to conceptualize the kind of interdependence she advocated until very late in the 20th century.

Chester Barnard: The First Organizational Communication Theorist?

Chester Barnard was a business executive, most notably the president of the New Jersey Bell Telephone Company, who published the first book on management without a prescriptive approach. *The Functions of the Executive* (1938) was a descriptive account of how organizations function, through a theory of formal organizations as cooperative systems with communication as the chief coordinating force. While Barnard was not an academic, he was well-read in political science, philosophy, sociology, anthropology, and psychology (as evidenced by citations in his work). Often labeled as the first text on organizational communication, the book focused on human relating and communication, with communication being the source of authority and cooperation a result of good communication. A high and consistent degree of cooperation, according to Barnard, is the key to organizational success and longevity. Barnard covers a comprehensive range of topics to create a well-integrated theoretic explanation of how organizations operate and, in turn, how executives can use this knowledge to ensure their organizations operate successfully. We will focus here on the elements of his theory that are most directly influential on management theory and later organizational communication theory, omitting those elements of the work that speak more directly to business operations (e.g., incentives, decision environments, opportunism, and moral leadership).

Effectiveness and Efficiency

Barnard (1938) was the first to use *effectiveness* and *efficiency* as primary metrics of organizational success. Effectiveness is defined as the attainment of organizational objectives and efficiency as the satisfaction of individual motives. Efficiency is twofold. First, an action is defined as efficient by its "unsought consequences" (p. 19). An efficient action's unanticipated outcomes are outweighed by its achievement of desired outcomes. Second, an efficient action satisfies the actors' motives without creating dissatisfaction. "This often happens; we find we do not want what we thought we wanted" (p. 20). Barnard explicitly defines *ends* as both material and social. Most important to our purposes is the centrality of communication and human relating to both organizational existence and success.

> Efficiency of a cooperative system is the resultant of the efficiencies of the individuals furnishing the constituent efforts, that is, as viewed by them. If the individual finds his motives being satisfied by what he does, he continues his cooperative effort; otherwise he does not. If he does not, this subtraction from the cooperative system may be fatal to it. ... Thus, the efficiency of a cooperative system is its capacity to maintain itself by the individual satisfactions it affords. This may be called its capacity of equilibrium, the balancing of burdens by satisfactions which results in continuance.
>
> (Barnard, 1938, pp. 56–57)

Informal Organization

Informal organization is Barnard's (1938) most notable influence on organizational studies, refers to "the aggregate of the personal contacts and interactions and the associated groupings of people" (p. 115). Barnard posits *informal organization* not only as a powerful source of organizational success but as the very stuff of the organization – a core idea in contemporary organizational communication theory. Barnard's (1938, p. 116) informal organization has two classes of effects: the establishment of "certain attitudes, understandings, customs, habits, institutions" (later used as the basis of theories of organizational culture); and the creation of "the conditions under which formal organizations may arise," which is quite similar to basic CCO claims. In another similarity, Barnard points out the mutually constitutive nature of formal and informal organization "Formal organizations arise out of and are necessary to informal organization; but when formal organizations come into operation, they create and require informal organizations" (p. 120). Informal organization is essential to both authority and the functioning of the executive.

Authority

Individual compliance and willingness to contribute to the organization are rooted in individual responsibility, and authority is rooted in communication. Authority is "the character of a communication (order) in a formal organization by virtue of which it is accepted by a contributor to or 'member' of the organization as governing the action he contributes" (Barnard, 1938, p. 163). In a significant departure from classical management, authority is not defined by position but by the extent to which the recipient of a directive accepts its legitimacy. Communication is authoritative under four conditions: the individual (1) understands the communication; (2) believes the communication is consistent with the purpose of the organization and (3) with their own personal interests; and that (4) they are able mentally and physically to comply. Barnard provides thorough consideration of gray areas in these four conditions.

Barnard also specifies the conditions under which persons can be said to *hold* authority. First, the communication of the person must lie in the *potentiality of assent* defined by organizational membership. There is no authority in directives to employees of another organization. Second, authority is presumed when the communication originates from a *center of communication* (a position or office) in the formal organization's structure, rather than from an individual (i.e., from *a manager* rather than *a person*). This *authority of position* is lost under two conditions: the directive is outside the scope of the position's function or the directive is not adjusted to the situation. *Authority of leadership* is quite different. Communication of individuals whose knowledge and understanding command respect will hold authority regardless of their positions because others will impute that authority. Here, Barnard is one of the first theorists to differentiate *positional authority* from *leadership*. Third, authority and responsibility are inseparable; those to whom authority is imputed are obligated to submit to the dominance of organizational ends, to *organization action* rather than *individual action*.

Several factors dictate the organization communication system's function as an authority system. First, channels of communication must be clear and known to all. This resembles Fayol's chain of command, but Barnard situates authority in communication rather than persons or positions. Second, objective authority requires that every organizational member be positioned in a clear and formal communication channel (a reporting relationship, similar to Fayol but again focused on communication and not persons). Third, these channels should be as short and direct as possible. Fourth, the complete line of communication must be used, not skipping over reporting relationships, to avoid conflicting communication and maintain responsibility. Fifth, persons serving as communication centers (officers, supervisors, heads, etc.) must be competent, both in personal skills (e.g., to assess situations and communicate clearly) and technical expertise. When the landscape is so complex that a single individual cannot be expected to personally hold the expertise or technical mastery of all processes involved, a staff may be relied on to provide that mastery. Here, we can see clearly that the *communication center* is the position or office, and not the person. Sixth, the line of communication should not be interrupted at times when the organization is expected to function. The line of authority must never be broken; this can be seen in operation when an interim manager is appointed during times when the regular manager must be absent. Finally,

> every communication should be authenticated. This means that the person communicating must be known actually to occupy the 'position of authority' concerned; that the position includes the type of communication concerned – that is, it is 'within its authority;' and that it actually is an authorized communication from this office.
>
> (Barnard, 1938, p. 180)

Functions of the Executive

The communication system creates a coordination system whereby individual actions are interlocked as organizational actions that achieve organizational goals.

> Such a system of communication implies centers or points of interconnection and can only operate as these centers are occupied by persons who are called

> executives. It might be said, then, that the function of executives is to service channels of communication so far as communications must passed through central positions. But since the object of the communication system is coordination of all aspects of organization, it follows that the functions of executives relate to all the work essential to the vitality and endurance of an organization so far, at least, as it must be accomplished through formal coordination. ... Executive work is not that *of* the organization, but the specialized work of *maintaining* the organization and operation.
>
> (Barnard, 1938, p. 215, emphasis in original)

Barnard (1938) clearly explains that the executive must maintain a system of cooperative effort, not manage people. The organization as a whole "is managed by itself, not by the executive organization, which is a part of it" (p. 216). He likens the executive organization to the body's nervous system, including the brain, which maintains the body by directing actions necessary for survival but is part of the body, and "can hardly be said to manage the body, a large part of whose functions are independent of it and upon which it in turn depends" (p. 217). Executives provide three essential complex functions: provide the system of communication; secure the efforts essential to its success; and formulate and define the organization's purpose.

PROVIDE THE SYSTEM OF COMMUNICATION

The system of communication is massive – the entirety of organizational design, Barnard's *scheme of organization* – organization charts, division of labor, duty specifications, etc. The executive must also specify the types and quantity of personnel that are needed and can be obtained, the incentives required, and the times and places for the work to be conducted. Once the organization is designed, personnel must be defined, identified, and secured. Finally, the informal organization requires maintenance of informal executive organization by careful selection of executives.

> The functions of informal executive organizations are the communication of intangible facts, opinions, suggestions, suspicions, that cannot pass through formal channels without raising issues calling for decisions, without dissipating dignity and objective authority, and without overloading executive positions; also to minimize excessive cliques of political types arising from too great divergence of interests and views, to promote self-discipline of the group; and to make possible the development of important personal influences in the organization.
>
> (Barnard, 1938, p. 225)

SECURE COOPERATIVE EFFORTS

The executive must secure essential services from the individuals who have been obtained as members, bringing individuals into the organization in a cooperative relationship and then eliciting services from them. The distinction from *managing persons* is subtle but important. The executive must function to define roles, attract individuals to fulfill those roles, and maintain an authoritative communication system that ensures a cooperative system of actions. It is the communication that must be managed, not the organization and not the people.

FORMULATE AND DESIGN THE ORGANIZATION'S PURPOSE

The organization's general purpose is composed of goals and objectives formulated in the cooperative system. The formulation and design of purpose is abstract and made up of smaller and increasingly more concrete goals and objectives. As such, the continual creation of the organization's purpose must be accomplished by the delegation of objective authority to positions in the communication system. At the lowest and most concrete levels of the organization, desired ends (which demand action) must be articulated with the more abstract objectives with which they correspond up the chain; it is the executive's function to achieve these articulations. For example, a factory worker might be tasked with a target production goal – to produce *x* number of widgets per week. Because (1) his job is to produce widgets, (2) he has the skills and materials to do so, and (3) he is directed to do so by a manager with acceptable authority, his cooperation is secured. Whether he is aware of it or not, his widgets are part of the larger set of production goals, matched with a larger set of sales goals, which correspond with corporate-level competitive goals (such as increasing market share), which in turn create a higher trading value for company stock, and so on. While workers on the floor may or may not be aware of the connections aligning their concrete personal production targets with such abstract things as the market share of the product or the value of the company's stock, their cooperation must be secured by an authoritative communication system designed and maintained by executives who, together, do perceive and understand all those connections.

Barnard's (1938) widely acclaimed book helped launch the HR movement. Heavily influenced by Mayo, Roethlisberger, and Follett, his ideas about motivation and communication were revolutionary. Barnard's ability to cross disciplines, particularly his psychological approach to leadership and employee motivation, was highly influential on management practices. The notion of the organization as a self-perpetuating communication system can still be seen in contemporary organizational communication theory.

Barnard's clear mandate to examine the human motivation to act toward organizational goals based on individual needs was not unique at the time, but it did serve to inspire the broad application of psychological theories of motivation to the theory and practice of management. As managers and theorists sought ways to motivate employees to cooperate, and thus be more productive, they turned to the psychology of human motivation. The most notably influential theory of human motivation cited by HR theorists is Maslow's (1943b) hierarchy of needs.

Abraham Maslow's Theory of Human Motivation

Maslow's (1943b) hierarchy of needs is one of the most well-known theories of human motivation, likely because of its ubiquity in the HR movement. Maslow rejected human motivation theory based on animal studies, largely because scholars commonly excluded *goals* from motivation theory because goals are unmeasurable in studies of rats. "Is it necessary to point out that we can ask a human being for his purpose?" (Maslow, 1943a, p. 89). Maslow's theory explains *motivations* for behavior rather than behavior itself.

Maslow's (1943a) fundamental propositions are: (1) theories of motivation must conceptually maintain the integrated wholeness of the human organism; (2) somatically based and localizable needs are atypical and should not be the center of any understanding of motivation; (3) ultimate goals (ends rather than means) should be the center, explicitly including unconscious motivations; (4) basic, unconscious goals are primary over local specific desires (culture often being an explanation for varying paths to the same goal); (5)

motivated behavior has multiple motivations and is a channel through which many basic needs are expressed and satisfied; (6) all states of the organism are motivated and motivating; (7) perhaps most importantly, *human needs are arranged in a hierarchy of prepotency* (the appearance of one resting on the prior satisfaction of another) and are not discrete or isolated (every drive is related to the state of others); (8) lists are theoretically and practically useless, and classifications of needs must encompass specificity and generalization of motives; (9) such classification must be based on goals; (10) motivation theory must be human, not based on animal research; (11) the situation (field) must be accounted for in the way that it is interpreted by the organism (but field theory is not motivation theory); (12) both integration and segmented reactions of the organism must be accounted for; (13) motivation theory is not behavior theory, motivations being just one class of behavioral determinant (others including biology, culture, and situation).

Maslow (1943b) classified human motivation into five categories of needs, each prepotent to the next – gratification of need low in the hierarchy creates the condition for the next higher-order need's appearance. *Potency* here means the capability to motivate. We do not feel a higher-order need, such as creative expression, when a lower-order need, such as a need for warmth, is potent. This is an important distinction that accounts for variations. It is the *potency* of needs and their *prepotency* in relation to each other that explain their motivational function, not the nature of the needs themselves. Maslow posits that his classification of basic human needs is universal but that needs only motivate behavior when their potency rises – which cannot occur in the face of an unmet prepotent need.

Deprivation and *gratification* are important concepts. When a prepotent need is unsatisfied, it will dominate to the point that other (higher) needs are disregarded or nonexistent. Gratification "releases the organism from the domination" of the prepotent need, "permitting the emergence of" higher goals (Maslow, 1943b, p. 375). For example, if hunger is prepotent to physical safety, starving people will disregard their physical safety to obtain food – but the potency of the unmet lower need must be such that the deprivation is sufficient to drive behavior. I will not run through a rain of bullets for food until the need for food reaches a level of potency that pushes my safety need to the background. Once the hunger is gratified to a certain (but variable) extent, my chief drive will be to meet my safety need. The higher need (safety) cannot be potent until the lower and prepotent need (hunger) is gratified sufficiently.

Maslow's five categories of needs are, in order of typical prepotency: physiological, safety, love, esteem, and self-actualization.

- The most prepotent category, *physiological*, is not as simple as it would seem. Maslow is quick to point out that things that meet physiological needs, such as food and eating, also meet cultural and emotional needs, so he cautions against universal generalizations. Such needs as sleepiness, physical activity, sexual desire, and maternal behavior are also subject to localizations and should not be considered definitively physiological.
- *Safety* needs include emotional and psychological safety as well as physical and must be defined by the individual's interpretation, not defined by any objective assessment of actual safety. In other words, the motivation is to *feel* safe. For example, sudden loud sounds may threaten a young child's feelings of safety in the absence of actual danger.
- *Love* includes affection, belongingness, and emotional intimacy – the need to have friends, be near family, or cultivate a romance. This last is an excellent example of Maslow's caution against localized needs. Since emotional intimacy is often achieved and expressed sexually, the sexual drive may be operating at either the physiological or love level of need, so localized expression cannot be generalized.

- *Esteem* is the need to attain stable positive evaluations of the self and others, and may be analyzed with a number of subcategories, such as achievement, independence, recognition, and appreciation.
- Finally, *self-actualization* "refers to the desire for self-fulfillment ... to become more and more what one is, to become everything that one is capable of becoming" (Maslow, 1943b, p. 382). The form and expression of self-actualization needs are highly individualized and deeply engrained in identity and culture.

Maslow discusses several important points often glossed over in summaries of the theory. First, the hierarchical order of the need categories themselves is not universal but varies by person. For some, esteem may be prepotent to love, for example. He claims only that the prepotent order of his hierarchy is typical for the individuals observed in the research literature. While Maslow does claim that he has identified categories of basic human need that transcend culture, the universality of the theory is found most powerfully in the claim of hierarchical prepotency and the way deprivation and gratification of needs continually create a new state of need. Thus, for some individuals, love may be prepotent to safety or creativity to hunger, but all individuals exist perpetually in a state of need, the gratification of which brings another (higher-order) need into prominence.

While behavior is universally driven by need gratification and deprivation, individualized prepotency variations can be explained by individual experience (such as a lifelong residence in a war zone that deadens the prepotency of safety), culture, personality, or pathology. Second, multiple-level need fulfillment is simultaneous and need not be total to reach the next-higher need's level of potency. A family meal, for example, may simultaneously fulfill physiological and love needs, but the hunger need will be prepotent until it reaches a state of sufficient gratification to open a place for the love need (assuming the prepotency of hunger). Partial satisfaction of a prepotent need is sufficient to create a state of potency for the next-level need, and this too can vary individually. For example, an impoverished artist accustomed to chronic hunger may develop such an atypically low level of sufficiency to satisfy that physiological need that she is able to crave creative expression. Need gratification predicts the emergence of other needs, but *how much* gratification does so is not universal.

The unconscious character of needs and motivations is particularly important to an understanding of human drive. Culture is also clearly accounted for and is the chief reason that basic human drives are used as the explanatory concept for motivation, rather than localized needs. Additionally, Maslow does not attempt to specify how needs are fulfilled. Maslow's discussion of other characteristics of basic needs includes the assertions that a single behavior has multiple motivations and that motivation is not the only determinant of behavior. Finally, Maslow's rejection of surface-level or fleeting desires as an explanation of motivation is important in applying the theory to psychopathology. "Thwarting of unimportant desires produces no psychopathological results; thwarting of a basically important need does produce such results" (1943b, p. 393).

The attention paid by management scholars and practitioners to Maslow's hierarchy (and other psychological treatments of human motivation) was a revolutionary departure from classical management. The recognition of the worker as a complex human being with needs, rather than a mechanistic component of the organizational machine, is the hallmark of the HR movement. Whether HR-theory-era managers personally cared about workers and their individual needs as humans is debatable, but the ubiquitous nature of their attention to Maslow's hierarchy is undeniable.

Douglas McGregor: Theory X and Theory Y

Douglas McGregor was a psychologist working as a professor of management. His Theory X and Theory Y are synopses of assumptions underlying traditional classical management philosophies and HR philosophies, respectively. McGregor (1957, 1960) offered an important distinction to Maslow's hierarchy between *lower-order needs* (physiological and safety) and *higher-order needs* (social, ego, and self-fulfillment), arguing that traditional, external methods of control can only work when the level of employee development is confined to the drives of lower-order needs. He also points out that satisfaction of those needs may keep people working but will not motivate increased productivity. Further, once the higher-order needs are in play, classical forms of management are detrimental because they offer deprivation rather than gratification. Traditional methods of managerial control rely on direction and command, with the means and methods of production dictated to the worker in conditions designed for them by management to serve organizational ends without regard to higher-order individual needs. McGregor argued that once the lower-order needs are satisfied and workers are driven by their social (and higher) needs, direction and control create conditions oppositional to human motivational needs. The current organizational condition was such that management was no longer directing a workforce acting out of fear for their subsistence and survival, but rather needed to motivate a workforce for whom those things had already been assured. His fundamental point was that the industrial workforce had developed to the point where traditional forms of management were not only useless but actively thwarting worker need-gratification and thus sabotaging organizational goals.

Theory X: The Conventional View of Management's Task

McGregor (1957) identified three basic propositions for traditional management, which he called *Theory X*. First, it is the responsibility of management to organize money, materials, equipment, and people – the elements of productive enterprise – in the interest of economic ends. Second, organizing people is "a process of directing their efforts, motivating them, controlling their actions, modifying their behavior to fit the needs of the organization" (p. 23). Finally, in the absence of such management intervention, people would be passive and resistant to meeting organizational needs. This means that they must be directed – persuaded, rewarded, punished, controlled. McGregor identified several implicit beliefs that underlie the propositions. First, people are fundamentally indolent with a desire to work as little as possible. People by nature lack ambition, dislike responsibility, want to be led, and are self-centered, indifferent to the needs of the organization, resistant to change, gullible, dull-witted, and easily duped. McGregor takes the position that conventional organization structures – as well as managerial policies, practices, and programs – reflected such assumptions.

Theory Y: The Contemporary Requirement

For Theory Y (essentially HR theory), McGregor identifies four fundamental propositions. The first one does not change: it remains the responsibility of management to organize the elements of productive enterprise (money, materials, equipment, and people) in the interest of economic ends. However, the remaining propositions recommend a revolution in the attitude of management. In his second proposition, McGregor argues that people are not *by nature* resistant to organizational needs but rather have been led to be so from their organizational experiences. Third, the motivation and capacity to develop, assume responsibility, and direct activities toward organizational goals are innate. Further, it is management's responsibility to create conditions in which people recognize and develop these human qualities in themselves. Finally, management's most fundamental task is to create organizational conditions and practices that allow people to achieve their own goals (satisfy their higher-order needs) by working toward organizational ends. McGregor acknowledges that creating such a system of management would face many obstacles but should not be perceived as a "soft" approach, which was a common criticism of HR practices at the time. Managers, he argues, must find ways to create opportunities and encourage growth in ways that release workers' potential. He sought not an abdication of management or lowering of standards but a wholly reinvented philosophy of leadership based on objectives rather than control.

Theories of Human Motivation: HR's Transition to HRM

By 1960, management theorists, industrial psychologists, and practitioners agreed that people are motivated to act on the organization's behalf when doing so meets their own needs, but two fundamental ideas had not yet matured. First, the link between individual and organizational needs holds only when the individual needs under consideration are at the level of *esteem/ego* or *self-actualization/self-fulfillment.* Second, the motivation in question can only be *internally* generated. A manager cannot provide motivation, only the conditions in which motivation will thrive. Higher-order needs cannot be met by external pressure, only by internal motivation to act on goals. HR practices continued to focus on workers' social needs, driven by the philosophy that management's goal was to drive employee compliance. However, social needs are simply the means through which ego (and then self-fulfillment) needs are activated.

Although McGregor's Theory Y was an excellent push in the right direction, scholars and practitioners of the time still had not learned that human beings do not work harder because they are satisfied; rather, it is the opposite. Human beings work harder when they have an internalized need that is met through that effort, and that hard work then results in satisfaction. Maslow is very clear: motivation is the *desire* to achieve an ungratified need, not the fulfillment derived from a previously met need. Yet, it is the previously met need that creates the appearance of the unmet need. So, motivation does not thrive by meeting needs, but rather by meeting needs in a way that provides both the next-level need and a path to achieve it. Furthermore, individual *social* needs do not align with *organizational* needs, so motivation to meet social needs does not translate to action that meets organizational needs. HR practices that created a friendlier and more humane workplace were just a start, but for several decades, HR practices stalled there – creating the complaint that HR management was "soft" (to which McGregor's Theory Y was in part a response).

Because the link between individual *development* and organizational goals had still not been made, HR practices focused on creating a positive climate and an enjoyable workplace that would lead to satisfied employees, under the faulty assumption that motivation to work harder would then follow from this satisfaction. While the first half of this linear sequence – from enjoyable workplace to worker happiness does indeed seem borne out by empirical research (e.g., Muchinsky, 1977), the second half – that improved productivity will be the final result – yields very mixed results (Brief, 1998), with the causal patterns among affect, job satisfaction, and productivity being neither linear nor clear (Côté, 1999; Herzberg, 1968). Moreover, HR practices were often used unethically as managerial manipulation (Argyris, 1964) rather than as a genuine attempt to motivate.

Chris Argyris and Worker Alienation

Chris Argyris, a management scientist with a background in psychology and economics, closely examined the fit between personality and organizational work to explore how organizational work might be designed to facilitate human development through alignment with higher-order needs. His work was foundational for organizational development, action research, and organizational learning, but had only marginal influence on organizational communication theory. His work is important to organizational communication scholars because it created revolutionary organizational practices that have profoundly shaped the phenomena we study in contemporary organizational communication research and because it deeply influenced organizational studies.

Argyris' (1964) theory of personality and organization is an extension of Maslow. Like McGregor, he was concerned with the ways hierarchical bureaucratic structures frustrate the needs of human development (Conrad, 1989). Argyris made several observations to illustrate that a fundamental shift in organizational design, management philosophy, and management practices was necessary. First, higher-order human needs are inconsistent with the dehumanizing external control exacted by vertical hierarchies. Such organizational structures are thus unhealthy for human development. Formal control structures, lack of attention to internal motivations and drives, specialized jobs, and paternalistic HR practices exacerbate these frustrations. Furthermore, bureaucratic structures and practices that create a competitive climate foster hostile rivalry and selfish employee attitudes focused on the short term, rather than cooperative attitudes focused on the long-term organizational good. Human beings, as adaptive organisms, naturally adjust to the stultifying environment of the vertical bureaucratic hierarchy with defensiveness, aggression, withdrawal, and apathy. They form social relationships with other alienated workers that feed on common frustrations and dilute their attention to work and to organizational goals. They often leave the organization or attempt to advance to less frustrating positions, but with their individual goals so displaced from the organization's goals, such advancement benefits neither the employee nor the organization. In the end, organizations lose the very employees they most need to retain – those who are most mature and psychologically healthy. Those who do stay become less and less effective over time.

Argyris' work is based on the presumption that human beings are driven according to Maslow's hierarchy of needs and will enact their drive to achieve more higher-order needs in ways appropriate to the situation at hand. If the organization provides opportunities for development that gratify employees' self-actualization needs, this basic human drive will lead to actions that will also serve the organization's needs. However, if the organization creates an environment in which self-actualization needs are frustrated and deprived, human behavior will fail to meet the needs of the organization. Argyris' observations are the fulfillment of Weber's admonition that bureaucracy would create a "polar night of icy darkness and hardness" (Weber, 1994, p. 368, see Chapter 5). Argyris produced a prodigious library of books and articles, with many collaborators, that launched the field of organization development (OD). OD theory and practices unite the internal drives and needs of human development with the needs of the organization, positing that like individual human beings, organizations need to learn, grow, and develop.

Herzberg's Theory of Job Satisfaction

Frederick Herzberg was a psychologist who applied mental health principles to industrial and organizational settings. Herzberg (1968) sharply criticized popular HR practices as enacting a poor understanding of HR principles. He devised an explanation of worker motivation that both explicates the murky waters of the mixed results of HR practices and serves as a launching point for HRM. Like Argyris, Herzberg focused on individual *development* rather than simple need-fulfillment, uniting individual growth with organizational goals in the form of concrete practices.

Herzberg (1968) used the acronym KITA (kick in the "pants," p. 54) to describe pressure applied by managers externally. A negative KITA is a push or threat, whereas a positive KITA is a pull or reward. Viewing contemporary HR practices as "soft," his descriptions of common personnel practices intended to be motivating are derisive – for example, his delightfully sarcastic critique of HR incentive programs that use time away from work:

> This represents a marvelous way of motivating people to work – getting them off the job!... An interesting variant of this approach is the development of off-hour recreation programs. The philosophy here seems to be that those who play together, work together. The fact is that motivated people seek more hours of work, not fewer.
>
> (Herzberg, 1968, p. 55)

He goes on to skewer practitioners' attempts to create motivational programs, pointing out that while external forces may get employees to move, they do so under the energy of the manager, so it is the manager who is motivated rather than the worker. When that energy is withdrawn, movement stops.

> Similarly, I can charge a man's battery, and then recharge it, and recharge it again. But it is only when he has his own generator that we can talk about motivation. He then needs no outside stimulation. He *wants* to do it.
>
> (Herzberg, 1968, p. 55, emphasis in original)

Herzberg's central argument is that external management-driven techniques to exact performance from employees completely miss the point that true motivation stems from the employee's *desire to work* as a means to achieve his/her own *individual goals*. The fault lies in a lack of attention to the individual worker's growth and development.

Herzberg's two-factor model of job satisfaction is based conceptually on Maslow's notion of lower- and higher-order needs and empirically on comprehensive field observations. His data from multiple studies (involving nearly 1700 diverse participants across a broad range of organizations and job types) indicates that *dissatisfaction* and *satisfaction* are not opposite poles of a linear continuum. Lack of dissatisfaction is not the same thing as satisfaction, and vice versa. Rather, gratification of lower-order needs, or *hygiene factors,* which relate to *job environment,* merely allows the employee to avoid dissatisfaction. Herzberg lists *social* needs in the hygiene area, rather than the motivating area. Hygiene factors include company policy and administration, quality of supervision, relationship with supervisor, work conditions, salary, relationship with peers, personal life, relationship with subordinates, status, and security. These things are stimuli that induce pain-avoidance behavior. When hygiene factors are good, the employee is not dissatisfied.

On the other hand, gratification of higher-order needs, or *motivators,* related to *job content*, drives satisfaction. It is this latter class of factors that creates the self-motivated employee whose job allows self-actualization. Motivators include achievement, recognition, challenge of the work itself, responsibility, advancement, and growth (Maslow's esteem and self-actualization). These factors induce individual development.

When motivators are good, the employee is satisfied. Motivators create the employee's internal generator. Herzberg points out that most HR applications had it backward. Satisfaction is not the cause of motivation but rather is its outcome.

Herzberg's system of *job enrichment* revolutionized the study of human motivation in industrial psychology. He cautioned against horizontal *job enlargement* practices, such as increased production targets, adding tasks, and rotating assignments – all of which simply enlarge the meaninglessness of the job. Successful *job enrichment*, on the other hand, increases the meaningfulness of the job to the employee's own growth and development. For example, vertical job enrichment practices that serve as motivators may include removing managerial controls while retaining employee accountability, increasing the individual's accountability for his/her own work, giving the employee complete responsibility for an entire unit of work (rather than distributing that unit's discrete tasks among several workers monitored by a supervisor), and introducing new and more difficult tasks as skills improve.

He gives the example of a secretarial pool required to produce a weekly quota of letters, all of which were proofread, approved, and signed by a supervisor who was also consulted on specialized and difficult questions. Herzberg critiques this as mere *job enlargement,* which does not provide the opportunity for growth and is thus not motivating. The letters did not *belong to* the secretaries because they were given no accountability for the outcomes or control of the process; the processes in place were external – controlling work process and output by shaping the job's environment. *Job enrichment,* on the other hand, took a very different form, controlling work processes and output by shaping the job content – allowing the secretaries to internalize the job's demands and their drive to meet them by enacting all of Herzberg's motivators. Subject matter experts were appointed in each unit so that its members consulted with one another instead of with the supervisor. Those writing the letters signed their own names, and letters went directly to the mailroom rather than across the supervisor's desk first. Proofreading was gradually reduced from 100% supervisor verification to 10% and was done at the secretary's desk rather than her supervisor's. Specific quotas were eliminated in favor of an expectation for "a full day's work" (Herzberg, 1968, p. 61), and each correspondent was held personally responsible for the quality and accuracy of letters.

Job enrichment is not a one-time practice but a "continuous management function" (Herzberg, 1968, p. 62), allowing the supervisor to spend less energy passively observing and correcting employees' performance and devote more time to administering thorough training and reviewing performance improvements. In this way, the organization develops in concert with the individual development of its employees. Moreover, job enrichment should progressively increase the challenge of the job to match the growing skills of the worker, allowing those with high ability to better demonstrate that ability and improve it and opening more opportunities for promotion. Because they promote individual development, motivators have a longer-term effect on employees' attitudes than hygiene factors.

By the waning of the HR era, academics' and practitioners' thinking about the nature of work, workers, organizations, and management had developed far beyond the mechanistic concerns of classical management. HR theory and practice humanized the workplace, and management mandates were well into the transition from exacting worker compliance to fostering worker development. The commitment to provide a humane workplace that fostered the social needs of employees and took care of their social needs likewise shifted from a production-oriented demand to an ethically oriented obligation.

Implications for Organizational Communication Theory

Classical management's bureaucratic structures and control practices remained in place throughout this era. HR theory should thus be seen as *highlighting* different aspects of communication, authority, and organization, but not in a way that replaces bureaucratic structures of authority or the priority of bureaucratic control.

Approach to Communication

HR theory examines the informal aspects of communication, with human psychology and emotion as primary concerns. Communication is treated relationally with a more transactional approach of two-way (but still linear) messaging between managers and employees. In HR theory, the treatment of communication is also enriched beyond mere messaging to also be seen as connecting and forging cooperative relationships. Communication, however, often remains cast as a management tool to accomplish worker productivity – not by establishing and maintaining organizational control vested in persons who hold authority as it was in classical theory, but as a tool to accomplish employee cooperation. The function of communication is both informational and relational and is still rooted in the capitalist presumption necessary for an elite management class.

The reciprocal relationship of the C–O cycle between deep enduring structures and daily practices is clear in the revolutionary change in American organizational life that can be traced to the HR movement, which introduced new practices that encouraged managers to communicate in humanizing ways. Over time, these practices became institutionalized to the point where entire bureaucratic units were deemed necessary to manage the HR function of the organization. HR has become such an enduring structure that *human resources* is now a thriving profession with its own professional career path, credentialing processes, and specializations. In addition, complex systems of labor regulations (such as requirements to provide health insurance and fair hiring practices) also appeared – again creating thriving professions with their own internal structures. You can see here how daily practices constitute enduring organizational structures in many ways. The original organization itself evolves as new structures emerge, but new formal organizations can also trace their emergence to these initial practices. For example, organizational entities such as degree programs in human resources, law firms specializing in labor law, human resources consulting firms, and government regulatory agencies could not exist without the HR practices initiated by the HR movement. Note, here, how colonial bureaucratic structures are replicated as HR principles are institutionalized. HR theory integrated our understanding of human activity and organizations as mutually constitutive. If daily practices perpetuate organizational development and work for individual higher-order need gratification, the C–O cycle increasingly improves both.

Approach to Organization and Authority

HR theory treats the organization more as an organism than a machine (Morgan, 1986), a metaphor that expanded with HRM. In HR theory, the organization is seen less as an external authoritative entity and more as a system of communication among its members. The managerial class is still ascribed with the authority to demand actions required of the labor class, but the managerial class had become larger with more internal layers and divisions, and authority was treated more as negotiated than dictated. Yet, the vertical hierarchy remained an engrained form for organizational structure. The focus turned from persons to positions, with more fluidity and flexibility. Despite Follett's and Barnard's admonitions that authority should be construed as *power with* rather than *power over*, the vertical metaphor for authority remained entrenched. On the other hand, our current organizational practices also show free communication up and down that hierarchy, work groups that freely communicate with one another with management's full approval, and dehumanization of work as a chief concern.

Cultural Implications

The HR movement changed work environments profoundly and permanently. Concerns for worker wellbeing remain an organizational priority, and the social needs of workers garner the attention required for a humane and enjoyable work environment. Today's employer-provided health insurance, organizational incentive programs, and employee wellbeing initiatives are all born of the HR movement. These programs are not just nice for employees. They are a means of meeting employees' lower-order needs as the foundation upon which management strategies for human development can foster the unification of individual and organizational needs, which has become a cultural imperative. Note, however, the enduring power of the corporate interest over the human.

Recommended Supplementary Readings

Acker, J., & Van Houten, D. (1974). Differential recruitment and control: The sex structuring of organizations. *Administrative Science Quarterly, 19*, 152–163.

This analysis provides an interesting and insightful gendered reading of the Hawthorne Studies, disrupting the common narrative about this piece of history.

Bruce, K. (2006). Henry S. Dennison, Elton Mayo, and human relations historiography. *Management and Organizational History, 1*, 177–199.

This article provides a thorough history of the Hawthorne Studies and the advent of the HR movement in management theory and practice.

Follett, M. P. (1919). Community is a process. *Philosophical Review, 28*, 576–588.

A reading of Mary Parker Follett's revolutionary ideas in their original source provides a first-hand experience of her visionary, ahead-of-her time ideas.

Herzberg, F. (1968). One more time: How do you motivate employees? *Harvard Business Review, 65*, 109–120.

Herzberg's irreverent style is interesting. The original had a sentence describing the motivation difference as that between rape and seduction (one "an unfortunate occurrence," the other a choice). Its 1968 acceptability, and subsequent deletion, can provoke a thoughtful classroom discussion.

Wrege, C. D. (1976). Solving Mayo's mystery: The first complete account of the origin of the Hawthorne Studies – the forgotten contributions of C. E. Snow and H. Hibarger. *Academy of Management Proceedings*, 12–16.

This article provides information on important contributors to the Hawthorne Studies who usually remain uncredited in contemporary accounts.

Important Concepts: Define and Discuss

Alienation
Eras of management theory
Hawthorne Studies
Job enlargement vs. job enrichment
Motivators vs. hygiene factors
Satisfaction vs. dissatisfaction
Theory X and Theory Y

Discussion Questions

1 Why should we classify the advancement of HR theory as an evolution from classical theory rather than a revolution against it?
2 Provide an example of a contemporary executive, and illustrate Barnard's three functions.
3 How does the contemporary landscape of electronic communication and social media accomplish the functions of informal organization?
4 How do contemporary communication media enhance the potential of implementing Follett's bottom-up coordination?
5 Why is it still so difficult to break away from top-down management to implement Follett's bottom-up thinking?
6 Discuss examples of contemporary programs and practices that have their roots in the HR movement. What functions do they serve?

Practitioners' Corner

Obvious applications of HR theories for communication practice include employee wellness and motivational programs. The distinction between hygiene factors and motivators based on an understanding of lower- and higher-order needs is particularly important both for designing programs that accomplish their intended purpose and for explaining those programs to organizational members and leaders. Clarity of expectations is key. A good understanding of what employee benefits and HR programs can accomplish is crucial to their success. Communication professionals have a role in providing this clarity to management.

More central to meeting organizational goals, however, is the important insight that managers and executives function as communication centers and that employee performance is a direct function of the quality of that communication. Getting things done requires the exercise of authority rooted in communication. Communication professionals are well-suited to support managers, either as internal communication officers or as consultants, to meet Barnard's four criteria for effective management communication, ensuring that employees understand the message and feel capable of compliance, believe the message to be consistent with organizational purposes, and perceive their own personal interests to be aligned.

References

Acker, J., & Van Houten, D. (1974). Differential recruitment and control: The sex structuring of organizations. *Administrative Science Quarterly*, *19*(2), 152–163. https://doi.org/10.2307/2393886
Argyris, C. (1964). *Integrating the individual and the organization*. Wiley.
Barnard, C. I. (1938). *The functions of the executive*. Harvard University Press.
Brief, A. P. (1998). *Attitudes in and around organizations*. Sage.
Bruce, K. (2006). Henry s. Dennison, Elton Mayo, and human relations historiography. *Management and Organizational History*, *1*(2), 177–199. https://doi.org/10.1177/1744935906064095
Conrad, C. (1989). *Strategic organizational communication* (2nd ed.). Holt, Rinehart and Winston.
Côté, S. (1999). Affect and performance in organizational settings. *Current Directions in Psychological Science*, *8*, 65–68. https://doi.org/10.1111/1467-8721.00016
Follett, M. P. (1919). Community is a process. *Philosophical Review*, *28*(6), 576–588. https://doi.org/10.2307/2178307
Follett, M. P. (1924). *Creative experience*. Peter Smith.
Greenwood, R. G., & Wrege, C. D. (1986). The Hawthorne studies. In D. A. Wren, & J. A. Pearce II (Eds.), *Papers dedicated to the development of modern management* (pp. 24–35). Academy of Management.
Herzberg, F. (1968). One more time: How do you motivate employees? *Harvard Business Review*, *65*(1), 53–62.
Maslow, A. H. (1943a). Preface to motivation theory. *Psychosomatic Medicine*, *5*(1), 85–92. https://doi.org/10.1097/00006842-194301000-00012
Maslow, A. H. (1943b). A theory of human motivation. *Psychology Review*, *50*(4), 370–396. https://doi.org/10.1037/h0054346
McGregor, D. (1957). The human side of enterprise. *Management Review*, *46*(11), 22–28.
McGregor, D. (1960). *The human side of enterprise*. McGraw-Hill.
Morgan, G. (1986). *Images of organization*. Sage.
Muchinsky, P. (1977). Organizational communication: Relationships to organizational climate and job satisfaction. *Academy of Management Journal*, *20*(4), 592–607. https://doi.org/10.5465/255359
Newman, M. A., & Guy, M. E. (1998). Taylor's triangle, Follett's web. *Administrative Theory & Praxis*, *20*(3), 287–297.
Roethlisberger, F. J., Dickson, W. J., & Wright, H. A. (1939). *Management and the worker: An account of a research program conducted by the Western Electric Company, Hawthorne Works, Chicago*. Harvard University Press.
Sethi, N. (1962). Mary Parker Follett: Pioneer in management theory. *The Journal of the Academy of Management*, *5*(3), 214–221.
Sethi, N. (1966). Coordination: The key to organizational engineering. *Industrial Management*, *8*(8), 9–14.
Weber, M. (1994). *Weber: Political writings*. Ed. P. Lassman. Trans. R. Speirs. Cambridge University Press.
Wrege, C. D. (1976). Solving Mayo's mystery: The first complete account of the origin of the Hawthorne Studies—The forgotten contributions of C. E. Snow and H. Hibarger. *Academy of Management Proceedings*, 12–16. https://doi.org/10.5465/AMBPP.1976.4975490

7 Human Resource Management Theory

Anne M. Nicotera

Human resource management (HRM) theory, as explained in Chapter 6, identified employee intelligence as a valuable resource, in a natural extension to the late HR focus on human development. As managers strived to align employee developmental needs with organizational goals, and scholars sought better evidence on how to best do so, the importance of worker participation in decision-making (PDM) became an important strategy, spurring the participation movement of the 1960s and 1970s, particularly in manufacturing. The humanism of the HR era functioned as an important transitional period from the mechanistic thinking and practices of the classical era to the more organismic thinking of HRM. As scholars and practitioners came to understand more about motivation and human development, the need to unite individual and organizational development became progressively clearer. Rather than neutral and static entities, organizations were increasingly seen as fluid, growing, learning organisms. It was soon a commonly accepted assumption that an organization could thrive and develop only through the developmental progress of its employees. In this chapter, we will focus on the early HRM theories that provide a conceptual link to the advent of organizational communication theory and research in the 1970s.

Participation strategies range from managers collecting employee input on decisions to fully delegating decision-making authority to employees (see Tannenbaum & Schmidt, 1958, for an early analysis of determining appropriate management strategy for decision-making on a continuum of autocratic to democratic to delegated). During this era in management theory, the field of Organizational Communication emerged as a separate and unique discipline (see Chapter 1). As such, we will not continue to trace the development of management theory after HRM. It is important to note, however, that by the 1990s, the idea of participation had expanded in the field of Management to widespread prescriptions for organizational restructuring to flatten hierarchies, decentralize authority, and create team-based environments characterized by self-managed groups. This was particularly prevalent in manufacturing.

The restructuring and teams movement in management is important for organizational communication scholars because it revolutionized the organizational environments we study, creating interesting communication phenomena, including paradoxes (Stohl & Cheney, 2001; see Chapter 3). There are sizable organizational communication literatures on groups, teams, leadership, and organizational democracy (in addition to numerous other areas) that document how the study of organizational communication shifted in response to the emergence of alternative organizational forms that for many organizations replaced the vertical authority hierarchy of traditional bureaucracy with flattened hierarchies encompassed by more circular organizational forms whose foundation lies in the mid-20th-century recognition of employee intelligence as a valuable organizational resource.

DOI: 10.4324/9781003484639-9

HRM theory is most fruitfully described through three fundamental themes: the integration of formal and informal organization, contingency, and participation. Each theme is explicated here with overviews of theories and practices that provide striking illustrations of that theme. However, all HRM theories and practices resonate with all three themes. Before summarizing the implications of HRM theory, the chapter then briefly reviews management theory developments that brought HRM ideals to fruition in the 1990s.

HRM Theme: Integrating Formal and Informal Organization

The two fundamental imperatives of HRM were to align individual and organizational development and to maximize the potential of employee intelligence. These could be accomplished only through fostering participative collaborative relationships across hierarchical levels. While relational communication was attended to by HR theory, the manager–employee relationship remained paternalistic and authoritarian. Under HRM, the definition of that relationship transformed. Although the character of the manager–employee relationship became more egalitarian, with greater respect for employee opinion fueled by increased recognition of the perspective gained from direct experience, managers retained positional authority rooted in the traditional hierarchical structure, maintaining the colonial presumption of a ruling class elite. Still, shared authority over organizational decision-making and goal-setting became more expected; employee performance targets and reward systems became more negotiable; and accountability became more decentralized. These formal aspects of the manager–employee relationship could not have been adjusted without a parallel reframing of the informal.

Rensis Likert: System IV

Rensis Likert was an organizational psychologist working in the U.S. Department of Agriculture in the 1940s, and later the director of the Institute for Social Research at the University of Michigan. Like McGregor, Likert (1961, 1967) provided descriptions of management systems he found undesirable to promote the system he advocated. Likert's primary focus was on decision-making.

System I: Exploitative Authoritative

Rooted in the ideals and practices of classical management (see Chapter 5), exploitative authoritative management utilizes top-down decision-making and threat-based motivation based on fear of losing physical and economic security. Organizational goals, and the methods by which to achieve them, are dictated by management. In such a system, management feels responsible for meeting organizational goals, whereas employees do not and welcome opportunities to behave in ways that defeat organizational goals. Individual employee goals and needs are ignored. As a result, Likert (1961) warns that employee attitudes are hostile to organizational goals. Communication is almost entirely downward. Employees are thus subservient to managers with some hostility. Hostility is also cultivated downward and with peers, and distrust is widespread. The informal organization usually opposes the goals of the formal organization; productivity is mediocre; and employees are generally dissatisfied. In this way, Likert describes the undesirable outcomes of the exploitative authoritative management system.

System II: Benevolent Authoritative

Still rooted in classical management ideals, but with a more considerate managerial attitude, System II is less controlling than System I, with employee motivation based on economic security and ego motives (e.g., a desire for status). While major decisions, such as setting organizational policies and goals, are made at the top, workers are afforded the opportunity to make some decisions within the limits of the framework provided by management. Organizational goals are set by management, with some employee opportunities for feedback. In this system, management feels responsible for organizational goals, whereas employees do not. Communication is mostly downward, but significant opportunities for upward communication do exist. Employees are subservient to and somewhat suspicious of managers, and the competition for managerial favor creates hostility among peers and condescension to subordinates. The informal organization partially opposes the goals of the formal organization; productivity is fair to good; and employees are only moderately satisfied. Likert's description of benevolent authoritative management shows how it begins to move management strategy in the right direction but does not go far enough.

System III: Consultative

The consultative management system is fundamentally based in the ideals and practices of HR theory (see Chapter 6). Employee motivation is based in economic, ego, and other employee-centered motives, such as the desire for new experiences. While employee input is actively sought by management as a key source of information necessary for goal-setting and decision-making, major decisions and the setting of organizational goals remain the territory of management. Lower level employees are afforded the freedom to make decisions only on specific things that directly impact their work. In this system, both managers and employees feel responsible for meeting organizational goals, and behavior counter to those goals is rare. Communication flows freely downward and upward, although upward communication is more limited. Employee attitudes are cooperative, albeit with some competition among peers. The informal organization is generally supportive of but somewhat resistant to the goals of the formal organization; productivity is good; and employees are moderately satisfied. Likert's description of System III shows it to be a vast improvement over Systems I and II, but not quite enough to maximize organizational goal-attainment.

System IV: Participative

Likert's System IV, which he argued was the most effective form of management, is an exemplar of HRM theory. System IV promotes full and genuine PDM and organizational goal-setting. Communication is free-flowing in all directions, with the skills, creativity, and intelligence of employees valued as key organizational resources. All organizational members feel responsibility for achieving organizational goals, and accountability is likewise high. Attitudes are favorable to organizational goals and foster cooperative relationships within and between levels. The informal and formal organizations are integrated; productivity is excellent; and satisfaction is high.

Likert (1967) provided detailed instructions for the successful implementation of System IV management. The achievement of System IV objectives is accomplished through shared authority, with clear systems of accountability in place. The role of management must shift to a facilitative function that monitors and coordinates rather than dictates.

Data collection must be constant, and participation must be facilitated effectively in groups rather than individual-to-individual. The reframing of *the organization as a system of groups* is crucial to Likert's advancements in managerial thinking. Collaborative high-performance goal-setting with employees, coupled with supportive communication with managers, is crucial to both organizational and individual success. Fundamentally, the central innovation contributed by Likert was the redefinition of the manager from an *authority who translates* organizational goals to employee activities to a *mediator who facilitates* participation in organizational goal-setting and negotiates the articulation of those goals with employee activities. Yet, the structural form of an elite class remained.

Blake and Mouton's Managerial Grid

Blake and Mouton were management theorists and consultants. Their Managerial Grid model is one of several HRM-era depictions of management and leadership as a set of practices integrating the task and relational dimensions of organization – the formal and informal organizations. The Managerial Grid has remained popular in practice and managerial training, with updates in terminology and flexibility of implementation. It was particularly influential in examining conflict management (Blake et al., 1964; see Chapter 16). Earlier considerations conceptualized leaders' task and relational behaviors as opposites, presuming each took something away from the other. Blake and Mouton (1964) were among the first scholars to posit task and relational behaviors of managers as independent dimensions, proposing five leadership styles according to the manager's *concern for production* and *concern for people*. Conceptualizations using this basic two-dimensional structure later became known as *dual-concern models*. In the Managerial Grid, each of these two dimensions is operationalized on a nine-point scale from low to high, with an accompanying self-report diagnostic scale covering numerous behavioral elements: initiative, inquiry, advocacy, decision-making, conflict, critique, and resilience. Similarly to Likert, Blake and Mouton describe four of their five styles as less effective than their preferred HRM ideal, *team management* (9,9) – high concern for both production and people, and thus an integration of formal and informal organization.

Impoverished management (1,1), with its low concern for both production and for people, is seen as negligent, an abdication of managerial responsibility. *Authority-compliance management* (9,1), characterized by a high concern for production with a low concern for people, is traditional classical management – ignoring the informal organization and thus losing the contributions of employee experience, creativity, and intelligence. *Country club management* (1,9) is the opposite. Blake and Mouton describe it in a way that reveals their contempt for HR practices that presume job performance can be improved by attention to employee happiness without a concomitant focus on task productivity (similar to the posture assumed by both McGregor and Herzberg). *Middle of the road management* (5,5) is seen as ineffective – its compromising stance pitting the two concerns against one another as oppositional ideals rather than mutually influential processes that can enhance one another. *Team management* (9,9), however, is the *sine qua non* of HRM, uniting employees' need for development with organizational goals, seeking full employee PDM, and pursuing a collaborative relationship between management and employees. Like other HRM theorists, Blake and Mouton (and, after their deaths, the consulting company they founded) produced a large library of publications designed to assist practitioners in implementing their system of management.

HRM Theme: Contingency

Contingency is another central theme in HRM theory and practice. *Contingency theory* is an umbrella term for management theory claiming there is no "one best way" to manage. Rather, different managerial strategies and skill sets fit different situations. One of the most pervasive assumptions of management theorists in this era (and since) was that one approach to managing employees was not advisable for all situations. Rather, the selection of appropriate and effective management strategies is presumed to be driven by contingent factors. As contingency thinking developed, flexibility of the leader emerged as a primary concern for the implementation of effective management strategies.

Fiedler's Situational Contingency Theory

One of the earliest contingency theories predicted group effectiveness from the match between leader style and situational demands, theorizing that leaders are most effective when the situation is modified to suit their strengths. Fiedler (1967) placed leader style into two categories, operationalized according to how the individual rates his or her *least preferred coworker* (LPC) on several bi-polar scales. Those who describe unfavorable coworkers in negative terms (low-LPC) are task-oriented, whereas high-LPC leaders are more motivated to maintain good interpersonal relations. This is a far less developed, bi-polar conceptualization of task and relational behavior than later HRM theories (such as Blake and Mouton's) would adopt. Fiedler also conceptually grounded leader style in personality traits, and therefore not subject to change. Rather than the leader's behavior, it is the contingent situational factors that are seen as malleable. Situational favorability (also called situational control) is defined by three contingencies: good leader–member relations (characterized by mutual trust and respect), clear task structures, and leader position power (ability to distribute resources) (Fiedler, 1967). Low-LPC leaders perform best in extreme situations – either highly unfavorable or highly favorable conditions. High-LPC leaders perform best in situations that are moderately favorable or unfavorable.

Later, the basic theory was expanded into *cognitive resource theory* (Fiedler, 1986). Two important leader cognitive resources – leaders' *intelligence* and *experience* (defined as knowledge and abilities gained over time in the organization) and an additional situational variable (*stress*) were included as leadership effectiveness contingencies. The theory predicts that a leader's direction is more likely to be followed when the leader has high intelligence and ability and when group members are supportive. In conditions of low stress (with leader's own supervisor, with the group members, or with the problem at hand), intelligence is applied more often and is more effective. On the other hand, in situations of high stress, leader experience (in the form of knowledge/skills gained over time) predicts high performance, and leader intelligence is either not important or can actually detract from the group's performance.

Fiedler's model was criticized because it neither accounted for nor advocated flexibility in the leader's style, presuming that leadership style was based in personality and was thus predetermined and stable. Fiedler, and those who joined his consulting practice, designed complex training programs to assist managers and executives in modifying organizational situational variables and matching leaders to appropriate assignments – but in the end, the only reliable solution offered to a mismatch between leader and situation was to change the leader. Fiedler's models also conceptualized task and relational concerns as oppositional styles and persisted in the narrow presumption that leadership is defined as giving direction, so it did not keep pace with the increasing demand for multidimensional conceptualizations of leadership concerns, delegation of authority, and participative decision-making. Note here, too, that the term *leader* means the designated manager, maintaining the formal authority hierarchy of classical management theory.

Hersey and Blanchard's Model of Situational Leadership

First introduced as the *life cycle theory of leadership* (Hersey & Blanchard, 1969), Situational Leadership Theory is an exemplar of contingency thinking in HRM theory because it both advocates flexibility in management strategy and links such leadership behavior to employee development to maximize organizational outcomes. Situational Leadership Theory is similar to Blake and Mouton's Managerial Grid in its two-dimensional structure of leader behavior. However, while Blake and Mouton focused on the concerns of the leader, Hersey and Blanchard concentrated on the type of support leaders offer to their followers. Hersey and Blanchard identified four main leadership styles, according to the extent of task and relationship support provided by the leader or manager, which should be adjusted contingent to the followers' task and relational needs. In early publications, these were referred to as *maturity* levels on the dimensions *ability* (task support need) and *willingness* (relational support need). Later versions of the theory (e.g., Blanchard et al., 1985; Hersey, 1985) refined the conceptualization of follower needs to focus on *development* (sometimes referred to as *readiness*), operationalized on the dimensions *competence* and *commitment*. This was an important theoretical advancement because this thinking introduced a dynamic character to the theory. The theory claims that the appropriate combination of task and relational support provided at levels adjusted over time – matched to followers' evolving needs – fosters follower development of independence and abilities that would, in turn, enable the leader to increasingly delegate responsibility in a way that advances organizational development and expansion. Further, the later iteration of the theory that replaced *willingness* with *commitment* provided a far more nuanced understanding of followers' relational support needs.

Followers with low competence but high commitment are the least developed, requiring the leader to practice a *Telling* (Style 1) leadership style that provides a high level of task direction and support and a low level of relational support. The initial version of the theory proposed the lowest level of employee maturity to be low on both ability and willingness, but data and field experience revealed that it was more typical for those new to a task to have initial enthusiasm that flags as their abilities increase. As they develop to the second level, followers remain less than fully competent and actually regress in their commitment level, realizing how much there is still to learn and feeling overwhelmed and/or disheartened. The second level of development is described as low competence and low commitment. This is the point when the manager needs to provide increasing relational support while maintaining high level of task support to continue building ability (Style 2, *Selling*). In the third level of development, competence is high. Followers now have the skills and abilities they need to perform independently. However, their commitment remains low or variable because they lack the confidence gained from independent performance, so the best leadership strategy reduces the level of task support while maintaining high relational support (Style 3, *Participating*). Finally, followers attain the highest level of development, with both the competence and commitment to perform independently. The leader can now greatly reduce both task and relational support, remaining involved to monitor and provide feedback, but distributing authority and accountability for the work to the follower (Style 4, *Delegating*). In a dynamic workplace, employees can be expected to repeat this process with each new set of tasks they encounter, as they increasingly develop to expand the domains of their ability to accomplish and expand organizational objectives. In this way, the Situational Leadership model demonstrates how attention to contingencies for appropriate management strategies also accomplishes the integration of individual and organizational development and champions the centrality of employee intelligence as an organizational resource. Again, like other models of its time, *leader* means manager in a formal authority hierarchy.

HRM Theme: Participation

Finally, all HRM theorists advocate employee PDM. Unlike HR theory, which does so with employees' need for belongingness as a central concern, HRM applications of PDM highlight the value of employee intelligence as a valuable resource. Under HR, participation is used to benefit the employee; under HRM, participation is used to benefit the organization. Whereas HR theory paternalistically involves employees to help them feel good, HRM theory involves employees because of the value brought by their intelligence and experience. PDM can thus be seen as an important conceptual bridge from HR to HRM. As the organizational value of the employee perspective came to be more recognized and valued, PDM practices already in place for the purposes of building morale provided a basis for HRM management strategies. Note here that the priority remains on the benefit to the organization, privileging the corporate interest over the human interest.

As mentioned at the outset of this chapter, HRM theory planted the conceptual seeds for the organizational restructuring movement several decades later that allowed numerous large organizations to dismantle vertical bureaucratic authority systems. PDM practices are at the heart of the ideas that manifested in such organizational redesign and the creation of new organizational forms. Decentralization of decision-making is fundamental to the flattening of hierarchies. As the authority to make decisions and the accountability for their outcomes were distributed horizontally, traditional authority structures in a significant number of industries were replaced by dynamic circular systems of independent business units composed of self-managed teams.

The distinction between HRM-era decentralization and later large-scale restructuring efforts is the type and scope of decision-making authority that was distributed. Work-related decision-making, rather than policy-level strategic decisions, was the stuff of PDM programs in the HRM era. These early efforts built into more large-scale participation in strategic decision-making in large organizational systems, such a government bureau (Bacharach & Aiken, 1977). According to Jablin (1987), early studies of participation in strategic decision-making lead to increased volume, frequency, and openness of communication across the organization (in all directions) and an increase in amount and quality of performance feedback. Seebold and Shea (2001) conducted a comprehensive summary of PDM programs, including the restructured or *new plant* approach. They analyzed the research literature on five voluntary formal participation systems, examining their effectiveness. The summary to follow is based on Seibold and Shea's (2001) analysis. The primary distinctions among PDM practices are the extent to which their influence on decisions ranges from consultative to full and the types of decisions involved (from concrete concerns of the work itself to organizational policy decisions). Note that all of these systems reproduce the dominance of the corporate interest.

Quality Circles

Quality circles (QCs) are a continuous improvement strategy. A QC is a discussion group of workers with similar jobs who identify, analyze, and solve task-related problems. QCs have a consultative role. They are led by supervisors and must present proposals to management for approval. Ordinarily, the workers are expected to implement the approved actions that result from their discussion. Their discussions are limited to the work itself and the immediate work area. There is a low degree of involvement and a low degree of effectiveness.

Quality of Work Life Programs

Quality of work life (QWL) is a broad term used to label structured programs that seek to involve employees in decisions affecting their work. QWL programs have a consultative role, functioning to provide important feedback to managers about the concerns of employees to inform their decision-making. The topics of discussion may be the work itself, working conditions, or even company policies. QWL programs can take many forms (e.g., employee surveys, town-hall-type meetings) and can include union representatives, workers, and managers. The degree of participation is relatively low, and effectiveness varies. The Total Quality Management (TQM) fad of the 1980s, an effort to create an organization climate of continuous improvement, followed the QWL philosophy.

Employee Stock Ownership Plans (ESOPs)

Employee stock ownership plans (ESOPs) were instituted in the 1970s to provide incentives to employees by making company stock part of the employee compensation and benefits system. The fundamental philosophy underlying ESOPs is the assumption that employees will internalize corporate profitability as a personal goal because they own a piece of the corporation and reap personal financial benefit from the value of the stock. ESOPs may take many forms but often allow voting among participating employees. The content of the decision-making varies but normally involves sending representatives to the board of directors. The degree of participation varies from low to moderate, depending on the type of ESOP. The influence of participating employees can vary from consultative only to full participation in company policy decisions. Their effectiveness is moderate.

Scanlon Plans

Scanlon gainsharing plans create a reward system linked to group and organizational performance. A Scanlon plan is a profit-sharing technique designed by Joseph Scanlon during the U.S. Great Depression to promote stability in labor–management relations during this volatile era. Employees share the financial rewards of cost savings and profit, based on their own effort according to a formalized incentive formula. Detailed periodic progress reporting and monitoring are necessary for implementation. Content of the decision-making can encompass the work itself, working conditions, company policy, and the design of financial bonuses. The degree of participation required is moderate to high. The influence can vary from consultative only to full participation in company policy decisions and may even include the privilege of implementing some decisions without prior management approval. Their effectiveness is high.

Self-Directed Work Teams

Self-directed work teams (SDWTs) manage themselves without the oversight of a traditionally authoritative manager. Teams are afforded full authority to make decisions over their own processes and production involving the work itself, working conditions, schedules, budgets, contracts, hiring (at the team level), and compensation. The degree of participation is very high, as is effectiveness when the program is implemented with appropriate training and is structured correctly. The use of SDWTs, or the *new plant* approach (Lawler, 1978, 1992), represents the most successful of the strategies that culminated in the restructuring movement of the 1990s. The new plant approach is reviewed in detail below to illustrate the kinds of large structural changes necessary to achieve the participation ideals of HRM. Research on the new plant approach provides evidence that the ideals of HRM are only fully attainable when formal structures are decentralized and hierarchies are flattened. However, without the appropriate cultural transition accomplished by thorough education and training, their implementation can result in adverse consequences (Barker, 1993; Stohl & Cheney, 2001; see Chapter 3).

Paradoxes of Participation

Through systematic examination of tensions and contradictions associated with worker participation programs, Stohl and Cheney (2001) derived four categories of paradox within which 14 specific types of paradox reside. *Paradoxes of structure* stem from the architecture of the participation program. *Paradoxes of agency* concern individual efficacy. *Paradoxes of identity* are about membership, inclusion, and boundaries. Finally, *paradoxes of power* are rooted in the locus, nature, and exercise of power.

Paradoxes of Structure

This category includes four types. First, imposed participation creates *paradoxes of design*. Driving employee input from above reproduces authority structures it was intended to replace. Middle managers feel threatened because they believe workers are given too much control, but workers feel controlled by management. Second, *paradoxes of adaptation* occur when restrictive rules dictate democracy, employees experience oppressive and rigid policies rather than the intended democratic, fluid, liberating process of participation. Third, *paradoxes of punctuation* develop from perceptions of causal sequencing (Stohl, 1995). Workers perceive the processes involved in teaching specific participatory processes (e.g., problem-solving agendas, discussion techniques) as inefficient, so they resist. Resistance slows the process and disconnects participation from "real work" (Stohl, 1995, p. 207). Finally, participants create *paradoxes of formalization* when they formalize participatory and democratic processes into institutional structures (e.g., decision-making rules, procedural formulas, codes of conduct) that negate their intended flexibility.

Paradoxes of Agency

This category of paradox is composed of four types. First, *paradoxes of responsibility* address reward and compensation. Incentives are commonly individually based, rewarding autonomous action and creating no motivation for the cooperative behavior required for effective team performance. Second, *paradoxes of cooperation* create acquiescence without compliance, a cycle in which workers increasingly play a role of accepting but not completing assignments. "To cooperate with the manager they must not participate and let the manager do the participating" (Stohl, 1995, p. 209). Third, *paradoxes of sociality* arise when organizational members are highly motivated and committed to participation, becoming involved in so many activities their performance suffers. The social aspect of participation can so overwhelm that personal lives also suffer (Stohl & Cheney, 2001). Finally, *paradoxes of autonomy* sacrifice individual agency to the collective. Rather than roles, *people* become absorbed by the organization, infringing on their efficacy and stultifying their ability to alter structures.

Paradoxes of Identity

This category contains three types. First, *paradoxes of commitment* occur when commitment is signified by obligatory conformance. Often, management views those who express reservations about participatory designs as uncommitted, needing to be persuaded, or saboteurs. Yet only those committed to organizational outcomes would dissent. Second, *paradoxes of representation* arise when participatory groups include worker representatives. Emergent networks and communication patterns change their views, so they no longer accurately represent worker experiences. Finally, *paradoxes of compatibility* occur when participation processes are incompatible with organizational culture, which is particularly problematic in international settings. Successful participation alters organizational culture (everyday practices, communicative expectations, and central values) by muting hierarchical patterns. "Participation works best in those organizations where the culture is already compatible with participatory goals" (Stohl, 1995, p. 211).

Paradoxes of Power

This category contains three types. First, in *paradoxes of control*, workers internalize and intensify organizational control mechanisms. In team-based structures, high identification, consensus on values, and personal connections "create a powerful system of 'concertive control' in which workers control and monitor themselves to an even greater extent that found a typical bureaucratic organization" (Stohl, 1995, p. 212). Participants internalize organizational control to the extent that self-discipline becomes a damaging force (see Chapters 11 and 12). Second, *paradoxes of leadership* express challenges of leading participation without controlling it. Finally, *paradoxes of homogeneity* function similar to groupthink, where consensus-seeking displaces fruitful disagreement (see Chapter 15). The homogeneity that provides efficacy blinds the group to alternative viewpoints, provides a sense of discomfort with disagreement, and discourages heterogeneity. When the group seeks to control heterogeneity, they lose fruitful disagreement.

Organizational Communication and Management Theory Developments

Theory and research on teams (Chapter 15) and on participation and democracy (Chapter 3) are rooted in HRM. Although it is beyond our scope to provide reviews of the ways HRM concepts were developed across organizational studies, it is important to discuss a body of management theory stemming from the implementation of employee participation programs that revolutionized organizational forms, creating the organizational landscape in which we currently live and work.

Management Theory that Extended HRM: Organizational Restructuring

In the 1990s, Edward E. Lawler III and his colleagues at the Center for Effective Organizations at the University of Southern California (USC) generated a theoretically rich empirically based body of prescriptive theory advocating the restructuring of vertical organizational designs with centralized authority structures to create flattened (or lateralized) participative designs with distributed authority (e.g., Galbraith et al., 1993; Lawler, 1991, 1992, 1999, 2000, 2001; Lawler et al., 1998; Mohrman et al., 1995; Mohrman et al., 1998). As stated previously, the HRM ideals cannot be realized in the presence of centralized hierarchical authority structures. Lawler's (1992) *new plant approach* provides an exemplar of this work. These so-called new ideas and practices were not altogether new. What was new was the business imperative demanding such practices for survival, the wide scale with which they were being applied, and the flattening of organizational authority structures (Lawler, 1992).

Lawler (2000) summarized six *new logic principles* for organizing, conceptualizing *new logic organizing* as a new era of management thinking. His conceptualization of new logic emerges from copious empirical descriptions in the prolific body of research generated by the Center for Effective Organizations at USC, providing a rich frame the new plant approach, established in practice prior to the articulation of these conceptual principles. Lawler (2000) contrasts his six new logic principles to the old logic principles of traditional bureaucratic organizing (see Table 7.1). Principles 2, 3, and 6 stem directly from HRM ideals. Principles 1, 4, and 5 specify how organizational structure must change to accomplish the promise of those ideals.

These integrating principles revolve around the dissemination of power, responsibility, and accountability – rooted in an explicit understanding that organizational form is the driving force. Lawler (1992) systematically reviews major structural features needed for high employee involvement. He then prescribes strategies to move beyond what had already been accomplished.

Table 7.1 Lawler's (2000) new logic principles

New logic principles	*Old logic principles*
1. Organization can be the ultimate source of competitive advantage.	1. Organization is a secondary source of competitive advantage.
2. Involvement is the most effective source of control.	2. Bureaucracy is the most effective source of control.
3. All employees must add significant value.	3. Top management and technical experts should add the most value.
4. Lateral processes are the key to organizational effectiveness.	4. Hierarchical processes are the key to organizational effectiveness.
5. Organizations should be designed around products and customers.	5. Organizations should be designed around functions.
6. Effective leadership is the key to organizational effectiveness.	6. Effective managers are the key to organizational effectiveness.

Source: Reprinted from Nicotera and Clinkscales (2003).

Lawler's High-Involvement Organization

Grounding his discussion in the assumption that a successful organization will have a management approach and design congruent with societal culture, Lawler (1992) differentiates two managerial/organizational design approaches: the control-oriented approach (vertical authority) rooted in old logic principles and the involvement-oriented approach (lateral authority) rooted in new logic principles. The involvement-oriented approach is "highly congruent with democratic values about decision-making and respect for individual rights ... [And] directly aligned with the strong entrepreneurial bent in the American culture" (pp. 43–44). Conversely, the control-oriented model is based on principles existing in opposition to such democratic ideals as participative decision-making, due process, freedom of speech, individual rights, and personal growth. Note, here, the parallel to the cultural shifts stimulated by the HR and HRM movements.

Lawler (1992) details organizational design features that can achieve the high-involvement organization, including alternative work designs, work that is highly involving, organization/improvement groups, person-based pay (as opposed to position-based), and performance rewards. Next, he discusses structural features necessary for the management of information and human resources, including open information channels, high-involvement management practices, support for positive managerial behavior, and union involvement. He closes with a synthesis, providing a comprehensive view of the high-involvement organization and discussing change strategies. A successful transition to a high-involvement organization is a massive change in organizational operation that completely replaces the bureaucratic form (Lawler, 1992). This theme is repeated throughout his work (e.g., Lawler, 1999, 2000, 2001). Integrated into such change must be managers, employees, union leaders, board members, and government.

THE NEW PLANT APPROACH

Based on case studies, the *new plant* is a description of business units to guide manufacturing companies in constructing new organizational units founded on the premise of participative management. Five prescriptions create the environment necessary for full employee participation: selection of employees, physical layout, job design, reward system and training, and organizational structure.

Selection of Employees. Lawler prescribes full disclosure to prospective employees about the nature of the job(s) and of the management style, offering empowerment pre-employment, a chance to decide for themselves whether they want to work in a participative environment, an expectation of involvement, and a good fit between employee culture and organizational form. Furthermore, "a great deal of the selection process is handled by production employees. They interview and interact with the job applicants and ultimately make the decision as to who will join the organization" (Lawler, 1992, p. 308). Often, applicants are hired long before the actual start-up of the new unit "so that they can be involved in determining personnel policies and establishing various procedures and work methods" (Lawler, 1992, p. 308). Here, we can clearly see a deeply participative process engrained in a lateralized authority structure.

Physical Layout. Echoing Frederick Taylor's admonition that the job must be physically arranged for optimum employee performance, but with a much different aim, Lawler advocates newly designed physical facilities. So-called *new plants* have an egalitarian physical workplace. Employees and managers tend to park in the same parking lots, enter through the same doors, and eat in the same cafeterias, and, in some cases, the managers have minimal offices or no offices. The physical layout of many new plants is designed to facilitate teamwork around particular products or services. For example, rather than having assembly lines, the plants often have manufacturing cells that build entire products (Lawler, 1992, pp. 308–309).

Job Design. New plant job design likewise emphasizes the egalitarian ideals of HRM.

> Employees perform jobs that are challenging, involving doing a whole piece of work, and allowing them to control how the work is carried out. Typically, this means that relatively self-managing work teams are responsible for the production of a whole product. They are self-managing in the sense that they make decisions about who performs which tasks on a given day; set their own production goals; and are often responsible for quality control, purchasing, and the control of absenteeism and employee behavior. Team members are expected to learn how to do all of the tasks that fall within the work area of the group.
>
> (Lawler, 1992, p. 309)

Reward System and Training. As noted, Lawler's (1992) design requires person-based pay structures, increasing pay with individual learning relevant to the organization's mission – creating a direct link between individual development and financial compensation.

> Most plants that adopt the new plant approach evaluate the skills of each individual and pay each person based on the number and kind of skills they have. Typically everyone starts at the same salary, and as people learn more, they are paid more. All employees are considered salaried employees and no time clocks are used. Job security also is typically offered to all employees.
>
> (Lawler, 1992, p. 309)

Reward structures are linked to *training*:

> All the new plants place a heavy emphasis on training, career planning, and personal growth. This emphasis is usually backed up with extensive in-plant training programs and strong encouragement for employees to take part in training outside of work. A strong commitment to training and development of the workforce is a cornerstone of the management practices in the new plant approach and is supported by the skill-based pay system.
>
> (Lawler, 1992, p. 310)

Organizational Structure. Because of fundamental shifts in organizational structure, the new plant approach is successful where previous HRM-based participation programs were not.

> One of the striking features of the new plants is their structure. These plants are characterized by very flat hierarchies and extremely wide spans of control. Typically, the traditional foreman's role is eliminated completely and multiple teams report to an area manager. Most plants have only two levels of supervision, although some

> large plants may have three levels. A flat structure is important because it helps assure that work teams will have the autonomy to manage themselves.... The new plant approach is also characterized by relatively lean staff groups. Work team members are given responsibility for areas such as quality control, employee selection, inventory management, and production scheduling that typically are done by staff specialists in traditional organizations.
>
> (Lawler, 1992, pp. 309–310)

Beyond the New Plant

Lawler (1992) emphasizes that such plants, although successful, "fall short of what can be done" (p. 313). Specifically, he identifies a *productivity involvement approach* to management that heavily emphasizes "being sure that individuals have control over and information about their piece of the production process" (p. 313). He recommends a significant step beyond this type of involvement to integrate individuals into the business process itself. In so doing, he recommends several organizational features.

He first identifies the required *organizational structure*: "a flat organizational structure and the extensive use of self-managing teams" (p. 314). He goes on to describe a structure in which teams operate as *mini-enterprises*, handling a full scope of business issues. This also requires integration of functions across the organization. It must be noted here that the term *flattened* is dated. The preferred terminology has shifted to *lateral*, fully replacing the presumption of verticality. Linguistically, *flat* connotes a vertical orientation, whereas *lateral* connotes a horizontal orientation.

In Lawler's model, a manufacturing team has responsibility for the entire process with respect to a particular customer. Customers order directly from the team, who deal directly with suppliers. Following delivery, the team deals directly with customers (e.g., via a toll-free telephone number printed on the product) regarding questions or problems with the product produced by the team. In addition, expertise in product development, design, manufacturing, marketing, and sales (for example) mutually inform one another in ways that enhance all of these areas. By linking team members directly to the business process from beginning to end, their productivity and the organization's mission drive one another. This is the kind of team-based organization studied by Barker (1993), who illustrated its potentially oppressive outcomes, which became concertive control theory (see Chapters 3, 11, and 12).

The total team environment expands teams beyond the production level to all parts of the organization.

> Managers, office personnel, and staff support individuals have different jobs than in a traditional plant because they have to deal with teams, but they are not in a team structure. This inconsistency has created some problems and, in some respects, has limited the effectiveness of the new plant approach because staff support groups do not have the same kind of flexibility and performance gains that are characteristic of the production area.
>
> (Lawler, 1992, p. 360)

Inherent in a total team environment is the application of *skill-based reward systems* across the organization, reward systems based on organizational performance (Lawler, 1992). For employees to achieve a high level of business involvement, they must be accountable for business performance. Such reward systems (gainsharing, profit-sharing, employee ownership, etc.) further deepen and strengthen convergences by integrating individuals with organizational structure and function.

Finally, Lawler (1992) discusses the use of new technologies to improve communication and quality. As information becomes widely available, with individuals across the organization more interconnected, their integration with organizational performance is enhanced. Because of technological advances that occurred since, this work is decidedly dated. In later works, this body of knowledge is vastly expanded in such areas as knowledge management (Lawler, 2001), organizational agility (Worley et al., 2014), and sustainability (Mohrman et al., 2015). There are also copious works (e.g., Mohrman et al., 1995) detailing the specifics of designing a team-based organization to replace the bureaucratic form. The especially accelerated use of technology resulting from the necessities created by the COVID-19 pandemic is not accounted for in the new plant literature.

While Lawler and his associates were developing prescriptive theory advocating wide-scale organizational restructuring, organizational communication theory and research examining participation flourished (see Chapter 3). Whereas management theory is prescriptive with an overarching aim to improve organizational performance with a view from the top, organizational communication theory is descriptive and far more diverse both in purpose and vantage point, with recommendations for organizational improvement taking a more holistic view of the organization. Stohl and Cheney's (2001) paradoxes of participation, reviewed above, can be traced to the fundamental incongruity between the activities required to fulfill the ideals of participation and the constraints of organizational authority structures that subvert those activities – the same fundamental problem identified by Lawler (1992, 2000, 2001). These two theories illustrate the differences between disciplines in their prescriptive and descriptive approaches, but they also show that it took decades of intervening conceptual developments and empirical study to implement the ideals of HRM – which can only be fully accomplished with a total reconfiguration of organizational structure that, as organizational communication research reveals, can create troublesome paradoxes for organizational members (see Chapter 3).

The restructuring movement of the 1990s, creating and implementing team-based organizational design, fundamentally altered the organizational landscape we study. Vertical hierarchy is central to our traditional understanding of formal organizations, and team-based organizing profoundly changes the nature of authority. As management theory and practice evolve, organizational communication theory and research must contend with these transformations in the objects of our scholarship. At heart, this is an ontological issue (see Chapter 2); team-based organizing and the disruption of vertical authority changes the nature of the phenomena. Our theory and research must develop to keep pace with and account for those changes. Moreover, vertical hierarchies are still prevalent. Contemporary organizations are commonly designed with hybrid authority structures.

Implications of HRM for Organizational Communication Theory

Prior to our brief review of restructuring in the 1990s, this chapter concluded our tracing of the management theory trends considered foundational to the field of Organizational Communication. Remember, however, that the study of organizational communication is multidisciplinary. Before beginning more focused examination of organizational communication literatures in Part III, we must take a moment to assess the implications of HRM theory for our thinking about communication, organization, authority, and culture. While classical management's bureaucratic structures and control practices remain in place for many organizations across a multitude of industries, HRM heralded the advent of lateralized, more democratic forms. These forms provide the ground for cultural changes highlighting different aspects of communication, authority, and organization.

Approach to Communication

HRM theory examines the intersections of formal and informal communication, with human intelligence and well-being as equally primary concerns for the benefit of the organization. Communication is treated holistically with a far more relational, constitutive, and less linear approach than that espoused by earlier philosophies. In HRM theory, the treatment of communication is enriched beyond messaging and relationship-forming to a process of meaning-creation. In contrast to HR models, communication is no longer treated as a mere management tool to accomplish worker productivity and cooperation, but as a meaning-creation process that integrates individuals, groups, and processes. The function of communication is informational, relational, constitutive, and productive.

Like HR, in HRM, the reciprocal relationship between deep enduring structures and daily practices is visible through its revolutionary changes to American corporate life. HRM practices introduced the expectation that all organizational members think for themselves and contribute to leadership and the design of organizational plans, practices, and processing. Today's workers expect opportunities for growth and development and expect to contribute their intelligence to organizational processes. Rooted in Argyris' learning organization, a vast industry of training and development has developed into its own set of institutionalized structures and practices. Like human resources, organizational development became, and continues to be, a booming profession with its own professional career path, credentialing processes, and specializations. Organizational practices that began to emerge in the 1970s are commonplace, such as visioning, strategic planning, continuous improvement, team-based management, and the configuration of business units as independently operating profit centers.

Approach to Organization and Authority

HRM theory treats the organization as a living, learning organism and a brain (Morgan, 1986). The lines dividing the managerial and labor classes become blurred as authority is distributed. The traditional management/labor class system has been replaced by other classification systems – defining professions according to blue-collar and white-collar categories, for example. Still, the vertical hierarchy of Fayol's organizational chart remains presumed, with the focus on organizational functions rather than either persons or positions. Moreover, organizational communication practices remain open and egalitarian, especially as communication technology has progressed.

Cultural Implications

The HRM movement democratized work environments. Concerns for worker development, and a corresponding expectation for employees to add value, have become organizational priorities. In large organizations, training and development opportunities abound in addition to employee benefits for well-being and incentives instituted in HR. Employees are increasingly expected to think for themselves and for the organization. Contemporary employees demand a wide range of educational and training opportunities, and organizations that do not provide these opportunities often fail to attract and retain the most qualified employees. Globally, workplace democracy is a vital concern (see Chapter 20). Alternative organizational forms, such as worker collectives, are advocated by many scholars (e.g., Parker et al., 2014).

The HRM movement also fundamentally altered the typical employment trajectory. The traditional presumption that one would be employed for a lifetime by a single organization has been replaced by a cultural imperative to advance our careers with frequent job changes. This shift is directly traceable to the culture of continual employee development created by HRM ideals. Many large corporations provide expensive employee training and education under the protection of a contractual obligation to remain with the corporation for a specified period following the training, to ensure that the development opportunities provided benefit the organization rather than one of its competitors. At the same time, the culture of large organizations has shifted to define the individual career advancements of former employees as an organizational accomplishment. In short, the meanings we now hold for career, employee development, meaningful work, and workplace democracy are a direct cultural consequence of HRM.

Recommended Supplementary Readings

Barker, J. R. (1993). Tightening the iron cage: Concertive control in self-managing teams. *Administrative Science Quarterly*, *38*(3), 408–437.

This case study was the foundation for concertive control theory. Barker compellingly illustrates the potential for self-imposed oppressive practices in team-based organizing.

Berry, G. (2006). Can computer-mediated, asynchronous communication improve team processes and decision-making? *Journal of Business Communication*, *43*(4), 344–366.

This article reviews 25 years of business and management literature to draw conclusions about the effect of asynchronous communication technology on teamwork and decision-making.

Cheney, G. (1995). Democracy in the workplace: Theory and practice from the perspective of communication. *Journal of Applied Communication Research*, *23*(3), 167–200.

Drawing from a multidisciplinary literature, this essay explores workplace democracy in the contemporary industrialized world, emphasizing issues that are particularly ripe for theoretical and practical contributions from a communication perspective. Cheney's now-classic case study of Mondragon worker cooperatives, in the Basque region of Spain, demonstrates the promise and problems of workplace democracy.

Cheney, G., & Cloud, D. L. (2006). Doing democracy, engaging the material: Employee participation and labor activity in an age of market globalization. *Management Communication Quarterly*, *19*(4), 501–540.

The two leading organizational communication scholars of workplace democracy engage each other in a compelling discussion ranging from the metatheoretical to the practical.

They examine the status of labor activity in organizational communication scholarship and consider important questions about workplace democracy in practice, with a goal of strengthening the field's engagement in robust democratic practices in a globalizing market economy, by using conceptualizations that venture beyond our comfortable discursive and symbolic constructionism to attend to practical and material concerns.

Coopman, S. J. (2001). Democracy, performance, and outcomes in interdisciplinary health care teams. *Journal of Business Communication*, *38*(3), 261–284.

This study of hospice care interdisciplinary teams demonstrates the central importance of perceived involvement in decision-making to the success of team-based organizing, as evidenced by several outcomes (cohesiveness, productiveness, satisfaction with the team, satisfaction with team communication, desire to stay with the team, team involvement, and job satisfaction).

Important Concepts: Define and Discuss

Contingency
Formal organization
Informal organization
Participation
Restructuring

Discussion Questions

1 Reflect on organizations of which you have been a part. Imagine you are a consultant who has been hired to align individual and organizational development and to maximize the potential of employee intelligence. Drawing from the models/theories summarized in this chapter, how would you advise your new client to foster participative and collaborative relationships across hierarchical levels?
2 We have demonstrated that it took several decades for HRM ideals of participation to be implemented with the advent of team-based organizing in the 1990s. How do you see the themes of formal-informal integration and contingency expressed in the new plant approach?
3 What aspects of classical management do you see as most difficult to transcend in order to implement HRM ideals, and why?
4 In general, what aspects of HRM do you recognize in our contemporary organizations?

Practitioners' Corner

As with HR, obvious applications of HRM principles can be seen in today's large organizations. Training and other employee skill development programs, collaborative leadership, team-based structures, and other opportunities for growth and for collaborative decision-making are now commonplace. Yet, as Barker (1993) and Stohl and Cheney (2001) illustrated, the culture of vertical authority is difficult to transcend, even when organizations are designed to eliminate or reduce it. Classical management principles and presumptions run deep in the cultural mindset, manifesting in organizational life. For example, executive-level managers often fail to involve front-line employees in problem-analysis when planning for organizational change to solve problems. Commonly, upon getting feedback from employees about daily problems, well-intentioned executive-level management enters a new software contract for broad organizational processes without consulting the end-users of that software about its implementation or details about their experience of the problems it purports to solve. Organizational members are then faced with implementing a change intended to solve their problems that actually brings new and more difficult problems to their daily functioning. Many front-line employees can tell horror stories about new software implementation that could have been avoided if only someone had consulted them about precisely what was needed before making the decision. In other words, some unanticipated problems with solutions might be anticipated via participation of the right people in the analysis of the original problem.

Communication professionals, either as internal communication officers or as consultants, are well-suited to support managers in understanding how authority structures may impede employee development as they seek to improve employee PDM, integrate employee development with organizational goals, and implement flexibility into their own leadership skills repertoire. A communication consultant, using a graphic like the C-O dynamic, can aid managers in understanding (a) the degree of collaboration that can be supported by the organizational structure; (b) how the way they communicate matters in the implementation of team-based structures; (c) how to design and implement reward and accountability structures that facilitate goal-achievement in a team-based structure; and (d) how to guide employees to let go of vertical authority presumptions and habits to develop team-based skills. Internal communication officers who construct and disseminate messaging in a team-based environment are likewise benefited by an understanding of the interplay among organizational design structures, expectations for organizational members' responsibilities and performance, and the content of messaging about internal organizational decision-making.

References

Bacharach, S. B., & Aiken, M. (1977). Communication in administrative bureaucracies. *Academy of Management Journal*, *20*(3), 365–377. https://doi.org/10.2307/255411

Barker, J. R. (1993). Tightening the iron cage: Concertive control in self-managing teams. *Administrative Science Quarterly*, *38*(3), 408–437. https://doi.org/10.2307/2393374

Blake, R., & Mouton, J. (1964). *The managerial grid: The key to leadership excellence*. Gulf Publishing Co.

Blake, R. R., Shepard, H., & Mouton, J. S. (1964). *Managing intergroup conflict in industry*. Gulf.

Blanchard, K. H., Zigarmi, P., & Zigarmi, D. (1985). *Leadership and the one minute manager: Increasing effectiveness through situational leadership*. Morrow.

Fiedler, F. E. (1967). *A theory of leadership effectiveness*. McGraw-Hill.

Fiedler, F. E. (1986). The contribution of cognitive resources and leader behavior to organizational performance. *Journal of Applied Social Psychology*, *16*(6), 532–548. https://doi.org/10.1111/j.1559-1816.1986.tb01157.x

Galbraith, J. R., & Lawler, E. E. Associates (1993). *Organizing for the future: The new logic for managing complex organizations*. Jossey-Bass.

Hersey, P. (1985). *The situational leader*. Warner.

Hersey, P., & Blanchard, K. H. (1969). *Management of organizational behavior: Utilizing human resources*. Prentice Hall.

Jablin, F. M. (1987). Formal organizational structure. In F. M. Jablin, L. L. Putnam, K. H. Roberts, & L. W. Porter (Eds.), *Handbook of organizational communication: An interdisciplinary perspective* (pp. 389–419). Sage.

Lawler, E. E. (1978). The new plant revolution. *Organizational Dynamics*, 6(3), 2–12. https://doi.org/10.1016/0090-2616(78)90044-X

Lawler, E. E. (1991). *High-involvement management: Participative strategies for improving organizational performance*. Jossey-Bass.
Lawler, E. E. (1992). *The ultimate advantage: Creating the high-involvement organization*. Jossey-Bass.
Lawler, E. E. (1999). *Rewarding excellence: Pay strategies for the economy*. Jossey-Bass.
Lawler, E. E. (2000). *From the ground up: Six principles for building the new logic corporation*. Jossey-Bass.
Lawler, E. E. (2001). *Organizing for high-performance: Employee involvement, TQM, reengineering, and knowledge management in the Fortune 1000*. Jossey-Bass.
Lawler, E. E., Mohrman, S. A., & Ledford, G. E. (1998). *Strategies for high-performance organizations—The CEO report: Employee involvement, TQM, and reengineering programs in Fortune 1000 corporations*. Jossey-Bass.
Likert, R. (1961). *New patterns of management*. McGraw-Hill.
Likert, R. (1967). *Human organization: Its management and value*. McGraw-Hill.
Mohrman, S. A., Cohen, S. G., & Mohrman, A. M. (1995). *Designing team-based organizations: New forms for knowledge work*. Jossey Bass.
Mohrman, S. A., Galbraith, J. R., & Lawler, E. E. Associates (1998). *Tomorrow's organization: Crafting winning capabilities in a dynamic world*. Jossey-Bass.
Mohrman, A. A., O'Toole, J., & Lawler, E. E. (Eds.) (2015). *Corporate stewardship: Achieving sustainable effectiveness*. Greenleaf Publishing.
Morgan, G. (1986). *Images of organization*. Sage.
Nicotera, A. M., & Clinkscales, M. J. (2003). *Understanding organization through culture and structure: Relational and other lessons from the African-American organization*. Erlbaum.
Parker, M., Cheney, G., Fournier, V., & Land, C. (Eds.) (2014). *The Routledge companion to alternative organization*. Routledge.
Seibold, D. R., & Shea, B. C. (2001). Participation and decision-making. In F. M. Jablin & L. L. Putnam (Eds.), *The new handbook of organizational communication: Advances in theory, research, and methods*. Sage.
Stohl, C. (1995). Paradoxes of participation. In P. Shockley-Zalabak & R. Cesaria (Eds.), *Organizzazioni e communicazione* [Organizations and communication] (pp. 145–167). Servizio Italiano Publicazioni Internazionali.
Stohl, C., & Cheney, G. (2001). Participatory processes/paradoxical practices: Communication and the dilemmas of organizational democracy. *Management Communication Quarterly*, *14*(3), 349–407. https://doi.org/10.1177/0893318901143001
Tannenbaum, R., & Schmidt, W. H. (1958). How to choose a leadership pattern. *Harvard Business Review*, *36*(5), 95–101.
Worley, C. G., Williams, T. D., & Lawler, E. E. (2014). *The agility factor: Building adaptable organizations for superior performance*. Jossey-Bass.

Part III

Topics in Theory and Research

This section provides comprehensive literature reviews of 14 areas of theory and research, each of which explains the trends over time in the area, major traditions, and contributions of organizational communication scholars. Chapters are authored by established scholars with specialized expertise. While it is not possible to cover every possible topic in the field, literatures that comprise the core knowledge base in the field are provided here. Each chapter applies the general conceptual models provided in Chapter 1 to explore the conceptual approaches of scholars in the area and to illustrate the reciprocally enabling and constraining relationship between organization and communication.

DOI: 10.4324/9781003484639-10

8 Socialization

Yejin Shin

Organizations are an integral part of society. People join and leave organizations several times during their lifespan. Organizational socialization refers generally to the process by which an individual becomes a knowledgeable organizational member; it is one of the most frequently studied topics in organizational communication. Encompassing a lifelong process of learning about work and occupations, specific jobs and organizations, joining and then leaving organizations, the socialization process is part of everyday discourse and a system of meaning about work and work life (Clair, 1996). While theory and research in organizational socialization began in the management and sociology fields, socialization is fundamentally communicative. This chapter provides an overview of socialization research, focusing on the role of communication throughout the process. Then, how socialization research comports with the conceptualizations of organization and communication that guide this book is addressed.

Organizational Socialization Models

First a Management Focus

Although scholarly interest in socialization began decades ago in the field of sociology (e.g., Giddings, 1897), it received substantive attention in management and organizational studies in the 1970s. Van Maanen and Schein (1979) provided a seminal model of the organizational socialization process, conceptualizing it as the process of individuals joining, participating in, and leaving organizations. Specifically, organizational socialization is "the process by which an individual acquires the social knowledge and skills necessary to assume an organization role" (Van Maanen & Schein, 1979, p. 211).

Van Maanen and Schein (1979) addressed socialization primarily from an organizational or management perspective, delineating organizations' various strategies to socialize new members. Their model includes six strategy pairs (Kramer, 2010). First, employees may be socialized using *formal* (e.g., formal training and orientation) or *informal* processes (e.g., begin tasks immediately with advice and feedback from interpersonal sources such as the supervisor and coworkers). Second, new employees may be socialized as a *group* (e.g., when cohorts are hired simultaneously) or as *individuals*. Third, socialization may occur *sequentially* (e.g., a newcomer must master one skill before moving on to the next) or *randomly* (e.g., employees learn in order of what is important to them). Fourth, newcomer socialization can be *serial* (e.g., the new employee is trained by someone experienced in the role) or *disjunctive* (e.g., no experienced employee is specifically assigned to train the newcomer). Fifth, timing in the socialization process may be *fixed* (e.g., newcomers are given a specific

DOI: 10.4324/9781003484639-11

amount of time to learn a particular aspect of their new role) or *variable* (e.g., newcomers spend as much time as needed to learn the various aspects of their new role). Finally, organizations may rely on *divestiture* (e.g., attempts to diminish the newcomer's unique individual characteristics, such as military boot camp) or *investiture* (e.g., the organization embraces the new employee's unique characteristics and talents and allows them to develop their new role) to socialize members.

Organizational Communication Enters

As exemplified by Van Maanen and Schein's (1979) model, much scholarship at the time approached socialization from an organizational (i.e., macro) perspective, conceptualizing the organization itself as an actor or agent. In 1984, Frederic Jablin provided a significant development by highlighting the important role of *communication* in individuals' socialization processes. His model brought socialization research squarely into the organizational communication field, bringing attention to the micro-level communication practices and processes that characterize organizational socialization.

Shifting to broader terminology, Jablin conceptualized *assimilation* as a reciprocal process in which both individuals and organizational structures have power and influence (Myers & Oetzel, 2003). Specifically, assimilation entails two simultaneous processes: (1) *socialization*, via which organizations socialize newcomers, attempting to instill organizationally desired attitudes, values, and behaviors, and (2) *individualization*, via which employees simultaneously seek to individualize their roles in the organization (or try to change the organization to meet their needs) as they learn organizational norms and values (Jablin, 2001; Jablin & Krone, 1987). Mignerey et al. (1995) similarly argued that assimilation is an active process that requires involvement of organizational attempts to form the newcomer as well as the newcomer's efforts to influence the organization.

As Myers and Gailliard (2016) argue, Jablin is considered the founder of socialization research in the field of organizational communication. Jablin's (1984) model has been widely used by scholars to examine the socialization experiences of various organization members such as managers (King et al., 2005), policemen (Van Maanen, 1975), volunteers (Kramer & Danielson, 2016), students (Powers & Myers, 2017), firefighters (Scott & Myers, 2005), and even family members (Maccoby & Martin, 1983).

Jablin's Assimilation/Socialization Model

Scholars across disciplines have examined organizational socialization and, not surprisingly, have developed different terms for the process. For instance, Kramer (2010) noted that "scholars frequently use the term *socialization* to refer to the overall process of individual becoming organizational members, which Jablin terms *assimilation*" (p. 4, emphasis added). In this section, for ease of reading and to maintain consistency with terms used in most of the literature, the term *socialization* refers to the overall process across the lifespan.

Jablin's model describes the socialization process across four phases: (1) anticipatory socialization, (2) encounter, (3) metamorphosis, and (4) exit/disengagement. Jablin (2001) emphasized that the model's phases should be understood as fluid and overlapping instead of a set of linear phases. For example, *encounter* and *metamorphosis* together can refer to one phase. Kramer and Miller (2014) also argued that despite the descriptions of these four phases appearing distinct from one another, they may not occur in separate, ordered sequences. With this caveat in mind, the phases in their most likely chronological order are addressed here. Also note that while Jablin's model might be applied to other kinds of organizations (e.g., volunteers, Kramer & Danielson, 2016; students, Powers & Myers, 2017), it specifically addresses the workplace.

Even before entering a new organization, individuals formulate expectations about work and occupations generally, as well as specific jobs and organizations (Jablin, 1982). This comprises the *anticipatory socialization* process – the process of learning about work before an individual begins a specific job. Jablin (2001) divided this phase into *vocational anticipatory socialization (VAS)* and *organizational anticipatory socialization (OAS)*. VAS refers to the process of individuals learning about work, careers, and occupations generally. OAS refers to the process of individuals learning about and choosing a specific job and organization to join. Kramer (2010) later used the term *role anticipatory socialization* for VAS, defining it as "the ongoing process of developing expectations for a role an individual wants to have in some organization" (p. 6).

The next phase, *encounter*, comprises individuals' experiences during the first few days, weeks, or months of organizational involvement through training or orientation (Feldman, 1976). Newcomers must learn the essentials of their organizational roles and responsibilities, such as how to perform their jobs, maintain relationships with coworkers, and learn the organization's cultural norms (Ostroff & Kozlowski, 1992). *Metamorphosis*, the third phase, is the period during which individuals perceive themselves as established organizational members rather than newcomers (Jablin, 1987). This stage can be considered a long-term settling in, during which employees experience the transition to full members of the organization (Myers & Oetzel, 2003). Last, *exit/disengagement* occurs when individuals leave organizations (Jablin, 1987). This phase can be divided into two different types: (1) voluntary exit, when individuals initiate the process, or (2) involuntary exit, when others initiate the process (Bluedorn, 1978). Grounded on Jablin's (1984) model, many scholars have focused on the role of communication in each phase. Below, an overview of this research organized by phase is provided.

Organizational Socialization Research

Anticipatory Socialization: VAS/OAS

Socialization is a *communicative* process that spans various experiences from early childhood, education, and initial/full-time employment (Jablin, 2001). Jablin (2001) identified five primary information sources influencing VAS via communication: family, education, friends, previous organization experience, and mass media. Most studies in this area focus on messages from different sources and how they are interpreted (Powers & Myers, 2017). Although VAS begins in early childhood and continues throughout one's lifetime, much research focuses on children and adolescents. Along these lines, Levine and Hoffner (2006) found that messages from parents, school, and part-time job employment were the most influential to an individual's learning about work requirements such as responsibility, deadlines, and other performance-related behaviors. Parents and friends were also more likely to express negative, rather than positive, aspects of work.

More recently, research has been done on emerging adults' socialization processes because members of Generation Z (born 1997–2012) are surpassing Baby Boomers (born 1946–1964) in the full-time workforce (Terrazas & Zhao, 2023). As Gen Zs and Millennials are seen as agents shaping the future of work, understanding their socialization processes is imperative. For example, Aley and Levine (2020) found that emerging adults actively utilize their social networks to create valuable VAS influence groups, with differences in the network characteristics, such as whether they know or do not know their career aspirations. Omilion-Hodges et al. (2019) found that VAS contributes to emerging adults' unrealistic job expectations and the evolving and generational nature of their VAS. In terms of information sources, Levine and Aley (2022) suggested the internet as an additional VAS source of career socialization information emerging adults utilize, in addition to five sources identified in previous VAS research (see Jablin, 2001). In addition, Gettings and Anderson (2021) found that young adults understand retirement similarly to older generations in their VAS processes, and the sources are associated mainly with those five sources (see Jablin, 2001).

OAS begins when individuals consider specific jobs in specific organizations and take steps to join an organization. Unlike VAS, which is a lifelong process, OAS usually lasts only as long as the job search itself (Kramer, 2010). Much OAS research focuses on the recruitment and selection process, including employment interviews and realistic job previews (RJPs) (Jablin, 2001). For example, Miller and Buzzanell (1996) noted that second interviews serve various purposes, including finding qualified applicants and providing the organization with an opportunity to enhance its reputation (i.e., a public relations function), as well as providing applicants with information about the position and organization.

Although the employment interview is fundamentally communicative, Jablin et al. (1999) noted that relatively little research has examined the interview communication *process*. That usually examines the interview from one of three approaches. Some studies identify patterns of "acts" (e.g., Babbitt & Jablin, 1985). Such studies identify general interaction patterns in employment interviews (e.g., "talk time" by interviewer and applicant, questions and answer patterns). A second approach examines "patterns of acts and interacts" (Jablin et al., 1999, p. 302) (e.g., Kacmar & Hochwarter, 1995). These studies focus on utterance types and interaction pairs to identify predictive patterns (e.g., how one person's dominance in the early part of an interview predicts overall control of the conversation). A third approach examines how the interviewer and applicant together enact the interview. Specifically, these studies conceptualize the employment interview "as a dynamic social system composed of interdependent beliefs and observable relations between recruiter and applicant that are produced and reproduced through the process of interaction" (Jablin et al., 1999, p. 305). These investigations examine how interactants exert mutual influence and socially construct their relationship, the interview structure, and various other outcomes. Cheepen (1988), for example, revealed how interviewers and applicants together socially constructed their relative status during employment interviews. Here, the C–O cycle (see Chapter 1) is evident, as the interaction constructs the structure of the interview, which then recursively enables and constrains that interaction.

Garnering more attention from scholars, much OAS research has focused on RJPs. Information provided to applicants during OAS tends to be positively skewed, giving applicants an inflated view of the position and organization by leaving out or minimizing drawbacks (Wanous, 1992). Such unrealistic previews lead to surprise and disappointment once an individual begins employment, in turn, leading to dissatisfaction and possibly turnover (Dugoni & Ilgen, 1981). To counter this, scholars argue for the use of RJPs as an alternative to the "seduction" method of recruiting. Baur et al. (2014) argue that RJPs help organizations decrease turnover and increase job satisfaction and stronger commitment when designed to provide realistic information about the job and organization. In a meta-analysis, Phillips (1998) found that RJPs were related to higher performance, lower recruitment attrition, and lower turnover.

Encounter

Perhaps the most often studied phase in Jablin's model, the *encounter* phase begins when an individual takes on a specific role or position in a specific organization. Research in this area is plentiful, examining various issues and processes, including uncertainty, information-seeking, and uncertainty management.

Van Maanen and Schein (1979) argued that newcomers need adequate information to understand their new roles and the organization to function effectively. The organizational encounter experience involves a high level of uncertainty, and much research examines newcomers' experiences of uncertainty and strategies used to reduce or manage that uncertainty. This research is typically grounded in uncertainty reduction theory (URT), which posits that when individuals experience uncertainty, they are motivated to seek information to reduce that uncertainty (Berger & Calabrese, 1975). The literature addresses the types of uncertainty newcomers experience, tactics they use to seek information to reduce that uncertainty, and factors that influence information-seeking tactic use.

Types of Uncertainty

Researchers have identified various types of newcomer uncertainty. Ostroff and Kozlowski (1992) identified the following four types of uncertainty: *task* (one's duties, assignments, and priorities), *role* (the boundaries of authority and responsibility, expectations and appropriate behaviors for different positions), *group* (coworker interaction, group norms and values, structure of the organization), and *organization* (the politics, power, mission/vision, leadership style, jargon). Similarly, scholars categorize newcomer uncertainty as (1) *referent uncertainty*, which refers to uncertainty about what one's tasks are and how they should be accomplished; (2) *appraisal uncertainty*, which refers to uncertainty regarding one's ability to do assigned tasks; and (3) *relational uncertainty*, which refers to uncertainty about relationships with other members of the organization and one's role in the group (Miller & Jablin, 1991; Sias & Wyers, 2001; Teboul, 1994).

Kramer (2010) organized uncertainty types into four main categories. *Task-related uncertainty* includes uncertainty about what tasks are expected, the norms regarding such tasks, and how such tasks are evaluated. *Relational uncertainty* involves uncertainty about who is in which workgroup, and how to develop relationships with others. *Organizational uncertainty* includes uncertainty about the organization's history, culture, norms, and rules. Finally, *political or power uncertainty* refers to uncertainty about who is influential in the organization and to whom one should talk in specific situations.

Information Sources

Newcomers rely on several sources of information to reduce or manage their uncertainty and make sense of their new surroundings. As Katz (1980) argued, the "new employee reduces uncertainty primarily through interpersonal and feedback processes and interactions" (p. 95). Primary among interpersonal sources are the newcomer's supervisor and coworkers (Morrison, 1993). Teboul (1994) also found newcomers rely on broader messages from the organization and sources external to the organization, such as friends, partners, and family members. Miller and Jablin's (1991) extensive list of sources includes information from others (e.g., peers, supervisors, other members, clients/customers) as well as written materials and the task itself.

As noted above, the newcomer's direct supervisor and coworkers are among the most important information sources during the encounter phase because they usually possess information relevant to the newcomer's concerns. Specifically, coworkers, especially those who work in the same or similar job, have useful referent/task information. Coworkers and supervisors also know the relational and cultural milieu of the workplace and can likely provide useful appraisal information. Access to these important information sources, however, requires the development of functional relationships with coworkers and the supervisor. Indeed, Sias (2005) found strong positive relationships between the quality of information an employee receives (e.g., accurate, relevant, timely, and useful information) and the quality of that employee's relationships with their supervisor and their peer coworkers. Thus, new employees should develop functional quality workplace relationships (see Chapter 10).

Information-Seeking Strategies

In addition to relying on different sources, newcomers use various methods to obtain information. Miller and Jablin (1991) identified seven newcomer information-seeking tactics. First, when newcomers feel comfortable soliciting information, they use overt questions involving direct interaction with information targets. On the other hand, if newcomers are not fully comfortable with the source, they may prefer *indirect questions*. Newcomers may prefer indirect questions because of their potential for saving face for both parties (Brown & Levinson, 1978). Specifically, the newcomer can mask the information-seeking intent of the message while the source can avoid responding to the request. Employees also use *third parties* to obtain information from a primary source. Newcomers tend to use this when the primary source is unavailable or when they feel uncomfortable asking for information from the primary source. *Testing limits or creating situations* in which the source must give information is the fourth tactic. In such cases, newcomers monitor sources' responses to gain insight into sources' attitudes. This tactic is unique because of its more-or-less specific stimuli and confrontational nature.

Newcomers may also *disguise conversations* by embedding the information request as a natural part of conversation. While putting information sources at ease, newcomers subtly encourage the sources to talk about certain issues. However, this tactic does not guarantee that sources will reveal the information newcomers seek because of the lack of control over sources' responses. The sixth tactic is *observing* information sources' behaviors. Newcomers use this tactic when they want to gain information unobtrusively. Observing discreetly provides information that may encourage newcomers to adjust their behaviors and attitudes. Last, *surveillance* involves retrospective sensemaking. Surveillance differs from observation in that observation is targeted, employees observe specific people or activities to acquire specific information, while surveillance involves indiscriminate attention to cues in the environment. In addition, surveillance involves integrating novel stimuli with past experiences (Miller & Jablin, 1991). As Weick (1979) pointed out, the accumulation of retrospective justifications can influence how one assigns meaning to present experiences and facilitates new cognitive maps over time (see Chapter 2).

Factors Affecting Information-Seeking

Various factors influence how newcomers seek information in the encounter phase (Miller & Jablin, 1991). First, seeking information entails *social costs*, such as harm to one's image by creating perceptions that one is incompetent or lacks confidence.

Newcomers are concerned with negative relational consequences or costs associated with observable information-seeking requests and try to minimize damage to their images (Miller & Jablin, 1991). Research indicates that perceived social costs associated with information-seeking are negatively associated with using direct questions to obtain the information (Miller & Jablin, 1991; Morrison, 1993). For example, Sias and Wyers (2001) found that social cost perceptions increased over time, leading to decreased information-seeking as the employees adjusted to their roles and organizations. This is consistent with the "honeymoon" period in which coworkers understand and tolerate information-seeking from newcomers (Jokisaari & Nurmi, 2009). But as the honeymoon comes to an end, coworkers expect the newcomers to have developed competence and confidence; thus, continued information-seeking can be interpreted as problematic (Sias & Wyers, 2001).

Relatedly, the amount and importance of uncertainty influence information-seeking. As Miller and Jablin (1991) noted, "uncertainty is considered a basic catalyst for newcomers' information-seeking behaviors" (p. 95). In general, the more uncertainty an individual experiences and the more important that uncertainty is to them, the more likely they will engage in information-seeking. This indicates that people may ignore uncertainty rather than seek information to reduce it. Along these lines, Kramer (2004) introduced the theory of managing uncertainty (TMU) as a contrast to the bulk of employee uncertainty studies that were grounded in URT.

TMU (see Kramer, 2004) acknowledges that newcomers do not always want to reduce uncertainty or gain certainty. Instead, they sometimes prefer to manage it. In contrast to the URT assumption that uncertainty is always negative, TMU contends that uncertainty may sometimes be preferable to certainty, similar to the concept of *strategic ambiguity*, which refers to situations in which organizations may purposefully use ambiguity as a tool to engender desired outcomes by manipulating how and when information is given to employees (Eisenberg, 1984). TMU entails two important points ignored by URT. First, TMU recognized that individuals often manage their uncertainty through internal or cognitive processes without seeking additional information. This is important to note, as TMU recognizes individuals' involvement as active participants. Second, TMU acknowledges competing motives that may reduce the impact of uncertainty on individuals' behaviors. Information-seeking will differ between individuals who are inherently inquisitive or less tolerant of uncertainty and those who are less inquisitive or more tolerant of uncertainty (Kramer, 2014). Therefore, TMU took a step forward in explaining how individuals *actively* participate in the socialization process; newcomers who successfully *manage* their uncertainty are more likely to be satisfied and stay in the organization. TMU offers a more complex understanding of uncertainty as multilayered, interconnected, and temporal, so the responses used to manage it will likely vary across contexts (Brashers, 2001).

Another theory used to address employee uncertainty during the encounter phase is Weick's sensemaking theory (1979, 1995). In contrast to URT's assumption of direct links between uncertainty, information, and uncertainty reduction, sensemaking addresses how individuals retrospectively assign meaning to their experiences. Sensemaking also differs from uncertainty management in that sensemaking typically involves assigning meaning to something that has already occurred while uncertainty management involves proactively seeking information to reduce uncertainty, rather than explain past events. In addition, uncertainty management can be accomplished individually via cognitive processes such as rationalization. Sensemaking, in contrast, is an intersubjective and interactive process. As Weick (1995) noted, (1) sensemaking is not an individual process but an intersubjective process as individuals create "agreed-upon meaning" with others through communication, (2) sensemaking is driven by plausibility rather than accuracy because a group can agree with the meaning incorrectly, and (3) sensemaking creates a certain identity by establishing a commitment to a specific interpretation. Overall, sensemaking focuses on how employees (both newcomers and veterans) communicatively create meaning regarding organizational experiences (see Chapter 2).

Metamorphosis

The third phase, *metamorphosis*, occurs when a newcomer "attempts to become an accepted, participating member of the organization by learning new attitudes and behaviors or modifying existing ones to be consistent with the organization's expectations" (Jablin, 1984, p. 596). In other words, this is when individuals no longer feel like newcomers but see themselves as established organizational members. Although uncertainty and information-seeking research tends to focus on newcomers in the encounter phase, Gallagher and Sias (2009) found that established members must adapt to new members and other organizational changes consistently; thus, members experience various types of uncertainty at varying levels throughout their membership. Metamorphosis involves *altering* one's attitudes and behaviors to be consistent with those of the organization, and this process is simultaneously coupled with individualization efforts by the member (Gibson & Papa, 2000). As Gibson and Papa (2000) noted, the metamorphosis phase is akin to actively adopting norms, rules, and behaviors, whereas the encounter phase could still be considered as a "feeling out" stage. Studies regarding the metamorphosis phase have dealt with how organizational members experience the organization's particular culture, relationships, and transitions as established members (Kramer, 2010).

Exit

The final phase in Jablin's (2001) model, disengagement or exit, involves members leaving the organization. Bluedorn (1978) divided exit into two categories: *voluntary exit* is when individuals perceive that they initiate the exit process by themselves, whereas *involuntary exit* is when individuals see that they have little or no choice because someone else forced them to leave. Lee et al. (1996) suggested four different paths to voluntary exit: planned exit (e.g., career progression, career change, or retirement), shock resulting in quitting, shock resulting in a job search before quitting, and gradual disenchantment. On the other hand, the employer's gradual disenchantment with the employee's performance over time can result in involuntary exit through termination. According to Kramer (2010), the exit process is steeped in social exchange evaluations. Individuals deliberate whether the cost-benefit ratio justifies staying at the organization; they attempt to make sense of their leaving and the consequences of that departure for themselves; and stayers attempt to make sense of their coworker's exit, which creates uncertainty about whether they too should leave the organization (Krackhardt & Porter, 1986).

Socialization Outcomes

The socialization process is critical to maintaining a dedicated workforce, as "how seriously the organization takes its obligation to socialize new members may determine the degree of turnover, and ultimately, productivity" (Modaff et al., 2012, p. 170). For instance,

Chao et al. (1994) noted that successful socialization results in high levels of performance proficiency, knowledge of organizational culture, understanding of organizational rules and language, and positive relationships with others. Saks et al. (2011) found that proactive information-seeking was positively related to task mastery, role clarity, and intention to stay in the organization.

Socialization can also influence an individual's identification with an organization (see Chapter 11). Identification generally refers to the extent to which an individual shares the values and decision premises of the organization (e.g., Cheney & Tompkins, 1987) or feelings of oneness/shared identity (Mael & Ashforth, 1992). Bullis and Bach (1989), for example, found that identification with the organization tended to increase when employees experienced reduction in relational and appraisal uncertainty, while newcomers who experienced disappointment were less likely to identify with the organization. Schaubroeck et al. (2013) also found that organizational identification increased as new employees developed relationships with their supervisor and coworkers during the encounter phase. Using a discursive approach, Barge and Schlueter's (2004) analysis revealed how both socialization and individualization processes are accomplished discursively via memorable messages. Their results also demonstrate the role of informal communication in constructing the individual–organization relationship during entry.

Socialization Contexts

Lester (1987) argued that successful socialization depends on the member's ability to manage uncertainty and perform proper behaviors in an appropriate organizational context. Most socialization research has centered on the more traditional workplace setting (e.g., full-time, permanent employees in an established organization). Increasingly, however, scholars have examined organizational socialization with different types of members and in different types of organizations, adding important insights to the literature. For instance, Kramer (1993) examined uncertainty and information-seeking tactics of job *transferees*, rather than organizational newcomers. Although job transferees are unique; they, in many ways, become newcomers again as they adjust to a new position or a new location. Kramer (1993) found that similar to newcomers, transferees used proactive strategies such as asking for feedback from peers and supervisors to reduce uncertainties. However, transferees tended to use more proactive communication behaviors than newcomers. Transferees were also less likely to feel they needed to prove themselves than newcomers. Sias et al. (1997) compared the experiences of *temporary* and permanent employees and found temporary employees were less concerned about their impression, less frequently sought appraisal information, and less involved in information-giving than newly hired, permanent employees.

In the case of *pilots* experiencing acquisition by another airline, Kramer et al. (2004) found that pilots experienced more uncertainty about specific job-related topics than broader organizational issues; they perceived that the acquisition changed their organization, but not their occupation. Pilots managed their uncertainty by focusing on their occupation instead of the company, but job satisfaction and commitment to their jobs remained constant. As a result, they experienced increases in job security while their attitude toward the acquisition declined.

Myers and McPhee (2006) examined socialization in a high-reliability organization – firefighting. They found that high-reliability workgroup assimilation also follows a general sequence, including involvement, development of trustworthiness, commitment, and acceptance. The firefighters in their study understood the importance of learning and following the norms of the culture that they believed were in place to protect them from harm.

Sias and Wyers (2001) examined socialization in newly formed organizations, asking the question, "What happens if everyone is a newcomer?" In a longitudinal study of several new branches that opened at the same time in a retail organization's expansion (i.e., newly formed expansion organizations or NFEOs), they found NFEO employees experienced the same types of uncertainty as newcomers in established organizations (e.g., task requirements), but they also identified a new type of uncertainty – viability uncertainty, or uncertainty about the new organization's ability to survive. They also found that supervisors were the most frequent sources that NFEOs' newcomers relied on and that newcomers relied on their prior work experience to reduce uncertainty.

Gallagher and Sias (2009) reconceptualized the role of newcomer from someone who experiences uncertainty to someone who *creates* uncertainty for veteran employees. They found that veterans experience several types of uncertainty about new employees, including uncertainty about the newcomers' competence, effect on the veteran employee's roles, and the possibility that the newcomer may disrupt the work environment's social milieu. They also found that veteran employees sought information to reduce such uncertainty via methods similar to newcomers (e.g., direct questions, indirect questions, and observation).

Influences of the COVID-19 Pandemic

The COVID-19 pandemic significantly affected newcomers' socialization due to the change in work. The high contagiousness and rapid spread of coronavirus diseases drastically increased remote and virtual work, and, in many cases, new hires were required to experience assimilation virtually, without even entering their physical workplace or meeting coworkers face-to-face (Scott et al., 2022). Much research on socialization has focused on face-to-face interactions in physical work settings, and the change in physical distancing has called upon novel socialization research, specifically adapting computer-mediated communication. For example, Wu et al. (2023) highlighted the importance of appropriate communication technologies for advice-seeking pairs that benefit newcomer adaptation. In addition, Woo et al. (2023) found that newcomers managed the uncertainties during the early stages of the COVID-19 pandemic in unique ways, such as organizing virtual small talks, initiating unsanctioned in-person meetings, asking overt and targeted questions, using digital repositories, unintentional limit testing, and anticipating future information-seeking.

The COVID-19 pandemic has expanded emerging socialization research, especially on virtual onboarding and remote and hybrid work. From a "new normal" of organizing, where organizations relied on remote work, society is now ushering in the "next normal," where flexible and hybrid work arrangements are welcomed (Wu et al., 2023). In this regard, future research needs to examine different ways to make remote socialization more effective and enable newcomers to be more proactive (Saks & Gruman, 2021). On the other hand, the limitation of remote socialization should be recognized as it will decrease newcomers' opportunities to interact with others face-to-face, which is necessary for their successful assimilation. Further research is needed due to challenges related to remote socialization, such as the lack of informal interactions, slower learning processes, hampered trust development, and newcomers' technostress (Russo et al., 2023).

Critiques

While organizational socialization research is prolific, it is not free from critique. A primary criticism centers on the stages of the model. Organizational socialization research focuses on the universal and developmental nature of the cycles of Jablin's (1987) model, which does not represent everyone's experiences (Bullis & Stout, 2000). "The stage model leads researchers away from understanding work activities and occupational choice as communication practices" (Clair, 1996, p. 265). She also claimed that stage models can only be applied to mainstream corporations, ignoring occupations such as artists, painters, and the self-employed. In addition, the four phases of the stage model are not as clear-cut as the model suggests (Allen, 1996). For instance, some individuals go back and forth between phases. Furthermore, Feldman (1981) argued that there could be overlap between stages; although the model suggests four stages occurring in the same way and order, socialization does not always occur in that way. Some newcomers have different experiences from others, but this model offers the stage model as a generalized process.

In addition, scholars have also criticized the literature for overlooking individual and diverse experiences. Bullis and Bach (1989) and Bullis (1993) argued that socialization theory and models tended to overemphasize the influence of the organization over the individual. In addition, Kramer and Miller (1999) noted, "A particularly sensitive issue concerns stage models' inattention to women's voices or other specific groups" (p. 362). Allen (2004) similarly noted that the model does not address the unique experiences of individuals of different races, socioeconomic statuses, religions, sexual identities, abilities, and ages. In this regard, some newcomers feel like they are "outsiders within" who never become established members of the organization (Bullis & Stout, 2000). Along these lines, Bullis and Stout (2000) argued that Jablin's model does not represent everyone's experiences. For example, Allen (1996) demonstrated how her socialization as a woman of color in academia differed from those of other men or women. From her experiences as an "outsider within," she advocated a positive social change in the diverse composition of the workplace as socialization research has given little attention to such situations (see Chapter 14).

However, a growing body of research recognizes the importance of socialization for various groups by examining the intersectional influences of diversity, such as gender, race, culture, and socioeconomic status. For example, Hall and Gettings (2020) examined women's experiences of marginalization during assimilation in male-dominated workplaces. Their findings show how women receive, interpret, and respond to workplace incivility, and that could work together to normalize marginalizing communication in the workplace over time. Scholars have also paid attention to particular groups' socialization. For example, Hoffmann-Longtin et al. (2021) suggested how the communication discipline can help graduate students socialize and identify through more effective teaching, mentoring, and career preparation.

Organizational members' inclusion is crucial to promoting positive socialization outcomes. Miller and Manata (2023) found a positive relationship between organizational members' feeling that they were included, both socially and while performing tasks, and assimilation outcomes, such as acculturation, job competencies, and coworker familiarity. Due to its significance, diversity, equity, and inclusion (DEI) during socialization deserves more attention from organizational communication scholars, especially for those experiences of women, minorities, and intersectional and less obvious identities, such as sexual orientation, veteran status, or having a disability (Rogers, 2020).

Like most areas of research in organizational studies, the organizational socialization literature is also steeped in the common bias that treats corporate and workplace settings neutrally as the only presumed organizational form, as well as all the other biases discussed in Chapter 1. Hence, we know little about how socialization functions for other kinds of organizational forms, processes, and structures. Moreover, owing to these biases, the literature is decidedly Western-centric and steeped in colonial assumptions (see Chapter 4). Great opportunities exist to expand our understanding of socialization beyond the Western workplace setting.

Approach to Communication and Organizations

Organizational socialization research has focused largely on the member's experience throughout the socialization process. In general, scholars conceptualize the experience as one of uncertainty and information acquisition. Toward this end, the vast majority of research in this area is grounded in a *transmission model of communication*. The encounter phase has arguably received the most research attention with most studies grounded in URT (Berger & Calabrese, 1975). Specifically, newcomers seek and receive information that reduces their uncertainty; that is, information is transmitted from others to the newcomer.

Unlike other areas (e.g., workplace relationship research – see Chapter 10), the interpretive turn (Putnam & Pacanowsky, 1983; see Chapter 2) did not lead to a substantial paradigm shift in conceptualizing the role of communication and socialization. While Jablin's (1984) model highlighted the role of communication in organizational socialization, it and subsequent versions (e.g., Jablin, 1987, 2001) were still largely grounded in a transmission model (see Chapter 1), treating the organization as a neutral entity rather than as constituted by the communication of members and others.

Some studies, however, do reflect a constitutive approach to communication, examining how interaction constructs or constitutes organization. OAS studies of employment interviews from an enactment perspective, for example, do not examine the transmission of messages between applicant and interviewer. Rather they examine how the interactants together communicatively create interview patterns and structures (i.e., the *organizationality* – organized structure, or O_2 – of the interview). Shaw (1983), for example, examined how applicant and interviewer "taken-for-granted assumptions" about employment interviews emerged through and structured the interview process. Although the authors of these studies did not use the term "constitutive," their studies exemplify how communication constitutes the employment interview. Barge and Schlueter (2004) examined how informal communication constitutes the individual–organization relationship during the organizational encounter phase. While not explicitly grounded in CCO theory, their study's fundamental assumptions about communication represent a constitutive conceptualization by demonstrating how informal interaction constitutes the organization and the newcomer's relationship to the organization. The C–O cycle presented in Chapter 1 refers to how communication constitutes organizations and the organization, in turn, constitutes communication. Here, you can clearly see this cyclic relationship between day-to-day communication practices and structured organizational patterns that then enable and constrain communication practices. Overall, however, organizational socialization has been and continues to be largely grounded in a transmission approach to communication.

Organizational socialization research centers on links between individuals and the organizations they join and exit. This body of work tends to emphasize an O_2 approach to organization. O_2 refers to the state of coordination/order (see Chapter 1). For example, socialization research examines how individuals learn about/become part of the organization (i.e., the order) via communication (e.g., information-seeking). Early work that approached socialization from a management or macro perspective by focusing on the strategies *organizations* use to socialize members represents an O_3 approach in which the organization is conceptualized as an entitative being or actor that acts upon its members (e.g., Van Maanen & Schein, 1979). The introduction of Jablin's model and subsequent focus on the communicative nature of socialization moved research toward an O_1 approach via research that examines how individuals coordinate with each other and organize their shared activities through their interactions (Chapter 1). Such studies, for example, identify how new members become knowledgeable veterans via interaction with others such as their supervisor and coworkers (Miller & Jablin, 1991).

Concerning the three expressions of organization presented in Chapter 1, both O_1 and O_2 socialization research tends to emphasize structure over agency; that is, individuals learn about organizational structures and norms, rather than changing or reconstituting them. This is consistent with critiques that socialization research tends to emphasize the organization over the individual (Bullis, 1993). The relatively few studies grounded in a constitutive conceptualization of communication (e.g., Barge & Schlueter, 2004) address how newcomers' roles and relationship to the organization are socially constructed through discourse. Such work exemplifies a greater emphasis on mutual constitution – the individual's relationship to the organization is not static nor imposed on the individual; rather it is socially constructed (and mutually constituted) via interaction, so the C–O cycle is explicitly examined in this body of work.

While the C–O cycle and the three expressions of organization can clearly be seen in organizational socialization processes, the dearth of socialization research that directly addresses these phenomena highlights an opportunity for communication scholars to make substantive contributions to the organizational socialization literature. As noted above, for example, workplace relationships are crucial for newcomer socialization. In fact, newcomers socially construct their relationships as they seek information and communicate with coworkers and their supervisors during the encounter phase and beyond. Much research demonstrates the socially constructed nature of workplace relationships (e.g., Sias & Cahill, 1998). Research examining how such relationships, in turn, constitute the organization would provide important insights regarding how newcomers influence the organization. Moreover, understanding how pre-existing organizational structures both enable and constrain workplace relationship development, and, therefore, influence workplace relationship development could generate useful insights into functional and dysfunctional relationship dynamics.

Cultural Implications

Becoming an established member of the organization requires learning the organizational culture as a successful socialization process. According to Van Maanen and Schein (1979), socialization "involves the transmission of information and values, it is fundamentally a *cultural* matter" (p. 210, emphasis added). Different organizations possess different cultures as members share substantially distinctive orientations to one another, their roles and missions of the organization (Louis, 1980). Along these lines, Alvesson (2002) argues "the cultural dimension is central in all aspects of organizational life; how people in a company think, feel, value, and act are guided by ideas, meanings and beliefs of a cultural (socially shared) nature" (p. 1).

However, socialization research has paid less attention to cultural diversity and international culture in the organizational socialization process. Although the body of research largely represents, at least implicitly, a white, Western perspective and experiences, there has been some active research at an international level more recently. Guo's (2019) exploratory qualitative study underlined the complex nature of emotion in Chinese newcomers working at a Chinese bureaucratic office because they adapted to and negotiated emotional rules and cultural assumptions in proactive group socialization. She found similarities between US and Chinese employees managing uncertainty using technologies (i.e., social media) and presenting impression management concerns during organizational assimilation. These results call for more attention to the impact of cultural differences on newcomers' socialization.

As globalization is one of the critical factors in how organizational communication is changing (see Chapter 20), examining cultural processes of socialization in an international context seems crucial. Organizational socialization research will benefit from understanding different cultural and organizational contexts.

Conclusion

The organizational socialization process occurs repeatedly over a person's lifetime. Given its ubiquity in our lives, it is unsurprising that socialization is among the most frequently studied topics in organizational communication research. This overview highlighted how the field developed over time from a management focus on how organizations socialize members to a communication focus on how socialization occurs communicatively. While we have learned much about socialization processes and practices, its complexities as people navigate increasingly global, diverse, and technologically complex organizational terrains remain much of a mystery. Examining how communication does not just play a role in socialization but constitutes the process and the organization itself would provide important insights into this important and ubiquitous aspect of human existence.

Recommended Supplementary Readings

Allen, B. J. (1996). Feminist standpoint theory: A Black woman's (re)view of organizational socialization. *Communication Studies*, *47*(4), 257–271.

A feminist critique of organizational socialization research emphasizes the experience of a black female academic as an "outsider within" a predominantly white organization.

Kramer, M. W., & Miller, V. D. (1999). A response to criticism of organizational socialization research: In support of contemporary conceptualizations of organizational assimilation. *Communication Monograph*, *66*(4), 358–367.

Bullis, C. (1999). Mad or bad: A response to Kramer and Miller. *Communication Monographs*, *66*(4), 368–373.

Clair, R. P. (1999). Ways of seeing: A review of Kramer and Miller's manuscript. *Communication Monographs*, *66*(4), 374–381.

Turner, P. K. (1999). What if you don't? A response to Kramer and Miller. *Communication Monographs*, *66*(4), 382–389.

Miller, V. D., & Kramer, M. W. (1999). A reply to Bullis, Turner, and Clair. *Communication Monographs*, *66*(4), 390–392.

The above five articles appeared in the 1999 Volume 66, Issue 4, of Communication Monographs. The authors engage in a spirited debate about the state of organizational socialization research at the time. Together, they provide useful insights into the primary conceptualizations and critiques of socialization research.

Wanberg, C. (Ed.). (2012). *The Oxford handbook of organizational socialization.* New York: Oxford University Press.

A relatively recent broad overview of organizational socialization, from a management/organizational behavior perspective.

Important Concepts: Define and Discuss

Anticipatory socialization (VAS and OAS)
Exit/disengagement
Information-seeking tactics
Metamorphosis
Organizational encounter
Realistic job previews
Social costs
TMU
URT

Discussion Questions

1 Think about the last organization you joined (e.g., as an employee, student). How did you feel when you first became a member? What types of uncertainty did you experience and how did you deal with them (e.g., information-seeking and uncertainty management)?
2 Who influenced your decision to pursue your current career choice? How did they influence you? What messages do you recall as particularly important?
3 Describe the process you used in your most recent job search. How did you learn about the position and company? To what extent did you rely on interpersonal communication and mediated communication (e.g., websites and online search)?

Practitioners' Corner

Employee turnover is a fact of life in organizations – veteran members leave and newcomers take their places. Consequently, practitioners devote much time to recruiting, hiring, and socializing new members. The large body of research on organizational socialization provides many useful insights for practitioners.

First, practitioners should ensure their recruitment and interview practices provide applicants with realistic and accurate portrayals of the job and the organization, conveying the negative aspects (e.g., long hours, little opportunity for advancement) along with the positive. Such information can be communicated in recruitment materials such as job announcements and during interviews. Providing RJPs can minimize newcomer shock, surprise, disappointment, and potentially turnover.

Once a newcomer begins their new position, understand that they are likely experiencing a great deal of uncertainty – uncertainty about their new tasks, their ability to do those tasks, their role in the organization's social network, and the organizational culture. Understand also that they may be hesitant to ask questions for fear of making a bad impression. Rather than waiting for newcomers to come to you with questions, ensure to provide unsolicited information you think they may need and check in with them regularly to ask if they have any questions or need any information.

Practitioners are also encouraged to recognize the importance of functional workplace relationships during the socialization process and create an environment that encourages and supports the formation of quality coworker and supervisory relationships. One way to do this is to provide opportunities for newcomers to communicate with others whenever possible (e.g., through collaborating on tasks and departmental lunches). See Chapter 10 for more regarding workplace relationships.

Finally, it is important to remember that uncertainty is not limited to newcomers. All employees experience uncertainty about various issues throughout their time in an organization. Practitioners are encouraged to check in frequently with all employees to ensure they are adequately informed about departmental and organizational issues and concerns.

References

Aley, M. R., & Levine, K. J. (2020). From whom do young adults actively seek career information? An ego-network analysis of vocational anticipatory socialization. *Communication Studies*, *71*(2), 351–367. https://doi.org/10.1080/10510974.2020.1735465

Allen, B. J. (1996). Feminist standpoint theory: A black woman's (re)view of organizational socialization. *Communication Studies*, *47*(4), 257–271. https://doi.org/10.1080/10510979609368482

Allen, B. J. (2004). *Difference matters*. Waveland Press.

Alvesson, M. (2002). *Understanding organizational culture*. Sage.

Babbitt, L. V., & Jablin, F. M. (1985). Characteristics of applicants' questions and employment screening interview outcomes. *Human Communication Research*, *11*(4), 507–535. https://doi.org/10.1111/j.1468-2958.1985.tb00058.x

Barge, J. K., & Schlueter, D. W. (2004). Memorable messages and newcomer socialization. *Western Journal of Communication*, *68*(3), 233–256. https://doi.org/10.1080/10570310409374800

Baur, J. E., Buckley, M. R., Bagdasarov, Z., & Dharmasiri, A. S. (2014). A historical approach to realistic job previews: An exploration into their origins, evolution, and recommendations for the future. *Journal of Management History*, *20*(2), 200–223. https://doi.org/10.1108/JMH-06-2012-0046

Berger, C. R., & Calabrese, R. J. (1975). Some explorations in initial interaction and beyond: Toward a developmental theory of interpersonal communication. *Human Communication Research*, *1*(2), 99–112. https://doi.org/10.1111/j.1468-2958.1975.tb00258.x

Bluedorn, A. C. (1978). A taxonomy of turnover. *The Academy of Management Review*, *3*(3), 647–651. https://doi.org/10.5465/AMR.1978.4305918

Brashers, D. E. (2001). Communication and uncertainty management. *Journal of Communication*, *51*(3), 477–497. https://doi.org/10.1093/joc/51.3.477

Brown, P., & Levinson, S. C. (1978). Universals in language usage: Politeness phenomena. In E. N. Goody (Ed.), *Questions and politeness: Strategies in social interaction* (pp. 56–311). Cambridge University Press.

Bullis, C. (1993). Organizational socialization research: Enabling, constraining, and shifting perspectives. *Communication Monographs*, *60*(1), 10–17. https://doi.org/10.1080/03637759309376289

Bullis, C., & Bach, B. W. (1989). Are mentor relationships helping organizations? An exploration of developing mentee-mentor-organizational identifications using turning point analysis. *Communication Quarterly*, *37*(3), 199–213. https://doi.org/10.1080/01463378909385540

Bullis, C., & Stout, K. R. (2000). Organizational socialization: A feminist standpoint approach. In P. M. Buzzanell (Ed.), *Rethinking organizational & managerial communication from feminist perspectives* (pp. 47–75). Sage.

Chao, G. T., O'Leary-Kelly, A. M., Wolf, S., Klein, H. J., & Gardner, P. D. (1994). Organizational socialization: Its content and consequences. *Journal of Applied Psychology*, *79*(5), 730–743. https://doi.org/10.1037/0021-9010.79.5.730

Cheepen, C. (1988). *The predictability of informal conversation*. Pinter.

Cheney, G., & Tompkins, P. K. (1987). Coming to terms with organizational identification and commitment. *Central States Speech Journal*, *38*(1), 1–15. https://doi.org/10.1080/10510978709368225

Clair, R. (1996). The political nature of the colloquialism, "a real job": Implications for organization socialization. *Communication Monographs*, *63*(3), 249–267. https://doi.org/10.1080/03637759609376392

Dugoni, B. L., & Ilgen, D. R. (1981). Realistic job previews and the adjustment of new employees. *Academy of Management Journal*, *24*(3), 579–591. https://doi.org/10.5465/255576

Eisenberg, E. M. (1984). Ambiguity as strategy in organizational communication. *Communication Monographs*, *51*(3), 227–242. https://doi.org/10.1080/03637758409390197

Feldman, D. C. (1976). A contingency theory of socialization. *Administrative Science Quarterly*, *21*(3), 433–452. https://doi.org/10.2307/2391853

Feldman, D. C. (1981). The multiple socialization of organization members. *The Academy of Management Review*, *6*(2), 309–318. https://doi.org/10.5465/AMR.1981.4287859

Gallagher, E. B., & Sias, P. M. (2009). The new employee as a source of uncertainty: Veteran employee information seeking about new hires. *Western Journal of Communication*, *73*(1), 23–46. https://doi.org/10.1080/10570310802636326

Gettings, P. E., & Anderson, L. B. (2021). An organizational socialization perspective on young adults' ideas about retirement: Examining sources of retirement information, meanings of retirement, and source-meaning associations. *Work, Aging and Retirement*, *7*(2), 90–106. https://doi.org/10.1093/workar/waaa019

Gibson, M. K., & Papa, M. J. (2000). The mud, the blood, and the beer guys: Organizational osmosis in blue-collar work groups. *Journal of Applied Communication Research*, *28*(1), 68–88. https://doi.org/10.1080/00909880009365554

Giddings, F. H. (1897). *The theory of socialization*. Macmillan.

Guo, Y. (2019). 'Let our emotions tell the story': An exploration of emotion management in Chinese proactive workgroup socialization. *Human Relations*, *72*(7), 1187–1208. https://doi.org/10.1177/0018726718796154

Hall, E., & Gettings, P. E. (2020). "Who is this little girl they hired to work here?": Women's experiences of marginalizing communication in male-dominated workplaces. *Communication Monographs*, *87*(4), 484–505. https://doi.org/10.1080/03637751.2020.1758736

Hoffmann-Longtin, K., Brann, M., Ridley-Merriweather, K. E., & Bach, B. W. (2021). Rethinking graduate student socialization and identification: How the communication discipline can help. *Communication Education*, *70*(1), 120–122. https://doi.org/10.1080/03634523.2020.1811361

Jablin, F. M. (1982). Organizational communication: An assimilation approach. In M. Roloff, & C. Berger (Eds.), *Social cognition and communication* (pp. 255–286). Sage.

Jablin, F. M. (1984). Assimilating new members into organizations. *Annals of the International Communication Association*, *8*(1), 594–627. https://doi.org/10.1080/23808985.1984.11678591

Jablin, F. M. (1987). Organizational entry, assimilation, and exit. In F. M. Jablin, L. L. Putnam, K. H. Roberts, & L. W. Porter (Eds.), *Handbook of organizational communication: An interdisciplinary perspective* (pp. 679–740). Sage.

Jablin, F. M. (2001). Organizational entry, assimilation, and disengagement/exit. In F. M. Jablin, & L. L. Putnam (Eds.), *The new handbook of organizational communication: Advances in theory, research, and methods* (pp. 732–818). Sage.

Jablin, F. M., & Krone, K. J. (1987). Organizational assimilation. In C. Berger, & S. Chaffee (Eds.), *Handbook of communication science* (pp. 711–746). Sage.

Jablin, F. M., Miller, V. D., & Sias, P. M. (1999). Communication and interaction processes. In R. W. Eder, & M. M. Harris (Eds.), *The employment interview handbook* (pp. 297–320). Sage.

Jokisaari, M., & Nurmi, J. E. (2009). Change in newcomers' supervisor support and socialization outcomes after organizational entry. *Academy of Management Journal*, *52*(3), 527–544. https://doi.org/10.5465/AMJ.2009.41330971

Kacmar, K. M., & Hochwarter, W. A. (1995). The interview as a communication event: A field examination of demographic effects on interview outcomes. *Journal of Business Communication*, *32*(3), 207–232. https://doi.org/10.1177/002194369503200301

Katz, R. (1980). *Time and work: Toward an integrative perspective*. In B. M. Staw, & L. Cummings (Eds.), *Research in organizational behavior* (Vol. 2, pp. 81–121). JAI Press Inc.

King, R. C., Xia, W., Campbell Quick, J., & Sethi, V. (2005). Socialization and organizational outcomes of information technology professionals. *Career Development International*, *10*(1), 26–51. https://doi.org/10.1108/13620430510577619

Krackhardt, D., & Porter, L. W. (1986). The snowball effect: Turnover embedded in communication networks. *Journal of Applied Psychology*, *71*(1), 50–55. https://doi.org/10.1037/0021-9010.71.1.50

Kramer, M. W. (1993). Communication and uncertainty reduction during job transfers: Leaving and joining processes. *Communication Monographs*, *60*(2), 178–198. https://doi.org/10.1080/03637759309376307
Kramer, M. W. (2004). *Managing uncertainty in organizational communication*. Lawrence Erlbaum.
Kramer, M. W. (2010). *Organizational socialization: Joining and leaving organizations*. Polity Press.
Kramer, M. W. (2014). *Managing uncertainty in organizational communication*. Taylor & Francis.
Kramer, M. W., & Danielson, M. A. (2016). Developing and re-developing volunteer roles: The case of ongoing assimilation of docent zoo volunteers. *Management Communication Quarterly*, *30*(1), 103–120. https://doi.org/10.1177/0893318915612551
Kramer, M. W., Dougherty, D. S., & Pierce, T. A. (2004). Managing uncertainty during a corporate acquisition: A longitudinal study of communication during an airline acquisition. *Human Communication Research*, *30*(1), 71–101. https://doi.org/10.1093/hcr/30.1.71
Kramer, M. W., & Miller, V. D. (1999). A response to criticisms of organizational socialization research: In support of contemporary conceptualizations of organizational assimilation. *Communication Monographs*, *66*(4), 358–367. https://doi.org/10.1080/03637759909376485
Kramer, M. W., & Miller, V. D. (2014). Socialization and assimilation: Theories, processes, and outcomes. In L. L. Putnam, & D. K. Mumby (Eds.), *The sage handbook of organizational communication: Advances in theory, research, and methods* (3rd ed., pp. 525–547). Sage.
Lee, T. W., Mitchell, T. R., Wise, L., & Fireman, S. (1996). An unfolding model of voluntary employee turnover. *The Academy of Management Journal*, *39*(1), 5–36. https://doi.org/10.2307/256629
Lester, R. E. (1987). Organizational culture, uncertainty reduction and the socialization of new organizational members. In S. Thomas (Ed.), *Culture and communication* (pp. 105–113). Ablex.
Levine, K. J., & Aley, M. (2022). Introducing the sixth source of vocational anticipatory socialization: Using the internet to search for career information. *Journal of Career Development*, *49*(2), 443–456. https://doi.org/10.1177/0894845320940798
Levine, K. J., & Hoffner, C. A. (2006). Adolescents' conceptions of work. *Journal of Adolescent Research*, *21*(6), 647–669. https://doi.org/10.1177/0743558406293963
Louis, M. R. (1980). Surprise and sense making: What newcomers experience in entering unfamiliar organizational settings. *Administrative Science Quarterly*, *25*(2), 226–251. https://doi.org/10.2307/2392453
Maccoby, E. E., & Martin, J. A. (1983). Socialization in the context of the family: Parent-child interaction. In E. M. Hetherington (Ed.), *Handbook of child psychology: Socialization, personality, and social development* (Vol. 4, pp. 1–101). Wiley.
Mael, F., & Ashforth, B. E. (1992). Alumni and their alma mater: A partial test of the reformulated model of organizational identification. *Journal of Organizational Behavior*, *13*(2), 103–123. https://doi.org/10.1002/job.4030130202
Mignerey, J. T., Rubin, R. B., & Gorden, W. I. (1995). Organizational entry: An investigation of newcomer communication behavior and uncertainty. *Communication Research*, *22*(1), 54–85. https://doi.org/10.1177/009365095022001003
Miller, M. J., & Manata, B. (2023). The effects of workplace inclusion on employee assimilation outcomes. *International Journal of Business Communication*, *60*(3), 777–801. https://doi.org/10.1177/2329488420976805
Miller, V. D., & Buzzanell, P. M. (1996). Toward a research agenda for the second employment interview. *Journal of Applied Communication Research*, *24*(3), 165–180. https://doi.org/10.1080/00909889609365449
Miller, V. D., & Jablin, F. M. (1991). Information seeking during organizational entry: Influences, tactics, and a model of the process. *Academy of Management Review*, *16*(1), 92–120. https://doi.org/10.5465/AMR.1991.4278997
Modaff, D. P., Butler, J., & DeWine, S. (2012). *Organizational communication: Foundations, challenges, and misunderstandings* (3rd ed.). Allyn & Bacon.
Morrison, E. W. (1993). Longitudinal study of the effects of information seeking on newcomer socialization. *Journal of Applied Psychology*, *78*(2), 173–183. https://doi.org/10.1037/0021-9010.78.2.173
Myers, K. K., & Gailliard, B. M. (2016). Organizational entry, socialization, and assimilation in health care organizations. In T. R. Harrison, & E. A. Williams (Eds.), *Organizations, health, and organizations* (pp. 31–48). Routledge.

Myers, K. K., & McPhee, R. D. (2006). Influences on member assimilation in workgroups in high-reliability organizations: A multilevel analysis. *Human Communication Research*, *32*(4), 440–468. https://doi.org/10.1111/j.1468-2958.2006.00283.x
Myers, K. K., & Oetzel, J. G. (2003). Exploring the dimensions of organizational assimilation: Creating and validating a measure. *Communication Quarterly*, *51*(4), 438–457. https://doi.org/10.1080/01463370309370166
Omilion-Hodges, L. M., Shank, S. E., & Packard, C. M. (2019). What young adults want: A multistudy examination of vocational anticipatory socialization through the lens of students' desired managerial communication behaviors. *Management Communication Quarterly*, *33*(4), 512–547. https://doi.org/10.1177/0893318919851177
Ostroff, C., & Kozlowski, S. W. J. (1992). Organizational socialization as a learning process: The role of information acquisition. *Personnel Psychology*, *45*(4), 849–874. https://doi.org/10.1111/j.1744-6570.1992.tb00971.x
Phillips, J. M. (1998). Effects of realistic job previews on multiple organizational outcomes: A meta-analysis. *The Academy of Management Journal*, *41*(6), 673–690. https://doi.org/10.2307/256964
Powers, S. R., & Myers, K. K. (2017). Vocational anticipatory socialization: College students' reports of encouraging/discouraging sources and messages. *Journal of Career Development*, *44*(5), 409–424. https://doi.org/10.1177/0894845316660627
Putnam, L. L., & Pacanowsky, M. E.(Eds.) (1983). *Communication and organizations: An interpretive approach*. Sage.
Rogers, M. S. (2020). Avoiding the issue: A critique of organizational socialization research from feminist and minority perspectives. *Organization Development Journal*, *38*(1), 75–88.
Russo, M., Morandin, G., & Manca, C. (2023). How can organizations improve virtual onboarding? Key learnings from the pandemic. In S. Bergum, P. Peters, & T. Vold (Eds.), *Virtual management and the new normal* (pp. 203–221). Palgrave Macmillan.
Saks, A. M., & Gruman, J. A. (2021). Employee engagement. In V. I. Sessa, & N. A. Bowling (Eds.), *Essentials of job attitudes and other workplace psychological constructs* (pp. 242–271). Routledge/Taylor & Francis Group. https://doi.org/10.4324/9780429325755-12
Saks, A. M., Gruman, J. A., & Cooper-Thomas, H. (2011). The neglected role of proactive behavior and outcomes in newcomer socialization. *Journal of Vocational Behavior*, *79*(1), 36–46. https://doi.org/10.1016/j.jvb.2010.12.007
Schaubroeck, J. M., Peng, A. C., & Hannah, S. T. (2013). Developing trust with peers and leaders: Impacts on organizational identification and performance during entry. *Academy of Management Journal*, *56*(4), 1148–1168. https://doi.org/10.5465/amj.2011.0358
Scott, C., Dieguez, T. A., Deepak, P., Gu, S., & Wildman, J. L. (2022). Onboarding during COVID-19: Create structure, connect people, and continue adapting. *Organizational Dynamics*, *51*(2), 100828. https://doi.org/10.1016/j.orgdyn.2021.100828
Scott, C., & Myers, K. K. (2005). The socialization of emotion: Learning emotion management at the fire station. *Journal of Applied Communication Research*, *33*(1), 67–92. https://doi.org/10.1080/0090988042000318521
Shaw, M. R. (1983). Taken-for-granted assumptions of applicants in simulated selection interviews. *Western Journal of Speech Communication*, *47*(2), 138–156. https://doi.org/10.1080/10570318309374112
Sias, P. M. (2005). Workplace relationship quality and employee information experiences. *Communication Studies*, *56*(4), 375–395. https://doi.org/10.1080/10510970500319450
Sias, P. M., & Cahill, D. J. (1998). From coworkers to friends: The development of peer friendships in the workplace. *Western Journal of Communication*, *62*(3), 273–299. https://doi.org/10.1080/10570319809374611
Sias, P. M., Kramer, M. W., & Jenkins, E. (1997). A comparison of the communication behaviors of temporary employees and new hires. *Communication Research*, *24*(6), 731–754. https://doi.org/10.1177/009365097024006006
Sias, P. M., & Wyers, T. D. (2001). Employee uncertainty and information-seeking in newly formed expansion organizations. *Management Communication Quarterly*, *14*(4), 549–573. https://doi.org/10.1177/0893318901144001
Teboul, J. B. (1994). Facing and coping with uncertainty during organizational encounter. *Management Communication Quarterly*, *8*(2), 190–224. https://doi.org/10.1177/0893318994008002003

Terrazas, A., & Zhao, D. (2023). Glassdoor's 2024 Workplace Trends. *Glassdoor*. Retrieved April 26, 2024, from https://www.glassdoor.com/research/workplace-trends-2024

Van Maanen, J. (1975). Police socialization: A longitudinal examination of job attitudes in an urban police department. *Administrative Science Quarterly*, *20*(2), 207–228. https://doi.org/10.2307/2391695

Van Maanen, J., & Schein, E. G. (1979). Toward a theory of organizational socialization. In B. M. Staw (Ed.), *Research in organizational behavior* (pp. 209–264). JAI Press.

Wanous, J. P. (1992). *Organizational entry: Recruitment, selection, orientation, and socialization of newcomers*. Prentice Hall.

Weick, K. E. (1979). *The social psychology of organizing* (2nd ed.). Addison-Wesley.

Weick, K. E. (1995). *Sensemaking in organizations*. Sage.

Woo, D., Endacott, C. G., & Myers, K. K. (2023). Navigating water cooler talks without the water cooler: Uncertainty and information seeking during remote socialization. *Management Communication Quarterly*, *37*(2), 251–280. https://doi.org/10.1177/08933189221105916

Wu, Y. J., Antone, B., DeChurch, L., & Contractor, N. (2023). Information sharing in a hybrid workplace: Understanding the role of ease-of-use perceptions of communication technologies in advice-seeking relationship maintenance. *Journal of Computer-Mediated Communication*, *28*(4), zmad025. https://doi.org/10.1093/jcmc/zmad025

9 Communication Networks

Lisa V. Chewning

Introduction

Throughout the text, we have focused on organizing as *the coordination of human activities for the purposes of achieving the accomplishment of tasks*. Such organizing is the foundation of network theory. Networks are the patterns of connection, called *ties*, among a set of actors (e.g., people, organizations), which are referred to as *nodes*. Put simply, networks are how we organize and have implications for important social and organizational outcomes, such as power, influence, access to resources, and collaboration. They can be defined in terms of the *ego*, or individual network of an actor, or as a *whole* network, which refers to all of the connections within a specific set of parameters, such as a neighborhood, organization, or supply chain. Networks can range from the individual level all the way to the societal level, as Castells (2000) claims that we are part of a network society based on the "organizational arrangement of humans in relationships of production/consumption, experience, and power, as expressed in meaningful interaction framed by culture" (p. 5).

While traditional network theory positioned networks as collectives based on *connection* or *interaction*, it is through *communication* that connection is enacted and given meaning. As emphasized throughout this text, a constitutive point of view posits that communication is about the creation of shared meaning. Thus, engaging in a network involves creating a series of connections with others through which shared meaning is negotiated and renegotiated through each instance of communicative action. Indeed, even as Castells (2000) talks about meaningful *interaction* framed by culture, because culture is socially and communicatively constructed, the basis of a network society is arguably communication.

There is a rich history of studying connections within and among organizations as networks. According to Nohria (1998, p. 290), "all organizations are, in important respects, social networks." Returning to the idea of networks being embedded, organizations *are* networks consisting of multiple subgroups, which can also be considered networks. Additionally, organizations are part of multiple networks, including, but not limited to, industries, the communities in which they operate, supply chains, and trade organizations. Organizations can also be connected through the individual ties of organizational members, such as when members of a board of directors sit on the boards of other organizations, creating *interlocks*. Each level of connection, and the communication that flows through those connections, has implications for the individual organizational member, the organization as a whole, and often, the macro system within which the organization exists. Thus, networks represent the intersection of communication, social organization, and the organization.

DOI: 10.4324/9781003484639-12

Defining Networks

Network theory has its own vocabulary, so to understand how networks impact organizations, it is important to understand how to define and measure networks. As defined earlier, networks are the patterns of connection among a set of individual and/or collective actors (see Chapter 1). Networks are not based on one-time communication but rather on repeated communication between members of a specific population. Network communication evolves as a natural progression shaped by both internal and environmental forces. Accordingly, network development is typically fluid, changing as the needs and circumstances of participants change. While the nature and frequency of the communication can vary within and among networks, network formation is rooted in the idea that (1) participants already have an idea of what to expect and how the other partner works, (2) trust has already been established (or is anticipated if this is the initial interaction) so each party does not have to look out for opportunism, and (3) participants are more willing to accommodate special requests/circumstances because of intended future interactions (Powell, 1990).

Networks can be studied through the lens of *social network theory*, which refers to "the mechanisms and processes that interact within network structures to yield certain outcomes for individuals and groups" (Borgatti & Halgin, 2011, p. 1), by *using social network analysis*, which uses graph theory to study the nature of the connections within a network, or by studying the communication that takes place within a given network. Networks emerge organically through social interaction and do not have natural boundaries (Borgatti & Halgin, 2011), so what constitutes a given network in social network analysis depends on the question being asked. To study a network, a researcher must identify what question they want to answer and then choose a set of actors (e.g., population) and type of connection to study (Borgatti & Halgin, 2011). For example, one could learn about the advice network in an organization by surveying all organizational members about whom they turn to within the organization for advice and then mapping the advice network. This network could then be examined in a variety of ways, including how it compares to the formal organizational chart or which members are most central in the network.

Networks can be studied from the ego, or individual, point of view or from a whole-network point of view. An *ego network* consists of all the recurring contacts that an individual actor has. One actor's ego network spans multiple other networks. For example, family, friends, coworkers, neighbors, and members of organizational affiliations (e.g., religious institutions, gyms, and clubs). A *whole network* considers all the contacts within a particular boundary, such as an organization. Within one organization there are often several smaller networks, or structural subgroups, that work together to keep the organization functioning. The composition and interaction of these subgroups are what create the overall organizational network.

Nodes and ties form the basis of the network. *Nodes* are the actors in the network and often represent individuals or organizations, but some studies examine how the co-occurrence of words in a body of text impact messages or how hyperlinks among websites can create representational networks on the organizational level as organizations indicate affiliation with other organizations (e.g., Fu et al., 2022; Humalisto et al., 2020). *Ties* are the connections, or possible lines of communication, among network members. Ties can be conceptualized in terms of strength (*weak, strong, affiliative*), activity (*active, latent, dormant*), and symmetry (*symmetrical* or *asymmetrical*). Strength and activity of ties can affect everything from the resources that pass through the individual tie and the frequency of communication to the structure of the overall network. For example, *strong ties* are generally found among people such as friends and family, who have a long-shared history, frequent communication, and communication around personal or intimate topics. Strong ties tend to be *homophilous*, or similar. Resources that typically flow through strong ties include personal advice, confidential information, social support, and even monetary or other types of tangible support. Homophily breeds connection, meaning that individuals with strong ties within a network often have direct connections with the same alters (i.e., other actors). Thus, networks that consist of mainly strong ties tend to be closed and cohesive networks, meaning that all members of the network, or portion of a network, are directly connected. This can be helpful, such as in situations where trust is important or when decisions have to be made quickly. However, it can stifle innovation and creativity, in that nodes that are similar often have access to similar resources and see things in a similar way. This can lead to *groupthink*, or a tendency toward group conformity that blinds group members to the importance of outside influence or alternative points of view. Groupthink can inhibit critical thinking and decision-making to the point of failure or even danger. For example, when organizational leadership fails to take into account advice from people outside of their inner circle, the status quo is often maintained, causing the organization to innovate less and ultimately be left behind. (See Chapter 15 for more on groupthink.)

Conversely, *weak ties* are connections between people who share a smaller range of information and communication topics and often do not have multiple contacts in common. This can lead to open networks, or networks that are not *densely connected*, meaning that members are "connected to many actors who are themselves unconnected" (Podolny & Baron, 1997, p. 673). Members of open networks often span several networks but are not deeply embedded in any given one, thus offering unique resources. While weak links and open network structures do not foster trust as quickly as a closed network, they may offer greater flexibility and innovation because of the diversity of their members, which provides easier access to a variety of resources. For individuals, having a large, sparse network of informal ties can lead to greater job mobility (Granovetter, 1984; Podolny & Baron, 1997). However, while an actor's ego network may be primarily strong or weak ties, it is unlikely that any overall network will be one or the other. Rather, there is evidence that a mix of strong and weak ties within a network structure leads to the most efficacy in the ability to obtain and leverage resources (Capaldo, 2007; Doerfel et al., 2010). Given these findings, being able to strategically adapt networks depending on internal and external needs is critical to both individual and organizational success. Additionally, while tie strength and overall network structure create opportunities for trust, resource mobilization, and innovation, the content of communication flowing through the network ties ultimately determines network outcomes.

It is worth noting that not all members within a given network need to be connected and that tie strength does not necessarily stay the same as networks evolve. Ties that connect two people are considered *active*. However, there is also the opportunity for *latent* ties, or ties for which a connection is possible but has not yet been activated, such as members of the same organization who have not met. Because they share the same boundary condition and are connected to others (either directly or indirectly) within that boundary condition, they still share the same social network. Additionally, because of the social identification that can come from being part of a shared social structure, unconnected members of the same network will likely still share a similar orientation to the overall network, although that orientation will be mediated by who they are connected to. Finally, *dormant* ties are those that were previously active but through which communication no longer flows, such as old friends or family members who have been out of communication for an extended period of time. However, dormant ties can be reactivated, start out as weak, and, over time, evolve into strong ties. Conversely, two members of an organization can be part of the same work unit and share a strong tie, but when one gets transferred to another part of the organization or leaves altogether, their tie could become weak or dormant.

Network Roles, Access, and Power

The number and connections of ties that actors have within a network have implications for both individual- and network-level issues of access, efficiency, and power. *Centrality* is a measure of how connected one is to other members of the network, either directly or indirectly (Borgatti et al., 2006; Freeman, 1978). An actor with high centrality is generally one who is optimally connected within the network, either in terms of direct ties or in their ability to connect other ties. Centrality is associated with power and influence, as one who is highly central has the most access to information and resources that flow throughout the network. This allows them not only to have high levels of institutional knowledge, both formal and informal, but also to become a "go-to" source of information or advice for coworkers. Briefly, there are four different types of centrality: degree, eigenvector, closeness, and betweenness (Borgatti & Everett, 1997; Borgatti et al., 2006).

Degree centrality measures the number of adjacent links to and from an individual, based solely on direct measures. *Eigenvector* centrality represents the degree measure of a node in terms of the centrality of adjacent nodes; that is, whether an actor is connected to other highly connected actors. *Closeness* centrality measures how close one is to all other members of a network by summing the lengths of the shortest paths from an individual to all other network members. *Betweenness* centrality measures the extent to which individuals occupy the position between other actors on the shortest paths that connect them. Networks can also be studied in terms of their degree of centralization, or the degree to which the majority of nodes cluster around a specific node or set of nodes. Highly centralized organizational networks have been shown to be the most efficient structure for completing tasks that are not complex, while less centralized networks are more efficient for tasks with higher complexity.

How many ties an actor has within the overall network and the composition of these ties in relation to the rest of the network have implications for the role they play within the network. The most common network roles are gatekeepers, liaisons, bridges, isolates, and stars. *Stars* are the network members with the most lines of communication, or highest degree centrality. As discussed earlier, they often have power and influence and are someone others seek out most for information or advice. While the designated leader can also be the opinion leader, the network star is most often the leader in emergent (e.g., advice, friendship) networks.

There are three different network roles that serve brokerage positions, or positions that connect and manage communication/resource flow among different parts of the organization. *Liaisons* connect groups without being a member of either group, such as a manager or coordinator who shares information among various workgroups contributing to the same project. *Bridges* play a similar role to liaisons, in that they connect otherwise unconnected groups; however, they share membership in one or more of the groups. An example of a bridge is someone who is a member of IT but also working on building the company website with members from the communication department. Finally, *gatekeepers* control the flow of information by strategically choosing with whom to share messages. Gatekeepers can be critical in the flow of messages through the organization, for example, in power differentials (e.g., an administrative assistant is a gatekeeper between employees and managers) and between the network and its environment (e.g., a client representative brokers information and goods between the organization and external stakeholders). Gatekeepers are important because they filter messages and can therefore prevent information overload (Rogers & Agarwala-Rogers, 1976), but they can also stymie or misdirect organizational communication by filtering or altogether withholding information. Thus, the role of gatekeeper can be a powerful one regardless of the number of direct or indirect ties a given gatekeeper has and regardless of their official position. For example, administrative assistants are the quintessential gatekeepers, as admins generally control the flow of information among managers and employees.

When discussing power related to social networks, it is critical to consider not only how network connections enable individuals or coalitions to become powerful, but also how they may serve to marginalize. Given the role of homophily, or similarity, in building strong ties and the related benefits of homophilous networks, marginalized populations may be left out of networks that offer access and power, thus perpetuating marginalization within the workplace. Research bears this out for both formal and informal organizational networks. For example, Falce and Watanabe (2020) found that women working in higher education have smaller research and friendship networks than male counterparts and were more likely to be on the periphery of research and friendship networks than men, who were more central. The exception to this trend was committee (service) networks, which showed no difference in structure between women and men. Looking at networks at a more macro level, Lobnibe (2018) proposed that institutional structures are characterized by systemic racism, which impacts outcomes for international graduate students and scholars who are expected to engage in the academic practice of networking with senior scholars to advance in their careers. Given the tendency to create networks of similar others, both structural advantages and disadvantages are replicated, potentially excluding international students from powerful networks that could help career advancement. Similarly, Lubbers (2022) argues that although "systemic forces now appear somewhat distanced from everyday interactions, social networks still reproduce, mitigate, or exacerbate systemic inequity" (p. 3) and proposes that in order to invoke structural resilience, network studies and practices should focus less on *who* is included in particular networks and more on *how* they are included (e.g., identifying microaggressions, exploitation, and control).

This section has highlighted the general ways in which network concepts can be applied to the study of organizational communication and touched on the real-world implications that these practices have for individuals and populations within networks. The following sections will dig deeper into the origins of, and subsequent advances in, organizational network studies and what this means in terms of social organization (O_2) related to the organization (O_3).

The Origin of Social Network Theory

Network concepts are interdisciplinary and international and have been adopted among a variety of fields, including communication, biology, mathematics, social science, anthropology, and computer science. Network theory as related to social and communication networks has roots in social science, psychological sciences, mathematics, and management communication. Scott (2000) traces three traditions in the development of social network analysis. The first is Harvard researchers in the 1930s who studied small groups and made advances in the mathematical basis of social network analysis, graph theory. These researchers were influenced by Gestalt theories in psychology, which stress "the patterns through which thought and perceptions are structured. These organized patterns are regarded as 'wholes' or systems that have properties distinct from those of their 'parts' which, furthermore, *determine* the nature of those parts" (Scott, 2000, p. 8, emphasis in original). Although Gestalt psychology was rooted in the idea of perception, researchers Jacob Moreno, Kurt Lewin, and Fritz Heider applied the concepts to study the influence of social contacts on one's actions, psychological development, and shared perception of the environment in which the group exists (Scott, 2000). Moreno is credited with developing the sociogram, or diagram where actors are represented as points, with the lines connecting the nodes representing the relationships (Fredericks & Durand, 2005; Scott, 2000, p. 16). This led to the birth of sociometry.

The sociogram, as seen in Figure 9.1, is still used in network theory and analysis today. From the 1930s to the 1940s, network concepts were applied to a number of settings, including organizational studies (e.g., the Hawthorne Studies (see Chapter 6) and geographic communities of place (Fredericks & Durand, 2005). Out of this tradition came the articulation of foundational structural concepts such as *cliques*, the tightly connected subgroups that exist within many networks, and the idea that larger networks can be studied by analyzing the connections within and between the smaller groups that serve as the building blocks of these structures.

The second tradition of network studies, rooted in work conducted by Manchester anthropologists, considered the role of conflict and power in the development of social structures. This work was heavily influenced by Radcliffe-Brown, whose theory of functionalism emphasized the interconnection of all aspects of society as vital to a functioning society, similar to the interdependence of biological functions. Using graph theory, researchers in this tradition used sociometrics to systemize the structural properties of social relations (Scott, 2000). Coining the term *network* as related to sociology, these researchers identified standard network properties, such as *density* (the number of actual connections out of the total number of possible connections within a network), *content* (the meaning or basis of relations within a network), tie reciprocity and strength, and *reachability* (the degree

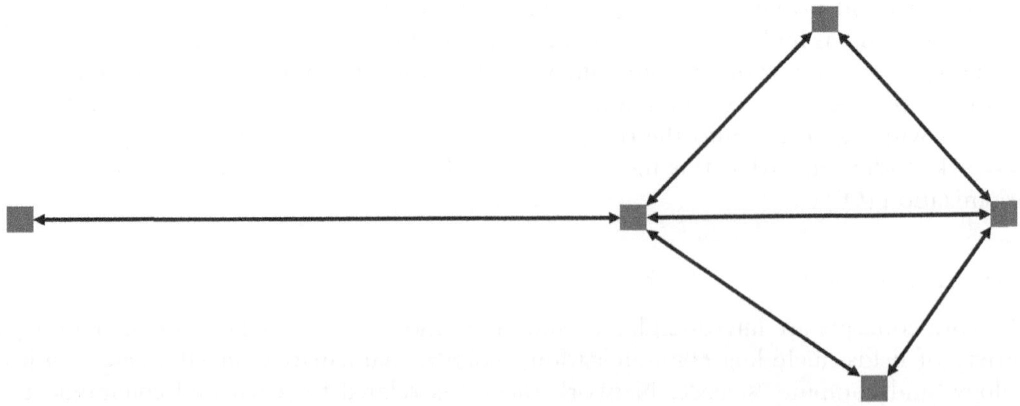

Figure 9.1 Example of a sociogram

to which all members can connect through a limited number of steps). Additionally, they formalized work on cliques and clusters and highlighted the importance of the *ego network* (Scott, 2000).

The third tradition, born out of work at Harvard, expanded the analytical capabilities of network studies through the inclusion of algebraic models and multidimensional scaling, allowing researchers to provide value and direction to the connections among actors, as well as calculate relationships in terms of social distance and map them in a social space (Scott, 2000). These advances allowed for a study of network properties regardless of context, thus moving network analysis out of purely interpersonal relations and into the study of other (nonhuman) actors such as organizations. As technology advanced, so did the ability to analyze larger networks from different perspectives, eventually leading to network analysis in its current form, in which networks are both a sociological construct and a mathematical object (Borgatti & Halgin, 2011).

As network theory spread into the field of communication, scholars began to focus on the importance of communication in understanding the implications of connections (Monge & Contractor, 2003), tying why and how we communicate to how networks are formed. For example, in studying network rebuilding after Hurricane Katrina, communication was enacted as an adaptive strategy, as shifts in how and why organizational leaders were communicating at different points in time affected network composition (Doerfel et al., 2011). Directly after the hurricane, organizational leaders reported communicating about safety and emergency needs, leading to networks composed primarily of personal contacts. However, once those needs were established, communication shifted outward to acquiring resources to get organizations functional, which included reaching out to partners outside of the immediate area, relying on indirect and weak ties, and then eventually returning to a new state of normalcy consisting of primarily pre-disaster ties with some post-disaster ties integrated into the network. Knowing what people were communicating about tells a fuller story and better explains the network development than does looking solely at structure.

Communication and Organizing in Social Networks

Communication and organizing are the building blocks of networks because, as stated in Chapter 1, it is through communication that we organize into social collectives. It is through our communication choices that we draw people into our networks. While sometimes this is based on convenience, such as proximity, we often make these communication choices strategically. Returning to the C-O cycle explored throughout the text, human agency is integral within networks because it is through actively seeking out others for specific purposes that networks are created. Related to organizations, this happens on both the intra- and interorganizational level. For example, emergency networks emerged after the Exxon Valdez oil spill that consisted of already existing organizations whose interactions were altered as a result of working together to respond to the Alaskan crisis (Topper & Carley, 1999). Some formed new alliances, while others altered their former relationships to fit the context of the new crisis. Such emergency interaction led to the creation of alternative network forms that best accommodated the parties involved.

Within social science, Burt's (1982) theory of structural action is a seminal approach to network studies that both illustrates and defines the interplay of network communication and structure. Earlier approaches to network studies, such as Blau's (1977) theory of macrosocial interaction, focused on the distributions of people in social positions. Blau (1977) argued that the relations between and among people of different positions are influenced by the frequency distributions of these people in the overall population. Alternatively, Burt's (1982) theoretical perspective of a structural theory of action posited both relational and positional motivations for social interaction. Burt (1982) based his theory on the premise that action is purposive. Actors are motivated by resources offering the greatest utility as revealed by evaluation of the alternatives. Structural action, the concept underlying Burt's theory, assumes that an actor evaluates the utility of alternatives independently and in regard to others. These actors, alternatives, and actions are all patterned by the context in which they exist. Thus, Burt's theory focuses on the idea of human agency as enabled or constrained by the macro-level environment in which the individual was embedded, and therefore, individuals are constrained by the very structure that their choices serve to reinforce. Similarly, Granovetter's view of embeddedness (discussed earlier) focuses on the reciprocal relationship that human agency and social structure share, through which communication choices both create and are guided by social organization.

Monge and Contractor's (2003) multi-theoretical multi-level (MTML) theorizing underscores this concept across social settings, as they argued for the application of a theoretical lens to examine the *why* behind the *how* actors come together to create networks within the context of broader, global systems. Such theorizing highlights the idea that "global organizations are processes, not places" (Monge & Contractor, 2003, p. 4), underscoring the connection between O_1 and O_2, both coincident with and distinct from O_3. The next section will examine how these network processes play out in the creation of formal and emergent networks.

Networks and Organizations

The development of network studies related to organizational communication has focused on applying the previously described network concepts in a variety of organizational settings with a focus on the interplay of formal and informal communication relationships and their effect on individual and organizational outcomes.

There have been some shifts in network research that have taken place as society has changed, most markedly with the rise of information and communication technologies (ICTs) and the accompanying shift from traditional hierarchies to a more horizontal organizational structure (see Chapter 7). ICTs have led to the ability to communicate across time and distance, allowing for organizations to operate on a global scale and a reconceptualization of how organizations communicate with both internal and external stakeholders. However, while the focus and scope of network studies have changed, one could argue that advances in ICTs only highlight the core concepts of social network theory. (See Chapter 19 for more information on ICTs.)

Formal and Emergent Networks in Organizations

Network research in organizational communication has focused on how a combination of the formal and informal ties in and between organizations can lead to power, influence, identification, innovation, alliances, and productivity. Formal and emergent networks coexist and complement each other (Monge & Contractor, 2003) on multiple, interdependent levels, including personal, group, organizational, and interorganizational (Stohl, 1995). Networks can take many forms related to organizations, such as personal contact networks, information flows within and between groups, strategic alliances among organizations, global network organizations, or employee networks supported by enterprise network software (Monge & Contractor, 2003, p. 3). According to Krackhardt and Hanson (1993, p. 104), while "the formal organization is the skeleton of a company, the informal is the central nervous system driving the collective thought processes, actions, and reactions of its business units."

The formal/informal dichotomy in network studies in some ways represents the implicit idea that the formal network is a predesignated entity. While the organization (O_3) is formed and sustained through communication links, the configuration of those links is often (but not always) treated as both a context for and direct result of the organizational communication. As we have discussed throughout this text, anytime there is O_3, O_1 and O_2 must be present. From this perspective, all organizational structures begin with rules for interaction designated by the individual(s) who conceptualize the organization (O_2). For example, the formal structure of the Ford Motor plant was created through officially sanctioned rules for communication (i.e., the organizational hierarchy) established by Henry Ford. These rules constituted the formal structure. When enacted and re-enacted by Ford and his employees, formal structure was "created" and reinforced. Because industries are also networks through which influence flows, it is worth noting that Ford's ideas were likely influenced by classical management theories, which were a common characterization of organizational structure during this timeframe and were broadly adopted (see Chapter 5).

Studies in intra-organizational networks primarily focus on how the O_1 and O_2 that take place "within" the organizations impact employees, as well as supporting or changing the overall organizational structure. Such studies focus on O_3 as the antecedent for organizational communication while simultaneously acknowledging that the organizational structure can be reinforced or changed by the communication that takes place within it. The main drivers for change in organizational networks are agency (motivation of actors to engage with the old/new partners), opportunity, inertia (e.g., pressures to stay the same or change), and external or random factors (Ahuja et al., 2012). Driven by these factors, organizational actors make decisions to create, maintain, or dissolve ties, which then changes both ego and whole-network structures. The ability to affect structural change can be enabled or constrained by issues such as organizational culture regarding who "can" talk to whom, individual preferences, and other factors.

A good example of the interplay of formal and emergent structure in organizational communication is found in early network literature focused on how the informal communication patterns engaged in by employees and managers often did not follow the organizational chain of command but rather created new, and sometimes more powerful, connections. For example, the *grapevine* is an emergent network that is temporarily created around specific messages, often gossip or informal organizational information (Davis, 1953). Despite the fact that the information is informal, it is often integral to both employee and management sensemaking can serve as an important feedback mechanism for organizational management (Davis, 1953, 1978; Goldhaber, 1993). Emergent networks within organizations can be mapped in several ways, including advice networks, trust networks, and communication networks (Krackhardt & Hanson, 1993). Ties in such networks are often stronger and more durable because they are based on personal connection, as opposed to formally designated organizational lines. As we tend to share more sensitive information with those to whom we are emotionally close, ties in emergent networks such as the grapevine or trust networks may provide access to exclusive or proprietary information that may not reach the same actors through formal network linkages.

However, not all ties in emergent networks are strong and durable, and not all strong and durable ties are advantageous. As previously mentioned, weak ties, or ties with those actors with whom individuals have *loose connections that are not connected to many similar contacts*. Weak ties can be part of a formal network (e.g., someone in an interdepartmental workgroup) or emergent, as employees become friends with members of the organization outside of their usual workgroup. Weak ties then fill a brokerage role between two densely connected (well-interconnected) groups, providing information that would not otherwise be available to members within dense subgroups. Such ties can be useful as they may provide information about opportunities outside of an individual's immediate group and can provide the impetus and connections to galvanize collective action (e.g., gathering support to unionize). That said, weak ties are not helpful in all situations. For example, weak ties between work units have been shown to speed up projects when knowledge is not complex but slow down work as knowledge increases in complexity (Hansen, 1999). In a study of interorganizational research and development, Michelfelder and Kratzer (2013, p. 1159) found that a combination of strong and weak ties can have a "mutually reinforcing effect on innovation outcomes if combined rather than considered separately."

Network Components, Overall Structure, and Organizational Outcomes

Tichy et al. (1979) identified three network properties as relevant to organizational communication: transactional content, the nature of links, and structural characteristics. Transactional content is what is exchanged among actors; for example, exchange of affect (such as friendship), exchange of power, exchange of information, and exchange of goods or services. Tichy et al. (1979) argue that networks can be developed for each of these types of content, that an individual's position or membership in each network may vary, and that these networks may or may not overlap. The nature of the links is the strength and qualitative nature of the ties, which can be conceptualized in terms of intensity (i.e., strength of the tie), reciprocity (whether ties are one-way or reciprocal), clarity of expectations (link agreement on overall network goals), and multiplexity (the degree to which links share one or more roles, such as friend *and* coworker vs. friend *or* coworker). Structural characteristics include the external network, the *total* internal network, *clusters* (subsections) within the organizational network, and individual roles within the network.

Similar to Granovetter's work on weak ties, Burt's (1982) theory emphasizes the importance of *structural holes*, or parts of the social structure in which people can serve as a broker between network clusters that would be otherwise unconnected. Burt argues actors who bridge structural holes have a "vision advantage that can translate into social capital" (Burt, 2004, p. 351). *Social capital* is a concept distinct from but directly related to networks, which captures the idea that benefits accrue from being part of a social network. Burt argues that position in the network can affect one's access to social capital. The actor's ability to broker information gives the actor the advantages commonly associated with weak ties: less amplified reciprocity, less inclination toward groupthink, and more access to novel information. Additionally, an actor filling a structural hole can enjoy the power that comes from connecting those who are otherwise unconnected. While many bridges spanning structural holes are also weak ties, Burt's theory posits that their power comes not from tie strength, but from the fact that they are non-redundant (i.e., filling a position that no other actor in the network fills). In fact, he suggests that if one can bridge a strong tie, there may be more advantage in the form of interpersonal influence. Multiple studies have emphasized the importance of structural holes for power, innovation, and knowledge sharing (Ahuja, 2000; Gargiulo & Benassi, 2000), but also highlight the importance of balance between network closure and opportunities for brokerage.

Organization and the Environment

Organizations operate as systems (see Chapter 2), both importing and exporting information and goods from the environment. Organizational network scholars in the 1980s and 90s introduced the core concepts of embeddedness and the networked organization to explain how organizations are essentially a form of network. In attempting to answer the question of how social relations impact the behavior and economics of organizations, Granovetter (1985) articulated the concept of embeddedness – the idea that organizations are so constrained by social relations that the traditional, rational view of organizational behavior does not accurately characterize organizational reality. Granovetter (1985) argued that embeddedness is ongoing and socially (re)constructed during each interaction with members of the organization and regular contacts outside of the organization (e.g., supply chains). Embeddedness guards against market opportunism as participants build relationships rooted in trust and reciprocity. Over time, these relationships are guided by a general knowledge of what one can expect from another partner, further embedding the actors within their shared network.

Powell (1990) formalized the idea that the network as an organizational form is neither market nor hierarchy. His work distinguished the contemporary organization as something distinct from the traditional governance structure of the hierarchy, which wards off opportunism at the cost of bureaucracy, and the opportunism of the market. Rather, he identified the basic assumption of network relations the idea that "one party is dependent on resources controlled by another, and that there are gains to be made by the pooling of resources" (Powell, 1990, p. 303). This dependency enters parties in a series of "reciprocal, preferential, [and] mutually supportive" interactions by which they are able to accomplish their own goals without sacrificing the goals of network partners (Powell, 1990, p. 303). As actors repeatedly interact in the same social patterns to drive resource acquisition and mutual gain, they create organizational and interorganizational structures. Unlike traditional hierarchies, these structures do not represent predetermined lines of communication but rather socially constructed pathways. Such structures are more flexible than traditional conceptualizations of the organization because they can be altered by changing communication to accommodate changing needs or conditions. Although he did not focus on communication per se, Powell's articulation of the organization as a network form was an articulation of the process of the CCO (see Chapter 3) approach related to organizations, with the C-O cycle clearly identifiable (see Chapter 1).

Interorganizational networks are the connections organizations have with other organizations, which can be studied in the same way as internal organizational networks. Interorganizational network scholarship that considers cooperation or competition across organizational boundaries developed alongside traditional organizational network research. The basic premise of interorganizational network research is that organizations form relationships in order to manage environmental uncertainty, share or leverage resources, and work together to address macro-level issues that affect their shared environment (Doerfel et al., 2010; Hannan & Freeman, 1977; Monge et al., 2008). Interorganizational network studies often examine how the connections among organizations lead to benefits for the involved organizations. Supply chains are a common example of interorganizational networks. Other examples include the contacts that organizations have in the community in which they operate, including community organizations, professional organizations, and the local government, as well as organizations that come together for a shared cause to advance macro-level interests. For example, nongovernmental organizations (NGOs) worked together, creating interorganizational networks to promote democratic elections in Croatia (Doerfel & Taylor, 2004). Although the NGOs normally competed for monies from the same agencies, they found that the benefits of promoting democracy in Croatia outweighed their individual needs for funding. Such interorganizational networks can be more temporary than interorganizational alliances formed around industry needs during stable times, as they are likely to return to at least some of their regular networking patterns after they accomplish their joint task, as was the case with NGOs in Croatia.

Toward the end of the 20th century, network studies began a natural shift toward examining the effect of ICTs on network development and evolution. As early as the 1990s, organizations were beginning to adopt email and other communication technologies to facilitate organizational communication (see Chapter 19). Recognizing this shift, network studies started to focus more on theoretical motives for network emergence that play out on multiple levels (e.g., Monge & Contractor, 2003; Su et al., 2010). As the development of ICTs progressed to offer more communicative capabilities, it became clear that the use of such technologies had a dramatic impact on both communication (O_1) and structuring (O_2), consequently affecting the organizational form (O_3).

Social Networks and Organizations in the 21st Century

Social networks in the 21st century are more likely to span boundaries than organizational networks in the past. This is largely fueled by ICTs such as the Internet, social media sites, and mobile phones but also relates to changing geopolitical contexts and generational shifts that require more nimble networks and more multiplex ties.

ICTs have dramatically altered the way that individuals communicate. We are no longer bound by geography and can use technology to *disembed* from traditional, geographically based networks and *re-embed* in new networks based on interest and opportunity. ICTs affect network structure in many ways, in that they allow for the creation of networks that are loosely coupled and flexible, with potentially unlimited boundaries. Strong ties can be reinforced by the communication redundancy offered by ICTs, while weak ties can be created and maintained, and even strengthened over time, by the structural opportunity provided by each medium (Haythornewaite, 2002). Additionally, latent, dormant, and indirect ties can be easily (re)activated via ICTs. Online platforms offer the structure to alter communication patterns in terms of increased frequency, the ability to direct communication to specific individuals, groups, or a mass audience, and often serve as a repository for information. Shifting social and organizational patterns supported by ICTs have given rise to workforces that are no longer co-located and rely strongly on technology to accomplish work tasks. While this trend was growing for several years before 2020, shutdowns related to COVID-19 and the capacities of Zoom (among other technologies) catapulted many people into remote work. While the remote worker population already existed, supported by technologies such as email, videoconferencing, intranet, and other enterprise management systems, COVID-19 forced an acceleration of this process for employees, even in industries such as education, where face-to-face communication was considered a necessity.

From a network point of view, there are drawbacks to a high number of employees working remotely. While employees can connect and facilitate work tasks via ICTs, they are much less likely to be part of the emergent networks that come from informal, spontaneous, and casual organizational communication, as online work communication tends to focus more on tasks than social interaction. The absence of social talk and access to emergent networks can impact employee identification with the organization, its values, and the employees' workgroup (Scott & Timmerman, 1999).

Thus, ICTs facilitate the ability to be part of the organizational network, but often at the risk of not sharing the same level or types of relationships that co-located employees have. For example, Yang et al. (2022) found that during COVID-19, collaboration among Microsoft employees became more static and siloed and had fewer bridges connecting various parts of the organization. Additionally, synchronous communication decreased, while asynchronous communication increased. As many organizations likely faced similar communication issues, they began instituting "return to office" policies in 2022 and beyond. Ironically, even the company that owns Zoom, the ultimate work-from-home technology, instituted a hybrid return-to-office policy in late 2023. While many people were happy to return to a physical workplace when shutdown restrictions were lifted, many others wanted to continue to work remotely, citing a better work/life balance and the ability to be as, or even more, productive than when working in an office setting. This has led to an ongoing negotiation between organizations that want the network benefits and control of having employees on-site and employees who seek more flexibility in their work.

Decreased network strength and utility in virtual organizational networks is not a given. That is, whether ICTs engage or distance people depends, in part, on how they are enacted. Although ICTs have established technological features, user agency comes into play because each user may decide to enact technology differently. This is influenced by a combination of the materiality of the technology, individual schema, and socio-cultural norms (e.g., organizational norms and group norms). Users can reinforce technical structures by continuing to use ICTs in designated ways or reinvent existing technological structures by reimagining the ICTs use for new or novel purposes (Orlikowski, 2008), such as using Zoom for an informal work "happy hour" to maintain personal connections during COVID-19. Thus, social organization dependent on ICTs becomes a *socio-technical* structure by which actors are connected via the shared enactment of technology.

ICTs have also changed the nature of organizations' external communication. Stakeholder networks are the social structure through which institutions both influence and are influenced by stakeholders. While traditional models of stakeholder networks position the organization at the center of a network of stakeholders who have no direct connections with each other, ICTs enable the ability for various stakeholder groups to *see* communication between the organization and other stakeholder groups, thus shifting the conceptualization of stakeholder networks to one where the focal organization is one node in an interconnected network of various stakeholders who also have connections with each other. To that end, social media has become an increasingly necessary communication tool for organizational public relations and marketing, enabling organizations to further develop their brand through content and engage in more "informal" communication with stakeholders, both one-on-one and as a mass audience. Social media also allows stakeholders to communicate directly with each other. This can help strengthen ties with the organization, as stakeholders come to the social media sites and comment or even dialogue with each other and the organization. It also enables stakeholders to form coalitions and pressure organizations, such as when the CEO of Barilla Pasta said Barilla would only use "traditional families" in Barilla advertising (Chewning, 2015, p. 139). Barilla received backlash, much of it in the form of stakeholder protests on their Facebook page that led to an apology and the creation of an advisory board to promote diversity. The company then planned a new, more inclusive advertising campaign. Using hashtags and hyperlinks, stakeholders can also organize around a specific cause related to an organization, either in protest or in support (e.g., adopting organizational hashtags (e.g., stakeholders' sharing Unilever's #ClearAPlate to promote their partnership with Oxfam).

Additionally, organizations are increasingly entering, or even being drawn into, social movements and controversies that don't directly connect to the organizations but rather reflect organizational values and/or stakeholder expectations about how the organization should engage with specific social issues. Known as Corporate Social Advocacy, such stances reflect the influence that ICTs have afforded stakeholder networks and the increased transparency demanded of organizations. It has also provided new opportunities for organizations to connect with stakeholders in a real-time and value-driven way. For example, utilizing social media, stakeholders have drawn organizations into politics, such as the Black Lives Matter movement (specifically around the time of protests related to the murder of George Floyd in 2020), and the conflict between Israel and Hamas in 2023. This level of access and transparency has changed not only the dynamics of the organizational/stakeholder relationship but also highlights the power of stakeholder networks and how they can influence the organization.

Finally, as we begin to encounter more crises related to climate change, organizations are relying heavily on networks consisting of a mix of personal, professional, and government/nonprofit contacts to help them recover from complex and cascading crises that pile on top of each other with few breaks (Chewning et al., 2024). For example, in some areas of the US, such as Florida, between 2020 and 2022, organizations had to adapt to COVID-19, hurricanes, and other climate-related flooding that happened in quick succession and even simultaneously. In 2024, the US South, Midwest, and Northeast had to deal with severe weather episodes with destructive and even devastating results in quick succession, with little chance to recover from one crisis before the next one hit. Simultaneously, organizations worldwide were dealing with supply chain issues and fluctuating economies related to COVID-19.

As such, we now see organizations taking a cue from high-reliability organizations (HROs), or organizations that operate in high-risk contexts, and as a result, have a strong focus on safety and reliability in terms of contingency planning and building internal/external networks able to provide access and resources when the inevitable next crisis arrives. This is a departure from more traditional types of crisis response that positioned a crisis (weather-related or otherwise) as something to be discretely handled and moved past. Organizations are now building networks that acknowledge that they are part of a larger system in crisis, thus decentering the focus on the singular organization and re-centering the focus of crisis recovery to resilience and the interdependence of individual, organizational, and system-level recovery as integral to organizational recovery (Chewning et al., 2024).

Conclusion

Networks richly illustrate the connections among O_1, O_2, and O_3. The interplay of formal and informal communication inherent to networks creates both bottom-up and top-down social structures that can be reified into organizations. The changing nature of the organizational landscape, fueled by the rise of ICT and an emphasis on employee feedback and collaboration, has loosened both internal and external organizational boundaries, highlighting the ways in which individual connections create pathways for collaboration, innovation, and change.

As networks are driven by our human communication choices, they are flexible and adaptive, changing as individual-, group-, and organization-level needs change. While traditional network literature was primarily concerned with the social structures resulting from these choices, focusing on the communication processes that underlie the choices provides a richer understanding of why organizational networks emerge and evolve and how organizational members and leaders can create networks that maximize benefits on individual, organizational, and interorganizational levels.

Recommended Supplementary Readings

Krackhardt, D., & Hanson, J. R. (1993). Information networks: The company behind the chart. *Harvard Business Review,* July–August, 104–111.

This is an easy-to-follow article that explains the importance of informal networks in the organization.

Putnam, R. D. (2000). *Bowling alone: The collapse and revival of American community.* New York, NY: Simon & Schuster.

Bowling Alone *demonstrates the importance of social ties to the creation of social capital. While Putnam does not go into depth about organizational networks, he does demonstrate the importance of participation in community organizations to stronger relations on both the individual and community levels, thus implicitly connecting micro-, meso-, and macro-structures.*

Doerfel, M., Kim, M., Kwestel, M., Hyunsook, Y., & Quow, J. (2022). Resilience organizing: A multilevel communication framework. *Journal of Communication, 72*(6), 605–618.

This article connects networks to organizational and individual resilience related to crisis communication. It touches on many of the issues discussed in the section on networks in the 21st century in this chapter.

Monge, P. R., & Contractor, N. S. (2003). *Theories of communication networks.* New York, NY: Oxford University Press.

This book provides a comprehensive overview of communication networks and directly ties communication and social science theories to network formation.

Important Concepts: Define and Discuss

Bridge
Centrality
Density
Formal network
Emergent network

Gatekeeper
Grapevine
Groupthink
Interorganizational Networks
Liaison
Homophily
Nodes
Ties
Sociogram
Star
Strong tie
Weak tie

Discussion Questions

1 There is an old adage that says: "It's not what you know, but who you know." Given what you learned about network structure, what do you think that means? How can you build and leverage networks that are advantageous to your future career plans?
2 Think about your own networks in terms of your strong and weak ties. What benefits do you glean from each? In what ways do they inhibit you?
3 How can organizational leaders purposely structure organizational communication to avoid groupthink and spur innovation and diversity while at the same time building relationships and trust among members? (Hint: think about the interplay of emergent and formal networks and open/closed network structures.)
4 Think about where you currently work or somewhere you have worked in the past. Was there a difference between the formal network and the way that information really traveled throughout the organization? If so, which had a stronger influence on workflow: the formal or emergent network? If there was an emergent network, did it undermine or complement the formal network?
5 What are some communicative ways that you can combat groupthink?

Practitioners' Corner

Social network theory provides direction for organizational leaders who want to increase overall network benefits and individual organizational members who want to maximize their organizational advantage. The following suggestions provide direction for how network theory can provide direction when creating organizational-level opportunities for interaction:

- Create opportunities for social interaction: Organizational communication research supports the importance of "watercooler" talk (informal communication). Company picnics, parties, and other social events provide opportunities for organizational members to strengthen their ties, which can increase personal and organizational social capital. Social networking site such as LinkedIn and X are a great way to connect with others within your industry.
- Strategically balance strong and weak ties: Network research has demonstrated the importance of both strong and weak ties for success in organizations. Dense, cohesive clusters, such as departmental work units, tend to develop strong ties based on frequent communication

around shared goals. This often leads to trust and cooperation, which can be conducive to productivity. However, as mentioned earlier in the chapter, it can also lead to groupthink, which can stymie innovation and change. Research has shown that dense, closed networks are more useful in times of change and uncertainty (Krackhardt, 1992), while weak ties are better at providing exposure to new information and resources. However, the usefulness of weak ties can be mitigated by the complexity of the information being transferred (Hansen, 1999). Ultimately, the optimal structure of network relations can be affected by the overall goals of the network members (Ahuja, 2000), emphasizing the need for making strategic communication choices on both the individual and organizational levels.

- Work with emergent networks: Organizational leaders should pay attention to emergent communication practices, such as who department/organizational members turn to for advice and where work gets done or stalls. If there is an emergent leader to whom people turn instead of the formally designated leader, consider giving that person a larger role in the organization. If the formal workflow is less productive or followed than an employee-created workaround, consider redesigning the process.
- Bring in outside influences: social network theory emphasizes the importance of weak ties to combat groupthink and spark innovation. Bringing in organizational consultants and speakers and being part of a trade organization or community business council are effective ways to bring weak ties into the organizational network.
- Remember the importance of communication: While a communication network point of view focuses on the advantages or disadvantages offered by a given network structure, the content that flows through the links has implications that go beyond structural advantages. Kind words, helpful information, genuine interest, collegiality, and emotional intelligence all play a large role in the success and happiness of the individual employee and overall network.

References

Ahuja, G. (2000). Collaboration networks, structural holes, and innovation: A longitudinal study. *Administrative Science Quarterly*, *45*(3), 425–455. https://doi.org/10.2307/2667105

Ahuja, G., Soda, G., & Zaheer, A. (2012). The genesis and dynamics of organizational networks. *Organization Science*, *23*(2), 434–448. https://doi.org/10.1287/orsc.1110.0695

Blau, P. M. (1977). A macrosocial theory of social structure. *American Journal of Sociology*, *83*(1), 26–54. www.jstor.org/stable/2777762

Borgatti, S., & Halgin, D. (2011, May). On network theory. *Organizational Science*. Papers in Advance, pp. 1–24. https://doi.org/10.2139/ssrn.2260993

Borgatti, S. P., Carley, K. M., & Krackhardt, D. (2006). On the robustness of centrality measures under conditions of imperfect data. *Social Networks*, *28*, 124–136. https://doi.org/10.1016/j.socnet.2005.05.001

Borgatti, S. P., & Everett, M. G. (1997). Network analysis of 2-mode data. *Social Networks*, *19*, 243–269. https://doi.org/10.1016/S0378-8733(96)00301-2

Burt, R. S. (1982). *Toward a structural theory of action: Network models of social structure, perception, and action*. Academic Press.

Burt, R. S. (2004). Structural holes and good ideas. *American Journal of Sociology*, *110*(2), 349–399. https://doi.org/10.1086/421787

Capaldo, A. (2007). Network structure and innovation: The leveraging of a dual network as a distinctive relational capability. *Strategic Management Journal*, *28*, 585–608. https://doi.org/10.1002/smj.621

Castells, M. (2000). *The rise of the network society*. Wiley-Blackwell.

Chewning, L. V. (2015). Measuring the enactment of IRT via social media: What are organizations and stakeholders saying during crisis? In J. Blaney, & L. Alwine (Eds.), *Putting image repair to the test*. Lexington Books.

Chewning, L. V., Doerfel, M. L., Ballard, D., & Harrison, H. (2024). From crisis response to hi-resilience organizing. In V. Miller & S. Poole (Eds.) *Organizational communication theory and research*, pp. 605–624. https://doi.org/10.1515/9783110718508-031

Davis, K. (1953). Management communication and the grapevine. *Harvard Business Review*, *31*(5), 43–49.

Davis, K. (1978). Methods for studying informal communication. *Journal of Communication*, *28*(1), 112–116. https://doi.org/10.1111/j.1460-2466.1978.tb01572.x

Doerfel, M., Lai, C.-H., & Chewning, L. (2010). The evolutionary role of communication: Modeling social capital in disaster contexts. *Human Communication Research*, *36* (2). https://doi.org/10.1111/j.1468-2958.2010.01371.x

Doerfel, M., Chewning, L. & Lai, C. (2011). The evolution of networks and the resilience of interorganizational relationships after disaster. *Communication Monographs*, 80(4). https://doi.org/10.1080/03637751.2013.828157

Doerfel, M., & Taylor, M. (2004). Network dynamics of interorganizational cooperation: The Croatian civil society movement. *Communication Monographs*, *71*(4), 373–394. https://doi.org/10.1080/0363452042000307470

Falce, C. D., & Watanabe, M. (2020). Network marginalization of women in the workplace: A case in academia. *Journal of Women and Minorities in Engineering*, *26*(2), 155–175. https://doi.org/10.1615/JWomenMinorScienEng.2020029186

Fredericks, K. A., & Durand, M. M. (2005). The historical evolution and basic concepts of social network analysis. *New Directions for Evaluation, Special Issue: Social Network Analysis in Program Evaluation*, *107*, 15–23. https://onlinelibrary.wiley.com/doi/abs/10.1002/ev.158

Freeman, L. C. (1978). Centrality in social networks conceptual clarification. *Social Networks*, *1*, 215–239. https://doi.org/10.1016/0378-8733(78)90021-7

Fu, P., Sarpong, D., & Meissner, D. (2022). Recalibrating, reconfiguring, and appropriating innovation: A semantic network analysis of China's mass innovation and mass entrepreneurship (MIME) initiatives. *Journal of Technology Transfer*, *47*, 1506–1523. https://doi.org/10.1007/s10961-021-09878-x

Gargiulo, M., & Benassi, M. (2000). Trapped in your own net? Network cohesion, structural holes, and the adaptation of social capital. *Organization Science*, *11*(2), 183–196. www.jstor.org/stable/2640283

Goldhaber, G. (1993). *Organizational communication* (5th ed.). Brown and Benchmark.

Granovetter, M. (1984). *Getting a job*. University of Chicago Press.

Granovetter, M. (1985). Economic action and social structure: The problem of embeddedness. *American Journal of Sociology*, *91*(3), 481–510. www.jstor.org/stable/2780199

Hannan, M. T., & Freeman, J. (1977). The population ecology of organizations. *American Journal of Sociology*, *82*(5), 929–964. www.jstor.org/stable/2777807

Hansen, M. T. (1999). The search-transfer problem: The role of weak ties in sharing knowledge across sub units. *Administrative Science Quarterly*, *44*(1), 82–111. https://doi.org/10.2307/2667032

Haythornewaite, C. (2002). Strong, weak, and latent ties and the impact of new media. *Information Science*, *18*, 385–401. https://doi.org/10.1080/01972240290108195

Humalisto, N., Valve, H., & Åkerman, M. (2020). Making the circular economy online: A hyperlink analysis of the articulation of nutrient recycling in Finland. *Environmental Politics*, *30*(5), 833–853. https://doi.org/10.1080/09644016.2020.1817291

Krackhardt, D. (1992). The strength of strong ties. In N. Nohria, & R. G. Eccles (Eds.), *Networks and organizations: Structure, form, and action* (pp. 216–239). Harvard Business School Press.

Krackhardt, D., & Hanson, J. R. (1993). Information networks: The company behind the chart. *Harvard Business Review*, July–August, 104–111. https://hbr.org/1993/07/informal-networks-the-company-behind-the-chart

Lobnibe, J. F. (2018). From networking to nepotism: Systemic racism and the paradox of academic networks. *Advances in Social Sciences Research Journal*, *5*(8), 156–167. https://doi.org/10.14738/assrj.58.3295

Lubbers, A. J. (2022). Social networks and the resilience of marginalized communities. In E. Lazega, T. Snijders, & R. Wittek (Eds.), *Social networks and social resilience* (pp. 1–16). Edward Elgar Publishing Limited. https://doi.org/10.4337/9781803925783.00006

Michelfelder, I., & Kratzer, H. (2013). Why and how combining strong and weak ties within a single interorganizational R&D collaboration outperforms other collaboration structures. *The Journal of Product Innovation Management*, *30*(6), 1159–1177. https://doi.org/10.1111/jpim.12052

Monge, P., Heiss, B. M., & Margolin, D. B. (2008). Communication network evolution in organizational communities. *Communication Theory*, *18*(4), 449–477. https://doi.org/10.1111/j.1468-2885.2008.00330.x

Monge, P. R., & Contractor, N. S. (2003). *Theories of communication networks*. Oxford University Press.

Nohria, N. (1998). Is a network perspective a useful way of studying organizations? In G. H. Hickman (Ed.), *Leading organizations: Perspectives for a new era* (pp. 287–301). Sage.

Orlikowski, W. (2008). Using technology and constituting structures: A practice lens for studying technology in organizations. In M. S. Ackerman, C. A. Halverson, T. Erickson, & W. A. Kellogg (Eds.), *Resources, co-evolution and artifacts: Computer supported cooperative work*. Springer.

Podolny, J. M., & Baron, J. N. (1997). Resources and relationships: Social networks and mobility in the workplace. *American Sociological Review*, *62*, 673–693. www.jstor.org/stable/2657354

Powell, W. W. (1990). Neither market nor hierarchy: Network forms of organization. *Research in Organizational Behavior*, *12*, 295–336. www.jstor.org/stable/2657354

Rogers, E. M., & Agarwala-Rogers, R. (1976). *Diffusion of innovations*. Free Press.

Scott, C., & Timmerman, C. E. (1999). Communication technology: Use and multiple workplace identifications among organizational teleworkers with varied degrees of virtuality. Paper presented at the International Communication Association Convention, May, San Francisco.

Scott, J. (2000). *Social network analysis: A handbook* (2nd ed.). Sage.

Stohl, C. (1995). *Organizational communication: Connectedness in action*. Sage.

Su, C., Huang, M., & Contractor, N. (2010). Understanding the structures, antecedents, and outcomes of organizational learning and knowledge transfer: A multi-theoretical and multilevel network analysis. *European Journal of International Management*, *4*(6), 576–601.

Tichy, N., Tushman, M., & Fombrun, C. (1979). Social network analysis for organizations. *The Academy of Management Review*, *4*(4), 507–519. https://doi.org/10.5465/amr.1979.4498309

Topper, C. M., & Carley, K. M. (1999). A structural perspective on the emergence of network organizations. *Journal of Mathematical Sociology*, *24*(1), 67–96. https://doi.org/10.1080/0022250X.1999.9990229

Yang, L., Holtz, D., Jaffe, S., Suri, S., Sinha, S., Weston, J., Joyce, C., Shah, N., Sherman, K., Hecht, B., & Teevan, J. (2022). The effects of remote work on collaboration among information workers. *Nature Human Behavior*, *6*, 43–54.

10 Workplace Relationships

Yejin Shin

Workplace relationships are central to organizational processes. In fact, some scholars conceptualize organizations as essentially systems of relationships (e.g., Wheatley, 1999). Thus, the quality of an organization is inextricably linked to the quality of the relationships among its members (Sias, 2014). The more functional the relationships among organizational members, the more functional the organization and vice versa. Workplace relationships are ongoing social entities characterized by patterned interdependent interaction (Keyton, 2017). Communication is, therefore, fundamental to workplace relationship dynamics (Sias, 2014). While there are many types of workplace relationships, this chapter addresses the workplace relationships that have been the primary focus of organizational communication research – supervisor–subordinate, peer, friendship, and romantic workplace relationships. For each relationship type, this chapter provides a brief overview of how research in that area has developed over time, highlighting the contributions of communication scholars. Consistent with the broader theme of this book, this chapter concludes with a discussion of how workplace relationship research has approached communication, organization, and culture.

Supervisor–Subordinate Relationships

Supervisor–subordinate relationships are among the most frequently studied topics in organizational research (Sias, 2009). The organizational communication discipline arguably began with the study of these relationships. As seen in Chapter 1, organizational communication can trace its roots to the 1940s, when research in management, industrial relations, and industrial psychology turned attention to supervisory communication (Redding, 1985). The goal of such research was to improve communication between supervisors (at that time referred to as *superiors*) and their employees in the service of organizational efficiency and effectiveness (see Chapter 6).

The Beginning: Supervisor–Subordinate Communication and Leadership

Early research on supervisor–subordinate relationships was conducted by leadership and management scholars and mainly focused on the supervisor (see Chapter 17), conceptualizing, at least implicitly, subordinate employees as passive recipients of leadership (Sias et al., 2002). Early theories, for example, centered on a leader's traits (e.g., intelligence, extroversion, attractiveness) and assumed leaders are born, not made (e.g., Ghiselli, 1963). Later theories centered leadership on behavior or styles, but still positioned employees as passive partners in the relationship (e.g., Blake & Mouton, 1964). Theoretical development

DOI: 10.4324/9781003484639-13

eventually acknowledged individual employees as relevant to leadership. For instance, situational leadership theory conceptualized employee readiness (i.e., ability and willingness) as central to effective leadership (Hersey & Blanchard, 1982). The supervisor, however, remained the dominant partner responsible for matching his or her leadership style to the employee (see Chapters 6 and 7).

A Turning Point: Leader–Member Exchange Theory

Vertical Dyad Linkage theory (Graen & Cashman, 1975) recognized the *dyadic relational* nature of supervisor-subordinate relationships. Unlike previous theories, it emphasized the employee's active and central role in the mutual negotiation of the supervisor-subordinate relationship. Later renamed leader–member exchange (LMX) theory (Graen & Scandura, 1987), the theory has had a significant impact on research about leadership and the supervisor–subordinate relationship.

LMX's primary contribution was conceptualizing the supervisor–subordinate (i.e., leader–member) relationship as an exchange relationship in which the partners mutually exchange resources – conceptualizing the dyad, not just the supervisor, as active agents. Different types of exchanges create different types of relationships. Thus, LMX theory introduced the notion that supervisors do not have an overall leadership style, but rather treat their employees differently and develop different types of relationships with their various subordinate employees (Graen & Scandura, 1987). According to LMX, supervisors form two primary types of relationships with their employees. *Leadership exchange* (high-quality exchange) relationships are characterized by open communication, trust, support, and negotiating latitude for the employee. *Supervisory exchange* (low-quality exchange) relationships, in contrast, are characterized by low levels of trust and support, less open communication, and direct supervision. Not surprisingly, employees who report having leadership exchange relationships enjoy many positive outcomes including access to higher-quality information (Sias, 2005), higher job satisfaction (Turban et al., 1990), and better job performance (Michael et al., 2006), than those who report having supervisory exchange relationships.

Another Turning Point: Communication and LMX

While much LMX research was, and continues to be, conducted by management scholars, communication scholars provided an important development by conceptualizing supervisor–subordinate relationships as socially constructed. Fairhurst and Chandler (1989), for example, studied how supervisor–subordinate relationships were distinguished communicatively. They found that higher-quality LMX relationships were characterized by mutual persuasion while lower-quality relationships were characterized by authority and accentuation of power distance. Similarly, Fairhurst (1993) found that low-quality LMX relationships were characterized by accentuation of power distance via monitoring, face-threatening acts, and conflict. In contrast, high-quality LMX relationships are characterized by insider talk, value convergence, and non-routine problem-solving.

Along these lines, Yrle et al. (2003) found high-quality LMX relationships are characterized by two distinct communication patterns: *Coordination* (i.e., an interaction that enables mutual coordination of activities) and *participation* (i.e., interaction by which subordinates participate in decision-making processes). Similarly, Fix and Sias (2006) found that high-quality LMX relationships are characterized by *person-centered communication*, which encourages employees to consider the complexities of situations, recognize themselves as autonomous agents, and participate in decision-making and problem-solving. Low-quality relationships, in contrast, are characterized by *position-centered communication*, which accentuates authority and direct supervision. They also found that employees whose supervisors used person-centered communication reported higher levels of job satisfaction than those whose supervisors used position-centered communication. Jian and Dalisay (2017) found that high-quality LMX relationships are associated with higher-quality communication (i.e., communication characterized by efficiency, coordination, and accuracy) and that quality LMX communication is positively associated with employee commitment to the organization. In sum, communication research indicates that communication patterns and practices distinguish LMX relationships and that this differential communication is associated with different employee outcomes.

Supervisor–Subordinate Relationship Functions

In addition to leadership, research has centered on three other primary functions of the supervisor–subordinate relationship – information exchange, feedback, and mentoring. Studies consistently identify the supervisor–subordinate relationship as an important site of *information exchange*. Employees rely on their supervisor for important information about tasks, performance, and organizational issues (Sias, 2009). Similarly, supervisors rely on their employees for information, using them as extra sets of eyes and ears (Ramaswami et al., 1997). The quality of a supervisor–subordinate relationship is positively associated with the quality of information exchanged by the relationship partners (Sias, 2005).

Employees also rely on their supervisor for constructive *feedback* about their job performance, which is key to professional and technical development (Ashford, 1993; Fedor, 1991). Research suggests high-quality supervisor–subordinate relationships are associated with effective performance feedback. Steelman and Rutkowski (2004), for example, found that employees with high-quality relationships with their supervisors (e.g., high levels of trust and likability) are more likely to listen to and accept negative feedback from them, and supervisors who maintain high-quality relationships with their employees tend to give constructive feedback. Lam et al. (2017) also found that because an employee's performance information needs tend to be met by supervisors with a quality LMX relationship, the employee engages in less frequent feedback-seeking behavior. These studies highlight the importance of developing high-quality LMX relationships for performance and professional development.

Because of their experience, knowledge, and positions of authority, supervisors are often important mentors for their employees. Mentoring is "a specific type of relationship in which the mentor functions as a type of 'guide' for the development and career advancement of the protégé/mentee" (Sias, 2009, p. 29). Mentoring relationships are unique in two ways: they emphasize unidirectional information flow from mentor to protégé, and they focus on the protégé's (rather than the mentor's) career. Organizations vary in whether they implement formal mentoring programs or whether mentoring emerges informally. In either case, research consistently demonstrates that mentoring benefits the protégé, including high levels of adjustment/satisfaction, career guidance, and role modeling (Jablin, 2001; Ragins & Scandura, 1997). LMX research indicates that mentoring is characteristic of high-quality leadership exchange relationships (Thomas & Lankau, 2009), highlighting another way employees who lack such relationships are disadvantaged.

Supervisor–Subordinate Relationship Development

Research has examined how and why these dynamic relationships develop. Much of this work is grounded in LMX theory, and several factors influence the likelihood that a supervisor–subordinate relationship will develop into a leadership exchange (high-quality) relationship. Among these are the employee's job competence (e.g., Bauer & Green, 1996) and the supervisor's ability to train and help employees (e.g., Cogliser & Schriesheim, 2000). Employees with an internal, rather than external, locus of control are also more likely to enjoy a high-quality relationship with their supervisor, while supervisors with authoritarian personalities are more likely to maintain supervisory (low-quality) LMX relationships (Kinicki & Vecchio, 1994).

Although leadership theories and models are often considered universally applicable and generalizable, scholars have pointed out the colonial nature of LMX development (see Chapters 14 and 17). Allen (2023) suggested differences in organizational relationships and experiences are influenced by privilege and power. For example, relative to dissimilarity, demographic similarity between supervisors and subordinates has been linked to a higher level of LMX, especially early in the relationship (Bauer & Green, 1996; Sergeant & Frenkel, 1998). Underrepresented group members (e.g., women, racial-ethnic minorities, LGBTQIA+ employees, and the disabled) experience negative stereotypes, resulting in compromised LMX development in the initial role-taking and subsequent role-making stages (Goldberg & McKay, 2015; Parker, 2005; see Chapter 14). In other words, dissimilarity leads to underrepresented or stigmatized groups experiencing low-quality LMX because they are more likely to be supervised by someone from a different demographic group.

Along these lines, minorities and women are disadvantaged in mentoring relationships because they are often absent from the upper echelons (Parker, 2005; Ragins, 2002). Underrepresented or stigmatized groups experience different organizational climates, and it may be difficult for a mentor or a protégé who does not share these "micro climates" (Ragins, 2002). This emphasizes the necessity for more research on differences and inclusive supervisor-subordinate research (see Chapter 14).

In sum, the supervisor–subordinate relationship is central to individual experiences and organizational processes. As such, it has long been a primary focus of organizational studies scholars and continues to hold its place as a central topic. Communication scholars were important in moving this literature forward by identifying and emphasizing the role of communication in constituting these relationships, enhancing our understanding of supervisor–subordinate relationships as dynamic entities.

Peer Coworker Relationships

Peer coworker relationships are relationships between employees at the same hierarchical level in the organization, neither of whom has formal authority over the other. With the large focus on supervisor–subordinate relationships, peer relationships have received comparatively less research attention (Sias, 2014). However, given the typical number of peers and the large amount of time peer coworkers generally spend with one another, they are an important workplace relationship type.

The Beginning: Alternatives to Formal Mentoring

Peer relationship research began with Kram and Isabella's (1985) study, which focused on identifying alternatives to formal mentors (i.e., supervisors) for employees. Their research revealed peer relationships as an important alternative to the traditional supervisor–subordinate mentoring relationship. Kram and Isabella (1985) identified three primary types of peer workplace relationships: information peers, collegial peers, and special peers. Most peer relationships are *information* peer relationships sharing superficial information regarding work-related topics and are characterized by low levels of trust and self-disclosure (Odden & Sias, 1997). While, in general, all peer relationships begin as information peers, some develop into closer friendship relationships. *Collegial* peers share moderate levels of trust, self-disclosure, emotional support, career feedback, and friendship. Some collegial peer relationships evolve into *special* peer relationships characterized by high levels of trust, self-disclosure, emotional support, career and personal feedback, and close friendship. Informal mentoring is an important function of collegial and special peer relationships (Kram & Isabella, 1985). In addition to mentoring, peers are important sources of information and support for one another. For example, employees exchange higher-quality information with their special and collegial peers than with their information peers (Sias, 2005), and employees tend to seek information more frequently from special peers than from information or collegial peers (Myers et al., 2018).

Odden and Sias (1997) found that collegial peer relationships are related to cohesive workplace climates in which employees like and help each other. Sollitto and Myers (2015) found that the peer types vary in the extent to which they express lateral dissent (express their complaints to employees at the same hierarchical level). Specifically, they found special and collegial peers engage in greater amounts of lateral dissent expression than do information peers, likely due to the higher levels of trust that characterize those relationships. Similarly, Myers et al. (2018) found that employees believe it is more appropriate to seek tasks, appraisal/performance, and social information from special peers than from information peers.

Peers are also important sources of information and support for new employees during the organizational socialization process (see Chapter 8). Coworkers help newcomers "learn the ropes," by teaching them the unwritten rules, providing insights into the unit's and the organization's distinctive cultural jargon and behavior patterns (Miller & Jablin, 1991). Peers are also important sources of social support because they share a unique understanding of workplace issues that others (e.g., family and friends outside of work) cannot (Ray, 1993). Hence, when employees face work-related stress, they tend to seek social support from their coworkers first (Cahill & Sias, 1997).

Peer relationships can be challenging and associated with negative experiences and outcomes (Fritz & Omdahl, 2006). Peer relationships are sometimes sites of destructive communication such as incivility, harassment, abuse of power, and bullying (Lutgen-Sandvik et al., 2009). Bullying refers to several destructive communication practices including "verbal abuse; offensive conduct and behaviors (including nonverbal) that are threating, humiliating, or intimidating; or work interference and sabotage that prevent work from getting done" (Lutgen-Sandvik et al., 2009, p. 27). Workplace bullying can impair productivity, decrease worker commitment and satisfaction, harm the organization's image, and increase operating costs (Lutgen-Sandvik et al., 2009). Similarly, Duffy (2018) argues that bullying leads to decreased communication, which damages relationships and harms the work environment and culture (see Chapter 16).

Workplace Friendships

Because of the time they spend together and their important roles as sources of information and social support, peers often develop friendships. These unique relationships are important for individual attitudes and adjustment, performance, and organizational processes.

Both supervisor–subordinate and peer relationships can develop into friendships. Unlike formally assigned relationships, workplace friendships are informal, voluntary workplace relationships. Workplace friendships develop and thrive in all types of organizations, at all hierarchical levels, and between all types of employees (Bridge & Baxter, 1992; Sias, 2009). Although workplace friendships are not represented in an organization's formal structure and are not mandated by management, they are crucial to organizational functioning and employee experiences (Sias, 2009). As Lincoln and Miller (1979) noted early on, friendship networks are "systems for making decisions, mobilizing resources, concealing or transmitting information, and performing other functions closely allied with work behavior and interaction" (p. 196).

The Beginning: Blended Relationships

Little research examined workplace friendship explicitly until the 1990s. Bridge and Baxter (1992) were among the first to focus on workplace friendships. Their study conceptualized workplace friendship as a *blended* relationship – a relationship that blends the coworker role with the friend role. They argued that the two roles carry unique expectations that conflict. Guided by dialectic theory (Baxter, 1988), Bridge and Baxter (1992) identified five dialectical tensions in blended relationships. Dialectical tensions are pairs of oppositional coexisting desires or pressures that characterize relationships. The *equality-inequality* tension refers to tensions between possible equality in friendship and inequality that characterizes workplace constraints and expectations. *Impartiality-favoritism* refers to tensions between organizational moral order without personal bias and friendship expectations of special treatment. The *openness-closedness* tension refers to expectations of openness and honesty as friends while honoring organizational expectations for confidentiality and caution about sharing information. The *autonomy-connection* tension refers to the advantages of contact for friends and the possibility that ongoing and daily contact among coworkers may provide too little autonomy or separation for the relationship parties. Last, *judgment-acceptance* refers to tensions between organizational requirements of the critical evaluation process and mutual affirmation and acceptance as friends. These tensions threaten the stability of the relationship and, if not managed, the individuals may choose to terminate the friendship either by one of them quitting their job or by returning the relationship to "just coworkers" (Sias et al., 2004).

Turning Point: Workplace Friendship

While Bridge and Baxter (1992) called scholars' attention to workplace friendship as a type of blended relationship, Sias and Cahill (1998) were among the first to study workplace friendship as a uniquely important workplace relationship. They noted that workplace friendships are unique in two ways. First, they are not imposed but *voluntary*. While supervisors and coworkers are typically assigned, employees voluntarily choose who they will befriend and voluntarily spend time with beyond what is required for task completion. Second, a *personalistic focus* characterizes workplace friendships. Workplace friends communicate with and understand one another as whole persons, not just role occupants.

Workplace friendship fulfills several important functions. First, they are sites of quality information exchange. Employees reported receiving higher-quality information (i.e., accurate, timely, relevant, and useful) from their workplace friends than from nonfriend coworkers (Sias, 2005). Second, friends are important sources of social support, providing advice and feedback regarding both work and personal problems and challenges. Constructive workplace friendships also help employees cope with uncertainty, stress, and anxiety (Sias & Cahill, 1998).

Yet, friendships can be associated with negative outcomes. Sias and Cahill (1998) found that high proportions of very close friendships in a workplace can indicate problems such as a problematic supervisor – the work-related problems draw coworkers into close friendships as they lean on one another for support. Methot et al. (2016) found that an employee's number of workplace friendships was positively associated with job performance, but also that emotional exhaustion resulting from the difficulty of maintaining such relationships offset the effect on job performance. Similarly, Shah et al. (2017) found a curvilinear relationship between friendships (i.e., multiplex relationships) and job performance; friendships were associated with improved job performance only to a point after which the excessive attention required to maintain relationships hurt performance.

Workplace Friendship Developmental Processes

Due to their important role in employee experiences and organizational processes, scholars have examined how and why employees become friends with one another. Sias and Cahill (1998) identified two primary types of developmental factors. *Individual* factors derive from the employees, including personality, perceived similarity, sex, race, and important life events. *Contextual* factors derive from the workplace context, including physical proximity, shared tasks, work-related problems, and socializing. Personality, proximity, shared tasks, and similarity are more important to initiating a friendship (i.e., moving from coworkers to friends). Life events, work-related problems, and socializing have a greater influence on transitioning from friends to close or best friends.

Recent studies have reconsidered the role of physical proximity in friendship initiation, given the increased use of information and communication technologies (ICTs) and telecommuting. Sias et al. (2012) examined the role of the developmental factors described above and found that, in contrast to Sias and Cahill (1998), respondents rated physical proximity as the *least* important factor in initiating a workplace friendship. Thus, the introduction of technologies that allow coworkers to communicate and work together virtually removed the necessity of physical proximity and face-to-face interaction for friendship initiation.

Conceptualizing relationships as socially constructed, Sias and Cahill (1998) and Sias et al. (2004) examined how communication enables relationship transitions from coworkers to friends and close friends. Specifically, they found that the transformation of a coworker relationship into a friendship is accomplished by increasingly frequent communication about a broader array of both work and personal topics, at increasingly intimate levels. The relationship partners also edit their communication less as the relationship grows closer. These results demonstrate how the coworkers communicatively produce the personalistic focus that characterizes friendship.

Although research emphasizes the positive side of workplace friendships (e.g., Feeley et al., 2008), maintaining these relationships can be difficult and complex. When the partners cannot manage these challenges, the friendship may deteriorate or even terminate. Sias et al. (2004) examined employees' narrative accounts of workplace friendship deterioration. They identified five primary causes of friendship deterioration. *Conflicting expectations* refer to the events in which coworkers behave differently than their partner expected (e.g., an employee may not support their coworker's proposal, but the coworker expects such support because they expect friends to support one another). This reflects the dialectical tensions that challenge workplace friendships (e.g., Bridge & Baxter, 1992). A *problem personality* can damage friendship when one finds he or she can no longer deal with another's annoying personality trait. While life events can bring coworkers closer together (Sias & Cahill, 1998), when those life events *distract* the employee to the point that their coworkers must pick up the slack, the friendship can be harmed. Since trust is central to friendship development and maintenance, *betrayal* of trust is another threat to workplace friendship. Finally, a workplace friendship may deteriorate if one of the relationship partners is *promoted* to formal authority over the other.

Again conceptualizing relationships as socially constructed, Sias et al. (2004) and Sias and Perry (2004) examined strategies individuals use to communicatively accomplish the deterioration of a workplace friendship. The most used strategy is *depersonalization*, which refers to limiting communication to work-related topics only. Recall that a personalistic focus characterizes workplace friendship and communicating about non-work topics helps coworkers develop friendships (Sias & Cahill, 1998). The depersonalization strategy effectively removes the relationship's personalistic focus, while enabling the employees to communicate as needed for task completion. Another form of depersonalization is *avoidance*. However, because this strategy involves avoiding any contact, it may be effective for ending the friendship but is less functional for employees and the organization as it harms the ability to accomplish tasks. Individuals may also use *cost escalation* to end the friendship. *Cost escalation* involves intentional negative acts toward the coworker such as criticism, snubbing, or talking to them in a condescending tone. Finally, individuals may address the issue *directly* with their coworker, explaining that they want to end the friendship or decrease the level of closeness in the relationship.

In sum, workplace friendship research has grown since the early 1990s. Studies have identified the unique nature of these relationships and their impact on individual experiences and organizational processes. Communication research has contributed to this body of research by conceptualizing workplace friendship as socially constructed and developing our understanding of the important and constitutive role of communication in workplace friendship dynamics.

Romantic Workplace Relationships

In a 2023 Society for Human Resource Management (SHRM) survey on workplace romantic relationships, over a quarter (27%) of U.S. employees reported they are or have been involved in a workplace romance. As this survey indicates, workplace romantic relationships are not unusual. However, relative to the other relationships addressed in this chapter, they have received little attention from organizational communication scholars (Sias, 2009). Romantic workplace relationship research was spurred into action in the 1970s when feminist movements led to an increase in women workers in U.S. organizations, leading to an increase in workplace romantic relationships (Sias, 2014).

Pierce et al. (1996) defined a workplace romantic relationship as "any relationship between two members of the same organization that entails mutual attraction" (p. 6). (Hence, in this literature, any relationship with a sexual component is defined as romantic.) Romantic relationships are voluntary and personalistic like friendships but are also characterized by their emotional and affective nature, incorporating love, affection, and intimacy. Thus, romantic workplace relationships are unique because they are emotional, physiological, and consensual (Sias, 2009). The *consensual nature* of these relationships distinguishes them from sexual harassment. There has been much research on sexual harassment (e.g., Clair, 1993; Dougherty & Smythe, 2004; also see Chapter 13). However, this chapter focuses on consensual romantic relationships.

Motives, Types, and Consequences

Early research centered on identifying the motives and types of workplace romantic relationships. Quinn (1977) identified three primary motives for engaging in a romantic relationship at work. The *job motive* refers to situations in which individuals engage in a romantic relationship for utilitarian reasons including job advancement and security, financial rewards (e.g., promotion, bonuses), and more efficient or easier tasks. The *ego motive* reflects personal desires such as excitement, ego gratification, and adventure. Finally, the *love motive* reflects genuine affection, respect, love, and companionship. Mainiero and Jones (2013) argued "most romantic relationships at work are sincere, love-motivated, and of the long-term companionate variety as opposed to the short-lived flings or job-motived utilitarian relationships" (p. 188).

Quinn (1977) found that different motives lead to different types of romantic relationships. Partners motivated by ego gratification and adventure tend to form *fling* relationships. Those who enter a romantic relationship due to the love motive form *companionate love* relationships. When one partner (usually male) is motivated by ego gratification and the other engages in the relationship due to the job motive, the partners form a *utilitarian* relationship. As Sias (2009) noted, this relationship type "represents the 'sleeping up the ladder' stereotype that has persisted over the years" (p. 134). Romantic workplace relationships have several consequences for relationship partners and their coworkers. Much research in this area centers on how coworkers perceive the romantic relationships of others. This indicates that when employees become aware of a romantic relationship between coworkers, that relationship becomes a topic of gossip, as the employees interpret and make attributions about the romance, particularly with respect to the relationship partners' motives (Michelson & Mouly, 2000). According to Dillard (1987), employees tend to make negative attributions about relationships that they perceive were formed for job motives. Chory and Hoke (2023) found that workplace romances resulted in more negative coworker perceptions and behaviors than workplace romance participants had expected, especially in hierarchical workplace romances. To be specific, attributions of motives for workplace romances led to decreased trust in the participants, resulting in less honest and accurate communication with them (Chory & Hoke, 2020).

In contrast, romances motivated by love tend to generate more positive attributions. An important factor in coworker perceptions of a romantic relationship is whether or not the relationship is between employees of the same or different hierarchical status. Specifically, employees tend to hold negative attitudes toward hierarchical romances (i.e., supervisor–subordinate) (Jones, 1999). Consistent with this, while not all organizations have policies forbidding workplace romance, those that do tend to forbid hierarchical romantic relationships, but are more lenient regarding non-hierarchical relationships (Wilson et al., 2003). Engaging in a workplace romance can have consequences for the relationship partners as well. Some studies indicate that employees are happier, have higher job satisfaction, and have better motivation when they are in a romantic workplace relationship (Dillard & Broetzmann, 1989; Mainiero, 1989; Pierce et al., 1996). This may result from looking forward to seeing one another, as well as putting in extra effort to avoid coworker perceptions that the relationship may hinder the partners' performance (Sias, 2009). Of course, the consequences depend in part on the nature of the relationship. An unhappy or unsatisfying relationship can, instead, harm the partners' morale, satisfaction, and performance (Pierce et al., 1996). More recently, Horan et al. (2024) found a more holistic view of workplace romances. Employees view workplace romances as inappropriate regardless of the sex of those involved and have concerns about gender-related differences and power imbalances. In line with past research, they also found both adverse effects (e.g., employees leaving, terminations) and positive or neutral views of workplace romance.

Romantic Workplace Relationship Development

Studies of romantic relationship development have focused on identifying factors that encourage relational development. Such research tends to conceptualize the organization as an "incubator" in which romantic relationships form and grow (Sias, 2009). Similar to other voluntary relationships (e.g., friendship), physical proximity primarily influences the initiation and development of a romantic workplace relationship; Quinn (1977) identified three types. *Geographical proximity* refers to individuals' physical closeness to one another in workspaces. *Ongoing work requirement proximity* refers to proximity resulting from various work-related activities such as employees working together on projects, business trips, and other tasks that bring the individuals close to one another. Finally, some situations cause *occasional contact* with one another, such as riding the elevator together or encountering each other in locations other than workspaces because of their work.

Attitude similarity is an important contributor to liking that can lead to workplace romance (Sias, 2009). This factor reflects the homophily principle, which refers to people being attracted to others who are similar to them. Pierce et al. (1996) argue that the homophily principle helps explain why workplace romantic relationships are likely to develop because hiring and selection processes tend to filter in individuals with similar attitudes and interests and filter out those who are dissimilar to the origination's general population.

Organizational *culture* or *climate* can also influence romantic relationship development. For instance, studies suggest that workplace romances are more likely to form in "liberal" organizations where people are more fast-paced, action-oriented, and dynamic than in "conservative" organizations, where such relationships tend to be discouraged (Mainiero, 1989; Pierce et al., 1996). Likewise, Mano and Gabriel (2006) examined workplace romantic relationships in "cold" and "hot" organizational climates. Impersonal, formal organizational structures characterize cold climates, while hot climates emphasize employees' physical appearance. They found that employees who work in hot workplace climates tend to talk more passionately about romantic stories in the workplace compared to those in cold climates. Horan et al. (2024) also found that employees in organizations with a workplace romance policy tend to have a more realistic view of workplace romance and are more likely to report positive reputational effects of hierarchical workplace romance.

Communication and Romantic Relationship Development

As noted earlier, organizational communication scholars have paid relatively little attention to romantic workplace relationships. Thus, much is unknown about the role of communication in romantic relationship dynamics. However, Yelvington (1996) identified flirting as key to romance initiation. They note that flirting is an indirect behavior, and the initiator risks the communication being misinterpreted as sexual harassment and/or risks rejection. Nonetheless, flirting tends to be "the first step in the initiation of a romantic relationship" (Sias, 2009, p. 135).

Scholars have also examined the role of ICT in workplace romantic relationships. For example, Hovick et al. (2003) found that employees tend to rely on face-to-face interaction to initiate romantic relationships and then rely more on email or other technologies as the relationship develops. Cowan and Horan's (2021) qualitative results revealed different reasons for ICT use in the stages of workplace romantic relationships (i.e., initiation, maintenance, dissolution); participants used technology due to privacy concerns in the two earlier stages, while avoidance of direct communication during the dissolution stage.

In sum, romantic relationships are common in organizations and, like the other relationships addressed in this chapter, play an important role in both employee experiences and organizational processes. Relative to other relationship types, however, they have received scant attention. In particular, we know little about the role of communication in romantic workplace relationships including the communication patterns that characterize romantic relationships and that characterize interaction between the partners and their coworkers. We also know little about how communication functions in romantic relationship initiation, development, and deterioration. Given the complexities and controversies associated with workplace romance, future studies should continue to examine this phenomenon in various contexts and cultures to understand the full implications of romantic workplace relationships.

Influences of the COVID-19 Pandemic

Due to its highly contagious nature and rapid spread, the COVID-19 outbreak forced organizations to reconsider their structures, including different approaches to nurturing workplace relationships. As employees experienced uncertainty and disrupted work routines, the research examined fostering and maintaining relationships in response to the external environmental jolt. Notably, the role of positive supervisor-subordinate relationships in various organizational attitudes (e.g., trust, creativity, employee resilience) was highlighted during the COVID-19 pandemic. For example, Men et al. (2022) found how leaders' use of motivating language affects employees' trusting attitudes toward the leader and the organization through satisfying psychological needs during the COVID-19 outbreak. Similarly, Lee and Kim (2023) found that family-supportive communication from leaders resulted in employees' creativity, which was mediated by positive affect and work-life enrichment. Focusing on internal communication at different levels during the COVID-19 outbreak, Qin and Men's (2023) study revealed the positive relationship between supportive peer communication and sustaining employee mental health. They also found the value of organizational trust regarding employee mental health; it fully mediated the relationship between corporate symmetrical communication and employee psychological well-being (Qin & Men, 2023).

The physical distancing requirement during the COVID-19 pandemic also focused scholarly attention on technology use and its impacts on various relationships. Regardless of the work context, communication in relationships remains crucial for the organization and its members. For example, Mikkelson et al.'s (2023) results suggested no difference in employees' perceptions of supervisor communication competence depending on remote, hybrid, and in-person work environments. In addition, Hu and Subramony (2022) found the buffering effect of friendships among teleworkers during the COVID-19 pandemic; friendship significantly decreased the negative effect of the perceived threat and professional isolation on well-being. The COVID-19 pandemic significantly affected organizational relationships research in two aspects: effective communication in crises and the impacts of technology. Research on these topics remains significant.

Approach to Communication

As noted earlier, organizational communication as a discipline began, in part, with the study of workplace relationships, particularly supervisor–subordinate relationships, focusing on supervisory practices that led to more effective organizational functioning (Redding, 1985). At that time, and consistent with other social science disciplines, research was grounded in a transmission model of communication, focusing largely on messages and message exchange. Jablin's (1979) literature review, for example, revealed that supervisor–subordinate communication research centered on identifying message exchange patterns such as openness in message sending and receiving, upward distortion (i.e., an employee's propensity to misrepresent information sent upward or withhold information from their supervisor), and semantic information distance (the extent to which supervisor and employees understanding of the employee's role responsibilities and knowledge are congruent). Later, Kram and Isabella's (1985) introduction of peer relationships to the literature examined message exchange between peers, particularly mentoring and advice-giving messages.

The interpretive turn (Putnam & Pacanowsky, 1983) initiated a different perspective on communication and social reality that, in turn, led to a shift in our understanding of workplace relationships. As noted in Chapter 2, the interpretive turn was grounded in a constructionist perspective that conceptualized social reality as socially constructed. This laid the foundation for constitutive approaches to communication and organizations (see Chapter 3). At this point, organizational communication scholars began focusing on relationship dynamics, examining how workplace relationships are communicatively created, maintained, and transformed. Fairhurst and Chandler's (1989) study of LMX relationships was grounded in such an approach, conceptualizing leader–member (i.e., supervisor–subordinate) relationships as socially constructed. That study and others that followed (e.g., Fairhurst, 1993; Sias & Cahill, 1998) centered on communication not as message exchange in the context of relationships, but as constitutive of relationships themselves.

Conceptualizing workplace relationships as dynamic communicative entities, Bridge and Baxter (1992) studied the role of communication in the dynamic management of dialectical tensions in "blended" relationships that combine work and friend roles. Sias and colleagues followed suit with respect to peer relationships. Sias and Cahill (1998), for example, examined how friendship development is accomplished communicatively. Sias et al. (2004) and Sias and Perry (2004) similarly studied the constitutive role of communication in friendship deterioration. Finally, Sias et al. (2012) conceptualized workplace relationships as dynamic even in times of stability, demonstrating how relationship maintenance requires continual communication to constitute a relationship at a desired level of closeness. While these studies were not explicitly grounded in communicative constitution of organizations (CCO) theory, nor did they often use the terms *constituted* or *constitutive*, their fundamental assumptions were squarely in the constitutive camp.

Approach to Organization

As micro-level phenomena, it is not surprising that the bulk of workplace relationship research uses an O_1 approach to organizations. As noted in Chapter 1, O_1 research "examines interaction processes by which members arrange themselves and manage their joint activities" (p. 5). Still, the O_3 presumption underlies this literature, as the organization is considered to be the context in which relationships occur.

Although the vast majority of workplace relationships center on dyadic interpersonal relationships, recent research on relationship networks has broadened our understanding of the role of workplace relationships in broader organizational structures, processes, and practices. Such studies represent an O_2 approach to organizations, i.e., "the state of a social collective's coordination/order" (Chapter 1). Feeley et al.'s (2008) study of peer relationship networks, for example, examines the broader network of workplace friendships and how such friendship networks are linked to turnover (an organization outcome). Shah et al. (2017) demonstrated how the nature of peer relationships (i.e., uniplex or multiplex) embedded in organization networks was linked to the organization's performance and capacity for creativity. Such studies illuminate the social order of an organization and the role of relationships in coordinating activities to maintain social order (see Chapter 9).

Workplace relationship research that uses a constitutive/social construction approach tends to explicitly emphasize the examination of a mutually constitutive communication-organization (C-O) cycle, as described in Chapter 1. That is, communication constitutes relationships, and those relationship structures enable and constrain communication. For example, peer relationships are communicatively transformed into friendships (via more personal, intimate, and frequent communication). Once the relationship becomes a friendship, the structures that characterize friendship (e.g., personalistic focus and openness) enable and constrain partner communication. The friendship structure, for instance, enables open discussion of broad topics and, at the same time, constrains employees from withholding information from one another that the organization prohibits them from sharing. This is just one example of the C-O cycle as explicated in organizational relationship research.

Cultural Implications

Early management and organizational communication theories and research centered on formal communication and formal reporting relationships. In fact, classical theories (e.g., bureaucracy, administrative management, and scientific management; see Chapter 5) intentionally excluded informal relationships and informal communication from their design of organizational processes. The focus on interpersonal relationships and informal relationships such as friendship was accompanied by cultural changes in business practices (compare, for example, IBM [International Business Machines Corporation, a technology company] in the 1960s to Google today). Peer relationships and friendships are now central to an organization's culture and climate, with many organizations becoming less authority-centered and instead more decentralized (see Chapter 7).

Globalization has increased the multicultural composition of organizations and their operation across multiple borders, suggesting the importance of various organizational relationships. Due to their significance across organizational studies, research has examined supervisor-subordinate relationships in different countries. Comparing the U.S. and India samples, Yue et al. (2022) found that leaders' motivating language use positively influences a healthy team culture and is positively related to quality relationships among the employees' working units in both countries. Furthermore, scholars have examined unique cultural aspects to understand cultural differences better. For example, Xing et al. (2020) examined how Guanxi, a fundamental relational construct in Chinese culture, was used in supervisor-subordinate relationships to strategically benefit organizations and enhance employee performance outcomes.

In addition, relationships in multinational corporations have received more attention as globalization made multinational corporations prevalent. Sergeant and Frenkel (1998) found that expatriate managers working with Chinese employees in an American subsidiary in China had difficulties developing high-quality LMX relationships due, in part, to Chinese cultural norms of respect for hierarchy and authority, which hindered the open communication, autonomy, and role negotiation that constitutes leadership exchange relationships. More recently, focusing on foreign-owned multinational businesses in the United States, Wyant and Kramer (2022) found how local employees make sense of their colleagues' (i.e., expatriates') roles and responsibilities in multinational enterprises.

Many organizations have a growing multicultural workforce, and it is crucial to understand their relationships in cross-cultural, global contexts. Typically, much focus on supervisor–subordinate relationships. However, future research should focus more on unique relationship types (e.g., virtual workers, expatriate workers, and interethnic friends) to improve our understanding of cross-cultural relationships.

The makeup of most organizations' employees is growing more diverse, which generates beneficial results (e.g., increased organizations' adaptability, innovation, creativity), but also concerns of gender, race, ethnicity, age, and generation (Omilion-Hodges & Ptacek, 2021). Since leaders can determine how they use diversity, equity, and inclusion (DEI) initiatives, organizational relationship researchers have investigated leaders' crucial role in diverse climates (Omilion-Hodges & Ptacek, 2021). Lee et al. (2021) found that racial minority employees' perceptions of fairness from the leader increase employee engagement and advocative behaviors, suggesting a positive relationship between diversity-oriented leadership and symmetrical internal communication. In addition, David et al. (2023) argued for the importance of developing multicultural workplace friendships (e.g., cross-sex, cross-race friendships) to increase one's social capital and performance.

Although the importance of DEI in workplace relationships has been highlighted, more research is required for organizations and employees to reap the benefits. For example, certain occupations and industries, such as blue-collar work and manual labor, are underexamined (Horan et al., 2021). Future research should also shed more light on its contemporary DEI issues, such as different generations (e.g., Omilion-Hodges & Sugg, 2019), LGBTQIA+ friendships (e.g., Rumens, 2017), immigrants, and employee activism (see Chapter 14). Finally, scholars should explore relationships more by incorporating various theoretical traditions, such as critical and rhetorical (see Deetz & Mumby, 1990). Research on workplace relationships has shown its profound impact on organizational members' experiences. Examining various settings, contemporary DEI issues, and integrating various theoretical approaches in DEI will advance the field.

Conclusion

As this overview demonstrates, workplace relationships matter. The field of organizational communication was founded on the study of supervisor–subordinate communication, and scholars over the following decades recognized workplace relationships' central role in organizations. As noted earlier, organizations are fundamentally systems of relationships. There is still much to learn, however. We encourage future scholars to examine workplace relationships in new and innovative ways, such as studies of relationships as they relate to O_2 and O_3 conceptualizations of organizations. Such studies would address, for example, how relationships structure the broader organization (O_2) and how relationships constitute organizations as entities (O_3). We also encourage studies that incorporate culture in all its forms (e.g., organizational culture, occupational culture, national culture, as well as demographic cultural features such as race, gender, and sexual orientation, and their intersections).

Recommended Supplementary Readings

Fritz, J. M. H., & Omdahl, B. L. (2006). *Problematic relationships in the workplace.* Peter Lang.

A thorough resource addressing the "dark side" of workplace relationships, covering the causes and outcomes of negative workplace relationships.

Graen, G. B., & Uhl-Bien, M. (1995). Relationship-based approach to leadership: Development of a leader–member exchange (LMX) theory of leadership over 25 years—Applying a multi-level multi-domain perspective. *Leadership Quarterly*, 62(2), 219–247.

An excellent review of the first 25 years of LMX theory development.

Jablin, F. M. (1979). Superior–subordinate communication: The state of the art. *Psychological Bulletin*, *86*(6), 1201–1222.

A classic article in the field of organizational communication, summarizing supervisor–subordinate communication research.

Kahn, W. A. (2001). Holding environments at work. *Journal of Applied Behavioral Science*, *37*(3), 260–279.

An interesting conceptualization of workplace relationships as sites of social support.

Omdahl, B. L., & Harden Fritz, J. M. (2012). *Problematic relationships in the workplace: Volume 2*. Peter Lang.

A follow-up to Fritz and Omdahl (2006) referenced above.

Rumens, N. (2013). *Queer company: The role and meaning of friendship in gay men's work lives*. Routledge.

An important book covering an under-studied area in organizational communication/ management research.

Important Concepts: Define and Discuss

Blended relationship
Bullying
Information, collegial, and special peers
Mentoring
Personalistic focus
Leader–member exchange theory

Discussion Questions

1 Reflect on a current or past workplace friendship. What dialectical tensions did you experience, and how did you manage them?
2 How might social media influence an employee's various workplace relationships?
3 Today's organizations are increasingly populated by employees from several different generations (e.g., Z generation, millennials, and late and early baby boomers). How might generational differences impact coworker communication and workplace relationships?
4 Reflect on your current or most recent job. How would you characterize your relationship with your supervisor (i.e., supervisory exchange or leadership exchange)? Explain your choice.

Practitioners' Corner

As this chapter demonstrates, workplace relationships matter. Employees are happier, more motivated, and more successful when they have functional high-quality relationships at work. Organizations reap many rewards from such relationships, including lower turnover and better performance. Practitioners should recognize workplace relationships' important role in organizational practices and processes and ensure the work environment is conducive and supportive of functional relationships.

Key to creating such an environment is understanding how and why relationships develop and deteriorate. LMX theory and research suggest the importance of high-quality (leadership exchange) relationships and indicate that supervisors tend to form such relationships with some, but not all, of their direct reports. However, as Graen and Uhl-Bien (1995) argued, there is no reason such relationships should be limited and supervisors should make efforts to forge and maintain leadership exchange relationships with all employees. First, employee competence is key to leadership exchanges. To warrant the trust and autonomy that characterizes such relationships, employees must demonstrate their ability and initiative. Hiring competent and responsible individuals, therefore, is the first step to a quality LMX relationship. The supervisor's ability to mentor, train, and help employees is also important. Managers should recognize their role as mentors and coaches, rather than simply supervisors, to help employees, both newly hired and veterans, with their professional development. Research also indicates that authoritarianism hinders LMX development. Supervisors must recognize that leadership exchange relationships require the sharing of power and authority with employees. Employees can also enable the development of such relationships by demonstrating competence and responsibility and being open in their communication and information-sharing with their manager.

Practitioners can also encourage the development of quality relationships among the employees themselves. HR professionals and managers should work collaboratively to provide opportunities for the kinds of interaction among coworkers that foster the development of collegial relationships. Managers can, and should, be aware of relationship quality among their employees, foster good quality communication, and find ways to allow those good relationships to support organizational goals (and vice versa). Providing employees with opportunities to work together on tasks and collaborate can help the coworkers initiate and maintain friendships. It is also important to provide opportunities for coworker interaction via physical proximity or virtual media such as information communication technologies and social networking systems.

Workplace romantic relationships are a fact of life. Despite their challenges and potential to disrupt organizational processes, they can also contribute to employee morale and performance. Practitioners are encouraged to review existing policies regarding workplace romance to ensure they are appropriate and effective with respect to differentiating between workplace romance and sexual harassment. This is especially important given recent societal changes spurred by the #MeToo movement. All employees should receive regular training in the organization's sexual harassment and consensual relationship policies, including mandatory reporting and disclosure, respectively. Employees who are unsure of policies are less likely to report or disclose, leaving the organization vulnerable.

References

Allen, B. J. (2023). *Difference matters: Communicating social identity* (3rd ed.). Waveland.

Ashford, S. J. (1993). The feedback environment: An exploratory study of cue use. *Journal of Organizational Behavior*, *14*(3), 201–225. https://doi.org/10.1002/job.4030140302

Bauer, T. N., & Green, S. G. (1996). Development of leader–member exchange: A longitudinal test. *Academy of Management Journal*, *39*(6), 1538–1567. https://doi.org/10.5465/257068

Baxter, L. (1988). A dialectical perspective on communication strategies in relationship development. In S. Duck (Ed.), *Handbook of personal relationships* (pp. 257–273). John Wiley & Sons.

Blake, R., & Mouton, J. (1964). *The managerial grid*. Gulf.

Bridge, K., & Baxter, L. A. (1992). Blended relationships: Friends as work associates. *Western Journal of Communication*, *56*(3), 200–225. https://doi.org/10.1080/10570319209374414

Cahill, D. J., & Sias, P. M. (1997). The perceived social costs and importance of seeking emotional support in the workplace: Gender differences and similarities. *Communication Research Reports*, *14*(2), 231–240. https://doi.org/10.1080/08824099709388665

Chory, R. M., & Hoke, H. (2023). Coworkers' perceptions of, and communication with, workplace romance participants: Proposing and testing a model. *International Journal of Business Communication*, *60*(4), 1290–1312. https://doi.org/10.1177/2329488420908321

Clair, R. P. (1993). The bureaucratization, commodification, and privatization of sexual harassment through institutional discourse: A study of the Big Ten universities. *Management Communication Quarterly*, *7*(2), 123–157. https://doi.org/10.1177/0893318993007002001

Cogliser, C. C., & Schriesheim, C. A. (2000). Exploring work unit context and leader–member exchange: A multi-level perspective. *Journal of Organizational Behavior*, *21*(5), 487–511.

Cowan, R. L., & Horan, S. M. (2021). Understanding information and communication technology use in workplace romance escalation and de-escalation. *International Journal of Business Communication*, *58*(1), 55–78. https://doi.org/10.1177/2329488417731860

David, N. A., Coutinho, J. A., & Brennecke, J. (2023). Workplace friendships: Antecedents, consequences, and new challenges for employees and organizations. In A. Gerbasi, C. Emery, & A. Parker (Eds.), *Understanding workplace relationships* (pp. 325–368). Palgrave Macmillan. https://doi.org/10.1007/978-3-031-16640-2_11

Deetz, S., & Mumby, D. (1990). Power, discourse, and the workplace: Reclaiming the critical tradition. *Annals of the International Communication Association*, *13*(1), 18–47. https://doi.org/10.1080/23808985.1990.11678743

Dillard, D. (1987). Money as an institution of capitalism. *Journal of Economic Issues*, *21*(4), 1623–1647. https://doi.org/10.1080/00213624.1987.11504717

Dillard, J. P., & Broetzmann, S. M. (1989). Romantic relationships at work: Perceived changes in job-related behaviors as a function of participant's motive, partner's motive, and gender. *Journal of Applied Social Psychology*, *19*(2), 93–110. https://doi.org/10.1111/j.1559-1816.1989.tb00047.x

Dougherty, D. S., & Smythe, M. J. (2004). Sensemaking, organizational culture, and sexual harassment. *Journal of Applied Communication Research*, *32*(4), 293–317. https://doi.org/10.1080/0090988042000275998

Duffy, M. (2018). The psychosocial impact of workplace bullying and mobbing on targets. In M. Duffy & D. C. Yamada (Eds.), *Workplace bullying and mobbing in the United States* (Vol. 1, pp. 131–150). ABC-CLIO.

Fairhurst, G. T. (1993). The leader–member exchange patterns of women leaders in industry: A discourse analysis. *Communications Monographs*, *60*(4), 321–351. https://doi.org/10.1080/03637759309376316

Fairhurst, G. T., & Chandler, T. A. (1989). Social structure in leader–member interaction. *Communication Monographs*, *56*(3), 215–239. https://doi.org/10.1080/03637758909390261

Fedor, D. B. (1991). Recipient responses to performance feedback: A proposed model and its implications. In G. R. Ferris & K. M. Rowland (Eds.), *Research in personnel and human resources management* (Vol. 9, pp. 73–120). JAI.

Feeley, T. H., Hwang, J., & Barnett, G. A. (2008). Predicting employee turnover from friendship networks. *Journal of Applied Communication Research*, *36*(1), 56–73. https://doi.org/10.1080/00909880701799790

Fix, B., & Sias, P. M. (2006). Person-centered communication, leader-member exchange, and employee job satisfaction. *Communication Research Reports*, *23*(1), 35–44. https://doi.org/10.1080/17464090500535855

Fritz, J. M. H., & Omdahl, B. L. (2006). *Problematic relationships in the workplace*. Peter Lang.

Ghiselli, E. E. (1963). Intelligence and managerial success. *Psychological Reports*, *12*(3), 898. https://doi.org/10.2466/pr0.1963.12.3.898

Goldberg, C., & McKay, P. F. (2015). Diversity and LMX development. In T. N. Bauer & B. Erdogan (Eds.), *The Oxford handbook of leader–member exchange* (pp. 381–396). Oxford University Press.

Graen, G. B., & Cashman, J. F. (1975). A role-making model of leadership in formal organizations: A developmental approach. In J. G. Hunt & L. L. Hunt (Eds.), *Leadership frontiers* (pp. 143–165). Kent State University Press.

Graen, G. B., & Scandura, T. (1987). Toward a psychology of dyadic organizing. In B. Staw & L. L. Cummings (Eds.), *Research in organizational behavior* (Vol. 9, pp. 175–208). JAI.

Graen, G. B., & Uhl-Bien, M. (1995). Relationship-based approach to leadership: Development of a leader-member exchange (LMX) theory of leadership over 25 years – Applying a multi-level multi-domain perspective. *Leadership Quarterly*, *6*(2), 219–247. https://doi.org/10.1016/1048-9843(95)90036-5

Hersey, P., & Blanchard, K. H. (1982). *Management of organizational behavior* (4th ed.). Prentice Hall.

Horan, S. M., Chory, R. M., Craw, E. S., & Jones, H. E. (2021). Blended work/life relationships: Organizational communication involving workplace peers, friends, and lovers. *Communication Research Trends*, *40*(2), 3–46.

Horan, S. M., Chory, R. M., Craw, E. S., & Mainiero, L. (2024). Workplace romance policies, behaviors, and reputational beliefs: Experiences of employees from major US cities. *Communication Quarterly*, *72*(2), 121–147. https://doi.org/10.1080/01463373.2023.2293969

Hovick, S. R. A., Meyers, R. A., & Timmerman, E. (2003). E-mail communication in workplace romantic relationships. *Communication Studies*, *54*(4), 468–482. https://doi.org/10.1080/10510970309363304

Hu, X., & Subramony, M. (2022). Understanding the impact of COVID-19 pandemic on teleworkers' experiences of perceived threat and professional isolation: The moderating role of friendship. *Stress and Health*, *38*(5), 927–939. https://doi.org/10.1002/smi.3146

Jablin, F. M. (1979). Superior–subordinate communication: The state of the art. *Psychological Bulletin*, *86*(6), 1201–1222. https://doi.org/10.1037/0033-2909.86.6.1201

Jablin, F. M. (2001). Organizational entry, assimilation, and disengagement/exit. In F. M. Jablin & L. L. Putnam (Eds.), *The new handbook of organizational communication: Advances in theory, research, and methods* (pp. 732–818). Sage.

Jian, G., & Dalisay, F. (2017). Conversation at work: The effects of leader–member conversational quality. *Communication Research*, *44*(2), 177–197. https://doi.org/10.1177/0093650214565924

Jones, G. E. (1999). Hierarchical workplace romance: An experimental examination of team member perceptions. *Journal of Organizational Behavior*, *20*(7), 1057–1072. https://doi.org/10.1002/(SICI)1099-1379(199912)20:7%3C1057::AID-JOB956%3E3.0.CO;2-O

Keyton, J. (2017). Communication in organizations. *Annual Review of Organizational Psychology and Organizational Behavior*, *4*, 501–526. https://doi.org/10.1146/annurev-op-04-030217-100001

Kinicki, A. J., & Vecchio, R. P. (1994). Influences on the quality of supervisor–subordinate relations: The role of time-pressure, organizational commitment, and locus of control. *Journal of Organizational Behavior*, *15*(1), 75–82. https://doi.org/10.1002/job.4030150108

Kram, K. E., & Isabella, L. A. (1985). Mentoring alternatives: The role of peer relationships in career development. *Academy of Management Journal*, *28*(1), 110–132. https://doi.org/10.2307/256064

Lam, L. W., Peng, K. Z., Wong, C., & Lau, D. C. (2017). Is more feedback seeking always better? Leader–member exchange moderates the relationship between feedback-seeking behavior and performance. *Journal of Management*, *43*(7), 2195–2217. https://doi.org/10.1177/0149206315581661

Lee, Y., & Kim, J. (2023). How family-supportive leadership communication enhances the creativity of work-from-home employees during the COVID-19 pandemic. *Management Communication Quarterly*, *37*(3), 599–628. https://doi.org/10.1177/08933189221144997

Lee, Y., Li, J. Y., & Sunny Tsai, W. H. (2021). Diversity-oriented leadership, internal communication, and employee outcomes: A perspective of racial minority employees. *Journal of Public Relations Research*, *33*(5), 314–334. https://doi.org/10.1080/1062726X.2021.2007388

Lincoln, J. R., & Miller, J. (1979). Work and friendship ties in organizations: A comparative analysis of relational networks. *Administrative Science Quarterly*, *24*(2), 181–199. https://doi.org/10.2307/2392493

Lutgen-Sandvik, P., Namie, G., & Namie, R. (2009). Workplace bullying: Causes, consequences, and corrections. In P. Lutgen-Sandvik & B. D. Sypher (Eds.), *Destructive organizational communication: Processes, consequences, and constructive ways of organizing* (pp. 27–52). Routledge.

Mainiero, L. A. (1989). *Office romance: Love, power and sex in the workplace*. Rawson Associates.

Mainiero, L. A., & Jones, K. J. (2013). Sexual harassment versus workplace romance: Social media spillover and textual harassment in the workplace. *Academy of Management Perspectives*, *27*(3), 187–203. https://doi.org/10.5465/amp.2012.0031

Mano, R., & Gabriel, Y. (2006). Workplace romances in cold and hot organizational climates: The experience of Israel and Taiwan. *Human Relations*, *59*(1), 7–35. https://doi.org/10.1177/0018726706062739

Men, L. R., Qin, Y. S., & Jin, J. (2022). Fostering employee trust via effective supervisory communication during the COVID-19 pandemic: Through the lens of motivating language theory. *International Journal of Business Communication*, *59*(2), 193–218. https://doi.org/10.1177/23294884211020491

Methot, J. R., Lepine, J. A., Podsakoff, N. P., & Christian, J. S. (2016). Are workplace friendships a mixed blessing? Exploring tradeoffs of multiplex relationships and their associations with job performance. *Personnel Psychology*, *69*(2), 311–355. https://doi.org/10.1111/peps.12109

Michael, J. H., Leschinsky, R., & Gagnon, M. A. (2006). Production employee performance at a furniture manufacturer: The importance of supportive supervisors. *Forest Products Journal*, *56*(6), 19–24.

Michelson, G., & Mouly, S. (2000). Rumour and gossip in organisations: A conceptual study. *Management Decision*, *38*(5), 339–346. https://doi.org/10.1108/00251740010340508

Mikkelson, A., Sloan, D., Walter, R., & Hinnenkamp, C. (2023). Supervisor communication competence and employee outcomes: Predictive effects in remote, hybrid, and in-person workplaces. *Business and Professional Communication Quarterly*, Advance online publication. https://doi.org/10.1177/23294906231167176

Miller, V. D., & Jablin, F. M. (1991). Information seeking during organizational entry: Influences, tactics, and a model of the process. *The Academy of Management Review*, *16*(1), 92–120. https://doi.org/10.5465/AMR.1991.4278997

Myers, S. A., Cranmer, G. A., Goldman, Z. W., Sollitto, M., Gillen, H. G., & Ball, H. (2018). Differences in information seeking among organizational peers: Perceptions of appropriateness, importance, and frequency. *International Journal of Business Communication*, *55*(1), 1–14. https://doi.org/10.1177/2329488415573928

Odden, C. M., & Sias, P. M. (1997). Peer communication relationships and psychological climate. *Communication Quarterly*, *45*(3), 153–166. https://doi.org/10.1080/01463379709370058

Omilion-Hodges, L. M., & Ptacek, J. K. (2021). *Leader-member exchange and organizational communication*. Palgrave Macmillan. https://doi.org/10.1007/978-3-030-68756-4_6

Omilion-Hodges, L. M., & Sugg, C. E. (2019). Millennials' views and expectations regarding the communicative and relational behaviors of leaders: Exploring young adults' talk about work. *Business and Professional Communication Quarterly*, *82*(1), 74–100. https://doi.org/10.1177/2329490618808043

Parker, P. S. (2005). *Race, gender, and leadership: Re-envisioning organizational leadership from the perspectives of African American women executives*. Lawrence Erlbaum.
Pierce, C. A., Byrne, D., & Aguinis, H. (1996). Attraction in organizations: A model of workplace romance. *Journal of Organizational Behavior*, *17*(1), 5–32. https://doi.org/10.1002/(SICI)1099-1379(199601)17:13.0.CO;2-E
Putnam, L. L., & Pacanowsky, M. E. (1983). *Communication and organizations*. Sage.
Qin, Y. S., & Men, L. R. (2023). Exploring the impact of internal communication on employee psychological well-being during the COVID-19 pandemic: The mediating role of employee organizational trust. *International Journal of Business Communication*, *60*(4), 1197–1219. https://doi.org/10.1177/23294884221081838
Quinn, R. E. (1977). Coping with cupid: The formation, impact, and management of romantic relationships in organizations. *Administrative Science Quarterly*, *22*(1), 30–45. https://doi.org/10.2307/2391744
Ragins, B. R. (2002). Understanding diversified mentoring relationships: Definitions, challenges, and strategies. In D. Clutterbuck & B. R. Ragins (Eds.), *Mentoring and diversity: An international perspective* (pp. 23–53). Butterworth Heinemann.
Ragins, B. R., & Scandura, T. A. (1997). The way we were: Gender and the termination of mentoring relationships. *Journal of Applied Psychology*, *82*(6), 945–953. https://doi.org/10.1037/0021-9010.82.6.945
Ramaswami, S. N., Srinivasan, S., & Gorton, S. A. (1997). Information asymmetry between salesperson and supervisor: Postulates from agency and social exchange theories. *Personal Selling and Sales Management*, *17*(3), 29–51. https://doi.org/10.1080/08853134.1997.10754098
Ray, E. B. (1993). When the links become chains: Considering dysfunctions of supportive communication in the workplace. *Communication Monographs*, *60*(1), 106–111. https://doi.org/10.1080/03637759309376301
Redding, C. W. (1985). Stumbling toward an identity: The emergence of organizational communication: Past and present tenses. In R. D. McPhee & P. K. Tompkins (Eds.), *Organizational communication: Traditional themes and new directions* (pp. 15–54). Sage.
Rumens, N. (2017). Researching workplace friendships: Drawing insights from the sociology of friendship. *Journal of Social and Personal Relationships*, *34*(8), 1149–1167. https://doi.org/10.1177/0265407516670276
Sergeant, A., & Frenkel, S. (1998). Managing people in China: Perceptions of expatriate managers. *Journal of World Business*, *33*(1), 17–34. https://doi.org/10.1016/S1090-9516(98)80002-3
Shah, N. P., Parker, A., & Waldstrom, C. (2017). Examining the overlap: Individual performance benefits of multiplex relationships. *Management Communication Quarterly*, *31*(1), 5–38. https://doi.org/10.1177/0893318916647528
Sias, P. M. (2005). Workplace relationship quality and employee information experiences. *Communication Studies*, *56*(4), 375–395. https://doi.org/10.1080/10510970500319450
Sias, P. M. (2009). *Organizing relationships: Traditional and emerging perspectives on workplace relationships*. Sage.
Sias, P. M. (2014). Workplace relationships. In L. L. Putnam & D. K. Mumby (Eds.), *The Sage handbook of organizational communication: Advances in theory, research, and methods* (3rd ed., pp. 375–399). Sage.
Sias, P. M., & Cahill, D. J. (1998). From coworkers to friends: The development of peer friendships in the workplace. *Western Journal of Communication*, *62*(3), 273–299. https://doi.org/10.1080/10570319809374611
Sias, P. M., Heath, R. G., Perry, T., Silva, D., & Fix, B. (2004). Narratives of workplace friendship deterioration. *Journal of Social and Personal Relationships*, *21*(3), 321–340. https://doi.org/10.1177/0265407504042835
Sias, P. M., Krone, K. J., & Jablin, F. M. (2002). An ecological systems perspective on workplace relationships. In M. L. Knapp & J. Daly (Eds.), *Handbook of interpersonal communication* (3rd ed., pp. 615–642). Sage.
Sias, P. M., Pederson, H., Gallagher, E. B., & Kopaneva, I. (2012). Workplace friendship in the electronically connected organization. *Human Communication Research*, *38*(3), 253–279. https://doi.org/10.1111/j.1468-2958.2012.01428.x
Sias, P. M., & Perry, T. (2004). Disengaging from workplace relationships: A research note. *Human Communication Research*, *30*(4), 589–602. https://doi.org/10.1111/j.1468-2958.2004.tb00746.x

Society of Human Resource Management. (2023). *New SHRM survey: Workplace romance 2023*. Retrieved from https://www.shrm.org/about/press-room/new-shrm-survey-workplace-romance-2023

Sollitto, M., & Myers, S. A. (2015). Peer coworker relationships: Influences on the expression of lateral dissent. *Communication Reports*, *28*(1), 36–47. https://doi.org/10.1080/08934215.2014.925569

Steelman, L. A., & Rutkowski, K. A. (2004). Moderators of employee reactions to negative feedback. *Journal of Managerial Psychology*, *19*(1), 6–18. https://doi.org/10.1108/02683940410520637

Thomas, C. H., & Lankau, M. J. (2009). Preventing burnout: The effects of LMX and mentoring on socialization, role stress, and burnout. *Human Resource Management*, *48*(3), 417–432. https://doi.org/10.1002/hrm.20288

Turban, D. B., Jones, A. P., & Rozelle, R. M. (1990). Influences of supervisor liking of a subordinate and the reward context on the treatment and evaluation of that subordinate. *Motivation and Emotion*, *14*(3), 215–233.

Wheatley, M. (1999). *Leadership and the new science: Discovering order in a chaotic world* (2nd ed.). Berrett-Koehler Publishers.

Wilson, R. J., Filosa, C., & Fennel, A. (2003). Romantic relationships at work: Does privacy trump the dating police? *Defense Counsel Journal*, *70*(1), 78–88.

Wyant, M. H., & Kramer, M. W. (2022). "They are nothing more than his spies on the floor": Local employees' sensemaking and interpretation of expatriates' roles and responsibilities. *Management Communication Quarterly*, *36*(1), 124–148. https://doi.org/10.1177/08933189211029561

Xing, Y., Liu, Y., Tarba, S., & Wood, G. (2020). A cultural inquiry into ambidexterity in supervisor–subordinate relationship. *The International Journal of Human Resource Management*, *31*(2), 203–231. https://doi.org/10.1080/09585192.2015.1137619

Yelvington, K. (1996). Flirting in the factory. *The Journal of the Royal Anthropological Institute*, *2*(2), 313–333. https://doi.org/10.2307/3034098

Yrle, A. C., Hartman, S. J., & Galle, W. P. (2003). Examining communication style and leader-member exchange: Considerations and concerns for managers. *International Journal of Management*, *20*(1), 92–100. https://doi.org/10.1108/13632540210807099

Yue, C. A., Thelen, P., & Verghese, A. K. (2022). Should I speak up? How supervisory communication, team culture, and team relationships determine employees' voice behavior. *International Journal of Business Communication*, Advance online publication. https://doi.org/10.1177/23294884221104794

11 Identity and Identification

Craig R. Scott and Rebecca J. Meisenbach

It is difficult to imagine a broader topic than *identity* when it comes to studying humans. Identity research has exploded across the social sciences in the past 30 years, in part due to the rise of the individual self in Westernized society where unique identities become increasingly possible in a globalized, diversified, mobile, media-intensive, and consumption-driven world (Larson & Gill, 2017). Focusing on communicative views of identity still leaves substantial literature to examine – because communication and language play significant roles in how we construct and manage multiple and fragmented identities.

Considering how fundamental identity is, it should not be surprising that it is especially relevant when talking about the organization (Gioia, 1998). Our identities are linked to the organizations we work for, belong to, and buy from. "Identity is increasingly constituted by public, profit-driven, and institutionalized discourses" (Tracy & Trethewey, 2005, p. 173). Those discourses are steeped in colonial, White, and Western assumptions. Furthermore, Deetz's (1992) argument that multinational corporations substantially influence people's daily lives still rings true today. Not only do organizational narratives shape individual identity, but organizations spend considerable resources on their own identities, as "identity has become a focused and professionalized enterprise, adopted by organizations in all sectors through the successive development of advertising, public relations, and marketing" (Cheney et al., 2014, p. 696). Identity issues have become even more central for organizations (Albert et al., 2000) amid the explosion of communication in our world and pressures for organizational transparency.

Inevitably, linkages between individual and organizational identities are crucial. This connection is usefully examined via organizational identification, which refers to the attachment between organizational members and the organization itself (Larson, 2017). These connections are shaped by and in turn influence various messages and broader discourses surrounding organizations and their members. These organizational memberships/affiliations become significant aspects of who we are (especially in a world where work organizations demand much of our time) but that identification also depends heavily on the identity of the organization and its values.

Thus, questions about *who am I?* and *who are we?* are not fully understood without also asking how those questions relate to one another. Cheney et al. (2014) have argued:

> Any comprehensive discussion of identity, identification, and organizational communication must consider at once (1) the grounds for and resources of identity construction and transformation in contemporary global society; (2) the articulation and promotion of corporate identities by institutions and organizations of all sorts;

DOI: 10.4324/9781003484639-14

and (3) the individual linkages to and bonds with organizations, industries, professions, brands, and other features.

(p. 695)

Thus, it is useful to collectively consider the powerful role of communication in shaping and revealing individual and organizational identities as well as in influencing identification processes between members and various collectives.

This chapter provides an overview of individual identities as relevant to contemporary organizations, organizational identities, and organizational identifications. For each, we describe them generally, examine relevant (meta)theoretical views and approaches, and highlight the constitutive role of communication. The chapter closes with a discussion about identity and identification as they pertain to organizing and communicating.

Individual Identity

At first glance, the construct of individual identity with its philosophical and psychological underpinnings may seem distant from communicating and organizing. However, a significant amount of organizational communication research focuses on aspects of individual identity. Organizations play a significant role in answering questions about *who am I?* for individuals even as those organizations are often struggling with that question (Larson & Gill, 2017).

One communication-focused definition of identity comes from Kuhn (2006): "the conception of the self reflexively and discursively understood by the self" (p. 1340). As Larson and Gill (2017) note, this definition is valuable because it positions discourse as central to the ongoing identity construction of the self. Cruz (2017) suggests that "identity is a complex concept that captures the multiple facets of the individual including personality, values, beliefs, roles, and, ultimately, how one perceives oneself in relation to others" (p. 1174). She adds that organizational communication scholars study various organizational and societal discourses (e.g., what it means to be a good worker or how to balance work and life) that impact how members view their identities generally and their organizational roles/jobs specifically.

Approaches/Perspectives

The relationship between identity and organizations can be examined through several metatheoretical lenses (Larson & Gill, 2017; also see Chapter 2). *Post-positivism* views identity as an essential, enduring set of traits or properties that distinguish one person from the next; this identity is measurable, and managers' communication helps shape these identities. The *social construction* perspective (an interpretive view) suggests language constructs reality, with identities created through, and reflected in, communication. *Critical* approaches see identities as sites of control and resistance. *Rhetorical* approaches examine how persuasive communication shapes identity and identification (discussed below). Such research also views identity work and management as a political resource that can be used to (de)legitimate arguments (Symon, 2005). A *postmodern* perspective draws attention to identities as fragmented, multiple, and contested where the experience of the self is constructed through power-laden language (although other metatheoretical views also allow for multiple identities). *Feminist* approaches emphasize the role of gender and other categories of sameness/difference; here again, identity is accomplished and (re)produced through communication and discourse. (See Chapter 13.)

Additionally, an intersectional approach to identity emphasizes how identities are constructed and resisted amid multiple intersections operating within a matrix of intertwined sources of oppression and privilege. Here, identities that other approaches might consider separately (e.g., race, gender, occupation) are viewed as inextricably interlocking. (See Chapter 14.) Decolonizing approaches to identity emphasize possibilities for distinct identities to confront and reform neoliberal policies, practices, and systems of power often intrinsic to nations and areas of the globe. (See Chapter 4.) Some scholars invoke combinations of the above approaches, such as Pal and Nieto-Fernandez (2024), who consider how identity scholarship discusses feminist transnationalism, intersectionality, and decolonizing approaches to the study of organizational communication. Other work in this space has connected intersectionality with the negotiation of managerial identity (Carrim & Nkomo, 2016).

Cutting across many of these perspectives is a *discursive* approach (Larson & Gill, 2017). This approach, which distinguishes little-d discourse (e.g., speech acts) from big-D Discourse (representing broader social narratives; see Chapter 3), views identities as discursively constructed and mediated, investigates the relationship between discourse and Discourse, considers the role of power, treats communication as constitutive, and sees identity and organizations as mutually constituted. Thus, a constitutive view of communication is highlighted. The methods used in such an approach include historical analyses, textual analysis, case studies, participant observation, ethnographic approaches, interviews, biographical/life narratives, and emerging methods such as photovoice (where participants provide visual images and then discuss them with the researcher).

Communication and Individual Identity

This discursive approach to identity highlights several overlapping areas where identity and organizations intersect. These include ideas related to *identity work, organizational/societal discourses* about identities, and work on the *crystallized self* as it pertains to organizational members.

Identity Work

Identity work describes how a sense of self is formed/reformed through our interactions amid existing societal and organizational discourses (Alvesson et al., 2008). Some scholars have recently considered the impacts of the COVID-19 pandemic on identity communication (see Spradley et al., 2020 for a collaborative autoethnography of negotiating mother/scholar identities during the pandemic). Others call for more work that considers how "individuals make sense of their selves and their legitimacy in relation to a collective-associative view of an occupational identity" – an approach that aligns with calls for postcolonial occupational identity research (Tian, 2023, p. 103; see also Cunha & Alcadipani Da Silveira, 2024). Definitions of the self are continuously formed, repaired, maintained, strengthened, or revised when a person's sense of self is challenged (Alvesson et al., 2008). Larson and Gill (2017) also point to organizational changes (e.g., restructuring job assignments) and destructive practices (e.g., workplace bullying) that require additional identity work.

As Cruz (2017) explains, many challenges to self-identity (e.g., face-threatening acts, role changes) require identity work. Kwon (2021) recently examined the unique identity work of employees with disabilities. Similarly, by analyzing identity struggles among Chinese women political leaders, Tian (2023) illustrated the value of highlighting both materiality and non-human agents in the performance of identity work amid cultural discourses of *suzhi* and *guanxi*. Negative statements about one's employer or occupation, especially if engaged in any form of "dirty work" (see Ashforth & Kreiner, 1999), may also necessitate identity work.

Organizational/Societal Discourses

Another way of framing research about individual identity and organizing highlights broader societal/organizational discourses. A discursive resource is a "concept, phrase, expression, trope, or other linguistic device that (a) is drawn from practices or texts, (b) is designed to affect other practices and texts, (c) explains past or present action, and (d) provides a horizon for future practice" (Kuhn et al., 2008, p. 162). These discursive resources "function as the building blocks for identity, the substance from which people imagine various possible identities … for themselves" (Larson & Gill, 2017, p. 65).

Such resources have been linked to the regulation of individual identities. For example, discourses of entrepreneurship and enterprise (e.g., Gill, 2013; Larson & Gill, 2017) and professionals and professionalism (e.g., Cheney & Ashcraft, 2007; Clair, 1996) are often studied in relation to identity regulation (see also Ferguson & Dougherty, 2022, for an analysis of how Black identity is not included in these discourses). Meisenbach and Feldner (2019) explain how television shows like *Undercover Boss* rhetorically construct a discursive resource of an ideal worker that organizational members then use to form their organizational identities. Other research explores how individuals embodying non-normative identities often experience tension between their own preferred identities and organizational norms (see Compton & Dougherty's, 2017, discussion of co-sexuality and Sahay & Dwyer's, 2023, analysis of hero discourses and nurses' identity management during the COVID-19 pandemic).

These discursive resources enable and constrain identity for organizational members, who may also resist these discourses. Mumby (2005) argues for a dialectic approach that highlights tensions and contradictions in identity control and resistance work. Holmer Nadesan's (1996) study of female service workers shows how resistance to identity regulation is enacted – and how that resistance can itself be controlling. Others have noted that responses to narratives about what makes for a "good mother" or an "ideal worker" can be resisted or integrated in creative ways to manage organizational attempts at identity regulation (e.g., Turner & Norwood, 2013; Wieland, 2010; see also Jammaers & Zanoni's, 2021, analysis of disabled workers resisting ideal worker discourses).

Crystallized Self

Work on real, fake, and crystallized selves is also relevant to a discursive approach to individual identity and organizing. Tracy and Trethewey (2005) argue that an employee's position in the organizational hierarchy offers unique, although often problematic, possibilities for identity construction. Their analysis suggests that some employees take extreme measures to align their seemingly real-self with a preferred organizational self (with one's best self reserved for work at the likely expense of nonwork relations and activities). In other cases, organizational members perform a seemingly fake, but organizationally preferred, identity (e.g., emotional labor; see Chapter 18). Tracy and Trethewey claim that these understandings of the real-self and the fake-self pervade popular understandings of identity and more scholarly discourse – to the detriment of organizational members.

Tracy and Trethewey (2005) challenge past conceptualizations of identity construction with the metaphor of the "crystallized self" to describe a unique whole that has many facets and "different shapes depending on the various discourses through which they are constructed and constrained" (p. 186). In this perspective, organizational members can begin to alter identities across work, home, and the spaces between through language – suggesting communication's constitutive role in shaping identities: "Rather than privileging work as the only productive realm of everyday experience, individuals might begin to elevate their nonprofessional selves alongside those that intersect with work" (e.g., home, community, or leisure; Tracy & Trethewey, 2005, p. 187). Similarly, Jones (2020) has analyzed the challenges experienced by individuals in minoritized groups, such as trans* persons, in trying to achieve a crystallized self understandable as authentic within work settings.

Intersectionality and postcoloniality are relevant here because they highlight how identities (e.g., race, gender, class) are inextricably intertwined with multiple Western systems of oppression and privilege (see Chapter 14). Intersectional identity work can be central to future organizational communication research that recognizes how power-laden identity categories come together (see Allen, 2023). Additionally, postcolonial and decolonial research can challenge identity-neutral approaches to diversity, equity, and inclusion (DEI) efforts, by promoting identity-conscious approaches that consider broad institutional, societal, and geographical contexts (e.g., Villamil et al., 2023). Such work invites organizational scholars to consider multiple facets of identities and the role of power-laden communication and colonial systems of oppression in their construction and expression.

Organizational Identity

Fields such as management, organization studies, and communication have examined organizational identity as a root construct addressing an essential question of existence (Pratt et al., 2016). Albert and Whetten (1985) classically define organizational identity as that which is central, distinct, and enduring about the collective. Questions of identity essentially ask, "Who are we?" or "Who is [organization]?" An organization's identity is revealed through its values and mission – as well as its name, products/services, physical location, and/or the people it employs (see Cheney et al., 2004). Furthermore, an organization's visual identity (e.g., logos, colors, architecture, and product packaging) provides visibility and recognizability (van den Bosch et al., 2006).

Several constructs are commonly linked to and overlap with organizational identity. Corporate identity focuses on how management represents the organization's identity symbolically to external audiences (see Hatch & Schultz, 2000). Balmer (2001) articulates an organization's actual, communicated, and conceived identities, noting the desire for alignment among them. Brown et al. (2006) consider four constructs: Organizational identity (who we are as an organization), intended image (what the organization wants others to think about it), construed image (what the organization believes others think about it), and reputation (what stakeholders actually think). Relations among identity, image, and reputation have been explored in a variety of theoretical models (Dukerich & Carter, 2000; Hatch & Schultz, 2000, 2003). Image matters because it represents our assessment of what others see when they look at the organization (Dutton & Dukerich, 1991), which may encourage the organization to adapt its identity to change its image. Reputations are associated with how well an organization communicates (Fombrun & Rindova, 2000). Reputations are revealed in multiple ways (e.g., company rankings, media coverage, consumer feedback, etc.);

furthermore, negative feedback threatens core identity and creates a high likelihood of response (Dukerich & Carter, 2000).

Wieland (2017) argues that organizational communication scholars have "approached organizational identity in three primary ways: (1) as a resource for individual identity; (2) as a collective sense of self that enables interpretation and action; and (3) as external stakeholders' interpretations of who the organization is" (p. 1). The first strand of research relates to processes of organizational identification, which will be covered later in the chapter. The second approach views organizational identity as similar to individual identity but at a higher level. The third strand emphasizes the communication of organizational identity for external stakeholders (e.g., consumers, competitors, media). Adding to those three views, Sheep et al. (2023) argue members can make the organization's identities into a discursive resource to help them explain or reject major organizational events.

Approaches/Perspectives

Organizational identity can be examined via all of the lenses discussed earlier: functionalist, interpretive, critical, feminist, postmodern, intersectional, and postcolonial. A wide range of methodologies have been used to investigate organizational identity: narrative discourse analysis, ethnographies, grounded theory, case studies, surveys, and secondary data analysis – with slightly more qualitative than quantitative approaches overall (especially recently) (Foreman & Whetten, 2016).

Wieland (2017) describes key tensions in conceptualizations of organizational identity. The first centers on organizational identity as an entity (an inherent, measurable property) or as a social construction. In the former, pre-existing identity is made visible through communication. In the constructionist view, identity itself is fundamentally communicative as it is constructed and negotiated. Gioia and Hamilton (2016) characterize this tension from a social actor perspective, which treats organizational identity as a set of claims about how the organization should be seen by internal and external stakeholders, and a social construction perspective, which views identity as subject to revisions as members interact with others. These authors advocate structurational thinking (see Chapter 3) to overcome tensions in potentially competing perspectives.

A second related tension asks whether organizational identity is advanced by organizational leaders or emerges from various stakeholders. As Scott (2013) contends, both exist; there is a preferred identity based on leadership strategies and an emergent identity resulting from the involvement of others assessing who the organization seems to be. As Wieland (2017) notes, the emergent perspective aligns with constructionist and constitutive views that value various organizational stakeholders.

Wieland's (2017) third tension focuses on internal vs. external audiences. Although several definitions privilege internal audiences, others have defined organizational identity as a view shared by internal and external stakeholders (e.g., Henderson et al., 2015). As more external views are considered, image and reputation become increasingly important. Yet, to understand organizational members' constructions and interpretations of organizational identity, we need to consider communication with internal and external audiences (Cheney & Christensen, 2001). Institutional perspectives (see Chapter 3) on organizational identity also consider forces at play in the broader social context in which organizations are embedded (Gioia & Hamilton, 2016).

Organizations, like individuals, have multiple identities that reflect different views about centrality, distinction, and endurance (Cheney, 1991; Pratt & Foreman, 2000). Views of organizations and identities as fragmented, fleeting, and conflicting reinforce the utility of a multiple-identities perspective. Pratt and Foreman (2000) offer a useful framework for the management of multiple (sometimes conflicting) identities. *Deletion* involves abandoning all but one main identity. *Integration* fuses several existing identities into a distinct new identity. *Compartmentalization* is when the organization retains all identities but keeps them separate (e.g., different identities for different audiences). *Aggregation* maintains and integrates all identities. Pratt (2016) claims that views emphasizing multiple organizational identities align with social constructionist views and attend to a range of stakeholders. Intersectionality approaches can consider how various organizational-level identities foster systems of privilege and oppression, seeking opportunities for transformation. For example, Eger (2018) studied how a transgender outreach organization operated via a crystallized organizational identity that sought to address its own and its members' interlocking facets of identities.

Communication and Organizational Identity

Communication is central to organizational identity. Organizational identity management has focused on communicating identity consistently and frequently – sometimes with *integrated marketing communications* – which attempts to create a unified impression via a single organizational voice. Such communication may involve the practical deployment of various vehicles (public relations, marketing, etc.) to disseminate identity features. Schinoff et al. (2016) argue that identity is communicated through *saying, showing*, and *staging*. Their typology of organizational identity communication is based on clarity of identity content and intentional communication of that content. With low clarity and low intention, an organization may not know its identity, so cannot *say*, *show*, or *stage* it. With high clarity but low intent an organization may not need to communicate its identity – and to the extent it does, it is mostly just *shown*. With low clarity but high intent, an organization may communicate who it wants to be, mostly through what is *said*. Finally, with high intent and high clarity, an organization can communicate who it is through what it *says*, *shows*, and *stages*.

When identity is viewed in more processual/constitutive terms, the focus is on how identities are regularly (re)negotiated based on interactions with various relevant others (see Cheney & Christensen, 2001). As Cheney et al. (2014) explain, in this sense organizations enact their identities through the stories they tell about themselves; organizational identities are seen as "volatile social constructions based in large part on the interpretive capabilities and preferences of their audiences" (p. 698). Cooren et al. (2011) argue that because communication constitutes organizations, "it only becomes possible to conceive and talk of an 'organizational identity' as grounded in language and as having no existence other than in discourse" (p. 1159).

Several empirical connections between organizational identity and constitutive views of communication have been offered in recent years. For example, Dobusch and Schoeneborn's (2015) study of the hacktivist group Anonymous extends work on organizational identity "by emphasizing the fundamental and formative role of identity claims in the communicative constitution of social collectives as organizational entities" (p. 1006) – suggesting the fluid rather than static nature of such collectives. Kopaneva and Sias (2015) take a constitutive view of identity in examining how organizational mission statements are constructed. Madsen's (2016) study of interactions in a Danish bank illustrates how members use internal social media (ISM) to challenge and negotiate organizational identity:

"Discussing *who we are* as an organization and *how we should act* as members of this organization are closely related and ISM introduce a new communication arena for negotiating rules, norms, and organizational identity" (p. 202, emphasis in original). Dawson's (2018) work also examines how organizational identity is constituted through conversation/interaction in a social media brand-based community – noting both identity-confirming and identity-disconfirming messages from stakeholders involved in the "social co-construction of organizational identity" (p. 8). Koschmann (2013) investigates the closely related notion of how communication constitutes collective identity among a collaboration of social service agencies. These examples illustrate that multiple communicators operating at multiple levels of the organization may be involved in the construction of organizational identity. "Identity management is carried out not only by managers with communication responsibilities but also by rank-and-file members who identify with the organization" (Cheney et al., 2004, p. 126). We next turn to a discussion of identification by organizational members.

Organizational Identification

Pratt (1998) suggests that identification involves an individual seeing some "other" as being definitive of one's self when beliefs about that other become self-referential or self-defining (through either a recognition of affinity or a changing of identity to emulate the other). Identification relates to specific aspects of identity more so than other forms of attachment (e.g., commitment). One's desire for identification stems from the need for safety, affiliation, self-enhancement, and more holistic (almost spiritual) goals.

Organizational identification refers to associations formed between organizational members/employees and the organization itself (Larson, 2017). Organizational identification is commonly defined as "the perception of oneness with or belongingness to [a collective], where the individual defines him or herself in terms of the [collective] in which he or she is a member" (Mael & Ashforth, 1992, p. 104). Barker (1998) argues identification "is not just a Western phenomenon; instead, it is *a characteristic of any organizing practice*" (p. 261, emphasis in original). Organizational identification describes both the process of becoming attached and the outcome of that process (Tompkins & Cheney, 1985).

Strong identification has been linked to a wide range of benefits (e.g., increased satisfaction, reduced turnover) for organizations and their members (see Ashforth et al., 2008). Affiliation with a highly regarded organization reflects positively on organizational members. Given such benefits, many organizations encourage member identification. Such efforts take on particular significance in societies where people spend increasing amounts of time with work organizations (Larson, 2017). Organizational identification also comes with downsides – most notably the control it may exert on members. Organizational identifications can also become an oversized part of who we are, evidenced by the many people who immediately mention their work or employer when first meeting others.

Indeed, individuals enact multiple identifications. People might identify – in general or in specific situations – with a work organization, a project team, a specific department, or a certain occupation/profession – in addition to various non-work identifications (religious organizations, family, etc.). Talk about multiple identifications often refers to *targets* of identification (where we aim to attach with various "others") and/or *resources* for identification (where we draw on those identities to shape our attachment) (Larson, 2017). Others have used the term identification *sources* to signify that identifications are simultaneously about targets and resources (Morgan et al., 2004). Although most research identifies specific targets/resources as other groups, organizations, or broader collectives, individuals may also identify with an organization's ideas, beliefs, and/or values.

Approaches/Perspectives

Scholarship on organizational identification comes primarily from two different disciplinary traditions (Scott, 2013). First, management scholars (e.g., Dutton & Dukerich, 1991; Mael & Ashforth, 1992; Pratt, 1998) have emphasized how individuals come to see themselves in terms of the organization's identity. The focus here is on a cognitive view of identification based on a member's beliefs and knowledge about the organization's identity. Some work in the management tradition has linked organizational identification to image and reputation. For example, the link between the attractiveness of an organization's image and the strength of member identification depends on the visibility of affiliation – with more visible/public roles in prominent organizations increasing organizational identification (Dutton et al., 1994). Management scholars have also paid attention to the dark side of member identification – including disidentification, deidentification, underidentification, overidentification, and schizo-identification (see Caprar et al., 2022). Another aspect of this work has examined identification among members engaged in "dirty work," where tasks have a physical, social, or moral taint associated with them (see Ashforth & Kreiner, 1999). If the dirty work is central to what the organization does, stronger identification may occur as compared to organizations where the dirty work aspects are less central to the overall identity (Kreiner et al., 2006). Relatedly, specific events (such as the COVID-19 pandemic) point toward a potential shift in salient worker identifications from their organizations to their occupations (Ashforth, 2020).

Much of the work in the management tradition draws on Social Identity Theory (SIT), a social-psychological approach to identification focusing on cognitive processes related to self-categorization (Tajfel & Turner, 1985). This approach has been described as one of the three primary schools of thought on organizational identification (Larson, 2017). SIT posits people have two aspects to their identities: a *personal identity* that concerns individual characteristics and beliefs and a *social identity* that includes associations with various groups including organizations. Organizational scholars primarily use SIT to better understand how organizational members come to identify with a collective via two processes (Pratt, 2001). *Categorization* involves clarifying in- and out-group boundaries and is more likely when the target organization is distinctive, outgroups are salient, and competition exists with other organizations. *Self-enhancement* suggests identification is more likely when an organization is prestigious, has an attractive image, and has an identity that increases members' esteem. SIT combines psychological and organizational views (Pratt, 2001) – but rarely mentions communication.

A second disciplinary-based research tradition examining organizational identification comes from organizational communication. Here we find Larson's (2017) other two research perspectives: rhetorical and structurational. Identification has frequently been traced back to the rhetorical strategies of Burke (1937), who described identification as part of the natural human desire to overcome divisions (see Cheney, 1983; Tompkins & Cheney, 1985). In this approach, organizations use specific rhetorical strategies (e.g., using collective "we" terms, uniting against a common enemy, and establishing common ground) to induce attachment and persuade members of their commonality and similar interests. Concertive control theory (Tompkins & Cheney, 1985) is also linked to this rhetorical tradition, explaining how members who are highly identified with an organization act "in concert" to hold each other accountable; this control is unobtrusive because it comes from peers rather than management (see Chapter 12). Recent work from the rhetorical perspective has also suggested that identification is ill-equipped to handle difference and alterity and that a focus on organizational subjectification can better attend to identity formation amid inequitable organizational conditions (Hanchey & Jensen, 2022).

In addition to SIT and rhetorically based views, Scott et al.'s (1998) structuration approach examines the mutually influential ways identification and identity relate. As they note, "most important indicators and expressions of identification are found in language. Thus, communicative manifestations of identification are emphasized as they occur in social interaction with others" (p. 305). Expressions of belonging or positive statements of membership represent important forms of member identification with the organization. They define identification as the "process of emerging identity," which implies "the forging, maintenance, and alteration of linkages between persons and groups" (p. 304). Scott et al. (1998) draw on several features of structuration theory in their model. The *duality of structure* suggests that structures (identities) are enabling and constraining when appropriated in the expressions of identifications that in turn serve to (re)create those identities. Additionally, the *regionalization of structure* helps to explain the ways in which multiple identities and identifications might relate to one another. *Situated activity* suggests that the identification process depends on what one is doing (and with whom they are doing it) and thus should be understood as changing based on context. Organizational identification research in the context of the COVID-19 pandemic illustrates situated activity (see e.g., Croucher et al., 2022; Sun et al., 2023). "Overall, the structural model of identification has proven useful in articulating the relationship between identity and identification as well as conceptualizing the complex, contextual, and communicative nature of identification" (Larson, 2017, p. 4) (see also Chapter 3).

Researchers have used varied methods to study organizational identification (e.g., questionnaires, interviews, observations, rhetorical analyses). In organizational communication, Cheney's Organizational Identification Questionnaire (OIQ) was widely used until critiques emerged of its considerable overlap with measures of organizational commitment (Miller et al., 2000). Mael and Ashforth's (1992) measure is prominent across fields. Scott and others have used select items from these two measures and extended them to other identification targets to assess multiple identifications (see Scott, 1997; Scott & Stephens, 2009). Qualitative approaches have begun to gain traction – focusing on interviews and textual analysis (Larson, 2017). We are beginning to see more sophisticated approaches when it comes to reconsidering organizational membership, challenging the desirability of identification, and questioning unitary expressions of identity. Future approaches should be culturally and historically informed, sensitive to time, multi-level, multi-methodological, and practical – but also critical/reflective and ethically aware (Cheney et al., 2014). Efforts to consider diversity climate and justice as they relate to organizational identification represent steps in this direction (see e.g., Asadullah et al., 2017; Rawski & Conroy, 2020).

Communication and Organizational Identification

Each of the perspectives discussed previously has implications for connecting communication to identification processes. In SIT, "direct reference to communication has been remarkably absent" (Postmes, 2003, p. 88); yet, even here, communication may play an important role. In SIT, simply talking about the collective or wearing a sign that signifies group membership can make group identity salient and foster identification. As Postmes explains, communication is possible because of our social identities and commonalities; it also helps shape those identities.

Bartel and Dutton (2001) argue for the need to move beyond psychic/cognitive views of identification to better understand "how a sense of membership in an organization is constituted through daily interactions with others" (p. 116). Scott (2007) has specifically noted five key linkages between communication and SIT that are relevant to organizational identification and identity: the salience of dual/multiple identifications, computer-mediated communication and virtual work related to identification, relationally focused work identities, organizational-level identities, and disidentification and related forms.

As already discussed, rhetorical and structurational perspectives have been used to describe how communication constitutes identification, how that identification may be expressed, and how those interactions influence identity and future identification processes. More recent efforts build on those traditions by specifically looking at how organizational identification communicatively constitutes an organization. For example, Chaput et al. (2011) view organizational identification as a "communicative process through which people develop a common basis for collective action and argue that this process of 'consubstantialization' is of central importance for the constitution of an organization" (p. 253). Their study shows how identification (and dis/mis-identification) occurs through communication and how that plays into the coproduction of a Canadian political organization.

Research has moved from simply studying multiple identifications to examining how communication influences the management of those identifications (Larson, 2017). Scott (1997) found that in decentralized, geographically dispersed organizations, members identify more strongly with local offices with whom they have greater interaction. Kuhn and Nelson (2002) found that those with more central places in a communication network tended to have stronger identification with multiple targets/sources. Larson and Pepper (2003) found three broad strategies for communicatively managing tensions between identifications: comparison (which uses rhetorical juxtaposition of competing identification targets to compare identity options), logic (which involves constructions of situationally and culturally logical arguments for identification choices), and support (which consists of communicative strategies referencing support from others to justify identifications).

Other work has looked at externally directed communication linked to identification. For example, Bartel et al. (2016) note that stakeholder identification is fostered through expressions of organizational identity. How identity is expressed through websites and other channels is part of the effort to craft a desired organizational image that facilitates identification. Cheney et al.'s (2014) notion of *auto-communication* (communication with self) is especially intriguing in explaining how communication about organizational identity influences identifications of internal audiences even though it is externally directed. Consider, for example, externally directed messages about corporate social responsibility that also influence employee identification with one's workplace (see Morsing, 2006). As Cheney notes, auto-communication can also be dysfunctional when there is an obsession with identity concerns.

Other strands of work suggest a need to reconsider how communication relates to identification. For example, efforts to communicatively manage multiple identifications challenge arguments favoring a "unified voice" when it comes to issues of identity and identification. Additionally, organizational members may have to reframe their thinking and their talk when dealing with the stigma surrounding dirty work or managing identifications with low-prestige organizations. Social media use and online relationships may influence identifications in expected and unexpected ways (see Bartels et al., 2019). Even recent work on hidden organizations suggests expressions of identification do not always suggest strong attachment; in some cases, silence reflects a stronger identification that does not reveal the hidden organization or its members (Scott, 2013).

Conclusion

As we think about individual identity, organizational identity, and organizational identification, it is clear communication is a vital element for all three. Clearly, various societal discourses influence the construction of identity at all levels and our interactions with various others influence the development of identity as we organize. More practically, communication is how we manage multiple identities and identifications, it allows for the induction of identification through various rhetorical strategies, and it is a vehicle for conveying and expressing identity to external and internal audiences. Thus, identity and identification are constructed as we organize (O_1); they display organizationality in their structuring (O_2); and organizational identity is crucial for entitative being (O_3; see Chapter 1).

To illustrate, imagine a member of a large company who is considering taking part in a corporate volunteering effort. Corporate communication about its identity as a good corporate citizen influences the development of a volunteer identity in employees and the identification of members with the corporation. How members talk to others shapes their own identification and influences the organization's identity. Although communication enables the development of various identities and identifications, it also constrains such efforts (e.g., when the company's volunteering-related messages seem hypocritical and lead members to avoid certain identities and resist organizational identification).

Communication is also seen in constitutive terms – implicitly and explicitly – in some of this work as well. Larson and Gill (2017) see communication as constitutive in discursive approaches to identity development. Organizational identity is clearly constructed and negotiated through communication (Wieland, 2017). Cooren et al. (2011) argue for a constitutive view of communication in the construction of organizational identity grounded in language; indeed, constitutive approaches among organizational communication scholars appear to be more common in studies of organizational identity than for the other constructs examined in this chapter. Having said that, Chaput et al. (2011) offer a very constitutive view of organizational identification. Even Scott et al. (1998) argue for constitutive-like processes related to communication and identity in their structurational model.

The C-O cycle (see Chapter 1) is also clear in this literature, as it is nearly impossible to separate organization and organizing from the communicative processes surrounding identity and identification. Indeed, a communication as constitutive view of organizations understands both constructs in terms of the other. This aligns with a process view of organizing, where the organization is best viewed as an ongoing construction composed largely of interactions with various others. Thus, it is organizing that helps to (re)create and (re)negotiate a fluid sense of identity at multiple levels. Views of organizational identification that emphasize its ongoing development in situated interactions with others fit here as well.

However, it is also useful to consider the ways in which organizations are understood as entities and structures when it comes to identity and identification. As entities, organizations are a pervasive aspect of our society, and each organizational entity has its own identities. This entity perspective is highlighted in one of Wieland's (2017) key tensions surrounding organizational identity. The view of organizations as entities also aligns with many views of organizational identification, where the organization is the "thing" to which we attach. Organizations are key storytellers, narrators, and sources of discourse that influence identity and identification. These collective entities are often powerful actors that strategically shape identity and identification and that may unobtrusively control members through such processes. As a form of structure, organizations provide important resources (discursive and otherwise) for members to appropriate in the creation of multiple identities/ identifications. Those structures may also sanction some identities as more or less preferred and can create challenges for identity (e.g., because of the nature of some forms of work). SIT is relevant here when it comes to organizational-based social identities. Structurational views also highlight ways in which organizations are structures that enable and constrain identity and identification.

Approaches that more closely consider the interplay between communicating and organizing are especially important for understanding personal identity, organizational identity, and organizational identification. As Larson and Gill (2017) conclude, "a discursive identity lens offers researchers an avenue to uncover necessary understandings about a fundamental factor and process of organizational life and to link identity to other important organizational constructs" (p. 171). Pratt et al.'s (2016) advice that future research should focus on process and deepen understanding of plurality and complexity also points to the importance of communication and constitutive views. It is vital that we consider not only the positive ways that organizations and communication construct identity and identification but also the ways communication deconstitutes organization as we resist, reframe, disidentify, and challenge certain identities and identifications (see Chapter 12). Although research in these areas is still largely US-based and has only recently begun to consider DEI issues, organizational communication scholars are in a position to do so as we continue offering valuable insights, useful theory, and informed research about identity and identification.

Recommended Supplementary Readings

Ashcraft, K. L. (2013). The glass slipper: "Incorporating" occupational identity in management studies. *Academy of Management Review*, *38*, 6–31.

This article redefines the current division of scholarly labor and, through the use of the glass slipper metaphor, theorizes collective occupational identity and its relation to other identities.

Barker, J. R., & Tompkins, P. K. (1994). Identification in the self-managing organization: Characteristics of target and tenure. *Human Communication Research*, *21*(2), 223–240.

This study examines worker identification with two targets simultaneously: one's self-managing team and the larger employing organization.

Meisenbach, R. J., & Kramer, M. W. (2014). Exploring nested identities: Voluntary membership, social category identity, and identification in a community choir. *Management Communication Quarterly*, *28*(2), 187–213.

This study explores how individuals articulate identities and identification sources in the context of joining or continuing to participate in a community choir.

Russo, T. C. (1998). Organizational and professional identification: A case of newspaper journalists. *Management Communication Quarterly*, *12*(*1*), 72–111.

This study, one of the first to study multiple targets of organizational identification, examines organizational and professional identification among journalists.

Scott, C. R., Connaughton, S. L., Diaz-Saenz, H., Maguire, K., Ramirez, R., Richardson, B., Shaw, S. P., & Morgan, D. (1999). The impacts of communication and multiple identifications on intent to leave: A multi-methodological exploration. *Management Communication Quarterly*, *12*(3), 400–435.

This study examines multiple targets of identification and how they influence turnover intentions – revealing complex relationships between three different types of identification and intent to leave.

Important Concepts: Define and Discuss

Discursive resource
Identity
Multiple identities/identifications
Organizational identification
Organizational identity

Discussion Questions

1 How do issues like work–life balance, diversity and equity, corporate colonization, and calls for transparency relate to identity and identification in organizations?
2 Can a transmission view of communication (using various channels and messages to induce identification or convey identity) exist alongside a constitutive view of identity and identification in organizations?
3 How stable are identities and identifications as they relate to organizations? How do situations like the COVID-19 pandemic influence identity and identification?
4 How are individual identities (as discursively constructed) constituting and constituted by organizational identities (which are themselves discursively constructed)?
5 How might communication serve to deconstitute identities and identifications related to organizations?

Practitioners' Corner

Tips for Effectively Managing Organizational Identities and Identifications

The responsibility for identity management falls not only to organizational leadership and those in professional communication roles, but every member plays a potential role in the creation and management of their own identities, the organization's identity, and their identifications. Recognition of that dispersed responsibility and power is important. A few additional key tips are suggested by the literature as they relate to communication:

- Individual and organizational identities are better thought of as fluid than stable. Thus, it is vital to think about how we communicate a tentative identity to various audiences in different situations and how interactions with those stakeholders influence those identities.
- Individual and organizational identities are almost always multiple. Thus, part of our identity work is about communicatively managing what are sometimes competing and sometimes compatible identities for individuals and organizations.

- Identity and reputation are different issues, but they are intimately tied when we remember that identity is communicatively constructed through our interactions with others. Our identity and our reputation are mutually influential and consideration of either requires efforts to manage and appreciate both.
- We should be conscious about ways in which organizational practices (e.g., certain tasks, harassment, organizational change) as well as broader societal discourses about work can challenge the self-identity of members and threaten the identity of the organization. The creation and communication of policies and practices that are sensitive to identity concerns are essential.
- Strong bonds of identification from employees, customers, and others depend in part on the organizational identity being one with which people can align their own identity. Thus, organizations and their members should strive to co construct mutually beneficial identities.
- Members and organizational leaders should recognize that there are downsides to obsessing too much about communicating identity or creating forms of control based on identifications. Even disidentifications and deidentifications may serve as important feedback about how people see themselves in relation to the organization.
- Our identity messages to external audiences may be heard by internal members in ways that influence their identification. This "auto-communication" can be used strategically – and we should recognize the challenges in creating entirely distinct messages for different audiences.

If we always keep in mind that issues of identity and identification can be quite consequential for organizations and their members, we can help remain alert to threats that challenge identity and opportunities for constructing strong identities and identifications.

References

Albert, S., Ashforth, B. E., & Dutton, J. E. (2000). Organizational identity and identification: Charting new waters and building new bridges. *Academy of Management Review*, *25*(1), 13–17. https://doi.org/10.5465/AMR.2000.2791600

Albert, S., & Whetten, D. A. (1985). Organizational identity. In L. L. Cummings & B. M. Staw (Eds.), *Research in organizational behavior* (Vol. 7, pp. 263–295). JAI Press.

Allen, B. J. (2023). *Difference matters: Communicating social identity* (3rd ed.). Waveland Press.

Alvesson, M., Ashcraft, K. L., & Thomas, R. (2008). Identity matters: Reflections on the construction of identity scholarship in organization studies. *Organization*, *15*(1), 5–28. https://doi.org/10.1177/1350508407084426

Asadullah, M. A., Akram, A., Imran, H., & Arain, G. A. (2017). When and which employees feel obliged: A personality perspective of how organizational identification develops. *Journal of Work and Organizational Psychology*, *33*, 125–135. http://dx.doi.org/10.1016/j.rpto.2017.02.002

Ashforth, B. E. (2020). Identity and identification during and after the pandemic: How might COVID-19 change the research questions we ask. *Journal of Management Studies*, *57*(8), 1763–1766. https://doi.org/10.1111/joms.12629

Ashforth, B. E., Harrison, S. H., & Corley, K. G. (2008). Identification in organizations: An examination of four fundamental questions. *Journal of Management*, *34*(3), 325–374. https://doi.org/10.1177/0149206308316059

Ashforth, B. E., & Kreiner, G. E. (1999). "How can you do it?" Dirty work and the challenge of constructing a positive identity. *Academy of Management Review*, *24*(3), 413–434. https://doi.org/10.5465/amr.1999.2202129

Balmer, J. M. T. (2001). From the Pentagon: A new identity framework. *Corporate Reputation Review*, *4*(11), 11–21. https://doi.org/10.1057/palgrave.crr.1540129

Barker, J. R. (1998). Managing identification. In D. A. Whetten & P. C. Godfrey (Eds.), *Identity in organizations: Building theory through conversations* (pp. 257–267). Sage.
Bartel, C. A., Baldi, C., & Dukerich, J. M. (2016). Fostering stakeholder identification through expressed organizational identities. In M. G. Pratt, M. Schultz, B. E. Ashforth, & D. Ravasi (Eds.), *Organizational identity* (pp. 474–493). Oxford University Press.
Bartel, C. A., & Dutton, J. (2001). Ambiguous organizational memberships: Constructing organizational identities in interactions with others. In M. A. Hogg & D. J. Terry (Eds.), *Social identity processes in organizational context* (pp. 115–130). Psychology Press.
Bartels, J., van Vuuren, M., & Ouwerkerk, J. W. (2019). My colleagues are my friends: The role of Facebook contacts in employee identification. *Management Communication Quarterly*, *33*(3), 307–328. https://doi.org/10.1177/0893318919837944
Brown, T., Dacin, P., Pratt, M., & Whetten, D. (2006). Identity, intended image, construed image, and reputation: An interdisciplinary framework and suggested methodology. *Journal of the Academy of Marketing Science*, *34*(2), 95–106. https://doi.org/10.1177/0092070305284969
Burke, K. (1937). *Attitudes toward history*. The New Republic Press.
Caprar, D. V., Walker, B. W., & Ashforth, B. E. (2022). The dark side of strong identification in organizations: A conceptual review. *Academy of Management Annals*, *16*(2), 759–805. https://doi.org/10.5465/annals.2020.0338
Carrim, N. M., & Nkomo, S. (2016). Wedding intersectionality theory and identity work in organizations: South African Indian women negotiating managerial identity. *Gender, Work and Organization*, *23*, 261–277. http://hdl.handle.net/2263/53359
Chaput, M., Brummans, B. H., & Cooren, F. (2011). The role of organizational identification in the communicative constitution of an organization: A study of consubstantialization in a young political party. *Management Communication Quarterly*, *25*(2), 252–282. https://doi.org/10.1177/0893318910386719
Cheney, G. (1983). The rhetoric of identification and the study of organizational communication. *Quarterly Journal of Speech*, *69*(2), 143–158. https://doi.org/10.1080/00335638309383643
Cheney, G. (1991). *Rhetoric in an organizational society: Managing multiple identities*. University of South Carolina Press.
Cheney, G., & Ashcraft, K. L. (2007). Considering "the professional" in communication studies: Implications for theory and research within and beyond the boundaries of organizational communication. *Communication Theory*, *17*(2), 146–175. https://doi.org/10.1111/j.1468-2885.2007.00290.x
Cheney, G., & Christensen, L. T. (2001). Organizational identity: Linkages between internal and external communication. In F. M. Jablin & L. L. Putnam (Eds.), *The new handbook of organizational communication: Advances in theory, research, and methods* (pp. 231–269). Sage.
Cheney, G., Christensen, L. T., & Dailey, S. L. (2014). Communicating identity and identification in and around organizations. In L. L. Putnam & D. K. Mumby (Eds.), *The Sage handbook of organizational communication* (pp. 695–716). Sage.
Cheney, G., Christensen, L. T., Zorn, T. E. Jr., & Ganesh, S. (2004). *Organizational communication in an age of globalization: Issues, reflections, practices*. Waveland.
Clair, R. P. (1996). The political nature of the colloquialism, "a real job": Implications for organizational socialization. *Communication Monographs*, *63*(3), 374–381. https://doi.org/10.1080/03637759609376392
Compton, C. A., & Dougherty, D. S. (2017). Organizing sexuality: Silencing and the push–pull process of co-sexuality in the workplace. *Journal of Communication*, *67*(6), 874–896. https://doi.org/10.1111/jcom.12336
Cooren, F., Kuhn, T., Cornelissen, J. P., & Clark, T. (2011). Communication, organizing and organization: An overview and introduction to the special issue. *Organization Studies*, *32*(9), 1149–1170. https://doi.org/10.1177/0170840611410836
Croucher, S. M., Kelly, S., Green, M., Homsey, D. M., Cullinane, J., Rocker, K. T., Nguyen, T., Anderson, K., Chen, H., Ding, G. G., Ashwell, D., Wright, M., & Palakshappa, N. (2022). The link between supervisor-subordinate computer-mediated immediate behaviors and organizational identification in U.S., English, and Australian organizations. *Management Communication Quarterly*, *36*(4), 688–709. https://doi.org/10.1177/08933189221076859
Cruz, D. (2017). Identity, individual. In C. R. Scott & L. Lewis (Eds.), *The international encyclopedia of organizational communication* (online edition). Wiley-Blackwell. https://doi.org/10.1002/9781118955567.wbieoc101

Cunha, V. B. D. C., & Alcadipani Da Silveira, R. (2024). A postcolonial critique of occupational identity research. *Academy of Management Proceedings*, *2024*(1), 19014. https://doi.org/10.5465/AMPROC.2024.86bp

Dawson, V. R. (2018). Fans, friends, advocates, ambassadors, and haters: Social media communities and the communicative constitution of organizational identity. *Social Media + Society*, *4*(1), 1–11. https://doi.org/10.1177/2056305117746356

Deetz, S. (1992). *Democracy in an age of corporate colonization: Developments in communication and the politics of everyday life*. SUNY Press.

Dobusch, L., & Schoeneborn, D. (2015). Fluidity, identity, and organizationality: The communicative constitution of anonymous. *Journal of Management Studies*, *52*(8), 1005–1035. https://doi.org/10.1111/joms.12139

Dukerich, J. M., & Carter, S. M. (2000). Distorted images and reputation repair. In M. Schultz, M. J. Hatch, & M. H. Larsen (Eds.), *The expressive organization: Linking identity, reputation, and the corporate brand* (pp. 97–112). Oxford University Press.

Dutton, J. E., & Dukerich, J. M. (1991). Keeping an eye on the mirror: Image and identity in organizational adaptation. *Academy of Management Journal*, *34*(3), 517–554. https://doi.org/10.5465/256405

Dutton, J. E., Dukerich, J. M., & Harquail, C. V. (1994). Organizational images and member identification. *Administrative Science Quarterly*, *39*(2), 239–263. https://doi.org/10.2307/2393235

Eger, E. K. (2018). *Communicating organizational and transgender intersectional identities: An ethnography of a transgender outreach center* [PhD thesis, University of Colorado at Boulder]. https://search.proquest.com/openview/b2e82725a6783ef2d355e856900ced56/1?pq-origsite=gscholar&cbl=18750

Ferguson, M. W., & Dougherty, D. S. (2022). The paradox of the Black professional: Whitewashing Blackness through professionalism. *Management Communication Quarterly*, *36*(1), 3–29. https://doi.org/10.1177/08933189211019751

Fombrun, C., & Rindova, V. (2000). The road to transparency: Reputation management at Royal Dutch/Shell. In M. Schultz, M. J. Hatch, & M. H. Larsen (Eds.), *The expressive organization: Linking identity, reputation, and the corporate brand* (pp. 77–96). Oxford University Press.

Foreman, P. O., & Whetten, D. A. (2016). Measuring organizational identity: Taking stock and looking forward. In M. G. Pratt, M. Schultz, B. E. Ashforth, & D. Ravasi (Eds.), *Organizational identity* (pp. 39–64). Oxford University Press.

Gill, R. (2013). The evolution of organizational archetypes: From the American to the entrepreneurial dream. *Communication Monographs*, *80*(3), 331–353. https://doi.org/10.1080/03637751.2013.788252

Gioia, D. A. (1998). From individual to organizational identity. In D. A. Whetten & P. C. Godfrey (Eds.), *Identity in organizations: Building theory through conversations* (pp. 17–31). Sage.

Gioia, D. A., & Hamilton, A. L. (2016). Great debates in organizational identity study. In M. G. Pratt, M. Schultz, B. E. Ashforth, & D. Ravasi (Eds.), *Organizational identity* (pp. 21–38). Oxford University Press.

Hanchey, J. N., & Jensen, P. R. (2022). Organizational rhetoric as subjectification. *Management Communication Quarterly*, *36*(2), 261–287. https://doi.org/10.1177/08933189211043253

Hatch, M. J., & Schultz, M. (2000). Scaling the Tower of Babel: Relational differences between identity, image, and culture in organizations. In M. Schultz, M. J. Hatch, & M. H. Larsen (Eds.), *The expressive organization: Linking identity, reputation, and the corporate brand* (pp. 11–35). Oxford University Press.

Hatch, M. J., & Schultz, M. (2003). Bringing the corporation into corporate branding. *European Journal of Marketing*, *37*(7/8), 1041–1064. https://doi.org/10.1108/03090560310477654

Henderson, A., Cheney, G., & Weaver, C. K. (2015). The role of employee identification and organizational identity in strategic communication and organizational issues management about genetic modification. *International Journal of Business Communication*, *52*(1), 12–41. https://doi.org/10.1177/2329488414560278

Holmer Nadesan, M. (1996). Organizational identity and space of action. *Organization Studies*, *17*(1), 49–81. https://doi.org/10.1177/017084069601700103

Jammaers, E., & Zanoni, P. (2021). The identity regulation of disabled employees: Unveiling the 'varieties of ableism' in employers' socio-ideological control. *Organization Studies*, *42*(3), 429–452. https://doi.org/10.1177/0170840619900292

Jones, S. E. (2020). Negotiating transgender identity at work: A movement to theorize a transgender standpoint epistemology. *Management Communication Quarterly*, *34*(2), 251–278. https://doi-org.proxy.mul.missouri.edu/10.1177/0893318919898170

Kopaneva, I., & Sias, P. M. (2015). Lost in translation: Employee and organizational constructions of mission and vision. *Management Communication Quarterly*, *29*(3), 358–384. https://doi.org/10.1177/0893318915581648

Koschmann, M. A. (2013). The communicative constitution of collective identity in interorganizational collaboration. *Management Communication Quarterly*, *27*(1), 61–89. https://doi.org/10.1177/0893318912449314

Kreiner, G. E., Ashforth, B. E., & Sluss, D. M. (2006). Identity dynamics in occupational dirty work: Integrating social identity and system justification perspectives. *Organization Science*, *17*(5), 619–636. https://doi.org/10.1287/orsc.1060.0208

Kuhn, T. (2006). A "demented work ethic" and a "lifestyle firm": Disclosure, identity, and workplace time commitments. *Organization Studies*, *27*(9), 1339–1358. https://doi.org/10.1177/0170840606067249

Kuhn, T., Golden, A. G., Jorgenson, J., Buzzanell, P. M., Berkelaar, B. L., Kisselburgh, L. G., Kleinman, S., & Cruz, D. (2008). Cultural discourses and discursive resources for meaning/ful work constructing and disrupting identities in contemporary capitalism. *Management Communication Quarterly*, *22*(1), 162–171. https://doi.org/10.1177/0893318908318262

Kuhn, T., & Nelson, N. (2002). Reengineering identity: A case study of multiplicity and duality in organizational identification. *Management Communication Quarterly*, *16*(1), 5–38. https://doi.org/10.1177/0893318902161001

Kwon, C. (2021). Resisting ableism in deliberately developmental organizations: A discursive analysis of the identity work of employees with disabilities. *Human Resource Development Quarterly*, *32*, 179–196. https://doi.org/10.1002/hrdq.21412

Larson, G. S. (2017). Identification, organizational. In C. R. Scott & L. Lewis (Eds.), *The international encyclopedia of organizational communication* (online edition). Wiley-Blackwell. https://doi.org/10.1002/9781118955567.wbieoc100

Larson, G. S., & Gill, R. (2017). *Organizations and identity*. Polity Press.

Larson, G. S., & Pepper, G. L. (2003). Strategies for managing multiple organizational identifications: A case of competing identities. *Management Communication Quarterly*, *16*(4), 528–557. https://doi.org/10.1177/0893318903251626

Madsen, V. T. (2016). Constructing organizational identity on internal social media: A case study of coworker communication in Jyske Bank. *International Journal of Business Communication*, *53*(2), 200–223. https://doi.org/10.1177/2329488415627272

Mael, F. A., & Ashforth, B. E. (1992). Alumni and their alma mater: A partial test of the reformulated model of organizational identification. *Journal of Organizational Behavior*, *13*(2), 103–123. https://doi.org/10.1002/job.4030130202

Meisenbach, R. J., & Feldner, S. B. (2019). Constructing the ideal worker identity: The rhetorical construction of discursive resources in Undercover Boss. *Western Journal of Communication*, *83*(4), 403–422. https://doi.org/10.1080/10570314.2019.1566564

Miller, V., Allen, M., Casey, M., & Johnson, J. (2000). Reconsidering the organizational identification questionnaire. *Management Communication Quarterly*, *13*(4), 626–658. https://doi.org/10.1177/0893318900134003

Morgan, J. M., Reynolds, C. M., Nelson, T. J., Johanningmeier, A. R., Griffin, M., & Andrade, P. (2004). Tales from the fields: Sources of employee identification in agribusiness. *Management Communication Quarterly*, *17*(3), 360–395. https://doi.org/10.1177/0893318903258169

Morsing, M. (2006). Corporate social responsibility as strategic auto-communication: On the role of external stakeholders for member identification. *Business Ethics: A European Review*, *15*(2), 171–182. https://doi.org/10.1111/j.1467-8608.2006.00440.x

Mumby, D. K. (2005). Theorizing resistance in organization studies: A dialectical approach. *Management Communication Quarterly*, *19*(1), 19–44. https://doi.org/10.1177/0893318905276558

Pal, M., & Nieto-Fernandez, B. (2024). Politics of transnational feminism to decolonize feminist organizational communication: A call to action. *Management Communication Quarterly*, *38*(1), 60–85. https://doi.org/10.1177/08933189231161620

Postmes, T. (2003). A social identity approach to communication in organizations. In S. A. Haslam, D. Van Knippenberg, M. J. Platow, & N. Ellemers (Eds.), *Social identity at work: Developing theory for organizational practice* (pp. 81–97). Psychology Press.

Pratt, M. G. (1998). To be or not to be? Central questions in organizational identification. In D. A. Whetten & P. C. Godfrey (Eds.), *Identity in organizations: Building theory thorough conversations* (pp. 171–207). Sage.

Pratt, M. G. (2001). Social identity dynamics in modern organizations: An organizational psychology/organizational behavior perspective. In M. A. Hogg & D. J. Terry (Eds.), *Social identity processes in organizational context* (pp. 13–30). Psychology Press.

Pratt, M. G. (2016). Hybrid and multiple organizational identities. In M. G. Pratt, M. Schultz, B. E. Ashforth, & D. Ravasi (Eds.), *Oxford handbook of organizational identity* (pp. 106–120). Oxford University Press. https://doi.org/10.1093/oxfordhb/9780199689576.013.28

Pratt, M. G., & Foreman, P. O. (2000). Classifying managerial responses to multiple organizational identities. *Academy of Management Review*, *25*(1), 18–42. https://doi.org/10.5465/amr.2000.2791601

Pratt, M. G., Schultz, M., Ashforth, B. E., & Ravasi, D. (2016). Introduction: Organizational identity, mapping where we have been, where we are, and where we might go. In M. G. Pratt, M. Schultz, B. E. Ashforth, & D. Ravasi (Eds.), *Oxford handbook of organizational identity* (pp. 1–18). Oxford University Press. https://doi.org/10.1093/oxfordhb/9780199689576.013.23

Rawski, S., & Conroy, S. (2020). Beyond demographic identities and motivation to learn: The effect of organizational identification on diversity training outcomes. *Journal of Organizational Behavior*, *41*(5), 461–478. https://doi.org/10.1002/job.2439

Sahay, S., & Dwyer, M. (2023). I am not a 'hero': U.S. nurses' identity overlaps and conflict during COVID-19. *Health Communication*, *38*(12), 2537–2548. https://doi.org/10.1080/10410236.2022.2088021

Schinoff, B. S., Rogers, K. M., & Corley, K. G. (2016). How do we communicate who we are? Examining how organizational identity is conveyed to members. In M. G. Pratt, M. Schultz, B. E. Ashforth, & D. Ravasi (Eds.), *Oxford handbook of organizational identity* (pp. 219–238). Oxford University Press. https://doi.org/10.1093/oxfordhb/9780199689576.013.8

Scott, C. R. (1997). Identification with multiple targets in a geographically dispersed organization. *Management Communication Quarterly*, *10*(4), 491–522. https://doi.org/10.1177/0893318997104004

Scott, C. R. (2007). Communication and social identity theory: Existing and potential connections in organizational identification research. *Communication Studies*, *58*(2), 123–138. https://doi.org/10.1080/10510970701341063

Scott, C. R. (2013). *Anonymous agencies, backstreet businesses, and covert collectives: Rethinking organizations in the 21st century*. Stanford University Press.

Scott, C. R., Corman, S. R., & Cheney, G. (1998). Development of a situated-action theory of identification in the organization. *Communication Theory*, *8*(3), 298–336. https://doi.org/10.1111/j.1468-2885.1998.tb00223.x

Scott, C. R., & Stephens, K. K. (2009). It depends on who you're talking to … predictors and outcomes of situated measures of organizational identification. *Western Journal of Communication*, *73*(4), 370–394. https://doi.org/10.1080/10570310903279075

Sheep, M. L., Rheinhardt, A., Hollensbe, E. C., & Kreiner, G. E. (2023). "Tearing the fabric" or "weaving the tapestry"? A discursive resources approach to identity-implicating organizational events. *Management Communication Quarterly*, *37*(1), 32–63. https://doi.org/10.1177/08933189221111911

Spradley, E., LeBlanc, S. S., Olson-Beal, H., Burrow, L., & Cross, C. (2020). Proving our maternal and scholarly worth: A collaborative autoethnographic textual and visual storying of mother-scholar identity work during the COVID-19 pandemic. *Journal of Motherhood Initiative*, *11*(2), 189–209.

Sun, R., Li, J.-Y. Q., Lee, Y., & Tao, W. (2023). The role of symmetrical internal communication in improving employee experiences and organizational identification during COVID-19 pandemic-inducted organizational change. *International Journal of Business Communication*, *60*(4), 1398–1426. https://doi.org/10.1177/23294884211050628

Symon, G. (2005). Exploring resistance from a rhetorical perspective. *Organization Studies*, *26*(11), 1641–1663. https://doi.org/10.1177/0170840605054626

Tajfel, H., & Turner, J. C. (1985). The social identity theory of intergroup behavior. In S. Worchel & W. G. Austin (Eds.), *Psychology of intergroup relations* (2nd ed., pp. 7–24). Nelson-Hall.

Tian, Z. (2023). Suzhi, guanxi, and the abject body: Nonhuman agents of paradox that perform identity work together with Chinese women political leaders. *Management Communication Quarterly*, *37*(1), 99–126. https://doi-org.proxy.mul.missouri.edu/10.1177/08933189221095615

Tompkins, P. K., & Cheney, G. (1985). Communication and unobtrusive control in contemporary organizations. In R. D. McPhee & P. K. Tompkins (Eds.), *Organizational communication: Traditional themes and new directions* (pp. 179–210). Sage.
Tracy, S. J., & Trethewey, A. (2005). Fracturing the real-self–fake-self dichotomy: Moving toward "crystallized" organizational discourses and identities. *Communication Theory*, *15*(2), 168–195. https://doi.org/10.1111/j.1468-2885.2005.tb00331.x
Turner, P. K., & Norwood, K. (2013). Unbounded motherhood: Embodying a good working mother identity. *Management Communication Quarterly*, *27*(3), 396–424. https://doi.org/10.1177%2F0893318913491461
van den Bosch, A. L. M., de Jong, M. D. T., & Elving, W. J. L. (2006). Managing corporate visual identity: Differences between profit and non-for-profit, and manufacturing and service organizations. *Journal of Business Communication*, *43*, 138–157. https://doi.org/10.1177/0021943605285476
Villamil, A. M., Mendoza, P., Hoyos Ensuncho, M., & Reina Zambrano, J. (2023). La inclusión relacional: Examining neoliberal tensions, relational opportunities, and fixed understandings in diversity, equity, and inclusion work in the Global South. *Human Communication Research*, *49*(2), 158–169. https://doi.org/10.1093/hcr/hqad011
Wieland, S. M. B. (2010). Ideal selves as resources for the situated practice of identity. *Management Communication Quarterly*, *24*(4), 503–528. https://doi.org/10.1177/0893318910374938
Wieland, S. M. B. (2017). Organizational identity. In C. R. Scott & L. Lewis (Eds.), *The international encyclopedia of organizational communication* (online edition). Wiley-Blackwell. https://doi.org/10.1002/9781118955567.wbieoc156

12 Power and Resistance

Heather M. Zoller and Zhuo Ban

A critical lens challenges some traditional approaches to understanding organizational communication by highlighting power and resistance dynamics. Rather than focusing primarily on shared meaning and cooperation, critical researchers view organizing as a site of conflict, both apparent and hidden. Critical studies are built on the interpretive turn in organizational communication and adopt a discourse of suspicion (Mumby, 1997). A central part of critical inquiry, therefore, is to question how certain meanings become dominant in the organizing process and whose interests are served by those symbolic constructions (see Chapter 2). As a result, many scholars theorize organizations as "social historical creations accomplished in conditions of struggle and power relations" (Deetz, 2001, p. 25), and as "political sites where various organizational actors and groups struggle to 'fix' meaning in ways that will serve their particular interests" (Mumby, 2004, p. 237). From this viewpoint, emphasizing consensus can hide conflicting interests in ways that create and reinforce relationships of domination and coloniality (Broadfoot & Munshi, 2007; Parker, 2003). At the same time, interrogating meaning structures affords possibilities of resistance and change.

The chapter begins by describing how researchers have conceptualized relationships among power, organizing, and communication. We then detail a range of theories related to both control and resistance. Finally, we demonstrate how these concepts operate in two areas: negotiating workplace health and well-being, and responses to corporate power in late capitalism.

Defining Power in Organizational Communication

First, we describe how scholars have theorized power from communication and organizational perspectives. Early conceptualizations of power drew from other disciplines, such as psychologists French and Raven's (1959) bases of social power. Their model theorized sources of social influence, including reward, coercive, legitimate, referent, and expert power. In political science, Dahl (1957) theorized a "one-dimensional" pluralist model, which construed power as a person's or group's direct influence over the behavior of others (e.g., an ability to make someone do something they would not otherwise do). Bachrach and Baratz (1962) introduced a two-dimensional model highlighting how elite groups control agendas to impede or suppress discussion of issues that might threaten their interests and preferences. Lukes' (1974) three-dimensional model added a more complex view of communication by observing that power operates in the absence of apparent conflict through the ability to shape and articulate the desires of others.

DOI: 10.4324/9781003484639-15

Organizational communication scholars expanded the three-dimensional model to conceptualize power as a centrally communicative phenomenon. As described in Chapter 2, some scholars integrated critical perspectives with hermeneutic theories of interpretation and social constructionist epistemologies to highlight how struggles over meaning are constitutive of organizational life (Clair, 1993; Conrad, 1983; Deetz, 1992; Mumby, 1993). For example, Hardy and Phillips (2004) suggested that dominant groups establish and maintain power by "articulating meaning in ways that legitimate their particular views as 'natural' and 'inevitable,' link the actions and preferences of other actors to the achievement of their interests, and make particular socially constructed structures take on a neutral and objective appearance" (p. 304). Scholars drawing from feminist and standpoint theorizing also highlight the role of power in communicative constructions of subjectivity (Allen, 1996; Nadesan, 1996; Parker, 2003). Mumby and Clair (1997) theorized that:

> The most effective use of power occurs when those with power are able to get those without power to interpret the world from the former's point of view. Power is exercised through a set of interpretive frames that each worker incorporates as part of his or her organizational identity.
>
> (p. 184)

Observing that extant feminist research often treated the subject as raceless and classless, Patricia Parker (2003) retheorized "… the gendered, raced, and classed communicative practices that constitute organizational control and resistance" (p. 260). Decolonial research highlights how identity constructions are tied to relations of domination between Western countries and the Global South (Pal et al., 2023).

Power and the Communicative Constitution of Organization

These definitions situate power in communicative terms. In addition, critical scholars have long theorized *organizing* as a fundamentally communicative and power-laden process. Critical organizational communication researchers were influenced by sociologist Anthony Giddens' (1979) theory of structuration (see Chapter 3). As we discuss below, Giddens emphasized the role of power and ideology in the recursive (mutually defining) processes of constituting individual agency and social structures, demonstrating how social structures can take on "objective" status.

This orientation reflects the *organization as grounded in action* perspective (Fairhurst & Putnam, 2004; also see Chapter 3) because it views organizational action and structure as mutually constitutive. Although contemporary CCO researchers draw from structuration to examine how micro-level, relational communication processes constitute and are constituted by organizational structures, this research often overlooks Giddens' focus on power and ideology. As such, much of the research in this area stopped short of considering how constructions systematically favor the interests of some groups over others. For example, some argued that CCO research treated workers and managers as equally capable of discursively constructing the organization (Cloud, 2005), or limited power to "… the competencies of individual actors; the effects of organizational structure on actors; or the concentration of power in authority figures" (Kwon et al., 2009).

CCO research does investigate authority and influence. For example, Kuhn (2008) theorized the "authoritative text." Recently, McDonald et al. (2020) drew from Deleuzian theory to conceptualize power in material rather than human-centered terms as "the capacity to set forces into particular relations" (p. 25), and force as "the capacity to affect and be affected" (p. 25). However, these differ from ideological approaches that address how organizing processes constitute and are constituted by larger cultural and political systems. For example, workplace policies about harassment are influenced by larger cultural and public policy discourses about race, gender, and sexuality, and changes in workplace policies recursively influence larger cultural discourses (Allen, 2009; Dougherty, 2023; Lewis, 2009). Critical theorists center power by interrogating how these communicative constructions evolve into enduring patterns that appear to be outside of our control, with the goal of facilitating change. Recently, scholars have forwarded feminist new materialism as a bridge between CCO and critical theories of power (see Harris, 2016; Kuhn et al., 2019; Zoller & Ban, 2024).

Significantly, much of the work defining power emerges from Western contexts. We describe below how research from the global south engages different frames related to domination and resistance. The next section discusses theories that expand our understanding of communication and control processes.

Conceptualizing Power and Control Processes

Drawing from multiple theoretical perspectives, researchers have created a rich conceptual repertoire for understanding relationships among communication, power, and control. In the following section, we describe ideology and hegemony, concertive control, systematically distorted communication, biopower and discipline, as well as intersectional theories of identity, and coloniality (see Chapter 4).

Ideology and Hegemony

Many critical theorists trace their roots to Karl Marx (1967). Marx was a German theorist who identified capitalism as the primary source of inequality and exploitation. In the 19th-century factory economy, capitalists made profits by paying the workers less than the value of what they produced. Marx described the ways in which ideologies served to hide workers' exploitation in this system, but he also theorized this exploitation as the source of a worker revolution aimed at the development of socialism. German scholars in the Frankfurt School (Institute for Social Research) sought to understand why workers continued to consent to exploitation. As they did so, they expanded Marx's approach to address multiple sources of inequality, including the economic, ideological, and cultural bases of power (see Chapter 2).

Contemporary critical research examines how ideologies, or shared belief systems, construct and reinforce the power of dominant groups in a range of social contexts. Anthony Giddens (1979) theorized the functions of ideology, including:

- Communicating the interests of certain groups as universal (e.g., "what is good for GM is good for America" or "free trade will lift all boats").
- Denying societal contradictions (e.g., U.S. politicians saying "we have the best healthcare in the world" ignores high costs and lack of access for many low and middle-income Americans).
- Reifying existing social relations (e.g., treating social hierarchies and inequities as natural and inevitable – "the rich got that way because they work hard.").

Antonio Gramsci (1971) was an Italian Marxist theorist who theorized linkages between ideology and *hegemony*. Hegemony entails a relationship in which a social group accepts subordination to a dominant group or groups as the norm. Subordinate groups "consent to and support belief systems and structures of power relations that do not necessarily serve – indeed, may work against – those groups' interests" (Mumby, 1997, p. 344). Dominant groups are able to articulate their own interests in ways that lead other groups to identify with them. For example, in the wake of the #MeToo movement calling attention to sexual harassment (as well as #WoYeShi in China, #MeTooGarçons in France, #MosqueMeToo in 2018 in Iran, and many others), we have seen women criticize victims who shared stories of harassment for being *too sensitive* or failing to come forward sooner. These criticisms identify with and support the dominant, masculine perspective.

However, as we discuss later, hegemony is not a matter of simple domination. It involves active struggles over meaning among multiple groups (Mumby, 1997). For example, women disagree about what constitutes harassment, and face different barriers in speaking out, leading to a situation where many conversations about gender equity center dominant groups' experiences (Parker, 2003).

Concertive Control

Concertive control is a related concept. Barker (1993) and Barker and Cheney (1994) expanded on Edwards' (1981) theorizing about simple (direct, authoritative), technological, and bureaucratic control (rules and hierarchical structures) to consider normative approaches (see Chapters 7 and 11). Barker observed that the creation of self-managing work teams allowed organizations to reduce layers of supervision, promote more flexible production practices, and increase production speed. Teams developed *concertive* or internalized forms of control, resulting in team members policing themselves more powerfully than supervisors had previously. Workers enforced stricter work expectations because they had internalized organizational values and felt a stronger commitment to apparently voluntary goals. An example of concertive control comes from the movie *Office Space*, when a manager in an Applebee's-type restaurant questions a server (played by Jennifer Aniston) about her *flair* (quirky buttons on her uniform): "I only see 15 pieces." He asks, "What do you think of someone who only does the bare minimum?" Aniston's character suggests that he should change the minimum to 30 if that is what he wants. The manager responds, "I thought you wanted to express yourself." Management hopes that employees will desire to "express themselves" in ways that support organizational goals. (You can search "Joanna Quits" to see the scene.)

Systematically Distorted Communication

A different strain of critical research examines the role of power in enabling or constraining democratic participation in meaning construction and decision-making. For example, researchers draw from German philosopher Jurgen Habermas' (1984) theorizing of distorted communication. Habermas posited an ideal speech situation in which communication follows a set of norms that facilitate open deliberation. In particular, participants:

- are able to evaluate each other's assertions on the basis of reason and evidence;
- are free from "non-rational" or coercive influences (physical or psychological);
- are motivated by the desire to achieve a rational consensus.

Although this model can be critiqued for its Western and gendered bifurcation of rationality and emotionality (Broadfoot & Munshi, 2007; Fraser, 1990/91), it provides a counterpoint for understanding *discursive closure*. Discursive closure occurs when a full evaluation of interests and claims is not possible, or certain people/perspectives are excluded from discussion. Communication becomes *systematically distorted* when these forms of closure are taken for granted and hidden from assessment (Deetz, 1992).

Groups with social and political power can use a variety of techniques to silence certain groups and ideas/positions. Discursive closure strategies include: neutralization, treating a value-based decision as though it were objective or value-free (*we had no choice but to downsize the company*); disqualification, using a rationale to rule out someone's ability to speak (*you are too emotional about this topic*); meaning denial, refusing to acknowledge valid interpretations of speech acts or events (*that was flirting, not harassment; I am not shouting!*), and denotative hesitance, refusing to label problems as such (*their behavior was inappropriate but not harassment*) (Clair, 1993; Deetz, 1992). For example, Lyon (2007) described how the pharmaceutical company Merck trained salespeople to use neutralization and topical avoidance to sell Vioxx despite well-established risks. Ban (2020) found that the garment industry's corporate social responsibility (CSR) discourses promoted "small steps of constant improvement" through discursively "open" discussions with labor rights groups that limited discussion of larger structural transformations.

Discursive closure prevents individuals and groups from actively participating in constructing meaning. As Deetz (1992) argued, "Democratic communication in these terms must be about the formation of knowledge, experience, and identity, not merely their expression" (p. 47). Some of our students have described this approach as going beyond making choices that were determined by others to actually "choose the choices."

Disciplinary Control

Critical discourses of suspicion can be contrasted with a postmodern "discourse of vulnerability" (Mumby, 1997), which questions foundational concepts and master narratives (e.g., objective truth, knowledge regimes, the unitary self), emphasizes contradiction and paradox (Ganesh, 2009), and treats power as shifting and diffuse. As described in Chapter 2, organizational communication scholars have drawn from Michel Foucault (1979, 1980) to theorize the productive role of power in forming the self, social norms, and structures of knowledge. Foucault addresses individuals (1) as *subjects* that actively make choices and (2) as *subject to* cultural and institutional efforts to shape knowledge and meaning. Foucault addresses both elements in theorizing *disciplinary power*. Discipline can be understood in terms of knowledge construction in defining fields of study and constituting professional practices (e.g., the discipline of communication, medical licensing). Discipline can also be understood in terms of discourses that inculcate standards for behavior. For example, institutions use surveillance technologies (e.g., tests and cameras) to observe and control the body in ways that become internalized by those controlled. Discipline operates through hidden and dispersed forms of power that render the individual highly visible. Foucault (1979) likened this process to Bentham's panopticon – a prison in which the guard is positioned to see all the prisoners. The prisoners internalize this gaze so that they discipline themselves even in the absence of the guard's direct observation. Disciplinary discourses work to create *docile bodies* that are ideal for particular economic/social arrangements, such as colonies, factories, military regiments, or knowledge work.

Digital technologies have forged new forms of panoptic control in the workplace, including productivity monitoring for remote workers and GPS tracking for gig workers (Berkelaar & Buzzanell, 2014; Ganesh, 2016). More broadly, Kellogg et al. (2020) described how digital media facilitates algorithmic control, which they argue is more comprehensive, interactive, and instantaneous than traditional and bureaucratic forms of control, with effects that are less easily discernable.

Emphasizing the embodied nature of disciplinary discourses, Foucault theorized biopower as a governmental technology "aimed at controlling life itself" (Dempsey & Gibson, 2017, p. 255) at the population level. For example, Dempsey and Gibson (2017) traced how popular discourses around school lunch construct the child's body and the problem of obesity in ways that reinforce class divisions and structure individualistic policy responses. Recent research also links biopolitical governmentality to *necropolitics*. Necropolitics results from intersecting colonial, carceral, capitalist, and military logics that render certain bodies vulnerable and mark them as "killable," facilitating the material destruction of populations (Banerjee, 2008b; Courpasson & Marti, 2019; Dempsey et al., 2022; Ganesh, 2018; Mbembe, 2019).

Organizing Marginalization: Otherness, and Intersectionality

As this discussion suggests, a range of scholars have linked domination with constructions of difference and identities (see Chapters 4 and 14). Research demonstrates how the organizing process constitutes and is constituted by inequities associated with gender, sexuality, race, class, nationality, and ability status (Biwa, 2021; Cruz, 2017; Fleming, 2007; Harris, 2017; McDonald et al., 2020; Parker et al., 2011; Pauly & Buzzanell, 2016). Postcolonial, feminist, anti-racist, and queer theorizing calls attention to the organizing of epistemological erasures as a mechanism of domination (Cruz, 2017).

Feminist research has described how gendered, binary distinctions such as subject/object, public/private, and emotionality/rationality devalue feminine experiences and ways of knowing (Ashcraft, 2009; Dougherty & Goldstein Hode, 2016). Queer theorizing calls attention to binary constructions of sexuality and gender that reinforce *heteronormativity*, the assumption that heterosexuality is fundamental and natural (Fleming, 2007; McDonald, 2015).

As discussed in Chapter 4, decolonial studies theorize marginalization resulting from projects of colonization and decolonization (Guha, 1983; Shome & Hegde, 2002; Spivak, 1988). Colonialism can be understood as an all-encompassing form of power and subjugation involving an assemblage of technologies and practices that achieve control over economic, political, and social processes in the colonies, including constructions of history and knowledge that justify domination and exploitation. By centering the voices of marginalized groups, decolonial perspectives trace the social and material consequences of ongoing colonialist logics (Ban et al., 2013; Cruz, 2017; Ganesh, 2018; Irigaray et al., 2021). This work also counters the epistemic erasures of communities of color and the Global South resulting from conformity to dominant knowledge regimes in academia (Cruz et al., 2020; Pal et al., 2022, 2023). As Munshi articulated (Broadfoot & Munshi, 2007),

> The ivory tower of reason, rationality, and rigid structures colonizes the world of lived experience. And as a result, those who seek academic legitimacy for their narratives from the heart end up echoing the sanitized tone of the Master Narrative.
>
> (p. 256)

As you will see in Chapters 13 and 14, *intersectionality* highlights how multiple systems of inequality overlap in complex ways (Crenshaw, 1989; Collins & Bilge, 2020). For example, McDonald et al. (2020) draw from queer intersectional theorizing to describe how gendered, racial, and class discourses (at personal, organizational, and political levels) influence how queer individuals manage disclosures about their sexuality. Researchers also investigate how racialized organizational power relations are intertwined with class and gender hierarchies (Ashcraft & Allen, 2003; Parker, 2013; Parker & Mease, 2009). For example, Gist-Mackey (2018) describes how unemployment support organizations reinforce inequities by requiring job seekers to communicatively assimilate to white and middle-class norms and failing to acknowledge their material struggles.

Engaging Resistance

These approaches to communication and control dynamics are closely connected to conceptions of resistance. Resistance entails contesting or withdrawing consent from existing power relations. We describe different ways that organizational communication researchers have theorized this concept.

A Dialectical Approach

A dialectical perspective (Mumby, 2005; Mumby & Ashcraft, 2004) emphasizes the simultaneity of control and resistance, domination and subordination (after all, there is no need for power without resistance and vice versa). Rather than view power as a relatively fixed and one-way relationship, a dialectical view investigates struggles over meaning among individuals and groups that shift over time. The perspective avoids privileging control (viewing resistance as ineffectual, merely reproducing existing power relations) or romanticizing the concept (overestimating its value).

Scholars have documented different types of resistance including overt, covert, individual, and collective forms. Ganesh et al. (2005) called for renewed attention to understanding how resistant communication links to changing power relations. However, understanding the effects of resistance is complicated for many reasons. One is that contesting power is risky and often hidden from view. Therefore, researchers have highlighted the significance of covert, "backstage" behaviors like humor, bitching, misbehavior, cynicism, and even sabotage in expressing opposition and asserting autonomy (Morrill et al., 2003). Another complication is that relatively hidden and indirect resistance may reinforce the status quo. For example, Tracy (2000) observed that "hidden transcripts" of private "bitching" among cruise ship workers gave employees the impression of control but largely left in place disciplinary expectations that made employees vulnerable to harassment and burnout. Similarly, Fleming and Spicer (2003) observed that although employee cynicism demonstrates a failure in the managerial colonization of employee identity (e.g., *we are a family*), many cynical employees still follow organizational rules and norms in their behavior. For example, a Disneyland cast member who gives a highly enthusiastic greeting to park guests is fulfilling the company's goals, even if she believes her performance is ironic. Furthermore, cynicism can actively promote behavioral consent because cynical employees may view themselves as agentic subjects in ways that excuse compliance with management (see Chapter 11). As Fleming and Spicer pointed out, management ultimately cares about employee behavior more than their internal attitudes.

As these examples show, another challenge in linking resistance with change is that resistance often results in partial or unanticipated outcomes. For example, Lutgen-Sandvik (2006) found that bullied employees may exit the organization as a sign of defiance to bullies and their enablers, but the departure may be the outcome desired by the bully (see Chapter 11); airline pilots may resist managerial encroachment on their status by reinforcing their (gendered and bureaucratic) power over others (Ashcraft, 2005). Those engaging in resistance may ultimately reinforce what they seek to contest.

Despite the challenges, scholars have investigated how relatively hidden forms of resistance relate to more confrontational and collective challenges (Ganesh et al., 2005). Gossett and Kilker (2006) analysis of the website "radioshacksucks" found that "hidden transcripts" of employee complaints on the site facilitated more overt, collective resistance by making complaints visible to management and encouraging members to participate in an ongoing lawsuit against the company. Dissent researchers shed light on factors that promote or impede overt expressions of concern about workplace policies, including whistleblowing (Garner, 2016; Kassing et al., 2018). Zoller and Fairhurst (2007) theorized the organizing of collective resistance as a form of leadership. Their research described how discursive leadership can transform hidden transcripts of resistance into collective shows of solidarity (see also Parker, 2020; Zanin & Bissell, 2018).

Resistance as Collective Action

Ganesh et al. (2005) called for renewed attention to larger-scale efforts that seek transformative social change. Organizational communication scholars investigate protest, grassroots organizing, social movements, and union campaigns, as well as governmental and corporate responses (Ganesh & Stohl, 2010; Heath et al., 2013; Kendall et al., 2007; Zoller & Casteel, 2021). Significantly, workers have forged new methods to overcome barriers to collective action resulting from the rise of precarious contracted, home-based, part-time, and outsourced labor (Chattopadhyay & Pandit, 2021; Dutta & Kaur-Gill, 2018; Gálvez et al., 2021). Research demonstrates how groups manage vulnerabilities through strategic forms of visibility *and* invisibility (Cruz, 2017; Ganesh, 2018).

Linking collective resistance with policy outcomes, Conrad and McIntush (2003) theorized a rhetorical approach to the punctuated equilibrium model of policymaking. The model suggests that business elites maintain policy monopolies – situations where the policy status quo serves their interests – because they have knowledge, resources, and connections that other groups do not have. However, non-dominant groups *can* assert their influence and interrupt elite control of policymaking when three things occur:

> (1) long-standing sociopolitical conditions become visible to the public and are defined as "*problems*" of sufficient import to demand action by policymakers, (2) potential *solutions* are made available to policymakers, and (3) *political pressures* are sufficiently intense to overcome the dominance by political and economic elites.
>
> (Conrad, 2004, p. 312, emphasis in original)

Conrad's (2004) rhetorical perspective highlights the use of framing by elites and non-elites to set agendas and shape policy processes favorable to their interests. Non-elites can outflank more powerful groups by exploiting differing interests among elites or capitalizing on galvanizing events and issues. For example, after several high-profile school shootings in the U.S., parents and high school students challenged the National Rifle

Association by promoting increased background checks for gun purchases and pressuring stores such as Field & Stream to stop selling AR-15-style rifles. Zoller and Casteel (2021) observed, though, that by targeting the National Rifle Association, *March for Our Lives* activists missed an opportunity to directly diagnose gun manufacturers as the cause of gun deaths.

Thus, just like more covert and individual forms of resistance, collective action is vulnerable to reinforcing dominant relations of power (D'Enbeau & Buzzanell, 2011; Harness et al., 2022; Lucas & Mitra, 2023; Zoller, 2024). For example, Ban's (2023) analysis of fan groups in China shows that anti-capitalist protests and boycotts can be exploited and co-opted by platform capital and political leaders. Hanchey (2023) demonstrates how dominant rationalities threaten avowedly decolonial organizing, as Western "allyship" in a Tanzanian NGO reinforced white savior tropes. In part for this reason, standpoint and decolonial studies call for dialogic processes to interrogate dominant logic as a part of reclaiming marginalized voices (Pal, 2016; Parker, 2003; see Chapter 4).

In addition to studying resistance, theorists directly engage resistance to colonization by developing communicative theories of power based on Global South organizing (Biwa, 2021; Broadfoot & Munshi, 2015). For example, Spiller et al. (2020) challenge Western theories of leadership by highlighting how Māori collective leadership crosses generations as well as living and non-living entities. Kang and Krone (2021) draw from Tibetan practices of *niamle* to re-conceptualize organized dissonance (Ashcraft, 2006) and the four flows (McPhee & Zaug, 2008). Cruz and Sodeke (2020) re-theorize the concept of liquidity as the work of shape-shifting and adapting among disenfranchised groups in the Global South (see Chapters 1 and 4).

Communication, Power, and Resistance in Context

In this section, we provide two extended examples of how the conceptual issues above have been applied to investigate organizational power and politics. We describe how critical perspectives have revised our theorizing of workplace health and well-being as well as corporate issues management and counter-organizing.

Power and Resistance in Communicating Workplace Health and Well-Being

Many scholars and practitioners promote the benefits of workplace health promotion (WHP) and wellness programs (Geist-Martin et al., 2003; Stephens & Zhu, 2016; Stephens et al., 2013). Initiatives, which may include on-site gyms or gym membership, health education, and/or medical testing and services, are often treated as a "win-win" for workers and management. However, critical scholarship questions whose interests programs serve (Dale & Burrell, 2014; Ford & Scheinfeld, 2016; Zoller, 2003; Zoller et al., 2023).

Critical scholars have situated WHP and wellness as a form of disciplinary biopower (Foucault, 1980), representing a governing technique aimed at producing productive and *less costly* bodies for work (Dale & Burrell, 2014; Ford & Scheinfeld, 2016; ; Zoller, 2003). Incentives, insurance surcharges (e.g., Walmart and PepsiCo charged workers deemed to be overweight or have high cholesterol), and digital wearable trackers afford management surveillance of employee's lives (Elmholdt et al., 2021). Some workplaces offer more extreme, cult-like fitness regimes such as CrossFit (James & Gill, 2018; James & Zoller, 2017).

These health discourses are constitutive of organizing (and organizing is constitutive of health) (Zoller et al., 2023). For example, by constructing knowledge regimes around what it means to be healthy and what causes illness, WHP programs legitimate and expand managerial control. Attributing the causes of illness entails selecting from a web of factors that produce ill health, and these choices construct and reinforce social hierarchies and shape interventions (Zoller et al., 2023). Focusing on employee lifestyles over genetic, environmental, and sociopolitical causes reinforces the status quo by drawing attention away from workplace sources of illness-generated risks (e.g., working long hours and exposure to workplace toxins and hazards). Programs also construct and reinforce hierarchies by stigmatizing employees whose health status and/or bodies do not conform to program ideals. For example, some wellness participants at an automobile manufacturer labeled nonparticipants as "[not] really car[ing] about themselves" (Zoller, 2003, p. 195) and suggested that injured workers were at fault because they did not work out.

At the same time, employees may avoid or actively resist WHP initiatives when the programs are not perceived to meet their needs (Dailey & Zhu, 2017; James & Zoller, 2017). Researchers have also developed alternative models that challenge the status quo. Harrison and Stephens (2019) promoted "wellness *in* work," reconfiguring the individualized focus of stress management programs. Observing that workplace wellness models often arise from Western "white collar" workplaces, Zoller et al. (2023) developed a Critically Holistic Framework based on a transnational farm labor rights initiative. The model promotes worker participation in managerial decision-making, paired with structural enforcement mechanisms to improve workers' physical, mental, social, economic, and environmental health.

This holistic and structural approach highlights the breadth of ways that organizational communication influences health. For example, organizational and occupational identification may promote consent to emotional labor norms, overwork, and physical health risks (Dale & Gibson, 2014; Villamil & D'Enbeau, 2021). Racial, sexual, and other forms of harassment influence physical and mental well-being (Akella & Lewis, 2019; Allen, 2009; Dougherty, 2023; Hollis, 2019; Ivancic & Ford, 2023). Given that income is a primary predictor of health status (Marmot, 2002; Rosengren et al., 2019), WHP should encompass equitable pay, stable employment, and unemployment supports, particularly for precarious contracted labor in the global supply chain and "gig" work in platform capitalism (Chattopadhyay & Pandit, 2021; de Souza, 2019; Dougherty et al., 2018; Dutta & Kaur-Gill, 2018).

Capitalism, Corporate Social Responsibility, and Alternative Organizing

Beyond the workplace, corporations are powerful sites influencing well-being, human rights, sustainability, and economic stability. Critical organizational communication examines different approaches to challenging extractive models of corporate organizing.

CSR is touted as one way to harness the power of corporations toward social good. The dominant "win-win" school of CSR (Porter & Kramer, 2011) suggests that corporations can/should use their economic prowess to create positive social change by pursuing policies beneficial to both business and society. Critical engagement with CSR, however, points out that these initiatives further expand corporate power (Ban, 2020; Munshi & Kurian, 2005; Ganesh, 2007). Viewing CSR discourse as "an ideological movement that intend[s] to legitimize and consolidate the power of large corporations," Banerjee (2008a, p. 51) argued that CSR programs represent "stakeholder colonialism" – a strategy to regulate stakeholder behaviors for the benefit of the business interests. CSR discourse normalizes capitalist governmentality. For example, promoting corporations' commitment to social welfare (ranging from developing supplier codes of conduct to organizing a marathon to cure cancer) may give the impression that corporations can take over the role of government and other social institutions. CSR discourse may justify a socio-political structure with limited government intervention on social issues and reduced regulations on corporate activities. In short, CSR discourses may not make corporations more socially responsible, but they can prevent other social actors from effectively challenging corporate power over social issues (Ban, 2016, 2020; Harness, 2023).

Activism, including subaltern collectives and grassroots solidarity networks, represents another route to challenging corporate dominance. Research has investigated the role of protest in organizing transnational resistance to neoliberal institutions (e.g., the occupy movement) as well as Indigenous rebellions (Ganesh & Stohl, 2010; Heath et al. 2013). Organizational communication research highlights the confluence of digital and IRL protest in contesting corporate control and neoliberal ideologies (Ganesh & Stohl, 2013; Heath et al., 2013; Jiang & Korczynski, 2016; Zoller & Casteel, 2021).

In addition to contesting capitalism, activists articulate equitable and regenerative alternatives (Cruz, 2017; Dutta & Thaker, 2019; Kang & Krone, 2021; Pal, 2016; Zoller, 2024). For example, Maingi Ngwu (2023) investigated how utu-feminist values in Kenyan migrant women's informal childcare practices defy capitalism's racial exploitation by emphasizing solidarity, reciprocity, sharing, and gifting. Research highlights how alternative economy organizers (e.g., cooperatives, land trusts, mutual aid) employ narratives, dialectical tension framing, and strategic capacity building to overcome inequities in access to capital, markets, and government support in order to communicate the plausibility of equitable and sustainable economic transformation (Gordon, 2024; Lucas & Mitra, 2023; Zoller, 2024). As these examples show, organizational communication is well-situated to investigate new and creative responses emerging from marginalized communities to rapidly expanding crises related to disinformation and technological change, climate change, and economic and social inequality.

Conclusion

In this chapter, we surveyed some key literature investigating the complex relationships among communication, control, and resistance. Understanding power is crucial to investigating the communicative constitution of the organizing process. Many scholars covered in the chapter have captured the way power organizes as it is communicatively produced and reproduced, whether through the lens of ideology and hegemony, disciplinary discourses, coloniality, or concertive control. This chapter has also shown the different ways communication facilitates resistance and social change.

From the CCO perspective (see Chapter 3), organizations are grounded in action. This includes communicative practices that are shaped by and further reify existing power structures. In this chapter, we have demonstrated how day-to-day communication/interaction and deep enduring processes/structures enable and constrain one another in a spiraling fashion in the context of power and resistance. From a dialectical approach, we have emphasized the simultaneity of control and resistance, domination and subordination, and have discussed how ideological control is never complete but is always embedded in everyday interactions and discursive struggles. As such, resistance in the form of day-to-day interactions may challenge, disrupt, or eventually rupture dominant systems of meaning, and bring about change at the institutional or structural level. Moving forward, we encourage continued attention to the interconnections among power dynamics at organizational, cultural, political, and economic levels.

Recommended Supplementary Readings

Cruz, J. M., & Sodeke, C. U. (2020). Debunking Eurocentrism in organizational communication theory: Marginality and liquidities in postcolonial contexts. *Communication Theory, 31*(3), 528–548.

Conceptualizing liquidity as adaptive and shape-shifting organizing, the authors demonstrate the critical role of motion, solvency, and permeability in managing power relations in postcolonial contexts. The work challenges Eurocentric biases in organizational communication theory by centering disenfranchised actors from the Global South.

Ganesh, S. (2016). Managing surveillance: Surveillant individualism in an era of relentless visibility. *International Journal of Communication, 10*(14), 164–177.

This article emphasizes the role of individual actions in shaping surveillance and countersurveillance and proposes new research directions for understanding its impact on organizational dynamics.

Munshi, D., Cretney, R., Kurian, P., Morrison, S. L., & Edwards, A. (2024). Culture and politics in overlapping frames for the future: Multi-dimensional activist organizing and communicating on climate change in Aotearoa New Zealand. *Organization, 31*(3), 477–495.

The authors examine how climate change activist groups in Aotearoa New Zealand resist the status quo by radically reimagining the future. The research identifies how key organizing frames (rebel, reform, rebuild, and ruin) create spaces for alternative organizing.

Zoller, H. M., & Ban, Z. (2024). Communication, Power, and Organizational Politics. In V.D. Miller & M. S. Poole (Eds.), *Organizational communication theory and research* (pp. 277–294). De Gruyter Mouton.

The chapter reviews trends in theorizing power, resistance, and political organizing in organizational communication.

Important Concepts: Define and Discuss

Biopolitics
Colonialism
Concertive control
Dialectical approach
Disciplinary power
Hegemony
Heteronormativity
Ideology

Necropolitics
Patriarchy
Power
Punctuated equilibrium model
Resistance
Resistance, a covert form of
Social movement
Systematically distorted communication

Discussion Questions

1 What is the difference between concertive control and other types of control? Have you had experience when you internalize the value and objectives of the organization you are in? Please reflect on how some socially accepted values (e.g., efficiency and rationality) work to regulate the behavior of social actors.
2 How do you see the dialectical approach to power and resistance playing out in your university? Do you see examples of ways that undergraduate and graduate students both comply with and resist relationships of power on campus?
3 What are some examples of everyday forms of resistance that you see operating in places where you have worked?
4 What are some examples of how corporate values influence your educational experience and professional goals?

Practitioners' Corner

Communication practitioners must navigate the power dynamics and relationships inside (and outside) the organization in designing, executing, and evaluating communication programs. We find that communication practitioners may adopt two problematic tendencies in relation to power. The first tendency is to ignore or elide power issues, assuming equity in communication processes and outcomes. The second tendency is to treat power and control as absolute, assuming that power structures are immutable even when positive change is possible. Taking the case of internal or external campaign designers, these tendencies may lead practitioners to treat value-based communication practices as though they were objective or value-free, and/or may design campaigns that exclude or discredit some people's voices.

For example, a marketing campaign that is based on assumptions about "generally accepted" normative values may trigger vehement objections from underrepresented, marginalized, or subaltern social groups. A best practice is to consciously incorporate a power perspective through conscious inclusivity, and through substantively designing, executing, and evaluating communication programs. In doing so, communication practitioners may have the potential to be part of positive change toward a more power-equitable society. To that end, we will offer some strategic and tactical considerations.

Strategic considerations:

- Understand the power aspects of communicative situations. Is the target audience a historically disempowered group? If some form of persuasion is used in the communication, is the target audience empowered to make sound and independent judgments about the promoted position? Whose voice is represented?

- Design power-sensitive communication plans. Does the plan involve discursive closure and systematically distorted communication in the form of neutralization, disqualification, and meaning denial? When trying to reach an agreement with a target group, is the objective of the plan to realize mutual benefit or exert concertive control? Has the plan been checked for normative assumptions (e.g., in some Asian countries, many skin product commercials highlight the "skin-lightening" functions, assuming that lighter skin tone is more desirable)? Is there a plan for resistance, either in collective or individual, overt or covert forms?
- Critically evaluate communication programs. This means evaluating the output and outcome of campaigns beyond economic indicators. Does the plan result in discursive closure and systematically distorted communication? What kinds of relationships are built? Is the relationship mutually beneficial?

Tactical considerations:

- At the planning stage, it is important to conduct research that considers relationships of power. Communication network analysis often helps you identify patterns of influence.
- Invite or form inclusive teams to check for normative assumptions in the communication plan.
- Reach out to audience members who keep silent, and make sure that they feel empowered enough to voice their concerns if they have any. Organizational members who feel disempowered to disagree openly may use more covert forms of resistance. With internal audiences treat humor and gossip seriously.

References

Akella, D., & Lewis, V. J. (2019). The modern face of workplace incivility. *Organization Management Journal*, *16*(2), 55–60. https://doi.org/10.1080/15416518.2019.1604202

Allen, B. J. (1996). Feminist standpoint theory: A black woman's (re)view of organizational socialization. *Communication Studies*, *47*(4), 257–271. https://doi.org/10.1080/10510979609368482

Allen, B. J. (2009). Racial harassment in the workplace. In P. Lutgen-Sandvik, & B. Davenport Sypher (Eds.), *Destructive organizational communication* (pp. 164–183). Routledge.

Ashcraft, K. L. (2005). Resistance through consent? Occupational identity, organizational form, and the maintenance of masculinity among commercial airline pilots. *Management Communication Quarterly*, *19*(1), 67–90. https://doi.org/10.1177/0893318905276560

Ashcraft, K. L. (2006). Feminist-bureaucratic control and other adversarial allies: Extending organized dissonance to the practice of "new" forms. *Communication Monographs*, *73*(1), 55–86. https://doi.org/10.1080/03637750600557081

Ashcraft, K. L., & Allen, B. J. (2003). The racial foundation of organizational communication. *Communication Theory*, *13*, 5–38. https://doi.org/10.1111/j.1468-2885.2003.tb00280.x

Bachrach, P., & Baratz, M. (1962). Two faces of power. *American Political Science Review*, *56*, 947–952. https://doi.org/10.2307/1952796

Ban, Z. (2016). Delineating responsibility, decisions and compromises: A frame analysis of the fast-food industry's online CSR communication. *Journal of Applied Communication Research*, *44*(3), 296–315. https://doi.org/10.1080/00909882.2016.1192290

Ban, Z. (2020). Open for change but closed for transformation: A communicative analysis of managerial corporate social responsibility discourse on the issue of labor. *Organization*, *27*(6), 900–923. https://doi.org/10.1177/1350508419867209

Ban, Z. (2023). Emotional communities in the economy of emotions: A study of discursive muscularity in networked mobilization of fan groups in China. In M. Pal, J. Cruz, & D. Munshi (Eds.), *Organizing at the Margins. New perspectives in organizational communication*. Palgrave Macmillan. https://doi.org/10.1007/978-3-031-22993-0_11

Ban, Z., Sastry, S., & Dutta, M. J. (2013). "Shoppers' Republic of China": Orientalism in neoliberal U.S. news discourse. *Journal of International and Intercultural Communication*, *6*(4), 280–297. https://doi.org/10.1080/17513057.2013.792941

Banerjee, S. B. (2008a). Corporate social responsibility: The good, the bad and the ugly. *Critical Sociology*, *34*(1), 51–79. https://doi.org/10.1177/0896920507084623

Banerjee, S. B. (2008b). Necrocapitalism. *Organization Studies*, *29*(12), 1541–1563. https://doi.org/10.1177/0170840607096386

Barker, J. (1993). Tightening the iron cage: Concertive control in self-managing teams. *Administrative Science Quarterly*, *38*, 408–437. https://doi.org/10.2307/2393374

Barker, J., & Cheney, G. (1994). The concept and practices of discipline in contemporary organizational life. *Communication Monographs*, *61*, 19–43. https://doi.org/10.1080/03637759409376321

Berkelaar, B. L., & Buzzanell, P. M. (2014). Cybervetting, person–environment fit, and personnel selection: Employers' surveillance and sensemaking of job applicants' online information. *Journal of Applied Communication Research*, *42*(4), 456–476. https://doi.org/10.1080/00909882.2014.954595

Biwa, V. (2021). African Feminisms and co-constructing a collaborative future with men: Namibian Women in Mining's discourses. *Management Communication Quarterly*, *35*(1), 43–68. https://doi.org/10.1177/0893318920973988

Broadfoot, K. J., & Munshi, D. (2007). Diverse voices and alternative rationalities: Imagining forms of postcolonial organizational communication. *Management Communication Quarterly*, *21*(2), 249–267. https://doi.org/10.1177/0893318907306037

Broadfoot, K. J., & Munshi, D. (2015). Agency as a process of translation. *Management Communication Quarterly*, *29*(3), 469–474. https://doi.org/10.1177/0893318915585158

Chattopadhyay, S., & Pandit, S. (2021). Freedom, distribution and work from home: Rereading Engels in the time of the COVID-19-pandemic. *tripleC: Communication, Capitalism & Critique. Open Access Journal for a Global Sustainable Information Society*, *19*(1), 140–153.

Clair, R. P. (1993). The bureaucratization, commodification, and privatization of sexual harassment through institutional discourse. *Management Communication Quarterly*, 7, 123–157. https://doi.org/10.1177/0893318993007002001

Cloud, D. L. (2005). Fighting words: Labor and the limits of communication at Staley, 1993 to 1996. *Management Communication Quarterly*, *18*(4), 543–592. https://doi.org/10.1177/0893318904273688

Collins, P. H., & Bilge, S. (2020). *Intersectionality*. John Wiley & Sons.

Conrad, C. (1983). Organizational power: Faces and symbolic forms. In L. L. Putnam, & M. E. Pacanowsky (Eds.), *Communication and organizations: An interpretive approach* (pp. 173–194). Sage.

Conrad, C. (2004). The illusion of reform: Corporate discourse and agenda denial in the 2002 "corporate meltdown". *Rhetoric & Public Affairs*, *7*(3), 311–338. https://doi.org/10.1353/rap.2005.0003

Conrad, C., & McIntush, H. G. (2003). Organizational rhetoric and healthcare policymaking. In T. L. Thompson, A. M. Dorsey, K. I. Miller, & R. Parrott (Eds.), *Handbook of health communication* (pp. 403–422). Lawrence Erlbaum Associates. https://doi.org/10.1177/08933189211000324

Courpasson, D., & Marti, I. (2019). Collective ethics of resistance: The organization of survival in the Warsaw Ghetto. *Organization*, *26*(6), 853–872. https://doi.org/10.1177/1350508418820993

Crenshaw, K. (1989). Demarginalizing the intersection of race and sex: A black feminist critique of antidiscrimination doctrine, feminist theory and antiracist politics. *University of Chicago Legal Forum*, *1989*, 139–167.

Cruz, J. M. (2017). Invisibility and visibility in alternative organizing: A communicative and cultural model. *Management Communication Quarterly*, *31*(4), 614–639. https://doi.org/10.1177/0893318917725202

Cruz, J. M., Gist-Mackey, A. N., Hanchey, J. N., Harris, K. L., Jensen, P. R., Kenney, S., & Leslie, K. J. (2020). ToneUpOrgComm-A Manifestx. *Departures in Critical Qualitative Research*, *9*(2), 152–154.

Cruz, J. M., & Sodeke, C. U. (2020). Debunking Eurocentrism in organizational communication theory: Marginality and liquidities in postcolonial contexts. *Communication Theory, 31*(3), 528–548. https://doi.org/10.1093/ct/qtz038

Dahl, R. (1957). The concept of power. *Behavioral Science*, *2*, 201–215. https://doi.org/10.1002/bs.3830020303
Dailey, S. L., & Zhu, Y. (2017). Communicating health at work: Organizational wellness programs as identity bridges. *Health Communication*, *32*(3), 261–268. https://doi.org/10.1080/10410236.2015.1120698
Dale, K., & Burrell, G. (2014). Being occupied: An embodied re-reading of organizational "wellness". *Organization*, *21*(2), 159–177. https://doi.org/10.1177/1350508412473865
Deetz, S. (1992). *Democracy in an age of corporate colonization: Developments in communication and the politics of everyday life*. SUNY Press.
Deetz, S. (2001). Conceptual foundations. In F. M. Jablin, & L. L. Putnam (Eds.), *The new handbook of organizational communication* (pp. 3–47). Sage.
Dempsey, S., & Gibson, K. E. (2017). Food, biopower, and the child's body as a scale of intervention. In P. Marcell, & F. Bosco (Eds.), *Food and place: A critical introduction* (pp. 253–269). Rowman & Littlefield.
Dempsey, S. E., Zoller, H. M., & Hunt, K. P. (2022). The meatpacking industry's corporate exceptionalism: Racialized logics of food chain worker disposability during the COVID-19 crisis. *Food, Culture & Society*, *26*(3), 571–590. https://doi.org/10.1080/15528014.2021.2022916
D'Enbeau, S., & Buzzanell, P. M. (2011). Selling (out) feminism: Sustainability of the ideology-viability tensions in a competitive marketplace. *Communication Monographs*, *78*, 27–52. https://doi.org/10.1080/03637751.2010.542472
de Souza, R. (2019). *Feeding the other: Whiteness, Privilege, and neoliberal stigma in food pantries*. MIT Press.
de Souza, R. (2022). Communication, carcerality, and neoliberal stigma: The case of hunger and food assistance in the United States. *Journal of Applied Communication Research*, 1–18. https://doi.org/10.1080/00909882.2022.2079954
Dougherty, D. (2023). *Sexual harassment in organizational culture: A transformative approach*. Cognella.
Dougherty, D. S., & Goldstein Hode, M. (2016). Binary logics and the discursive interpretation of organizational policy: Making meaning of sexual harassment policy. *Human Relations*, *69*(8), 1729–1755. https://doi.org/10.1177/0018726715624956
Dougherty, D. S., Schraedley, M. A., Gist-Mackey, A. N., & Wickert, J. (2018). A Photovoice study of food (in)security, unemployment, and the discursive-material dialectic. *Communication Monographs*, 1–24. https://doi.org/10.1080/03637751.2018.1500700
Dutta, M. J., & Kaur-Gill, S. (2018). Precarities of migrant work in Singapore: Migration, (im)mobility, and neoliberal governmentality. *International Journal of Communication*, *12*, 4066–4084.
Dutta, M. J., & Thaker, J. (2019). 'Communication sovereignty' as resistance: Strategies adopted by women farmers amid the agrarian crisis in India. *Journal of Applied Communication Research*, *47*(1), 24–46. https://doi.org/10.1080/00909882.2018.1547917
Edwards, R. C. (1981). The social relations of production at the point of production. In M. Zey-Ferrell, & M. Aiken (Eds.), *Complex organizations: Critical perspectives* (pp. 156–182). Scott Foresman.
Elmholdt, K. T., Elmholdt, C., & Haahr, L. (2021). Counting sleep: Ambiguity, aspirational control and the politics of digital self-tracking at work. *Organization*, *28*(1), 164–185. https://doi.org/10.1177/1350508420970475
Fairhurst, G. T., & Putnam, L. L. (2004). Organizations as discursive constructions. *Communication Theory*, *14*(1), 5–26. https://doi.org/10.1111/j.1468-2885.2004.tb00301.x
Fleming, P. (2007). Sexuality, power, and resistance in the workplace. *Organization Studies*, *28*(2), 239–256. https://doi.org/10.1177/0170840606068307
Fleming, P., & Spicer, A. (2003). Working at a cynical distance: Implications for power, subjectivity, and resistance. *Organization*, *10*(1), 157–179. https://doi.org/10.1177/1350508403010001376
Ford, J. L., & Scheinfeld, E. N. (2016). Exploring the effects of workplace health promotion: A critical examination of a familiar organizational practice. *Annals of the International Communication Association*, *40*(1), 277–305. https://doi.org/10.1080/23808985.2015.11735263
Foucault, M. (1979). *Discipline and punish: The birth of the prison* (Trans. A. Sheridan). Vintage.
Foucault, M. (1980). *The history of sexuality: An introduction* (Trans. R. Hurley, Vol. 1). Vintage.
Fraser, N. (1990/91). Rethinking the public sphere: A contribution to the critique of actually existing democracy. *Social Texts*, *25/26*, 56–80. https://doi.org/10.2307/466240

French, J., & Raven, B. (1959). The bases of social power. In D. Cartwright (Ed.), *Studies in social power*. University of Michigan Press.
Gálvez, A., Tirado, F., & Alcaraz, J. M. (2021). Resisting patriarchal cultures: The case of female Spanish home-based teleworkers. *Work, Employment and Society*, *35*(2), 369–385. https://doi.org/10.1177/0950017020987390
Ganesh, S. (2007). Sustainable development discourse and the global economy: Promoting responsibility, containing change. In S. May, G. Cheney, & J. Roper (Eds.), *The debate over corporate social responsibility* (pp. 379–390). Oxford University Press.
Ganesh, S. (2009). Organizational communication: Postmodern approaches. *Encyclopedia of communication theory* (pp. 1–5). Sage.
Ganesh, S. (2016). Managing surveillance: Surveillant individualism in an era of relentless visibility. *International Journal of Communication*, *10*(14). https://ijoc.org/index.php/ijoc/article/view/4544
Ganesh, S. (2018). Logics of mobility: Social movements and their networked other. *International Journal of Communication*, *12*(14). https://ijoc.org/index.php/ijoc/article/view/9660
Ganesh, S., & Stohl, C. (2010). Qualifying engagement: A study of information and communication technology and the global social justice movement in Aotearoa, New Zealand. *Communication Monographs*, *77*(1), 51–74. https://doi.org/10.1080/03637750903514284
Ganesh, S., & Stohl, C. (2013). From Wall Street to Wellington: Protests in an era of digital ubiquity. *Communication Monographs*, *80*(4), 425–451. https://doi.org/10.1080/03637751.2013.828156
Ganesh, S., Zoller, H. M., & Cheney, G. (2005). Transforming resistance: Critical organizational communication meets globalization from below. *Communication Monographs*, *19*(2), 169–191. https://doi.org/10.1080/03637750903514284
Garner, J. T. (2016). Open doors and iron cages: Supervisors' responses to employee dissent. *International Journal of Business Communication*, *53*(1), 27–54. https://doi.org/10.1177/2329488414525466
Geist-Martin, P., Horsley, K., & Angele, F. (2003). Working well: Communication and individual and collective wellness initiatives. In T. L. Thompson, A. M. Dorsey, K. I. Miller, & R. Parrott (Eds.), *Handbook of health communication* (pp. 423–443). Erlbaum.
Giddens, A. (1979). *Central problems in social theory: Action, structure and contradiction in social analysis*. University of California Press.
Gist-Mackey, A. N. (2018). (Dis)embodied job search communication training: Comparative critical ethnographic analysis of materiality and discourse during the unequal search for work. *Organization Studies*, *39*(9), 1251–1275. https://doi.org/10.1177/0170840617736936
Gordon, C. (2024). Learning mutual aid: Food justice public pedagogy and community fridge organizing online. *Journal of Applied Communication Research*, *52*(2), 158–178. https://doi.org/10.1080/00909882.2024.2327417
Gossett, L., & Kilker, J. (2006). My job sucks: Examining counterinstitutional web sites as locations for organizational member voice, dissent, and resistance. *Management Communication Quarterly*, *20*, 63–90. https://doi.org/10.1177/0893318906291729
Gramsci, A. (1971). *Selections from the prison notebooks* (Trans. Q. Hoare & G. N. Smith). International Publishers.
Guha, R. (1983). *Elementary aspects of peasant insurgency in colonial India*. Oxford University Press.
Habermas, J. (1984). *The theory of communicative action: Reason and the rationalization of society* (Trans. T. McCarthy, Vol. 1). Beacon Press.
Hanchey, J. N. (2023). *The center cannot hold: Decolonial possibility in the collapse of a Tanzanian NGO*. Duke University Press.
Hardy, C., & Phillips, N. (2004). Discourse and power. In D. Grant, C. Hardy, C. Oswick, & L. L. Putnam (Eds.), *The Sage handbook of organizational discourse* (pp. 299–316). Sage.
Harness, D. (2023). The constant report: Everything, everywhere, all at once? *Public Relations Review*, *49*(5), 102387. https://doi.org/10.1016/j.pubrev.2023.102387
Harness, D., Ganesh, S., & Stohl, C. (2022). Visibility agents: Organizing transparency in the digital era. *New Media & Society*, 14614448221137816. https://doi.org/10.1177/14614448221137816
Harris, K. L. (2016). Feminist dilemmatic theorizing: New materialism in communication studies. *Communication Theory*, *26*(2), 150–170. https://doi.org/10.1111/comt.12083
Harris, K. L. (2017). Re-situating organizational knowledge: Violence, intersectionality and the privilege of partial perspective. *Human Relations*, *70*(3), 263–285. https://doi.org/10.1177/0018726716654745

Harrison, M. A., & Stephens, K. K. (2019). Shifting from wellness at work to wellness in work: Interrogating the link between stress and organization while theorizing a move toward wellness-in-practice. *Management Communication Quarterly*, *33*(4), 616–649. https://doi.org/10.1177/0893318919862490

Heath, R. G., Fletcher, C. V., & Munoz, R. (Eds.) (2013). *Understanding occupy from Wall Street to Portland: Applied studies in communication theory*. Lexington Books.

Hollis, L. P. (2019). Something to lose sleep over? Predictive analysis of Black men's and White men's Insomnia issues due to workplace bullying in higher education. *Journal of Black Sexuality and Relationships*, *5*(4), 1–19. https://doi.org/10.1353/bsr.2019.0007

Irigaray, H. A. R., Celano, A., Fontoura, Y., & Maher, R. (2021). Resisting by re-existing in the workplace: A decolonial perspective through the Brazilian adage "For the English to See". *Organization*, *28*(5), 817–835. https://doi.org/10.1177/13505084211022666

Ivancic, S. R., & Ford, J. L. (2023). (Dis) organizing sexual harassment: Patterns of bystander communication. *Management Communication Quarterly*, 38(2), 331–358. https://doi.org/10.1177/08933189231179653

James, E. P., & Gill, R. (2018). Neoliberalism and the communicative labor of CrossFit. *Communication & Sport*, *6*(6), 703–727. https://doi.org/10.1177/2167479517737036

James, E. P., & Zoller, H. M. (2017). Resistance training: (Re)shaping extreme forms of workplace health promotion. *Management Communication Quarterly*, *32*(1), 60–89. https://doi.org/10.1177/0893318917696990

Jiang, Z., & Korczynski, M. (2016). When the 'unorganizable' organize: The collective mobilization of migrant domestic workers in London. *Human Relations*, *69*(3), 813–838. https://doi.org/10.1177/0018726715600229

Kang, D., & Krone, K. J. (2022). Organising dissonance on the Tibetan plateau: Insights from the wisdom of nonduality. *Culture and Organization*, *28*(1), 25–45. https://doi.org/10.1080/14759551.2021.1963963

Kassing, J. W., Fanelli, S. A., & Chakravarthy, L. (2018). Full- and part-time dissent: Examining the effect of employment status on dissent expression. *International Journal of Business Communication*, *55*(4), 455–465. https://doi.org/10.1177/2329488415597518

Kellogg, K. C., Valentine, M. A., & Christin, A. (2020). Algorithms at work: The new contested terrain of control. *Academy of Management Annals*, *14*(1), 366–410.

Kuhn, T. (2008). A communicative theory of the firm: Developing an alternative perspective on intra-organizational power and stakeholder relationships. *Organization Studies*, *29*(8–9), 1227–1254. https://doi.org/10.1177/0170840608094778

Kuhn, T., Ashcraft, K. L., & Cooren, F. (2019). Introductory essay: What work can organizational communication do? *Management Communication Quarterly*, *33*(1), 101–111. https://doi.org/10.1177/0893318918809421

Kwon, W., Clarke, I., & Wodak, R. (2009). Organizational decision-making, discourse, and power: Integrating across contexts and scales. *Discourse & Communication*, *3*(3), 273–302. https://doi.org/10.1177/1750481309337208

Lewis, A. (2009). Destructive organizational communication and LGBT workers' experiences. In P. Lutgen-Sandvik & B. Davenport Sypher (Eds.), *Destructive organizational communication* (pp. 203–226). Routledge.

Lucas, A., & Mitra, R. (2023). Entrepreneurial support organization (ESO) narratives and transitional entrepreneurship in Detroit. *New England Journal of Entrepreneurship*, *26*(2), 130–151. https://doi.org/10.1108/NEJE-08-2022-0060

Lukes, S. (1974). *Power: A radical view*. Macmillan.

Lutgen-Sandvik, P. (2006). Take this job and… quitting and other forms of resistance to workplace bullying. *Communication Monographs*, *73*(4), 406–433. https://doi.org/10.1080/03637750601024156

Lyon, A. (2007). "Putting patients first": Systematically distorted communication and Merck's marketing of Vioxx. *Journal of Applied Communication Research*, *35*(4), 376–398. https://doi.org/10.1080/00909880701611052

Maingi Ngwu, N. (2023). Alternative economic discourses from the margins: Kenyan migrant women's informal childcare organizing as an alternative economic discourse in the contemporary U.S. context. In M. Pal, J. Cruz, & D. Munshi (Eds.), *Organizing at the margins: Theorizing organizations of struggle in the global south* (pp. 63–90). Springer International Publishing. https://doi.org/10.1007/978-3-031-22993-0_5

Marmot, M. (2002). The influence of income on health: Views of an epidemiologist. *Health Affairs*, *21*(2), 31–46. https://doi.org/10.1377/hlthaff.21.2.31
Marx, K. (1967). *Capital* (Trans. S. Moore & E. Aveling). International Publishers.
Mbembe, A. (2019). *Necropolitics*. Duke University Press. https://doi.org/10.1215/08992363-15-1-11
McDonald, J. (2015). Organizational communication meets queer theory: Theorizing relations of "difference" differently. *Communication Theory*, *25*(3), 310–329. https://doi.org/10.1111/comt.12060
McDonald, J., Harris, K. L., & Ramirez, J. (2020). Revealing and concealing difference: A critical approach to disclosure and an intersectional theory of "closeting". *Communication Theory*, *30*(1), 84–104. https://doi.org/10.1093/ct/qtz017
McPhee, R. D., & Zaug, P. (2008). The communicative constitution of organizations: A framework for explanation. In L. L. Putnam & A.M. Nicotera (Eds.). *Building theories of organization: The constitutive role of communication* (pp. 21–47). Routledge.
Mease, J. J. (2021). Techniques and forces and the communicative constitution of organization: A Deleuzian approach to organizational (in)stability and power. *Management Communication Quarterly*, *35*(2), 226–255. https://doi.org/10.1177/0893318920969969
Morrill, C., Zald, M., & Rao, H. (2003). Covert political conflict in organizations: Challenges from below. *Annual Review of Sociology*, *29*, 391–415. https://doi.org/10.1146/annurev.soc.29.010202.095927
Mumby, D. K. (Ed.) (1993). *Narrative and social control: Critical perspectives*. Sage.
Mumby, D. K. (1997). The problem of hegemony: Rereading Gramsci for organizational communication studies. *Western Journal of Communication*, *61*, 343–375. https://doi.org/10.1080/10570319709374585
Mumby, D. K. (2004). Discourse, power and ideology: Unpacking the critical approach. In D. Grant, C. Hardy, C. Oswick, & L. L. Putnam (Eds.), *The Sage handbook of organizational discourse* (pp. 237–258). Sage.
Mumby, D. K. (2005). Theorizing resistance in organizational studies: A dialectical approach. *Management Communication Quarterly*, *19*(1), 19–44. https://doi.org/10.1177/0893318905276558
Mumby, D. K., & Ashcraft, K. L. (2004). *Reworking gender: A feminist communicology of organization*. Sage.
Mumby, D. K., & Clair, R. P. (1997). Organizational discourse. In T. A. van Dijk (Ed.), *Discourse studies, volume 2: Discourse as social interaction* (Vol. 2, pp. 181–205). Sage.
Munshi, D., & Kurian, P. (2005). Imperializing spin cycles: A postcolonial look at public relations, greenwashing, and the separation of publics. *Public Relations Review*, *31*(4), 513–520. https://doi.org/10.1016/j.pubrev.2005.08.010
Nadesan, M. H. (1996). Organizational identity and space of action. *Organization Studies*, *17*, 49–81. https://doi.org/10.1177/017084069601700103
Pal, M. (2016). Organization at the margins: Subaltern resistance of Singur. *Human Relations*, *69*(2), 419–438. https://doi.org/10.1177/0018726715589797
Pal, M., Cruz, J., & Munshi, D. (2023). Decolonizing knowledge: Cultural aspirations, political self-determination and social rights in knowledge making. In L. Tuhiwai Smith & D. Munshi (Eds.), *Organizing at the margins: Theorizing organizations of struggle in the global south* (1 ed., pp. 15–33). Palgrave Macmillan. https://doi.org/10.1007/978-3-031-22993-0
Pal, M., Kim, H., Harris, K. L., Long, Z., Linabary, J., Wilhoit Larson, E., Jensen, P. R., Gist-Mackey, A. N., McDonald, J., Nieto-Fernandez, B., Jiang, J., Misra, S., & Dempsey, S. E. (2022). Decolonizing organizational communication. *Management Communication Quarterly*, *36*(3), 547–577. https://doi.org/10.1177/08933189221090255
Parker, P. S. (2003). Chapter 9: Control, resistance, and empowerment in raced, gendered, and classed work contexts: The case of African American women. *Communication Yearbook*, 27(1), 257–291. https://doi.org/10.1207/s15567419cy2701_9
Parker, P. S. (2013). Difference and organizing. In L. L. Putnam, & D. K. Mumby (Eds.), *Handbook of organizational communication* (pp. 619–641). Sage.
Parker, P. S. (2020). *Ella Baker's catalytic leadership a primer on community engagement and communication for social justice*. University of California Press.
Parker, P. S., & Mease, J. (2009). Beyond the Knapsack: Disrupting the production of White racial privilege through organizational practices. In L. A. Samavor, R. E. Porter, & E. R. McDaniel (Eds.), *Intercultural communication: A reader* (12th ed.). Wadsworth.

Parker, P. S., Oceguera, E., & Sanchez, J. (2011). Intersecting differences: Organizing [ourselves] for social justice research with people in vulnerable communities. In D. K. Mumby (Ed.), *Reframing difference in organizational communication studies* (pp. 219–244). Sage.

Pauly, J. A., & Buzzanell, P. M. (2016). Considering difference in diversity management: A critical take on practices and policies around the world. *Scandinavian Journal of Management*, *32*(2), 114–118. https://doi.org/http://dx.doi.org/10.1016/j.scaman.2016.03.001

Porter, M. E., & Kramer, M. R. (2011). Creating shared value. *Harvard Business Review*, *89*(1/2), 62–77. https://doi.org/10.1007/978-94-024-1144-7_16

Rosengren, A., Smyth, A., Rangarajan, S., Ramasundarahettige, C., Bangdiwala, S. I., AlHabib, K. F., Avezum, A., Bengtsson Bostrom, K., Chifamba, J., Gulec, S., Gupta, R., Igumbor, E. U., Iqbal, R., Ismail, N., Joseph, P., Kaur, M., Khatib, R., Kruger, I. M., Lamelas, P.,…, & Yusuf, S. (2019). Socioeconomic status and risk of cardiovascular disease in 20 low-income, middle-income, and high-income countries: The Prospective Urban Rural Epidemiologic (PURE) study. *The Lancet Global Health*, *7*(6), e748–e760. https://doi.org/10.1016/S2214-109X(19)30045-2

Shome, R., & Hegde, R. S. (2002). Postcolonial approaches to communication: Charting the terrain, engaging the intersections. *Communication Theory*, *12*(3), 249–270. https://doi.org/10.1111/j.1468-2885.2002.tb00269.x

Spiller, C., Maunganui Wolfgramm, R., Henry, E., & Pouwhare, R. (2020). Paradigm warriors: Advancing a radical ecosystems view of collective leadership from an Indigenous Māori perspective. *Human Relations*, *73*(4), 516–543. https://doi.org/10.1177/0018726719893753

Spivak, G. C. (1988). Can the subaltern speak? In C. Nelson, & L. Grossberg (Eds.), *Marxism and the interpretation of culture* (pp. 271–313). University of Illinois Press.

Stephens, K., Goins, E., & Dailey, S. (2013). Organizations disseminating health messages: The roles of organizational identification and HITs. *Health Communication*, *29*(4), 398–409. https://doi.org/10.1080/10410236.2012.759896

Stephens, K. K., & Zhu, Y. (2016). Organizational identification and using technology to communicate about health. In T. H. E. Williams (Ed.), *Organizations, communication, and health* (pp. 204–222). Routledge. https://doi.org/http://doi.org/10.4324/9781315723020-7

Tracy, S. J. (2000). Becoming a character for commerce: Emotion labor, self-subordination, and discursive construction of identity in a total institution. *Management Communication Quarterly*, *14*(3), 90–128. https://doi.org/10.1177/0893318900141004

Villamil, A. M., & D'Enbeau, S. (2021). Essential work in the U.S. during COVID-19: Navigating vulnerability–sustainability tensions. *Sustainability*, *13*(19), 10665. https://www.mdpi.com/2071-1050/13/19/10665

Zanin, A. C., & Bisel, R. S. (2018). Discursive positioning and collective resistance: How managers can unwittingly co-create team resistance. *Management Communication Quarterly*, *32*(1), 31–59. https://doi.org/10.1177/0893318917717640

Zoller, H. M. (2003). Working out: Managerialism in workplace health promotion. *Management Communication Quarterly*, *17*(2), 171–205. https://doi.org/10.1177/0893318903253003

Zoller, H. M. (2024). Pragmatic utopianism in the union cooperative movement: (Dis)organizing transformative social change. *Communication Monographs*, 1–29. https://doi.org/10.1080/03637751.2024.2399137

Zoller, H. M., & Ban, Z. (2024). Communication, power, and organizational politics. In D. M. Vernon & P. Marshall Scott (Eds.), *Organizational communication theory and research* (pp. 277–294). De Gruyter Mouton. https://doi.org/doi:10.1515/9783110718508

Zoller, H. M., & Casteel, D. (2021). #March for Our Lives: Health activism, diagnostic framing, gun control, and the gun industry. *Health Communication*. https://doi.org/10.1080/10410236.2020.1871167

Zoller, H. M., & Fairhurst, G. T. (2007). Resistance leadership: The overlooked potential in critical and leadership studies. *Human Relations*, *60*(9), 1331–1360. https://doi.org/10.1177/0018726707082850

Zoller, H. M., Strochlic, R., & Getz, C. (2023). An employee-centered framework for healthy workplaces: Implementing a critically holistic, participative, and structural model through the Equitable Food Initiative. *Journal of Applied Communication Research*, *51*(2), 164–184. https://doi.org/10.1080/00909882.2022.2106579

13 Engaging Feminist Organizational Communication Scholarship and Activism for Our Times

Patrice M. Buzzanell

Feminist organizational communication scholarship and activism have always shifted based on geopolitical locations and contemporary issues (Buzzanell, 2021; James, 2024; Pal & Nieto-Fernandez, 2024). In concert with its interdisciplinary roots, it engages with differing notions of gender, has expanded from U.S.- and Western-centric emphases on knowledge and organizing, and has broadened to encompass Black, Indigenous, and People of Color (BIPOC) more fully by retaining its focus on multiple forms of gender and aligning with diversity, equity, and inclusion (DEI) and country-specific legislation (see Nkomo et al., 2019; Örtenblad et al., 2017). Despite these concerns and goals, feminist organizational communication and its interdisciplinary counterparts remain incredibly practical. The issues change as researchers and organizational members struggle to constitute equitable sites of labor and organizing and as they counter movements that aim to stifle gender justice. Even as feminisms address war, artificial intelligence, and gender disparities resulting from the Covid-19 pandemic and right-wing populism (e.g., see Khrebtan-Hörhager & Pyatovskaya, 2024; Nkomo et al., 2019; Toupin, 2024), there are continuities in feminist organizational communication rooted in the constitutive nature of gender, power, and organizing.

At the heart of this chapter are questions about what gender equality means. The meaning has shifted over time. In the West, early rights to vote and attention to laws focused on persuasive messages and institutional structures (also known as First and Second Wave Feminisms, respectively, as discussed below). These issues have shifted to subtle nuances, ambiguities, and contradictions in sensemaking and organizing consistent with more recent Third Wave and subsequent feminist movements, but the narratives of progress are uneven and nonlinear (Pal & Nieto-Fernandez, 2024). Indeed, basic human rights for women are still being sought and some rights for women's bodily integrity have been rescinded (e.g., Fuentes, 2023; Mitra, 2023). Gender equality is one of numerous contemporary movements labeled social justice focused on distribution of privilege (advantages), individual and cultural survival, and individual-societal relationships (Deer et al., 2021).

Regardless of what era and meaning of gender equality to which individuals subscribe, this chapter maintains that equality is valuable and advantageous for everyone but can be challenging to communicate and enact as part of DEI initiatives (see Leslie et al., 2024). On the personal level, we might consider how we would feel if we knew that our own family members, neighbors, and friends were not paid fairly, could not earn educational degrees or attend school, could not obtain life-saving medical care, and could not own property, have credit, speak in public, drive cars, obtain the job titles commensurate with what they do in their jobs, and so on. On broader levels, gender equality is advantageous so that all can participate fully in personal and work life, regardless of gender identities. These rights

DOI: 10.4324/9781003484639-16

include the opportunities both to contribute meaningfully to the organizations with which they identify and to choose what careers they want and how they might best "balance" work and personal life considerations. These reasons align with human agency, choice, and dignity presented in other chapters of this book (see Chapters 2–4, 12, 14, and 20).

This chapter discusses why and how agency is constrained and enabled in ways that align with sex (biological difference) and gender (psychological and socially constructed identities). The earliest research on gender and feminisms sought to understand the many different reasons why sex and gender were and continue to be primary ways of organizing societies and individual identities. Put simply, this research sought to uncover why, how, and in what contexts traditional sex and gender prevail (i.e., women should act feminine and do women's work of caring at home and in the office, just as men should act masculine and do men's work of leading, directing, being breadwinners, and forming governments). Early Western gender and feminist scholarship and activism focused on finding strategies to enable women's voice to enter into governmental policies and decisions (such as rights to vote in elections) and on rewriting scientific, literary, and communication histories. The process of rewriting and including women is ongoing. For instance, it was only recently that films such as *Hidden Figures* (2016, the story of Black mathematicians and engineers, Katherine Johnson, Dorothy Vaughan, and Mary Jackson) depicted contributions made by these women decades earlier at NASA, along with the gender and racial discrimination they faced (Sumarsono et al., 2023). Their insights and hard work were crucial for humans orbiting the earth.

Ironically, when women did accomplish work or discoveries, their efforts and outcomes were considered unusual, irregular, and non-normative. In these ways, women and men maintained the current gendered order, an order and set of gendered stereotypes codified in the Bem Sex Role Inventory (BSRI; Bem, 1974), which enabled researchers to test how and in what contexts conventional gender stereotypes were associated with particular behaviors, values, and attitudes. U.S. Supreme Court judge Ruth Bader Ginsburg built her career arguing that gender-based discrimination on pay, partner benefits for men, ability of women to buy beer at the same age as men, and other cases were unconstitutional (Vacca & Bartow, 2023). Today, men's household contributions are still valued higher than those of women (Peretz, 2023).

Our discussion explores the myriad and complicated considerations through which sex and gender are intertwined with how people do their everyday lives and structure their worlds. Over time, these relationships between sex and gender have explored the contradictions, ironies, and tensions in research and everyday practice. Despite extensive documentation, *sexism* or gender-based stereotyping and discrimination persist. The Everyday Sexism Project (ESP) invites and catalogues women's (and some men's) accounts of sexism to promote feminist solidary and resistance to such acts; the ESP reports that the largest number of entries into this transnational global Internet-enabled platform reports and promotes individual and collective agency against assault, harassment, and discrimination in the workplace (Vachhani & Pullen, 2019). Similarly, Kudumbashree is a state-instituted and bottom-up program in India for poverty reduction and economic empowerment for women who are lower caste and class, or subaltern women, that ironically embraces gender rights using market language (Kandathil & Chennangodu, 2024). Kudumbashree "metaphorically stands for married woman glorified as prosperity and light for a family within the predominantly patriarchal culture of [the Indian state of] Kerala" (an Indian state, p. 118). The collective members worked to better their family's living conditions while also being vulnerable to larger political and neoliberal patriarchal forces that served to disempower them.

These types of contradictions form the contemporary bases of feminist solidarity as gendered interactions and organizing retain tradition while enveloping change for individual women, families, and communities.

We begin this chapter by differentiating among sex, gender, and feminisms in communication and interdisciplinary studies on gender and feminist theory. We do so to establish fundamental conceptualizations for discussion in this chapter. We present studies in these areas and show where there are continuities and discontinuities, such as sustained and changing attention to messages that equate sex (biology) with gender (social construction). We discuss current expansion beyond binary male-female models prominent in earlier studies, such as transgender scholarship that disrupts sex=gender equations. We also discuss how scholarship and organizing have expanded to online organizing that encourages politicized action in ways that reconstitute particular forms of masculinity and networked feminisms.

In the second part, we explore organizational communication scholars' contributions to gender studies and feminisms. In this section, we describe how organizational communication scholars have contributed to, or advanced, gender studies and feminisms in three main ways. In each of these three areas, we attend to theoretical developments and new insights from empirical studies as well as strategies for research-to-practice considerations.

Sex, Gender, and Feminisms

To begin, we differentiate among sex, gender, and feminisms. In doing so, we lay out the continuities of traditional assumptions and everyday practices based on beliefs that sex and gender are equivalent, meaning for example that someone who is female is also feminine (and heterosexual). Second, we elaborate upon core feminist values and how they manifest differently over time, space, and organizational research. We close this section by noting that the present is a time of profound contestations centering on sex, gender, and feminisms that call into question how individuals enact agency, choice, and dignity.

Differentiating Categorizations

First, we *differentiate among sex, gender, and feminisms* and provide an example of organizational communication research that touches upon these categorizations. *Sex* is the traditional binary biological classification into male and female, as assigned through genitalia, genetics, and hormones. Sex categories on surveys have expanded to include "other" for those whose bodies exhibit prominent anatomical and physiological factors that are both male and female. In contrast, *gender* conveys the wide range of socially constructed groupings associated with masculinity and femininity, as well as LGBTQ+ and non-binary identities, that result from socialization, identity, norms, and cultural processes about appropriate roles, communication, and expectations. To understand how gender is socially constructed, we might consider how what is feminine or masculine and normative for people in the United States today is vastly different in appearance and roles from what would be appropriate in China during the Ming Dynasty, in rural vs. urban and Northern vs. Southern alignments during the U.S. Civil War, and in other contexts. Gender scholars in communication continue to include *sex* as a demographic variable or means of comparing and contrasting practices (activities) and enduring structures (see Figure 1.2, this volume) without politicizing sex=gender difference by engaging in discussions about choice and human agency. Feminist scholars maintain that sex and gender are central organizing structures and *modus operandi* in societies. Feminist organizational communication scholars seek to disrupt the linear depiction of privilege that accords male=masculine with benefits such as advancement, leadership, status, power, and control. This privilege does not happen in all situations, as we discuss later in this chapter. Instead, privilege is always co-constituted with marginalization, which means that based on our social identities, we might accrue advantages (e.g., given the benefit of the doubt about our competence before we even open our mouths) or might be disadvantaged (e.g., automatically dismissed as not the person in power) as a group member.

Feminisms explore gender with pragmatic and advocacy approaches called *praxis* (see Chapter 2) both to create and change awareness of how gender organizes everyday life in ways that are inequitable and that require transformation in all processes of the communication-organization-dynamic cycle (Figure 1.2). For students, the awareness-advocacy engagement known as praxis would mean incorporation of voices not typically part of the classic organizational communication readings and calling out instructors and writers for not incorporating BIPOC concerns and lived experiences-their ways of knowing (epistemologies), being (ontologies), and valuing (praxiologies) in the world – in complex and intersectional ways (Walker & Muñoz Rojas, 2021). Walker and Muñoz Rojas' call to change the curriculum and pedagogical techniques opens up understandings about how structural racism, sexism, and other forms of silencing people and opportunities are complicit in disenfranchising all people. Walker and Muñoz Rojas urge incorporation of diverse feminisms and change efforts.

To show how Walker and Muñoz Rojas, among others, call to decolonize feminist organizational communication (e.g., Kang & Long, 2024; Pal & Nieto Fernandez, 2024), we first overview the canon or some of most common feminist approaches (for overview, see Buzzanell, 1994; see also Ashcraft & Mumby, 2004), and then we present more recent feminisms and theorizing for praxis that complicates notions of materialities, cultures, national/transnationalities, gender, occupations, and knowledge production (e.g., Biwa, 2021; Branton & Compton, 2021; Freedman et al., 2024; Maingi Ngwu, 2023; Tian, 2023).

For instance, *liberal feminists* find that the root of women's subordination lies in exclusion from legal and policy (structural) equality, with the idea that showing how and where such exclusions occur can then lead to equalizing rules (laws, policies, and practices). *Radical feminists* believe that change to existing structures is too difficult. They advocate the revamping of society and alternative organizing structures based on feminist values. Still other feminists, known as *standpoint feminists*, study how groups are systematically advantaged and disadvantaged by the socio-political-cultural and material aspects of their lives such that they construct knowledge from their awareness of these commonalities to make change.

The advantage of understanding the different feminisms is that they provide insight into how and why gender inequality exists and is so complex – insight that cannot be obtained by referencing only one feminism or promoting only one set of strategies to benefit women and men. Instead, a feminist metatheoretical matrix enables dialogue within and across the different feminisms for a rich and powerful basis for studying organizations and proposing changes (Buzzanell, 1994).

Combining these feminist approaches, Harris (2017) analyzed how federal laws and institutional policies and procedures coalesce around "mandated reporting" of sexual violence in U.S. universities in ways that prioritize (or privilege) masculinity, whiteness, and heteronormativity. In discussing a first-year student orientation skit, Harris described how the audience and skit actors ironically constructed understanding of sexual violence and its reporting from white heterosexist and homophobic positions through techniques of humiliation and humor, thus continuing to "prioritize privileged perspectives" (p. 274). Methods of reporting violence also may buffer colleges against more complete knowledge. For example, she overheard students talk about date rape but lacked names and details. This lack of detail meant that she was not mandated to report the occurrence to officials, thus legitimating non-responsiveness. Furthermore, organizational members' knowledge depended on the production of power as associated with their social locations (e.g., student vs. administrator, a standpoint feminist approach) and difference (e.g., interlocking systems of power and inequality predicated on discourses and structures of difference such as race, class, gender, sexuality, an intersectional feminist approach; see also Chapter 14). Although not stated in Harris' article, a radical feminist implication based on her findings might be to scrap current mandated reporting practices and start from the ground up, or everyday experiences and feminist values, to generate more viable procedures. These examples combine messages and meaning such that procedures of mandated reporting are contradictory in process and in their institutionalization as policy.

In addition, more recent feminisms and theorizing for praxis complicate notions of materialities, cultures, national/transnationalities, gender, occupations, and knowledge production. Biwa (2021) describes how Namibian women collaborate with men and utilize African women feminist values, such as care and interdependence with men, God, and nature, to promote their rights as women and as workers. Branton and Compton (2021) describe how gay bars in Midwestern U.S. towns try to stay true to their identities and ideologies while also creating consumer bases that enable them to be financially viable. They queer or destabilize space for both non-binary and straight gender enactment that disrupts gender normativity but prompts patrons to feel both welcome and excluded. In occupations, contradictions emerge as current media representations of women in STEM (science, technology, engineering, and math) portray the persistence of gender stereotypes and biases that still focus more on traditional gender such as family and household work than scientific accomplishments (Freedman et al., 2024). For Chinese political leaders, women negotiate their political, gendered, and symbolic bodies within both feminine and masculine boundaries to gain and retain power and achieve their goals (Tian, 2023). In short, current feminist organizational communication scholarship delves into the complexities of everyday life that are entangled with culture, material conditions, and intersections of politicized and complicated identity performances.

Core Feminist Values

Second, we *elaborate upon core feminist values* and how they manifest differently over time, space, and organizational research. To do so, we provide an overview of feminist waves (phases of theoretical advancements). Then, we delve more fully into feminist communication research to note how communication theories and research about everyday organizing extend and enrich ideas about sex, gender, and feminisms.

Like our earlier discussion about gender, feminisms have shifted over time and space both in political contestations and in communication theory and research. As can be seen in the example of Harris' (2017) study on mandated reporting of sexual violence, one feminist approach often is inadequate to describe and remedy situations that preclude women's and men's full participation in organizational life. As a result, we use *feminisms* rather than the singular form, *feminism*, to indicate the numerous movements and theoretical bases for feminist organizational communication theory. However, core feminist commitments transcend these individual approaches. Core commitments include the following: analyses of how local and global conditions can be changed to create greater equality (research for praxis), engagement in ongoing and mindful self- and other-critique (self-reflexivity and analyses), and moral obligations to advocate for change (Buzzanell, 1994). Seeing these commitments through a spatio-temporal lens can indicate how and why individuals and collectivities have acted as agents in the past and how people continue to advocate for constituting an organizational world predicated on equality.

Feminist Waves

In taking a spatio-temporal lens to feminisms, we note how feminist waves have made changes in our worlds and in organizing processes. Starting with social movements to incorporate women's voice in public venues, the suffrage movements around the world fought to gain the right to vote in political elections. Suffrage movements differed nationally and globally in time periods based on activism, demands, and effectiveness. They differed (and still do differ) for particular groups of women such as members of Indigenous tribes and minority groups (Örtenblad et al., 2017). The U.S. feminist First Wave ended in 1920 after decades of activism when women achieved the right to vote. However, Black women in the Southern United States could not exercise this right until the Voting Rights Act of 1965 (Waxman, 2020). Samoa adopted universal suffrage in 1990 (Schaeffer, 2020).

In the United States, the Second Wave began in the 1960s and expanded activism in the 1970s and later for women's rights, inclusion in public and private arenas, incorporation of color and sexualities, and protections against discrimination and harassment (e.g., acts against pregnancy discrimination in the workplace; rights to education, equal pay, and ability to have one's own credit). Consistent with Second Wave politics and practices, organizational communication scholars engaged in examination and critique of doing gender and structuring gendered institutions, as well as policies and laws formed to promote gender equality. These studies examine every day micro-practices of inequity and macro-discourses of gendered organizing (e.g., masculine ethics of equal treatment and policy use that privilege work over family in tension with feminine ethics of care, nurturing, and family and fairness) and societal notions of gendered identities and relations (e.g., traditional gender roles in and boundaries between family and work or career). This history is contested. In other parts of the world, such as Turkey, the Second Wave began in the 1980s; the wave metaphor and timeline are inconsistent with the political realities. Implications of the wave grand narrative are as follows: as one feminist form peaks another feminism emerges; periods of progress are followed by backlash and "barren years"; and those involved in political and societal change on behalf of women must call themselves "feminist" (Adak & Çağatay, 2023).

Moreover, race, class, sexuality, gender identity, and other forms of difference emerged during (and affected the transition from) Second Wave Feminist organizational communication studies and still challenge the gender-neutrality of organizational relationships, policies, and ideal (white, male, heterosexual) workers and bodies, unencumbered with dependents such as children (e.g., Long et al., 2023). These studies have developed new theoretical insights about organizational communication. Embedded within and extending Second Wave organizational communication studies are investigations about the paradoxical organizational relationships and structures established to provide gender equality that often fail to achieve goals (see summary, Putnam & Ashcraft, 2017).

The Third Wave and subsequent iterations expand upon activism for women's and men's rights and have enriched feminisms through explicit incorporations of, and theorizing about, paradox, ambiguity, embodiment, ethics, culture, and online and global feminist organizing. Current scholarship aligns with the structurational process depicted in Figure 1.2. Postmodern sensibilities are destabilizing notions of sex, gender, feminisms, sexuality, organizing, and organization. Decolonizing efforts in organizational communication and feminist interdisciplinary scholarship critique the wave imagery as promoting visions of linear feminist progress focused on women in Western nations: "Such a linear sequence of temporality draws boundaries around each wave, obscuring possibilities of coinciding and conflicted intellectual movements," while "the result is a narrow racialized, nation-centered view of feminist thought in the U.S." (Pal & Nieto Fernandez, 2024, pp. 67, 68). Like the wave critique, "the decolonial feminist perspective sees the effect of multiple relations of power rooted in the coloniality/modernity nexus, criticizing the assumption that the term *woman* has a uniform meaning, irrespective of context and history" (Fotaki & Pullen, 2024, p. 606). These recent feminist manifestations are discussed in the next section of this chapter.

In summary, throughout these different waves, notions about sex, gender, and feminisms have become more complicated. They have been contested in different ways in politics, in the home, in workplaces, and in the communication discipline. Organizational communication scholars continue to investigate sex differences because there still exists a need to demonstrate inequitable treatment and material consequences for those men and women who both conform to and violate sex role expectations. Contemporary sex difference research conducted on micro- (individuals), meso- (workplaces, project teams, organizations), and macro-levels (societal, global) has uncovered complex dynamics of privilege and marginalizations that defy easy conclusions, invalidating assumptions that women always experience disenfranchisement and men always are privileged or benefit in the public sphere.

Contestations

Third, organizational communication scholars are addressing *profound contestations centering on sex, gender, and feminisms* that call into question how people enact agency, choice, and dignity. These contestations surface in scholarship on work, occupations, and careers, and on online organizing, including local and transnational social movements.

Gendered Scholarship on Work, Occupations, and Careers

Instead of the somewhat simplistic notions about different behaviors, qualities, and styles aligned with the sex=gender equation, current sex and gender difference research contributes complicated and contradictory or paradoxical insights about difference and intersectionalities in work, occupations, and careers. For instance, privilege-marginalization, ideal-real, "majority"-difference are politicized tensions that erupt in discursive and material ways. Whereas meritocracy beliefs (namely, that the cream rises to the top, everyone has an equal chance, hard work and competence can insure employability) form the core of organizational rules, structures, and advancement, the reality is that meritocracy does not account for difference.

For instance, wage-earning mothers across nations work and live within contradictory policies and results. Countries and organizations that provide family-friendly benefits such as extended parental leaves, flexible work arrangements, and publicly funded childcare assistance find lower gender equality. Women opting out of the workforce with even temporary labor force detachments incur long-term wage inequalities and lower value retirement amounts (e.g., Herbst-Debby & Achouche, 2023) as well as gender gaps depending on parenting and disruptions like the Covid-19 pandemic (Qian & Fuller, 2020). A 2023 Pew Research Center report documents the growing trend for stay-at-home parents, with one in five U.S. parents caring for family and not engaging in paid labor now being fathers (Fry, 2023). Yet the long-term economic and familial consequences are unknown, especially in a society that equates masculinity with success in the public realm of work and career. Interdisciplinary scholars have looked at labor force trends through sociological, cross-national and global, gendered, economic, and political lenses. Organizational communication researchers have begun to delve deeply into contradictions and disparities in their examinations of messages, meanings, and the constitution of organizing in labor force trends.

These literatures portray the tangled relationships among gender identities and hegemonic conceptualizations of career and personal life in processes of doing and undoing gender. Medved (2016) described how women breadwinners engage in doing-undoing gender in several ways: Resisting career-primary assumptions of breadwinning; creating parallel obligations that primary obligations need not be "earner" for men or "caregiver" for women; positioning themselves as fitting their roles invoking masculine qualities and language; and challenging traditional gendered relationships by disrupting power-money associations and identities. In these disruptive and reintegrative communication strategies, people struggle with the meanings and boundaries of career and personal life. They engage in tension-filled change for themselves through language, social interaction, and reformulations of social institutions.

Likewise, Branicki et al. (2023) describe the difficulties that female entrepreneurs face in every phase of creating, prototyping, obtaining financial investments, securing patents, and commercializing and marketing their products. In a film about a semi-fictionalized entrepreneur, Joy Mangano (performed by Jennifer Lawrence) invents and brings to market the "Miracle Mop," a self-wringing mop that can be cleaned by placing the fabric head into a washing machine. The film, *Joy* (2015), shifts from exaggerated traditionally feminine spaces (children's bedroom, kitchen), activities (cleaning), and attire (dresses) and instrumental masculinities (Joy dressed in black pants and behaving assertively) as well as traditionally masculine scenarios (man ineptly trying to use the mop on a TV commercial) to subvert gendered expectations and open conversation for change. *Joy* was selected because it is one of the few recent films to depict a female entrepreneur and because it was distributed world-wide, viewed by a large audience, and grossed over 100 million USD. The movie, *Barbie* (2023), also depicts situations in which Barbie (performed by Margot Robbie) and Ken (performed by Ryan Gossling) move back-and-forth from the fictionalized world in which women rule, to the real world in which men and masculinities are dominant. The slogan, "She's everything. He's just Ken," summarizes the key tensions and opportunities as the characters strive for greater recognition and equity by conforming to and resisting gender norms.

Work in doing-undoing gender (McDonald, 2013; Medved, 2016) extends past scholarship by transcending complicated and tension-filled sex and gender differences in individual, workplace, work-family, occupational, and societal sites. The articles typically are theoretically based, problem-centered in orientation, and strategic in implications for everyday life.

Online Organizing and Social Movements

This section on online organizing and social movements discusses organization and organizing centered around hashtag activism and network feminisms discussed at the start of this chapter with attention to women's and men's rights, dignity, choice, and well-being.

To these, we add *material feminisms* that seek to understand the confluence of social arrangements that result in particular forms of gender relations and structures in a specific time and place.

As of this writing, sex, gender, and feminist contestations depicted in this section are being played out in local, national, and global social media and in scholarship focused on gender harassment and with other media, reports, and scholarship exposing transgender violence, pathologization, arrests, killings, and exclusions in organizing (e.g., Eger et al., 2022; United Nations, 2023). When facing exclusion based on gender such as women in engineering majors and trans employees in organizations, they create spaces, often called third spaces, where they and others embrace their identities and create strategies to pursue their goals (Buzzanell et al., 2023; Eger, 2021). These are feminist organizational communication issues because they affect the abilities of men, women, non-binary, and LBGTQ+ persons to participate fully in society and different organizations – thus affecting membership, activity, organizing, and organizational structure.

Moreover, online organizing for men trying to protect masculinities in a world where traditional gender markers, economic advantages, and other benefits of mainstream (white) hegemonic masculinity seem to have eroded is creating an uneasy space of contestation. These alt-right movements from the manosphere (clusters of numerous Internet-enabled men's rights organizing spaces) attempt to reconcile and establish a male-dominated order that is technologically sophisticated, anti-feminist, misogynist, pro-fathers' rights, and founded in precarious labor markets locally and globally, such as The Red Pill (Eddington, 2020). There are different readings for what is happening and why. The alt-right's anti-feminist perspective is that they need to redress political correctness and discriminations against straight White men and their rights, so that men can resume their places at the heads of the tables at home and in the public sphere. They, like members of the Spanish manosphere, argue that men around the world are "wounded" by feminisms (García Mingo & Díaz Fernández, 2023).

In contrast, other networked organizing movements serve as digital micro-publics, in which people create safe spaces and online discussions about issues, with outreach labeled "hashtag activism" (e.g., #blacklivesmatter and #alllivesmatter; Sobieraj, 2018, p. 1702; see also #MeToo in Austin et al., 2023; #girls help girls# in Yang & Hu, 2024; and #WhyIStayed in Linabary et al., 2020). These online collectivities self-organize to promote particular activities and ideologies through social network platforms, conventional mass media, and face-to-face organizing. For instance, a two-year interview study of digital sexism (processes and practices of online abuse based on gender) uncovered three patterns that mitigate against women's safety: Strategies designed to limit women's impact in digital publics (intimidating, discrediting, and shaming); invocation of femininity to undermine women's contributions; and attention directed to women's physicality in exchanges to divert attention and develop fear (Sobieraj, 2018). These patterns are instantiated in verbal messages, visual imagery, online organizing, and embodiment (e.g., physical responses to hostility and online and offline attacks on women's bodies).

Network feminisms involve people dedicated to women's safety, economic empowerment, and retention of women's rights who have formed online organizing processes and collectivities. *Transnational feminist* network scholars engage in problem-centered research and practice that cross national boundaries but manifest differently depending on women's regional concerns, human rights, labor organizing, not-for-profit and nongovernmental organizing, effects of global neoliberalism, and other activities built on affective engagement (Vachhani, 2024). In organizational communication, this work has focused on how men and women organize online and globally to construct and sustain safe spaces for women who have experienced violence. For example, #WhyIStayed offers feminist activist strategies to counter victim-blaming (Linabary et al., 2020). The constitution of contested terms like "safety" and attention to materialities has been incorporated into online and hybrid social movement-self-organizing collectivities. For instance, how do people self-identified as women, men, non-binary, and LBGTQ+ living under the threat of sexual violence and death self-organize and reach out to others for support when there exist possibilities for harm even with privacy safeguards?

Regarding this last point, *material feminism* reincorporates the body and other physical conditions of everyday life both as "real," not entirely constituted through language and interaction, and as agentic: "this new *materialism* attempts to avoid dualisms and/or privileging discourse over matter, and thus interweaves materialities and discourses...[as] inextricably fused" (Cozza & Gherardi, 2023, pp. 56–57). It is here that the organizing and organization online and offline are interrelated theoretically and practically. Violence against women and men is not only symbolic, but it has also material consequences for well-being. Thus, material feminist organizational communication scholars explore knowledge developed through epistemologies (or ways of knowing through social constructionism) and ontologies (or ways of being and connections with the physical as grounded in nature, technologies, bodies, places, and spaces) to indicate how our relationships and organizing are co-constituted as more-than discourse and materiality. Researchers' onto-epistemological mappings "allow something new [to] emerge" (p. 58). Agency flows – "spreading from and circulating within—affective-material-discursive practices" (p. 61).

In short, the present is an exciting time to explore sex, gender, and feminisms not only as communication scholars and students, but also as members of societies that are dealing with the tensions and paradoxes about what it means to be men and women of varied sexual orientations and organizations. Simply because businesses are relatively new, decentralized, agile, Internet-enabled, and labeled part of the "share economy" – such as Uber's ride-sharing and Airbnb's lodging sharing – or simply because businesses promote social justice through presumably "gender-free" technologies does not mean that people constitute businesses and other organizing efforts that exhibit equality. Simply because gender normative patterns become replicated does not mean that the practices/activities (communication) and enduring structures (organization, see again Figure 1.2) are deterministic. Instead, this chapter highlights how choice/strategy and human agency are explored in gender and feminist organizational communication theory and research about how the kind of world that could and does move more toward gender equality for members of all genders is constituted.

Organizational Communication Scholars' Contributions to Gender Studies and Feminisms

Gender and feminist organizational communication scholars have explored and advanced gender studies and feminisms in particular ways. These ways include the focus on: (1) the communication-organization cycle, (2) enactment of gender in in/equitable ways materially and discursively, (3) transnational and Second World feminist politics, and (4) contradiction-and/or tension-based lenses.

Communication-Organization Cycle

First, gender and feminist organizational communication scholars focus on the ***communication-organization cycle*** or *how* agents constitute organization (structure) and organizing (process) as relatively enduring systems and practices that are gendered and that affect the welfare of individuals, communities, and ecological systems (see Figure 1.2).

With regard to structure, Mumby and Putnam's (1992) now-classic piece on bounded emotionality (see Chapter 18) deconstructed how organizational practices deemed rational and normal were based on masculine underpinnings that replicated traditional hierarchies, reward structures, and ideal worker norms (24/7 White male employee without caregiving responsibilities) to exert control and benefit few. In exploring feminist ways of knowing, being, and valuing the world as organizing principles, they constructed an organizational framework that could thrive on contradiction and construct businesses and other types of organizations based on care, mutual respect, reflexivity, empathy, and other values. Similarly, Putnam and Kolb (2000) constructed viable ways of reconstructing negotiation from ideals of empathic and collaborative dialogue in which sharing of perspectives and asking of questions rather than posturing and positioning could establish feminist ways of changing conflicts to result in mutually beneficial solutions. This hybrid framework enables women working in managerial positions to negotiate maternity leaves effectively since they incorporate the instrumental perspectives of their bosses to keep work flowing and the relational and embodied needs of themselves and others such as their direct reports and unborn children (Buzzanell, 2024).

As example of organizing-organization co-constitution, Cruz (2015; see also Biwa, 2021) contends that "feminist organizational communication scholarship remains rooted in Western assumptions in the ways in which it approaches organizational forms, values, and subjectivities of organizational members" (p. 23). She discusses classic Western bureaucratic structures, rationalities in terms of audit mentalities and accountabilities, and which communication and identities are valued. In contrast to Western organizing, she describes African feminist organizing as rooted in praxis or change in terms of economic agency, immediacy with regard to material conditions for survival, and foundations of holism, collectivity, and situationality. Holism counters Western dualistic worldviews, including work-family boundaries. Collectivity is oriented to group or communal life and harmony, whereas situationality portrays the shifting meanings and nature of relationships including flexible categories such as a "'male daughter' institution, [in which] a daughter could become an honorary male if her father did not have a male heir" (Cruz, 2015, p. 29). Building on this and others' scholarship, greater incorporation of feminist organizational communication scholarship from around the globe can help people to locate different ways of constructing messages, meanings, and organizing around gender and Indigenous knowledge (Na'puti & Cruz, 2022).

In summarizing this section, whereas many members of other organizational disciplines focus upon distinctions between female and male managers and leaders, and between employees in terms of horizontal (occupational) and vertical (advancement) sex segregations and career content and trajectories, organizational communication scholars often explore how difference itself is constituted communicatively in organizing processes and structures as well as how alternative ways of theorizing and embodying gender individually and organizationally, such as that found in African and Indigenous feminisms, can be produced.

Moreover, gender and feminist organizational communication scholars working in alternative organizational space confront assumptions that organization must be done a particular way; organizing and organization are and should be designed around particular values or else they are not serious or legitimate; and survival, profit, and growth are the ultimate indicators of organizational success. Some of these assumptions seem outdated given corporate social responsibility (CSR) and Corporate Social Advocacy (CSA).

But the organizing-organization tensions remain and become replicated in the hopes and ideals surrounding online organizing, sharing economy, and even feminist transnational networks that strive to disrupt and resist deeply embedded patterns of relating, structuring, and valuing members and organizations as a whole. In these ways, feminist organizing has the burden of proof against the normalization or presumption of mainstream organizing and organization even as network and material feminisms provide proof of concept. Of interest in these Internet-enabled feminist collectives are challenges about whether these are simply social movements in online (and often offline hybrid) formats or whether they are new organizational forms predicated on feminist solidarity and resistance.

Gender Enactment

Second, besides the focus on the communication-organizational cycle in general, most gender and feminist organizational communication scholars attend to the *enactment of gender in in/equitable material and discursive ways*. In other words, they focus on *how* gender and feminist change takes place within and through linguistic choices, interactions, and (relational network and institutional) structures as well as *what* is changed (discursive-material) online and offline. Organizational communication scholars delve into gendered embodiment (birth, male, and female bodies, breastfeeding), work and personal life spaces (hospital rooms, classrooms, labs, apartments, online platform work), and artifacts (grades, computers, lab equipment, project timetables, bottles, toys, play areas) that reproduce and disrupt traditional organizing in particular spaces and institutions.

Transnational and Second World Feminist Politics

Pal and Nieto-Fernandez (2024) describe women's and children's lives of poverty and violence that result from exploitation of land and other resources as well as complex and changing historical and structural forms of oppression and violence. For instance, women in the Global South often are employed in the lowest paying jobs with no representation (e.g., clothing, footwear) while also engaging in the unpaid labor of cooking, finding fuel, transporting water to homes, and childcare. Challenges for scholars working within the transnational feminist agenda are "to understand the location of the other in the transnational—a space within structures of global capital and geopolitical arrangements" (p. 68) and to transform living and economic conditions produced by rampant neocapitalism (e.g., toxic waste sites; deforestation; human trafficking; contamination, depletion, and/or diversion of water supplies) and by knowledge colonization by and for Western interests. As Fotaki and Pullen (2024) point out, the Covid-19 pandemic pushed women further into precarity, further normalizing violence against women. In advocating for self-reflection and transnational solidarity, Pal and Nieto-Fernandez (2024) turn scholars and organizational members' gaze to everyday struggles for social justice to redress past injustices and claim futures of care, democracy, and viable living conditions world-wide.

In arenas of feminist geopolitical struggles, Khrebtan-Hörhager and Pyatovskaya (2024) expose the Russian and Soviet histories and current "events of the Russia-Ukraine war [that] reveal profound suffering of Russian women as double victims: of the war and Putin's truly draconian patriarchal militarism" (p. 10). Despite previous popular media that used to convey Russian/Soviet women as equal to men, practices continue that subjugate women's voices and rights while erasing differences among these women. Khrebtan-Hörhager and Pyatovskaya focus on Russian feminism within the broader category of Second World Feminism as historically and culturally situated (in discursive space and materialized place, bodies, and artifacts) form of advocacy on behalf of women. They advocate for reinvigorating failed feminist alliances that have isolated and "sidestepped [Russian feminism] by transnational feminism" (p. 16). They hope "that our essay will serve as a humble cultural and feminist attempt to shift the discourse and to work together toward a common goal of peace, gender equality, and social justice" (p. 30).

Contradiction and Tension

Finally, many gender and feminist organizational communication scholars leverage *contradiction- and/or tension-based lenses* to develop practices and processes that can have value in how people make sense of a chaotic world (Fairhurst & Putnam, 2024). For instance, D'Enbeau (2017) wanted to know how organizational members confronted with dilemmas of sexual violence in U.S. university campuses came to understand how such complex behaviors and policies established for clarity in ambiguous and threatening situations, and stakeholder roles and practices were constituted ironically in specific socio-material conditions. Occupation and action orientations to dilemmas with their advocacy-compliance and proactive-reactive tensions provided insight into how viable strategies for approaching sexual assault on campuses could be constructed. These strategies go well past mandatory reporting regulations and encourage diverse response and prevention procedures.

Furthermore, typical models for changing the gendered status quo have been "fix the women"/"change the culture" or sameness/difference and control/resistance strategies – all rational, coherent, and ultimately unsatisfying models for change. These models reflect the kinds of dilemmatic thinking about which D'Enbeau (2017) and Harris (2015) write. Harris combines material feminism and a tension-centered approach to describe persistent dilemmas in feminist theory. These dilemmas include the following: desires to explain and change the world, to demarcate biological sex and socially constructed gender, to preserve and trouble identity categories, to celebrate agency while noting constraints, to envision and use the personal as political, and to depict feminisms, particularly the waves, as linear and less complex than they were and are. She situates communication as a site for agency. This move is picked up by Putnam and Ashcraft (2017) who encourage innovative both/and mergers to deal with multiple dilemmas in organizing.

So what does feminist dilemmatic scholarship mean for organizations? In particular, what does it mean for organizational difficulties in fostering talent regardless of difference, encouraging innovation that comes from integration of diverse opinions and knowledge, and embedding creative logics and difference into corporate boards and the C-suite? The two main strategies for incorporating women and people of color have been "fix the woman" and "fix the culture" with their contradictory sameness and difference orientations. We explore these strategies to challenge readers and scholars to engage in dilemmic – material and tension based – feminisms for change.

In particular, "fix the woman" strategies are based on deficit models, meaning that women are different from men, but this movement strives to signal key similarities that could affect desired individual and organizational outcomes. In other words, these models are based on what women were lacking – they lack masculine bodies, single-minded devotion to work and organization because they do not have "wives" (caretakers and caregivers), and sometimes prioritized relationships and family. The male developmental model strove to break free of relationships and be autonomous, independent, strong, and self-reliant (Marshall, 1993). To be successful, namely, to advance in organizations and industry and to attain leadership positions, means that women (and communal men) supposedly need to emulate hegemonic males. They need to leave anything feminine and collectively oriented behind to pursue success. Even so, they could never be what they are not. They could not meet the criteria for success because the criteria advantage careerist men by making excuses for lack of qualifications or by shifting criteria. "Fix the woman" orientations are based on the notion that awareness of inequities would be sufficient to make changes without fully addressing how deeply sedimented the categorical male=masculine and female=feminine equations are (even with acknowledgment of variations within and between these equations).

"Fix the woman" strategies seek rational solutions to the "problems" called by various names: Glass ceiling, vertical and horizontal sex segregation in occupations, gender pay gaps, motherhood penalty and fatherhood bonus, family-friendly (originally women-friendly) policies, lack of mentoring, clarity and reporting in sexual assault policies and procedures, and other inequalities. Even as gains were made in terms of laws, policies, and formulated standard operating procedures, as for which liberal feminists advocated, the gains were relatively small because they often did not achieve goals and/or were not sustainable or alienated men. However, they were significant because they established the foundations for equality. They named inequality and they legitimized the need for interventions. In "fix the woman" strategies, however, the interventions made women different but not equal.

The contradictions in "fix the culture" surface some of the same arguments (see Arendt & Nuru, 2023). The culture is deficient and can be readily fixed, thus ignoring a vast literature of organizational communication scholarship that indicates just how difficult changing cultures are and how long such change would take. In "fix the culture" (as in "fix the woman"), celebrating difference as a message strategy assumes that all women (or communal men) are similar. Creating equal opportunities, as discussed earlier in this chapter, again assumes that all men and women are fundamentally the same. It also assumes that the structure – and not people – creates gender inequalities. Gendered and feminist organizational communication scholarship indicates that this locus of change (structure) is not the case, or at least not the whole means of creating change. Instead, using the process, structure, organization model (O_1, O_2, and O_3,) depicted in Chapter 1 enables us to understand how language, social interaction, structuring activities, and organization can recreate and offer opportunities to challenge the status quo (e.g., through alternative settings or organizational forms, authority and community processes, and diverse organizational membership).

Conclusion

The most outrageous contribution of feminist organizational communication theorists is overlying lenses that *call into question everyday organizing and organization.* When taking a feminist analytic lens, everything looks different – because the lens confronts everyday normative assumptions about organizing and organization. This lens is not just about critique but about building a new vision, with the vision of gender equality involving ethics, embodiment, and multiple pathways for constructing better quality lives for women and men. In recognizing feminist contributions to everyday practice and scholarship, we return to the core feminist values, particularly the one that says that gender equality is a moral obligation (Buzzanell, 1994). It is a moral obligation to engage in the constitution of organizing and structuring of organization in ways that are in women's and men's best interests overall and in their particular socio-political and economic locations. Core feminist values and individual feminisms formed a metatheoretical matrix, or structure that enabled dialogue about feminist theory, root causes for and strategies for agency, and praxis in organizational communication (Buzzanell, 1994) bringing together process, structure, and entity (O_1, O_2, and O_3).

Recent work in network and material feminisms promises to engage in these discussions in local through global spaces, online and offline. Networked feminisms can be viewed organizing processes or online mobilizing (O_1). It is through these processes that structures are organized or assembled (O_2) to form the entities that we call organization. Hashtag feminisms function as organizations (entities or O_3) insofar as they operate as social collectives that focus on specific issues and that have the authority and agency to speak out on behalf of members and offer remedies or strategies for combatting particular forms of gender violence. As noted in Chapter 1, ethical considerations about who and what is represented, whether the organization fairly represents members' concerns, and how accountability for actions can be assessed are important questions. To address these questions, material feminisms offer insights today into the social and material conditions that recreate, modify, and disrupt gendered arrangements in any particular gendered spatio-temporal-cultural location. These locale-specific inquiries and activisms can be linked transnationally through online affordances to continuously engage in generating feminist processes, structures, and organization. It is an exciting time to learn how to enact choice, agency, and dignity for self and others from gender and feminist organizational communication.

Recommended Supplementary Readings

Eddington, S., Jarvis, C., & Buzzanell, P. M. (2023). Constituting affective identities: Understanding the communicative construction of identity in online men's rights spaces. *Organization*, *30*(1), 116–139.

Through analyses of Reddit posts in an online men's rights community, Eddington et al. found that these men constructed their identities and identified with others in this community through gendered and affective organizing.

LeBlanc, S., Spradley, E., Olson Beal, H., Burrow, L., & Cross, C. (2023). Toward a communication theory of coping: COVID-19 and the MotherScholar. *Atlantic Journal of Communication*, *31*(4), 354–371.

Given the multiple demands on mothers who also were scholars (MotherScholars) during the Covid-19 and lockdowns, five women academicians asked how they constituted coping. Drawing from a collaborative autoethnography in which they recounted and analyzed their personal, professional, and family lives, these MotherScholars found several coping stages. Their coping meant that they first needed to acknowledge the trigger event of the Covid-19 pandemic and associated disruptions. They then adjusted and prioritized behaviors, even as they questioned themselves and finally resolved themselves simply to surviving.

McDermott, T., Gee, J., & May, A. (2022). *Women of the wild: Challenging gender disparities in field stations and marine laboratories*. Lexington.

This edited collection describes how women who work in field stations and marine laboratories (FSMLs) continue their work despite personal, relational, and environmental challenges. Through detailed stories, survey results, case studies, and chapters using other methods, the authors show how women empower themselves and what cultures of support grounded in positive communication and leadership can look like in male-dominated fields.

Pauly, J., Hernández, L., & Munz, S. (Eds.) (2023). *Feminist mentoring in academia*. Lexington.

This compilation attests to the need for feminist mentoring throughout individuals' educational journeys in terms of one-on-one, collaborative, and spaces dedicated to mentoring women from intersectional, queer, disability, and other perspectives. Multiple conceptualizations and applications of feminist mentoring are presented.

Van Gilder, B., Austin, J., & Bruscella, J. (Eds.). (2023). *Communication and organizational changemaking for diversity, equity, and inclusion: A case studies approach*. Routledge.

This edited collection of case studies offers a range of controversial topics – trans athletes; intersectionalities of race/ethnicity, class, and gender; AI in hiring – handled in depth and with feasible practical applications.

Important Concepts: Define and Discuss

Core feminist commitments
Hashtag feminism
Liberal feminism
Material feminism
Network feminism
Radical feminism
Standpoint feminism

Discussion Questions

1 What communication strategies and organizing processes could enable people to transcend the dilemma of "fix the woman" and "fix the culture" strategies?
2 Please debate the different sides of alt-right men's online movements and network feminisms? How could different stakeholders' needs and interests be addressed?

Practitioners' Corner

Gender and feminist organizational communication has always been both theoretical and practical. Because praxis is based on understanding and change, there are multiple ways in which gender inequality has been discussed to raise and/or change consciousness about equality for men and for women. There also have been multiple ways to redress causes and promote action. The practical applications of gender and feminist organizational communication have been flexible work arrangements, parental leave and anti-discrimination and anti-harassment policies, and services on the corporate grounds to help manage work-life considerations (e.g., childcare, eldercare, clinics, take-home dinners, technologies to work from home). Particularly with regard to services, some experts contend that corporations have included these services to better control workers and increase productivity. Still others point out that use of these policies and services is considered a choice, meaning that those who request them need special treatment to do their work and that their top priority is not paid labor but some other aspect of their lives. The implications are that gender and feminist organizational communication scholarship ironically can both enable and constrain choice, agency, and dignity.

Xandra was a top student in her major and was encouraged by her engineering instructors and undergraduate advisors to consider graduate school. To help build her application, her professor offered her an opportunity to do research in his lab. Xandra was thrilled by this chance to understand more about what graduate school and, perhaps, a professorial career would entail. She also was excited about contributing to papers that might be published from her lab contributions. After a few weeks in the lab, Xandra's best friend tweeted her wedding and pregnancy announcement. Xandra immediately FaceTimed with her friend and accepted the invitation to be the "person of honor" at the ceremony a few weeks later. The ceremony and her person of honor duties would require that she miss school and her lab work for a week. Xandra was shocked when her professor questioned her commitment to the lab project and to an academic career. If you were Xandra, how would you handle this situation?

References

Adak, S., & Çağatay, S. (2023). Revisiting feminist historiography on women's activism in Turkey: Beyond the grand narrative of waves. *Women's History Review*, *32*(5), 723–744. https://doi.org/10.1080/09612025.2023.2198107

Arendt, C., & Nuru, A. (2023). The glass treadmill and the gender leadership gap. *Women & Language*, *46*(2), 369–391.

Ashcraft, K., & Mumby, D. (2004). *Reworking gender: A feminist communicology of organization*. Sage.

Austin, J. T., Wong, N., & Owens, A. C. (2023). The hashtag heard around the world: Social media users' perceptions and responses to the #MeToo hashtag. *Atlantic Journal of Communication*, *31*(5), 389–403. https://doi.org/10.1080/15456870.2022.2083136

Barbie. (2023), Directed by Greta Gerwig. Warner Brothers.

Bem, S. L. (1974). The measurement of psychological androgyny. *Journal of Consulting and Clinical Psychology*, *42*, 155–162.

Biwa, V. (2021). African feminisms and co-constructing a collaborative future with men: Namibian women in mining's discourses. *Management Communication Quarterly*, *35*(1), 43–68. https://doi.org/10.1177/0893318920973988

Branicki, L., King, E., & Norbury, K. (2023). Joy and the mop: The role of film in doing and undoing gender in entrepreneurship. *Gender, Work & Organization*, *30*(6), 1960–1979. https://doi.org/10.1111/gwao.13031

Branton, S., & Compton, C. (2021). There's no such thing as a gay bar: Co-sexuality and the neoliberal branding of queer spaces. *Management Communication Quarterly*, *35*(1), 69–95. https://doi.org/10.1177/0893318920972113

Buzzanell, P. M. (1994). Gaining a voice: Feminist organizational communication theorizing. *Management Communication Quarterly*, *7*(4), 339–383. https://doi.org/10.1177/0893318994007004001

Buzzanell, P. M. (2021). Reflections on feminist organizational communication. *Management Communication Quarterly*, *35*(1), 127–141. https://doi.org/10.1177/0893318920975211

Buzzanell, P. M. (2024). Motherhood at work: Positive communication and maternity leave negotiations (un)bounded by job types. *International Journal of Business Communication*, 61(4), 853–875. https://doi.org/10.1177/23294884241263558

Buzzanell, P. M., Arendt, C., Dohrman, R., Zoltowski, C., & Rajan, P. (2023). Engineering emotion sustainably: Affective gendered organizing of engineering identities and third space. *Sustainability*, *15*(6), 5051. https://doi.org/10.3390/su15065051

Cozza, M., & Gherardi, S. (2023). Posthuman feminism and feminist new materialism: Towards an ethico-onto-epistemology in research practices. In *Handbook of feminist research methodologies in management and organization studies* (pp. 55–71). Edward Elgar Publishing.

Cruz, J. (2015). Reimagining feminist organizing in global times: Lessons from African feminist communication. *Women & Language*, *38*(1), 23–41.

D'Enbeau, S. (2017). Unpacking the dimensions of organizational tension: The case of sexual violence response and prevention among college students. *Journal of Applied Communication Research*, *45*, 237–255.

Deer, S., Byrd, J., Mitra, D., & Haley, S. (2021). Rage, indigenous feminisms, and the politics of survival. *Signs: Journal of Women in Culture and Society*, *46*(4), 1057–1071. https://doi.org/10.1086/713294

Eddington, S. (2020). Alt-resilience: A semantic network analysis of identity (re) construction in an online men's rights community. *Journal of Applied Communication Research*, *48*(1), 114–135. https://doi.org/10.1080/00909882.2019.1706099

Eger, E. (2021). Co-constructing organizational identity and culture with those we serve: An ethnography of a transgender nonprofit organization communicating family identity and identification. *International Journal of Business Communication*, *58*(2), 254–281. https://doi.org/10.1177/2329488419893738

Eger, E., Litrenta, M., Kane, S., & Senegal, L. (2022). LGBTQ+ workers. In *Oxford research encyclopedia of communication*. https://doi.org/10.1093/acrefore/9780190228613.013.1247

Fairhurst, G. T., & Putnam, L. (2024). *Performing organizational paradoxes*. Routledge.

Fotaki, M., & Pullen, A. (2024). Feminist theories and activist practices in organization studies. *Organization Studies*, *45*(4), 593–616. https://doi.org/10.1177/01708406231209861

Freedman, G., Moutoux, I., Hermans, I., & Green, M. (2024). "She made a mean beef stroganoff": Gendered portrayals of women in STEM in newspaper articles and their effects. *Communication Monographs*, *91*(2), 261–282. https://doi.org/10.1080/03637751.2023.2285989

Fry, R. (2023, August 3). *Almost 1 in 5 stay-at-home parents in the U.S. are dads*. Policy Commons. Pew Research Center. https://policycommons.net/artifacts/4572202/almost-1-in-5-stay-at-home-parents-in-the-us/5395773/

Fuentes, L. (2023, January 17). *Inequality in US abortion rights and access: The end of Roe is deepening existing divides*. Guttmacher Institute. https://www.guttmacher.org/2023/01/inequity-us-abortion-rights-and-access-end-roe-deepening-existing-divides?utm_source=Guttmacher+Email+Alerts&utm_campaign=cc2e29b4b9-equity-lizapiecegupdate&utm_medium=email&utm_term=0_-cc2e29b4b9-%5BLIST_EMAIL_ID%5D

García Mingo, E., & Díaz Fernández, S. (2023). Wounded men of feminism: Exploring regimes of male victimhood in the Spanish manosphere. *European Journal of Cultural Studies*, *26*(6), 897–915. https://doi.org/10.1177/13675494221140586

Harris, K. L. (2015). Feminist dilemmatic theorizing: New materialism in communication studies. *Communication Theory*, *26*(2), 150–170. https://doi.org/10.1111/comt.12083

Harris, K. L. (2017). Re-situating organizational knowledge: Violence, intersectionality and the privilege of partial perspective. *Human Relations*, *70*(3), 263–285. https://doi.org/10.1177/0018726716654745

Herbst-Debby, A., & Achouche, N. (2023, September). Double jeopardy: Gendered social policy for two risky life periods in six welfare state contexts. In *Women's studies international forum* (Vol. 100, p. 102814). Pergamon.

James, A. (2024). Platform work-lives in the gig economy: Recentering work–family research. *Gender, Work & Organization*, *31*(2), 513–534. https://doi.org/10.1111/gwao.13087

Joy. (2015). Directed by David O. Russell. Fox 2000 Pictures.

Kandathil, G., & Chennangodu, R. (2024). Postfeminist individuating of a women collective and the strugglesome emergence of a relational collective feminist solidarity: The story of Kudumbashree, a Kerala state-instituted women empowerment program. *Gender, Work & Organization*, *31*(1), 115–132. https://doi.org/10.1111/gwao.13057

Kang, D., & Long, Z. (2024). Organizing as Tong (通): Decolonizing organizational communication from the roots. *Management Communication Quarterly*, *38*(3), 595–622. https://doi.org/10.1177/08933189231223424

Khrebtan-Hörhager, J., & Pyatovskaya, E. (2024). Russian women, Ukraine war, and (neglected) writing on the wall: From the (im)possibility of world traveling to failing feminist alliances. *Journal of International and Intercultural Communication*, *17*(1), 9–38. https://doi.org/10.1080/17513057.2023.2265992

Leslie, L., Flynn, E., Foster-Gimbel, O., & Manchester, C. (2024). Happy talk: Is common diversity rhetoric effective diversity rhetoric? *Academy of Management Journal*, *67*(3), 595–624. https://doi.org/10.5465/amj.2021.1402

Linabary, J., Corple, D., & Cooky, C. (2020). Feminist activism in digital space: Postfeminist contradictions in #WhyIStayed. *New Media & Society*, *22*(10), 1827–1848. https://doi.org/10.1177/1461444819884635

Long, Z., Buzzanell, P. M., & Selzer King, A. (2023). Pivoting multiple liminalities in working parenthood: Communicative negotiations of transitional, permanent, and limbo liminalities. *Management Communication Quarterly*, *37*(2), 225–250. https://doi.org/10.1177/08933189221095093

Maingi Ngwu, N. (2023). Alternative economic discourses from the margins: Kenyan migrant women's informal childcare organizing as an alternative economic discourse in the contemporary US Context. In M. Pal, J. Cruz, & D. Munshi (Eds.), *Organizing at the margins: Theorizing organizations of struggle in the Global South* (pp. 63–90). Springer International Publishing.

Marshall, J. (1993). Viewing organizational communication from a feminist perspective: A critique and some offerings. *Annals of the International Communication Association*, *1*, 122–143. https://doi.org/10.1080/23808985.1993.11678848

McDonald, J. (2013). Conforming to and resisting dominant gender norms: How male and female nursing students do and undo gender. *Gender, Work & Organization*, *20*(5), 561–579. https://doi.org/10.1111/j.1468-0432.2012.00604.x

Medved, C. E. (2016). The new female breadwinner: discursively doing and un doing gender relations. *Journal of Applied Communication Research*, *44*(3), 236–255. https://doi.org/10.1080/00909882.2016.1192286

Mitra, D. (2023). The Report, or, whatever happened to Third World Feminist Theory? *Signs: Journal of Women in Culture and Society*, *48*(3), 557–584. https://doi.org/10.1086/723270

Mumby, D., & Putnam, L. (1992). The politics of emotion: A feminist reading of bounded rationality. *Academy of Management Review*, *17*, 465–486. https://doi.org/10.2307/258719

Na'puti, T., & Cruz, J. (2022). Mapping interventions: Toward a decolonial and indigenous praxis across communication subfields. *Communication, Culture and Critique*, *15*(1), 1–20. https://doi.org/10.1093/ccc/tcab064

Nkomo, S., Bell, M., Roberts, L., Joshi, A., & Thatcher, S. (2019). Diversity at a critical juncture: New theories for a complex phenomenon. *Academy of Management Review*, *44*(3), 498–517. https://doi.org/10.5465/amr.2019.0103

Örtenblad, A., Marling, R., & Vasiljević, S. (Eds.) (2017). *Gender equality in a global perspective*. Routledge.

Pal, M., & Nieto-Fernandez, B. (2024). Politics of transnational feminism to decolonize feminist organizational communication: A call to action. *Management Communication Quarterly*, *38*(1), 60–85.

Peretz, T. (2023). A male feminist walks into a bar, because it was set so low: The pedestal effect and the economy of gratitude in feminist spaces. *Sociology Compass*, *17*(11), e13151. https://doi.org/10.1111/soc4.13151

Putnam, L., & Ashcraft, K. (2017). Gender and organizational paradox. In M. Lewis, W. Smith, P. Jarzabkowski, & A. Langley (Eds.), *Handbook of organizational paradox: Approaches to plurality, tensions, and contradictions* (pp. 333–352). Oxford University Press.

Putnam, L., & Kolb, D. (2000). Rethinking negotiation: Feminist views of communication and exchange. In P. M. Buzzanell (Ed.), *Rethinking organizational and managerial communication from feminist perspectives* (pp. 76–106). Sage.

Qian, Y., & Fuller, S. (2020). COVID-19 and the gender employment gap among parents of young children. *Canadian Public Policy*, *46*(S2), S89–S101.

Schaeffer, K. (2020, October 5). Key facts about women's suffrage around the world, a century after U.S. ratified 19th Amendment. Pew Research Center. https://www.pewresearch.org/short-reads/2020/10/05/key-facts-about-womens-suffrage-around-the-world-a-century-after-u-s-ratified-19th-amendment/

Sobieraj, S. (2018). Bitch, slut, skank, cunt: Patterned resistance to women's visibility in digital publics. *Information, Communication & Society*, *21*, 1700–1714. https://doi.org/10.1080/1369118X.2017.1348535

Sumarsono, I., Darmajanti, P., Lestari, C., Fanani, U. Z., Pratita, I., Suprihatien, S., … & Sopaheluwakan, Y. (2023). Racial and gender discrimination reflected in Theodore Melfi's *Hidden Figures*. *World Journal of English Language*, *13*(5), 67–75. https://doi.org/10.5430/wjel.v13n5p67

Tian, Z. (2023). *Suzhi, guanxi*, and the abject body: Nonhuman agents of paradox that perform identity work together with Chinese women political leaders. *Management Communication Quarterly*, *37*(1), 99–126. https://doi.org/10.1177/08933189221095615
Toupin, S. (2024). Shaping feminist artificial intelligence. *New Media & Society*, *26*(1), 580–595. https://doi.org/10.1177/14614448221150776
United Nations. (2023). The struggle of trans and gender-diverse persons. *United Nations Human Rights*. https://www.ohchr.org/en/special-procedures/ie-sexual-orientation-and-gender-identity/struggle-trans-and-gender-diverse-persons
Vacca, R., & Bartow, A. (Eds.) (2023). *The jurisprudential legacy of Justice Ruth Bader Ginsburg*. NYU Press.
Vachhani, S., & Pullen, A. (2019). Ethics, politics and feminist organizing: Writing feminist infrapolitics and affective solidarity into everyday sexism. *Human Relations*, *72*(1), 23–47. https://doi.org/10.1177/0018726718780988
Vachhani, S. J. (2024). Networked feminism in a digital age—Mobilizing vulnerability and reconfiguring feminist politics in digital activism. *Gender, Work & Organization*, *31*(3), 1031–1048. https://doi.org/10.1111/gwao.13097
Walker, T., & Muñoz Rojas, L. (2021). Teaching and gaining a voice: A rhetorical intersectionality approach to pedagogy of feminist organizational communication. *Management Communication Quarterly*, *35*(1), 17–42. https://doi.org/10.1177/0893318920972692
Waxman, O. (2020, August 17). *It's a struggle they will wage alone. How Black women won the right to vote. Time*. https://time.com/5876456/black-women-right-to-vote/
Yang, X., & Hu, N. (2024). #girls help girls#: Feminist discussions and affective heterotopia in patriarchal China, *24*(6), 1298–1313. *Feminist Media Studies*, 1–16. https://doi.org/10.1080/14680777.2023.2229967

14 Engaging Scholarship on Difference and Intersectionality in Challenging Times

Jamie McDonald

The claim "people are different than each other" (Sedgwick, 2008, p. 22) seems banal. Of course, people are different from each other. However, behind this claim lie enormous complexities that scholars across disciplines seek to understand. In Organizational Communication, scholars explore these complexities with questions as follows: which differences matter and shape our organizational experiences? How do these differences intersect with each other and shape power relations? How are some intersecting differences privileged in organizational settings? How are other differences marginalized and/or stigmatized? How are work and occupations organized around these differences? And how is difference a constitutive feature of organizing? As we shall see in this chapter, a rich body of research addresses these questions.

The first edition of *Difference Matters* (Allen, 2004) helped to institutionalize difference as a key concern for Organizational Communication scholars. *Difference* is broadly conceptualized as a power-laden social construction referring "to the ways in which people differ from each other along the lines of socially significant identities such as gender, race, and sexuality" (McDonald, 2015, p. 310). Difference can also be conceptualized in terms of behaviors or characteristics in addition to identities (Buzzanell, 2018). As such, Organizational Communication scholars attend to all forms of difference that "matter" – that is, differences that shape organizational interactions and experiences in ways that are related to power and privilege (Allen, 2023; see Chapter 12). Examples of differences that are reviewed in this chapter and particularly salient in contemporary public discourse include race, gender, sexuality, and nation.

Decades of scholarship and activism have demonstrated that power-laden differences are interrelated and experienced simultaneously. This is the main premise of *intersectionality*, which "investigates how intersecting power relations influence social relations across diverse societies as well as individual experiences in everyday life" (Collins & Bilge, 2020, p. 2). Coining the term *intersectionality*, legal scholar Kimberlé Crenshaw (1991) referred to a case of discrimination where women of color were discriminated against not on the basis of either gender or race alone, but at the intersection of both gender and race. While Crenshaw's (1991) work was vital in naming intersectionality and institutionalizing the term in academia, intersectional sensibilities have a longer history with origins in activist circles. African American feminist and activist Francis Beal (1969/1995) noted intersecting oppressions in the 1960s when critiquing patriarchy within the Black Power movement and racism in the women's liberation movement (Collins & Bilge, 2020). Moreover, the Combahee River Collective (1977/2019) issued a statement in the 1970s condemning their struggle against interlocking systems of oppression related to race, gender, sexuality, and class.

DOI: 10.4324/9781003484639-17

As an analytical concept in academia, *intersectionality* has been so taken up in interdisciplinary circles that intersectionality studies is becoming its own field of inquiry (Cho et al., 2013). Intersectional sensibilities made their way to Organizational Communication in the 1990s with Allen's (1996, 1998, 2000) work on Black feminist standpoints (see Chapter 13), as well as a landmark article critiquing how structural oppression on the basis of intersectional differences is experienced in the academy (Allen et al., 1999; see Chapter 2). Yet, much feminist research centering on gender oppression did not attend to intersecting differences, which eventually led to a call for a moratorium on research examining gender without adopting an intersectional approach (Ashcraft, 2011). Today, it is widely agreed that analyses of difference must address intersectionality to account for the complexities of interlocking oppressions (Linabary et al., 2021). As the #ToneUpOrgComm Collective (2020) affirms, "the time for intersectionality is now" (p. 153; see Chapter 1).

The time for intersectionality is now because interlocking structures of oppression such as cisheteronormativity, patriarchy, and white supremacy remain firmly in place in contemporary organizations (O_3), embedded in their structures (O_2) and organizing processes (O_1), while efforts to recognize and dismantle these structures have been increasingly met with backlash as our social and political context has shifted. For example, the rise of populist discourse around the world has fueled anti-intellectual sentiments, an increased distrust of the academy, and hostility related to diversity, equity, and inclusion (DEI) initiatives (Butler, 2024). This averseness to DEI is reflected in President Trump's executive order to ban DEI in the federal government and in announcements by the CEOs of several major corporations, including Meta, Amazon, McDonald's, Walmart, and Target, that they are rolling back their DEI programs. Even when DEI initiatives exist, they are sometimes cast in neoliberal terms that are used to tell "happy stories" (Banerjee & Tedmanson, 2010, p. 150), which brand institutions as diverse, inclusive, and welcoming, even as oppressive institutional logics go unchallenged (Collins & Bilge, 2020). Because at its core intersectionality is about systematic oppression, power, and privilege, it is needed to ensure that diversity initiatives focus on social inequality and social justice (Collins & Bilge, 2020).

Recent events in the discipline of communication and the subfield of Organizational Communication highlight the urgent need for intersectionality. Even as scholars of color have repeatedly drawn attention to the field's structural racism and whiteness (Chakravartty et al., 2018) and the paucity of communication research that critically interrogates race (Orbe & Allen, 2008), the Distinguished Scholars controversy and the 2019 NCA Organizational Communication Division top paper panel respondent's claim that she didn't "have time for intersectionality" (see Chapter 1) demonstrate that, like academic institutions, the field can be unwilling to engage with difference and intersectionality. Moreover, there is reticence to recognize the field's role in perpetuating oppression along the lines of intersecting differences (Ashcraft, 2024). Intersectional sensibilities are also needed as the field works toward decolonizing and challenging the Western-centrism at the foundation of organizational communication scholarship (Pal et al., 2022; see Chapter 4).

In light of these challenges, this chapter first positions difference as a constitutive feature of organizing that has implications for all scholars of organizational communication, regardless of focus area. Conceptualizing difference in this way exposes oppressive logics in both our scholarship and organizing practices, which is imperative to move beyond them. Second, the chapter reviews recent developments in Organizational Communication scholars' approaches to intersectionality. Third, it reviews recent research that shows how intersecting differences matter in organizational life, particularly as they relate to race, gender identity, sexuality, and nation. In so doing, it interrogates and critiques normative ideologies such as whiteness, cisnormativity, heteronormativity, and Western-centrism. The chapter concludes by reflecting on how we might begin to organize in ways that are more socially just and emancipatory.

Difference as a Constitutive Feature of Organizing

A constitutive approach views difference as central to organizing, rather than considering categories of difference as merely demographic variables that affect organizational outcomes. Nkomo (1992) offered a landmark critique of functionalist approaches that treat categories of difference as only demographic variables. Treating race as merely a demographic variable relies heavily on racial stereotypes, assumes that it is only relevant if it can be objectively measured, presumes organizations to be race-neutral, overlooks oppressive structures by viewing discrimination as function of personal bias, and tends to rely on binaries (e.g., Black/White) (see Chapter 1). Organizational Communication scholars now favor constitutive approaches to difference that are attentive to the socially constructed nature of difference and power dynamics.

Conceptualizing difference from a constitutive approach underscores that intersecting differences shape all organizing processes (Mumby, 2011). As such, organizational communication research and theory is biased when it does not address difference in critical, substantive ways and consider how difference is embedded into organizational foundations, hierarchies, and processes (Allen, 2007; Parker, 2003; Ray, 2019). Rather than considering difference as merely one topic to examine among others, difference can be engaged across all topics pertaining to organizational communication, including socialization, relationships, leadership, emotion, and conflict (Alvarez et al., 2015).

Allen's (1996, 1998, 2000) critiques of organizational socialization research provide a poignant illustration of the need to consider the implications of intersecting differences. Drawing from her standpoint as a Black woman in the academy, she exposes how a model of organizational socialization hailed as universal presumes a White organizational subject. Her work illustrates the need to account for difference and intersectionality in organizational communication theory. Similarly, dominant models of leadership are based almost exclusively on studies of White women and men, yet presented as universal and generalizable (Parker, 2005). Parker's (2005) critical feminist approach to leadership highlights the leadership practices of African American women executives and illustrates the imperative of accounting for intersecting differences in leadership research (Parker, 2001, 2002, 2003; see Chapter 13).

Difference can also be seen as a constitutive feature of work itself (Mumby, 2011). Put differently, we know work through its associations with bodies that are gendered, raced, classed, and sexualized. These associations shape the value and meaning of this work (Ashcraft, 2011). Ashcraft's (2013) *glass slipper* metaphor explains how arbitrary and socially constructed meanings of work become associated with embodied and intersectional differences. The glass slipper is a metaphor for occupational identity – the identity *of* work. Ashcraft (2013) shows how particular occupations have been discursively and strategically associated with certain forms of difference to shape the meaning and value of this work. As such, some work is made to "fit" certain people but not others, just like shoes are designed to fit only some people's feet. For example, Ashcraft's research on airline pilots shows that to bolster claims of professionalism and secure higher salaries, post-World War II pilots sought to associate their occupational identity with a particular form of white, heterosexual masculinity (Ashcraft, 2007; Ashcraft & Mumby, 2004). Intersectional differences thus permeate our understandings of how work is organized and understood (Ashcraft, 2011).

McFarland and Larson's (2024) account of reproducing violence, racism, and erasure in research offers another powerful illustration of the importance of viewing intersectional differences as constitutive features of organizing and thus as central to research practices. In their reflexive account, they discuss the initial aim of their project: examine how midwives in Alabama advocated for the legitimacy of their occupation and how their professional identities were constructed in legislative efforts to decriminalize midwifery. While their research initially received accolades, subsequent reflection led them to expose the logics of white supremacy embedded in their initial research account. By excluding race from the initial rendering of their research, they realized they had overlooked how contemporary efforts to legitimize midwifery perpetuated racist assumptions about the rich history of Black lay midwifery in Alabama. They also acknowledge that they failed to critically interrogate gender by tacitly assuming that all midwives identify as women and without considering the experiences of pregnant trans and nonbinary folks. McFarland and Larson (2024) vividly demonstrate the imperative of critically interrogating difference and adopting intersectional sensibilities in research to avoid reproducing oppressive logics such as white supremacy and cisheteronormativity.

In addition to viewing difference and intersectionality as central features of organization, work, and research, constitutive approaches view intersecting differences as socially constructed. Categories of difference emerge in particular sociohistorical contexts, leading meanings of difference to vary across time and space (Allen, 2023). A social constructionist lens underscores that the concept of *race* was invented by European colonizers with categories used to denote race that are arbitrary, constantly evolving, and contextually specific (Parker et al., 2017; see Chapter 1). Although arbitrary, socially constructed meanings of difference have real and sometimes devastating consequences. Indeed, socially constructed meanings of race have been deployed throughout history to justify horrific practices such as colonialism, slavery, and genocide (see Chapters 1 and 4).

Drawing from constitutive and social constructionist approaches, we can examine the implications of difference and intersectionality for different expressions of organization. Meanings of intersectional differences are embedded into the organizing processes through which members of a social collective coordinate meaning (O_1). This approach to understanding organization is particularly evident in research examining how work is organized around difference and how particular intersections of difference come to matter in everyday organizational life. Examining how difference operates as a key organizing principle that shapes the "meaning, structure, practice, and economy of work" (Ashcraft, 2011, p. 4) is also consistent with O_1. Further, scholarship on difference conceptualizes organization as a coordinated entity (O_3), enabling us to examine how intersectional differences are experienced in these contexts. Last, difference and intersectionality research can conceive of organization as the state of a social collective's coordination (O_2) by interrogating how meanings of difference are embedded in organizational policies and structures.

Approaches to Intersectionality

While intersectionality is a critical concept drawing our attention to how interlocking, power-laden differences shape organizational life, it is also a complex concept that can be difficult to operationalize in empirical studies. One key tension that arises in intersectional analyses pertains to the impossibility of accounting for all intersecting differences that may be relevant (Parker, 2014). Intersectional scholarship that attends to gender and race can inadvertently gloss over additional intersections that matter, such as sexuality, age, and nation (Holvino, 2010; McDonald, 2015; Rodriguez et al., 2016). Moreover, intra-group complexities exist within all categories of difference, creating another tension inherent in intersectional scholarship: making political claims on behalf of marginalized groups without also falling into the essentialism that reifies what it means to be part of a particular group (Harris, 2015). Indeed, it is challenging to foreground particular categories of difference while at the same time not "negating or undermining the complexities and particular character of an individual, group, system of oppression, or culture" (Parker, 2014, p. 625).

Tensions inherent to intersectional scholarship must be managed rather than resolved (Harris, 2015). One tension-management strategy is practicing reflexivity, reflecting upon why we foreground certain forms of difference and what our analysis enables and does not enable us to claim, recognizing the merits and limitations of the chosen approach to intersectionality (Cunliffe, 2003). It is also imperative to conceive of categories such as fluid, changing, and interwoven with each other (Cho et al., 2013), which underscores that, even as we may foreground particular intersections of difference, these categories should not be assumed to be stable and fixed features of social life, nor as the only ones that matter (Harris, 2015). Indeed, certain intersections of difference can be more or less salient in particular contexts and interactions (Wells et al., 2015).

Holvino's (2010) simultaneity framework offers one approach to manage tensions related to operationalizing intersectionality. Drawing from socialist, poststructural, and transnational feminisms (see Chapter 13), Holvino (2010) suggests that intersectionality can be simultaneously examined at multiple levels of practice: institutional, identity, and social. *Institutional practice* refers to the ways inequalities related to intersectional differences are embedded into organizational forms and structures; *identity practice* refers to the processes through which some intersecting identities are constructed in ways that are valued over others; and *social practice* refers to the ways dominant societal ideologies and beliefs reproduce inequalities on the basis of intersectional differences (Holvino, 2010). She suggests that intersectional scholarship consider how "meanings of gender, race, class, ethnicity, sexuality, and nation are built into and manifested in organizational structures and policies, dominant societal beliefs and ideologies, and everyday work interactions" (Holvino, 2010, p. 262). Simultaneously examining processes of institutional, identity, and social practices complicates the study of intersectionality, but the goal of intersectionality should not be to simplify complex processes and phenomena (Holvino, 2010).

Although intersectionality is an interdisciplinary concept, Organizational Communication scholars have developed disciplinary-specific approaches. One such approach is grounded in the communicative constitution of organizations (CCO) concept of *ventriloquism*, the processes by which human and nonhuman agents are mobilized and made present (Cooren et al., 2013; see Chapter 3). Long et al.'s (2018) ventriloqual approach to intersectionality examines intersecting differences and power relations as figures made present in interactions. A ventriloqual approach to intersectionality offers a clear, grounded-in-action approach to determine which intersectional differences matter and should be foregrounded in each context, as emphasis is placed on intersections that are mobilized – or ventriloquized – in interactions (Long et al., 2018). A ventriloqual approach does not require analysts to pre-determine which intersections of difference to highlight.

Closeting, which refers to "the communication processes through which individuals navigate the revelation and concealment of stigmatized, invisible differences" (McDonald et al., 2020, p. 85), is another disciplinary-specific approach to intersectionality.

The intersectional theory of closeting has implications for a host of intersectional differences that can be concealed and are stigmatized such that disclosure risks negative consequences (Harris & McDonald, 2018; McDonald et al., 2020). Drawing from queer theory, it specifically highlights non-normative differences; that is, those that contrast with what is typically assumed and taken-for-granted (McDonald, 2015). For example, individuals may negotiate closeting in relation to non-normative family structures (Dixon, 2018), transgender identities (Eger, 2018), communities of origin (Ferguson, 2018), citizenship statuses (McDonald, 2018), health and lifestyle behaviors (Romo, 2018), and parenthood in graduate school (Long et al., 2024). Approaching intersectionality through the lens of closeting highlights hard-to-see non-normative intersectional differences. Moreover, it enables analysts to consider how individuals simultaneously negotiate closeting in relation to multiple stigmatized differences, thereby showing how multiple closeting processes intersect with each other to shape experiences in power-laden ways (McDonald & DeTurk, 2022).

Difference and Intersectionality Matter

So far, we have conceptualized *difference* as constitutive of organizing and *intersectionality* as a critical sensitizing concept. Race, gender identity, sexuality, and nation are four power-laden intersectional differences that shape organizational experiences. Foregrounding these differences reflects some of the key axes of differences most salient in contemporary public discourse, but this focus does *not* negate others. Rather, a focus on these four intersecting differences highlights two tensions that are constitutive of writing review chapters on difference, intersectionality, and organizing. First, any list of differences that matter invariably ends in an "embarrassed 'etc.'" (Butler, 2006, p. 196). Second, doing justice to all intersectional differences that "matter" is an exceedingly difficult, if not impossible, task to accomplish in one chapter (Ashcraft, 2024). Although this chapter focuses primarily on race, gender identity, sexuality, and nation, organizational scholars also consider how class, age, and disability are among the other intersecting, power-laden differences that create differential experiences in organizations (Allen, 2023).

Race and Organizing

While calls to critically interrogate race and organizing date back decades (Allen, 1995, 2007; Allen et al., 1999; Ashcraft & Allen, 2003; Grimes, 2001; Orbe & Allen, 2008), the field has been painfully slow to take them up (see Chapter 1). The body of unanswered calls to critically interrogate race is even ironically cited as evidence that the field has addressed race (Ashcraft, 2024).

The reluctance of Organizational Communication to critically interrogate race illustrates its overall whiteness. Whiteness is the subtle construction of white racial identity as the dominant, taken-for-granted norm through everyday practices and communication (Grimes, 2002). Because of these practices, white racial identity becomes invisible and race becomes associated with what is *not* white (see Chapter 1). As such, white racial identity is unmarked and invisible in dominant societal and organizational contexts (i.e., a CEO), whereas the race of people of color is marked and visible (i.e., a Black CEO) (Nkomo, 1992).

Macalpine and Marsh's (2005) study illustrates how whiteness functions. When White participants were asked what it was like to be White in their organization, the taken-for-grantedness of whiteness was evident: "There's nothing I can say, I don't think about it";

"It's the norm – I take it for granted"; "Not an issue you talk about" (Macalpine & Marsh, 2005, p. 440). White racial identity thus enables the development of a unique standpoint through which one understands the world – a privileged standpoint from which individuals are not likely to think about their race and from which race appears to be a non-issue (Allen, 2007). Organizational Communication has been reluctant to critically interrogate race because the field's whiteness makes it appear as though race is irrelevant to organizing and organizations are race-neutral structures, despite being embedded in racialized power relations (Grimes, 2001; Liu, 2022; Ray, 2019).

Grimes (2002) identified three perspectives on whiteness in diversity management literature written by and for practitioners: re-centering whiteness, masking whiteness, and interrogating whiteness. *Re-centering* whiteness relies on racial stereotypes to treat whiteness as a universal, taken-for-granted norm. Although racial difference is acknowledged, re-centering does not problematize power relations embedded in whiteness. *Masking* whiteness maintains the status quo by denying racial difference and white privilege, keeping whiteness invisible, and treating race as a non-issue. Grimes (2002) calls on the field to *interrogate* whiteness by naming, unmasking, and de-centering whiteness as a privileged standpoint. This can be accomplished by interrogating "the ways writers talk about race when it is not the topic about which they claim to write" (Grimes, 2001, p. 136). Because whiteness is a normative ideology operating through invisibility, exposing implicit racialized assumptions embedded in discourse that may not be explicitly about race is a key way to make whiteness visible, the first step in challenging it (Grimes, 2001).

While the field has been reluctant to critically interrogate race (Ashcraft, 2024), Parker (2001, 2002, 2003, 2005) has made important contributions that expose whiteness in dominant understandings of leadership. Parker (2002) notes that the very presence of African American women senior executives in positions of authority challenges normative preconceptions of organizational leaders as both White and male. Participants noted two salient contexts in which they faced challenges: interacting with White male colleagues and interacting with African American coworkers and clients (Parker, 2002). Parker (2001) examines how the *standpoint* (see Chapter 13) of African American women executives informs and shapes their experiences of leadership. In so doing, she reconceptualizes *collaboration* and *instrumentality* in leadership research, viewing directness and control as a means of collaboration and associating instrumentality with both strategic message transmission and dialogue. Parker (2001) thus challenges the whiteness of traditional views of leadership and expands our understanding of leadership in a way that is grounded in the experiences of African American women executives. Parker (2020) has also examined the leadership practices of the late civil rights activist Ella Baker to coin the concept of *catalytic leadership*, an approach that refers to "a concrete set of communication practices for doing social justice leadership in equitable partnership with, instead of on, communities" (p. 11).

Ferguson and Dougherty (2022) also critically interrogate whiteness by examining experiences of Black professionals. While it has long been established that professionalism is associated with maleness, creating a paradox for women professionals (Wood & Conrad, 1983), Ferguson and Dougherty (2022) show how normative conceptions of professionalism are also embedded in whiteness. Black professionals experience double binds as they are unable to physically and discursively embody dominant discourses of professionalism. It is thus crucial to interrogate how contemporary discourses of professionalism are based in racist assumptions as well as engage in a more "mindful, meaning-centered, and co-constructed approach" (Ferguson & Dougherty, 2022, p. 25) that abandons the racist and gendered assumptions underpinning the term *professionalism*.

Gender Identity and Organizing

Organizational Communication has a long and rich history of feminist research critically interrogating gender as a communicative accomplishment (see Chapter 13). Yet, most research has been presumptively cisnormative, glossing over trans* and intersex experiences by presuming gender's binary alignment with sex as assigned at birth (Köllen & Rumens, 2022). Following Köllen and Rumens (2022), I use the term *trans** with an asterisk "for its contemporary currency as an inclusive term that denotes a dazzling array of gender diverse people including, but not limited to, those who identify as transgender, transexual, non-binary, genderqueer and genderfluid" (p. 703) and intersex to refer to people, "whose genetic/chromosomal, gonadal and/or phenotypic sex is misaligned within the binary model of being either male or female" (p. 705). In organizational research, intersex experiences have largely been ignored, with Blithe and Hanchey's (2015) analysis of gendered physiological discrimination in sex verification testing for athletes being an important exception. There is, however, a nascent body of research that begins to expose and challenge cisnormativity as it examines trans* experiences in organizational life.

One particularly poignant way to see cisnormativity in organizational research is to note how cisgender identity is silently assumed. In the literature, the unqualified use of the terms *women* and *men* almost always assumes cisgender identity but is rarely labeled such, a key way cisnormativity is constructed (Köllen & Rumens, 2022). As a normative and taken-for-granted ideology, cisnormativity functions in a similar way to whiteness. To counter cisnormativity, Jones (2020) developed a transgender standpoint epistemology, defined as "the net realities available to a transgender employee based upon conscious reflections on the nature of oppression and discrimination constituted through cisnormative expectations of organizational performance" (p. 256). Trans* employees are hyperaware of cisnormativity, which fuels both covert and overt forms of discrimination and is manifested in both everyday interactions (e.g., intentional misgendering) and organizational structures (e.g., the unavailability of gender-neutral restrooms) (Jones, 2020).

Highlighting embodied experiences of trans* individuals in cisnormative organizational contexts challenges cisnormativity (Jones, 2023). In this regard, organizational entry and the job search process can be particularly difficult for trans* people (Eger, 2018; Goryunova et al., 2022). Because of rampant employment discrimination, trans* jobseekers may engage in closeting communication (Eger, 2018), communicatively negotiating revealing and/or concealing trans* identity. Closeting communication is complex because individuals do not fully control identity disclosures. Trans* people may be outed without their consent, as background checks by potential employers may reveal former names and inconsistent gender markers on identification documents (Eger, 2018). Many who come out as trans* and embrace their trans* identity during the job search process experience retribution and discrimination (Goryunova et al., 2022). Indeed, trans* individuals are chronically underemployed and face difficulties gaining employment (Eger, 2018; O'Shea, 2020). As O'Shea (2020) recounts in an evocative autoethnography of their experiences as a nonbinary transgender academic, "in the last 15 months I have applied for over 250 jobs and have had a handful of interviews, all but one since I stopped declaring that I am a transgender person" (p. 1443).

Trans* people entering cisnormative organizations negotiate closeting communication with different levels of outness and strategies for managing their trans* identity visibility. Some are fully out to peers and supervisors, while others conceal their identities and pass as cisgender (Goryunova et al., 2022). Organizational context is a key factor shaping strategy.

Workplace supportiveness is positively related to outness, such that trans* people are more likely to disclose their identities when they perceive their organization to be supportive (Baumler, 2024). Conversely, lower perceptions of workplace supportiveness lead to trans* identity closeting (Baumler, 2024). In another study, Muhr et al. (2016) examined how one trans woman manages her identity as she moves across different contexts. While she is actively political and transgressive in contexts outside of work, she de-emphasizes her transgender identity in professional contexts.

Another important factor shaping trans* experiences at work is the extent to which gender enactment falls in line with normative conceptions of masculinity/femininity. Jeanes and Janes (2021) found that trans men doing gender in ways perceived as stereotypically masculine tend to be more accepted by colleagues than those whose gender performances are more ambiguous. Moreover, some trans men felt compelled by others to do gender in more stereotypically masculine ways and reinscribe the gender binary (Jeanes & Janes, 2021). Because nonbinary transgender individuals do not fit the gender binary, they face additional challenges (O'Shea, 2018). As O'Shea (2020) notes, they can face a choice between erasing their nonbinary identity to select a binary label and losing employment.

Schilt (2006) found that post-transition, some trans men who enact gender in line with normative conceptions of masculinity may experience newfound privilege, including higher respect and pay, upon being read as a man by colleagues. This newfound privilege was more common for White trans men in white-collar jobs; men of color in blue-collar jobs faced resistance from employers and colleagues (Schilt, 2010). Schilt and Connell (2007) examined both trans men and trans women, finding that post-transition opportunities for enacting gender in alternative ways that disrupt the gender binary may be limited. Individuals "who cross over at work find themselves either anchored to their birth gender through challenges to the authenticity of their destination gender, or firmly repatriated into 'the other side' of the gender binary" (Schilt & Connell, 2007, p. 597). However, remote workers may have more freedom to enact gender in liberatory and transgressive ways in their everyday organizational lives. Individuals who came out as nonbinary or gender fluid while working remotely during the COVID-19 pandemic reported, "reduced perceptions by others of one's gender, or reduced external assessments of gender accountability, create(ing) more space for the cultivation of nonbinary subjectivities" (Stone & Gallin-Parisi, 2024, p. 379).

While organizational researchers are beginning to interrogate cisnormativity by highlighting the experiences of trans* individuals, much remains to be done. de Souza and Parker (2022) propose that moving forward, the field must think *with* trans in a way that disrupts binary cisnormative assumptions and dualisms by promoting practices of freedom. Rather than seeking simply to make organizations hospitable to trans* people, their concept of *transorganizing* suggests that we "organize gender and other identities across and beyond dualisms, rearrange ourselves differently, organizing gender beyond the either/or, producing new subjectivities and perhaps new ways to make lives liveable" (de Souza & Parker, 2022, p. 79).

Sexuality and Organizing

Heteronormativity refers to localized systemic practices that cast heterosexuality as the dominant and taken-for-granted norm, casting all other forms of sexuality as deviant and non-normative (Yep, 2003). Because these practices are taken-for-granted and invisible, heteronormativity functions similarly to whiteness and cisnormativity, maintaining dominance through invisibility. Critique of heteronormativity is a defining element of queer theory, a dynamic and heterogeneous body of thought from which organizational scholars have increasingly drawn to explore how sexuality matters in organizational contexts (McDonald, 2015; Rumens, 2018).

Rooted in queer theory and co-cultural theory, Compton (2020) proposes *co-sexuality* as a helpful framework for interrogating negotiation of norms regarding expression of sexuality. Co-sexuality is the "process of communicatively organizing around sexuality" (Compton, 2020, p. 1014) and examines how certain norms regarding sexuality are socially constructed as normative and others as deviant. By focusing on communicative processes through which norms regarding sexuality are constructed among people of all sexual identities, analyses of co-sexuality make heteronormativity visible. For example, Compton and Dougherty's (2017) study of co-sexuality processes in the Midwestern United States shows individuals discipline themselves to discuss sexuality only in ways that align with heteronormative understandings, silencing any discussion of sexuality that challenges dominant understandings and reifying norms about how sexuality can be discussed at work. Branton and Compton (2021) draw from co-sexuality to examine how patrons communicatively organize around sexuality in two gay bars, traditionally queer spaces. They highlight tensions regarding the communicative negotiation of sexual norms, particularly in terms of which expressions of sexuality are celebrated and normative (e.g., gay male sexuality) and which disrupt these norms (e.g., heterosexuality).

As individuals negotiate norms regarding sexuality at work, a key consideration is the extent to which individuals disclose non-normative sexual identities or seek to closet them. Because of heteronormativity, LGBTQ+ workers must continually negotiate the closet, as coming out is risky (Eger et al., 2022; McDonald et al., 2020). Negotiating the closet can be particularly difficult because of mixed messages that individuals may receive (Compton, 2016). For example, some LGBTQ+ workers in organizations with supportive policies reported that communication from their colleagues and coworkers often negated the supportive policies, leading them to closet their sexual identities. Conversely, some LGBTQ+ workers perceived messages from their coworkers and managers as supportive, despite the lack of supportive policies at the organizational level. Overall, "policies and practices related to sexuality often seem to be at odds, leading to feelings of confusion and frustration for employees" (Compton, 2016, p. 416) as they receive mixed messages and communicatively negotiate the closeting of their sexual identities. Because of these mixed messages, LGBTQ+ workers can be subject to a heavy mental load burden that requires them to be continually mindful about how their identities may be unintentionally displayed to colleagues and managers who may not be supportive (Minei et al., 2024). For example, LGBTQ+ workers may be particularly mindful about whether to display family pictures in their offices. Indeed, individuals whose family structures deviate from heteronormative expectations may find that their families are unwelcome in the workplace, preventing them from engaging in workplace conversations about family as they continually negotiate the closeting of their family (Dixon, 2018; Dixon & Dougherty, 2014).

While heteronormativity is a key feature of contemporary organizations, there has been an emergence of organizations that openly brand themselves as "gay-friendly" (Rumens, 2015; Williams et al., 2009). While "gay-friendly" might be a welcome change to prohibitions of non-normative sexual identity disclosure, heteronormativity is often reproduced. Rumens and Kerfoot (2009) found that gay men working in "gay-friendly" organizations still needed to conform to heteronormative norms regarding the expression of sexuality because sexuality is incompatible with dominant discourses of professionalism. Whereas LGBTQ+ sexuality is visible, heterosexuality is normative, taken-for-granted, and thus consistent with discourses of professionalism. As such, "gay-friendly" organizations enable individuals to publicly come out as gay only to the extent that they appear "normal" like their heterosexual colleagues (Connell, 2015; Williams et al., 2009). Even in industries that are considered "gay-friendly," such as the performing arts, normative expressions of gay male sexuality are cast in homogenized, limited ways that reinforce heteronormativity. As such, heteronormativity is a dominant ideology actively reproduced even within "gay-friendly" organizations and industries (Rumens & Broomfield, 2014). Moreover, the term "gay-friendly" should be scrutinized and deconstructed for failing "to convey the complexity of social diversity within and between sexual minorities" (Rumens, 2015, p. 187). Indeed, the term erroneously presumes that organizations welcoming gay men are also welcoming to all sexual minorities. Research has shown that even organizations with supportive policies for gay, lesbian, and bisexual individuals can dismiss and exclude trans* identities (Dixon, 2015; Dixon & Dougherty, 2014).

Nation and Organizing

Organizational communication research and practice is heavily Eurocentric (Cruz & Sodeke, 2021; see Chapters 1–4). With some mostly recent exceptions, organizational communication scholarship silently presumes a normative, Western (mostly US) subject who is a citizen of the country in which they reside. In this section, I use "nation" as a broad term to review research that shows how national origin, language fluency, and citizenship status interlock with race and other differences to shape organizational experiences.

A significant amount of work examines immigrant scholars' intersectional identities related to national origin and citizenship status. An intersectional perspective is imperative to differentiate experiences among immigrant scholars; differences such as race, country of origin, native language, gender, and sexuality greatly shape how immigrant scholars experience privilege and/or disadvantage (Cruz et al., 2020). Among immigrant academics in Australia and New Zealand, Sang and Calvard (2019) found that while some experience disadvantages, "for Anglo white male senior academics, considerable privilege is (re) produced through the migration experience" (p. 1507). Moreover, in the UK, Johansson and Śliwa (2014) show that immigrant women academics experience privilege and/or disadvantage differently on the basis of gender, ethnicity, and country of origin.

As their identity is not immediately visible or known, immigrant scholars negotiate revealing and/or concealing citizenship status and national origin. For example, McDonald (2018) showed that immigrant scholars in the US job market negotiate closeting as it relates to their citizenship status, particularly in light of concerns of discrimination on the basis of their need for immigration sponsorship. Similarly, Fernando et al. (2020) discuss how the first author engages in identity work in Australia as a non-White immigrant business scholar from Sri Lanka, avoiding stigmatization by accenting certain parts of his identity while covering others. Long et al. (2024) showed that international graduate student parents at US institutions also negotiate closeting processes at the intersection of nation, citizenship status, and parenthood. International graduate student parents find themselves doubly stigmatized on the basis of both citizenship and parenthood status because academic institutions construct a norm of "single, dependent-free, self-reliant graduate workers who tend to concentrate on work over other life aspects" (Long et al., 2024, p. 2) and who do not require visa sponsorship (Buzzanell, 2018).

The experiences of immigrant workers are heavily shaped by multiple intersections. In their study of women entrepreneurs in China, Denmark, and the US, Long and Buzzanell

(2022) show how, in addition to gender, race, and class, "power relations of age, expertise/knowledge, work experience, education, family/marital status, economic power, nationality/immigrant status, culture, and so on, co-constitute interlocking structures that constrain and enable women's entrepreneurial agencies" (p. 227). In highly skilled scientific work, Wells et al. (2015) found that "national origin and alignment with Western modes of organizing and communication were more salient in constructing workplace privilege and inequalities than characteristics such as education, occupational tenure, and/or gender" for immigrant workers (Wells et al., 2015, p. 547). As such, some intersections of difference can shape privilege and/or disadvantage more than others.

Linguistic fluency is a rarely discussed intersection of difference relevant to experiences of immigrant workers. In their study of Polish migrants in the UK, Johansson and Śliwa (2016) found that "language is inextricably intertwined with other differentiating processes such as gender, class and nationality... it might play a role in the perpetuation of power relations and systems of domination in globalized social and organizational settings" (p. 297). Linguistic fluency is a particularly salient difference because it can determine immigrant workers' ability to access employment and social services (Johansson & Śliwa, 2016). Linguistic fluency is also intertwined with whiteness because certain accents and dialects of English are stigmatized (Liu, 2022). Speaking English alone is not enough, as individuals may experience discrimination or negative comments for not speaking English in a normative accent aligned with whiteness (Kothiyal et al., 2018). Particularly in academic contexts, English has a hegemonic status such that non-English-speaking voices are silenced. Decolonizing organizational communication – a central theme framing this volume – requires challenging the hegemony of the English language in our scholarship and valuing linguistic plurality (Pal et al., 2022; see Chapter 4).

Moving Forward: Reflections on Organizing Differently

One overarching theme of this chapter is that normativity, broadly defined as the extent to which certain identities and practices are positioned as the taken-for-granted norm (Yep, 2003), shapes organizing (O_1) and organization (O_2 and O_3) in power-laden ways. Whiteness, cisnormativity, heteronormativity, and Western-centrism are examples of normative ideologies that maintain the status quo and reify dominant power relations on the basis of intersecting differences (see Chapter 4). The pervasiveness of these normative ideologies constrains agency by shaping the ways individuals think about and organize around difference. Interrogating normative ideologies is thus a challenging, but critical, step in imagining how we might organize in ways that account for the diversity of human experiences.

Because the goal of difference and intersectionality research is ultimately emancipatory to create more just and equitable organizations, an important question is how scholarship might be translated into organizational settings. Many organizations have practitioners tasked with organizational interventions related to DEI; yet, diversity work is a tension-filled process that sometimes reinscribes the normative ideologies it seeks to challenge (Kenney, 2024; Mease, 2016). For example, Kenney (2024) shows that diversity work is premised on the assumption that organizations are merely containers for individual exploration of diversity, which functions to leave oppressive organizational structures and ideologies intact while reinscribing inequitable relations on the basis of difference. Moreover, a constitutive tension of diversity work consists in determining which groups to include in organizational interventions (Mease, 2016). In this regard, diversity work typically proceeds by identifying groups said to be diverse (e.g., women, people of color, people with disabilities), which can reify binary notions of identity as well as constrain individuals within fixed subject positions (Bendl & Hofmann, 2015; Bendl et al., 2008; Just & Christiansen, 2012).

As an alternative, Kenney's (2024) queer approach to diversity work seeks to fundamentally disrupt the status quo and interrogate normativity. Rather than taking identity groups as the starting point, he suggests practitioners encourage participants to identify organizational norms and reflect on who creates these norms, who they exclude and benefit, and what becomes possible when these norms are challenged (Kenney, 2024). Reconceptualized as such, diversity work is not about individual exploration but about interrogating and reconfiguring oppressive organizational norms in liberatory ways. Kenney's (2024) approach to diversity work thus has immense promise for positive organizational transformation.

This chapter has explored how difference and intersectionality matter in both Organizational Communication as a discipline and organizational life. Recent exciting developments in the field are a testament to the vitality of critical approaches to difference and intersectionality. Yet, the field continues to face challenges as it grapples with how it has and continues to reify normative ideologies, such as whiteness, cisnormativity, heteronormativity, and Western-centrism. Such challenges are normal, as breaking with normative ideologies is difficult by virtue of their taken-for-grantedness and invisibility. Thinking about the future of organizational communication scholarship, I leave us with a not-so-modest challenge and goal: a review chapter on difference and intersectionality written in ten years will show that we have collectively interrogated how difference and intersectionality matter in all of our scholarship, normative ideologies have been challenged, and our research has contributed to transforming organizational life in ways that are more just and emancipatory.

Recommended Supplementary Readings

Allen, B. J. (2023). *Difference matters: Communicating social identity* (3rd ed.). Waveland.

The first edition of Difference Matters, *published in 2004, helped to institutionalize difference as a key area of concern in organizational communication research. The most recent edition has been updated with contemporary examples that reflect cultural and sociopolitical developments since the first edition.*

Ashcraft, K. L. (2024). Can we meet at the alter? Doing justice through Organizational Communication. In V. D. Miller & M. S. Poole (Eds.), *Organizational communication theory and research* (pp. 45–64). De Gruyter Mouton.

This recent handbook chapter reflects on how critical approaches to differences are unsettling and transforming the foundational scholarly practices of the Organizational Communication discipline.

McDonald, J. (2021). Difference, intersectionality, and organizing. In J. F. Nussbaum (Ed.), *Oxford Research Encyclopedia of Communication* (pp. 1–29). Oxford University Press.

This encyclopedia article reviews key theoretical approaches to the study of difference, intersectionality, and organizing, as well as empirical studies that adopt intersectional approaches.

Mumby, D. K. (Ed.). (2011). *Reframing difference in organizational communication studies: Research, pedagogy, practice*. Sage.

This edited collection contains influential contributions from key difference scholars and has helped shape the agenda for contemporary organizational communication research on difference.

Parker, P. S. (2014). Difference and organizing. In L. L. Putnam & D. K. Mumby (Eds.), *The SAGE handbook of organizational communication: Advances in theory, research, and methods* (pp. 619–643). Sage.

This chapter provides an excellent and comprehensive overview of the key theoretical approaches to difference in Organizational Communication.

Important Concepts: Define and Discuss

Cisnormativity
Difference
Heteronormativity
Intersectionality
Nation
Normativity
Whiteness

Discussion Questions

1 How can you apply what you've learned in the chapter to what you've learned so far in this book? That is, how can scholarship on difference and intersectionality help us better understand topics such as classical management theory, human relations theory, human resource management theory, organizational socialization, workplace relationships, organizational identity, and power and resistance?
2 What does it mean to say that difference and intersectionality are *constitutive* features of both work and organizing? How are meanings of intersectional differences embedded into the ways in which we know and understand work and organizing?
3 In an organization of which you are a member, reflect on which intersecting differences are normative and non-normative. How are these (non)normative differences constructed and communicated in ways that privilege some and disadvantage others?
4 Tensions are embedded into the writing of any review chapter on difference and intersectionality because of the impossibility of doing justice to all intersecting differences that matter. How is my writing of this chapter a political process that involves making difficult choices about what to foreground? How would you have organized the chapter if you had been tasked with writing it?

Practitioner's Corner

As discussed in the chapter, organizational interventions to foster DEI are tension-laden and can unwittingly function to reinscribe inequitable relations on the basis of difference without challenging oppressive organizational logics and norms (Kenney, 2024). To counter these logics and norms, Sean Kenney (he/him) and Kathryn Leslie (they/them), founders of the consulting group Project Deviate, approach diversity work by encouraging participants to identify and interrogate organizational norms that can perpetuate and reify racism, sexism, cisheteronormativity, and ableism. By centering normative processes rather than identity categories, their approach is theoretically grounded in Kenney's (2024) queer approach to diversity work and a model for practitioners seeking to create more just and equitable organizations. Their approach to diversity work is described below and copied from their website with permission:

> *Our framework asks organizational members to individually and collectively examine policies, practices, and personal assumptions that limit ways of being and working in the organization. We approach this by asking two deceptively simple questions:* ***What counts as normal? Who or what does that exclude?***
>
> *The texture of our work is oriented around norms, and what happens when we make them visible. To examine what counts as normal in our organizations is to look at the taken for granted assumptions that undergird our policies and practices. These norms can perpetuate racism, sexism, cisheteronormativity, and ableism by protecting the status quo that makes oppression and marginalization seem invisible. Thus, to question what counts as normal in our organizations is to not only examine our privilege, but also intervene in the -isms and -phobias that explicitly and/or implicitly shape our organizations.*

References

#ToneUpOrgComm Collective (2020). #ToneUpOrgComm: A manifestx. *Departures in Critical Qualitative Research*, 9(2), 152–154.

Allen, B. J. (1995). "Diversity" and organizational communication. *Journal of Applied Communication Research*, 23(2), 143–155. https://doi.org/10.1080/00909889509365420

Allen, B. J. (1996). Feminist standpoint theory: A Black woman's (re)view of organizational socialization. *Communication Studies*, 47(4), 257–271. https://doi.org/10.1080/10510979609368482

Allen, B. J. (1998). Black womanhood and feminist standpoints. *Management Communication Quarterly*, 11(4), 575–586. https://doi.org/10.1177/0893318998114004

Allen, B. J. (2000). "Learning the ropes": A Black feminist standpoint analysis. In P. M. Buzzanell (Ed.), *Rethinking organizational and managerial communication from feminist perspectives* (pp. 177–208). Sage.

Allen, B. J. (2004). *Difference matters: Communicating social identity*. Waveland Press.

Allen, B. J. (2007). Theorizing race and communication. *Communication Monographs*, 74(2), 259–264. https://doi.org/10.1080/03637750701393055

Allen, B. J. (2023). *Difference matters: Communicating social identity* (3rd ed.). Waveland.

Allen, B. J., Orbe, M. P., & Olivas, M. R. (1999). The complexity of our tears: Dis/enchantment and (in)difference in the academy. *Communication Theory*, 9(4), 402–429. https://doi.org/10.1111/j.1468-2885.1999.tb00206.x

Alvarez, W., Bauer, J. C., & Eger, E. K. (2015). (Making a) difference in the organizational communication undergraduate course. *Management Communication Quarterly*, 29(2), 302–308. https://doi.org/10.1177/0893318915571352

Ashcraft, K. L. (2007). Appreciating the 'work' of discourse: Occupational identity and difference as organizing mechanisms in the case of commercial airline pilots. *Discourse & Communication*, 1(1), 9–36. https://doi.org/10.1177/1750481307071982

Ashcraft, K. L. (2011). Knowing work through the communication of difference: A revised agenda for difference studies. In D. K. Mumby (Ed.), *Reframing difference in organizational communication studies: Research, pedagogy, practice* (pp. 3–29). Sage.

Ashcraft, K. L. (2013). The glass slipper: 'Incorporating' occupational identity in management studies. *Academy of Management Review*, 38(1), 6–31. https://doi.org/10.5465/amr.2010.0219

Ashcraft, K. L. (2024). Can we meet at the alter? Doing justice through organizational communication. In V. D. Miller & M. S. Poole (Eds.), *Organizational communication theory and research* (pp. 45–64). De Gruyter Mouton.
Ashcraft, K. L., & Allen, B. J. (2003). The racial foundation of organizational communication. *Communication Theory*, *13*(1), 5–38. https://doi.org/10.1111/j.1468-2885.2003.tb00280.x
Ashcraft, K. L., & Mumby, D. K. (2004). *Reworking gender: A feminist communicology of organization*. Sage.
Banerjee, S., & Tedmanson, D. (2010). Grass burning under our feet: Indigenous enterprise development in a political economy of whiteness. *Management Learning*, *41*(2), 147–165. https://doi.org/10.1177/1350507609357391
Baumler, R. (2024). Negotiating trans identity and boundaries at work: How situational and personal factors affect workplace identity communication. *Western Journal of Communication*, 1–23. https://doi.org/10.1080/10570314.2024.2324380
Beal, F. (1969/1995). Double jeopardy: To be Black and female. In B. Guy-Sheftall (Ed.), *Words of fire: An anthology of African American feminist thought* (pp. 146–155). The New Press.
Bendl, R., Fleischmann, A., & Walenta, C. (2008). Diversity management discourse meets queer theory. *Gender in Management*, *23*(6), 382–394. https://doi.org/10.1108/17542410810897517
Bendl, R., & Hofmann, R. (2015). Queer perspectives fuelling diversity management discourse: Theoretical and empirical-based reflections. In R. Bendl, I. Bleijenbergh, E. Henttonen, & A. J. Mills (Eds.), *The Oxford handbook of diversity in organizations* (pp. 195–217). Oxford University Press.
Blithe, S. J., & Hanchey, J. N. (2015). The discursive emergence of gendered physiological discrimination in sex verification testing. *Women's Studies in Communication*, *38*(4), 486–506. https://doi.org/10.1080/07491409.2015.1085474
Branton, S. E., & Compton, C. A. (2021). There's no such thing as a gay bar: Co-sexuality and the neoliberal branding of queer spaces. *Management Communication Quarterly*, *35*(1), 69–95. https://doi.org/10.1177/0893318920972113
Butler, J. (2006). *Gender trouble: Feminism and the subversion of identity*. Routledge.
Butler, J. (2024). *Who's afraid of gender?* Farrar, Straus and Giroux.
Buzzanell, P. M. (2018). Legitimizing and transforming the closet/closeting. *Management Communication Quarterly*, *32*(2), 297–300. https://doi.org/10.1177/0893318917742518
Chakravartty, P., Kuo, R., Grubbs, V., & McIlwain, C. (2018). #CommunicationSoWhite. *Journal of Communication*, *68*(2), 254–266. https://doi.org/10.1093/joc/jqy003
Cho, S., Crenshaw, K. W., & McCall, L. (2013). Toward a field of intersectionality studies: Theory, applications, and praxis. *Signs*, *38*(4), 785–810. https://doi.org/10.1086/669608
Collins, P. H., & Bilge, S. (2020). *Intersectionality* (2nd ed.). Polity.
Combahee River Collective. (1977/2019). Black feminist statement: The Combahee River Collective. *Monthly Review: An Independent Socialist Magazine*, *70*(8), 29–36.
Compton, C. A. (2016). Managing mixed messages: Sexual identity management in a changing U.S. workplace. *Management Communication Quarterly*, *30*(4), 415–440. https://doi.org/10.1177/0893318916641215
Compton, C. A. (2020). Co-sexuality and organizing: The master narrative of "normal" sexuality in the Midwestern workplace. *Journal of Homosexuality*, *67*(7), 1–27. https://doi.org/10.1080/00918369.2019.1582220
Compton, C. A., & Dougherty, D. S. (2017). Organizing sexuality: Silencing and the push–pull process of co-sexuality in the workplace. *Journal of Communication*, *67*(6), 874–896. https://doi.org/10.1111/jcom.12336
Connell, C. (2015). Reconsidering the workplace closet: The experiences of lesbian and gay teachers. In F. Colgan & N. Rumens (Eds.), *Sexual orientation at work: Contemporary issues and perspectives* (pp. 42–57). Routledge.
Cooren, F., Matte, F., Benoit-Barné, C., & Brummans, B. H. J. M. (2013). Communication as ventriloquism: A grounded-in-action approach to the study of organizational tensions. *Communication Monographs*, *80*(3), 255–277. https://doi.org/10.1080/03637751.2013.788255
Crenshaw, K. W. (1991). Mapping the margins: Intersectionality, identity politics, and violence against women of color. *Stanford Law Review*, *43*(6), 1241–1299. https://doi.org/10.2307/1229039
Cruz, J. M., McDonald, J., Broadfoot, K., Chuang, A. K.-C., & Ganesh, S. (2020). "Aliens" in the United States: A collaborative autoethnography of foreign-born faculty. *Journal of Management Inquiry*, *29*(3), 272–285. https://doi.org/10.1177/1056492618796561

Cruz, J. M., & Sodeke, C. U. (2021). Debunking Eurocentrism in organizational communication theory: Marginality and liquidities in postcolonial contexts. *Communication Theory*, *31*(3), 528–548. https://doi.org/10.1093/ct/qtz038

Cunliffe, A. L. (2003). Reflexive inquiry in organizational research: Questions and possibilities. *Human Relations*, *56*(8), 983–1003. https://doi.org/10.1177/00187267030568004

de Souza, E. M., & Parker, M. (2022). Practices of freedom and the disruption of binary genders: Thinking with trans. *Organization*, *29*(1), 67–82. https://doi.org/10.1177/1350508420935602

Dixon, J. (2015). Organizational communication – The workplace socialization of gender identity: A phenomenological exploration of being transgender at work. In L. G. Spencer & J. C. Capuzza (Eds.), *Transgender communication studies: Histories, trends, and trajectories* (pp. 19–31). Lexington.

Dixon, J. (2018). Looking out from the family closet: Discourse dependence and queer family identity in workplace conversation. *Management Communication Quarterly*, *32*(2), 271–275. https://doi.org/10.1177/0893318917744067

Dixon, J., & Dougherty, D. S. (2014). A language convergence/meaning divergence analysis exploring how LGBTQ and single employees manage traditional family expectations in the workplace. *Journal of Applied Communication Research*, *42*(1), 1–19. https://doi.org/10.1080/00909882.2013.847275

Eger, E. K. (2018). Transgender jobseekers navigating closeting communication. *Management Communication Quarterly*, *32*(2), 276–281. https://doi.org/10.1177/0893318917740226

Eger, E. K., Litrenta, M. L., Kane, S. R., & Senegal, L. D. (2022). LGBTQ+ workers. In I. N. West (Ed.), *Oxford encyclopedia of queer studies and communication*. Oxford University Press. https://doi.org/10.1093/acrefore/9780190228613.013.1247

Ferguson, M. W. (2018). (Re)negotiating organizational socialization: Black male scholarship and the closet. *Management Communication Quarterly*, *32*(2), 282–286. https://doi.org/10.1177/0893318917741990

Ferguson, M. W., & Dougherty, D. S. (2022). The paradox of the Black professional: Whitewashing Blackness through professionalism. *Management Communication Quarterly*, *36*(1), 3–29. https://doi.org/10.1177/08933189211019751

Fernando, M., Reveley, J., & Learmonth, M. (2020). Identity work by a non-white immigrant business scholar: Autoethnographic vignettes of covering and accenting. *Human Relations*, *73*(6), 765–788. https://doi.org/10.1177/0018726719831070

Goryunova, E., Schwartz, A. K., & Turesky, E. F. (2022). Exploring workplace experiences of transgender individuals in the USA. *Gender in Management: An International Journal*, *37*(6), 732–750. https://doi.org/10.1108/GM-02-2020-0055

Grimes, D. (2001). Putting our own house in order: whiteness, change and organization studies. *Journal of Organizational Change Management*, *14*(2), 132–149. https://doi.org/10.1108/09534810110388054

Grimes, D. S. (2002). Challenging the status quo? Whiteness in the diversity management literature. *Management Communication Quarterly*, *15*(3), 381–409. https://doi.org/10.1177/0893318902153003

Harris, K. L. (2015). Reflexive voicing: A communicative approach to intersectional writing. *Qualitative Research*, *16*(1), 111–127. https://doi.org/10.1177/1468794115569560

Harris, K. L., & McDonald, J. (2018). Introduction: Queering the "closet" at work. *Management Communication Quarterly*, *32*(2), 265–270. https://doi.org/10.1177/0893318917742517

Holvino, E. (2010). Intersections: The simultaneity of race, gender and class in organization studies. *Gender, Work & Organization*, *17*(3), 248–277. https://doi.org/10.1111/j.1468-0432.2008.00400.x

Jeanes, E., & Janes, K. (2021). Trans men doing gender at work. *Gender, Work & Organization*, *28*(4), 1237–1259. https://doi.org/10.1111/gwao.12675

Johansson, M., & Śliwa, M. (2014). Gender, foreignness and academia: An intersectional analysis of the experiences of foreign women academics in UK business schools. *Gender, Work & Organization*, *21*(1), 18–36. https://doi.org/10.1111/gwao.12009

Johansson, M., & Śliwa, M. (2016). 'It is English and there is no alternative': Intersectionality, language and social/organizational differentiation of Polish migrants in the UK. *Gender, Work & Organization*, *23*(3), 296–309. https://doi.org/10.1111/gwao.12049

Jones, A. (2023). "It's hard out here for a unicorn": Transmasculine and nonbinary escorts, embodiment, and inequalities in cisgendered workplaces. *Gender & Society*, *37*(5), 665–698. https://doi.org/10.1177/0891243220965909

Jones, S. E. (2020). Negotiating transgender identity at work: A movement to theorize a transgender standpoint epistemology. *Management Communication Quarterly*, *34*(2), 251–278. https://doi.org/10.1177/0893318919898170
Just, S. N., & Christiansen, T. J. (2012). Doing diversity: Text-audience agency and rhetorical alternatives. *Communication Theory*, *22*(3), 319–337. https://doi.org/10.1111/j.1468-2885.2012.01407.x
Kenney, S. C. (2024). Kaleidoscopic inquiries: Queering approaches to organizational diversity work. *Management Communication Quarterly*. https://doi.org/10.1177/08933189241239175
Köllen, T., & Rumens, N. (2022). Challenging cisnormativity, gender binarism and sex binarism in management research: Foregrounding the workplace experiences of trans* and intersex people. *Gender in Management*, *37*(6), 701–715. https://doi.org/10.1108/GM-01-2022-0022
Kothiyal, N., Bell, E., & Clarke, C. (2018). Moving beyond mimicry: Developing hybrid spaces in Indian business schools. *Academy of Management Learning and Education*, *17*(2), 137–154. https://doi.org/10.5465/amle.2015.0137
Linabary, J. R., Cruz, J. M., Allen, B. J., Chalupa, J. A., Dempsey, S. E., Glenn, C. L., Harris, K. L., Long, Z., McDonald, J., Musleh, S., Oktaviani, F. H., Parker, P. S., & Sobande, F. (2021). Envisioning more equitable and just futures: Feminist organizational communication in theory and praxis. *Management Communication Quarterly*, *35*(1), 142–168. https://doi.org/10.1177/0893318920973598
Liu, H. (2022). How we learn whiteness: Disciplining and resisting management knowledge. *Management Learning*, *53*(5), 776–796. https://doi.org/10.1177/13505076211061622
Long, Z., & Buzzanell, P. M. (2022). Constituting intersectional politics of reinscription: Women entrepreneurs' resistance practices in China, Denmark, and the United States. *Management Communication Quarterly*, *36*(2), 207–234. https://doi.org/10.1177/08933189211030246
Long, Z., Buzzanell, P. M., & King, A. S. (2024). International graduate student parenthood: Engaging in closeting labor to constitute productive work-family negotiation during transitions to parenthood. *Communication Studies*, 1–19. https://doi.org/10.1080/10510974.2024.2320752
Long, Z., King, A. S., & Buzzanell, P. M. (2018). Ventriloqual voicings of parenthood in graduate school: An intersectionality analysis of work-life negotiations. *Journal of Applied Communication Research*, *46*(2), 223–242. https://doi.org/10.1080/00909882.2018.1435901
Macalpine, M., & Marsh, S. (2005). 'On being white: There's nothing I can say': Exploring whiteness and power in organizations. *Management Learning*, *36*(4), 429–450. https://doi.org/10.1177/1350507605058138
McDonald, J. (2015). Organizational communication meets queer theory: Theorizing relations of "difference" differently. *Communication Theory*, *25*(3), 310–329. https://doi.org/10.1111/comt.12060
McDonald, J. (2018). Negotiating the "closet" in U.S. academia: Foreign scholars on the job market. *Management Communication Quarterly*, *32*(2), 287–291. https://doi.org/10.1177/0893318917740428
McDonald, J., & DeTurk, S. (2022). Social justice organizing through the closet metaphor. In S. J. Blithe & J. C. Bauer (Eds.), *Badass feminist politics: Exploring radical edges of feminist theory, communication, and activism* (pp. 241–255). Rutgers University Press.
McDonald, J., Harris, K. L., & Ramirez, J. (2020). Revealing and concealing difference: A critical approach to disclosure and an intersectional theory of 'closeting'. *Communication Theory*, *30*(1), 84–104. https://doi.org/10.1093/ct/qtz017
McFarland, C. S., & Larson, E. W. (2024). Reproducing violence, racism, and erasure in research. *Communication and Critical/Cultural Studies*, *21*(2), 226–242. https://doi.org/10.1080/14791420.2024.2325145
Mease, J. J. (2016). Embracing discursive paradox: Consultants navigating the constitutive tensions of diversity work. *Management Communication Quarterly*, *30*(1), 59–83. https://doi.org/10.1177/0893318915604239
Minei, E. M., Hastings, S. O., & Warren, S. (2024). The LGBTQ+ employee mental load dilemma: Captive identity and adaptive responses. *Management Communication Quarterly*. https://doi.org/10.1177/08933189241245133
Muhr, S. L., Sullivan, K. R., & Rich, C. (2016). Situated transgressiveness: Exploring one transwoman's lived experiences across three situated contexts. *Gender, Work & Organization*, *23*(1), 52–70. https://doi.org/10.1111/gwao.12093

Mumby, D. K. (2011). Organizing difference: An introduction. In D. K. Mumby (Ed.), *Reframing difference in organizational communication studies: Research, pedagogy, practice* (pp. vii–xiii). Sage.

Nkomo, S. M. (1992). The emperor has no clothes: Rewriting "race in organizations". *Academy of Management Review*, *17*(3), 487–513. https://doi.org/10.5465/AMR.1992.4281987

O'Shea, S. C. (2018). This girl's life: An autoethnography. *Organization*, *25*(1), 3–20. https://doi.org/10.1177/1350508417703471

O'Shea, S. C. (2020). Working at gender? An autoethnography. *Gender, Work & Organization*, *27*(6), 1438–1449. https://doi.org/10.1111/gwao.12513

Orbe, M. P., & Allen, B. J. (2008). "Race matters" in the Journal of Applied Communication Research. *Howard Journal of Communications*, *19*(3), 201–220. https://doi.org/10.1080/10646170802218115

Pal, M., Kim, H., Harris, K. L., Long, Z., Linabary, J., Wilhoit Larson, E., Jensen, P. R., Gist-Mackey, A. N., McDonald, J., Nieto-Fernandez, B., Jiang, J., Misra, S., & Dempsey, S. E. (2022). Decolonizing organizational communication. *Management Communication Quarterly*, *36*(3), 547–577. https://doi.org/10.1177/08933189221090255

Parker, P. S. (2001). African American women executives' leadership communication within dominant-culture organizations: (Re)conceptualizing notions of collaboration and instrumentality. *Management Communication Quarterly*, *15*(1), 42–82. https://doi.org/10.1177/0893318901151002

Parker, P. S. (2002). Negotiating identity in raced and gendered workplace interactions: The use of strategic communication by African American women senior executives within dominant culture organizations. *Communication Quarterly*, *50*(3–4), 251–268. https://doi.org/10.1080/01463370209385663

Parker, P. S. (2003). Control, resistance, and empowerment in raced, gendered, and classed work contexts: The case of African American women. *Annals of the International Communication Association*, *27*(1), 257–291. https://doi.org/10.1080/23808985.2003.11679028

Parker, P. S. (2005). *Race, gender, and leadership: Re-envisioning organizational leadership from the perspectives of African American women executives*. Lawrence Erlbaum.

Parker, P. S. (2014). Difference and organizing. In L. L. Putnam & D. K. Mumby (Eds.), *The SAGE handbook of organizational communication: Advances in theory, research, and methods* (pp. 619–643). Sage.

Parker, P. S. (2020). *Ella Baker's catalytic leadership: A primer on community engagement and communication for social justice*. University of California Press.

Parker, P. S., Jiang, J., McCluney, C. L., & Rabelo, V. C. (2017). Race, gender, class, and sexuality. In *Oxford Research Encyclopedia of Communication*. Oxford University Press. https://doi.org/10.1093/acrefore/9780190228613.013.204

Ray, V. (2019). A theory of racialized organizations. *American Sociological Review*, *84*(1), 26–53. https://doi.org/10.1177/0003122418822335

Rodriguez, J. K., Holvino, E., Fletcher, J. K., & Nkomo, S. M. (2016). The theory and praxis of intersectionality in work and organisations: Where do we go from here? *Gender, Work & Organization*, *23*(2), 201–222. https://doi.org/10.1111/gwao.12131

Romo, L. K. (2018). Coming out as a non-drinker at work. *Management Communication Quarterly*, *32*(2), 292–296. https://doi.org/10.1177/0893318917740227

Rumens, N. (2015). Is your workplace 'gay-friendly'?: Current issues and controversies. In F. Colgan & N. Rumens (Eds.), *Sexual orientation at work: Contemporary issues and perspectives* (pp. 181–196). Routledge.

Rumens, N. (2018). *Queer business: Queering organization sexualities*. Routledge.

Rumens, N., & Broomfield, J. (2014). Gay men in the performing arts: Performing sexualities within 'gay-friendly' work contexts. *Organization*, *21*(3), 365–382. https://doi.org/10.1177/1350508413519766

Rumens, N., & Kerfoot, D. (2009). Gay men at work: (Re)constructing the self as professional. *Human Relations*, *62*(5), 763–786. https://doi.org/10.1177/0018726709103457

Sang, K. J. C., & Calvard, T. (2019). 'I'm a migrant, but I'm the right sort of migrant': Hegemonic masculinity, whiteness, and intersectional privilege and (dis)advantage in migratory academic careers. *Gender, Work & Organization*. https://doi.org/10.1111/gwao.12382

Schilt, K. (2006). Just one of the guys?: How transmen make gender visible at work. *Gender & Society*, *20*(4), 465–490. https://doi.org/10.1177/0891243206288077

Schilt, K. (2010). *Just one of the guys? Transgender men and the persistence of gender inequality*. University of Chicago Press.

Schilt, K., & Connell, C. (2007). Do workplace gender transitions make gender trouble? *Gender, Work & Organization*, *14*(6), 596–618. https://doi.org/10.1111/j.1468-0432.2007.00373.x
Sedgwick, E. K. (2008). *Epistemology of the closet*. University of California Press.
Stone, A. L., & Gallin-Parisi, A. (2024). What happens when gender accountability is reduced? The experiences of nonbinary and genderfluid people during the COVID-19 pandemic. *Gender & Society*, *38*(3), 379–407. https://doi.org/10.1177/08912432241244805
Wells, C. C., Gill, R., & McDonald, J. (2015). "Us foreigners": Intersectionality in a scientific organization. *Equality, Diversity and Inclusion*, *34*(6), 539–553. https://doi.org/10.1108/EDI-12-2014-0086
Williams, C., Giuffre, P., & Dellinger, K. (2009). The gay-friendly closet. *Sexuality Research & Social Policy*, *6*(1), 29–45. https://doi.org/10.1525/srsp.2009.6.1.29
Wood, J. T., & Conrad, C. (1983). Paradox in the experiences of professional women. *Western Journal of Speech Communication*, *47*(4), 305–322. https://doi.org/10.1080/10570318309374128
Yep, G. A. (2003). The violence of heteronormativity in communication studies: Notes on injury, healing, and queer world-making. *Journal of Homosexuality*, *45*(2–4), 11–59. https://doi.org/10.1300/J082v45n02_02

15 Groups, Teams, and Decision-Making

Dawna I. Ballard, Dron M. Mandhana, and Yohanna Tesfai

The research and theorizing on teamwork and decision-making in organizational communication has been shaped by multidisciplinary perspectives that intersect around the processual and structural aspects of group interaction. As such, the study of groups and teams across disciplines – such as psychology, sociology, management, information studies, education, social work, political science, public policy, and urban planning – reflects a deeply communication-focused site of scholarship. Indeed, Poole (1998) argues that the small group should be *the* fundamental unit of analysis in communication research because of its key characteristics related to interaction: individual actors can be easily discerned (unlike at macro-levels of analysis) and yet social context comes into play (unlike at micro-levels of analysis). Poole's provocative argument is even more apt for organizational communication scholarship because groups are a site where organizational scholars and practitioners can discern agency, varying cultures, and see the constitutive aspects of communication in organizations up close. Notably, McPhee and Zaug (2000) highlight subgroup processes as central to activity coordination – one of the four message flows that constitute organizations (see Chapter 3).

In this chapter, we offer an overview of the group and teamwork literature, especially as it relates to decision-making. We begin by defining groups and teams and pay particular attention to theoretical developments over time, specifically the contributions of communication theorists. Throughout, we consider the approaches taken to communication and to organization, noting the attention to culture, and trace how various literatures consider the communication-organization cycle and the role of agency that shapes groups, teamwork, and decision-making in organizational contexts.

Groups, Teams, and Decision-Making in Organizational Life

A consideration of groups, teams, and decision-making in organizational life highlights the role of smaller social collectives in organizing – like formal teams and informal coalitions – and the divergent objectives each may have that often require difficult decisions about which goals to privilege, when to execute them, and how to do so.

Across the literature, membership in a *group* is defined by shared dependence on a common resource base. This dependence can arise through assignment to a formal team that holds a particular budget to fund members' activities. The common resources that members of a group share can also be informal. For example, members may seek social resources – perhaps they gather to talk about parenting issues or social justice and DEI (diversity, equity, and inclusion) – or skill-based resources, as when organizational members come together as communities of practice (Wenger, 1998) to solve a problem shared across various teams.

DOI: 10.4324/9781003484639-18

In this chapter, we discuss methods and approaches to studying each of these types of groups (i.e., formal and informal).

In addition to relying upon shared resources, *team* members' activities also evidence commitment to a shared purpose. So, all teams are groups – an entity designation (O_3) – but not all groups are teams, which reflects both structural (O_2) and processual (O_1) designations. Additionally, teams rely upon formal and informal structures to accomplish their tasks: this is observed, in popular parlance, as *teamwork*. Their communication is both task-oriented and concerned with managing the social and emotional needs of group members. In terms of these formal and informal communication structures and the processes that they enable and constrain, then we can also say, more precisely, that while not all groups carry out teamwork processes, all teamwork necessarily arises through group interaction.

The related decision-making focus that characterizes much of the group literature is owed to the fact that teams often face multiple and often incompatible instrumental and interactive goals and objectives. Nonetheless, not all of the literature focuses solely on decision-making in teams. Below we choose three prominent traditions in group and team communication research – one focused on decision-making and formal task-oriented groups, the second focused on the role of communication in creating the team itself, and the last focused on both formal and informal team membership. Throughout, we pay particular attention to how instrumental and interactive goals and objectives are communicatively managed. See Table 15.1 for an overview of the three perspectives – *functional approaches to group decision-making*, *symbolic-interaction perspective*, and *network approaches*.

Table 15.1 The Treatment of Communication, Organization, Agency, and Culture Across Traditions

Tradition	*Communication (message, meaning, constitutive)*	*Organization (process, structure, entity)*	*C-O Cycle with Agency*	*Culture*
Functional perspective and decision-making	The focus on communication as message is reflected in early models of communication that were prominent at the time that this perspective emerged.	The primary focus is on the decision-making process, and structure is considered in the ways that it informs process.	Early treatments addressed agency; however, the focus in much research is on outcomes and not agency.	Culture is generally not considered.
Symbolic-interpretive perspective	This perspective pays special attention to meaning creation given its focus on symbol use. It also views the group as communicatively constituted through members' symbolic activities.	The interplay among structure, process, and entity is vital. The focus is on how the entity is (re)shaped through symbolic processes. This process (re) produces structures that enable and constrain members' interaction.	The role of agency is central to this perspective.	Culture is relevant as it is part of the lens we use to constitute meanings. It is one of the structural factors that enable and constrain agency.

(*Continued*)

Table 15.1 (Continued)

Tradition	*Communication (message, meaning, constitutive)*	*Organization (process, structure, entity)*	*C-O Cycle with Agency*	*Culture*
Network perspective	The focus is on the tie among and between individuals and groups – rather than a particular message or meaning – as the constitutive feature of social collectives.	Structure and entity are considered simultaneously. Process is not the focus of the network perspective, with notable exceptions.	Communication and organization are highlighted. Agency is often overlooked in this perspective, with notable exceptions (e.g., MTML, Monge).	Culture is considered as one of the many factors which shapes networks and characterize different systems.

Multiple Traditions of Group and Team Scholarship in Organizational Communication

The study of teamwork and group decision-making was highly influenced by early work at the Tavistock Institute in T-groups, or training groups, popularized within the human relations tradition of management scholarship (see Chapter 6). The focus originally centered on psychological variables, but interest among group scholars soon moved into decision-making and influence.

Based on this backdrop, we begin our review below with the earliest tradition and describe new developments in the study of groups, teams, and decision-making over time. However, this is not primarily a chronological review because the perspectives have origins in different disciplines that developed without reference to (or knowledge of) the others in some cases, often in parallel or overlapping fashion. (In fact, because so many different group and team scholars were working in similar areas without opportunities to learn or benefit from work in other fields, the Interdisciplinary Network for Group Research [INGRoup] was formed in 2006 to remedy this problem and integrate group research.) Thus, in the following pages, the prominent organizing principle for our review highlights differences in the treatment of communication (such as message, meaning, or constitutive), organization (entity [O_3], process [O_1], and structure [O_2]), culture, and the communication-organization cycle with agency. Particularly, we begin with perspectives that historically took more limited conceptions of communication and organization and move on to perspectives that more clearly attend to the mutually constitutive nature of communication and organization.

Functional Approaches to Group Decision-Making

Origins

The functional perspective and interest in group decision-making can be traced over time through the early work of philosopher John Dewey (1910), sociologist Robert Freed Bales (1950), and psychologist Irving Janis (1972). First, Dewey's reflective thinking method was used to teach group discussion. The method contained five steps – it begins with identifying a felt difficulty, determining its cause and definition, suggesting potential solutions, problematizing the solutions, and concluding the best course forward.

Next, Bales' work on problem-solving groups (which began in the 1940s) led to the development of Interaction Process Analysis (IPA) as a method to study group performance. IPA epitomizes the functional perspective and is still widely used by group researchers today. Bales proposed that groups strive for equilibrium and that varied communication acts – both verbal and nonverbal – indicate either a lack of equilibrium or are used by group members to (re)establish equilibrium. IPA was a means through which recorded group interaction could be classified into 12 different categories that reflect a variety of functions – including 3 categories concerning positive reactions, 3 concerning negative reactions, 3 concerning the task, and 3 concerning responses to questions – all of which supported this ultimate goal of equilibrium.

Finally, Irving Janis' popular work on groupthink centered on decision-making and, particularly, the reasons for faulty decision-making among governmental groups. Janis (1972, 1982) highlighted that groups often make faulty, unsound decisions even when they appear to be well-informed. Groups and teams are goal-oriented, information-processing entities. However, they are vulnerable to information-processing failures (Schippers et al., 2014). Herbert Simon (1982) found that individual members of groups or teams are restricted by their cognitive abilities to process all of the information and make decisions under the constraints of *bounded rationality*. Bounded rationality refers to the finding that – under conditions of limited processing capabilities, knowledge, and time – individuals are unable to behave and interact according to early models of problem-solving, such as Dewey's reflective thinking. Members' ability to follow models that suggest the idealized rational actor (one who carefully weighs all options, is fully informed and expert, and has unlimited time to make a decision) is, in fact, bounded by the limits of their processing capabilities, knowledge, and time (Simon, 1982). While it seems logical that team or group members should be able to complement each other's information-processing lacunae, group dynamics such as withholding information, proclivity to seek consensus, and selective information-processing biases lead to groupthink and poor decision-making (Janis, 1972, 1982; Schippers et al., 2014).

Key Assumptions

Together, these strands of scholarship helped to establish the functional approach to group decision-making. The core assumptions of a functional perspective are that groups are (a) goal-oriented entities (b) whose performance varies, and (c) this variation is a function of internal and external influences on group interaction. It is still the most common approach taken to the study of groups and centers on discerning which inputs and processes shape team effectiveness in the form of particular outputs (or outcomes).

Key Scholarship

Some examples of this perspective include groupthink theory, the functional theory of group decision-making, and the social combination approach.

GROUPTHINK THEORY

Groupthink is such a popular concept with mainstream purchase that you can find this term in the Oxford English Dictionary (among other dictionary sources). Irving Janis (1972) proposed groupthink theory to explain the faulty and sound decision-making processes during global political and economic crises. Through a qualitative analysis, he compared the faulty decision-making processes that led to disasters such as the invasion of North Korea, the escalation of the Vietnam War, and the attack on Pearl Harbor with the effective decision-making processes that took place during the Cuban Missile Crisis and the Marshall Plan. Based on these comparisons, Janis (1972, p. 9) defined groupthink as "a mode of thinking that people engage in when they are deeply involved in a cohesive in-group, when the members' strivings for unanimity override their motivation to realistically appraise alternative courses of action." Janis (1972) further observed that groupthink occurs in a team when the drive toward unanimity leads to suppressing or discounting dissenting voices and perspectives. This loss of information weakens the inputs and processes needed for effective decision-making and results in poor-quality decisions. Groupthink is more likely in groups when three conditions are present: (a) high levels of cohesion; (b) high levels of insulation from outside ideas and information; and (c) high-pressure (competitive or time-constrained) environments.

Janis (1982) developed a unified, five-stage model of groupthink and proposed groupthink as a decision-making process. Although this model included certain organizational and situational conditions as antecedents to groupthink, Janis (1982) maintained that group cohesiveness was the primary predictor of groupthink (Cline, 1990). Per Janis, this concurrence-seeking tendency resulted in eight symptoms of groupthink that lead to faulty decision-making among groups. To loosely categorize these symptoms, the first two are outcomes of overconfidence in group's abilities, the next two are due to the lack of exploration of alternative views, and the remaining symptoms stem from the pressures of group conformity. Below we list the eight symptoms and related tendencies or outcomes:

1 *The illusion of invulnerability:* Members engage in reckless risk-taking due to optimistic biases.
2 *Belief in the inherent morality of the group:* Members believe in the rightness of their cause with a lack of regard for the moral consequences.
3 *Collective rationalization:* Members operate based on their preconceived assumptions, unwilling to reconsider alternatives.
4 *Out-group stereotypes:* Members respond to intergroup conflict ineffectively due to negative stereotypes of out-group members.
5 *Self-censorship:* Members avoid raising concerns that deviate from the perceived consensus of the group.
6 *Illusion of unanimity:* Members believe that the decisions are agreed upon by all members.
7 *Direct pressure on dissenters:* Members are dissuaded from making counterarguments to the group's view.
8 *Self-appointed mindguards:* Members keep the group and leaders in the dark from problematic information.

FUNCTIONAL THEORY OF GROUP DECISION-MAKING

The functional theory developed by Gouran and Hirokawa (1983, 1996, 2003) identifies five requisite communication functions needed for effective decision-making.

First, *problem analysis* includes using available information to understand (a) the nature of the problem, (b) its magnitude or seriousness, (c) its probable cause, and (d) potential consequences of not resolving it. The second requisite function is to *establish evaluation criteria*. What standards does the group need to meet – by its own and others' judgment? Herbert Simon's (1982) concept of satisficing is relevant here. Satisficing concerns making a decision that is adequate but not optimal. It typically occurs when resources (material or time-based) are low or when it is difficult to determine an optimal solution because of highly ambiguous or constantly changing events. The third requisite function is to *generate alternative solutions*. Groups should identify a number of potential resolutions, rather than limiting themselves to one idealized "best" choice. The fourth requisite function focuses on *evaluating the positive consequences of solutions*. What is the best-case scenario for each proposed decision? The fifth requisite function focuses on *evaluating the negative consequences of solutions*. What is the worst-case scenario for each proposed choice? The ability of a group to carry out each of these requisite functions predicts their ability to perform well.

SOCIAL COMBINATION APPROACH

This approach is based on social decision scheme theory and centers on predicting how members of a group will combine their unique contributions for a given task type (Davis, 1973; Lorge & Solomon, 1955). It is only relevant for task settings in which a group must agree on a pre-specified set of possible decision alternatives. Studies also show that the best decision rule depends on the task (Davis, 1973). Thus, the findings are highly specific, making it useful to understand group decision-making in particular contexts, such as with jury decisions (Davis et al., 1989).

The social combination approach, or social decision schemes, has been utilized to study decision-making processes involved in the execution of a range of task types. For example, Laughlin and Ellis (1986) found that groups use a truth-wins decision scheme on tasks that have demonstrably correct responses (e.g., mathematical problems). For decision tasks that do not have explicitly visible correct solutions, a majority-wins decision scheme is used by group members (Davis, 1982). The social combination approach has also been used to explain how groups come to a decision based on the inputs from expert group members. For instance, Bonner (2004) studied the influence of expert members on decision-making and found that experts wield more influence than other group members.

Approaches Taken to Communication

The majority of research in this line of scholarship regards communication as a message and focuses on its role in making meaning, which shapes group process. This is consistent with its narrow focus on task-oriented decision-making. For example, how does a given message fulfill the requisite functions needed for team success? Hirokawa and Poole (1996) explicitly delineate nine functions of communication in groups: information processing, analytical processing, procedural functions, goal-oriented functions, synergistic functions, rhetorical, conflict management, control, and creation and maintenance of group cultures and climates. This focus on messages and meaning is consistent with transmissive models of communication that were prominent at the time this perspective emerged (see Chapter 1). Similarly, much of the work in this tradition ignores the role of culture except as it shapes the ability of the group to fulfill its requisite functions.

Approaches Taken to Organization and Agency in the Communication-Organization Cycle

Three core assumptions of the functional perspective are that groups are goal-oriented; group performance varies and can be evaluated; and internal and external factors influence group performance. Structure (seen as an input) is considered in the ways it informs process and is viewed as a predictor of team performance. Theories that draw on a functional perspective mainly focus on communication and influence. For instance, the COVID-19 pandemic impacted how team members collaborated over dispersed locations. Particularly, in a work-from-home context, Breideband and colleagues (2023) compared how the location of workers, whether in a nonprivate/private room versus working at the office, impacted team conflict. Their findings revealed those who worked in private rooms at home had significantly lower perceptions of team conflict, likely due to the ability to control disruptions.

Other work from this perspective includes a deliberate focus on the role of agency in the communication-organization cycle. Homans' (1950) work on the external systems orientation highlights the dynamic construction of groups and teams. Rather than viewing groups as a static entity, Homan considers continuing cycles of interaction with the environment and ways in which positive or negative feedback loops shape groups through their ability to adapt to external conditions. This focus on interaction with the environment is unique among group theories that draw on a functional perspective, illustrating how a range of approaches can be described as functional.

The Symbolic-Interpretive Perspective

Origins

The symbolic-interpretive perspective has its origins in hermeneutics and phenomenology (see Chapter 2). Hermeneutics was founded based on a pre-20th-century concept called *verstehen*, or understanding. Similarly, phenomenology is the study of knowledge that arises from understanding, consciousness, and experience. Ultimately drawn from theoretical and methodological influences across a range of literatures and disciplines – including Schutz's social phenomenology, Heidegger's hermeneutic phenomenology, Garfinkel's ethnomethodology, as well as seminal work by Mead, Blumer, Langer, and Burke – the symbolic-interpretive approach takes communication to be the key social process that shapes our reality. Within a group perspective, it bears on team members' shared reality.

Key Assumptions

A fundamental assumption of the symbolic-interpretive perspective is that groups are socially constructed and the group as an entity exists only through members' interaction. Following from this basic understanding of groups as communicatively constituted, groups are also readily acknowledged to be fluid in terms of their boundaries and to exhibit interdependence with the external environment. It shares this in common with Homans' (1950) work, which discussed the functional perspective. However, it typically departs from the external systems orientation in terms of its empirical focus. Scholarship conducted from a symbolic-interpretive perspective focuses on group members' symbolic activities, ranging from the stories members tell to the written organizational rules they follow or reject in their daily interactions.

Key Scholarship

Exploring symbolic convergence theory, structuration theory, the dialectic perspective, and adaptive structuration theory helps to further explicate the key assumptions and methods used in symbolic-interpretive research.

SYMBOLIC CONVERGENCE THEORY (SCT)

SCT concerns how group consciousness is created through symbol use. The communication process that leads them to converge as a group around a given fantasy is a central point of investigation for this theory. Scholars drawing on this theoretical perspective study group fantasy chains that derive from members' shared interpretations of events that fulfill particular social or psychological needs (Bormann, 1996). Fantasies reflect the creative and imaginative interpretations of everyday events that converge in a shared group understanding (i.e., chain reaction). Additionally, symbolic convergence theory highlights the ways in which group members' behavior is shaped and guided by this shared understanding (Bormann, 1973, 1996).

For example, Aghazadeh's (2022) study grounded in symbolic convergence theory examines how the National Eating Disorders Association's (NEDA) social media utilizes a symbolic "warrior" fantasy to frame eating disorder recovery as a heroic journey. Besides their ongoing use of social media hashtags, such as #recoverywarriors or #edwarrior, NEDA also engages members through using visual and rhetorical cues of the warrior fantasy that prompts multiple users to engage in chaining behaviors. This is seen in one of their posts of a recovery-themed tattoo with the caption: "Do you have a recovery tattoo? Show us your ink, recovery warriors!" (Aghazadeh, 2022, p. 111). In response, members shared their tattoos, stories, and messages of hope – indicating a shared reality.

Groups may converge around cultural identity, norms, and traditions. For example, Klett and Arnulf (2020) discuss how myths around Chinese and Western management teams lead scholars to overlook the impact of Indigenous Chinese leadership theories and philosophical systems on team processes. For example, traditional Chinese philosophies – such as Confucianism, Legalism, and Daoism – can mediate Chinese business leaders' actions regarding team processes. A Chinese leader may manage their team as a culturally hierarchical, Confucian "imperial court," which may lead their team to become more synergistic and high-performing in "an Indigenous Chinese manner and not in an essentialist Western way" (Klett & Arnulf, 2020, p. 9). This implies that while Chinese and Western teams may experience similar phenomena, contextual variables produce distinct communicative processes. Therefore, understanding these cultural contexts, stories, and histories can enrich team research by offering alternative perspectives on team structure and performance.

STRUCTURATION THEORY

The focus of structuration theory extends well beyond the confines of the group as an entity. A sociological theory, structuration is concerned with the role of larger societal structures in shaping human behavior (see Chapter 3). However, this theory found a home in group communication research as scholars from the functional perspective began to look further outside the boundaries of group process to consider the larger role of structure – the *rules* and *resources* that group members draw on to accomplish everyday activities – as well as the role of human agency in decision-making. In terms of structure, examples of organizational rules include an employee handbook or stories told to newcomers about what to do or not to do in order to succeed. Resources range from things like the raw materials used in production to the training and certification needed to obtain a job (see Chapter 3).

Unlike a functional perspective, structures alone are not viewed as determining group outcomes. Group members make decisions – implicitly or explicitly – about whether to draw on these structures in their daily practices. For instance, a meeting agenda is a structure designed to introduce a particular order to group interaction. Members may only loosely follow that agenda, however. This reflects human agency, which is enabled and constrained by structures (such as the agenda) – making some things more likely and others less likely – not solely determined by the structures. Therefore, structures are both the medium and the outcome of human interaction and symbolic activity.

DIALECTIC PERSPECTIVE

Continuing the example about whether group members closely follow a meeting agenda, the dialectic perspective highlights the frustration members may feel about how their agenda item is treated, rushed, or even skipped altogether. The dialectic perspective concerns the tensions that arise in group interaction because of the continual need to choose between two different, and seemingly, contradictory choices. The ways that team members manage these ever-present tensions through their symbolic activity is the focus of this perspective (Johnson & Long, 2002; see also Chapter 3).

ADAPTIVE STRUCTURATION THEORY (AST)

In the 1990s, Poole and DeSanctis (1990) further refined aspects of structuration theory to bear on the use of information and communication technologies (ICTs) to facilitate the work of groups and teams. AST theorizes that the influence of ICTs (on teamwork, for example) depends upon the structure built (i.e., designed) into the technology and the structures that emerge when users try to incorporate the ICTs in their work. Structure refers to both the *features* and the *spirit* of the ICTs. The features are made up of the specific rules and resources embedded in the material aspects of the ICT. The spirit is made up of the broader aim concerning the values and goals that underlie a certain feature.

The closer the alignment between the way a given technology is appropriated by its users and the spirit of the technology, the more likely it is that the technology may provide benefits. If the meeting agenda described above is delivered via any number of the popular digital meeting applications, its success will depend upon a combination of the structural features, the spirit of the app, and how members use it. For instance, in a healthy team, if members use it to keep the meeting moving and productive without privileging the voices of particular people, then it will be more likely to be adopted and used by members. If, however, it is appropriated to suppress dissent, then it may become a contested ICT that some members refuse to use altogether (see Chapters 3 and 19).

Additionally, ICT adoption is impacted by macro-level events, such as the COVID-19 pandemic, where team members had to quickly learn to exclusively collaborate via technology (see Chapter 19). This pivot exemplifies how teams adjusted their activity coordination around ICTs in order to effectively complete both individual and team-level work (Whillans et al., 2021). For example, some organizational members quickly learned to work on shared digital documents versus locally saved ones to improve communication speed and team performance (Klonek et al., 2022). Macro-level events can also impact how technology is adopted to enhance belongingness and community across temporal and geographic distances (Abelsen et al., 2023).

Approaches Taken to Communication

The symbolic-interpretive perspective pays special attention to meaning creation, given its focus on symbol use. It also views the group as communicatively constituted through members' symbolic activities. Group fantasy chains are key to the symbolic-interpretive perspective. They begin with dramatizing messages, which contain at least one of the following: analogy, anecdote, parable, allegory, fable, narrative, wordplay, double entendre, or a figure of speech. If these messages elicit an affirmative response among members, a chain reaction (i.e., a fantasy chain) is created in which others join in and participate, shaping the group culture (Bormann, 1973, 1996; Bormann et al., 2001).

Approaches Taken to Organization and Agency in the Communication-Organization Cycle

The interplay between entity and process is vital to the symbolic-interpretive perspective. The focus is on how the entity arises and is (re)shaped through symbolic processes. These symbolic representations then structure future interactions. However, while symbolic representations enable and constrain group members' interactions, this perspective centers on the ways in which group members continually (re)create these representations through exercising their own agency. This reflects the concept of *duality of structure* in structuration.

The agentic nature of fantasy chains offers an illustrative example: fantasy themes are never faithful representations of some past experience – they always project a particular experience that has a unique spin, thus recreating the group to suit their purposes. Also, multiple fantasy themes are often shared among group members as a way to account for different versions of the same experience and can develop into stock scenarios that are repeated over and over again. Sometimes these themes get integrated by characters into a larger rhetorical vision that captures the group's imagination. Thus, the group (and larger organization of which it is a part) is literally created through their members' everyday symbolic communication practices. Culture plays an important role in this perspective because organizational groups and teams are sites of organizational subcultures. These fantasy themes and rhetorical visions mark divisions across these subcultures and serve to bind members within a subculture even more tightly.

The Network Perspective

Origins

The network tradition of group scholarship dates back to at least the 1930s and was developed across multiple disciplines, including anthropology, social psychology, communication, sociology, mathematics, epidemiology, political science, and economics. It derives from theories of mutual or collective interest, theories of self-interest, theories of homophily, social exchange or dependency theories, and cognitive theories – all of which have contributed to the diverse schools of thought within the network approach. Two distinct lines of work emerged across time. The first line of work was conducted between 1930 and 1960, and a new line of research emerged in the 1990s that reflects strides made in network software as well as a burgeoning interest in social capital. Consistent with the timing and tradition of the functional perspective, in the 1950s, one of the earliest and most famous experiments that leveraged a network approach to small groups examined the ideal network structure to support group performance (Bavelas, 1950; Bavelas & Barrett, 1951). More centralized groups, those focused around a few primary group members, performed better than others on complex tasks. More decentralized groups performed better on simple tasks.

Key Assumptions

Unity across the varied perspectives is found in five underlying principles identified by Wellman (1988). First, individuals' social networks – e.g., reflected in their group membership – are a better predictor of individual behavior than their drives, attitudes, or demographic characteristics. Second, the relationship among units – such as among members of a group or among groups in an organization – should be the analytical focus of network research rather than characteristics of the units themselves, e.g., individual or group characteristics. Third, the methods used to study networks should not rely upon the assumption of independence among units or groups. Fourth, we cannot understand a social system, such as a group or a network of groups, through the dyadic ties within that system. All units within a system are interdependent; therefore, the whole system must be studied. Finally, organizations are not made up of clearly demarcated groups, but of overlapping networks. This is due to the fuzzy, permeable, and shifting boundaries of groups which is owed, in part, to the fact that individuals maintain multiple group memberships.

Within a network perspective, a group is considered either (a) an emergent characteristic of a network that reflects a particular structural "grouping" or (b) a formally imposed category or designation about a set of actors. Also frequently referred to as a clique, within the emergent view, a group reflects the connection among various nodes in a population. In this view, network analyses often focus on various types of connections among nodes within a system, based on any number of characteristics, including culture, expertise, trust, and collaboration. In contrast, when a group is considered as an imposed designation or boundary, such as a political party, network analysis often focuses on comparing communication patterns within and outside of that network (see Chapter 9).

Key Scholarship

Some examples of this perspective include theories of self-interest, social exchange and dependency, and theories of mutual or collective interest.

THEORIES OF SELF-INTEREST

This school of thought assumes that individuals are driven by a rational self-interest and form dyadic or group ties in order to pursue these interests (an assumption critiqued below). A central influence in this research tradition was the work of sociologist James Coleman (1988) who illustrated how dyadic interactions – where each actor tries to maximize their self-interest – form the basis of a social system (like a small group). Against this backdrop of self-interest, Coleman's work showed that the interdependence shared by the individuals acts as a limit or constraint on the extent to which each person will pursue their self-interests. Ultimately, each person receives access to more rewards by working together than could be obtained by unchecked self-seeking.

From a self-interest theoretical perspective, individuals also earn social capital from their investments in particular relationships that can be leveraged for a variety of rewards. Sociologist Pierre Bourdieu defines social capital as the "sum of the resources, actual or virtual, that accrue to an individual or group by virtue of possessing a durable network of more or less institutionalized relationships of mutual acquaintance and recognition" (Bourdieu & Wacquant, 1992, p. 119). One of the ways that people may gain further social capital is through filling structural holes, or places in a network where connections are missing. Making those connections for others can be a "profitable" way to invest one's social capital and earn returns on one's investment.

The theory of self-interest warrants critiques for its Western bias that asserts people are primarily self-motivated and seek to maximize their personal value through relationships and resources. Beyond the Western context, social groups often work together toward mutual benefits. In theorizing various environmental justice models that are specific to Africa, Ssebunya and colleagues (2019) focus on communitarian societies that emphasize mutual dependence and relationality. For instance, the Buganda region of Uganda practices *bulungibwansi*, meaning "for the good of the country," and in Kenya, the concept of *harambee*, or "pooling efforts together," reflects a similar ethos. This does not suggest all non-Western cultures are focused on interdependence and collectivism, but it does render Western logics visible within the groups and teams literature.

SOCIAL EXCHANGE AND DEPENDENCY

Homans' (1950) work was central to the social exchange school, as he argued that people proactively seek to build ties to others with whom they can reap benefits through the exchange of valuable resources. Relationships are continued to the extent that they continue to yield such resources and ended when they no longer do so. Because of the explicit focus on external resources (and resource dependency) within the study of groups, Homans (1950) helped to link micro (i.e., individual) and macro (i.e., organizational) levels of analysis and show how structure arises from interaction (as we discussed with regard to structuration theory). Emerson (1972a, 1972b) also studied the social exchange of resources and observed that it was enabled by a large-scale network of relationships in which individuals, dyads, and groups are embedded. Thus, he also considered the role of intergroup communication and relationships. In contrast to theories of self-interest, the social exchange and dependency perspective highlights how individuals are motivated to create ties in order to minimize their dependence on others and to maximize the dependence of others on them.

THEORIES OF MUTUAL OR COLLECTIVE INTEREST

Public goods theory (Samuelson, 1954) is a well-developed theory of collective action that focuses on how the potential benefits that accrue from coordinated action typically outweigh individual self-interests. Its original focus centered on the economics of public versus private ownership of public goods, like material resources, but it has been applied to a range of public goods, including intellectual property (Fulk et al., 1996). Research in this tradition identifies the conditions under which group members are more likely to aid collective action aimed at creating and maintaining public goods that benefit everyone. It addresses the *free-rider* problem, wherein all members of the group will benefit from this public good whether or not they help to create or maintain it. Findings suggest that individuals are motivated to act in ways that maximize their shared ability to use these resources, despite the free-rider problem. This runs counter to both the self-interest and social exchange theories.

Approaches Taken to Communication

Major network theories are concerned with how communication ties and networks are created rather than a particular message or meaning. For instance, *public goods theory* highlights the conditions under which group members are motivated to form ties and build networks. Communication networks are also based on *homophily*, the finding that ties are more likely to form among group members who share things in common. Individuals strategically form ties with others who are similar in order to reduce conflict, foster trust, and offer predictability. *Transactive memory system* is another theoretical perspective that concerns how group members develop communication networks to benefit from the expertise and skills of others in the group. For each of the varied network perspectives, while the focus is on the constitutive features of the ties within a network, scholars also consider the nature of the ties, which inheres in the messages or meaning associated with the tie. This includes

> communication ties (such as who talks to whom, or who gives information or advice to whom), formal ties (such as who reports to whom), affective ties (such as who likes whom, or who trusts whom), proximity ties (who is spatially or electronically close to whom), and cognitive ties (such as who knows who knows whom).
>
> (Katz et al., 2004, p. 308)

Scholars are also considering how network analysis can benefit research on human-autonomy teams (HATs), or teams involving humans and one or more autonomous computerized agents (Baker et al., 2021). Over time, this emerging form of teaming will impact how teams construct trust, develop shared mental models, and coordinate tasks. Because this work is in its earliest stages, further research is needed to clarify relevant constructs for theory development (O'Neill et al., 2023).

Approaches Taken to Organization and Agency in the Communication-Organization Cycle

While structure and entity are considered simultaneously, process is typically not the focus of the network perspective. Therefore, in most network studies, network content is rarely a variable under investigation. Podolny and Baron (1997) are among the few who emphasize and explore the effects of network content and its interaction with network structure. Instead, a prominent – although contested – view is that formal organizational structure influences the communication interactions and the content of those interactions. These formal roles should determine the individuals with whom the member communicates, what they should communicate, and the operating procedure for communication. This view is debated because it fails to take into account the active part that individuals play in creating and shaping organizational structure. Following the weaknesses and inconclusive findings relating formal networks to organizational behaviors (Johnson, 1992), there is growing interest in the role of informal networks. For example, Kalra and Szymanski (2023) show how an "us versus them" dynamic can exist not only in globally distributed teams but also within linguistically homogenous teams, such as in India, where dialect differences can impact team cohesion. This research also highlights the need to acknowledge diversity as more than race and gender, as Minbaeva and colleagues (2021) argue, and to shift focus away from US and Western European research contexts. Indeed, Miike (2007) brings an Asiacentric perspective to bear on the Eurocentric bias in communication theory, while work by Meyer and colleagues (2014) and Emich and colleagues (2020) points to the growing literature on groups and teams globally.

Moreover, there is a need to develop more complex, multi-level theoretical models of diversity within groups and teams in order to better understand the interdependence of interactions and processes across different levels of analyses (McLeod & Yuan, 2021). An example can be seen in Tasheva and Hillman's (2019) multi-level analysis which distinguishes between team-level and individual diversity to predict how various sources of diversity (including surface- and deep-level) can influence team effectiveness.

All of this work illustrates that informal networks are driven and shaped by factors not captured by formal organizational structure analysis. Informal networks involve more discretionary patterns of interaction, where the content of relationships may be work-related, social, or both. Early network research (e.g., Brass, 1984) also takes a relational approach to organizations, rooted in modern systems theory (see Chapter 2), and considers the emergence of structure as bottom-up, individually motivated, and dynamic. The impact of informal networks on various organizational outcomes, such as job effectiveness, commitment, turnover rate, career mobility, and satisfaction, has been examined in this tradition.

Some scholars recommend studying formal and informal networks together in the context of each other as way of understanding the interdependencies between formal and informal networks. Not surprisingly, formal workplace interactions often develop into informal, friendship networks due to similarity, proximity, and constant interaction among organizational members (see Chapter 10). When these formal and informal networks overlap, they create multiplex ties, which means they interact in multiple contexts. In addition to the idea that formal ties naturally lead to informal ones, the reverse is also true. For instance, we may recommend our friends for jobs within our organization, or we may befriend a colleague from another department and this informal tie may influence the way we vote on interdepartmental matters. The key issue with formal and informal ties is to explore each within the context of the other (see Chapter 9).

Conclusion

Across the varied research traditions focused on groups, teams, and decision-making, the concept of organization is viewed and studied in diverse ways – including as process (O_1), as structure (O_2), and as entity (O_3). Beginning with the functional perspective, organization is largely treated as structure (O_2, seen as an input) and is investigated in terms of the ways it informs process (rather than organization being investigated *as* a process). While Homans' (1950) approach sheds light on the ways in which communication and organization are mutually constituted, most theories that draw on a functional perspective mainly focus on the relationship between communication and influence. In contrast, the symbolic-interpretive perspective highlights the communication-organization spiral through considering the interplay between entity and process. Research from this perspective considers how the entity (i.e., the group and/or organization) arises and is (re)shaped through symbolic processes as well as the ways in which group members continually (re) create symbolic representations through exercising their own agency. Finally, for research within the network perspective, structure and entity are considered simultaneously, but process is typically not studied.

The study of groups, teams, and decision-making in organizations is fundamental to the study of organizational communication processes. It is a multidisciplinary area of study, yet the varied fields coalesce around communication and interaction as the key driver of group formation and process, exhibiting the conceptual pattern of the C-O dynamic that is so prevalent in organizational communication theory.

Recommended Supplementary Readings

Functional Perspective

Hirokawa, R. Y. (1985). Discussion procedures and decision-making performance: A test of a functional perspective. *Human Communication Research, 12*, 203–224.

Orlitzky, M., & Hirokawa, R. Y. (2001). To err is human, to correct for it divine: A meta-analysis of research testing the functional theory of group decision-making effectiveness. *Small Group Research, 32*(3), 313–341.

Wittenbaum, G. M., Hollingshead, A. B., Paulus, P. B., Hirokawa, R. Y., Ancona, D. G., Peterson, R. S., Jehn, K. A. & Yoon, K. (2004). The functional perspective as a lens for understanding groups. *Small Group Research, 35*(1), 17–43.

These readings provide a good overview of the functional perspective, specifically as it relates to groups performing tasks. They include the early work in the area (Hirokawa, 1985), reviews of the work (Cummings & Ancona, 2005; Wittenbaum et al., 2004), as well as a meta-analysis of empirical research on functional groups (Orlitzky & Hirokawa, 2001).

Symbolic-Interpretive Perspective

Bormann, E. G. (1996). Symbolic convergence theory and communication in group decision making. In R. Y. Hirokawa & M. S. Poole (Eds.), *Communication and group decision making* (2nd ed., pp. 81–113). Sage.

DeSanctis, G., & Poole, M. S. (1994). Capturing the complexity in advanced technology use: Adaptive structuration theory. *Organization Science, 5*, 121–147.

Frey, L. R., & Sunwolf. (2004). The symbolic-interpretive perspective on group dynamics. *Small Group Research, 35*, 277–306.

Seibold, D. R., & Meyers, R. A. (2007). Group argument: A structuration perspective and research program. *Small Group Research, 38*, 312–336.

These readings focus on the symbolic-interpretive perspective and how it applies to the study of groups. Bormann (1996) uses symbolic convergence theory to explain how individuals create a common ground through a chain of fantasies. DeSanctis and Poole (1994) explain the tenets of adaptive structuration theory and how it explains the relationship between the structures of advanced technologies and the emergent structures of social action that emerge using these technologies. Seibold and Meyers (2007) provide a review of research on group argument from a structuration perspective. Finally, Frey and Sunwolf (2004) review the foundations of the symbolic-interpretive perspective and propose a composite model of group processes, practices, products, and predispositions.

Network Perspective

Cummings, J. N., & Cross, R. (2003). Structural properties of work groups and their consequences for performance. *Social Networks, 25(3)*, 197–210.
Balkundi, P., & Harrison, D. A. (2006). Ties, leaders, and time in teams: Strong inference about network structure's effects on team viability and performance. *Academy of Management Journal, 49*, 49–68.
Contractor, N., & Su, C. (2011). Understanding groups from a network perspective. In A. Hollingshead & M.S. Poole (Eds.), *Research methods for studying groups and teams: A Guide to approaches, tools, and technologies* (pp. 284–310). Routledge.
Katz, N., Lazer, D., Arrow, H., & Contractor, N. (2004). Network theory and small groups. *Small Group Research, 35*, 307–332.

These readings focus on the study of small groups from a network perspective. They include pragmatic approaches to studying small groups from a network perspective (Contractor & Su, 2011), a detailed review of network research on small groups (Katz et al., *2004), a meta-analysis of research on the effects of network structures on team effectiveness (Balkundi & Harrison, 2006), and an empirical study on the effects of group network structure on team performance (Cummings & Cross, 2003).*

Important Concepts: Define and Discuss

Bounded rationality
Cohesion
Duality of structure
Feedback loops
Free-rider problem
Group fantasy chains
Homophily
Phenomenology
Problem analysis
Satisficing
Social capital

Practitioners' Corner and Discussion Questions

Contributions to Multidisciplinary Teams (MDTs) at the Children's Advocacy Centers

In any given organizational context, each of the three major research traditions we describe here may be leveraged to yield insights on teamwork and decision-making. Below, we describe a recent multi-year large-scale research project undertaken by a research team (which include the present authors) and ask you to consider how each of the scholarly traditions could assist in the study.

Background: The Children's Advocacy Center (CAC) Movement

The Children's Advocacy Center (CAC) movement changed the individual and institutional landscape for child abuse investigations around the globe through leveraging the power of multidisciplinary teams (MDTs) in the service of children and their families.

The CAC MDT refers to the various individuals from a myriad of core child abuse disciplines who provide the front-line and immediate supervisory services involved in child abuse investigations, assessment, intervention, and prosecution. Those core disciplines include law enforcement, child protective services, prosecution, medical, mental health, and the CAC itself (forensic interviewers, family advocates, mental health clinicians, and MDT coordination staff).

Joint investigation of child abuse cases by MDTs is foundational to the mission of children's advocacy centers. The success of this approach is shaped by the quality and timeliness of communication among team members from different agencies and professions. A number of intra- and interorganizational factors come together to enable and constrain effective coordination in this setting. Our team – comprising experts in communication, time-based coordination, team interaction, and organizational science – conducted a comprehensive analysis of the MDT model. Our objective was to determine what factors influence MDT performance in the complex environment they face.

Discussion Questions

PRACTITIONER LENS – *In an effort to better understand the teams you will study, what kinds of questions would you ask during initial meetings with the organizational leadership?*

RESEARCHER LENS – *Can each of the three research traditions described in this chapter be of assistance in a project of this nature? Describe specific contributions that each of the varied traditions can make to address this research objective.*

Fieldwork at the CAC

To understand the multiple factors that shape best practices for joint investigations, we took a multi-tiered approach to studying MDT communication dynamics. To offer a complete and exhaustive account of the life of MDTs, we systematically analyzed and compared three different – yet complementary – types of observations:

- MDT members' language and communication patterns as exhibited in focus group conversations (in both 10 intra-disciplinary settings and 17 multi-disciplinary settings);
- MDT members' shared views and considerations about the issues of greatest import to high-quality work (discussed in concert with other members of their MDT during 17 multidisciplinary focus groups); and
- MDT members' personal reports about a range of individual, team, and agency-related factors that shape their ability to be effective as an MDT member (as reflected in a statewide survey of 1424 members).

Our primary objective was to identify systemic barriers to effective collaboration and information sharing. Through reviewing emergent themes from the participant observation, archival data, focus groups, and interviews, we developed a survey to assess MDT members' experiences around issues that included factors such as the role of task design and feedback, training, supervisory support, team psychological safety, task cohesion, social cohesion, individual attraction to the group, and work method autonomy in team performance.

Discussion Questions

Practitioner lens – *As a practitioner, how would you approach the fundamental question of what constitutes MDT performance? On what particular outcomes would you focus as you spoke with MDT members and as you reviewed relevant organizational documents?*

Researcher lens – *Taking the perspective of a researcher trained in each of the three traditions, which of the previous types of data would be of most interest to you? How would you design a study that collects the types of information needed to understand MDT performance?*

Culture at the Children's Advocacy Centers

Because the MDTs were made up of occupational groups with unique cultures – most notably law enforcement, doctors and nurses, therapists, child protective services, and prosecutors – we studied how members of each occupational group perceived the other occupational groups through both focus groups and survey data. In the occupational focus groups, each focus group was constituted entirely of members belonging to a given profession or from a given agency – i.e., where the members were largely homogenous in terms of their work focus. This allowed us to view differences in interagency perceptions of the MDT model.

Discussion Questions

Practitioner lens – *What questions would you ask participants in the occupational focus groups?*

Researcher lens – *What insights, if any, could each research tradition offer to help you better understand the impact of occupational culture on MDT performance?*

Research Findings about MDT Effectiveness

Based upon our triangulation of the multiple data sources, several prominent themes emerged about what shapes MDT effectiveness (both in terms of existing practices associated with strong case development and outcomes as well as existing barriers to effective collaboration and information sharing):

- *Social support predicts resilience and positive case outcomes.* We found positive case outcomes for child abuse investigations are associated with strong MDTs. At the same time, this social support not only leads to improved case outcomes but expressly allows MDT members to carry out their work more effectively and to have more longevity in their careers within an agency.
- *Institutional barriers weaken MDTs. Institutional support strengthens MDTs.* A number of structural and professional barriers exist inside the various partner agencies. These institutional barriers may serve to systematically weaken team processes and create impediments for team members' full participation on the MDT. When partner agencies support the model, MDTs are more effective.
- *Proximity facilitates information sharing and collaboration.* Proximity served as a powerful predictor of information sharing, collaboration, and identity, and diminished barriers associated with professional identity. Physical distance increased these barriers and reduced the ease of information sharing and collaboration.

Discussion Questions

Practitioner lens – *(a) Based on these findings, what advice would you offer to children's advocacy centers about how to foster social support among MDT members? (b) How can children's advocacy centers communicate and leverage these findings to cultivate greater institutional support among partner agencies? (c) In settings without physical proximity, how can children's advocacy centers address the barriers we found associated with physical distance?*

Researcher lens – *(a) Which of these findings would you predict based on extant research in any of the three traditions? Are any of the findings unexpected? (b) Based on these findings, can you design a follow-up study to collect more data to shed even greater insight into team dynamics at children's advocacy centers? What research tradition(s) would offer the most utility given these findings?*

References

Abelsen, S. N., Vatne, S. H., & Mikalef, P. (2023). Digital working during the COVID-19 pandemic: How task-technology fit improves work performance and lessens feelings of loneliness. *Information Technology & People*, *36*(5), 2063–2087. https://doi.org/10.1108/ITP-12-2020-0870

Aghazadeh, S. A. (2022). "Recovery warriors": The National Eating Disorders Association's online community and rhetorical vision. *Public Relations Inquiry*, *11*(1), 103–119. https://doi.org/10.1177/2046147X211014083

Baker, A. L., Fitzhugh, S. M., Huang, L., Forster, D. E., Scharine, A., Neubauer, C., Baker, A. L., Fitzhugh, S. M., Huang, L., Forster, D. E., Scharine, A., Neubauer, C., Lematta, G., Bhatti, S., Johnson, C. J., Krausman, A., Holder, E., Schaefer, K. E., & Cooke, N. J. (2021). Approaches for assessing communication in human-autonomy teams. *Human-Intelligent Systems Integration*, *3*(2), 99–128. https://doi.org/10.1007/s42454-021-00026-2

Bales, R. F. (1950). *Interaction process analysis*. Addison-Wesley.

Bavelas, A. (1950). Communication patterns in task-oriented groups. *Journal of the Acoustical Society of America*, *22*, 723–730. https://doi.org/10.1121/1.1906679

Bavelas, A., & Barrett, M. (1951). An experimental approach to organizational communication. *Personnel*, *27*, 386–397.

Bonner, B. L. (2004). Expertise in group problem solving: Recognition, social combination, and performance. *Group Dynamics: Theory, Research, and Practice*, *8*, 277–290. https://doi.org/10.1037/1089-2699.8.4.277

Bormann, E. G. (1973). The Eagleton affair: A fantasy theme analysis. *Quarterly Journal of Speech*, *59*, 143–159. https://doi.org/10.1080/00335637309383163

Bormann, E. G. (1996). Symbolic convergence theory and communication in group decision making. In R. Y. Hirokawa, & M. S. Poole (Eds.), *Communication and group decision making* (2nd ed., pp. 81–113). Sage.

Bormann, E. G., Cragan, J. F., & Shields, D. C. (2001). Three decades of developing, grounding, and using symbolic convergence theory (SCT). *Annals of the International Communication Association*, *25*, 271–313. https://doi.org/10.1080/23808985.2001.11679006

Bourdieu, P., & Wacquant, L. J. D. (1992). *An invitation to reflexive sociology*. University of Chicago Press.

Brass, D. J. (1984). Being in the right place: A structural analysis of individual influence in an organization. *Administrative Science Quarterly*, *29*(4), 518–539. https://doi.org/10.2307/2392937

Breideband, T., Moulder, R. G., Martinez, G. J., Caruso, M., Mark, G., Striegel, A. D., & D'Mello, S. (2023). 'Location, location, location': An exploration of different workplace contexts in remote teamwork during the COVID-19 Pandemic. *Proceedings ACM Human-Computer Interaction*, 7(CSCW1), 1–22. https://doi.org/10.1145/3579504

Cline, R. J. W. (1990). Detecting groupthink: Methods for observing the illusion of unanimity. *Communication Quarterly*, *38*, 112–126. https://doi.org/10.1080/01463379009369748

Coleman, J. (1988). Social capital in the creation of human capital. *American Journal of Sociology*, *94*, S95–S120. Retrieved from www.jstor.org/stable/2780243

Davis, J. H. (1973). Group decision and social interaction: A theory of social decision schemes. *Psychological Review*, *80*, 97–125. https://doi.org/10.1037/h0033951

Davis, J. H. (1982). Social interaction as a combinatorial process in group decision. In H. Brandstatter, J. H. Davis, & G. Stocker-Kreichgauer (Eds.), *Group decision making* (pp. 27–58). Academic Press.

Davis, J. H., Kameda, T., Parks, C., Stasson, M., & Zimmerman, S. (1989). Some social mechanics of group decision making: The distribution of opinion, polling sequence, and implications for consensus. *Journal of Personality and Social Psychology*, *57*, 1000–1012. https://doi.org/10.1037/0022-3514.57.6.1000

Dewey, J. (1910). *How we think*. D. C. Heath.

Emerson, R. M. (1972a). Exchange theory: Part I. A psychological basis for social exchange. In J. Berger, M. Zelditch, & B. Anderson (Eds.), *Sociological theories in progress* (pp. 38–57). Houghton Mifflin.

Emerson, R. M. (1972b). Exchange theory: Part II. Exchange relations and networks. In J. Berger, M. Zelditch, & B. Anderson (Eds.), *Sociological theories in progress* (pp. 58–87). Houghton Mifflin.

Emich, K. J., Kumar, S., Lu, L., Norder, K., & Pandey, N. (2020). Mapping 50 years of small group research through small group research. *Small Group Research*, *51*(6), 659–699.

Fulk, J., Flanagin, A. J., Kalman, M. E., Monge, P. R., & Ryan, T. (1996). Connective and communal public goods in interactive communication systems. *Communication Theory*, *6*(1), 60–87. https://doi.org/10.1111/j.1468-2885.1996.tb00120.x

Gouran, D. S., & Hirokawa, R. Y. (1983). The role of communication in decision-making groups: A functional perspective. In M. S. Mander (Ed.), *Communications in transition* (pp. 168–185). Praeger.

Gouran, D. S., & Hirokawa, R. Y. (1996). Functional theory and communication in decision-making and problem-solving groups: An expanded view. In R. Y. Hirokawa, & M. S. Poole (Eds.), *Communication and group decision-making* (2nd ed., pp. 55–80). Sage.

Gouran, D. S., & Hirokawa, R. Y. (2003). Effective decision making and problem solving in groups: A functional perspective. In R. Y. Hirokawa, R. S. Cathcart, L. A. Samovar, & L. D. Henman (Eds.), *Small group communication* (pp. 27–38). Roxbury.

Hirokawa, R. Y., & Poole, M. S. (Eds.). (1996). *Communication and group decision making*. Sage.

Homans, G. (1950). *The human group*. Harcourt, Brace.

Janis, I. L. (1972). *Victims of groupthink*. Houghton-Mifflin.

Janis, I. L. (1982). *Groupthink: Psychological studies of policy decisions* (2nd ed.). Houghton Mifflin.

Johnson, J. D. (1992). Approaches to organizational communication structure. *Journal of Business Research*, *25*(2), 99–113. https://doi.org/10.1016/0148-2963(92)90010-9

Johnson, S. D., & Long, L. M. (2002). "Being a part and being apart": Dialectics and group communication. In L. R. Frey (Ed.), *New directions in group communication* (pp. 25–42). Sage.

Kalra, K., & Szymanski, M. (2023). Alike yet distinct: The effect of language diversity on interpersonal relationships within national and multinational project teams. *Management and Organization Review*, *19*(4), 627–654. https://doi.org/10.1017/mor.2023.4

Katz, N., Lazer, D., Arrow, H., & Contractor, N. (2004). Network theory and small groups. *Small Group Research*, *35*(3), 307–332. https://doi.org/10.1177/1046496404264941

Klett, T. C., & Arnulf, J. K. (2020). Are Chinese teams like Western teams? Indigenous management theory to leapfrog essentialist team myths. *Frontiers in Psychology*, *11*(1758), 1–16. https://doi.org/10.3389/fpsyg.2020.01758

Klonek, F. E., Kanse, L., Wee, S., Runneboom, C., & Parker, S. K. (2022). Did the COVID-19 lock-down make us better at working in virtual teams? *Small Group Research*, *53*(2), 185–206. https://doi.org/10.1177/10464964211008991

Laughlin, P. R., & Ellis, A. L. (1986). Demonstrability and social combination processes on mathematical intellective tasks. *Journal of Experimental Social Psychology*, *22*, 177–189. https://doi.org/10.1016/0022-1031(86)90022-3

Lorge, I., & Solomon, H. (1955). Two models of group behavior in the solution of eureka-type problems. *Psychometrika*, *20*, 139–148. https://doi.org/10.1007/bf02288986

McLeod, P. L., & Yuan, Y. C. (2021). Diversity and team communication: A critical review and call for broadened representation. *The Emerald handbook of group and team communication research*, 391–405.

McPhee, R. D., & Zaug, P. (2000). The communicative constitution of organizations: A framework for explanation. *The Electronic Journal of Communication*, *10*, 1–15. Retrieved from www.cios.org/EJCPUBLIC/010/1/01017.html

Meyer, B., Glenz, A., Antino, M., Rico, R., & González-Romá, V. (2014). Faultlines and subgroups: A meta-review and measurement guide. *Small Group Research*, *45*(6), 633–670. https://doi.org/10.1177/1046496414552195

Miike, Y. (2007). An Asiacentric reflection on Eurocentric bias in communication theory. *Communication Monographs*, *74*(2), 272–278. https://doi.org/10.1080/03637750701390093

Minbaeva, D., Fitzsimmons, S., & Brewster, C. (2021). Beyond the double-edged sword of cultural diversity in teams: Progress, critique, and next steps. *Journal of International Business Studies*, *52*(1), 45. https://doi.org/10.1057/s41267-020-00390-2

O'Neill, T. A., Flathmann, C., McNeese, N. J., & Salas, E. (2023). Human-autonomy teaming: Need for a guiding team-based framework? *Computers in Human Behavior*, *146*, 107762. https://doi.org/10.1016/j.chb.2023.107762

Podolny, J. M., & Baron, J. N. (1997). Resources and relationships: Social networks and mobility in the workplace. *American Sociological Review*, *62*(5), 673–693. www.jstor.org/stable/2657354

Poole, M. S. (1998). The small group should be the fundamental unit of communication research. In J. S. Trent (Ed.), *Communication: Views from the helm for the 21st century* (pp. 94–97). Allyn & Bacon.

Poole, M. S., & DeSanctis, G. (1990). Understanding the use of group decision support systems. In J. Fulk, & C. Steinfield (Eds.), *Organizations and communication technology* (pp. 173–193). Sage.

Samuelson, P. (1954). The pure theory of public expenditure. *The Review of Economics and Statistics*, *36*(4), 387–389. https://doi.org/10.2307/1925895

Schippers, M. C., Edmondson, A. C., & West, M. A. (2014). Team reflexivity as an antidote to team information-processing failures. *Small Group Research*, *45*, 731–769. https://doi.org/10.1177/1046496414553473

Simon, H. A. (1982). *Models of bounded rationality*. MIT Press.

Ssebunya, M., Morgan, S. N., & Okyere-Manu, B. D. (2019). Environmental justice: Towards an African perspective. In M. Chemhuru (Ed.), *African Environmental ethics: A critical reader* (pp. 175–189). Springer.

Tasheva, S., & Hillman, A. J. (2019). Integrating diversity at different levels: Multilevel human capital, social capital, and demographic diversity and their implications for team effectiveness. *Academy of Management Review*, *44*(4), 746–765.

Wellman, B. (1988). Structural analysis: From method and metaphor to theory and substance. In B. Wellman, & S. Berkowitz (Eds.), *Social structures: A network approach* (pp. 19–61). Cambridge University Press.

Wenger, E. (1998). *Communities of practice: Learning, meaning, and identity*. Cambridge University Press.

Whillans, A., Perlow, L., & Turek, A. (2021). Experimenting during the shift to virtual team work: Learnings from how teams adapted their activities during the COVID-19 pandemic. *Information and Organization*, *31*(1), 100343, 1–12. https://doi.org/10.1016/j.infoandorg.2021.100343

16 Organizational Conflict

Chandler Marr and Jessica Katz Jameson

Conflict is often defined as "the interaction of interdependent people who perceive opposition of goals, aims, and values, and who see the other party as potentially interfering with the realization of these goals" (Putnam & Poole, 1987, p. 552). Given that interdependence is fundamental to defining the organization itself (see Chapter 1), conflict should be seen as an omnipresent – even necessary – part of organizational life as people coordinate activities to achieve individual, group, and organizational goals. Indeed, interdependence among organizational members, teams, policies, and exogenous forces produces a complex social system requiring constant negotiation of interests, tasks, and relationships. Consistent with the CCO perspective, there is a mutual influence between formal conflict management policies (structure/text) and everyday conflict interaction among organizational members (agency/conversation). In this way, organizational structures (e.g., policies, dispute procedures, and task norms) are both a medium for and a product of the conflicts they produce (i.e., the duality of structure; see Chapter 3).

Moreover, conflict should be seen as a fundamental part of organizing because social systems often have contradictory or incompatible goals. For example, consider how an employee's salary goals inherently conflict with corporate goals to minimize costs and maximize profits, or the ways in which an employee's desire for job stability is at odds with the organization's need to be flexible and adapt to the ever-changing environment. Such overlapping and paradoxical goals create conflict laced with issues of power, control, and resistance (see Chapter 12). Put simply, conflict is an inevitable part of organizational life.

Conflict has been examined by organizational communication scholars in a myriad of ways that contribute to the larger field of conflict studies. We begin by reviewing various levels of organizational analysis. We then discuss how conflict has been studied from the three dominant paradigms of communication studies (see Chapter 2). Overall, our review emphasizes the communication cycle – that is, how conflict communication behaviors emerge from, (co)create, and (re)produce organizational relationships, culture, policies, norms, structures, and so on.

Levels of Conflict

Interpersonal-level conflict between two or more organizational members often has a significant impact on workgroups and the organization as a whole. Conversely, conflict at superordinate levels, such as between organizations or institutions, shapes organizational members' expectations and interactional norms. Although conflict often spans several levels of organizational analysis, conflict research has traditionally studied this phenomenon at a single level. Focus on a single level of analysis is especially common among post-positivist

DOI: 10.4324/9781003484639-19

perspectives on organizational conflict, which understand conflict as something that happens *inside* organizations (O_3). Such research examines conflict communication in dyadic (e.g., coworkers or supervisor–supervisee); group/team (e.g., departments, work teams, or professional or demographic identity groups); and inter-organizational contexts (e.g., between corporations and environmental groups). We briefly provide examples of research at each level below.

Dyadic/Interpersonal (Micro)

Interpersonal research examines how organizational members interact with coworkers or supervisors/supervisees, succumbing to the container bias (see Chapter 1) by viewing interpersonal conflict as occurring *within* organizations (O_3). Organizational conflict research often examines the effectiveness of communication and conflict styles on individual outcomes such as employee satisfaction, burnout, or supervisor–supervisee relationships. For example, Weider-Hatfield and Hatfield (1995) found supervisors using collaborative conflict styles were more likely to be promoted, receive raises, and have satisfied employees than those using other styles.

Intercultural scholars have examined the impact of cultural differences on conflict behavior. Cheng and Chen (2020) used a survey method and found a positive relationship between perceived supervisor support and employee willingness to articulate dissent. In another study, Moreland and Apker (2016) used an open-ended survey instrument and found nurses' conflict communication is often characterized by exclusionary and unsupportive language, leading to a conflict-stress cycle. The authors conclude that focusing on responses to conflict through using respectful communication can improve conflict outcomes and ameliorate negative impacts on the work environment.

Group (Meso)

While group communication is a sub-discipline often considered distinct from organizational communication (see Chapter 15), organizations are made up of subsystems such as teams, committees, and hierarchies (e.g., labor vs. management), as well as identity groups based on occupation (e.g., accountants vs. attorneys), or demographics (e.g., North American vs. Japanese employees). Scholars interested in group communication generally see organizations as a set of interdependent structures (O_2), and thus conflicts within and across groups impact and are impacted by larger organizational contexts. For instance, Kuhn and Poole's (2000) study of 11 naturally occurring workgroups across two US organizations found that groups with collaborative conflict management norms made better decisions than those with competing or avoiding styles, as well as those with no consistent conflict style.

Organizational/Institutional (Macro)

Conflict among organizations and institutions is often about policies and divergent stakeholder interests. The diversity of inter-organizational relationships (e.g., cross-sector partnerships, buyer–supplier agreements, and strategic alliances) provides fertile ground for conflict when the activities of one organization threaten the interests, goals, or values of another (Lumineau et al., 2015). For instance, public relations scholars often study inter-organizational conflict. Plowman et al. (1995), analyzed conflict that Walgreens experienced with healthcare providers, pharmaceutical companies, and customers, finding that each of these conflicts included unique sets of interests and required different conflict resolution approaches. Similarly, Murphy and Dee's (1992) examination of the conflict between DuPont and Greenpeace determined that negotiations were largely unsuccessful because it was in the best interests of Greenpeace to appease its stakeholders by maintaining the conflict.

Toward a Multilevel Approach: Transcending Conflict Levels

Concentrating on one level fails to capture conflict's dynamic and transformational nature as organizational levels interpenetrate and influence each other. Indeed, conflict at one level of analysis often leads to or is the result of conflict at another. Focusing solely on one level of analysis risks oversimplifying and neglecting the contextually situated nature of communication and organizing.

For example, Ashforth and Reingen's (2014) explored how a duality of *idealism* and *pragmatism* in a natural food cooperative led to conflict over organizational identity (see Chapter 11). Using ethnographic methods, they found that the idealism–pragmatism duality manifested across interpersonal, group, and organizational levels. Members experienced discomfort arising from ambiguity in the organization's mission, which led to the formation of ingroup/outgroups and heated conflicts over whether or not to adhere to the ideals of the collective or ensure the viability of the business. Extreme members of each out-group were cast as stereotypes, paradoxically facilitating cooperation among more moderate members of each group. Moreover, relational repair rituals and shifts in power between idealist and pragmatist groups worked to sustain the organization. This study highlights the interconnectedness of conflict across levels, with mutual influence between organizational-level and interpersonal-level tensions. Here, a myopic focus on a single level could have hindered the researchers' ability to identify how the interpersonal conflicts involving the idealism–pragmatism dualism were institutionalized (e.g., in the organization's mission and policies) and became competing interpretive frames that members internalized. Focusing on how interpersonal conflict is connected to other levels of organizational analysis also avoids the pitfall of framing conflict as a private problem to be managed individually (Mikkelsen & Clegg, 2019). Overall, comprehensively addressing and managing conflict requires that researchers and practitioners adopt a holistic approach, acknowledging the interplay between interpersonal, group, and structural factors.

Similarly, focusing on the level where conflict manifests overlooks conflicts that transcend traditional levels of analysis. Indeed, individuals may find themselves in conflict not only with their immediate peers or supervisors but also with the overarching organizational structures, norms, or ideologies. These conflicts can arise when individuals perceive misalignment between personal values, goals, or interests and those espoused or enforced at the organizational level – for example, when organizational policies or practices contradict employees' ethical principles or when hierarchical power dynamics impede their ability to voice concerns or enact change. This was seen in Moreland and Apker's (2016) study of nurses' conflict-stress cycle, which became a structural impediment to collaborative conflict management. Elsewhere, a case study of a Brazilian technology park demonstrated how different interpretations of organizational norms among partner organizations intersected with informal norms and social preferences (Mattar et al., 2022). Ambiguous communication expectations impacted the development of interpersonal networks critical to collaboration and innovation.

Paradigmatic Approaches to Studying Conflict

The three traditional paradigmatic approaches (see Chapter 2) represent different assumptions about the nature of conflict and organizations/organizing that shape how scholars study conflict as it occurs across various levels of analysis (i.e., micro, meso, macro). The studies described below illustrate how scholars using each paradigm conceptualize organizational conflict differently, leading to different research questions and study designs.

Post-Positivism

Early organizational conflict scholars examined interpersonal communication *inside* organizational boundaries, primarily from a variable-analytic post-positive perspective, and with a container view (O_3). Examples of post-positivist conflict research include topics such as conflict styles, organizational dissent, intercultural conflict, and the role of technology in conflict.

Conflict Styles

Conflict styles are individual *preferences for using some conflict management approaches more frequently than others* (Thomas & Kilmann, 1974). Thomas and Kilmann (1974) adapted Blake and Mouton's (1964) dual concern model framework (see Chapter 7) to describe conflict behavior on two dimensions: *assertiveness*, attempts to satisfy their own concerns, and *cooperativeness*, attempts to satisfy the other person's concerns. The resulting five styles are avoiding, accommodating, competing, collaborating, and compromising. *Avoiding* is unassertive and uncooperative, not addressing the issue. *Accommodating* has low assertiveness and high cooperativeness, giving in to the other. High assertiveness and low cooperativeness characterize a *competing* style, a focus on one's needs while disregarding others'. *Collaborating* includes high assertiveness and cooperativeness, seeking to meet all parties' needs. *Compromising* is moderately assertive and cooperative, meeting some of everyone's needs. The Thomas-Kilmann Conflict Mode Instrument (TKI; Thomas & Kilmann, 1974) is most widely used by training and development professionals to identify individual conflict styles.

On the other hand, the ROCI-II (Rahim & Bonoma, 1979) is the most commonly implemented conflict styles *research* instrument, in which the dual concerns *concern for self* and *concern for other* result in the same five styles with slightly different names (avoiding, obliging, dominating, integrating, and compromising). Decades of organizational research using the ROCI-II (Rahim, 1983) have demonstrated that integrating is most often perceived as the most appropriate and effective conflict style (Friedman et al., 2000; Gross & Guerrero, 2000; Trudel & Reio, 2011). Guerrero and Gross (2014) examined relationships among argumentativeness, verbal aggressiveness, and conflict styles, finding the five styles are shaped by individual traits and interactions among interactants' traits. Their findings suggest greater nuance to conflict styles than suggested by the dual concerns model.

A special issue of *Management Communication Quarterly* (Putnam, 1988) emphasized the relationship between communication and conflict style. Therein, Womack's (1988) review of communication research demonstrated that individuals use all five conflict styles depending on the context. Putnam and Wilson (1982) had earlier addressed this concern with the Organizational Conflict Communication Index (OCCI), a measure of conflict communication strategies identifying three communicative approaches to conflict management. Collapsing the original five styles in dual concern models resulted in: *non-confrontation* (avoidance and accommodating); *solution-oriented* problem-solving (compromising and collaborating); and *controlling* (competing). OCCI research revealed an important relationship between hierarchical position and conflict communication. Organizational members are more likely to use controlling strategies with subordinates than superiors, more likely to use non-confrontation strategies with superiors than peers or subordinates, and more likely to use solution-oriented strategies with peers and superiors than subordinates (Wilson & Waltman, 1988). These early studies elucidated the important relationship between power and organizational conflict communication (see Chapter 12).

The managerial bias of early organizational communication research led to significant interest in conflict across levels of organizational hierarchy. Noted above, Weider-Hatfield and Hatfield (1995) found that supervisors who used collaborative strategies were more likely to be promoted, receive raises, and have satisfied employees than those who used other styles. While employees in this study perceived more conflict overall when supervisors used collaborative strategies, these results validate the idea that conflict is not problematic when managed effectively. Hopeck et al. (2014) examined whether conflict styles predicted student use of an ombuds process in conflicts with professors. Like other conflict style studies, they found that individuals with a collaborative, solution-oriented conflict style were more likely to have positive perceptions of procedural justice and indicate intent to use an ombuds system.

Employee Satisfaction and Organizational Dissent

Infante and Gordon (1985) found a positive relationship between conflict communication, managerial success, and employee satisfaction. Contrasting *argumentativeness*, the use of facts and data to support one's position, with *verbal aggressiveness*, the tendency to attack the other personally, they found that argumentativeness increased career satisfaction, achievement, and relationship satisfaction. Another study found that lower-quality leader-member relationships lead to increased employee defensiveness, associated with low satisfaction and burnout (Becker et al., 2005). In a study of the relationship between conflict-prone organizations and external communication during the COVID-19 pandemic, a survey of 476 full-time employees in the US found that those who reported high conflict-prone organizations and active concerns about COVID-19 were more likely to engage in negative external communication during the crisis and more likely to report turnover intentions (Chon et al., 2021). The implication of this study is that organizational leaders need to manage contentious issues through proactive and continuous communication.

Organizational dissent is defined as the communication of disagreement with an organizational decision or policy (Kassing, 1998, 2011). The way members communicate dissent influences how dissent is received and responded to and whether conflict occurs. Dissent communication may be *upward* (i.e., to supervisors), *lateral* (i.e., to peers), or *displaced* (i.e., to someone external to the organization, such as a friend, partner, or the media, as in *whistleblowing*; Kassing, 2002). Kassing (2002) identified five common upward dissent tactics. *Direct-factual appeal* brings facts and evidence to support employee concerns, while *solution-orientation* presents problems and solutions. Given that solution-oriented tactics are most likely to have positive outcomes, these are referred to as *prosocial dissent*. Prosocial dissent strategies are consistent with *argumentativeness* – they are most likely to create an environment that welcomes employee *voice* (the ability to speak up and participate) and collaborative conflict management. Redmond et al. (2016) found that prosocial dissent tactics were correlated with the use of a collaborative conflict style, whereas repetition, circumvention, and threatening resignation were correlated with the dominating conflict style. Although no direct relationship was found between leader–member relationships and dissent strategies, Redmond and colleagues' study confirmed that higher superior–subordinate relationship quality is related to integrating conflict management style. Kassing's other upward dissent strategies include *repetition, circumvention*, and *threatening resignation*. These strategies tend to be *face-threatening* to supervisors or management and have been found to have less positive results (see Garner, 2012 for an extended list of additional dissent strategies).

In a cross-cultural study of organizational dissent, employee burnout, and work-family balance, Zeng and Chen (2020) surveyed 203 workers in China and Finland and found that emotional fatigue was positively related to latent dissent (dissenting to coworkers or peers) and negatively related to articulated dissent (dissent to direct supervisor). This relationship was mitigated by supervisors who provided support. They also found a relationship between National culture and burnout, work-family balance, and dissent. "Finnish employees significantly express more dissent, experience less burnout, and perceive a more supportive organizational culture than their Chinese counterparts" (pp. 642–643). This example demonstrates the importance of cross-cultural organizational communication research for understanding appropriate and effective conflict communication patterns.

Intercultural Conflict

Drawing from Erving Goffman's (1956) concept of *face* – the public persona or identity people present to others – *Face Negotiation Theory* explains intercultural communication in conflict (Ting-Toomey, 1988). Ting-Toomey's theory integrates intercultural communication with conflict styles research, noting that certain conflict styles are more face-supportive or face-threatening. Hence, individuals' conflict style and attention to others' faces are related to the culture in which they were raised. For example, people from collectivist cultures, typically found in the Eastern part of the world, may be more concerned with *other-face*, protecting the face of others, than *self-face*, or protecting their own identity needs, and as a result tend toward conflict styles such as avoidance and accommodation. Oetzel and Ting-Toomey (2003) conducted a cross-cultural study of 768 students from four nationalities (China, Japan, Germany, and the US) in which participants were asked to recall a specific conflict and then answer a series of questions about this experience. People who emphasize interdependence (collectivity), focus more on other-face and are more likely to use integrating and avoidance conflict styles, while those who emphasize their independence are more focused on self- than other-face and more likely to use dominating conflict styles. Another study examined the complex relationship between culture and conflict styles by testing the relationship between the level of interaction an immigrant has with a host culture and their preferences for different conflict styles (Oommen, 2017). This study concluded that more host involvement led to preferences for integrating and accommodating styles, while more home involvement (interaction with others from their home country) led to a preference for avoiding. Findings such as these demonstrate that organizations must pay attention to the role of cultural differences in organizational communication, both in terms of how difference impacts interpersonal communication as well as how they constitute the culture of the organization.

Technology and Conflict Management Effectiveness

One consequence of adaptations made during the height of the COVID-19 pandemic is an increase in remote work and flexible hours, thus more attention is being given to the role of technology in organizational conflict. Boundary conflicts may occur when employees are asked to use devices after "typical" work hours (van Zoonen et al., 2020). As a sign of how work expectations may be changing, cell phone use after hours was not negatively associated with work-life conflict and was positively associated with organizational identification (see Chapters 11 and 19). In a study of mobile instant messaging use in South Korea, an online survey of 434 office workers revealed a relationship between instant messaging and information overload, which often led to role ambiguity, role conflict, and employee burnout (Cho et al., 2019). In a survey-based study of information communication technologies at work, Lyu et al. (2023) found that online voice (the expression of concerns or suggestions through online tools) was positively correlated with online bullying in a sample of 152 full-time Chinese workers. When an employee expresses concerns, it may induce change that is rejected or resisted by coworkers, leading to online bullying. This may also be explained by coworkers perceiving the person who articulated the dissent to be less competent or trustworthy. Studies such as these remind us of the benefits and limitations of communication technologies (see Chapter 19).

Interpretivism

Interpretive approaches to studying conflict embrace organizing as a process (O_1). In the 1980s, scholars began to focus on how conflict was enabled and constrained by structural and cultural contexts, examining how the ongoing (re)production of collective values, norms, and assumptions contributed to conflict. Put simply, interpretive scholars believe that "conflict is part of the social fabric of organizations" (Bartunek et al., 1992, p. 217) and cannot be separated from its context. Here, conflict can only be understood by examining the local meanings and interpretations that constitute organizations and the tensions they produce.

Organizational conflict research from this approach focuses on how conflict is talked into being – that is, how communication among organizational actors and their interpretations give rise to conflict. This is an important distinction, as "people in organizations can be in conflict without labeling their relationship as such" (Mikkelsen & Clegg, 2019, p. 171). Interpretive scholarship emphasizes the communication-organization cycle (O_1). Common topics from this approach include paradox, contradiction, tensions, organizational dissent, and metaphors for conflict.

Paradox, Contradictions, and Tensions

One of the major trends of interpretive theorizing maintains that conflict is produced through paradoxical or contradictory meaning systems (see Chapter 3 for a discussion of paradox and contradiction). For instance, when supervisors view employees' requests for family time as conflicting with their productivity at work, they reinforce the notion that work and family are incompatible. According to Putnam et al. (2016),

> Conflict can emerge from dualling expectations. From a constitutive view of organizing, paradoxes emanate from social actions and interactions as organizational members respond to and process contradictions in ways that create systematic patterns. These patterns become embedded in routines and structures, are brought from the past into the future, and evolve as organizing continues across time and space.
>
> (p. 14)

Said another way, contradictions arise from conflicts between foundational structural elements (e.g., norms that attempt to routinize creativity and innovation) that are interlinked in their creation and perpetuation. Contradictory meaning systems may trigger conflict as people consider a multitude of opposing choices.

Huang and Zhang (2019) examined the contradictory impacts of instant messenger use (WeChat) on organizational outcomes in China. This interview study found paradoxes related to engagement, formality, and visibility. Factors contributing to these paradoxical outcomes included differences in organizational norms, coworker expectations, and conflicts in individual understandings of WeChat. For example, WeChat allowed workers to connect with coworkers with whom they had not been formally introduced, which could improve connectivity while creating unwanted connections. WeChat simultaneously enabled workers to be more visible to their managers. While this has positive implications, it creates stress and pressure to perform or meet expectations for responsiveness.

Woo et al. (2017) interviewed 40 interns and found three communicative tensions underlying their identity management, including being inexperienced while wanting to be deemed competent; focusing on present vs. future, and desire for close or distant supervision. While *either/or* approaches to tension management are not recommended, interns may not have the skills to navigate tensions using a *both/and* approach without support. *More-than* approaches might generate options for the tension to bring benefit to both the intern and the organization.

Structurational divergence explains how contradictory and paradoxical meaning systems can lead to conflict (Nicotera & Clinkscales, 2010; see Chapter 3). People enmeshed in a structurationally divergent system tend to engage in dysfunctional communication behaviors such as verbal aggression and competitive conflict management (Nicotera & Mahon, 2013). In these cases, managing conflict may be perceived as so futile that people disengage altogether. Malterud and Nicotera (2020) explored how intractable conflict cycles escalated from a structurational divergence nexus of contradictory meanings. They found that the degree to which people take conflict personally (specifically with feelings of stress and persecution) and non-confrontational conflict management style may be critical factors in creating recurrent cycles of intractable conflict. Relatedly, employees who perceive an SD-nexus (see Chapter 3) engage in defensive silencing about formal organizational power holders (Millender et al., 2023). When employees engage in defensive silencing and non-confrontational conflict management, deeper structural concerns driving conflict remain unaddressed. As a result, structural contradictions may spiral into conflict cycles that further entrench paradox.

Organizational Dissent

Organizational dissent research has typically taken the perspective of the dissenter (Garner, 2013); this perspective neglects how dissent and the context in which it occurs is produced through continuous interactions between dissenters, coworkers, and managers. Garner (2013) conceptualized dissent as "an organizational stream of interaction punctuated by particular moments" (p. 377) and sought to demonstrate how ongoing organizational communication patterns create an organizational culture that supports or obstructs employee voice and dissent effectiveness. Through interviews and observations with a nonprofit organization's members, Garner sought to better understand how managers' responses to dissent influenced future employee decisions regarding whether and how to dissent. This study revealed important differences in how managers and coworkers talk about dissent (e.g., an employee described as making a *valiant effort* vs. being a *whiny employee*). Dissent discourse results in *residual communication* that stays with organizational members and (re)produces a narrative that supports or impedes dissent.

Garner (2013) offers a processual view of dissent, where three stages unfold sequentially. During the *precipitation stage*, the potential dissenter makes sense of their grievances and weighs the pros and cons of expressing dissent. What constitutes a "grievance" worthy of dissent is contoured by organizational meaning systems. Other organizational members, such as supervisors and colleagues, "interact with the would-be dissenter to shape the experience of any potential disconnect with managerial expectations, part of what defines an act as dissent" (p. 380). For example, employees accustomed to expectations for long hours and response to emails after hours may not feel disgruntled with their circumstances (Kunda, 1992) or may be hesitant to speak up for fear of sanction (Barker, 1993). Other organizational members can shape the dissenter's beliefs about outcomes of dissent expression (e.g., change to the system vs. stasis) based on previous dissent experiences.

During the *initial conversation stage*, the dissenter expresses their grievance and receives reactions from the dissenting audience (Garner, 2012). These reactions play a significant role in (co)constructing what counts as a legitimate or illegitimate complaint. For instance, a manager may frame dissent as "whining" or "constructive feedback." Framing dissent as whining may lead to sanctions, but framing dissent as constructive feedback legitimizes the complaint. "How the audience labels dissent exerts a force on the outcome of the dissent conversation" (p. 381). The way people respond to dissent is based on both how the dissenter communicates frustration (Garner, 2012), as well as the audience's exogenous goals (e.g., profit, maintaining power; Shore & Strauss, 2008) and relationship to the dissenter (Kassing, 2000).

The final stage, *residual communication*, involves all interactions after dissent expression. The outcome of dissent materializes as structural change or reification of the status quo. Consistent with a process orientation, residual communication is influenced by previous interactions and can include stories portraying dissent expression as necessary and effective at bringing about organizational change. Stories help orient newcomers to the norms of appropriate dissent in organizations, influencing when and how dissent is expressed. Even when nothing changes in the short term, residual communication can prompt a delayed response (Gossett & Kilker, 2006). We can see here how conflict – in the form of dissent – is a co-constructed process shaped by systems of shared meaning.

Conflict Metaphors

Metaphors are linguistic expressions that compare one thing, person, or experience to another. The metaphors we use for certain experiences shape how we approach and interact with(in) that experience:

> Metaphors make realities for us, especially social realities. A metaphor may thus be a guide for future action. Such actions will, of course, fit the metaphor. This will, in return, reinforce the power of the metaphor to make experience coherent. In this sense, metaphors can be self-fulfilling prophecies.
>
> (Lakoff & Johnson, 1981, p. 156)

Metaphors are not only linguistic embellishments – they fundamentally constitute our realities and the ways we experience the world. Metaphors "provide an account of how respondents' view themselves as participants in the conflict process, how they envision the conflict process itself, and how others'... perceived roles are enacted" (Burrell et al., 1992, p. 123). Simply put, it is through metaphors that we can understand what conflict means to people (Buzzanell & Burrell, 1997). Metaphors reveal assumptions about the appropriate approaches to conflict management and whether such interventions will be effective. For instance, if participants describe conflict as a battle or war, they may implicitly endorse confrontational strategies and take a win/loss orientation. Therefore, exploring the conflict metaphors individuals employ constitutes potential pathways for (dys)functional conflict management.

In one of the earliest uses of metaphor analysis to understand conflict, Smith and Eisenberg (1987) analyzed root metaphors used to make sense of conflict at Disneyland. They found differences in the metaphors used by management and employees, with management using a drama metaphor (i.e., putting on a show that makes money) and employees favoring a family metaphor (i.e., we are all a family who take care of each other). Different metaphors may lead to differing expectations that might help explain the labor strike. Another more recent study explored how nurses perceived being called "heroes" to describe their work with COVID-19 patients (Sahay & Dwyer, 2023). In a thematic analysis of interviews with 23 nurses, Sahay and Dwyer (2023) found that nurses reported experiencing self-doubt and failure, which impacted their own well-being at work. The authors also used this study to demonstrate the role of communication in constituting and shaping employee identity during the pandemic.

Metaphors are a useful tool for understanding what conflict *feels* like for involved parties. For example, Tracy et al. (2006) analyzed metaphors for workplace bullying to understand how exactly it is experienced by targets. Participants described the experience of bullying as a game or battle, a nightmare, torture, or a toxic substance. Targets of bullies described themselves as abused children, enslaved persons, animals, prisoners, and heartbroken lovers, framing their bullies as demons, dictators, and two-faced backstabbers. Metaphors are helpful for understanding people's subjective experiences of workplace bullying and can capture the emotional pain associated with these conflicts that may otherwise be difficult to express. It is through metaphors that we can better understand how people experience, construct, and make sense of the emotional dynamics of conflict (see Chapter 18).

Studies on conflict metaphors have also been used to capture how people experience conflict differently based on their social identity and demographic characteristics. Turner and Shuter (2004) compared European-American and African-American women's perceptions of conflict at work, asking 51 working women to complete the sentence "To me conflict is like..." (p. 174). Their analysis of metaphors concluded that while all the participants experienced conflict as negative, African-American women's metaphors were more passive, less focused on resolution, and more intense than metaphors used by European Women, suggesting different experiences of conflict across members of the two groups. (See Chapters 1 and 4.)

Critical-Interpretivism

The critical-interpretive approach considers how histories of power shape ways of talking and knowing, assuming that our understanding of the world is produced through systems of domination and that organizational life is constructed to privilege some identities, bodies, and ideologies over others. From this approach, communication and the conflict it engenders are both a product and outcome of these histories of domination. As such, conflict cannot be "isolated from ongoing organizational struggles, perceptions and values related to organizational change, control and justice" (Morrill, 2000, p. 639).

Critical-interpretive scholarship is ultimately grounded in an optimistic hope for more equitable and just social practices (Banet-Weiser, 2013) and acknowledges that conflict and disruption of the status quo is an inherent part of achieving emancipation (Mumby & Kuhn, 2021). Critical scholarship fundamentally "encourages the exploration of alternative communication practices that allow greater democracy and more creative and productive cooperation among stakeholders through reconsidering organizational governance and decision-making processes" (Deetz, 2005, p. 85). Conflict cannot be eliminated, as organizing is inherently an ideological struggle (Mumby, 2015). However, critical scholars try to imagine how conflict can be a catalyst for social justice and deeper human connection. See Chapter 12 for a full explanation of organizational power, control, and resistance.

Conflict across Difference

Organizational communication patterns contribute to the emergence of conflict across differences (see Chapter 14), as well as the ways in which these conflicts are managed. According to the critical-interpretive perspective, intercultural conflicts are often skewed in favor of the dominant group. For example, in a study of how people communicate about employee mistreatment in a culturally diverse workplace, Meares and colleagues (2004) found that strategic ambiguity was used to prevent marginalized employees from speaking out about their abuse. Through strategic ambiguity (see Chapter 2), mistreatment became hidden and silenced as individuals lacked a shared understanding of what constitutes it. This lack of shared understanding was a result of unclear definitions and policies that left employees without language to describe their abuse. Narratives that showed little confidence in satisfactory conflict resolution were muted in favor of narratives that demonstrated confidence in management's ability to handle mistreatment. Strategic ambiguity is thus a way that dominant groups can maintain power by creating hegemonic knowledge regimes that privilege certain narratives of conflict over others.

MICROAGGRESSIONS

Microaggressions are "the everyday verbal, nonverbal, and environmental slights, snubs, or insults, whether intentional or unintentional, that communicate hostile, derogatory, or negative messages to target persons based solely upon their marginalized group membership" (Sue, 2010, p. 3). Holling (2019) explains how microaggressions toward scholars of color, such as "you intimidate me," create a controlling image of Black women (Hill Collins, 1990). By framing Black women as difficult, hostile, and underperforming, these microaggressions absolve aggressors of responsibility, create "clashing realities" (p. 108), and impose (post)colonial relations on faculty of color. Microaggressions reinforce historical power dynamics where marginalized groups in the academy are seen through stereotypical lenses and blamed for the actions of others (see Chapter 4). Holling's work demonstrates how microaggressions are intersectional in nature – that is, they are rooted in overlapping structures of oppression that are constituted through communication.

Similarly, immigrant professionals in the United States experience microaggressions from their colleagues through behaviors such as imitating accents (i.e., verbal microaggressions), stereotyping (i.e., attitudinal microaggressions), and questioning credentials (i.e., professional microaggressions; Shenoy-Packer, 2015). In response to these microaggressions, immigrant professionals engage in a variety of critical sensemaking strategies. To combat verbal and attitudinal microaggressions, targets rationalized perpetrators' actions through perspective-taking, overlooking lack of cross-cultural knowledge, and humor. Targets also created alternative selves to make "critical sense of the power dynamics embedded within majority–minority, or rather dominant–nondominant, communication" (p. 268). These alternative selves were constructed by limiting their contributions, dissociating from coworkers, and silencing tokenized elements of their identity. In response to professional microaggressions that disparaged their qualifications, immigrant workers blamed themselves and internally normalized skepticism from others. Their self-blame is a result of hegemonic structures of power that privilege certain cultural performances (e.g., whiteness) over others at work.

Conflict across differences ultimately occurs due to organizational communication patterns that marginalize certain bodies, identities, and cultures. As explained by Ferdman (2017), "without rules for positive interaction across difference, then anything goes and differences could easily spiral out of control into overt and destructive conflict" (p. 251). Overall, communication between members, as well as policy texts, organizes workplace relationships in such a way that perpetuates biases and exclusionary practices for historically marginalized groups. The unequal distribution of social and material resources can be the source of conflict, resistance, and dissent.

Sexual Harassment

According to the US Equal Employment Opportunity Commission (Equal Employment Opportunity Commission (EEOC), 1997), sexual harassment is defined as

> unwelcome sexual advances, requests for sexual favors, and other verbal or physical conduct of a sexual nature constitutes sexual harassment when submission to or rejection of this conduct explicitly or implicitly affects an individual's employment, unreasonably interferes with an individual's work performance or creates an intimidating, hostile or offensive work environment.

This definition encompasses two forms of sexual harassment: hostile environment and quid pro quo. In hostile environment interactions, sexual advances become so persistent or severe that they create a harmful work environment that hinders the targets' well-being. With quid pro quo sexual harassment (i.e., "something for something"), a person, typically with more authority, offers to improve the work circumstances of another in exchange for sexual favors. This could include behaviors such as offering promotions for sexual favors or giving important tasks to employees who accept sexual advances. Sexual harassment and the behaviors/circumstances it constitutes are created through communication (Dougherty, 2009; Keyton & Menzie, 2007).

Through the lens of feminist and queer organizational scholarship (see Chapters 13 and 14), sexual harassment is facilitated by gendered, heteronormative organizational structures, cultures, and processes (e.g., Dougherty & Smythe, 2004; Foley et al., 2022; Gómez-González et al., 2023). Sexual harassment is not an isolated issue in an otherwise functional organization; rather, sexual harassment is embedded in and enabled by sociopolitical systems of meaning that constitute how organizational members relate to and interact with one another. Organizational efforts to address harassment can unintentionally perpetuate sexist norms by prioritizing certain experiences, thereby normalizing some behaviors (Brewis, 2001). Hlavka (2014) and Hennekam and Bennett (2017) found that normalized sexism underpins harassment in adolescent and creative industry settings. Phipps and Young (2015) linked persistent harassment in higher education to entrenched "lad cultures." These norms persist through their repetitive nature, but they can be contested and changed. Understanding the performativity of norms reveals their rhetorical nature – they are sustained as long as they are persuasive.

Unfortunately, bureaucratic structures often impede the effective resolution of conflict, especially sexual harassment (Ahmed, 2021; Malvini Redden & Scarduzio, 2024). Bureaucracy relies on rationality to govern people's behavior, banning emotional and personal expressions in decision-making processes (see Chapter 5). Adherence to bureaucratic rules sediments them and makes them increasingly more rational – sometimes so much so that the rules themselves become irrational and contradictory. As evidence, consider the notorious idea of "red tape," in which no movement can be made on certain tasks due to adherence to deeply entrenched and complicated systems of rules. Such convoluted bureaucratic structures are one reason targets of sexual harassment choose not to go through formal channels, describing the process of reporting as a battle or game (Burrell et al., 1992; Clair et al., 2019; Malvini Redden & Scarduzio, 2024). Unfortunately, some sexual harassment policies inadvertently harm the target while avoiding accountability for the perpetrator (Ahmed, 2021).

Conclusion

Conflict is (co)constructed through the communication-organization cycle, which represents the ways in which people's responses to conflict are both a medium and outcome of organization structures. Conflict is a multifaceted phenomenon that permeates every level of organizational life. From interpersonal disagreements to inter-organizational tensions, conflicts arise from the inherent interdependence among organizational members and the complex interplay of goals, values, assumptions, and structures within which they operate.

We hope that our discussion of conflict through various theoretical lenses has underscored the diverse ways in which scholars approach the study of conflict and its management. Each of these paradigms offers unique insights into the nuances of organizational conflict and emphasizes different aspects such as communication patterns, meaning systems, and/or power dynamics. In the future, it is imperative for researchers and practitioners alike to continue exploring the nuances of organizational conflict and its implications for organizational members and their relationships.

There is a rich and expansive literature on organizational dispute resolution, mediation, and restorative justice that is beyond the scope of this chapter. This literature demonstrates that conflict is not inherently negative; rather, it is an inevitable consequence of the dynamic and contradictory meaning systems that constitute organizational life. By recognizing conflict as an inherent aspect of organizational life and harnessing its constructive potential, people can transform conflicts into opportunities for growth and engage in functional communication practices that foster collaboration and mutual understanding.

Recommended Supplementary Readings

Bodtker, A. B., & Jameson, J. K. (2001). Emotion in conflict formation and its transformation: Application to organizational conflict management. *The International Journal of Conflict Management*, *12*(3), 259–275.

Provides a conceptual argument for the role of emotion in organizational conflict; presents ideas for confronting emotions in organizations.

Gayle, B. M., & Preiss, R. W. (1998). Assessing emotionality in organizational conflicts. *Management Communication Quarterly*, *12*(2), 280–302.

One of few organizational communication studies to empirically examine emotion in organizational conflict; study discusses the impact of conflict memory on communication.

Harrison, T. R., & Morrill, C. (2004). Ombuds processes and disputant reconciliation. *Journal of Applied Communication Research*, *32*(4), 318–341.

Discusses the role of ombuds in an organizational setting.

Jameson, J. K. (1999). Toward a comprehensive model for the assessment and management of intraorganizational conflict. *International Journal of Conflict Management*, *10*(3), 268–294.

Presents a model to illustrate the complexity of choosing among possible conflict management approaches.

Kirby, E., & Krone, K. J. (2002). "The policy exists but you can't really use it": Communication and the structuration of work-family policies. *Journal of Applied Communication Research*, *30*, 50–77.

Speaks to the relationship between organizational policy and how employee interaction impacts how employees interpret the policy, which impacts trust in organizational conflict management options.

Knapp, M. L., Putnam, L. L., & Davis, L. J. (1988). Measuring interpersonal conflict in organizations: Where do we go from here? *Management Communication Quarterly*, *1*, 414–429.

Credited for setting the initial research agenda for communication scholarship in organizational conflict.

Kolb, D. M., & Putnam, L. L. (1992). The multiple faces of conflict in organizations. *Journal of Occupational Behavior*, *13*, 311–324.

This interdisciplinary work increased the visibility of organizational communication for the field of conflict studies.

Putnam, L. L. (2005). Discourse analysis: Mucking around with negotiation data. *International Negotiation*, *10*, 17–32.

Discusses insights gleaned from qualitative, discourse-based approaches.

Putnam, L. L. (2010). Communication as changing the negotiation game. *Journal of Applied Communication Research*, *38*(4), 325–335.

Provides points of communication practice for negotiators in all types of settings.

Oetzel, J. G., & Ting-Toomey, S. (2013). *The Sage handbook of conflict communication: Integrating theory, research, and practice* (J. G. Oetzel & S. Ting-Toomey, Eds.) (2nd ed., pp. 267–292). Sage.

This handbook provides a comprehensive overview of conflict communication scholarship and surveys key concepts related to this topic of study.

Important Concepts: Define and Discuss

Assertiveness
Conflict
Conflict metaphors
Conflict styles

  Accommodating
  Avoiding
  Collaborating
  Competing
  Compromising

Cooperativeness
Face
Intercultural conflict
Interdependence
Microaggressions
Organizational dissent
Sexual harassment
Structurational divergence
Workplace bullying
Verbal aggressiveness

Discussion Questions

1 How might dominant organizational ideologies shape the way employees experience and manage conflict? How might these ideologies contour employees' perspectives on various forms of conflict, such as dissent, intercultural conflict, or sexual harassment?
2 Brainstorm productive and unproductive metaphors for organizational conflict. In each of these metaphors, consider: (a) what role does the metaphor user take on? (b) How does the metaphor cast their conflict partner? (c) How does this metaphor represent power dynamics at play between the two conflict parties? (d) What conflict management strategies would be encouraged by this conflict metaphor?
3 Discuss a situation in which you or a coworker felt you were not being treated fairly by your supervisor or you disagreed with an organizational policy. Did anyone talk to the supervisor or a manager? Why or why not? Provide some examples of how you might voice your concerns, with a focus on the characteristics of organizational dissent. Then, describe what you could do as an organizational leader to promote employee voice.
4 You and a coworker rely on each other for information and task coordination to help the team achieve its goals. Your coworker is often unavailable, arriving late, leaving early, and taking long breaks. You told this coworker it would be helpful to touch base daily, but your coworker just said "yeah" and laughed it off. Based on ideas from this chapter, what would be your next step in trying to address this conflict?

Practitioner's Corner

Robbie is a Certified Registered Nurse Anesthetist (CRNA) at a private hospital in North Carolina. Her job is to prepare patients, provide anesthesia during surgery, and stay with the patient through their post-op recovery. Hospital and state rules require an anesthesiologist to supervise anesthesia administration. The anesthesiologist checks in during surgery in case complications arise or the CRNA needs assistance. Anesthesiologists and CRNAs meet at the beginning of each shift to review that day's patients. One day, Robbie met with an anesthesiologist, Dr. Don Dolan, to discuss the anesthesia plan for a patient who was having surgery. They agreed on the process for administering anesthesia and knew when the surgery was scheduled; however, at the appointed time, Robbie learned that the patient had eaten within the last 2 hours, and she recommended a delayed start to the surgeon to adapt to this new information. The surgeon was irritated that the surgical schedule was thrown off and reprimanded Dr. Dolan. Dr. Dolan was embarrassed and furious that Robbie's actions were inconsistent with the agreed-upon plan. Dr. Dolan lodged a complaint against Robbie to the Chief Nurse, who began an investigation of the incident to decide whether a new policy needs to be put in place to prevent such conflict in the future.

The above conflict demonstrates how interdependence among organizational levels constructs an environment requiring constant negotiation of interests, tasks, and relationships. The conflict between Robbie and Dr. Dolan impacts their relationship, affects the surgical team, and influences future policies that structure communication between CRNAs and anesthesiologists at this hospital. Moreover, the conflict influences (and is influenced by) communication outside of this specific organization, such as a nationwide tension between CRNAs and anesthesiologists regarding ambiguous CRNA supervision policies. In some hospitals, for example, CRNAs occasionally give anesthesia without supervision and without harm (Dulisse & Cromwell, 2010). However, anesthesiologists often argue that their depth of medical expertise is required to assure patient safety. Given uncertainties of surgery, potential drug interactions, or other unknowns, they contend CRNAs must always be under the anesthesiologist's supervision. CRNAs often find this insulting to their knowledge and expertise. This interpersonal/occupational group conflict plays out at several organizational and institutional levels as hospital administrations must construct policies consistent with the statewide policies, which must comply with federal legislation. In fact, the professional associations of each group, the American Society of Anesthesiologists (ASA) and the American Association of Nurse Anesthetists (AANA), have actively lobbied legislators on the issue of supervision. Members of each organization promote their positions with politicians, administrators, and colleagues (see Jameson, 2003, 2004). The conflict between Robbie and Dr. Dolan demonstrates how conflict is interwoven across micro, meso, and macro levels.

Recall that formal conflict management policies and the everyday conflict interactions among organizational members are mutually constitutive of one another. Robbie found herself in a challenging situation; the goals of patient safety clashed with surgical efficiency. Despite adhering to safety protocols, the decision to delay surgery caused friction among the surgical team. This conflict has the potential to alter future policies that inform the surgical process, illustrating the recursive nature of the communication-organization cycle (see Chapter 1). The policy enables and constrains decision-making, and everyday talk alters the interactional norms among anesthesiologists and CRNAs, shapes future interactions between parties, and influences change in organizational culture and policies.

Consider the dynamics and effects of the conflict between Robbie and Dr. Dolan: How might this incident affect future interactions between CRNAs and anesthesiologists in the hospital, both in their (in)formal interactions and the norms that structure them? Similarly, how might this incident affect the professional identities and responsibilities of CRNAs and anesthesiologists within the hospital? What existing cultural norms within medical institutions might shape the way conflicts like this are handled? How might this incident challenge or reinforce those norms? What new policies would be developed that could either stifle or encourage professional judgment and the expression of dissent? If you were an organizational consultant tasked with managing this conflict, what advice might you give to conflict stakeholders (e.g., the individuals in conflict, hospital administrators, and other policymakers)?

References

Ahmed, S. (2021). *Complaint!* Duke University Press. https://doi.org/10.2307/j.ctv1v7zdh2

Ashforth, B. E., & Reingen, P. H. (2014). Functions of dysfunction: Managing the dynamics of an organizational duality in a natural food cooperative. *Administrative Science Quarterly*, *59*(3), 474–516. https://doi.org/10.1177/0001839214537811

Banet-Weiser, S. (2013). Locating critique. *Communication and Critical/Cultural Studies*, *10*(2–3), 229–232. https://doi.org/10.1080/14791420.2013.806140

Barker, J. (1993). Tightening the iron cage: Concertive control in self-managing teams. *Administrative Science Quarterly*, *38*(3), 408–437. https://doi.org/10.2307/2393374

Bartunek, J. M., Kolb, D. M., & Lewicki, R. J. (1992). Bringing conflict out from behind the scenes: Private, informal, and nonrational dimensions of conflict in organizations. In D. M. Kolb & J. M. Bartunek (Eds.), *Hidden conflict in organizations: Uncovering behind-the-scenes disputes* (pp. 209–228). Sage. https://doi.org/10.4135/9781483325897

Becker, J. A. H., Halbesleben, J. R. B., & Dan O'Hair, H. (2005). Defensive communication and burnout in the workplace: The mediating role of leader–member exchange. *Communication Research Reports*, *22*(2), 143–150. https://doi.org/10.1080/00036810500130653

Blake, R., & Mouton, J. (1964). *The managerial grid: The key to leadership excellence*. Gulf Publishing Company.

Brewis, J. (2001). Foucault, politics and organizations: (Re)-constructing sexual harassment. *Gender, Work & Organization*, *8*(1), 37–60. https://doi.org/10.1111/1468-0432.00121

Burrell, N. A., Buzzanell, P. M., & McMillan, J. J. (1992). Feminine tensions in conflict situations as revealed by metaphoric analyses. *Management Communication Quarterly*, *6*(2), 115–149. https://doi.org/10.1177/0893318992006002001

Buzzanell, P. M., & Burrell, N. A. (1997). Family and workplace conflict: Examining metaphorical conflict schemas and expressions across context and sex. *Human Communication Research*, *24*(1), 109–146. https://doi.org/10.1111/j.1468-2958.1997.tb00589.x

Cheng, Z., & Chen, M. (2020). An exploration of the relationships between organizational dissent, employee burnout, and work-family balance: A cross-cultural comparison between China and Finland. *Communication Studies*, *71*(3), 1–16. https://doi.org/10.1080/10510974.2020.1749864

Cho, J., Lee, H. E., & Kim, H. (2019). Effects of communication-oriented overload in mobile instant messaging on role stressors, burnout, and turnover intention in the workplace. *International Journal of Communication*, *13*, 1743–1763. https://ijoc.org/index.php/ijoc/article/view/9290/2623

Chon, M. G., Tam, L., & Kim, J. N. (2021). Effects of organizational conflict history and employees' situational perceptions of COVID-19 on negative megaphoning and turnover intention. *Journal of Communication Management*, *25*(3), 298–315. https://doi.org/10.1108/JCOM-10-2020-0114

Clair, R. P., Brown, N. E., Dougherty, D. S., Delemeester, H. K., Geist-Martin, P., Gorden, W. I., …, & Turner, P. K. (2019). # MeToo, sexual harassment: An article, a forum, and a dream for the future. *Journal of Applied Communication Research*, *47*(2), 111–129. https://doi.org/10.1080/00909882.2019.1567142

Deetz, S. (2005). Critical theory. In S. May & D. K. Mumby (Eds.), *Engaging organizational communication theory & research: Multiple perspectives* (pp. 85–111). Sage.

Dougherty, D., & Smythe, M. J. (2004). Sensemaking, organizational culture, and sexual harassment. *Journal of Applied Communication Research*, *32*(4), 293–317. https://doi.org/10.1080/0090988042000275998

Dougherty, D. S. (2009). Sexual harassment as destructive organizational process. In P. Lutgen-Sandvik & B. D. Sypher (Eds.), *Destructive organizational communication* (pp. 219–242). Routledge. https://doi.org/10.4324/9780203928554-19

Dulisse, B., & Cromwell, J. (2010). No harm found when nurse anesthetists work without supervision by physicians. *Health Affairs*, *29*(8), 1469–1479. https://doi.org/10.1377/hlthaff.2008.0966

Equal Employment Opportunity Commission (EEOC). (1997). *Fact sheet: Sexual harassment discrimination*. US EEOC. https://www.eeoc.gov/laws/guidance/fact-sheet-sexual-harassment-discrimination

Ferdman, B. M. (2017). Paradoxes of inclusion: Understanding and managing the tensions of diversity and multiculturalism. *The Journal of Applied Behavioral Science*, *53*(2), 235–263. https://doi.org/10.1177/0021886317702608

Foley, M., Oxenbridge, S., Cooper, R., & Baird, M. (2022). 'I'll never be one of the boys': Gender harassment of women working as pilots and automotive tradespeople. *Gender, Work & Organization*, *29*(5), 1676–1691.

Friedman, R. A., Tidd, S. A., Currall, S. C., & Tsai, J. C. (2000). What goes around comes around: The impact of personal conflict style on work conflict and stress. *The International Journal of Conflict Management*, *11*(1), 32–55. https://doi.org/10.1108/eb022834

Garner, J. T. (2012). Making waves at work: Perceived effectiveness and appropriateness of organizational dissent messages. *Management Communication Quarterly*, *26*(2), 224–240. https://doi.org/10.1177/0893318911431803

Garner, J. T. (2013). Dissenters, managers, and coworkers: The process of co-constructing organizational dissent and dissent effectiveness. *Management Communication Quarterly*, *27*(3), 373–395. https://doi.org/10.1177/0893318913488946

Goffman, E. (1956). *The presentation of self in everyday life*. University of Edinburgh, Social Sciences Research Centre.

Gómez-González, A., Girbés-Peco, S., González, J. M. J., & Casado, M. V. (2023). "Without support, victims do not report": The co-creation of a workplace sexual harassment risk assessment survey tool. *Gender, Work & Organization*, *30*(4), 1354–1386. https://doi.org/10.1111/gwao.12840

Gossett, L. M., & Kilker, J. (2006). My job sucks: Examining counterinstitutional web sites as locations for organizational member voice, dissent, and resistance. *Management Communication Quarterly*, *20*(1), 63–90. https://doi.org/10.1177/0893318906291729

Gross, M. A., & Guerrero, L. K. (2000). Managing conflict appropriately and effectively: An application of the competence model to Rahim's organizational conflict styles. *The International Journal of Conflict Management*, *11*(3), 200–226. https://doi.org/10.1108/eb022840

Guerrero, L. K., & Gross, M. A. (2014). Argumentativeness, avoidance, verbal aggressiveness, and verbal benevolence as predictors of partner perceptions of an individual's conflict style. *Negotiation Conflict Management Research*, 7(2), 99–120. https://doi.org/10.1111/ncmr.12029

Hennekam, S., & Bennett, D. (2017). Sexual harassment in the creative industries: Tolerance, culture and the need for change. *Gender, Work & Organization*, 24(4), 417–434. https://doi.org/10.1111/gwao.12176

Hill Collins, P. (1990). *Black feminist thought: Knowledge, consciousness, and the politics of empowerment*. Routledge. https://doi.org/10.4324/9780203900055

Hlavka, H. R. (2014). Normalizing sexual violence: Young women account for harassment and abuse. *Gender & Society*, *28*(3), 337–358. https://doi.org/10.1177/0891243214526468

Holling, M. A. (2019). "You intimidate me" as a microaggressive controlling image to discipline womyn of color faculty. *Southern Communication Journal*, *84*(2), 99–112. https://doi.org/10.1080/1041794X.2018.1511748

Hopeck, P., Desrayaud, N., Harrison, T. R., & Hatten, K. (2014). Deciding to use organizational grievance processes: Does conflict style matter? *Management Communication Quarterly*, *28*(4), 561–584. https://doi.org/10.1177/0893318914549811

Huang, L. V., & Zhang, K. (2019). Engagement, formality, and visibility: Managing paradoxes of using mobile instant messaging for work. *International Journal of Communication*, *13*, 1919–1938. https://ijoc.org/index.php/ijoc/article/view/7782/2633

Infante, D. A., & Gordon, W. I. (1985). Superiors' argumentativeness and verbal aggressiveness as predictors of subordinates' satisfaction. *Human Communication Research*, *12*(1), 117–125. https://doi.org/10.1111/j.1468-2958.1985.tb00069.x

Jameson, J. K. (2003). Transcending intractable conflict in health care: An exploratory study of communication and conflict management among anesthesia providers. *Journal of Health Communication*, *8*(6), 563–582. https://doi.org/10.1080/716100415

Jameson, J. K. (2004). Negotiating autonomy and connection through politeness: A dialectical approach to organizational conflict management. *Western Journal of Communication*, *68*(3), 257–277. https://doi.org/10.1080/10570310409374801

Kassing, J. W. (1998). Development and validation of the organizational dissent scale. *Management Communication Quarterly*, *12*(2), 183–229. https://doi.org/10.1177/0893318998122002

Kassing, J. W. (2000). Investigating the relationship between superior-subordinate relationship quality and employee dissent. *Communication Research Reports*, *17*(1), 58–69. https://doi.org/10.1080/08824090009388751

Kassing, J. W. (2002). Speaking up: Identifying employees' upward dissent strategies. *Management Communication Quarterly*, *16*(4), 187–209. https://doi.org/10.1177/089331802237234

Kassing, J. W. (2011). *Dissent in organizations*. Polity Press.

Keyton, J., & Menzie, K. (2007). Sexually harassing messages: Decoding workplace conversation. *Communication Studies*, *58*(1), 87–103. https://doi.org/10.1080/10510970601168756

Kuhn, T., & Poole, M. S. (2000). Do conflict management styles affect group decision-making? Evidence from a longitudinal field study. *Human Communication Research*, *26*(4), 558–590. https://doi.org/10.1111/j.1468-2958.2000.tb00769.x

Kunda, G. (1992). *Engineering culture: Control and commitment in a high-tech corporation*. Temple University Press. https://doi.org/10.1287/orsc.6.2.228

Lakoff, G., & Johnson, M. (1981). *Metaphors we live by*. University of Chicago Press. https://doi.org/10.2307/430414

Lumineau, F., Eckerd, S., & Handley, S. (2015). Inter-organizational conflicts: Research overview, challenges, and opportunities. *Journal of Strategic Contracting and Negotiation*, *1*(1), 42–64. https://doi.org/10.1177/2055563614568493

Lyu, M., Sun, B., & Zhang, Z. (2023). Linking online voice to workplace cyberbullying: Roles of job strain and moral efficacy. *Kybernetes*, *52*(5), 1778–1794. https://doi.org/10.1108/K-03-2021-0246

Malterud, A. S., & Nicotera, A. M. (2020). Expanding structurational divergence theory by exploring the escalation of incompatible structures to conflict cycles in nursing. *Management Communication Quarterly*, *34*(3), 384–401. https://doi.org/10.1177/0893318920912738

Malvini Redden, S., & Scarduzio, J. A. (2024). Mysteries, battles, and games: Exploring agency in metaphors about sexual harassment. *Management Communication Quarterly*, *38*(1), 117–146. https://doi.org/10.1177/08933189231172427

Mattar, L., Higgins, S. S. S., & Neves, J. A. B. (2022). Diversity and autonomy in the structuration of a multilevel organizational social network in a technology park. *Social Networks*, *68*, 346–355. https://doi.org/10.1016/j.socnet.2021.08.009

Meares, M. M., Oetzel, J. G., Torres, A., Derkacs, D., & Ginossar, T. (2004). Employee mistreatment and muted voices in the culturally diverse workplace. *Journal of Applied Communication Research*, *32*(1), 4–27. https://doi.org/10.1080/0090988042000178121

Mikkelsen, E. N., & Clegg, S. (2019). Conceptions of conflict in organizational conflict research: Toward critical reflexivity. *Journal of Management Inquiry*, *28*(2), 166–179. https://doi.org/10.1177/1056492617716774

Millender, L. G., Bisel, R. S., & Zanin, A. C. (2023). Why do employees choose defensive silence?: How concerns with formal powerholders undermine self-efficacy to dissent. *Communication Research Reports*, *40*(4), 216–225. https://doi.org/10.1080/08824096.2023.2236926

Moreland, J. J., & Apker, J. (2016). Conflict and stress in hospital nursing: Improving communicative responses to enduring professional challenges. *Health Communication*, *31*(7), 815–823. https://doi.org/10.1080/10410236.2015.1007548

Morrill, C. (2000, September). Using conflict in organizations. *Administrative Science Quarterly*, *45*(3), 638–640.

Mumby, D. K. (2015). Organizing power. *Review of Communication*, *15*(1), 19–38. https://doi.org/10.1080/15358593.2015.1015245

Mumby, D. K., & Kuhn, T. R. (2021). *Organizational communication: A critical introduction*. Sage.
Murphy, P., & Dee, J. (1992). Du Pont and Greenpeace: The dynamics of conflict between corporations and activist groups. *Journal of Public Relations Research*, *4*(1), 3–20. https://doi.org/10.1207/s1532754xjprr0401_02
Nicotera, A. M., & Clinkscales, M. J. (2010). Nurses at the nexus: A case study in structurational divergence. *Health Communication*, *25*(1), 32–49. https://doi.org/10.1080/10410230903473516
Nicotera, A. M., & Mahon, M. M. (2013). Between rocks and hard places: Exploring the impact of structurational divergence in the nursing workplace. *Management Communication Quarterly*, *27*(1), 90–120. https://doi.org/10.1177/0893318912458214
Oetzel, J. G., & Ting-Toomey, S. (2003). Face concerns in interpersonal conflict: A cross-cultural empirical test of the face negotiation theory. *Communication Research*, *30*(6), 599–624. https://doi.org/10.1177/0093650203257841
Oommen, D. (2017). A test of the relationships between host and home national involvements and the preferences for intercultural conflict management styles. *Journal of Intercultural Communication Research*, *46*(4), 314–329. https://doi.org/10.1080/17475759.2017.1329159
Phipps, A., & Young, I. (2015). Neoliberalisation and 'lad cultures' in higher education. *Sociology*, *49*(2), 305–322.
Plowman, K. D., ReVelle, C., Meirovich, S., Pien, M., Stemple, R., Sheng, V., & Fay, K. (1995). Walgreens: A case study in health care issues and conflict resolution. *Journal of Public Relations Research*, *7*(4), 231–258. https://doi.org/10.1207/s1532754xjprr0704_01
Putnam, L. L. (1988). Communication and interpersonal conflict in organizations. *Management Communication Quarterly*, *1*(3), 293–301. https://doi.org/10.1177/0893318988001003002
Putnam, L. L., Fairhurst, G. T., & Banghart, S. (2016). Contradictions, dialectics, and paradoxes in organizations: A constitutive approach. *Academy of Management Annals*, *10*(1), 65–171. https://doi.org/10.5465/19416520.2016.1162421
Putnam, L. L., & Poole, M. S. (1987). Conflict and negotiation. In F. M. Jablin, L. L. Putnam, K. H. Roberts, & L. W. Porter (Eds.), *Handbook of organizational communication: An interdisciplinary perspective* (pp. 549–599). Sage.
Putnam, L. L., & Wilson, C. (1982). Communication strategies in organizational conflicts: Reliability and validity of a measurement scale. In M. Burgoon (Ed.), *Communication yearbook 6* (pp. 629–652). Routledge. https://doi.org/10.1080/23808985.1982.11678515
Rahim, A., & Bonoma, T. V. (1979). Managing organizational conflict: A model for diagnosis and intervention. *Psychological Reports*, *44*(3), 1323–1344. https://doi.org/10.2466/pr0.1979.44.3c.1323
Rahim, M. A. (1983). A measure of styles of handling interpersonal conflict. *Academy of Management Journal*, *26*(2), 368–376. https://doi.org/10.5465/255985
Redmond, V., Jameson, J. K., & Binder, A. R. (2016). How superior–subordinate relationship quality and conflict management styles influence an employee's use of upward dissent tactics. *Negotiation and Conflict Management Research*, *9*(2), 164–172. https://doi.org/10.1111/ncmr.12072
Sahay, S., & Dwyer, M. (2023). I am not a 'hero': U.S. nurses' identity overlaps and conflict during COVID-19. *Health Communication*, *38*(12), 2537–2548. https://doi.org/10.1080/10410236.2022.2088021
Shenoy-Packer, S. (2015). Immigrant professionals, microaggressions, and critical sensemaking in the US workplace. *Management Communication Quarterly*, *29*(2), 257–275. https://doi.org/10.1177/0893318914562069
Shore, T., & Strauss, J. (2008). The political context of employee appraisal: Effects of organizational goals on performance ratings. *International Journal of Management*, *25*(4), 599–612.
Smith, R. C., & Eisenberg, E. M. (1987). Conflict at Disneyland: A root-metaphor analysis. *Communication Monographs*, *54*(4), 367–380. https://doi.org/10.1080/03637758709390239
Sue, D. W. (2010). *Microaggressions and marginality: Manifestation, dynamics, and impact*. John Wiley & Sons.
Thomas, K. W., & Kilmann, R. H. (1974). *Thomas-Kilmann conflict MODE instrument*. Xicom.
Ting-Toomey, S. (1988). Intercultural conflict styles: A face-negotiation theory. In Y. Y. Kim & W. Gudykunst (Eds.), *Theories in intercultural communication* (pp. 213–235). Sage.
Tracy, S. J., Lutgen-Sandvik, P., & Alberts, J. K. (2006). Nightmares, demons, and slaves: Exploring the painful metaphors of workplace bullying. *Management Communication Quarterly*, *20*(2), 148–185. https://doi.org/10.1177/0893318906291980

Trudel, J., & Reio, T. G. Jr. (2011). Managing workplace incivility: The role of conflict management styles: Antecedent or antidote? *Human Resource Development Quarterly*, *22*(4), 395–423. https://doi.org/10.1002/hrdq.20081

Turner, L. H., & Shuter, R. (2004). African American and European American women's visions of workplace conflict: A metaphorical analysis. *Howard Journal of Communications*, *15*(3), 169–183. https://doi.org/10.1080/10646170490479787

van Zoonen, W., Sivunen, A., & Rice, R. E. (2020). Boundary communication: How smartphone use after hours is associated with work-life conflict and organizational identification. *Journal of Applied Communication Research*, *48*(3), 372–392. https://doi.org/10.1080/00909882.2020.1755050

Weider-Hatfield, D., & Hatfield, J. D. (1995). Relationships among conflict management styles, levels of conflict, and reactions to work. *Journal of Social Psychology*, *135*(6), 687–699. https://doi.org/10.1080/00224545.1995.9713972

Wilson, S. R., & Waltman, M. S. (1988). Assessing the Putnam-Wilson organizational communication conflict instrument (OCCI). *Management Communication Quarterly*, *1*(3), 367–388. https://doi.org/10.1177/0893318988001003006

Womack, D. F. (1988). A review of conflict instruments in organizational settings. *Management Communication Quarterly*, *1*(3), 437–445. https://doi.org/10.1177/0893318988001003010

Woo, D., Putnam, L. L., & Riforgiate, S. E. (2017). Identity work and tensions in organizational internships: A comparative analysis. *Western Journal of Communication*, *81*(5), 560–581. https://doi.org/10.1080/10570314.2017.1312510

Zeng, C., & Chen, M. (2020). An exploration of the relationships between organizational dissent, employee burnout, and work–family balance: A cross-cultural comparison between China and Finland. *Communication Studies*, *71*, 1–16. https://doi.org/10.1080/10510974.2020.1749864

17 A Communicative Approach to Leadership

J. Kevin Barge

This chapter focuses on two key questions: "What counts as leadership?" and "What is the relationship between communication and leadership?" A common definition used by communication scholars describes leadership as "a co-created, performative, contextual, and attributional process where the ideas articulated in talk or action are recognized by others as progressing tasks that are important to them" (Barge & Fairhurst, 2008, p. 232). It is within the flows of communication that social understandings of what counts as leadership and expectations regarding its effectiveness within situations are generated. At face value, this simple definition seems to provide solid answers to both questions, defining leadership as a collective activity that progresses tasks that are important to people and establishing that communication is the primary social activity that creates our understanding of what constitutes leadership within situations and facilitates organizing to accomplish tasks.

While conceptual definitions are useful for demarcating the domain of study for a particular area such as leadership, they oftentimes obscure important distinctions, differences, and issues that differentiate scholars who work within an area. For example, several leadership scholars identify themselves as working within a social constructionist framework that examines the way that language, communication, and discourse constitute leadership within conversational episodes as well as the worldviews that inform what counts as leadership within organizations and societies. However, Fairhurst and Grant (2010) observe there is not a monolithic social constructionist approach to leadership. Rather, there are a number of dimensions that distinguish leadership scholars who take a social constructionist approach to leadership: whether it focuses on the social construction of reality or the construction of social reality; whether communicative approaches to leadership should focus on theory or praxis; to what degree communicative leadership approaches should attend to issues of power; or whether leadership research should be monomodal (focusing on language) or multimodal focusing on both the symbolic aspects of leadership and other "means of generating meaning through, for example, the use of space, the body, clothing, technology, and so on" that are more material or institutional (Fairhurst & Grant, 2010, p. 190). While definitions may highlight commonalities among theorists and researchers, they can also obscure important distinctions.

To answer the question, "What counts as leadership?," it is important to distinguish between individualistic and relational approaches to leadership that center on what counts as the appropriate unit of analysis for leadership theory and research. To answer the second question, "What is the relationship between leadership and communication?," it is crucial to differentiate between leadership communication as transmissive and leadership communication as the management of meaning. While such questions and distinctions are useful, the ultimate question is not whether an individualistic or relational approach to leadership

DOI: 10.4324/9781003484639-20

is better or whether a transmissive or constitutive approach to communication is superior, the ultimate question is how these distinctions can be employed by researchers and practitioners in useful ways to generate knowledge and action.

Individualistic and Relational Approaches to Leadership

The study of leadership has been of interest to writers, philosophers, and researchers for over 2000 years. Grint (2011) points out that some of the earliest written treatises on leadership focused on the conduct of war such as Sun Tzu's *The Art of War*, as well as the importance of civic and political leadership as reflected in the writings of Plato and Aristotle. The focus of studying leadership within military and political contexts was expanded to organizational contexts in the late 1800s and early 1900s by scholars such as Max Weber, Frederick Taylor, and Elton Mayo who were interested in the way that leadership influences the way individuals experience organizations (see Chapters 5 and 6). Contemporary leadership studies have continued to focus on the way that leadership is practiced in military, civic, governmental, and business contexts. While context can serve as one dimension to distinguish among leadership research and scholars, leadership studies may be more profitably distinguished by the unit of analysis it employs in its inquiry into leadership – whether it focuses on the characteristics of organizational leaders or whether it focuses on leadership as a relational practice that is accomplished through the interaction of organization actors.

Individualistic Leadership Approaches

Individualistic leadership approaches tend to focus on the individual traits, competencies, and actions that allow people to create and sustain leadership roles within organizations, communities, and societies. Such individuals are typically viewed as being privileged and are often characterized as either being "heroes" that can engage the major problems confronting a human system or as imbued with particular authority by an organization or institution. The former is illustrated in the lectures by Thomas Carlyle, one of the first modern writers of leadership in the 1800s, who equated leadership with individualistic heroism. As Grint (2011, p. 8) observes, "In the beginning was perhaps not god, but rather the god-like creatures that peppered the 1840 lectures of Thomas Carlyle, whose fascination with the 'Great Men' of history effectively reduced the role of mere mortals to 'extras'." The emphasis on individualistic heroism is reflected by the traditional focus of leadership studies and practice on military and political leaders such as Sun Tzu, Machiavelli, Napoleon, and Abraham Lincoln. While the traditional focus on military and political leaders has been broadened over the past few decades to include corporate and sports leaders such as Steve Jobs (founder of Apple), Jack Ma (founder of Alibaba), and Gregg Popovich (NBA basketball coach), "heroic" approaches to leadership remain focused on identifying men who seem to possess superhuman qualities and to a much lesser degree female business (e.g., Sheryl Sandberg), political (e.g., Angela Merkel), and sports leaders (e.g., Dawn Staley).

The historical concentration on "heroic" leadership was complemented in the early 1900s by a focus on administrative leadership that occurred within formal hierarchies. While both foci share an assumption that leadership should focus on individuals, the basis for leadership authority changes as administrative leadership (1) is equated with the power and influence that are granted to leaders given their roles as managers or administrators within organizational systems and (2) places emphasis on rationality with a key concern for logically understanding the context to ensure that the leadership responds appropriately to the social and structural constraints of the situation. Grint (2011) observes that this emphasis on administrative leadership and its concern with rationality can be traced from the early 1900s with its emphasis on scientific management, to the 1950s with the emergence of contingency analysis and systems analysis, to the 1970s and 1980s with its focus on Total Quality Management and Quality Circles, to contemporary leadership approaches that give attention to distributed leadership and followership (see Chapters 5–7).

"Heroic" and administrative models engaged leadership as an individually centered phenomenon. However, differences exist among specific leadership theories and models associated with an individualist leadership approach according to the following: (1) whether the theory or model focuses on identifying the traits or behaviors associated with leadership; (2) whether the theory or model assumes that a set of leadership traits and behaviors are universally effective across contexts or whether the effectiveness of a set of leadership traits and behaviors depends on the situation; and (3) whether the analytical focus should be placed on a single leader or a distributed set of leaders.

Traits versus Behaviors

One way to distinguish among individualistic leadership theories is whether they use traits or behaviors to explain how individuals create and sustain positions of leadership. Trait-based leadership theories focus on identifying the underlying communicative, social, physical, cognitive, or personality characteristics that explain how and why individuals create and sustain leadership positions. Behavior-based leadership theories focus on the overt verbal utterances or nonverbal behaviors that are performed by leaders and how they affect an individual's ability to act as a leader. Behavior-based leadership theories often rely on the concept of style, a pattern of messages and nonverbal acts that serve as a distinctive behavioral signature, to explain leadership. Regardless of whether a leadership theorist focuses on traits or behaviors, the underlying assumption is that individual differences should be correlated with various outcomes such as leadership effectiveness and emergence, follower motivation and satisfaction, and organizational productivity and efficiency.

Trait-based leadership approaches began by identifying the motives, traits, and abilities that distinguish leaders from non-leaders and contribute to leadership effectiveness. For example, Ensari et al. (2011) were interested in identifying the individual differences that predicted who would emerge as a leader and found that extraversion and authoritarian personality were strong predictors of leadership emergence. Leadership researchers such as Hoffman et al. (2011) have distinguished between trait-like and state-like individual differences where the former are viewed as more distal dispositional qualities such as motives, traits, and abilities that an individual is born with and that remain with a person for a lifetime with the latter being viewed as proximal situated differences such as knowledge and skills that can be learned and are particularly relevant for specific kinds of tasks and contexts. Rather than get caught in a "nature-nurture" debate over whether leaders are born or made, more contemporary research adopts a "both-and" position where both trait-like and state-like individual differences are expected to influence leadership and organizational performance with the question becoming which one exercises the most influence and when.

Behavior-based leadership approaches have focused on identifying the behavioral styles associated with leadership and have taken three distinct paths. One path may be characterized as "two-factor" theories of leadership where the behavior leaders exhibit to others can be characterized by two global dimensions – task and relational. Inspired by the 1950s Ohio State Leadership Studies, the task dimension focuses on behaviors that facilitated goal achievement, while the relational dimension centers on behaviors that indicate trust, warmth, support, empathy, and two-way communication. "Two-factor" theories of leadership typically use these two dimensions to create a grid where the factors are integrated to differentiate among competing behavioral styles a leader may employ. For example, Blake and Mouton's (1994) Managerial Grid Theory identified five different styles of leadership, including Country Club Management (high relationship, low task), Impoverished Management (low relationship, low task), Middle-of-the-Road Management (moderate relationship, moderate task), Authority-Compliance (low relationship, high task), and Team Management (high relationship, high task). Hersey and Blanchard (Hersey et al., 2012) identified four styles of leadership, including Telling (moderate to high task, low to moderate relationship), Selling (moderate to high task, moderate to high relationship), Delegating (low to moderate task, low to moderate relationship), and Participating (low to moderate task, moderate to high relationship). While the names of a particular style vary according to a specific theory or model, the assumption that leadership styles can be arrayed along the dual dimensions of task and relationship orientation remains the same (see Chapter 7).

A second stream of leadership style research can be traced to the 1930s Iowa Child Welfare Studies, which examined the consequences of autocratic, democratic, and laissez-faire leadership (Lewin et al., 1939). Autocratic leadership is associated with leaders having high levels of power, who employ centralized decision-making, and who direct their followers' behavior through one-way communication. Democratic leadership is typically associated with shared power and decentralized decision-making where leaders and followers employ two-way communication to jointly make decisions and pursue particular lines of action. Laissez-faire leadership is typically viewed as a "hands off" approach to leadership as leaders are relatively uninvolved with the activity of their followers. The notion that leadership styles can be differentiated along the dimensions of autocratic-democratic leadership has informed several approaches to leadership such as Likert's System IV, Vroom and Yetton's Contingency Theory of Leadership, and team leadership (see Chapter 7).

A third stream of research focuses on transformational leadership approaches. Initially conceptualized by James T. Burns (1978) and subsequently revised by Bernard Bass (1985), transformational leadership is concerned with explaining how leaders create changes in their followers' beliefs, needs, and attitudes through appeals to their higher-order needs using the strength of their personality and the creation of a compelling vision. Dimensions of transformational leadership include idealized influence, inspirational motivation, intellectual stimulation, and individualized consideration. Transformational leadership differs from transactional leadership as the latter is based on the notion that the relationship between leaders and followers is based on social exchange whereby leaders use contingent and noncontingent rewards to gain followers' compliance. Transformational leadership research has been interested in exploring the relationships between transformational leadership dimensions and outcomes such as performance, innovation, job satisfaction, organizational identification, and organizational citizenship behavior, yet the relationships between these individual behavioral dimensions and outcomes, as well as moderating and mediating variables that may influence these relationships, are not clear (van Knippenberg & Sitkin, 2013).

Universal versus Contextual

A second way that individualistic leadership theories or models are differentiated centers on whether the theory or model assumes that a single set of traits or leadership style is universally effective or whether the traits or behaviors needed to help progress tasks vary according to the situation. For example, some two-factor leadership behavioral theories such as Blake and Mouton's Managerial Grid Theory suggest that a single leadership style such as Team Management is universally effective across situations, while Hersey and Blanchard's Situational Leadership Theory suggests that job and psychological maturity determines whether a Selling, Telling, Consulting, or Participating leadership style is most appropriate for the situation. Similarly, while "heroic" theories of leadership presume that particular traits are effective across situations, situational trait-based theories such as Fiedler's Contingency Theory (1967) assume that there needs to be a match between leader traits and the situation in order for leadership to be effective. Fiedler identified three situational variables that can be used to determine whether more task-oriented or relationship-oriented traits are needed: (1) position power, (2) task structure, and (3) leader-member relationships. Depending on how these different dimensions are configured, they can generate different levels of favorableness where some situations are viewed as highly favorable, some highly unfavorable, and some in the middle. Fiedler's theory predicts that highly favorable or unfavorable situations require leaders to have task-oriented traits and those that are moderately favorable/unfavorable require leaders to have more relationally oriented traits. Any number of contextual variables such as culture, leader and follower gender, economic conditions, task and job characteristics, temporal factors, and social networks can influence the type of leadership that is needed to manage situations as well as moderate or mediate the relationship between leadership traits or behaviors and outcomes (Oc, 2018) (see Chapter 7).

A contextual variable that has been a central focus for leadership researchers is national culture. Comparative leadership studies have focused on the differences and similarities between the kinds of traits, values, and behaviors that characterize leaders and followers among differing national cultures. The GLOBE (Global Leadership and Organizational Behaviour Effectiveness) Project has focused on the interrelationships among culture, leadership, and effectiveness developing a network of more than 200 researchers representing 62 countries to systematically explore these interrelationships (see https://globeproject.com/foundation). The GLOBE studies have focused on developing a culturally endorsed theory of leadership (CLT) that is based on implicit leadership theory (Dorfman et al., 2012). Implicit leadership theories "represent the cognitive structures or schemas that specify what people expect from leaders in terms of leader traits or attributes" (Offermann & Coats, 2018, p. 513). The GLOBE studies are grounded in the belief that CLTs are an important phenomenon that cultures and societies rely on to socialize individuals into a particular set of values that make them more accepting of certain leadership practices than others. For example, if individuals have been socialized into a culture that is more egalitarian and emphasizes shared decision-making, they may prefer organizational leadership styles that are more democratic, emphasizing participatory and consultative decision-making.

The starting point for the GLOBE studies was to identify the key attributes that are perceived to facilitate or inhibit outstanding leadership which could then be used to develop leadership profiles to characterize nations or clusters of nations. The six dimensions that were used to construct CLT leadership profiles were as follows: (1) charismatic/value-based, (2) team-oriented, (3) participative, (4) humane-oriented, (5) autonomous, and (6) self-protective. Differences among these dimensions were then used to create clusters of nations that have a distinctive profile such as Latin Europe, Confucian Asia, the Middle East, and sub-Saharan Africa.

The GLOBE studies suggest that leadership attributes exist that are universal facilitators and inhibitors of leadership effectiveness. For example, Dorfman et al. (2012, pp. 507–508) state, "ideal leaders are expected to develop a vision, inspire others, and create a successful performance-oriented team within their organizations while behaving with honesty and integrity" regardless of culture. At the same time, Javidan et al. (2010) identified several dimensions that were culturally specific: status consciousness, bureaucratic, autonomous, face saving, humane, self-sacrificial/risk taking, and internally competitive. Culturally specific dimensions may be facilitative in some cultures, but inhibitive in others. Javidan et al. (2010) offer a compelling example of the way that status consciousness may play out in different cultures observing, "While it may be a good idea in an American organization to directly contact anyone with the right information regardless of their level, such behavior may be seen as a sign of disrespect to those in formal positions in a Brazilian organization" (p. 76).

The GLOBE studies provide a nuanced analysis of culture that explores both similarities and differences among various cultures using multiple dimensions. For leaders who wish to work in different cultures than their home culture, Dorfman et al. (2012) offer the following advice. First, match and exceed the expectations that are associated with a particular culture. The idea is for leaders, at a minimum, to match their behaviors with cultural expectations, and if they are to be highly successful, exceed them. Second, given that some leadership attributes are universal, if a leader is not sure what to do, then a leader should focus on "developing a vision, inspiring others, demonstrating integrity, being decisive, and creating a performance oriented culture" (Dorfman et al., 2012, p. 514).

Single versus Distributed Leadership

Individualistic approaches have tended to view leadership as either an individual-level phenomenon performed by a single individual or a distributed phenomenon performed by a group of individuals. The former attempts to identify the traits or behaviors that enable an individual to perform a leadership role. While studies of followership have grown in recent years as an attempt to conceptualize leadership as more of a relational phenomenon (Uhl-Bien, 2021a), they reinforce the notion that there are certain individuals who are leaders, and others who are followers and, further, that a person can be either a leader or a follower at a particular moment in time but not both. While some leadership approaches such as Leader-Member Exchange Theory (see Chapter 10) suggest that we need to look at the relationships leaders may form with followers, they still presume that there is an individual who is a leader within the network of relationships within an organization and others are non-leaders. Leaders may individualize their relationships with others forming either in-group relationships with followers characterized by closeness, trust, and support or out-group relationships characterized by distance, a lack of trust, and low levels of support (Martin et al., 2016), but they remain in a leadership position, while others enact followership roles.

In response to increasingly complex organizational systems, the notion that a single person can be a leader and direct the activities of an organization or team was complemented with the notion that leadership needed to be shared or distributed throughout members within a system. Denis et al. (2012) refer to this as "leadership in the plural" where focus is placed on "the combined influence of multiple leaders in specific organizational situations" (p. 211). Although different approaches to shared and distributed leadership exist, many of these approaches focus on individual leaders and the pattern of distribution of particular leadership roles or functions within a system. Denis et al. (2012) observe that leadership may be shared to enhance team effectiveness, leadership may be pooled at the top of organizations (e.g., senior management teams) to lead others, and leadership may be shared sequentially where leadership is spread across levels over time. For example, Manz and Sims' (2001) concept of super-leadership is premised on the idea that the formal team leader needs to adopt an empowering style that enables others within the team to also act as leaders. Distributed approaches to leadership recognize that leadership can be distributed vertically throughout various levels of a hierarchy as well as horizontally within a particular level of grouping of individuals. The analytical interest is on how varied configurations of distributed leadership generate different outcomes.

Focus of Individualist Leadership Approach

An individualistic leadership approach has a specific mindset that focuses on the mechanisms that explain how and why individual leaders act the way they do, determines whether the traits and behaviors that are needed to progress tasks cut across situations or must be tailored to the unique qualities of situations, and explores the way that individual leaders or distributed leadership affect various outcomes. Individualistic leadership approaches tend to view organization as a structure (O_2) by focusing on the way leadership is coordinated within organizations, the way that leadership structures such as distributed leadership influence organizations, and how other aspects of an organization's structure such as task structure, leader-member relationships, and national culture moderate or mediate the relationships between leadership and organizational outcomes.

Relational Approaches to Leadership

Starting in the early 2000s, relational approaches to leadership began to develop which offered a contrasting perspective to individualistic leadership approaches (Uhl-Bien & Ospina, 2012). Numerous lines of theorizing and research have emerged within a relational approach, including discursive leadership (Fairhurst, 2007), systemic constructionist leadership (Barge, 2012), and leadership-as-practice (LAP) (Raelin, 2016a). Although these lines of theorizing and research on leadership vary, relational leadership approaches tend to make one or more of the following assumptions: (1) relational leadership focuses on mundane interaction and practices; (2) relational leadership focuses on the role of symbolic and material actors within organizational systems; and (3) relational leadership needs to consider multiple agencies that constitute organizational systems.

Mundane Interaction and Practice

Rather than center attention on knowledge, skills, and actions that individual leaders need to possess to perform their role, relational approaches suggest leadership is located "in the ways actors engage, interact, and negotiate with one another to influence organizational understandings and produce outcomes" (Fairhurst & Uhl-Bien, 2012, p. 1044). This means that leadership theory and research should focus attention on the process and temporality of communication recognizing that different configurations of messages and utterances among individuals and groups in organizations are likely to create various leadership arrangements. Both quantitative and qualitative methods can be used to examine the relationships among communication processes, leadership, and outcomes. For example, the former is illustrated by Fairhurst et al. (1987), who used relational control theory to conceptualize individual messages in leadership conversations as one-up (asserting a relational definition), one-down (accepting a relational definition offered by another), and one-across messages (neither offering nor accepting a relational definition) that could be used to identify sequential control patterns and subsequently correlated with relational judgments regarding leadership. The latter is illustrated by Cooren and Fairhurst's (2004) use of discourse analysis to examine how control is exercised in conversations by the way that individuals initiate and close off sequences of interaction. Whether a quantitative or qualitative approach is employed, the focus is on unpacking the sequence and organization of talk using a variety of discourse analytic methods, including interaction analysis, critical discourse analysis, conversation analysis, narrative analysis, and membership categorization (Fairhurst & Uhl-Bien, 2012).

The focus on leadership talk-in-interaction does more than simply dissolve the leader-follower binary by viewing leadership as a processual phenomenon where individuals may move in and out of leadership positions or share leadership positions several times over the duration of an interaction; it also views leadership interaction as culturally, historically, and temporally situated. Raelin (2016b) observes, "we can see that it [leadership] has a cultural and grammatical history that can be traced to an origin that is humanly constructed (Grint, 2005; Hersted & Gergen, 2013)" (p. 132). Leadership talk acts from context and invites new contexts. Simply, pre-existing worldviews, perspectives, and stories as well as material realities exist which create a context that shapes the way that individuals interact within conversation. At the same time, the way individuals interact may alter and reframe the context, inviting new possibilities for meaning-making and action. For example, Barge (2004) examined how leaders can use "systemic stories" to create an understanding of the context that they are engaging in to make choices regarding how to intervene and reshape the context.

Human and Nonhuman Actants

Leadership studies have tended to focus on the way human actors create and sustain leadership. Inspired by approaches such as Actor-Network Theory (ANT) (Latour, 1999; see Chapter 3), some relational approaches have argued that the creation of leadership cannot be solely reduced to the interactions among human actors, and the influence of nonhuman actors must also be considered (Fairhurst & Cooren, 2009). For example, participative leadership involves more than leaders inviting others to give their opinion or jointly deliberate over important issues. The ability to create participative leadership also depends on nonhuman technologies that can be used to share data, poll organizational members, and make decisions as well as the physical or electronic space to convene meetings. Even if an individual wants to act as a participative leader, it would be difficult to pull off this performance unless other technologies and spaces are present that support this impulse. ANT uses the term *actants* as opposed to *actors* to capture both the human and nonhuman elements that contribute to the accomplishment of a social activity such as leadership.

Understanding a social activity requires articulating the network of human and nonhuman actants associated with the activity and how the actants' interrelationships contribute to its performance. For example, the authority presented by a university professor is composed of several human actants such as the professor's communication style as well as other professors and students collaborating with the professor on research and nonhuman actants such as the professor's title (e.g., endowed professorship) and framed degrees and awards prominently displayed in the professor's office. The authority of a university professor is not simply an individual characteristic; rather, it is supported, created, and enabled by the configuration of a larger network of human and nonhuman actors.

The use of ANT to inquire into leadership is nicely illustrated by Fairhurst's (2007) analysis of Rudy Giuliani's performance of charisma in his response to the 9/11 attacks on

New York's World Trade Center. Most studies of charismatic leadership tend to suggest that leadership charisma is a function of some combination of individual traits and behaviors that foster an impression that the leader is charismatic. From an ANT perspective, most studies of charismatic leadership tend to "black box" charisma attributing it to the contribution of a single actant, the individual leader, and ignore the other actants that are part of a network of human and nonhuman actants that contribute to the construction of charismatic leadership. Fairhurst (2007) demonstrates how the network of actants was orchestrated in such a way to create the attribution that Giuliani acted as a heroic and charismatic leader. Her analysis explored how human actants (e.g., needs and emotions of New York citizens), nonhuman actants such as architectural actants (e.g., where news conferences were held), and technological actants (e.g., telephone and geographical information systems) contributed to peoples' attribution that Giuliani was a charismatic leader.

Plurality and Relational Agency

Meindl et al. (1985) observed over three decades ago that the agency of leaders to create change within organizations is exaggerated. He argued that our fascination with the "romance of leadership" tends to move organizational members to ascribe important changes within an organization to the acts of leaders as opposed to other concepts such as organizational culture or technical systems. While it may be premature to dismiss completely the agency of individuals, the notion that human and nonhuman actors constitute networks that enable leadership suggests that agency is plural; that agency may best be located in the joint action among human and nonhuman actants in a network. This means that leadership researchers should not focus on the individual agency of organizational members and how their sense of agency enables or constraints available choices regarding actions and meaning-making. Rather, the focus needs to be on the practice that emerges among individuals. Raelin (2016c, p. 125) argues, "a practice is a coordinative effort among participants who choose through their own rules to achieve a distinctive outcome. It is, accordingly, less about what one person thinks or does and more about what people may accomplish together." This suggests that patterns of interaction become an actant when people talk and act together. Moreover, a distinct logic emerges from the interaction pattern that enables and constrains people from taking certain actions or making particular social choices. For example, sometimes when people engage in a heated argument that neither wants, they often feel that the argument itself acted as a third-party in the conversation that initiated and sustained the argument.

Raelin's (2016b, p. 137) notion of collaborative agency as aligning thoughts, actions, and interpretations reflects the notion that agency is an intersubjective accomplishment among people. Within his LAP framework, activities become attached to a practice, which cannot be reduced to single individuals, but instead focus on the relationality of leadership, making "the unit of analysis in collaborative agency…the intersubjective interaction among parties to the practice rather than the individuals who are presumably mobilizing the practice" (Raelin, 2016b, p. 142). For example, Raelin (2016b) has identified several leadership activities, including task (scanning, signaling, weaving, stabilizing) and relational (inviting, unleashing, reflecting) whose performance is not associated with a particular individual, but rather with the activity of multiple actants and authorities. As a result, agency is not singular; it is plural as each actant carries its own sense of agency that intertwines with other actants to create a hybrid agency that reflects different elements of its network.

Summary Relational Leadership Approach

A relational approach to leadership differs from an individualistic approach given its emphasis on everyday interaction, human and nonhuman actants, and the notion of collaborative agency. A relational approach to leadership clearly engages organization as a process (O_1) where the mundane interaction of human and nonhuman actants creates and invites different patterns of organizing. These patterns of organizing may become institutionalized over time – in the form of ideologies, ritualistic or normative interaction, stories, and the like – which give rise to organized patterns within organizations such as networks and role structures (O_2). As organizational members interact, they may explicitly reference these organized patterns or these organized patterns may enter the interaction as silent actors who nonetheless exert influence within the ongoing conversation. For example, a team member may "Call the question" to end discussion over an issue and take a vote. Other team members recognize this utterance as being tied to a historical nonhuman actant, Robert's Rules of Order, a normative parliamentary model for conducting meetings, that only must be indirectly referenced in order to shape the discussion.

Leadership and Communication

Fairhurst and Connaughton (2014a, 2014b) suggest that leadership research has viewed communication as both a transmissive and meaning-making (constitutive) phenomenon. These two conceptualizations of communication represent complementary alternatives regarding the function and purpose of leadership communication. Herein, the term *constitutive* is used as the counterpart to *transmissive*, to maintain consistency with the framework of this book.

Leadership Communication as Transmission

A transmissive approach to leadership communication views communication as a form of information transfer where messages are encoded by a source, through a channel or conduit, and are decoded by a receiver. Communication effectiveness is judged according to message fidelity where effective communication is clear and that the message and the meaning the source intended to send are received and clearly understood by the receiver. Barriers that may frustrate the ability to accurately decode the message may include obstacles that block or interfere with the transmission of the message as well as perceptual filters that may influence the interpretation of the message (see Chapter 1).

Transmissive models tend to use an input-process-output orientation with communication frequently conceptualized as a process. For example, Chaudhry and Joshi's (2018) model of transformational leadership and commitment to change identified transformational leadership as its key concept and then identified five types of transformative leadership communication – organizational vision, inspiration, change information, feedback, and emotional support. Moving from a focus on input-process to process-outcome, they then hypothesized that these types of communication would influence affective commitment to change and organizational identification. Studies that examine the process-outcome link operationalize communication in a variety of ways, including interaction coding or self-report surveys that capture perceptions of communication processes. The former is illustrated by Lehman-Willenbrock et al.'s (2015) study where they coded interaction within team meetings in terms of problem-solving and solution-focused communication and discovered that transformational leadership was positively related to problem-solving communication. The latter is represented by Men's (2014) study that revealed that transformational leadership influenced an organization's symmetrical internal communication channels and that transformational leaders tended to use rich face-to-face channels to communicate with employees.

Fairhurst and Connaughton (2014a, 2014b) observe that leadership scholars who employ transmissional models of communication, knowingly or unknowingly, view communication as a message that is encoded by a source, transmitted through a channel, and decoded by a receiver. They do not problematize the meaning-making process, which leads them to focus on issues relating to message clarity, the frequency and timing of communication, informational adequacy, communication effectiveness, the way that messages are used to formulate and convey vision, and message characteristics such as message complexity. For example, they note that several studies relating to transformational leadership and visionary leadership focus on elements of communication that have a transmissional flavor such as idea density and grammatical complexity (Balthazard et al., 2009) and the importance of being careful encoders (transmitters) and decoders (listeners) of messages (Berson & Avolio, 2004).

Leadership Communication as the Management of Meaning

Leadership communication as the management of meaning focuses on the way communication is employed by individuals and organizations to make sense of situations and centers attention on the formative power of language and communication to shape meaning. For example, Grint (2005) argued that the kinds of situations that leaders must respond to are not separate from the actions they undertake. Rather than assume that situations dictate how leaders respond to contextual demands, Grint contended that leaders use communication to shape the very situation that they find themselves engaging. In an analysis of President Bush's rhetoric prior to the decision to invade Iraq, he concluded the Bush administration used communication in a way to frame the situation as a crisis, which would mandate and legitimate his use of a command style of leadership. The appropriateness and effectiveness of leadership communication is both constrained by the pre-existing situation and can also be altered through communication.

Leadership communication research that operates within a communication as the management of meaning framework focuses attention on how individuals position themselves to make meaning from within the flow of communication, the strategies that individuals may use to influence the meaning-making process, and the consequences of patterns of meaning-making. For example, Shotter (2011) and his associates have been interested in creating an approach to leadership grounded in social poetics that centers attention on how individual leaders may pick up on the way that meaning is made from within the flow of conversation and alter it. Rather than assume that leaders only cognitively plan their responses, Shotter argues for the importance of embodied ways of knowing and using preconscious feelings to explore how leaders use their body to notice important elements of the unfolding conversation as the basis for additional inquiry and to act in ways that both pick up on what has been previously uttered and gesture toward new possibilities for meaning-making. Fairhurst's (Fairhurst, 2011; Fairhurst & Sarr, 1996) research program on leadership as framing has explored the ways that individual leaders may use frames such as spin, comparison/contrast, metaphors, and stories to create ways of interpreting and making sense of persons, situations, and events. Her research examines not only the kinds of frames that leaders may employ to influence the meaning-making power but also the processes such as mental models that influence how leaders make sense of the situation and select frames as well as the consequences of employing different frames on the way that future action and power relationships are constructed.

Within recent years, there has been a growing interest in leadership studies that focus on the management of meaning. For example, Fairhurst's (Fairhurst, 2011; Fairhurst & Sarr, 1996) program of research has examined the variety of tactics that leaders may use to frame issues and problems and how that can facilitate organizing processes. Her more recent research focuses on how "discursive knots," intersecting discursive formations, constitute tensions and paradoxes and how they may be untangled (Fairhurst & Putnam, 2023). Barge (2004) has explored how inquiry – through questioning and story making – can shape the way that leaders and organizational members co-create meaning. Leadership scholars who operate from the communication as the management of meaning model focus on addressing questions that relate to the way that individuals make sense of situations and communication, how they can intervene in the process of meaning-making, and the consequences that are generated by shaping the meaning-making process in particular ways.

The Changing Focus of Leadership Theory and Research

This chapter is organized around two key questions: "What counts as leadership?" and "What is the relationship between communication and leadership?" The first question focuses on the appropriate unit of analysis for leadership studies with individualistic approaches focusing attention on individual organizational leaders or networks of organizational leaders and the personal qualities, traits, and behaviors that distinguish leaders from non-leaders and enable leaders to create and sustain leadership positions and achieve excellence. Relational approaches center attention on the everyday interactional processes of organizational members and how their symbolic interaction is connected with material actants within the organization to create varied forms of leadership. The second question focuses on the ways that leadership scholars have conceptualized communication and the perspectives of communication as transmissive message-centered process and communication as a constitutive meaning-making phenomenon are both represented in the research.

The answers to the two questions generate four distinct research orientations for leadership theory and research, presented in Figure 17.1: (1) individual-transmissive, (2) individual-constitutive, (3) relational-transmissive, and (4) relational-constitutive. These research orientations provide a working vocabulary for approaching leadership recognizing that (1) certain orientations might be more appropriate given the kinds of research questions scholars pose or the types of problems that individual leaders engage, and (2) these alternative orientations may be integrated or blended in ways to address different problems. For example, consider an organization that is a victim of a cyberattack releasing sensitive employee personal information. A scholar or practitioner employing a relational-transmissive approach would pay attention to the way that leaders disseminate information through various communication channels and networks to update people about the cyberattack and how the organization planned on addressing it. Scholars or practitioners focused on relational-constitutive would pay attention to the role of communication in shaping organizational identity and culture and how that facilitates or inhibits relational coordination among individuals and units. Organizational leadership may take this opportunity to reinforce that it cares for its employees and will go above and beyond to mitigate harms caused

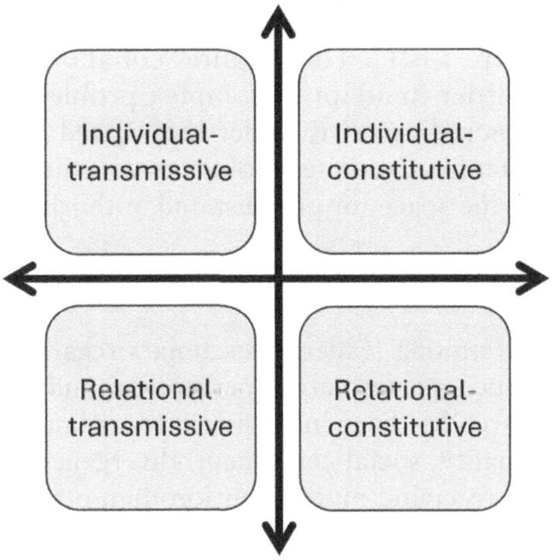

Figure 17.1 Research Orientations for Leadership Theory and Research

by the cyberattack and protect them in the future. It is not that one orientation is superior to another; they simply draw attention to different aspects of leadership communication and both may be important to pursue in order to fully address the problem.

The kinds of communication puzzles and problems that intrigue leadership theorists, researchers, and practitioners are a product of the sociopolitical environment. The focus on democratic leadership in the 1930s (see Chapter 6) was in part a response to the rise of authoritarian and fascist forms of leadership in Germany, Italy, and Japan. Leadership theorists' preoccupation with visionary and transformative leadership approaches in the 1980s was in response to societal and economic challenges in the United States with a concern regarding how to build organizations that could be innovative, productive, and competitive. The rise of leadership theory and research that focused on meaning-making during the 1980s and 1990s emerged from a larger interpretive and discursive turn in the social sciences.

How might we describe the current sociopolitical environment? Spector (2020) notes that the Western world currently seems to be in a state of upheaval given climate change, "waves of migration, the rise of would-be authoritarians in democratic societies, terrorist attacks, foreign interference in domestic elections, voter suppression, children in cages, #BlackLivesMatter and #MeToo movements .... And then the pandemic struck!" (Spector, 2020, pp. 203–304). The current sociopolitical environment highlights three important research areas that require renewed attention given the "new normal" of the historical moment: (1) leadership and complex uncertain environments, (2) leadership and difference, and (3) leadership and internationalization.

Leadership and Complex Uncertain Environments

The COVID-19 pandemic along with other persistent sociopolitical issues highlights that many of the problems that leadership engages are "wicked problems," complex, potentially unsolvable, and rapidly changing (Grint, 2020; Tourish, 2020). Uhl-Bien (2021a) observes, "In a complex world, research and practice must focus on how we can enable leaders and organizations to adapt more quickly in the face of complexity challenges and pressures" (p. 1401). This requires collaborative leadership approaches that facilitate learning in order to adapt to complex problems. This has renewed interest in a variety of topics, including crisis leadership, shared and collaborative leadership, rapid change, and the use of information technology to coordinate dispersed work activities as well as how crises create the space for populist and authoritarian forms of leadership.

Leadership and Difference

There is a growing concern among leadership scholars regarding the role that social difference plays in the emergence, performance, perception, and consequences of leadership. Leadership theory and research has been inconsistent regarding its focus on the dynamics of race, ethnicity, gender, sexuality, social class, neurodivergence, and (dis)ability with some social groups and identities receiving more attention than others. For example, the role of gender in leadership studies has received a great amount of attention exploring how gender influences the way that men and women create and sustain leadership positions, how gender influences the appropriateness and effectiveness of certain leadership traits and styles, and the consequences of gendered leadership (Shen & Joseph, 2021).

On the other hand, race has received scant attention by leadership scholars, remaining on the margins of leadership theory and research (Ladkin & Patrick, 2022). A notable exception in the communication discipline is Patricia Parker's (2004, 2020) research on African American women leaders. She was one of the first researchers to focus on the intersectionality of gender and race. Future leadership research should explore a broad range of social differences, categories, and identities with a focus on studying social identities in an intersectional fashion as most studies of leadership tend to view social categories such as race and gender in isolation (Begeny et al., 2021; see also Chapter 14 and Parker, 2014). A second opportunity for future inquiry is to heighten our focus on inclusive leadership. Inclusive leadership is an approach that centers on developing practices that embrace difference and strive to create culture of belonging (Buzzanell & Pyatovskaya, in press). If we accept the notion that difference is the natural state of our social worlds, then leadership approaches that embrace and work with difference in all its forms need to be developed.

Internationalization and Culture

Studies that explore the role of internationalization in leadership have centered mainly on how cultural differences and dimensions characterize leadership in particular countries as highlighted by the GLOBE studies. Given the international flow of labor and the fact that global organizations have employees in multiple countries, leadership studies need to expand their focus to investigate how internationalization affects the relationships between leadership and the international composition of work teams, how leadership intersects with immigration and visa status, the role of leadership in managing expats, how leadership manages peoples' feelings of precarity due to outsourcing and flexible labor arrangements, and the way that leadership employs technology to manage international teams.

The study of leadership remains an important topic that occupies the attention of organizations, communities, and societies. There are many ways that scholars can engage the communicative dynamics of leadership and recent sociopolitical shifts in the environment suggest a renewed interest in the intersections among leadership, complex disruptive environments, difference, and internationalization. The ongoing challenge for leadership scholars and practitioners is creating and adapting communication practices that engage an always evolving set of communication problems and shifting sociopolitical environment.

Recommended Supplementary Readings

Fairhurst, G. T., & Connaughton, S. (2014). Leadership. In L. L. Putnam & D. K. Mumby (Eds.), *The SAGE handbook of organizational Communication* (pp. 401–423). Sage.
Fairhurst, G. T. (2001). Dualisms in leadership communication. In L. L. Putnam & F. M. Jablin (Eds.), *The new handbook of organizational communication* (pp. 379–439). Sage.
Jablin, F. M., Putnam, L. L., Roberts, K., & Porter, L. (1987). *The handbook of organizational communication: An interdisciplinary perspective*. Sage.

These handbook chapters provide state-of-the-art reviews on the relationship between communication and leadership. They trace the historical evolution of leadership from being primarily grounded in leadership psychology (1987), to a dialectical view of communication and leadership (2004), to a complex view of leadership communication (2014) as a relational process that embraces both transmission and meaning-centered models of communication, that needs to take into account human-material organizing, and that recognizes that organizing is infused with power dynamics, reflexivity, and moral accountability.

Grant, D., Fairhurst, G. T., Grint, K., & Jackson, B. (Eds.). (2010). Social constructionist views of leadership. *Management Communication Quarterly, 24*(2).

This special issue focuses on the way that social constructionist approaches have been used to reconceptualize leadership. The opening essay by Gail Fairhurst and David Grant provides a valuable framework for teasing apart the many dimensions of social constructionism and highlighting the many faces that social constructionism may take in leadership studies.

Jian, G., & Fairhurst, G. T. (in press). *The Routledge handbook of organizational leadership communication*. Routledge.

This state-of-the-art review explicitly explores leadership communication and its relationship to a variety of theoretical perspectives, including critical, constitutive, dialectical, dialogical, and leadership-as-practice as well as contemporary issues such as ethics, diversity, technology, collaboration, and strategy.

Uhl-Bien, M., & Ospina, S. M. (2012). *Advancing relational leadership theory: A conversation among perspectives*. Information Age Publishing.

Relational leadership is an alternative perspective to traditional individualistic approaches to leadership. This book provides a wide-ranging overview of relational leadership from a variety of perspectives including communication, critical leadership studies, and psychodynamic theory as well as examines the way that relational leadership engages with issues of social change, shared leadership, and working with diverse staff in organizations.

Bryman, A., Collinson, D. L., Grint, K., Jackson, B., & Uhl-Bien, M. (Eds.). (2011). *The SAGE handbook of leadership*. Sage.

It provides an excellent overview of the history of leadership as well as coverage of macro and sociological perspectives, political and philosophical perspectives, and psychological perspectives on leadership. Fairhurst's chapter on discursive leadership helps situate what a communicative approach offers in relation to existing perspectives within leadership studies.

Grint, K. (2010). *Leadership: A very short introduction*. Oxford University Press.

An excellent introduction to the study of leadership that is organized around key questions such as what is leadership, are leaders born or bred, what is followership, and is leadership important to organizations?

Northouse, P. G. (2021). *Leadership theory and practice* (9th ed.). Sage.

An introductory text that provides an overview of general leadership approaches such as trait, skills, and behaviors as well as specific theories and types of leadership such as leader-member exchange, authentic leadership, and servant leadership.

Johnson, C. E., & Hackman, M. Z. (2018). *Leadership: A communication perspective* (7th ed.). Waveland Press.

An introductory text to leadership with a distinctive communication approach that examines how leadership communication in terms of styles, behaviors, and messages relates to issues of power, influence, and crisis management within various contexts such as teams, organizations, and the public.

Important Concepts: Define and Discuss

Actants
Administrative leadership
Autocratic leadership
Behavior-based leadership
Collaborative agency
Democratic leadership
Distributed leadership
Environment
Heroic leadership
Individualistic approach to leadership
Internationalization
Leadership
Relational approach to leadership
Race
Trait-based leadership
Transactional leadership
Transformational leadership

Discussion Questions

1. Compare and contrast individualistic and relational approaches to leadership. Imagine that you have been asked to design a leadership training program for mid-level managers in an organization. If you adopted an individualistic approach to leadership, what knowledge, skills, and abilities would you emphasize in your training program? What knowledge, skills, and abilities would you emphasize if you adopted a relational approach?
2. When is it more useful to view leadership as primarily a transmission or meaning-making process? Are there particular kinds of situations or problems where it may be helpful to view communication through a transmission lens? A meaning-making lens? Both simultaneously?
3. Make a list of the various elements (e.g., task structure, culture, history, and gender) that may serve as a context for leadership communication. What elements do you consider to be most important? Least important? When do particular elements become more or less important? Why?
4. Information and communication technologies (ICTs) have dramatically altered modes of organizing. How might the prevalence of ICTs in contemporary life alter our conceptualizations of individualistic and relational approaches to leadership? Our conceptualizations about leadership communication as a transmission or meaning-making process?

Practitioner's Corner

The study of leadership is marked by a number of varied approaches and perspectives, each generating a distinct take regarding what leadership activities need to be taken to facilitate organizing. For example, the GLOBE leadership studies move individuals to think about the importance of culture, while Hersey and Blanchard's Life Cycle theory focuses attention on the maturity and capacity of the people we are leading and how that might affect the kind of leadership style that is needed to facilitate organizing. Distributed leadership approaches focus our attention on the configuration of individual leaders within an organization and how they are connected with the process of organizing. None of these approaches is necessarily incorrect and the advice that flows from a particular perspective is not inherently wrong. Taken collectively, these various approaches, perspectives, and theories simply provide different lenses to make sense of situations and determine what actions need to be performed.

It is more useful to think of these different perspectives as providing a variety of resources that organizational leaders may use to engage situations and make wise choices about how to act. Simply, organizational leaders need to become mindful of the situation they are engaging, reflective of their ethical stance that they use when making decision about how to act, and endeavor to create lines of action that fit with the demands of the situation and align with their ethical stance. Scharmer (2016) suggests that leaders need to engage in the activity of "presencing" versus "downloading" as the former directs leaders to attune to the unique qualities of situations and to be open to reconfiguring their perspective on the situation, whereas the latter suggests that organizational leaders use a set of *a priori* fixed frameworks to understand and engage situations. Operating from a communication as design perspective, Barge (2012, 2015) suggests that leaders and individuals undertaking leadership activities need to determine what communication problem(s) they are trying to address in the situation, brainstorm various options that might address the problem(s), and select actions that reflect the leader's sensibility or core values regarding how to work with people and manage the problem(s).

Differing leadership frameworks should not necessarily be viewed as competing; rather, they can be viewed as complementary each providing a different way to read a situation and offering a different repertoire of actions to perform. From this perspective, organizational leaders need to ask themselves four important questions:

1 What values inform my approach to relating and organizing?
2 How do I frame the problems in the present situation?
3 What communicative actions can I make to address the problems I have named?
4 What communicative actions best fit with my value system and the needs of the situation to progress tasks?

The first question requires individuals to reflect on the key values that inform their approach toward relating to people and organizing activity. Questions 2–4 have people draw on their past experience as well as the theoretical frameworks to view the potential problems, actions, and solutions from a variety of perspectives. For example, what problems do I give attention to if I view the situation through Fiedler's Leadership Contingency Theory? Raelin's practice theory? Fairhurst's leadership framing approach? Rather than rely on one's pet theories regarding leadership, an approach based on "presencing" has people examine a situation from multiple perspectives, assuming that the more alternative readings of situations that can be generated, the more likely it is that a leader will select one that fits with the unique characteristics of the situation and will progress tasks. By aligning potential actions simultaneously with a leader's core values and the unique particulars of a situation, leaders can create patterns of interaction over time that are both consistent with their core values and uniquely adapted to the demands of the situation.

References

Balthazard, P. A., Waldman, D. A., & Warren, J. E. (2009). Predictions of the emergence of transformational leadership in virtual decision teams. *Leadership Quarterly*, *20*, 651–663. https://doi.org/10.1016/j.leaqua.2009.06.008

Barge, J. K. (2004). Antenarrative and managerial practice. *Communication Studies*, *55*, 106–127. https://doi.org/10.1080/10510970409388608

Barge, J. K. (2012). Systemic constructionist leadership and working from within the present moment. In S. Ospina & M. Uhl-Bien (Eds.), *Advancing relational leadership theory: A conversation among perspectives* (pp. 107–142). Information Age Publishing.

Barge, J. K. (2015). Consulting as collaborative co-inquiry. In G. Bushe & R. Marshak (Eds.), *Dialogic organizational development: Theory and practice* (pp. 177–196). Berrett-Koehler.

Barge, J. K., & Fairhurst, G. F. (2008). Living leadership: A systemic constructionist approach. *Leadership*, *4*, 227–251. https://doi.org/10.1177/1742715008092360

Bass, B. M. (1985). *Leadership and performance beyond expectations*. Free Press.

Begeny, C., Wong, C. Y. E., Kirby, T. A., & Rink, F. (2021). Gender, race, & leadership. In *Oxford Research Encyclopedia of Psychology*. https://doi.org/10.1093/acrefore/9780190236557.013.450

Berson, Y., & Avolio, B. (2004). Transformational leadership and the dissemination of organizational goals: A case of a telecommunication firm. *Leadership Quarterly*, *15*, 625–646. https://doi.org/10.1016/j.leaqua.2004.07.003

Blake, R. R., & Mouton, J. S. (1994). *The managerial grid*. Gulf Publishing Company.

Burns, J. M. (1978). *Leadership*. Harper.

Buzzanell, P. M., & Pyatovskaya, E. (in press). Leadership communication and diversity, equity, and inclusion. In G. Jian & G. T. Fairhurst (Eds.), *The Routledge handbook of organizational leadership communication*. Routledge.

Chaudhry, S., & Joshi, C. (2018). Effect of transformational leader communication on affective commitment to change. *International Journal of Leadership*, *6*, 27–35. https://www.i-scholar.in/index.php/ijl/article/view/172880

Cooren, F., & Fairhurst, G. T. (2004). Speech timing and spacing: The phenomenon of organizational closure. *Organization, 11*, 797–828. https://doi.org/10.1177/1350508404047252
Denis, J., Langley, A., & Sergi, V. (2012). Leadership in the plural. *The Academy of Management Annals*, *6*, 211–283. https://doi.org/10.1080/19416520.2012.667612.
Dorfman, P., Javidan, M., Hanges, P., Dastmalchian, A., & House, R. (2012). GLOBE: A twenty year journey into the intriguing world of culture and leadership. *Journal of World Business*, *47*, 504–518. https://doi.org/10.1016/j.jwb.2012.01.004
Ensari, N., Riggio, R. E., Christian, J., & Carslaw, G. (2011). Who emerges as a leader? Meta-analyses of individual differences as predictors of leadership emergence. *Personality and Individual Differences*, *51*, 532–536. https://doi.org/10.1016/j.paid.2011.05.017
Fairhurst, G. T. (2007). *Discursive leadership*. Sage.
Fairhurst, G. T. (2011). *The power of framing: Creating the language of leadership*. Jossey-Bass.
Fairhurst, G. T., & Connaughton, S. (2014b). Leadership. In L. L. Putnam & D. Mumby (Eds.), *The SAGE handbook of organizational communication* (pp. 401–423). Sage.
Fairhurst, G. T., & Connaughton, S. L. (2014a). Leadership: A communicative perspective. *Leadership*, *10*, 7–35. https://doi.org/10.1177/1742715013509396
Fairhurst, G. T., & Cooren, F. (2009). Leadership as the hybrid production of presence(s). *Leadership*, *5*, 469–490. https://doi.org/10.1177/1742715009343033
Fairhurst, G. T., & Grant, D. (2010). The social construction of leadership: A sailing guide. *Management Communication Quarterly*, *24*, 171–210. https://doi.org/10.1177/0893318909359697
Fairhurst, G. T., & Putnam, L. L. (2023). *Performing organizational paradoxes*. Taylor & Francis.
Fairhurst, G. T., Rogers, L. E., & Sarr, R. A. (1987). Management-subordinate control patterns and judgements about the relationship. In M. McLaughin (Ed.), *Communication yearbook 10* (pp. 395–415). Sage.
Fairhurst, G. T., & Sarr, R. A. (1996). *The art of framing: Managing the language of leadership*. Jossey-Bass.
Fairhurst, G. T., & Uhl-Bien, M. (2012). Organizational discourse analysis (ODA): Examining leadership as a relational process. *The Leadership Quarterly*, *23*, 1043–1062. https://doi.org/10.1016/j.leaqua.2012.10.005
Fiedler, F. E. (1967). *A theory of leadership effectiveness*. McGraw-Hill.
Grint, K. (2005). Problems, problems, problems: The social construction of leadership. *Human Relations*, *58*, 1467–1494. https://doi.org/10.1177/0018726705061314
Grint, K. (2011). A history of leadership. In A. Bryman, D. Collinson, K. Grint, M. Uhl-Bien, & B. Jackson (Eds.), *The SAGE handbook of leadership* (pp. 3–14). Sage. https://doi.org/10.1177/0018726705061314
Grint, K. (2020). Leadership, management and command in the time of the Coronavirus. *Leadership*, *16*(3), 314–319. https://doi.org/10.1177/1742715020922445
Hersey, P., Blanchard, K. H., & Dewey, E. J. (2012). *Management of organizational behavior* (10 ed.). Pearson.
Hersted, L., & Gergen, K. J. (2013). *Relational leading: Practices for dialogically based collaboration*. Taos Institute Publications.
Hoffman, B. J., Woeher, D. J., Maldagen-Youngjohn, R., & Lyons, B. D. (2011). Great man or great myth? A quantitative review of the relationship between individual differences and leader effectiveness. *Journal of Occupational and Organizational Psychology*, *84*, 347–381. https://doi.org/10.1348/096317909X485207
Javidan, M., Dorfman, P. W., Howell, J. P., & Hanges, P. J. (2010). Leadership and cultural context: A theoretical and empirical examination based on project GLOBE. In N. Nohria & R. Khurana (Eds.), *Handbook of leadership theory and practice* (pp. 335–376). Harvard Business Press.
Ladkin, D., & Patrick, C. B. (2022). Whiteness in leadership theorizing: A critical analysis of race in Bass' transformational leadership theory. *Leadership*, *18*(2), 205–223. https://doi.org/10.1177/17427150211066442
Latour, B. (1999). *Pandora's hope: Essays on the reality of science studies*. Harvard University Press.
Lehman-Willenbrock, N., Meinecke, A. L., Rowold, J., & Kauffeld, S. (2015). How transformational leadership works during team interactions: A behavioral process analysis. *The Leadership Quarterly*, *26*, 1017–1033. https://doi.org/10.1016/j.leaqua.2015.07.003
Lewin, K., Lippitt, R., & White, R. K. (1939). Patterns of aggressive behavior in experimentally created "social climates. *Journal of Science Psychology*, *10*, 271–299.

Manz, C. C., & Sims, H. P. Jr (2001). *The new super-leadership: Leading others to lead themselves*. Berrett-Koehler.
Martin, R., Guillaume, Y., Thomas, G., Lee, A., & Epitropaki, O. (2016). Leader-member exchange (LMX) and performance: A meta-analytic review. *Personnel Psychology*, *69*, 67–121.
Meindl, J. R., Ehrlich, S. B., & Dukerich, J. M. (1985). The romance of leadership. *Administrative Science Quarterly*, *30*, 78–102. https://doi.org/10.2307/255897
Men, L. R. (2014). Strategic internal communication: Transformational leadership, communication channels, and employee satisfaction. *Management Communication Quarterly*, *28*, 264–284. https://doi.org/10.1177/0893318914524536
Oc, B. (2018). Contextual leadership: A systematic review of how contextual factors shape leadership and its outcomes. *The Leadership Quarterly*, *29*, 218–235. https://doi.org/10.1016/j.leaqua.2017.12.004
Offermann, L. R., & Coats, M. R. (2018). Implicit theories of leadership: Stability and change over two decades. *The Leadership Quarterly*, *29*, 513–522. https://doi.org/10.1016/j.leaqua.2017.12.003
Parker, P. S. (2004). *Race, gender, and leadership: Re-envisioning organizational leadership from the perspectives of African American women executives*. Routledge.
Parker, P. S. (2014). Difference and organizing. In L. L. Putnam & D. K. Mumby (Eds.), *The SAGE handbook of organizational communication: Advances in theory, research, and methods* (pp. 619–643). Sage.
Parker, P. S. (2020). *Ella baker's catalytic leadership: A primer on community engagement and communication for social justice* (Vol. 2). University of California Press.
Raelin, J. A. (Ed.) (2016a). *Leadership-as-practice: Theory and application*. Routledge.
Raelin, J. A. (2016b). Imagine there are no leaders: Reframing leadership as collaborative agency. *Leadership*, *12*, 131–158. https://doi.org/10.1177/1742715014558076
Raelin, J. A. (2016c). It's not about the leaders: It's about the practice of leadership. *Organizational Dynamics*, *45*, 124–131.
Scharmer, O. C. (2016). *Theory U: Leading from the future as it emerges* (2nd ed.). Berrett-Koehler.
Shen, W., & Joseph, D. L. (2021). Gender & leadership: A criterion-focused review and research agenda. *Human Resource Management Review*, *31*. https://doi.org/10.1016/j.hrmr.2020.100765
Shotter, J. (2011). *Getting it: Withness-thinking and the dialogical... in practice*. Hampton Press.
Spector, B. (2020). Even in a global pandemic, there's no such thing as a crisis. *Leadership*, *16*(3), 303–313. https://doi.org/10.1177/1742715020927111
Tourish, D. (2020). Introduction to the special issue: Why the coronavirus crisis is also a crisis of leadership. *Leadership*, *16*(3), 261–272. https://doi.org/10.1177/1742715020929242
Uhl-Bien, M. (2021a). Complexity and COVID-19: Leadership and followership in a complex world. *Journal of Management Studies*, *58*(5), 1400–1404. https://doi.org/10.1111/joms.12696
Uhl-Bien, M. (2021b). Complexity leadership and followership: Changed leadership in a changed world. *Journal of Change Management*, *21*(2), 144–162. https://doi.org/10.1080/14697017.2021.1917490
Uhl-Bien, M., & Ospina, S. M. (2012). *Advancing relational leadership theory: A conversation among perspectives*. Information Age Publishing.
Van Knippenberg, D., & Sitkin, S. B. (2013). A critical assessment of charismatic-transformational leadership research: Back to the drawing board? *The Academy of Management Annals*, *7*, 1–60. https://doi.org/10.1080/19416520.2013.759433

18 The Structuration of Emotion

Sarah J. Tracy and Shawna Malvini Redden

Suffering at work – from burnout, compassion fatigue, emotional abuse, and emotive dissonance – has motivated a wealth of research and theorizing on emotion in the field of organizational communication. This chapter reviews macro discourses of Western rationality and masculinity as well as organizational feeling rules that discipline workplace emotion; reviews forms of emotional communication in organizations, via phenomena such as emotional labor, compassion, and workplace bullying; and analyzes how employees resist, reify, and transcend emotion rules and emotional constructions through humor, social support, bystander intervention, resilience, and more. The chapter closes by synthesizing how this research contributes to a structuration model of emotion and organizational communication. Auxiliary materials illustrate key concepts through discussion questions and a mini case analysis of the emotion-charged organizational environment of an airport.

Organizations and organizing processes are typically presented rationally, often focused on maximizing financial gains and efficient production (Riforgiate & Tracy, 2023). The reigning Western discourse of rationality privileges reason, implying that emotions interfere with goal-directed economic processes (Dougherty & Drumheller, 2006). Most workplaces expect employees to behave *professionally*, to practice self-control and mask non-prescribed emotions at work (Cheney & Ashcraft, 2007), as well as whitewash Blackness (Ferguson & Dougherty, 2022). Together, these expectations create a disease model of emotions that suggests strong feelings and expressed emotions threaten the health of the workplace and require management (Paul & Riforgiate, 2015).

Indeed, getting emotional is linked to being unprofessional, feminine, and/or even mentally unstable (Waldron, 2012), which helps explain why most early organizational research either ignored emotion or subsumed it under bland variables such as job satisfaction, morale, or commitment (Kramer & Hess, 2002). In the popular imagination, emotion has historically been deemed useful when coupled with masculine characteristics like being tough or showing anger to control others (Lutgen-Sandvik & Tracy, 2012). When employees get upset, stressed, or burned out, Western discourses of rugged individuality and meritocracy pressure them to deal with these issues on their own time, privately, without whining (Lutgen-Sandvik & McDermott, 2008). Indeed, prior to the COVID-19 pandemic, which brought burnout and grief to center stage for a time (Stanley et al., 2021), emotional anguish was all but absent in society's grand narratives about work where successful employees gallantly "pull themselves up by their bootstraps" rather than admit feeling burned out due to unmanageable workloads or abusive bosses.

DOI: 10.4324/9781003484639-21

Through the 1990s, management research treated emotion as incompatible with desired workplace behaviors because emotion was viewed as damaging to productivity (Mayer et al., 2016). Meanwhile, communication scholars of organizations and emotions primarily ignored one another. Case in point, the index of the *Handbook of Communication and Emotion* (Andersen & Guerrero, 1998) did not include the word *organization*, and the index of the *Handbook of Organizational Communication* (Jablin et al., 1987) did not include the word *emotion*.

Arguably the first and most influential communication article to question the rationality-emotionality duality was Mumby and Putnam's (1992) research on *bounded emotionality*. They offered bounded emotionality as an alternative to Herbert Simon's (1982) *bounded rationality* (see Chapter 15), suggesting that organizations should encourage employees to experience a range of emotions, including nurturance, care, and supportiveness. From a feminist perspective, Mumby and Putnam (1992) argued that emotion should not be used as a rational organizational instrument, but rather that *work feelings* are integral to organizing. Concurrently, organizational psychologists and management scholars started exploring *emotional intelligence*. This literature suggested that well-timed emotional displays, empathy, and emotion regulation are important characteristics of good leadership and effective organizing (Mayer et al., 2016). Most emotional intelligence research remains siloed in management and organizational psychology, with critical organizational and communication researchers arguing that emotional intelligence research is flavored with instrumental rationality (Murphy, 2014).

Returning to Mumby and Putnam's (1992) plea to support a range of work feelings, communication scholars now highlight the value of positive organizational communication research (Leach et al., 2024) and emotions like compassion (Leach et al., 2023; Miller, 2007; Tietsort et al., 2023). Research about emotions like kindness and nurturance shows that care work is undervalued and associated with private, unpaid, often feminized labor (Tracy, 2008). Most organizational communication emotion research has focused on the negative, framing emotion as the problematic result of employee conditions (e.g., emotional exhaustion); something used by the organization for rational ends (e.g., emotional labor); feminized care work that is naturalized and under-rewarded; racialized and to be "toned down" and controlled (Cruz et al., 2020; Davis & Ernst, 2017); and something that when weaponized (e.g., emotional abuse) is an individual rather than an organizational issue.

We begin this chapter by explaining the pragmatic impetus for emotion and organizing research. Second, we review organizing structures and macro discourses that discipline workplace emotion. Third, we explain the central communicative actions of emotion at work. Fourth, we analyze how employees resist, reify, and sometimes transcend emotion rules and processes. Along the way, we highlight how organizational communication has extended parallel work from management, organizational psychology, and sociology, and how culture intersects with emotion and organizing. The chapter closes with a structuration model of emotion and organizational communication.

Suffering at Work: The Impetus for Organizational Communication and Emotion Theorizing

Much organizational communication and emotion theorizing is designed to practically explain and ameliorate suffering at work, including burnout, compassion fatigue, emotive dissonance, and emotional abuse.

Burnout

Chronologically, burnout was the first problem that motivated organizational communication theorizing related to emotion. Usually considered the general "wearing down" from work pressures, burnout features emotional exhaustion, depersonalization, cynicism, and decreased personal accomplishment. To cope, emotionally exhausted employees distance themselves from work. But, as a result, they experience increased cynicism, callousness, and alienation, which contributes to decreased job performance and satisfaction (Tracy, 2017).

The most widely used inventory to measure burnout was developed by social psychologist Christina Maslach (1982). The earliest organizational communication studies used this inventory to explore communication variables that cause, mitigate, or reduce burnout (Miller et al., 1988). Most burnout research centers caring professions – like nursing (Way & Tracy, 2012), corrections (Tracy, 2009), and teaching (Kamrath, 2018) – which require high levels of interpersonal contact and *toxin management* (Frost, 2004), or managing the negative emotions of others. Such work is typified by conflicting work expectations (e.g., caring for clients while controlling them), work overload, and caring deeply for a job as a calling despite its increasing professionalization. Given the COVID-19 pandemic and abrupt, world-wide changes to work and life, burnout research will likely continue to flourish (Stanley et al., 2021).

Compassion Fatigue

Related to burnout is *compassion fatigue*, or the cost of caring. This concept emanated from nursing, sociology, and traumatology and is similar to vicarious traumatization and secondary traumatic stress as it refers to discomfort resulting from caring for others experiencing trauma (Radey & Figley, 2007). Like second-hand smoke, certain types of workers regularly bear witness to trauma and are quite susceptible to its ill-effects. Research cautions that when "our hearts go out to our clients through our sustained compassion, our hearts can *give* out from fatigue" (Radey & Figley, 2007, p. 207, emphasis in original). Concern about compassion fatigue has spurred organizational communication research with volunteers (McAllum, 2014) and healthcare personnel – especially during the COVID-19 pandemic (Leach et al., 2023).

Discomfort of Faking Emotions

A third source of organizational suffering is expressing inauthentic emotion as a requirement of work. Coined by sociologist Arlie Hochschild (1983), *emotive dissonance* is the discomfort that emanates when employees' inner feelings clash with inauthentic outward expression. Many jobs ask employees to amplify, suppress, or transform emotions they deem inappropriate, as when service employees are expected to smile and suppress irritation (Tracy, 2000), and security employees are expected to maintain stoicism and suspicion (Malvini Redden, 2021). Such work can be alienating when people feel like they are creating false selves. The pain of emotion work is exacerbated when it conflicts with identities that employees deem authentic or preferred. For instance, most correctional officers prefer to perceive themselves as tough and masculine, finding it difficult to show deference to convicted criminals (Tracy, 2005). Indeed, being kind or compassionate to stigmatized populations can be challenging, as with border patrol officers whose work includes caring for undocumented immigrants (Rivera, 2015).

Emotional Abuse and Bullying

A fourth problem motivating emotion and organizational communication research involves workplace emotional abuse. Workplace bullying refers to "persistent verbal and nonverbal aggression at work... includ[ing] personal attacks, social ostracism... painful messages and hostile interactions" (Lutgen-Sandvik, 2006, p. 406). More than 25 percent of working adults will experience bullying during their careers, and at any given time, between 7 and 8 percent are actively being bullied (Keashly, 2018). Bullying is linked to psychosomatic illnesses, suicidal ideation, increased medical expenses, and reduced productivity (Lutgen-Sandvik & Tracy, 2012). Targets of workplace bullying describe it as an unending nightmare, full of torture and humiliation (Tracy et al., 2006a). Bullying also harms larger workgroups and bystanders who feel terrified, muted, guilty, and powerless (Lutgen-Sandvik, 2006).

In summary, four main areas of organizational suffering have motivated emotion and organizational communication theorizing – burnout, compassion fatigue, emotive dissonance, and workplace bullying. To address and ameliorate suffering, researchers have investigated the organizational and institutional norms that produce and discipline emotional problems; how problems manifest in employee interactions; and how employees resist, reify, or transcend them – topics we synthesize next. Together, these processes make up the communication-organization spiral dynamic that frames this book.

Organizational and Institutional Structures That Discipline and Construct Emotion

Organizations are typically considered rational, masculine enterprises where employees should be professional and merit-focused. Discourses of rationality, Whiteness, masculinity, individuality, and meritocracy produce and shape organizational norms about emotions and their (im)proper place at work.

Feeling Rules

Many organizations institute blatant or subtle feeling rules that discipline employees' emotions (Hochschild, 1983). Most organizational settings expect workers to suppress and restrict communication about stress and burnout, producing *communicatively restricted organizational stress* (Boren & Veksler, 2015). In this model, employees simply put up with hard work and, if they feel stressed, cope privately or leave the organization. In addition to this blanket organizational expectation, some roles have specific feeling rules, as described by Waldron (2012):

- boundary spanners, like receptionists, should show interest and patience;
- emotional believers, such as clergy, should show calm and faith;
- emotional elicitors, like comedians, should create laughs;
- resilience builders, such as soldiers, should be tough and stoic;
- orchestrators, such as sales team leaders, should amplify personal emotion and motivate it in others;
- coolers and soothers, such as 911 call-takers, should suppress personal anxiety and neutralize others;
- moral emoters, such as activists, should show outrage.

These feeling rules appear formally and informally in employee recruitment materials (Rivera, 2015), socialization rituals (Hanners & Malvini Redden, 2021), training (Foss & Foss, 2011), and performance evaluations (Tracy, 2000).

Gendered and Raced Emotion Norms

Since Hochschild's (1983) groundbreaking research with flight attendants, feeling rules remain gendered, classed, and raced. Black employees are asked to conform their identities to fit whitewashed and westernized notions of professionalism and civility (Ferguson & Dougherty, 2022). Employees (especially women) in feminized occupations, such as teaching, nursing, social work, and service, are expected to express care and concern. Much care work goes unnoticed and under-rewarded (McAllum et al., 2024). And when marginalized peoples express resistance and anger, they are often tone-policed (Cruz et al., 2020; see Chapter 4). Likewise, when jobs involve caring for low-status clients (e.g., children, the elderly, criminals, undocumented immigrants), employees must manage contagious stigma and emotional taint (Rivera, 2015). Meanwhile, men (especially White men) typically enjoy a "status shield" that protects them from the "displaced feelings of others" (Hochschild, 1983, p. 163). Due to their greater social status, dominant group members (Razzante & Orbe, 2018) are more likely to be shielded from anger, verbal abuse, and complaints compared to women and people of color.

People in masculine professions, such as policing, creative arts, and executive leadership, are allowed and even glorified for being tough and verbally abusive (e.g., a reality television star turned U.S. President, famous for yelling, "You're fired!") (Razzante et al., 2018). However, even when marginalized group members hold masculinized or high-status positions, they are not afforded the same luxury as dominant group members in expressing a range of emotions. Instead, they are often sexualized, ignored, or exemplified as angry (Davis, 2019). As Collins (1998) argues, "Black and Hispanic men are seen as dangerous, not powerful" when aggressive, rather than "masculine," while "women of color and working class and poor White women are [excluded by universal gender symbolism]" (pp. 217–218). In sum, feeling rules, along with racial and gendered discourses, allow more privileged employees freedom to perform a full range of emotions at work.

Empathy, Care, and Emotional Intelligence Are Underrated

Empathy, care, and emotional intelligence are largely underrated and under-rewarded in organizational settings. *Emotional intelligence* refers to capabilities that include emotional self-awareness, emotional self-regulation, motivating oneself and others, leveraging emotion, understanding cultural differences in emotion, and empathizing with others (Mayer et al., 2016). These capabilities are linked with stronger relationships, trust, and higher productivity (Harvard Business Review, 2015), despite rarely being rewarded by organizations.

Emotional Abuse Is Enabled by Workplace Structures

Organizational structures produce and enable emotional abuse at work. Lutgen-Sandvik and McDermott (2008) argue that employee abuse emerges from discourses that "come from an amalgamation of economic theory, religious and secularized ideals of work, the merger of corporate interests and governing bodies, ... [belief in] rugged individualism, [the dogma of] meritocracy, and the ideology of entrepreneurialism" (p. 317). Such discourses penalize employees perceived as weak or thin-skinned, and link tough treatment to increased productivity and "just the way the world works." Women in male-dominated workplaces are especially at risk for marginalizing communication (Dorrance Hall & Gettings, 2020). When bad behavior is too blatant to ignore, workplaces tend to focus on bad apples rather than organizational structures. However, individual "bad apple" behavior spills into larger work processes and, therefore, can spoil the barrel (Thoroughgood et al., 2011).

Most workplace bullies are supervisors. When targets seek help, human resource (HR) professionals are often at a loss because they view workplace abuse as competitive rather than hostile (Cowan, 2012). Workplace policies (or lack thereof) often condone abusive behavior (Keashly, 2018). In more than 70 percent of cases, bullying targets believe that upper management is complicit in abuse, whether due to inaction or through intervention that worsens the situation (Namie & Lutgen-Sandvik, 2010). Indeed, HR policies are largely ineffective at punishing "equal opportunity" workplace jerks who are abusive without obvious demographic-specific discrimination. Even when companies institute wellbeing programs, they tend to focus on individual rather than collective concerns of employee health (Ganesh & McAllum, 2010). In short, numerous organizational and societal structures enable emotional suffering at work.

Employee Communicative Action in Relationship to Emotion and Organizing

Employees respond to organizational structures and larger societal discourses via emotional labor, care work, empathic concern, and workplace bullying.

Emotional Labor

Emotional labor is the commodification of emotion, where people manage their emotions in line with organizational expectations and training (Hochschild, 1983). In practice, emotional labor involves people shaping their emotional communication, frequently to suppress negative emotions and amplify emotions that foster organizational goals. For instance, customer service workers are usually trained to conduct "service with a smile" – suppressing anger with rude customers while amplifying cheerfulness. However, in some occupations like law enforcement, organizationally preferred emotion management may look stoical, where people cultivate composure in difficult situations even when they feel anxious or scared.

Hochschild (1983) differentiated between types of emotional labor, including deep and surface acting. Employees engage in *surface acting* when they force emotions they do not actually feel, like when airport security officers perform an intimidating "commanding presence" when they actually feel bored, or compassionate (Scarduzio & Malvini Redden, 2015, p. 7). Discrepancies in felt and expressed emotions result in *emotive dissonance*, which promotes tension and strain (Ashforth & Humphrey, 1993). When employees feel compelled to generate inauthentic emotions they do not agree with – "faking in bad faith" (Rafaeli & Sutton, 1987) – they are likely to experience more significant consequences, such as burnout, depression, and cynicism. Surface acting is associated with decreased psychological wellbeing and physical health (Riforgiate et al., 2022). When employees both feel and demonstrate required emotion, they may engage in *deep acting,* which is an effortful process of changing internal feelings to match organizational requirements. Over time, deep acting can lead to alienation from personal feelings (Hochschild, 1983) but is not as closely associated with increased burnout as surface acting (Powers & Myers, 2020).

Examining power relations is vital to understanding whether employees will feel discomfort with emotional labor. Faking low-status emotions that conflict with preferred identities can be much more difficult than feigning those that align with dominant, affirmative organizational discourses (Tracy, 2005). Simulating low-status emotions is easier when employees engage in interpersonal resistance, something we explain when discussing employee agency below.

While most research focuses on employee experiences of emotional labor, some scholarship considers the complex interplay between organizational members and patrons. In compulsory interactions in airport security checkpoints, patrons in low-power positions are required to demonstrate emotions in line with organizational expectations, which are negotiated through interactions with security officers in positions of power rather than spelled out in policies (Malvini Redden, 2021). These emotional performances or *emotional taxes* are similar to financial penalties – required for everyone – but can vary depending upon interpersonal interactions and personal identity.

Compassion

Compassion is another important emotional process in organizations (Miller, 2007) and includes three primary components: (a) Recognizing verbal and nonverbal cues from others, as well as the context and subtext of interactions; (b) relating, which involves "identifying with, feeling for, and communicatively connecting with another to enable sharing of emotions, values, and decisions"; and (c) reacting, which involves communicating compassionately (Way & Tracy, 2012, p. 307). Compassion in organizations can improve relationships, customer service, productivity, and reputation (Men, 2014). However, some compassion work involves burnout-inducing toxin management (Frost, 2004).

Although the emotional labor literature portrays feminized care work as low status and exhausting, some populations like hospice nurses seem to thrive. Rather than their hearts giving out due to strain, their hearts actually get stronger and more capable through work (Way & Tracy, 2012). This may be due to the hospice context, where the overall goal is to provide comfort rather than cure, and suggests that organizational visions, structures, and norms influence whether the same behavior (e.g., caring) is experienced as exhausting or enriching (Leach et al., 2023). Compassion is communicated variously through embodied togetherness (Huffman, 2017), collective creation of hope (Tracy & Huffman, 2017), compassionate coaching during sustained crisis (Kim et al., 2024), and earnest script-breaking and collective communication where employees can "spiral" through trauma together (Leach et al., 2023).

Workplace Emotional Abuse, Bullying, and Microaggressions

Employee communicative action becomes very difficult when organizational structures enable antisocial behaviors like microaggressions, emotional abuse, and workplace bullying. *Microaggressions* are "subtle, intentional, or unintentional prejudicial or discriminatory words or behaviors" (Shenoy-Packer, 2015, p. 258). These small actions can cause serious emotional consequences as they are often tied to critical identity markers like race/ethnicity, gender, culture, size, and ability. For example, over time, questions and comments like "What are you?" or "You speak such good English" can *other* racial minorities, similar to how questions like "Who is this little girl they hired?" marginalizes women's experiences in male-dominated workplaces (Dorrance Hall & Gettings, 2020). Microaggressions often contribute to workplace bullying.

Bullying is a communicative process that involves ongoing, escalating, and repeated significant physical or psychological harm between a bully and a target with disparate power positions in organizations (Lutgen-Sandvik & Tracy, 2012). Bullying comes in many communicative forms, including spreading rumors, public humiliation, abusive language, and constant criticism. Furthermore, bullying behaviors are accomplished with a persistence that intensifies abuse, differentiating it from incivilities or microaggressions. Occasionally yelling at a coworker does not equate to bullying. However, continually screaming, swearing at, and isolating the same coworker day after day does. Targets of abuse usually perceive that bullies are acting purposefully (Tracy et al., 2006a). Abusive behaviors – whispering, insults, gossip, sneering, eye-rolling – can be traumatizing over time. Bullying victims often have trouble describing the abuse, although narratives show that targets experience significant loss, isolation, and lack of social support from bystanders who are more likely to ignore bullying than intervene (Tye-Williams & Krone, 2015).

Employees Sediment, Resist, and Transcend Emotion Issues at Work

Despite the grim picture emerging from much emotion research, organizational communication scholarship has also examined how employees shape their emotional constructions and organizational emotion rules. Employee action can involve (a) sedimenting and reinforcing, (b) resisting, and (c) transcending.

Sedimenting and Reinforcing

As structuration theory posits (Giddens, 1984), structures are constructed and reinforced by action. Organizational communication research shows that employees can also reinforce and sediment emotion norms and related discourses. For instance, employees tend to reinforce the dichotomy between emotionality and rationality by carefully controlling their emotions in organizations, denying emotions altogether, reframing experiences to depersonalize emotions, discussing emotions in rationalized ways, and relegating emotions to private spaces (Dougherty & Drumheller, 2006). By de-emphasizing emotion and repeating rationalist and white discourses about professionalism, prevailing norms are reinforced and sedimented.

Employees also reinforce emotional labor expectations via cynicism and disidentification. For instance, the idea of distancing or making fun of one's work role may appear to be resistance. However, disidentification can ironically facilitate emotional labor expectations. Consider a disgruntled fast-food worker who wears a "McShit" T-shirt under her uniform to show that her "real" self sees through the absurdity of minimum wage work. However, her secret act of rebellion might actually preclude more blatant or consequential resistance (Fleming & Spicer, 2003) and, therefore, may strengthen the organization's feeling rules. Likewise, correctional officers who view work as "just a job" and find identity and success validation outside of work appear to more successfully engage in emotion labor without undue discomfort (Tracy, 2005). As noted by Fleming and Spicer (2003, p. 160), "when we dis-identify with our prescribed social roles we often still perform them – sometimes better, ironically, than if we did identify with them."

Emotional abuse can also be sedimented through activity at the workgroup level. Consider workplace bullying bystanders who join in to mock a colleague, through distortion or further terrorizing targets (Ivancic & Ford, 2023). Their actions reinforce problematic emotion cycles and make it difficult to change organizational culture. Hareli and Rafaeli (2008) describe emotion cycles as a "double-interact social process" (p. 37) where a person's emotion is communicated, shared, and made sense of by another, who then reciprocates with an emotional process that can continue or change the cycle. Emotion cycles can reinforce emotion norms or give sense about organizational processes to others (Scarduzio & Tracy, 2015). For instance, in municipal courtrooms, bailiffs function as intermediaries in the emotion cycle–downplaying a judge's anger to help a defendant, or laughing at a judge's unfunny joke to keep a positive mood.

With complex emotion cycles like workplace bullying, opportunities for agency and control are complicated. Followers are likely to endure abuse when the organizational climate tolerates or ignores negative leader behavior (Thoroughgood et al., 2011). Sometimes bullying targets go through official channels to seek justice and find HR professionals who frame bullying as a direct manager's issue, not an organizational problem (Cowan, 2012). Likewise, well-intentioned peers may offer bad advice by recommending that the bullied employee simply "keep calm" and "stay rational." Such advice discounts the severity of abuse, de-emphasizes organizational responsibility, and constrains individual agency (Tye-Williams & Krone, 2017). What's more, it ignores the ways that civility is regularly invoked to protect privilege and silence resistance (Kisselburgh & Dutta, 2009; see Chapter 4).

Resistance

Although employees can sediment and reinforce feeling rules and emotional abuse, they also resist in ingenious ways. In stressful, stigmatized, and rule-bound work, employees can draw on larger discourses to create positive identities, as with restaurant workers who create identities of flexibility, empathy, and composure in the face of stigma (Hanners & Malvini Redden, 2021). Employees can also refuse to buy into feeling rules by blatantly ignoring them via emotional deviance, which is "the opposite of emotional dissonance because the organizational member expresses inner feelings and disregards feeling rules" (Rafaeli & Sutton, 1987, p. 33). Examples of emotional deviance include a pastor who giggles during a funeral or a server who rolls her eyes at a customer's ridiculous request. Emotional deviance can serve several agentic purposes, including providing employees with distance, a break from emotion rules, and relief from monotonous tasks.

Some employees are able to deviate from emotion rules without penalty more than others. People in high-power professions associated with masculinity and Whiteness, such as law, medicine, and academia, more easily deviate. Such is the case with judges who enact "robe-itis," and let the power of their formal black robe go to their heads. Via what Scarduzio (2011) calls *privileged deviance*, judges regularly break from expectations of solemnity and neutrality, and instead joke with defendants. People with marginalized identities like women and people of color are more likely to feel compelled to play by the rules (Razzante & Tracy, 2019) as consequences for deviating from emotional expectations are greater for minoritized people (Malvini Redden & Scarduzio, 2018). For example, employees report more intentions to resist and blow the whistle on abusive leaders when the leader is female (Thoroughgood et al., 2011).

Employees also find creative ways to resist workplace bullying and emotional abuse. Although ambiguous HR policies discourage intervention (Cowan, 2012), bullying bystanders, witnesses, and supervisors can intercede in bullying. Critically, traditionally powerful employees may impede and dismantle abuse (Razzante & Orbe, 2018). When supervisors encourage employee autonomy and social support, they also effectively discourage bullying as a response to job stressors (Goodboy et al., 2022). Moreover, interpersonal and procedural acts of justice reduce burnout and enhance employee engagement (Kim & Leach, 2021).

Some organizations have also instituted bystander training, where employees learn to increase affirmative communication, report observed bullying, and resource problematic behavior (Foss & Foss, 2011). Depending on the context, effective bystander intervention affirms positive behavior, corrects emotionally abusive behavior, and may include immediate intervention (Bowes-Sperry & O'Leary-Kelly, 2005). Interference could be directly calling for bullying to stop or redirecting to a new topic, e.g., *conversational pivoting* (Foss & Foss, 2011). A bystander or leader could also comfort suffering targets (Tietsort et al., 2023). This last type of action may not immediately change bullying behavior but would help the organization maintain high-quality connections (Dutton, 2003) and support coping – a topic we turn to next.

Coping

Employees engage in many coping techniques – another form of enacting agency in response to emotional pressures at work. To practice compassion without fatigue, employees balance involvement with detachment. This is accomplished by feeling *for* others via empathic concern (Miller, 2007) rather than feeling *with* others via emotional contagion which is connected to burnout (Powers & Myers, 2020). When people are in deep despair, caregivers should generally avoid joining them. Showing concern without feeling others' negative emotions is a balancing act, however. Some workers descend into depersonalization or aloofness that, while useful for self-protection, does not usually accomplish organizational goals (Miller et al., 1988).

Compassion is also best accomplished by setting boundaries, making sure the compassion-giver has privacy, and ensuring social support (Miller, 2007). Indeed, being able to discuss workplace stressors can help employees make sense of frustrating, identity threatening, or demanding work. When employees feel constricted in talking about workplace frustrations, this results in *communicatively restricted organizational stress* (CROS) (Boren & Veksler, 2015). However, excessive negative talk and co-rumination can exacerbate burnout when people focus on problems rather than potential solutions (Boren, 2014).

Similar to bystander intervention, the effectiveness of social support depends on context. As Tracy (2009) describes,

> Instrumental support (an exchange of time, resources or labor) helps prevent emotional exhaustion and depersonalization, and as such, may enhance the care and treatment of clients. Informational support (related to role definition, general information about job, skills training) is related to increased retention. Emotional support (empathy, caring, acceptance and assurance) is directly related to retention, commitment and all dimensions of burnout.
>
> (p. 88)

Support from like-minded peers can be more effective than help from researchers, family, or friends (Lutgen-Sandvik, 2006). Peer support is especially ameliorative in terms of gender and race, reducing the problematic effects of harassment through commiseration and reframing (Ivancic & Ford, 2023) and providing a sensemaking haven in the face of racial injustice (Davis, 2019). Organizational superiors also can help alleviate emotional exhaustion by decreasing workloads, providing recognition and rewards, fostering fairness, and increasing employee participation in decision-making (Leiter & Maslach, 2011). Indeed, employees who help "create their work environment feel more powerful and accomplished.

Further, having a voice ... helps them deal with rules or regulations that would otherwise be framed as debilitating constraints or irritating hassles" (Tracy, 2017, p. 5).

Social support is especially useful for bullying targets because abusive interactions "linger in a hundred conversations as members of the original audience re-encounter one another and negotiate the meaning of the original event" (Waldron, 2000, p. 68). Rehashing can affect workplace productivity, re-victimize targets, and poison organizational climates (Lutgen-Sandvik & McDermott, 2008). However, when bullied employees make sense of experiences with coworkers or other bullying targets, they feel less isolated (Tracy et al., 2006). Some employees even construct elaborate collective revenge fantasies (Tye-Williams & Krone, 2015), which may not transform bullying but can help reframe problems and create preferred identities (Lutgen-Sandvik, 2008). Leaders play a critical role in providing social support and access to resources, particularly in creating climates where employees feel comfortable disclosing suffering (Tietsort et al., 2023).

Thriving and Overcoming

Prosocial emotions can also be cultivated at work to help people thrive. Flourishing is different than simply surviving. It's an agentic activity that allows employees to transcend emotional suffering. For example, organizational members use humor to manage stress and bond with coworkers, which fosters organizational identification and reduces job-related stress (Tracy et al., 2006b). Humor and affirmative behaviors like praise and acknowledgment create healthy organizational cultures (Bowes-Sperry & O'Leary-Kelly, 2005) and support trusting and respectful peer connections (Dutton, 2003). For instance, joking helps public safety employees cope with dangerous work and eases the tension of worrying family members (Bochantin, 2017). Prosocial communicative processes, when they involve regular, positive experiences, help people feel important and included, building resilience (Lutgen-Sandvik et al., 2011).

Psychologically speaking, resilience is an important skill involving the ability to bounce back from challenges or recover from crisis (Richardson, 2002). Resilience involves maintaining social ties and creatively reframing difficulties through storytelling, rituals, networks, and social media messaging (Buzzanell, 2018) while maintaining dialectics and cultivating dignity (Wieland, 2020). One way people cultivate resilience is through mindfulness practices. Individually, this might include setting aside judgment to "practice acceptance, kindness, and openness, even when what is occurring ... is contrary to deeply held wishes or expectations" (Shapiro et al., 2006, p. 377).

An orientation of "nonattachment" encourages people to reframe their subject positions to reduce personal ego and see themselves and their coworkers as interdependent (Brummans & Hwang, 2010). This orientation can enable compassion, flexibility, attention, discipline, and wisdom. What's more, leaders who practice mindfulness are better able to manage paradox and contradiction (Town et al., 2023). Employees who practice resilience – such as rape crisis advocates – buffer against vicarious trauma and construct work as meaningful (Biss & Barrett, 2023). Finally, consider the strength of calls for self-care (Rodino-Colocino, 2021) and "quiet quitting" (Lawless, 2023) that emerged in the pandemic to challenge organizational norms of emotional repression, efficiency, and rationality.

Culture, Gender, and the Constitution of Organizing via Emotion

Chapter 1 defined organizational communication "a complex set of processes and structures through which people interact to coordinate action and accomplish goals." In the current chapter, emotion and organizational communication literature conceptualize communication as a method to attend to organizational feeling rules, a way emotional abuse manifests due to larger structural norms that value rationality and expertise over emotional intelligence, and how organizations help employees know the meaning of their work through specific feeling rules. In this section, we return to issues of culture and gender, and examine emotion and the communicative constitution of organizing and organization.

Culture and Gender

Despite the importance of culture in understanding emotion at work, organizational communication literature on these topics has been largely constrained to research in the Global North – primarily in the United States, Western Europe, Australia, and Aotearoa New Zealand – and focused on White professional and human service populations with neurotypical and normatively abled employees. There is much value to expanding this focus as organizational emotion processes are embedded in and shaped by discourses of culture, race, coloniality, (dis)ability, and gender.

Indeed, emotional experiences can be spurred by cultural and identity differences such as gender, ethnicity, race, or class (Malvini Redden & Scarduzio, 2018) (see Chapters 11–14). For example, while typically masculine emotional expressions of irritation, neutrality, aggression, or sarcasm are privileged, feminized displays of care and compassion are stigmatized; women must often go above and beyond to show their expertise (Zanin et al., 2023). Organizational processes perpetuate discriminatory and difficult emotion practices such as racialized feeling rules (Wingfield, 2010) and training that prioritizes cheerful Western emotion norms (Leach et al., 2024), revealing the postcolonial legacy of organizational practices (see Chapter 4). When marginalized people become emotional, they are often subjected to tone policing – especially if they are challenging privileged notions of Whiteness or colonial norms of oppression (Cruz et al., 2020; Davis & Ernst, 2017; see Chapter 4). Additionally, current conceptualizations of social support and compassion feature neurotypical approaches to empathy and relating (Way & Tracy, 2012) – with little attention to how neurodivergent people express and recognize care.

Understanding emotional abuse at work requires consideration of identity, as gender, ethnicity, (dis)ability, and race are historically stigmatizing markers that contribute to workplace bullying. Marginalized workforce members are easier targets for bullying and enjoy less flexibility in acceptable emotional displays (Meares et al., 2004). Indeed, women and people of color experience a range of negative social phenomena (Davis, 2019) and ideologies that make emotional work more difficult (Ferguson & Dougherty, 2022). Thankfully, engagement in resilience processes like reframing, humor, and new routines can help moderate the negative effects of marginalization (Dorrance Hall & Gettings, 2020). Within the emotion and organizing literature, scholars examine culture and gender as they influence individuals as well as larger organizational structures. So, how do these communicative practices constitute organizing and organization?

O_1: Organizing

Consider organizing as a verb or, as explained in Chapter 1, the process of coordinating/ordering among persons and things. What does this look like in the emotion and organizational communication literature? Emotion research shows how work feelings cycle through workgroups and organizational contexts (Hareli & Rafaeli, 2008). For example, judges sometimes express sarcasm to misbehaving defendants. The defendants' responses affect whether bailiffs amplify harsh emotion or compensate through comforting behavior (Scarduzio & Tracy, 2015). This cycling of emotion through organizational workgroups is accomplished through verbal and nonverbal messaging, as well as material items such as the judge's black robe. Organizational communication scholarship shows how emotion is contagious, rippling through mentoring sessions, hallway conversations, and employee trainings. For instance, teachers communicatively construct resilience in response to burnout via collective sensemaking and storytelling that frames organizational challenges as meaningful growth opportunities (Kamrath, 2018).

O_2: *Organizationality*

This chapter also illuminates O_2, *organizationality*, which is the "state of coordination or order, or extent to which a social collective's activities seem organized" (see Chapter 1). Emotion research explicates the structuring of workplace coordination showing, for example, that emotion rules are strongest when employees identify with and buy into organizational norms. Furthermore, emotion and organizing research has illuminated concepts like emotional intelligence, which frequently appears in trainings and performance reviews (Harvard Business Review, 2015) as employees are rewarded for expressing emotion appropriately, listening, and empathizing with others.

Workplace bullying was an almost unheard-of term at the turn of the century. Now the term returns more than 75 million Google hits in .59 seconds (as of Spring 2024). Increasing numbers of workplaces have policies about bullying, such as University of California, Berkeley's Workplace Bullying Prevention Policy, instituted in 2016 and updated in 2023 (University of California, Berkeley, 2023). This policy mirrors conceptualizations of workplace bullying from a range of scholarship, including organizational communication. Years earlier, the Berkeley ombudsman office publicly posted a white paper, now book chapter, by communication scholars Tracy et al. (2007) called "How to Bust the Office Bully."

Emotional labor, despite its dominance in organizational communication research, is not as clearly powerful as other concepts in its impact on organizational constitution. Despite calls to do so, emotional labor is curiously missing from most performance reviews (Poly, 2015). This is not surprising as societal discourses tend to naturalize emotion work (especially feminized care work) so that *emotional labor* may be almost invisible to organizational practitioners.

O_3: *Organizations*

Chapter 1 discusses organizations as nouns, or as coordinated and ordered entities arising from O_1 and O_2. Emotion and organizational communication scholarship tends to implicitly treat organizations as neutral environments. Mirroring central biases pointed out in Chapter 1, much emotion and organizational communication research focuses on interactional behavior of specific employed members situated within the organization as a container or backdrop. That said, critical scholars have examined how organizational histories and genealogies affect emotion labor norms (e.g., Tracy, 2000) and how organizational climates and policies affect workplace bullying (Cowan, 2012).

The research reviewed herein has also constituted academic organizations such as specialized emotion conferences, institutes, and LISTSERVs, including the now 1400-member Emonet. Research centers have sprung up such as the Center for Positive Organizations at the University of Michigan and the Greater Good Center at UC Berkeley. Public scholarship has led to documentaries, specialized institutes like the Workplace Bullying Institute, and movement toward anti-bullying laws (Yamada, 2015).

Finally, continued attention on workplace burnout and stress has arguably contributed to wellness and employee assistance programs that feature activities ranging from fitness challenges to chair massages to anger management. Such programs, although popular, tend to focus on individual rather than collective employee health concerns (Ganesh & McAllum, 2010), as do products like the "fidget cube," essential oils, and adult coloring books. However, increasingly organizations are paying attention to employee mental health and self-care (Rodino-Colocino, 2021).

Conclusion

As demonstrated, the emotion and organizing literature exemplifies the C-O cycle in many ways. The literature shows how larger discourses, organizational policies, and employee talk create organizational feeling rules that enable and constrain emotional expression. Meanwhile, institutional HR processes enable the destructive communication of "equal opportunity" jerks, and employee resistance can ironically result in even harsher treatment in organizations.

Taken together, the complex and varied literature about emotion in organizations contributes to organizational practices and the ways employees, supervisors, and the general public interpret such practices. The research hopefully has helped people see that emotion at work is not only something that gets in the way of organizing but also as something that can enhance the workplace experience. Furthermore, when people are better able to name and define various types of emotional suffering (e.g., compassion fatigue, burnout, bullying, emotive dissonance), they know they are not alone and might even have avenues to survive or transcend suffering.

Recommended Supplementary Readings

Bochantin, J. E. (2017). "Ambulance thieves, clowns, and naked grandfathers": How PSEs and their families use humorous communication as a sensemaking device. *Management Communication Quarterly, 31*(2), 278–296.

An exemplar of humor, sensemaking, and work–life balance among public safety employees.

Dougherty, D. S., & Drumheller, K. (2006). Sensemaking and emotions in organizations: Accounting for emotions in a rational(ized) context. *Communication Studies, 57*(2), 215–238.

Critiques the priority of rationality over emotionality in organizations.

Hareli, S., & Rafaeli, A. (2008). Emotion cycles: On the social influence of emotion in organizations. *Research in Organizational Behavior, 28*, 35–59.

The original discussion of emotion cycles in organizations, focusing primarily on negative emotion cycles.

Hochschild, A. R. (1983). *The managed heart: Commercialization of human feeling.* University of California Press.

The book that coined key terms of emotional labor, surface and deep acting, and emotive dissonance.

Huffman, T. P. (2017). Compassionate communication, embodied aboutness, and homeless young adults. *Western Journal of Communication, 81*(2), 149–167.

Drawing upon experiences of homeless youth, Huffman depicts the embodied enactment of compassion.

Malvini Redden, S., & Scarduzio, J. A. (2018). A different type of dirty work: Hidden taint, intersectionality, and emotion management in bureaucratic organizations. *Communication Monographs, 85*(2), 224–244.

This study shows how professional occupations can involve difficult, identity-, and emotion-related dirty work.

Rivera, K. D. (2015). Emotional taint: Making sense of emotional dirty work at the U.S. Border Patrol. *Management Communication Quarterly, 29*(2), 198–228.

Rivera coins the term "emotional taint" to describe work that is "dirty" by virtue of the emotion it requires.

Tracy, S. J., & Huffman, T. P. (2017). Compassion in the face of terror: A case study of recognizing suffering, co-creating hope, and developing trust in a would-be school shooting. *Communication Monographs, 84*(1), 30–53.

This article provides a vivid picture for communicating compassion when sufferers are angry, threatening, or resisting help.

Tracy, S. J., Lutgen-Sandvik, P., & Alberts, J. K. (2006). Nightmares, demons, and slaves: Exploring the painful metaphors of workplace bullying. *Management Communication Quarterly, 20*, 148–185.

Using drawing and metaphor analysis, this article shows what workplace bullying feels like.

Important Concepts: Define and Discuss

Bounded emotionality
Burnout
Compassion (fatigue)
Communicatively restricted organizational stress (CROS)
Deep acting, surface acting
Discourses of individualism, meritocracy, rationality, and masculinity
(dis)Identification

Emotional deviance
Emotional Intelligence
Emotional labor
Emotive dissonance
Emotional taint and dirty work
Emotional taxes
Feeling rules/emotion norms
Microaggressions
Resilience
Workplace bullying

Discussion Questions

1 Identify cultural, organizational, and professional discourses that shape emotional experiences for employees (e.g., rationality, individuality). How do these structures shape emotion at personal, organizational, and societal levels?
2 How have you resisted or participated in emotion management norms?
3 How can workplace policy and/or employee communication improve workplace emotional experiences?
4 What emotional cycles have you experienced? How does considering emotion socially, and in relationship to organizational and discursive structures, shape your understanding of how emotions influence organizing?

Practitioners' Corner

Emotion and Communication Go to the Airport

Since the September 11, 2001 terrorist attacks and subsequent creation of the Transportation Security Administration (TSA), airport security is steeped with discourses about terrorism, safety, privacy, and authority. On one hand, macro-level conversations about security are rife with critiques of security policies. However, millions of people submit to TSA procedures daily in order to fly. In doing so, they are complicit in practices that curb personal freedoms.

For Transportation Security Officers (TSOs), emotional experiences are complicated by organizational training and mandates; many require difficult, sustained emotional performances of intimidation and composure. TSOs are trained to prevent terrorist attacks with the mantra "not on my watch" and are bombarded with pseudo-military and patriotic messaging regarding duty to country. However, the material reality of TSO work is physically processing thousands of people and constantly managing emotions. Furthermore, TSOs do not enjoy many affirmative discourses about their occupation outside of organizational training.

Consider a typical trip to the airport. People regularly worry about long lines, security screenings, and missing flights. It's not uncommon for people to be sleep deprived and anxious about being late. Imagine a tired, uncertain passenger – irritated by long, winding lines and fellow passengers who take forever loading their belongings for screening – being confronted by a TSO who says they've done something wrong. They will need a bag search and full body pat-down. The passenger – now angry because they've flown before, know what they're doing, and are very worried about the extra time – starts rudely ranting about feeling unfairly singled out. The TSO explains that something in the passenger's bag looked suspicious and protocol dictates extra screening.

The passenger belittles the officer, shouting about how their taxes pay TSO salaries and that TSOs are glorified security guards who couldn't make it into "real" law enforcement. In turn, the officer stays outwardly neutral, sharing that they only enforce and do not create rules. But the TSO moves slower now, performing the pat-down with unnecessary thoroughness. The passenger runs to make the plane, careening through airport crowds while the TSO, still seething but amused that the passenger will probably miss the flight, turns to the next person in line.

The passenger barely makes it, lucky to gain admittance as they were past the airline's boarding deadline. Instead of acting grateful, however, the passenger scans packed overhead bins and doesn't see a single available space. While trying to cram a duffel bag into an overfull bin, a flight attendant says the bag must be checked. The passenger laments that it is unfair since security caused the delay and tells the flight attendant to stop being such a "bitch" and just help already. The flight attendant keeps a placid grin plastered on and explains how it would be unfair to move the luggage of people who arrived on time. It's the fifth passenger meltdown today, and there are still two more legs before the flight attendant is off work. It's no wonder that a Jet Blue flight attendant lost it and, after a profanity-laced rant over the public address system, grabbed a beer and exited the plane via an inflatable ramp (Newman & Rivera, 2010)!

In this mini case study, inspired by past research (Malvini Redden, 2013, 2021), it's easy to see how emotion influences communication at many levels and is shaped by organizational and institutional structures. For passengers, emotional management is informed by personal experiences of airport security and air travel, as well as macro-level discourses like news about security. Likewise, the airport context is surrounded by broad social discourses about terrorism and how airport security is meant to ensure national safety. The reality of flying involves significant anxiety and embodied time pressures. When passengers are primed to be unsettled, it's not surprising that security lines provoke further negative feelings.

Think about the downstream effects of interactions described in the case. Will the emotion cycle co-created in security promote positive emotions? How will the passenger treat fellow travelers on the plane or interact with flight attendants who might issue more directions that seem "unfair?" How will the TSO cope with passenger ranting? Will the officer seek social support from coworkers? If so, will those conversations involve co-rumination that will make the situation feel worse? Or, perhaps their talk will contribute to negative discourses about passengers who "check their brains with their baggage." What if the passenger complained to the TSO's manager who, unbeknownst to the passenger, is an emotionally abusive bully? If the interaction had been racially charged, would the passenger or TSO perhaps feel singled out because of ethnicity? Now think about the organizational structures and processes that shape security interactions – the requisite emotional performances for TSOs and the processes purposefully meant to provoke passenger anxiety (Malvini Redden, 2013). Certainly, these organizational processes constrain agency for patrons and employees alike.

References

Andersen, P. A., & Guerrero, L. K. (Eds.), (1998). *Handbook of communication and emotion: Research, theory, applications, and contexts*. Academic Press.

Ashforth, B. E., & Humphrey, R. H. (1993). Emotional labor in service roles: The influence of identity. *Academy of Management Review*, *18*, 88–115. https://doi.org/10.2307/258824

Biss, D. C., & Barrett, A. K. (2023). Exploring resilience and meaningful work in rape crisis advocacy. *Paper presented at the 2023 National Communication Association annual convention.*

Bochantin, J. E. (2017). "Ambulance thieves, clowns, and naked grandfathers": How PSEs and their families use humorous communication as a sensemaking device. *Management Communication Quarterly*, *31*, 278–296. https://doi.org/10.1177/0893318916687650

Boren, J. P. (2014). The relationships between co-rumination, social support, stress, and burnout among working adults. *Management Communication Quarterly*, *28*(1), 3–25. https://doi.org/10.1177/0893318913509283

Boren, J. P., & Veksler, A. E. (2015). Communicatively Restricted Organizational Stress (CROS) I: Conceptualization and overview. *Management Communication Quarterly*, *29*, 28–55. https://doi.org/10.1177/0893318914558744

Bowes-Sperry, L., & O'Leary-Kelly, A. M. (2005). To act or not to act: The dilemma faced by sexual harassment observers. *Academy of Management Review*, *30*(2), 288–306. https://doi.org/10.5465/AMR.2005.16387886

Brummans, B. H., & Hwang, J. M. (2010). Tzu Chi's organizing for a compassionate world: Insights into the communicative praxis of a Buddhist organization. *Journal of International and Intercultural Communication*, *3*(2), 136–163. https://doi.org/10.1080/17513051003611610

Buzzanell, P. M. (2018). Organizing resilience as adaptive-transformational tensions. *Journal of Applied Communication Research*, *46*(2), 14–18. https://doi-org.ezproxy1.lib.asu.edu/10.1080/00909882.2018.1426711

Cheney, G., & Ashcraft, K. L. (2007). Considering "the professional" in communication studies: Implications for theory and research within and beyond the boundaries of organizational communication. *Communication Theory*, *17*(2), 146–175. https://doi.org/10.1111/j.1468-2885.2007.00290.x

Collins, P. H. (1998). Toward a new vision: Race, class, and gender as categories of analysis and connection. In M. L. Anderson & P. H. Collins (Eds.), *Race, class, and gender: An anthology* (pp. 213–223). Wadsworth.

Cowan, R. L. (2012). It's complicated: Defining workplace bullying from the human resource professional's perspective. *Management Communication Quarterly*, *26*, 377–403. https://doi.org/10.1177/0893318912439474

Cruz, J. M., Gist-Mackey, A. N., Hanchey, J. N., Harris, K. L., Jensen, P. R., Kenney, S. C., & Leslie, K. J. (2020). #ToneUpOrgComm: A manifestx. *Departures in Critical Qualitative Research*, *9*(2), 152–154. https://online.ucpress.edu/dcqr/article-abstract/9/2/152/110317/ToneUpOrgCommA-Manifestx

Davis, A. M., & Ernst, R. (2017). Racial gaslighting. *Politics, Groups, and Identities*, *7*(4), 761–774. https://doi.org/10.1080/21565503.2017.1403934

Davis, S. M. (2019). When sistahs support sistahs: A process of supportive communication about racial microaggressions among Black women. *Communication Monographs*, *86*(2), 133–157. https://doi.org/10.1080/03637751.2018.1548769

Dorrance Hall, E., & Gettings, P. E. (2020). "Who is this little girl they hired to work here?": Women's experiences of marginalizing communication in male-dominated workplaces. *Communication Monographs*, *87*(4), 484–505. https://doi.org/10.1080/03637751.2020.1758736

Dougherty, D. S., & Drumheller, K. (2006). Sensemaking and emotions in organizations: Accounting for emotions in a rational(ized) context. *Communication Studies*, *57*(2), 215–238. https://doi.org/10.1080/10510970600667030

Dutton, J. (2003). *Energizing your workplace*. University of Michigan Press.

Ferguson, M. W. Jr, & Dougherty, D. S. (2022). The paradox of the Black professional: Whitewashing Blackness through professionalism. *Management Communication Quarterly*, *36*(1), 3–29. https://doi.org/10.1177/08933189211019751

Fleming, P., & Spicer, A. (2003). Working at a cynical distance: Implications for power, subjectivity and resistance. *Organization*, *10*(1), 157–179. https://doi.org/10.1177/1350508403010001376

Foss, S. K., & Foss, K. A. (2011). *Inviting transformation: Presentational skills for a changing world*. Waveland Press.

Frost, P. J. (2004). Handling toxic emotions: New challenges for leaders and their organizations. *Organizational Dynamics*, *33*, 111–127. https://doi.org/10.1016/j.orgdyn.2004.01.001

Ganesh, S., & McAllum, K. (2010). Well-being as discourse: Potentials and problems for studies of organizing and health inequalities. *Management Communication Quarterly*, *24*(3), 491–498. https://doi.org/10.1177/0893318910370274

Giddens, A. (1984). *The constitution of society: An outline of the theory of structuration*. Polity.

Goodboy, A. K., Martin, M. M., Mills, C. B., & Clark-Gordon, C. V. (2022). Workplace bullying in academia: A conditional process model. *Management Communication Quarterly*, *36*(4), 664-687. https://doi.org/10.1177/08933189221103625

Hanners, K. A., & Malvini Redden, S. (2021). Communicating values to cultivate sustainable occupational identity: How restaurant workers resist service work stigma. *Sustainability*, *13*(15), 8587. https://doi.org/10.3390/su13158587

Hareli, S., & Rafaeli, A. (2008). Emotion cycles: On the social influence of emotion in organizations. *Research in Organizational Behavior*, *28*, 35–59. https://doi.org/10.1016/j.riob.2008.04.007

Harvard Business Review. (2015). *HBR's 10 must reads on emotional intelligence*. Harvard Business Review Press.

Hochschild, A. R. (1983). *The managed heart: Commercialization of human feeling*. University of California Press.

Huffman, T. P. (2017). Compassionate communication, embodied aboutness, and homeless young adults. *Western Journal of Communication*, *81*(2), 149–167. https://doi.org/10.1080/10570314.2016.1239272

Ivancic, S. R., & Ford, J. L. (2023). (Dis)Organizing sexual harassment: Patterns of bystander communication. *Management Communication Quarterly* (online first). https://doi.org/10.1177/08933189231179653

Jablin, F. M., Putnam, L. L., Roberts, K. H., & Porter, L. W. (Eds.) (1987). *Handbook of organizational communication*. Sage.

Kamrath, J. K. (2018). *The social construction and reciprocity of resilience: An empirical investigation of an organizational context*. Arizona State University.

Keashly, L. (2018). Prevalence of workplace bullying and mobbing among US working adults: What do the numbers mean. *Workplace Bullying and Mobbing in the United States*, *1*, 25–51.

Kim, H., & Leach, R. B. (2021). Mitigating burnout through organizational justice: Customer support workers' experiences of customer injustice and emotional labor. *Management Communication Quarterly*, *35*(4), 497–517. https://doi-org.ezproxy1.lib.asu.edu/10.1177/08933189211012040

Kim, H., Stanley, L., Harms, B., & Michaelides, A. (2024). Enacting compassion in mHealth: Communicative subprocesses of compassionate coaching and their relationships to resilience during a prolonged pandemic. *Journal of Applied Communication Research*, *52*(3), 297–317. https://doi.org/10.1080/00909882.2024.2338836

Kisselburgh, L. G., & Dutta, M. J. (2009). The construction of civility in multicultural organizations. In P. Lutgen-Sandvik & B. D. Sypher (Eds.), *Destructive organizational communication: Processes, consequences, & constructive ways of organizing* (pp. 121–142). Routledge.

Kramer, M. W., & Hess, J. A. (2002). Communication rules for the display of emotions in organizational settings. *Management Communication Quarterly*, *16*, 66–80. https://doi.org/10.1177/0893318902161003

Lawless, B. (2023). Performative enactments of resistance to academic neoliberalization: Quiet quitting as educational transgression and sustainability. *Communication Education*, *72*(3), 316–319. https://doi.org/10.1080/03634523.2023.2207144

Leach, R. B., Tracy, S. J., & Wong, T. (2024). Refreshing the positive: Bridging positive organizational communication and critical scholarship with Buddhist philosophies. *Communication Theory*, *15*. https://doi.org/10.1093/ct/qtad015

Leach, R. B., Zanin, A. C., Tracy, S. J., & Adame, E. A. (2023). Collective compassion: Responding to structural barriers to compassion with agentic action in healthcare organizations. *Management Communication Quarterly* (online first). https://doi-org.ezproxy1.lib.asu.edu/10.1177/08933189231209724

Leiter, M. P., & Maslach, C. (2011). *Banishing burnout: Six strategies for improving your relationship with work*. Wiley.

Lutgen-Sandvik, P. (2006). Take this job and… quitting and other forms of resistance to workplace bullying. *Communication Monographs*, *73*(4), 406–433. https://doi.org/10.1080/03637750601024156

Lutgen-Sandvik, P. (2008). Intensive remedial identity work: Responses to workplace bullying as trauma and stigma. *Organization*, *15*(1), 97–119. https://doi.org/10.1177/1350508407084487

Lutgen-Sandvik, P., & McDermott, V. (2008). The constitution of employee-abusive organizations: A communication flows theory. *Communication Theory*, *18*(2), 304–333. https://doi.org/10.1111/j.1468-2885.2008.00324.x

Lutgen-Sandvik, P., Riforgiate, S., & Fletcher, C. (2011). Work as a source of positive emotional experiences and the discourses informing positive assessment. *Western Journal of Communication*, *75*(1), 2–27. https://doi.org/10.1080/10570314.2010.536963

Lutgen-Sandvik, P., & Tracy, S. J. (2012). Answering five key questions about workplace bullying: How communication scholarship provides thought leadership for transforming abuse at work. *Management Communication Quarterly*, *26*, 3–47. https://doi.org/10.1177/0893318911414400

Malvini Redden, S. (2013). How lines organize compulsory interaction, emotion management, and "emotional taxes": The implications of passenger emotion and expression in airport security lines. *Management Communication Quarterly*, *27*, 121–149. https://doi.org/10.1177/0893318912458213

Malvini Redden, S. (2021). *101 pat-downs: An undercover look at airport security and the TSA*. Potomac Press.

Malvini Redden, S., & Scarduzio, J. A. (2018). A different type of dirty work: Hidden taint, intersectionality, and emotion management in bureaucratic organizations. *Communication Monographs*, *85*(2), 224–244. https://doi.org/10.1080/03637751.2017.1394580

Maslach, C. (1982). *Burnout: The cost of caring*. Prentice Hall.

Mayer, J. D., Caruso, D. R., & Salovey, P. (2016). The ability model of emotional intelligence: Principles and updates. *Emotion Review*, *8*(4), 290–300. https://doi.org/10.1177/1754073916639667

McAllum, K. (2014). Meanings of organizational volunteering: Diverse volunteer pathways. *Management Communication Quarterly*, *28*(1), 84–110. https://doi.org/10.1177/0893318913517237

McAllum, K., Elvira, M. M., & Villamor Martin, M. (2024). "I only tell them the good parts:" How relational others influence paid careworkers' descriptions of their work as meaningful. *Management Communication Quarterly*, *38*(1), 171–202. https://doi.org/10.1177/08933189231180133

Meares, M. M., Oetzel, J. G., Derkacs, D., & Ginossar, T. (2004). Employee mistreatment and muted voices in the culturally diverse workforce. *Journal of Applied Communication Research*, *32*, 4–27. https://doi.org/10.1080/0090988042000178121

Men, L. R. (2014). Strategic internal communication: Transformational leadership, communication channels, and employee satisfaction. *Management Communication Quarterly*, *28*, 264–284. https://doi.org/10.1177/0893318914524536

Miller, K. (2007). Compassionate communication in the workplace: Exploring processes of noticing, connecting, and responding. *Journal of Applied Communication Research*, *35*, 223–245. https://doi.org/10.1080/00909880701434208

Miller, K. I., Stiff, J. B., & Ellis, B. H. (1988). Communication and empathy as precursors to burnout among human service workers. *Communication Monographs*, *55*(3), 250–265. https://doi.org/10.1080/03637758809376171

Mumby, D. K., & Putnam, L. L. (1992). The politics of emotion: A feminist reading of bounded rationality. *Academy of Management Review*, *17*, 465–486. https://doi.org/10.5465/amr.1992.4281983

Murphy, K. R. (Ed.) (2014). *A critique of emotional intelligence: What are the problems and how can they be fixed?* Routledge.

Namie, G., & Lutgen-Sandvik, P. E. (2010). Active and passive accomplices: The communal character of workplace bullying. *International Journal of Communication*, *4*, 343–373.

Newman, A., & Rivera, R. (2010, August 9). Fed-up flight attendant makes sliding exit. *The New York Times*. www.nytimes.com/2010/08/10/nyregion/10attendant.html

Paul, G. D., & Riforgiate, S. E. (2015). "Putting on a happy face," "getting back to work," and "letting it go": Traditional and restorative justice understandings of emotions at work. *Electronic Journal of Communication*, *25* (3/4). www.cios.org/getfile/025303_EJC

Poly, A. (2015). Emotional labour and employee performance appraisal: The missing link in some hotels in south east Nigeria. *International Journal of Hospitality and Tourism Systems*, *8*(2). https://pdfs.semanticscholar.org/2263/7ac93bd9f255064a19f540238d70b7e1a695.pdf

Powers, S. R., & Myers, K. K. (2020). Work-related emotional communication model of burnout: An analysis of emotions for hire. *Management Communication Quarterly*, *34*(2), 155–187. https://doi-org.ezproxy1.lib.asu.edu/10.1177/0893318919893765

Radey, M., & Figley, C. (2007). The social psychology of compassion. *Clinical Social Work Journal*, *35*(3), 207–214. https://doi.org/10.1007/s10615-007-0087-3

Rafaeli, A., & Sutton, R. I. (1987). Expression of emotion as part of the work role. *Academy of Management Review*, *12*(1), 23–37. https://doi.org/10.5465/amr.1987.4306444

Razzante, R., & Tracy, S. J. (2019). Co-cultural theory: Performing emotional labor from a position of exclusion. In C. J. Liberman, A. S. Rancer, & T. A. Avtgis (Eds.), *Casing communication theory* (pp. 117–130). Kendall Hunt.

Razzante, R., Tracy, S. J., & Orbe, M. P. (2018). How dominant group members can transform workplace bullying. In R. West & C. Beck (Eds.), *Routledge handbook of communication and bullying* (pp. 46–56). Routledge.

Razzante, R. J., & Orbe, M. P. (2018). Two sides of the same coin: Conceptualizing dominant group theory in the context of co-cultural theory. *Communication Theory*, *28*(3), 354–375. https://doi.org/10.1093/ct/qtx008

Richardson, G. E. (2002). The metatheory of resilience and resiliency. *Journal of Clinical Psychology*, *58*, 307–321. https://doi.org/10.1002/jclp.10020

Riforgiate, S., & Tracy, S. J. (2023). Management, organizational communication, and emotion. In G. L. Schiewer, J. Altarriba, & B. C. Ng (Eds.), *Handbook on language and emotion* (pp. 1853–1871). De Gruyter.

Riforgiate, S. E., Howes, S. S., & Simmons, M. J. (2022). The impact of daily emotional labor on health and well-being. *Management Communication Quarterly*, *36*(3), 391–417. https://doi-org.ezproxy1.lib.asu.edu/10.1177/08933189211041352

Rivera, K. D. (2015). Emotional taint: Making sense of emotional dirty work at the U.S. Border Patrol. *Management Communication Quarterly*, *29*, 198–228. https://doi.org/10.1177/0893318914554090

Rodino-Colocino, M. (2021). A pand(acad)emic plea for self-care and shorter hours. *Communication, Culture & Critique*, *14*(2), 315–319. https://doi.org/10.1093/ccc/tcab018

Scarduzio, J. A. (2011). Maintaining order through deviance? The emotional deviance, power, and professional work of municipal court judges. *Management Communication Quarterly*, *25*, 283–310. https://doi.org/10.1177/0893318910386446

Scarduzio, J. A., & Malvini Redden, S. (2015). *The positive outcomes of negative emotional displays: A multi-level analysis of emotion in bureaucratic work. Electronic Journal of Communication*, *25*(3/4).

Scarduzio, J. A., & Tracy, S. J. (2015). Sensegiving and sensebreaking via emotion cycles and emotional buffering: How collective communication creates order in the courtroom. *Management Communication Quarterly*, *29*, 331–357. https://doi.org/10.1177/0893318915581647

Shapiro, S. L., Carlson, L. E., Astin, J. A., & Freedman, B. (2006). Mechanisms of mindfulness. *Journal of Clinical Psychology*, *62*(3), 373–386. https://doi.org/10.1002/jclp.20237

Shenoy-Packer, S. (2015). Immigrant professionals, microaggressions, and critical sensemaking in the U.S. workplace. *Management Communication Quarterly*, *29*(2), 257–275. https://doi.org/10.1177/0893318914562069

Simon, H. A. (1982). *Models of bounded rationality: Empirically grounded economic reason* (Vol. 3). MIT Press.

Stanley, B. L., Zanin, A., Avalos, B., Tracy, S., & Town, S. (2021). Collective emotion during collective trauma: A metaphor analysis of the COVID-19 global pandemic. *Qualitative Health Research*, *31*, 1890–1903. https://doi.org/10.1177/10497323211011589

Thoroughgood, C. N., Hunter, S. T., & Sawyer, K. B. (2011). Bad apples, bad barrels, and broken followers? An empirical examination of contextual influences on follower perceptions and reactions to aversive leadership. *Journal of Business Ethics*, *100*(4), 647–672. https://doi.org/10.1007/s10551-010-0702-z

Tietsort, C. J., Tracy, S. J., & Adame, E. A. (2023). "You just don't talk about certain topics": How concerns to disclose suffering to leaders constrain compassion at work. *Sustainability*, *15*(5), 4628. https://doi.org/10.3390/su15054628

Town, S., Fairhurst, G. T., & Tracy, S. (2023). Processing organizational paradox: The role of mindfulness. *Academy of Management Proceedings*, *2023*(1), 13144. https://doi.org/10.5465/AMPROC.2023.13144abstract

Tracy, S. J. (2000). Becoming a character for commerce: Emotion labor, self subordination and discursive construction of identity in a total institution. *Management Communication Quarterly*, *14*, 90–128. https://doi.org/10.1177/0893318900141004

Tracy, S. J. (2005). Locking up emotion: Moving beyond dissonance for understanding emotion labor discomfort. *Communication Monographs*, *72*(3), 261–283. https://doi.org/10.1080/03637750500206474

Tracy, S. J. (2008). Care as a common good. *Women's Studies in Communication*, *31*, 166–174. https://doi.org/10.1080/07491409.2008.10162529

Tracy, S. J. (2009). Power, paradox, social support and prestige: A critical approach to addressing correctional officer burnout. In S. Fineman (Ed.), *Le emozioni nell'organizzazione*. Rafaello Cortina Editore.

Tracy, S. J. (2017). Burnout. In C. Scott & L. Lewis (Eds.), *The international encyclopedia of organizational communication* (online edition). Wiley-Blackwell. https://doi.org/10.1002/9781118955567.wbieoc015

Tracy, S. J., Alberts, J. K., & Rivera, K. D. (2007). *How to bust the office bully: Eight tactics for explaining workplace abuse to decision-makers*. https://staffombuds.berkeley.edu/sites/default/files/how_to_bust_the_office_bully.pdf
Tracy, S. J., & Huffman, T. P. (2017). Compassion in the face of terror: A case study of recognizing suffering, co-creating hope, and developing trust in a would-be school shooting. *Communication Monographs*, *84*, 30–53. https://doi.org/10.1080/03637751.2016.1218642
Tracy, S. J., Lutgen-Sandvik, P., & Alberts, J. K. (2006a). Nightmares, demons, and slaves: Exploring the painful metaphors of workplace bullying. *Management Communication Quarterly*, *20*(2), 148–185. https://doi.org/10.1177/0893318906291980
Tracy, S. J., Myers, K. K., & Scott, C. W. (2006b). Cracking jokes and crafting selves: Sensemaking and identity management among human service workers. *Communication Monographs*, *73*(3), 283–308. https://doi.org/10.1080/03637750600889500
Tye-Williams, S., & Krone, K. J. (2015). Chaos, reports, and quests: Narrative agency and co-workers in stories of workplace bullying. *Management Communication Quarterly*, *29*(1), 3–27. https://doi.org/10.1177/0893318914552029
Tye-Williams, S., & Krone, K. J. (2017). Identifying and reimagining the paradox of workplace bullying advice. *Journal of Applied Communication Research*, *45*(3), 218–235. https://doi.org/10.1080/00909882.2017.1288291
University of California, Berkeley. (2023). *New presidential policy on abusive conduct (bullying) in the workplace*. https://evcp.berkeley.edu/news/new-presidential-policy-abusive-conduct-bullying-workplace
Waldron, V. R. (2000). Relational experiences and emotions at work. In S. Fineman (Ed.), *Emotion in organizations* (pp. 64–82). Sage. https://doi.org/10.4135/9781446219850.n4
Waldron, V. R. (2012). *Communicating emotion at work*. Polity Press.
Way, D., & Tracy, S. J. (2012). Conceptualizing compassion as recognizing, relating and (re)acting: An ethnographic study of compassionate communication at hospice. *Communication Monographs*, *79*, 292–315. https://doi.org/10.1080/03637751.2012.697630
Wieland, S. M. (2020). Constituting resilience at work: Maintaining dialectics and cultivating dignity throughout a worksite closure. *Management Communication Quarterly*, *34*(4), 463–494. https://doi.org/10.1177/0893318920949314
Wingfield, A. H. (2010). Are some emotions marked "whites only"? Racialized feeling rules in professional workplaces. *Social Problems*, *57*(2), 251–268. https://doi.org/10.1525/sp.2010.57.2.251
Yamada, D. C. (2015). Workplace bullying and the law: US legislative developments 2013-15. *Employee Rights and Employment Policy Journal*, *19*, 49.
Zanin, A. C., Marr, C., & Avalos, B. L. (2023). Sport officiating as aggression work: A positioning analysis of gendered emotion management. *Management Communication Quarterly* (online first). https://doi/10.1177/08933189231200240

19 Technology and Organizational Communication

Keri K. Stephens and Kerk F. Kee

Organizational life is lived, and communication is shaped through and around information and communication technologies (ICTs). That might be a bold statement, but for scholars who study ICTs, organizations, and organizing, as well as people who lived through the COVID-19 pandemic, this realization grounds many current studies and lived experiences. This chapter includes a body of research that is interdisciplinary, showcasing the contributions of organizational communication scholars. It begins by providing a historical perspective on ICTs and organizational life that includes theories and empirical work from the 1980s to current day. It also examines concepts related to the adoption and diffusion of ICTs into organizational practices at the individual and organization levels. The chapter ends by suggesting areas of research that offer promise for further scholarly explorations as well as have societal implications.

Technology is a vague term with multiple meanings. For example, a refrigerator is a technology, and now that many interface with smart devices, they can actually "communicate" with the humans who need to restock them. But to understand how technology functions in an organizational context, there needs to be a more specific definition that reflects issues relevant for our field. In keeping with the communicative constitution of organization (CCO) perspective (see Chapter 3), this chapter uses a definition that encompasses communication with technology but also considers that information (referred to as *data* in the discussion of *big data* later in the chapter) is a key structure found in organizational life. *Computer-mediated communication* (CMC) is a term commonly used in several communication fields. Although CMC does combine the concepts of communication and technologies, the term *ICTs* is used throughout this chapter because it more closely aligns with organizational communication.

ICTs define the tangled nature of technologies that enable and constrain communication as well as various forms of organizational information. This approach assumes that ICTs – while not openly biased – are not necessarily neutral objects: Information and communication are inherently entwined with power and control (Beniger, 1989). This means that ICT use can influence and be influenced by a host of organizational variables and processes, including organization/organizing type, hierarchies, policies, individual preferences, job roles, and coworkers. ICTs are also linked to power in complex ways (see Chapter 12). Technologies in organizations are often controlled by higher-ranking members, reinforcing their decision-making power. Leaders may have access to advanced communication technologies or data, allowing them to control information flows, decision-making, and visibility (Stephens, 2018). Conversely, new technologies can enable lower-power individuals or groups to challenge the status quo. Digital platforms, for example, provide opportunities for employees to organize, collaborate, or challenge hierarchical norms outside formal structures (Gossett & Kilker, 2006).

DOI: 10.4324/9781003484639-22

In the past decade, exciting changes have occurred in how organizational communication scholars study technology: We have embraced prior calls to move beyond studying how communication happens *through* ICTs (Rice & Leonardi, 2014) and we now study how communication and organizing happen *around* ICTs (e.g., Bimber et al., 2012; Ganesh & Stohl, 2010; Leonardi, 2009; Stephens, 2018). This has helped the sub-discipline of organizational communication contribute to the growing perspective that technology is an integral part of the communicative constitution of organizational life. When organizational communication scholars study technology, we use our field's theoretical assumptions and frameworks to guide our research, but we also build on theories found in other disciplines. Thus, today we focus less on specific technologies and their features, which will likely change over time, and more on structures and processes that will shape and are shaped by communication technologies.

Therefore, the frame used in this chapter to understand the role technology plays in organizational communication is the following: *Organizational life is lived, and communication is shaped, through and around ICTs*. This framework follows the communication-organization cycle guiding this book and reflects the mutual enabling and constraining relationship between communication and organization seen in ICTs. For example, in some organizations, email (an ICT) is understood by the communication practices that shape its use, but it also constrains communication because it is not feasible or advisable to copy many people on every email. Furthermore, email can be a flexible ICT for asynchronous communication; people can read and respond at their own leisure. However, users can become too dependent on the convenience of asynchronous email communication and thus use it as a substitute for much needed face-to-face (FtF) communication, sometimes under the wrong circumstances. Here we can see how daily communication through and with ICTs and enduring organizational structures enable and constrain one another over time.

Because it was not always this way in studies of technology and organization, this chapter begins with a historical perspective on ICTs and organizational life. The early theorizing around ICTs began in the field of management, but organizational communication scholars quickly joined these efforts and created a robust set of early conversations to address the explosive growth in communication technology in organizational contexts.

This chapter is organized as follows. First, we provide an overview of the three foundational perspectives on understanding ICTs' use in organizational life. Second, we discuss organizational communication research in understanding the adoption and diffusion of ICTs into organizational practices at the individual and organizational levels. Third, we explore the various ways scholars have studied communication with and through ICTs in organizational processes. Fourth, we examine how cultures manifest in the integration of ICTs into organizational life. Finally, we conclude with a reflection of the ways organizational communication scholarship and ICTs help us answer the three central questions of communication, organization, and the communication-organization cycle guiding this book.

Historical Perspective on ICTs and Organization

Many organizational scholars have focused on how technology can structure communication (e.g., Barley's, 1986, work on CT scanners). With the 1980s growth in forms of communication technologies, it was also important to develop an understanding of how the material devices functioned for communication. Between the 1980s and early 2000s, developing theories and empirical studies progressed from viewing technology as being the key deciding factor in how communication *should happen* to a more social constructivist view, where other people are a dominant influence in using technology to communicate. This chapter adopts a waves metaphor to explain these shifting perspectives. We begin with a focus on the technology-deterministic wave.

The Technology-Deterministic Wave

Imagine a time when organizations did not rely on email and smartphones to coordinate and communicate. Although ICTs like computers, documents, and landline phones have been a part of organizational life for more than 60 years, this is still a young and rapidly changing area of study. In the early 1970s, the telecommunication field began explaining the presumed magic present in FtF communication that did not exist as fully when communicating over the telephone and videoconferencing. The theory of *social presence* (Short et al., 1976) identified that magic and defined it as the "degree of salience of the other person in the interaction and the consequent salience of interpersonal relationships" (p. 65). Short and his colleagues (1976) placed ICTs on a continuum of their ability to convey social presence. There was an assumption that some tasks required a high degree of social presence, so communicators should match their tasks and ICTs. Notice that this is not an organization-specific theory, but it forms the foundation for the next major theoretical development around ICTs in the field of management.

Many ICTs were not ubiquitous in the 1980s, and most of them had distinct features that allowed scholars to categorize these technologies into what was considered their inherent communication potentials. As these communication tools diffused into organizations, management scholars created new theories to help managers optimize their time and use them effectively, building theories around *information* and *media richness* (Daft & Lengel, 1984, 1986). Management scholars and social psychologists often focused on organizational environments as being uncertain (Weick, 1979), unpredictable, and having vast information-processing needs (Daft & Lengel, 1984). Media richness theory (MRT) – the popularized term from the original work on information richness – became a logical, structured roadmap for managers needing to make difficult ICT use decisions.

Richness is a set of properties that an ICT possesses, with four criteria that determine an ICT's richness (capability to convey robust details): (1) Feedback timeliness; (2) multiple cues available for interpretation; (3) language variety; and (4) personal focus. FtF communication is considered the richest medium because of access to immediate feedback, nonverbal cues, language variation, and emotional message tailoring to make the conversation more personal. Much like the continuum found in social presence theory, a continuum of ICTs ranges from richest (i.e., FtF) to leanest (i.e., print documents).

Since the goal of MRT was to help managers be more efficient in handling complex organizational realities, the theory also proposed that managers should match their communication needs with the ideal ICT, following an optimizing strategy. Imagine these two examples of a mismatch in communication needs and efficiency in communicating:

- You walk seven blocks to a person's office to ask for a copy of a report that is available online. When you get to her office, you chat for 30 minutes, and walk back to your office, spending an unnecessary hour.
- Your colleague sends you a text message asking why you are rejecting a proposal to restructure your department and lay off four of your staff. You roll your eyes and respond, "duh!" Seven text messages later you realize that your colleague was concerned about his friend losing her job.

MRT suggests considering two main factors before choosing the ICT to use. First, if the request is meant to answer a question (reduce uncertainty), a leaner ICT, like email, would optimize efficiency. Second, if the request is complex and involves emotions (an equivocal task), a richer medium, such as FtF communication, will likely be needed to leverage the features of a rich ICT. Building on MRT, Trevino et al. (1987) expanded this theory to align with a symbolic interactionist framework, highlighting ICTs as carriers of symbolic meaning. For example, a written letter symbolizes formality. These types of extensions, and some early empirical comparisons, reveal the incompleteness of a rational task-matching ICT framework. Rice's (1992) comprehensive comparative studies provided direct tests of social presence theory and MRT finding that while FtF was consistently ranked the highest in richness and social presence, the continuum broke down with added gradations of new ICTs.

Multidisciplinary Nature of Early Theorizing and Empirical Work

While much of the early research on ICTs was conducted in the field of management, organizational scholars across disciplines were regular contributors to these bodies of literature. For example, Rice conducted empirical tests of early theories (e.g., Rice, 1992, 1993), and communication scholars Fulk and Poole were regular coauthors with management professor DeSanctis. Together, these partnerships created some of the most foundational theoretical works in organizational communication and technology, grounded in a multidisciplinary perspective. Fulk partnered with Steinfield to edit one of the most grounding books in this area: *Organizations and Communication Technology* (1990). She engaged in several additional partnerships that yielded a pivotal contribution with the social influence model (Fulk, 1993; Fulk et al., 1990). DeSanctis and Fulk's (1999) edited book, *Shaping Organization Form: Communication, Connection, and Community*, set the stage for the explosive use of ICTs and how they shaped (and were shaped by) organizational life. DeSanctis and Poole (1994) embraced a more structurational approach, explaining that different groups use ICTs differently, which developed into adaptive structuration theory (see Chapters 3 and 15). Therefore, considering social aspects of ICT use became the norm. The topics of media richness and social presence became more salient during the pandemic when the whole world transitioned to virtual work quickly, solely depending on ICTs.

The Social Construction and Emergent Perspectives Wave

As more scholars began to question whether the richness and ICT-matching approach provides extensive explanatory value, new theories, models, and perspectives entered the field. These theories claimed that people and social considerations matter more than the ICTs themselves; thus, a wave of social-construction-oriented theories emerged. In their social influence model, Fulk and colleagues (1990) built their claims by relying on theories of social learning, organizational norms, and social-information processing. They included ICT features as part of their model, but also included peoples' experiences and skills in using the ICTs along with task features, and situational factors. Of particular relevance for organizational communication, Fulk identified four social factors that influence ICT perceptions and use: (1) direct statements by coworkers in organizations; (2) vicarious learning – observing others; (3) organizational norms for how ICTs should be evaluated and used; and (4) social definitions of rationality. This socially oriented theory did not lend itself to then-popular quantitative methods and experimental research; yet it garnered support. For example, Fulk's (1993) measure of social influence was found to predict individuals' ICT attitudes as well as when they choose to use a particular ICT. Furthermore, research concluded that large enough groups of people need to use specific ICTs to reach *critical mass* (Markus, 1990) before the technologies will naturally diffuse widely. Yet, the general feeling was that something was still missing in this ICT-use puzzle.

There was growing evidence that individuals, groups, and organizations use what appears to be the exact same ICTs in very different ways. DeSanctis and Poole (1994) drew from the macro, societal-level metatheoretical perspective of structuration theory, to develop what they called adaptive structuration theory (see Chapters 3 and 15). They theorized that a combination of technologies and social influences explain why some groups adapt technology in unexpected, novel ways. Their theory has since been used extensively in organizational communication, information systems, and management.

Carlson and Zmud (1999) pivoted from understanding how people select specific ICTs to expand Fulk and colleagues' notion of experience, arguing that users can expand their perception of a specific ICT. These scholars, along with researchers like D'Urso and Rains (2008) have tested the value of channel expansion theory and found that as users become more experienced with a given ICT, they will view it as richer. Other scholars, primarily in management, argued that the materiality of ICTs – like features – were so entwined with the social and organizational environment that it was impossible to examine them independently; thus, the concept of sociomateriality emerged (Orlikowski, 2007). In response to these claims, Leonardi (2009) and colleagues pushed back to demonstrate that even though both material and social factors matter, materiality can play a key role in enabling and constraining organizational communication.

To this point in ICT theorizing most theories assumed that people used a single ICT for each task, but there was growing evidence this assumption was false (e.g., Rice et al., 2004), especially when mobile devices appeared and included multiple ICTs in a single tool. For example, is a smartphone a telephone, email, an Internet-access device, or a texting tool? It serves all these functions, and how users draw from the affordances of these tools further explains ICT use. While web conferencing has long been studied (e.g., Stephens & Mottet, 2008), during the pandemic platforms like Zoom and Microsoft Teams offered users different ICTs on one platform, integrating features such as video-conferencing, chat, screen share, collaborative whiteboard, breakout groups, and document sharing. Organizational members used these features based on observing others and kept their cameras on or off during meetings (Stephens et al., 2020); these behaviors provide modern examples of the social construction of ICT use.

Combinatorial ICT Use Wave

The third wave of understanding how ICTs are used in an organizational context focused on sequential and simultaneous use. Stephens (2007) developed ICT succession theory to illustrate how people build and expand on the material and social considerations of ICT use when they chain them over time. She and her colleagues further illustrated how this functioned by explaining patterns in sequential ICT-use pairs (Stephens et al., 2008). Browning et al. (2008) presented narratives collected between 1999 and 2003 of combinatorial ICT use in Norway and the U.S., connecting these narratives to organizational theories that explained and situated their interviewees' experiences with ICTs.

Simultaneous ICT use also began emerging as people multitasked and multicommunicated in various organizational contexts. Multicommunicating is a theoretically derived term describing what happens when people use technology to carry on multiple conversations simultaneously (Reinsch et al., 2008). Simultaneous conversations are more cognitively taxing than multitasking, or doing two things at once (Reinsch et al., 2008). This practice is often on display during organizational meetings, whether in person or through an online conferencing system.

Cyberinfrastructure

Simultaneous and sequential ICT use also occurs in the emerging concept of cyberinfrastructure. Cyberinfrastructure can be understood as an interwoven collection of ICTs, specialized software, computing hardware, remote instruments, big data, high speed networks, virtual processes, organizational policies, and human experts (Hayes et al., 2023; Kee & Browning, 2010). Scholars in this area argue we need to understand the larger infrastructure in which the ICTs are embedded to avoid studying ICTs out of context. Furthermore, increasingly the use of one ICT is dependent on an infrastructure of many other ICTs and technologies available for combinatorial use. Therefore, to manage effective organizational infrastructure, particularly when organizing virtually, we need to understand when and how technologies are simultaneously and sequentially used to achieve organizational goals.

Affordances of Communication Technologies

Work on the affordances of communication technologies builds on the ideas that materiality matters, social parameters are influential, and contemporary tools provide many options. Affordances are material features that individuals and groups can choose to use to accomplish relational communication objectives (Evans et al., 2017). The concept of affordances did not originate in the field of communication, but organizational-, interpersonal-, and mobile-communication researchers have embraced it because it provides conceptual framing that helps technology discussions move beyond deterministic assumptions (e.g., Evans et al., 2017; Rice et al., 2017; Stephens, 2018; Treem & Leonardi, 2012). While management and information systems scholars have also embraced the concept of affordances, this chapter focuses on contributions by organizational communication researchers.

Evans and her team (2017) reviewed the literature to date on technology affordances, noting that researchers often identify affordances, but then fail to conceptually develop them. Conceptual development is a strength in much organizational communication research because our scholars are now leading the effort to conceptualize and theorize around affordances of technologies. For example, one group of researchers has focused on the affordances of social media (Treem & Leonardi, 2012) and linked these concepts to expertise and knowledge-sharing (Ellison et al., 2015). Stephens (2018) elaborated the affordance of reachability and dimensionalized this affordance into the temporal variables *frequency* and *predictability*. In addition, Rice and colleagues (2017) have looked beyond the individual level to argue that there are organizational media affordances that exist beyond an individual ICT and which are associated with practices found in organizational life.

Enterprise Social Media

Organizational communication scholars have focused their work on affordances around enterprise social media. This type of social media is different from personal platforms, such as Facebook, because they are tools used only by organizational members (the enterprise). Treem and Leonardi (2012) identified and elaborated four affordances that often exist in social media tools: visibility, persistence, editability, and association. These affordances are not necessarily unique to enterprise social media, but they reflect relational perspectives and the importance of human agency found in and around these forms of technology. Leonardi (2014) further developed the affordance of visibility into a grounded theory that reveals how organizational members experience the tensions of being open and sharing information while also managing their own impressions.

Table 19.1 A timeline of ICT use theories situated in organizational life[a]

Social presence theory	Short et al. (1976)
Media richness theory	Daft and Lengel (1984) Trevino et al. (1987)
Social influence model	Fulk (1993) Fulk et al. (1990)
Critical mass	Markus (1990)
Adaptive structuration theory	DeSanctis and Poole (1994)
Channel expansion theory	Carlson and Zmud (1999)
ICT succession theory	Stephens (2007)
Multicommunicating	Reinsch et al. (2008)
Sociomateriality	Orlikowski (2007)
Materiality matters	Leonardi (2009)
Affordances of enterprise social media	Treem and Leonardi (2012)

[a] Please note that these do not include many of the group-communication, interpersonal, or information-systems theories that are related, but not discussed in this chapter.

Table of Theories

This chapter has covered a host of theories so far. To facilitate understanding of this breadth of the field, Table 19.1 summarizes them before we move into our next section. Look back into the sections that describe these theories and see if you can find how they build on and diverge from earlier work.

ICT Diffusion into Organizational Practices

It is not a given that ICTs designed and developed by technologists and software companies will become integrated into organizational life. Many ICTs are tried and rejected, and only some are adopted into organizational contexts. Furthermore, some ICTs become staples, while others are discontinued or replaced by newer ICTs. We now turn the discussion to understanding how ICTs are adopted and diffused in modern organizational contexts.

When examining technology through the three lenses of organizational communication (as an organizing process, as organized structures, and as an entity), another branch of theoretical and empirical research on structures emerges. This area of research also has a long history, and it can be considered macro-organizational because most of the scholarship has focused on how organizational entities acquire and deploy technology to enable communication and coordination.

Adoption and Diffusion

Adoption is defined as an individual organizational member's decision to accept, reject, and/or discontinue using a new technology, while diffusion refers to the systemic phenomenon of the spreading of a new technology as it integrates within organizational life (Kee, 2017a). The literature on adoption and diffusion is multidisciplinary, including research from sociology (Ryan & Gross, 1943), public health (Valente & Pumpuang, 2007), and most importantly communication (Rogers, 1962, 2003). Everett Rogers, a pioneer in the field of communication, is the key figure who is most identified with diffusion and adoption research, including in organizational communication.

Originally trained in rural sociology, Everett Rogers spent most of his career as a Professor of Communication. Rogers published the first edition of his classic text, *Diffusion of Innovations* (1962), to describe a theory of how innovations are adopted and diffused, as he recognized a striking general pattern documented by researchers across diverse fields. Rogers explicitly defined *diffusion* as a communication process through which an innovation spreads in social systems via various communication channels over time. In the fifth and last edition of his classic text, Rogers (2003) described how the Internet was the fastest adopted and diffused innovation in human history. In 2024, our field is witnessing the rapid adoption of AI tools, such as ChatGPT and Copilot with Microsoft, Bard/Gemini with Google.

Individual-Level Adoption

Diffusion researchers interested in understanding individual adoption of technologies focused on identifying innovation attributes, such as relative advantage, compatibility, complexity, trialability, and observability perceived by individual adopters (Rice, 2009; Rogers, 2003). Different types of adopters of technology have unique socio-psycho profiles: *innovators* (2.5%), *early adopters* (13.5%), *early majority* (34.0%), *late majority* (34.0%), and *laggards* (16.0%). This line of research helps researchers better understand why some organizational members tend to be the first to adopt and experiment with a new ICT, while some take longer to use it, and others never really get on board. Understanding different adopter groups in organizations is important, because these group differences can lead to digital divides (Van Dijk, 2020) and knowledge gap bias (Kee, 2017a) within the workplace. For example, some employees may have a greater ability to adopt and benefit from technology due to economic status, prior education, or early exposure, placing others at a disadvantage. Moreover, organizational policies (such as "bring your own device" [BYOD] or remote work setups) often favor certain employees who can afford high-quality personal devices or faster internet connections, further entrenching inequality (Stephens, 2018).

Taking a deterministic perspective, the case of ICT adoption and diffusion in organizational contexts can be metaphorically described as *the ripple effect* or *the domino effect* (Kee, 2017a). However, organizational members have agency. An important concept in diffusion research is *reinvention*, which refers to the repurposing of a technology in creative ways unintended by the original designer. Rice and Rogers (1980) argued that reinvention is natural, showing ordinary users in their adaptation and modification of an innovation as they struggle to give meaning(s) to technology in the organizational contexts of their local problems and cultures. Furthermore, diffusion research also examines how individuals in social networks, especially opinion leaders with many *weak ties* (Granovetter, 1973, see also Chapter 9), naturally spread new technologies within social systems. This body of literature sheds light on how word-of-mouth and interpersonal communication are more powerful in persuading about the value of a new technology than official advertising messages from vendors and other sources.

Organization-Level Adoption

Organizational communication researchers also study organizational adoption of ICTs, in addition to individual adoption, because of *contingent adoption decisions* (Rice, 2009). Individuals only have access to an ICT after the organization has adopted it. Moreover, individuals do not always make adoption decisions by personal choice because they can be an organizational requirement. The adoption of Zoom or MS Teams during the pandemic, as required by organizations or managers, is a case in point. Therefore, organizational adoption of ICTs is key to understanding the relationship between technology and organizational communication.

Organizational adoption of ICTs is usually driven by observations of practices in peer organizations and trends in the industries. Subsequently, drawing upon institutional theory, Zorn et al. (2011) illustrated that organizational adoption of ICTs is driven by isomorphic pressure – conforming to industry norms. This pressure also stems from the perceived need for achieving organizational power derived from social and institutional legitimacy. Zorn and his team (2011) concluded that isomorphic pressures are most predictive of organizational adoption of ICTs, stronger than other factors such as budget and company size.

When the COVID-19 pandemic radically changed how knowledge workers could communicate by removing FtF as an option, several rapid ICT adoptions occurred. Organizations adopted video-based platforms, such as Zoom and Teams, and employees either taught themselves (e.g., Stephens, 2022) or attended training the learn this new way of communicating, teaching, and socializing (McGloin et al., 2022). Communication practices between work colleagues and supervisors changed as people used text messages to build rapport (McGloin et al., 2022) and photos to participate in visual discussions (Näsi, 2023).

When an innovation is adopted and integrated into organizational life, change often occurs. It is human nature to resist organizational change, although some people recognize the need to constantly innovate and adapt to new challenges. Lewis (2014) offers an alternative to treating organizational change as a reaction to new technologies by arguing that internal and environmental sensemaking usually occur simultaneously and are mutually influential. Thus, change in the external environment often influences the change resulting from the adoption and diffusion of ICTs in organizational life, and vice versa. This insight reveals that sensemaking, communication, and interaction during ICT diffusion are complex relationships, especially during reinvention (see Chapter 21).

The Future of ICTs and Organizational Life

Big Data

Big data is a relatively new term that describes the immense amount of data (structured, semi-structured and unstructured) that now inundates organizations and outpaces the capabilities of traditional data management tools and practices. Big data is increasingly important for organizational communication. For example, a social network analysis of email exchanges can reveal the most central communicators in the organization (Kossinets & Watts, 2009). Big data is defined often by characteristics such as volume, variety, velocity (Laney, 2001), variability, veracity, and value (Gandomi & Haider, 2015). *Volume* refers to the size of data while *variety* denotes the diversity of data formats. *Velocity* describes data's production and processing speed, but *variability* expresses the fluctuating and erratic data flow rates. *Veracity* means despite imprecision and inexactitude, big data possess hidden insights. *Value* implies the significance of big data. Although the literature has discussed these six different characteristics, big data is generally defined in industry by what has become known as the "five Vs," omitting variability (Kee, 2017b).

Kee (2017b) recommends understanding the big data movement through a factory metaphor: data are being generated in a standardized, predictable, centralized, and efficient manner – akin to how goods were produced during the Industrial Revolution. Standardization and predictability can reduce the challenges of big data's variety and variability. Having centralized data repositories and efficient computing resources to process big data can support big data's volume and velocity. As noted in Chapter 5, classical management emerged during the Industrial Revolution due to the invention of steam engines and emergence of factories. A re-emergence of classical management principles and practices may inform how big data are integrated into organizational life in the third decade of the 21st century.

Many organizational processes continuously generate data, and in turn, use that data to guide decisions like changes to products, people, and processes. This is one reason we link information with communication when we have addressed technologies, or ICTs, in this chapter. ICTs are dynamic; software is continuously updated; and the latest smartphone today is old news tomorrow.

The future of communication technologies as a part of the fabric of organizational structures is the integration of robots, artificial intelligence, and virtual reality. These technologies are studied in other fields (e.g., Stone et al., 2018) and in areas of interpersonal communication, persuasion, and human–computer interaction (e.g., Lee & Liang, 2016). Imagine human paramedics and rescue robots working together as a team to save lives during a crisis or disaster. Customers enter an instant messenger chat with an artificial intelligence agent, or chatbot, for screening and pre-scripted answers before being escalated to a human agent. Knowledge workers use AI chatbots, such as ChatGPT, to brainstorm ideas and draft company reports. Dispersed workers use virtual reality to enable a robust collaboration as if they are co-located, especially in multinational organizations.

However, cultural power dynamics, including how ICT adoption can vary across cultural contexts, particularly in multinational organizations and global teams (Boyraz, 2019), where technologies might privilege Western managerial styles over other culturally rooted practices should be considered. Technology might impose structures that favor one group while marginalizing others, thus embedding power inequities across different regions and employee groups.

Moreover, with the rise of AI, those with access to AI tools are better equipped to handle large data volumes and make predictive decisions, reinforcing power in certain roles. Additionally, global organizations may experience varying levels of access to ICTs based on their location's cyberinfrastructure. Employees in developing countries might face limited bandwidth or restricted access to software tools, making it harder to compete or collaborate equally with colleagues from more developed regions. These are examples of the digital divide and knowledge gap bias on a global scale. Therefore, it is crucial to consider how technologies like robots, artificial intelligence, and virtual reality can enable, constrain, and assist humans in their organizational life, as they will be significant areas of study for our field.

We observe that most theories and literature cited in this chapter are US- and Western-based. This may reflect that, among all conferences attended by technology researchers in organizational communication, only the International Communication Association annual conference includes some scholars from the Global South and other non-Western regions. However, their numbers are relatively small compared to attendees from the US and Western countries. A head count of the editorial board of *Management Communication Quarterly*, the premier journal for organizational communication, shows about 93% of members are scholars based in North America, followed by Europe (7%), Asia (3%), Australasia (2%), and Latin America (1%). These trends highlight the lack of non-US theories on technology adoption and use in the workplace summarized in this chapter. We hope this observation inspires the next generation of organizational communication scholars to move towards a more globalized future, especially in studying workplace technology, as virtual organizations and remote work teams in the post-pandemic era know no boundaries.

Communicating With and Through Technology in Organizing Processes

Many of the ICT use theories shared in the historical timeline can and likely do apply to organizing practices. Yet, there are important considerations of contemporary organizing, especially when groups are dispersed, loosely connected, and their communication and coordination practices are displayed visually through organizing software and platforms. When groups draw upon communicative affordances, like visibility found through social media (Treem & Leonardi, 2012), new connections can emerge and so can opportunities. ICTs also play a vital role in organizing and coordinating collective action in diverse organizations (Bimber et al., 2012). While this growing body of research often is addressed separately from ICTs and organizational life, these ideas are becoming entwined, thus, this chapter puts them in conversation with one another. Let us expand this idea and briefly discuss some core literature around networks, emergent groups, and ICT use.

Networks and Organizing

Networks connect people and provide opportunities for communication and organizing (see Chapter 9). Communication networks were rather invisible until ICTs, such as email and social media, became ubiquitous in organizations. Now connections and information flows are more easily seen and are linked often to the collection of and sensemaking around big data. Shumate and Contractor (2014) define communication networks as "relations among various types of actors that illustrate the ways in which messages are transmitted, exchanged, or interpreted" (p. 449). A unique contribution of this definition is the notion of "multidimensional networks" – networks consisting of different types of human and non-human nodes (e.g., individuals, organizations, and technologies) and different types of linkages (e.g., information transmission, collaborations) (Contractor et al., 2011). Drawing from an earlier example in the MRT section of this chapter, instead of walking seven blocks to a person's office to ask for a copy of a report (i.e., a person–person link in the form of a communication request), you can download the report directly from the web (i.e., a person–technology link in the form of information retrieval). Both forms of networks are valid, and the latter is multidimensional.

Shumate and Contractor (2014) describe three types of infrastructure networks that relate clearly to how ICTs are discussed in this chapter. First, *technological* networks support the message flow among technologies, such as telephone networks and Internet connections. Second, *physical* networks refer to how close or proximate organizational members are to each other in time and space. For instance, the locations and physical distance between offices demonstrates a physical network. Finally, *affiliation* networks imply the relation between members and their organizational entities. For example, organizations' memberships in the same consortium suggest a particular affiliation among them. These communication and infrastructure networks connect members and ICTs in a complex multidimensional web and provide opportunities for communication and organizing.

Online and Emergent Groups

Groups that organize online, rather than in a physical space, are often called virtual groups, online groups, and digital groups. Organizational communication and crisis informatics scholars, as one relevant example, have studied how online groups emerge, organize, and coordinate their actions – often on a temporary basis – using ICTs during disasters and emergencies (e.g., Chewing et al., 2013; Smith et al., 2018; Starbird & Palen, 2011). Urgent situations are infused with uncertainty; official responses often vary, and community groups want to help (Smith et al., 2018). Starbird and Palen (2011) have coined the term "digital volunteers" to explain how dispersed volunteers self-organize through online platforms, like social media, to provide a collective response. In addition, ICTs often work hand-in-hand with organizing practices like information sharing, connecting people, and acquiring resources (Chewing et al., 2013). Furthermore, formal and informal groups use ICTs differently depending on the stage of a crisis and the recovery to that crisis (Chewing et al., 2013).

Research on online and emergent groups is highly interdisciplinary and organizational scholars are in an ideal place to understand the role that structure – including ICTs – plays as online groups continue to self-organize and dissolve right before our digital eyes. ICTs play key roles in the global social justice movement, providing opportunities to connect people who are not co-located (Ganesh & Stohl, 2010). These findings suggest more research is needed in this area.

Culture and ICTs

Throughout this chapter, elements of culture have appeared. Whether in an understanding of how ICT adoption and diffusion is shaped by local culture, in models such as Fulk et al.'s (1990) social influence model or in DeSanctis and Poole's (1994) adaptive structuration theory, many aspects of culture are entwined with ICTs. Culture can be defined as "a negotiated set of shared symbolic systems that guide individuals' behaviors and incline them to function as a group" (Chen & Starosta, 1998, p. 26). When organizational communication scholars examine culture, we consider more than artifacts, belief, values, and norms; we examine how individuals perceive these cultures as well as they cultural roots of perceptual differences. Next, we address two additional ways notions of culture intersect with ICTs and organizational communication: work/life and occupational differences.

Work/Life

Culture considerations infuse the body of communication scholarship known as work/life, and ICTs have helped further complicate issues of agency and boundaries. In their handbook chapter on work/life, Kirby and Buzzanell (2014) highlight the myriad ways ICTs are entwined with work/life concerns and practices. For example, work practices like telework – meaning people who work either fully or partially out of their home – offer clear examples of the cultural complexity present when some employees are not physically present in the workplace. Leonardi et al. (2010) studied these issues and found workers who used ICTs to work remotely experienced what they termed *the connectivity paradox*. The ICTs that appear to afford benefits of flexibility and working remotely are negated by the very ICTs that make the telework arrangement possible. In response, teleworkers use ICTs to create the impression they are working just like when they were co-located at a physical office.

Another intersection between ICTs, work-life, and culture concerns mobile communication. Through personal mobile devices, employees and coworkers are reachable regardless of whether it is during their work hours (Stephens, 2018). Further, most organizations have adopted some form of BYOD to Work policy because some employees, and information technology departments, want people to provide and use their same communication tools for work and personal life (Stephens, 2018; Stephens et al., 2017). Coworkers and managers can pressure peers to be available when the team needs their help, and this expectation can develop into cultural norms (Stephens, 2018). During the COVID-19 pandemic, Portugal and other countries in Europe enacted laws to help employees deal with the loss of context between home and work and personal and professional ICT use, but it was less common in the United States (Stephens, 2023), and many employees had to make it work in this time of rapid ICT change (Stephens et al., 2020). When mobile communication devices enter organizational life, they enable and constrain both communication practices and organizational processes and structures.

Occupational Differences

Another culture-related consideration for ICTs and organizational life involves understanding that people in different occupations will often use ICTs in disparate ways. Bailey and Leonardi (2016) examined the question of technology choices among three different groups of engineers: structural engineers, hardware engineers, and automotive engineers. Although the three types of engineering work are equally complex, they approach their technology use differently. For example, structural engineers minimize the role of computers but prefer to depend on pen and paper, hardware engineers maximize their use of computers, and automotive engineers maintain a balance between relying on computer simulated crash tests versus physical crash tests for automotive design. Their study reveals that technologies are not universal, and workers vary in their embrace of technologies primarily based on their occupations and occupational cultures.

In her longitudinal study of people from 35 different occupations, Stephens (2018) found there were also differences in the policies and cultural practices surrounding ICT-use expectations depending on people's job roles. People in more powerful or knowledge worker positions had fewer restrictions than people in manual labor or customer service roles. However, Stephens (2018) ultimately finds that regardless of occupation, most people have negotiated control over their communication with their friends and family, and some of those negotiations tie back to work-life issues.

Conclusion

Let us revisit the framework used in this chapter: *Organizational life is lived, and communication is shaped, through and around ICTs*. In this chapter, technology use and communication are constitutive components of organizational life, and we narrowed our discussions of ICTs to situate how organizational communication scholars have played an integral role in developing theories and understanding. ICT use is a practice and a process where organizational members use multiple ICTs concurrently and sequentially to achieve myriad goals, such as information, persuasion, or organizing.

Organization is conceptualized and used by ICT scholars in myriad ways, and sometimes the same scholars use different approaches depending on the goals of their research. Early researchers – discussed in this chapter as those associated with the technological determinism wave – often viewed this as more of an entity (O_3); a place where technology was used (e.g., Daft & Lengel, 1984). This did not change substantially during the social construction wave, as scholars viewed ICT use as heavily shaped by people in and around organizations (O_3). During the third wave, when combinations of ICTs were studied, organization became viewed as a process (O_1); this was especially in the case in virtual organizations and as enterprise social media were included in the ICT mix.

Diffusion researchers, as well as many more contemporary scholars, view organization as an organizing process (O_1), sometimes considering how organizing occurs in, around, and through technologies over time (e.g., Smith et al., 2018). In that sense, diffusion is inherently organizational in nature, in that it can be understood as an organizing process (O_1) in the entity of an organization (O_3). For scholars who study big data, organizations and their members *are* the data sources for pattern recognition, detection, and/or prediction. Organizations are once again treated as an entity (O_3), but they also become the target to which conclusions are applied with the goal of improving organizing (O_1) and the structures associated with being organized (O_2). While in Chapter 1 O_3 is understood as the result of O_1 and O_2, here we see how O_3 can feed back to O_1 and O_2. Furthermore, many researchers discussed in this chapter consider organization as a structure (O_2) (DeSanctis & Poole, 1994; Ganesh & Stohl, 2010; Shumate & Contractor, 2014).

Finally, in keeping with the core questions considered in this book, this chapter acknowledged all three organization perspectives, but focused on how people have some choices in how they communicate, organize, and use ICTs. This chapter has both used and applied the C-O cycle introduced in Chapter 1 to illustrate the complexities of ICT use in organizational life, and to stress the mutual enabling and constraining relationship between communication and organization seen in ICTs. The examples and ideas shared here should illustrate the role that human agency plays as the communication and organization spiral incorporates ICTs into organizational life.

Recommended Supplementary Readings

Applied

Barley, S. R., Myers, D. E., & Grodal, S. (2011). E-mail as a source and symbol of stress. *Organization Science, 22*, 887–906.

A thought-provoking look at how we blame email for our stress.

Berkelaar, B. L. (2014). Cybervetting, online information, and personnel selection: New transparency expectations and the emergence of a digital social contract. *Management Communication Quarterly, 28*, 479–506.

Rich study examining the process of cybervetting – snooping online about employees.

Stephens, K. K., Jahn, J., Fox, S., Charoensap-Kelly, P., Mitra, R., Sutton, J., Waters, E. D., Xie, B., & Meisenbach, R. J. (2020). Collective sensemaking around COVID-19: Experiences, concerns, and agendas for our rapidly changing organizational lives.

A thought-provoking reflection on how COVID-19 changed people's use of ICTs and their lives.

Historical Theory

Stephens, K. K., & Mandhana, D. M. (2017). Media choice/use in organizations. In C. R. Scott & L. K. Lewis (Eds.), *The international encyclopedia of organizational communication* (online edition). Wiley-Blackwell.

This encyclopedia entry provides an accessible look at how the foundational theories have changed over time.

DeSanctis, G., & Fulk, J. L. (1994). *Shaping organization form: Communication, connection, and community*. Sage.
Fulk, J., & Steinfield, C. (1990). *Organizations and communication technology*. Sage.

These books provide a grounding in organizational communication and technology.

Important Concepts: Define and Discuss

Adoption
Affordances
Big data
BYOD
Channels
Combinatorial ICT use
Cyberinfrastructure
Diffusion
Enterprise social media
ICTs
Materiality
Mobile devices
Multicommunicating
Networks
Online (social) movements
Social media
Technology
Also see Table 19.1 for a list of the core theories.

Discussion Questions

1 Skim the Internet for 5 minutes and identify the popular topics being discussed that are related to this chapter. Choose one topic and share how the research literature could help elevate and/or clarify this popular discourse.
2 Choose one theory in this chapter and apply it to your personal use of technology. If you can put it into an organizational context then that will help with the application.
3 Now it is time to debate agency and technology use. Write a one to two-paragraph argument for how you have agency in your use of communication technologies in organizational life. Next, write a one to two-paragraph argument discussing the limits and tensions you face concerning agency. You might want to refer to Chapter 1 and examine the communication and organization spiral that is driven by agency.

4 In contrast to early management research, summarize and briefly describe the unique contributions by organizational communication researchers to the understanding of technology and organizing.
5 Given the metaphor of "factory" to describe the phenomenon of "big data," how can classical management or a modified version of classical management guide the organizing processes around data? Discuss the advantages and/or disadvantages of the classical approach.
6 If you were teaching an undergraduate course in organizational communication and technology, what are the top five topics you would cover in the class?
7 If you were covering a unit on technology in an undergraduate organizational communication class, what are the three topics you would include?
8 Consider how AI tools such as ChatGPT and Copilot from Microsoft and Bard/Gemini from Google present new examples for the theories and concepts discussed in this chapter. Pick one theory/concept and elaborate it using your own example.

Practitioners' Corner

As a practitioner, you probably find yourself interfacing with ICTs on a regular basis. Here we share two scenarios useful for you to consider outside of a specific situation. By using the material in this chapter to think through these scenarios (often with your team), you can be better prepared to address organizational issues that arise. Finally, we share some take-aways that invite you to consider that not all people in your organization have access or use ICTs in the same ways.

Scenario 1: You have been asked to evaluate a new ICT – e.g., an enterprise social media system, a big data analytics software, or an AI tool – for organization-wide adoption. Consider evaluating it with the five innovation attributes of relative advantage, compatibility, complexity, trialability, and observability. Discuss with your organizational decision-makers about the likelihood of the ICT being fully adopted, implemented, and optimized by majority, if not all, of the members. Explore possible ways for reinventions to better fit the ICT to local problems and/or organizational culture.

Scenario 2: Many organizations are complaining about being overloaded with email today. Use MRT's four factors of feedback timeliness, multiple cues available for interpretation, language variety, and personal focus to rate and rank the ICTs available in your organizational life. Evaluate when to use which ICT for a given communication situation. Remember the two factors to consider: Is the request meant to answer a question, otherwise known as reducing certainty? Is the request complex enough that emotions will be involved and you will need to interact to determine how to respond, known as an equivocal task? Work with your team to design a one-page guide of how you might establish rules to help you more effectively, and more meaningfully communicate through ICTs. Could these mutually agreed upon guidelines help you address email overload?

Take-away thoughts: When organizing a diverse group of collaborators (diverse in terms of occupations and job roles), design policies and encourage practices that strike a balance between being universal and being sensitive to cultural differences among occupational groups and/or individuals with different roles in the collective organizational life. Resist the desire to be overly universal at the detriment of becoming a barrier for some occupations and/or roles. Keep in mind that individuals, teams, occupations, and entire organizations vary in how they like to use ICTs to organize, collaborate, and share information.

Finally, consider investigating the policies in your organization that encourage and discourage ICT use. Researchers are finding that these policies can marginalize some workers and that not only affects those individuals, but it can harm productivity as well (see Stephens & Ford, 2016 for an example).

References

Bailey, D. E., & Leonardi, P. M. (2016). *Technology choices: Why occupations differ in their embrace of new technology*. MIT Press.

Barley, S. R. (1986). Technology as an occasion for structuring: Evidence from observations of CT scanners and the social order of radiology departments. *Administrative Science Quarterly*, *31*, 78–108. https://doi.org/10.2307/2392767

Beniger, J. (1989). *The control revolution: Technological and economic origins of the information society*. Harvard University Press.

Bimber, B., Flanagin, A., & Stohl, C. (2012). *Collective action in organizations: Interaction and engagement in an era of technological change*. Cambridge University Press.

Boyraz, M. (2019). Faultlines as the "earth's crust": The role of team identification, communication climate, and subjective perceptions of subgroups for global team satisfaction and innovation. *Management Communication Quarterly*, *33*, 581–615. https://doi.org/10.1177/0893318919860799

Browning, L. D., Sætre, A. S., Stephens, K. K., & Sørnes, J. O. (2008). *Information & communication technologies in action: Linking theory and narratives of practice*. Routledge.

Carlson, J. R., & Zmud, R. W. (1999). Channel expansion theory and the experiential nature of media richness perceptions. *Academy of Management Journal*, *42*, 153–170. https://doi.org/10.2307/257090

Chen, G., & Starosta, W. J. (1998). *Foundations of intercultural communication*. Allyn and Bacon.

Chewing, L. V., Lai, C.-H., & Doerfel, M. L. (2013). Organizational resilience and using information and communication technologies to rebuild communication structures. *Management Communication Quarterly*, *27*, 237–263. https://doi.org/10.1177/0893318912465815

Contractor, N., Monge, P., & Leonardi, P. M. (2011). Multidimensional networks and the dynamics of sociomateriality: Bringing technology inside the network. *International Journal of Communication*, *5*, 682–720. http://ijoc.org/index.php/ijoc/article/view/1131

Daft, R. L., & Lengel, R. H. (1984). Information richness: A new approach to managerial behavior and organization design. In B. M. Staw & L. L. Cummings (Eds.), *Research in organizational behavior* (pp. 191–233). JAI Press.

Daft, R. L., & Lengel, R. H. (1986). Organizational information requirements, media richness and structural design. *Management Science*, *32*, 554–571. https://doi.org/10.1287/mnsc.32.5.554

DeSanctis, G. & Fulk, J. (Eds.) (1999). *Shaping organization form: Communication, connection, and community*. Sage.

DeSanctis, G., & Poole, M. S. (1994). Capturing the complexity in advanced technology use: Adaptive structuration theory. *Organization Science*, *5*, 121–147. https://doi.org/10.1287/orsc.5.2.121

D'Urso, S. C., & Rains, S. A. (2008). Examining the scope of channel expansion: A test of channel expansion theory with new and traditional communication media. *Management Communication Quarterly*, *21*, 486–507. https://doi.org/10.1177/0893318907313712

Ellison, N. B., Gibbs, J. L., & Weber, M. S. (2015). The use of enterprise social network sites for knowledge sharing in distributed organizations: The role of organizational affordances. *American Behavioral Scientist*, *59*, 103–123. https://doi.org/10.1177/0002764214540510

Evans, S. K., Pearce, K. E., Vitak, J., & Treem, J. W. (2017). Explicating affordances: A conceptual framework for understanding affordances in communication research. *Journal of Computer-Mediated Communication*, *22*, 35–52. https://doi.org/10.1111/jcc4.12180

Fulk, J. (1993). Social construction of communication technology. *The Academy of Management Journal*, *36*, 921–950. https://doi.org/10.2307/256641

Fulk, J., Schmitz, J., & Steinfield, C. W. (1990). A social influence model of technology use. In J. Fulk & C. Steinfield (Eds.), *Organizations and communication technology* (pp. 117–140). Sage.

Fulk, J., & Steinfield, C. W. (Eds.) (1990). *Organizations and communication technology*. Sage.

Gandomi, A., & Haider, M. (2015). Beyond the hype: Big data concepts, methods, and analytics. *International Journal of Information Management*, *35*, 137–144. https://doi.org/10.1016/j.ijinfomgt.2014.10.007

Ganesh, S., & Stohl, C. (2010). Qualifying engagement: A study of information and communication technology and the global social justice movement in Aotearoa/New Zealand. *Communication Monographs*, *17*, 51–74. https://doi.org/10.1080/03637750903514284

Gossett, L. M., & Kilker, J. (2006). My job sucks: Examining counter institutional web sites as locations for organizational member voice, dissent, and resistance. *Management Communication Quarterly*, *20*, 63–90. https://doi.org/10.1177/0893318906291729

Granovetter, M. S. (1973). The strength of weak ties. *American Journal of Sociology*, *78*, 1360–1380. https://doi.org/10.1086/225469

Hayes, C., Kulkarni, C., & Kee, K. F. (2023). The situational window for boundary-spanning infrastructure professions: Making sense of cyberinfrastructure emergence. *Journal of Professions and Organization*. https://doi.org/10.1093/jpo/joad007

Kee, K. F. (2017a). Adoption and diffusion. In C. Scott & L. Lewis (Eds.), *International encyclopedia of organizational communication* (online edition). Wiley-Blackwell. https://doi.org/10.1002/9781118955567.wbieoc058

Kee, K. F. (2017b). The 10 adoption drivers of open source software that enable e-research in data factories for open innovation. In S. Matei, N. Julien, & S. Goggins (Eds.), *Big data factories, computational sciences: Collaborative approaches* (pp. 51–65). Springer. https://link.springer.com/chapter/10.1007/978-3-319-59186-5_5

Kee, K. F., & Browning, L. D. (2010). The dialectical tensions in the funding infrastructure of cyberinfrastructure. *Computer Supported Cooperative Work*, *19*, 283–308.

Kirby, E. L., & Buzzanell, P. M. (2014). Communicating work-life issues. In L. L. Putnam & D. K. Mumby (Eds.), *The SAGE handbook of organizational communication: Advances in theory, research, and methods* (3rd ed., pp. 351–373). Sage.

Kossinets, G., & Watts, D. J. (2009). Origins of homophily in an evolving social network. *American Journal of Sociology*, *115*, 405–450. https://doi.org/10.1086/599247

Laney, D. (2001). 3D data management: Controlling data volume, velocity and variety. *META Group Research Note*, *6*, 70. https://blogs.gartner.com/doug-laney/files/2012/01/ad949-3D-Data-Management-Controlling-Data-Volume-Velocity-and-Variety.pdf

Lee, S. A., & Liang, Y. (2016). The role of reciprocity in verbally persuasive robots. *Cyberpsychology, Behavior, and Social Networking*, *19*, 524–527. https://doi.org/10.1089/cyber.2016.0124

Leonardi, P. M. (2009). Why do people reject new technologies and stymie organizational changes of which they are in favor? Exploring misalignments between social interactions and materiality. *Human Communication Research*, *35*, 407–441. https://doi.org/10.1111/j.1468-2958.2009.01357.x

Leonardi, P. M. (2014). Social media, knowledge sharing, and innovation: Toward a theory of communication visibility. *Information Systems Research*, *25*(4), 667–891. https://doi.org/10.1287/isre.2014.0536

Leonardi, P. M., Treem, J. W., & Jackson, M. H. (2010). The connectivity paradox: Using technology to both decrease and increase perceptions of distance in distributed work arrangements. *Journal of Applied Communication Research*, *21*, 82–105. https://doi.org/10.1080/00909880903483599

Lewis, L. K. (2014). Organizational change and innovation. In L. L. Putnam & D. K. Mumby (Eds.), *The SAGE handbook of organizational communication* (3rd ed., pp. 503–524). Sage.

Markus, M. L. (1990). Toward a "critical mass" theory of interactive media. In J. Fulk & C. Steinfield (Eds.), *Organizations and communication technology* (pp. 194–218). Sage.

McGloin, R., Coletti, A., Hamlin, E., & Denes, A. (2022). Required to work from home: Examining transitions to digital communication channels during the COVID-19 pandemic. *Communication Research Reports*, *39*(1), 44–55. https://doi.org/10.1080/08824096.2021.2012757

Näsi, A. (2023). Visual discussion as part of internal organizational communication—Functions and significance. *Journalism and Media*, *4*, 6–74. https://doi.org/10.3390/journalmedia4010005

Orlikowski, W. J. (2007). Sociomaterial practices: Exploring technology at work. *Organizational Studies*, *28*, 1435–1448. https://doi.org/10.1177/0170840607081138

Reinsch, N. L., Turner, J. W., & Tinsley, C. H. (2008). Multicommunicating: A practice whose time has come? *Academy of Management Review*, *33*, 391–403. https://doi.org/10.5465/amr.2008.31193450

Rice, R. E. (1992). Task analyzability, use of new media, and effectiveness: A multi-site exploration of media richness. *Organization Science*, *3*, 475–500. https://doi.org/10.1287/orsc.3.4.475

Rice, R. E. (1993). Media appropriateness: Using social presence theory to compare traditional and new organizational media. *Human Communication Research*, *19*, 451–484. https://doi.org/10.1111/j.1468-2958.1993.tb00309.x

Rice, R. E. (2009). Diffusion of innovations: Theoretical extensions. In R. Nabi & M. B. Oliver (Eds.), *Handbook of media effects* (pp. 489–503). Sage.

Rice, R. E., Evans, S. K., Pearce, K. E., Sivunene, A., Vitak, J., & Treem, J. W. (2017). Organizational media affordances: Operationalization and associations with media use. *Journal of Communication*, *67*, 106–130. https://doi.org/10.1111/jcom.12273

Rice, R. E., Hiltz, S. R., & Spencer, D. (2004). Media mixes and learning networks. In S. R. Hiltz & R. Goldman (Eds.), *Learning together online: Research on asynchronous learning* (pp. 215–237). Erlbaum.

Rice, R. E., & Leonardi, P. M. (2014). Information and communication technology use in organizations. In L. L. Putnam & D. K. Mumby (Eds.), *The SAGE handbook of organizational communication* (3rd ed., pp. 425–448). Sage.

Rice, R. E., & Rogers, E. M. (1980). Reinvention in the innovation process. *Science Communication*, *1*, 499–514. https://doi.org/10.1177/107554708000100402

Rogers, E. M. (1962). *Diffusion of innovations*. Free Press.

Rogers, E. M. (2003). *Diffusion of innovations* (5th ed.). Free Press.

Ryan, B., & Gross, N. C. (1943). The diffusion of hybrid seed corn in two Iowa communities. *Rural Sociology*, *8*, 15–24.

Short, J. A., Williams, E., & Christie, B. (1976). *The social psychology of telecommunications*. John Wiley & Sons.

Shumate, M., & Contractor, N. S. (2014). Emergence of multidimensional social networks. In L. L. Putnam & D. K. Mumby (Eds.), *The SAGE handbook of organizational communication* (3rd ed., pp. 449–474). Sage.

Smith, W. R., Stephens, K. K., Robertson, B. W., Li, J., & Murthy, D. (2018). Social media in citizen-led disaster response: Rescuer roles, coordination challenges, and untapped potential. In K. Boersma & B. Tomaszewski (Eds.), *Proceedings of the 15th International ISCRAM Conference*. Rochester, NY, May 2018.

Starbird, K., & Palen, L. (2011). Voluntweeters: Self-organizing by digital volunteers in times of crisis, *Proceedings of CHI 2011* (pp. 1071–1080), Vancouver, Canada.

Stephens, K. K. (2007). The successive use of information and communication technologies at work. *Communication Theory*, *17*, 486–509. https://doi.org/10.1111/j.1468-2885.2007.00308.x

Stephens, K. K. (2018). *Negotiating control: Organizations and mobile communication*. Oxford University Press.

Stephens, K. K. (2022). The COVID-19 pandemic: Self-organizing at the edges of chaos and stability. In L. D. Browning, J.-O. Sørnes, & P. J. Svenkerud (Eds.), *Organizational communication in the time of Coronavirus: Ethnographies and the future of work* (pp. 83–104). Palgrave.

Stephens, K. K. (2023). Mobile work, mobility, and mobile devices: Responding to a societal shift. *Mobile Media & Communication*, *11*(1), 118–124. https://doi.org/10.1177/20501579221126956

Stephens, K. K., & Ford, J. L. (2016). Unintended consequences of a strategically ambiguous organizational policy selectively restricting mobile device use at work. *Mobile Media & Communication*, *4*, 186–204. https://doi.org/10.1177/2050157915619211

Stephens, K. K., Jahn, J., Fox, S., Charoensap-Kelly, P., Mitra, R., Sutton, J., Waters, E. D., Xie, B., & Meisenbach, R. J. (2020). Collective sensemaking around COVID-19: Experiences, concerns, and agendas for our rapidly changing organizational lives. *Management Communication Quarterly*, *34*(3), 426–457. https://doi.org/10.1177/0893318920934890

Stephens, K. K., & Mottet, T. M. (2008). Interactivity in a Web conferencing training context: Effects on trainers & trainees. *Communication Education*, *57*(1), 88–104. https://doi.org/10.1080/03634520701573284

Stephens, K. K., Sørnes, J. O., Rice, R. E., Browning, L. D., & Sætre, A. S. (2008). Discrete, sequential, and follow-up use of information and communication technology by managerial knowledge workers. *Management Communication Quarterly*, *22*, 197–231. https://doi.org/10.1177/0893318908323149

Stephens, K. K., Zhu, Y., Harrison, M., Iyer, M., Hairston, T., & Luk, J. (2017). *Bring your own mobile device (BYOD) to the hospital: Layered boundary barriers and divergent boundary management strategies*. Proceedings of the Fiftieth Annual Hawaii International Conference on Social Systems, Computer Society Press, 2017.

Stone, C. B., Neely, A. R., & Lengnick-Hall, M. L. (2018). Human resource management in the digital age: Big data, HR analytics and artificial intelligence. In P. N. Melo & C. Machado (Eds.), *Management and technological challenges in the digital age* (pp. 13–42). CRC Press Taylor & Francis.
Treem, J. W., & Leonardi, P. M. (2012). Social media use in organizations: Exploring the affordances of visibility, editability, persistence, and association. In C. T. Salmon (Ed.), *Communication yearbook 36* (pp. 143–189). Routledge.
Trevino, L. K., Lengel, R. H., & Daft, R. L. (1987). Media symbolism, media richness, and media choice in organizations: A symbolic interactionist perspective. *Communication Research*, *14*, 553–574. https://doi.org/10.1177/009365087014005006
Valente, T. W., & Pumpuang, P. (2007). Identifying opinion leaders to promote behavior change. *Health Education & Behavior*, *34*, 881–896. https://doi.org/10.1177/1090198106297855
Van Dijk, J. (2020). *The digital divide*. John Wiley & Sons.
Weick, K. E. (1979). *The social psychology of organizing* (2nd ed.). Addison-Wesley.
Zorn, T. E., Flanagin, A. J., & Shoham, M. D. (2011). Institutional and noninstitutional influences on information and communication technology adoption and use among nonprofit organizations. *Human Communication Research*, *37*, 1–33. https://doi.org/10.1111/j.1468-2958.2010.01387.x

20 Globalization and Organizational Communication

Jennifer L. Gibbs and Shiv Ganesh

Globalization has been defined as the increasing interconnectedness of the world in terms of four dimensions: extensity (expanding scale), intensity (growing magnitude), velocity (speeding up), and impact (deepening consequences of interregional flows and patterns of social interaction) (Held & McGrew, 2003). It is a process of "intensification of worldwide social relations and interactions such that distant events acquire very localized impacts and vice versa" (Held & McGrew, 2007, p. 2). For instance, viral outbreaks such as Covid-19 are harder to isolate and are more likely to turn into global pandemics due to the increased movement of people around the globe. Similarly, social justice movements have also become widespread through the dissemination of ideas in traditional and social media, integrating local concerns and events into global movements.

As such, globalization is fundamentally communicative and has important implications for organizational communication. Indeed, scholars of Organizational Communication have been actively studying global organizing processes for the past three decades, which have given rise to new global organizational forms such as global virtual teams, global social movements, and global network organizations. A unique feature of these new organizational forms is that they have no physical instantiation, such that they are entirely constituted through communication practices. Further, they allow for new forms of collective action and collaboration across time, space, and other boundaries.

Research on Globalization spans a variety of disciplines, including sociology, anthropology, political science, management, and communication. We treat Globalization here as an umbrella term that includes research on related terms reflecting worldwide trends, such as transnationalism, international and multinational teams and organizations, and colonization/decolonization.

Organizational Communication scholars have drawn on these broader social traditions to study global patterns of interaction and new organizing forms in a variety of ways. Topics of study in Organizational Communication include global team collaboration (Connaughton & Shuffler, 2007; Gibbs, 2009), networks and network organizations (Fulk et al., 2005; Shumate & O'Connor, 2010), social movements (Dempsey et al., 2011; Ganesh & Stohl, 2010, 2013), corporate social responsibility (CSR) (Stohl et al., 2007; Zoller, 2004), use of communication technologies (Monge, 1998; Monge & Fulk, 1999), global crises and pandemics (Stephens et al., 2020), and organizational culture (Stohl, 2001; Wieland, 2011). Many studies of Globalization have either explicitly or implicitly documented tensions that play out in various ways.

DOI: 10.4324/9781003484639-23

Dialectical Tensions in Globalization

Given its complexity, globalization involves multiple inherent tensions. A prominent tension is between convergence and divergence (Held et al., 1999; Stohl, 2001). On one hand, globalization involves processes of standardization that result in similar organizational structuring across nations; on the other, it involves processes of polarization as the centrifugal forces of cultural diversity and identity push back against the centripetal forces of convergence. It involves the interlacing of the global and the local, also known as "glocalization" (Robertson, 1992).

Precisely because globalization is a complex and multidimensional process consisting of economic, political, technological, cultural, and environmental dimensions and imperatives, it is also uneven, playing out differently in different spheres, with some countries or regions being more globalized than others and various dimensions of globalization interacting differently even in highly globalized regions. Thus, it involves restructuring of social relations and new patterns of global stratification and power relations at both supra- and sub-state levels (Scholte, 2005). Key features of multidimensional globalization include (1) time-space distantiation, in which those in different locations can experience the same event through the compression of time and space, (2) the disembedding of events and institutions and new realignments and restructuring of social interaction across time and space, enabling collective action in new ways, and (3) an increase in global consciousness through processes of reflexivity as we establish our position in relation to the global system, heightening local politics and identity (Giddens, 1991; Monge, 1998).

While networks have been a key focus of Globalization scholars (e.g., Castells, 1996, 2012; González-Bailón & Wang, 2016; Stohl & Stohl, 2007), more recent work has argued that global organizational environments have moved away from network forms and are better characterized by fluid hybridity, in which fluid communicative conditions give rise to hybrid organizing that is a mix of form and formlessness (Ganesh & Stohl, 2020). Globalization research has also been reshaped by the rise of visibility and visibility management (Albu, 2023). Ganesh et al. trace four generations of globalization, which they call the generations of uncertainty, connectivity, ubiquity, and visibility, arguing that globalization has moved from the foreground to the background of study and is looping back again in a fourth wave that involves highly visible global crises, attenuated by processes of magnification, monitorization, distortion, and refraction (Ganesh et al., 2024).

Organizational Communication scholars have begun to regard tensions, paradoxes, and contradictions as normal, ubiquitous features of organizing (Fairhurst & Putnam, 2024; Putnam et al., 2016; see Chapter 3). A dialectical tension is defined as an opposition between two conflicting or competing poles, such that both poles (goals, needs) are equally necessary and desired, and it is not possible to make a simple either-or choice between one or the other. Productive strategies for managing dialectical tensions require the development of communicative practices that find a way to mutually attend to both poles in a way that acknowledges each one as well as overcoming or transforming the contradiction through "both-and" approaches (Putnam & Boys, 2006).

The dialectical tensions inherent in globalization can be framed in terms of three broad categories: ontological, epistemological, and axiological (see Chapter 2). Ontological tensions refer to how globalization has been defined and what it is. Epistemological tensions spotlight how globalization has been studied. Axiological tensions refers to how globalization is judged and evaluated. Commitments are not necessarily aligned. Similar ontological commitments may produce very different epistemological or axiological assessments. In the rest of the chapter, we will discuss each category of tensions both in terms of (1) how each pole of the tension has been studied in the literature and (2) how framing the field through the lens of dialectical tensions can help us better conceptualize connections among interrelated phenomena that have previously been studied separately by communication scholars. In this way, we hope to help integrate and frame the field as well as provide a call to action for communication scholars to make more concerted efforts to place diverse and opposing views into dialogue with one another.

Ontological Tensions

Ontological tensions are evident both in terms of what globalization "is" and its impact, as well as how it has been defined. We examine two types of ontological tensions: transformationalist vs. skeptical and totalizing vs. particularistic.

Transformationalist vs. Skeptical

The first ontological tension concerns the degree to which globalization represents a novel phenomenon. Scholars often take one of two perspectives: *transformationalists* argue that globalization is fundamentally reshaping the world, while skeptics see it as a continuation of social, economic, or political processes that have been occurring for hundreds of years. Held and McGrew (2007) distinguish between the *globalists* and the *skeptics*. The globalists regard globalization as a process of growing convergence or interconnectedness in which global markets, governance, and civil society are replacing nation states and national economies as dominant power structures. Scholars in this camp take both utopian and dystopian perspectives: Neoliberals celebrate world unification and seamless global markets ("global village") (McLuhan & Powers, 1989; Negroponte, 1995; Ohmae, 1995), while Neomarxists critique global capitalism and corporations for creating growing inequalities and cultural imperialism ("global pillage") (Sklair, 1991; Wallerstein, 1974).

This debate has played out in public policy around the Washington Consensus, a neoliberal policy agenda consisting of 10 policy points proposed by the economist John Williamson in 1989 (Williamson, 2002) and designed to help facilitate globalization in developing countries. Its points consist of financial and trade liberalization, deregulation, and privatization of state enterprises, among other things. Globalization has thus become largely synonymous with neoliberalism, the view that free and open markets will provide for equality and social change (see Chapter 4), and while its impacts are hotly contested, it is generally regarded as a transformational process that is changing society in significant ways. Other scholars recognize that globalization is not a process of homogenization but may be an uneven process of transformation that is characterized by new patterns of global stratification that reinforce some power structures while reconfiguring others (Appadurai, 1990; Featherstone, 1990; Giddens, 2003; Tomlinson, 1999). Scholars in both of these camps agree that fundamental change is occurring due to globalization.

On the other hand, the *skeptical* view regards the world as less interdependent than in the 1890s (Held et al., 1999) and as characterized by divergence and fragmentation, discounting notions of global markets or global civil society (Johnson, 1991; McGee, 1990; Scott, 1997). In this view, some regionalization is occurring, but overall the nation state is not dying, and national economies and governments retain their power. Scholars taking a skeptical view argue that capitalism may have taken on new shape, but that a powerful class antagonism between employers and workers still exists (Cloud, 2001). Skeptics point to the increasing digital divide and marginalization of the Global South and developing countries (Hirst & Thompson, 1996), as well as the resurgence of nationalism and religious fundamentalism that has led to increasing conflicts among and within civilizations (Barber, 1995; Huntington, 1996; Kotkin, 1992). While the globalist/transformationalist view was the dominant one in the 1990s, post-9/11 the skeptical view has come to the forefront due to heightened ethnic, religious, and political polarization. In recent years, the increasing rise of protectionism in trade policies has also resulted in some commentators declaring the "end" of globalization or the emergence of a "post-global" era (e.g., Flew, 2019).

Totalizing vs. Particularistic

Another difference in how globalization has been conceptualized has been in terms of either a totalizing process or a particularistic phenomenon. This relates to the tensions between convergence and divergence mentioned above (Stohl, 2001). Scholars who take a *totalizing* view tend to study Globalization in terms of a universal set of processes or phenomena that transcends particular local contexts. For instance, Perlmutter's (1969) geocentric orientation describes a management style that is oriented to the world rather than to the company's home country (an ethnocentric orientation) or to the host country (a polycentric orientation). Multinational organizations taking a geocentric orientation attempt to find the best managers and workers to perform their work from across the globe, regardless of nationality. They also engage in collaboration between headquarters and subsidiaries to establish universal standards and policies, allowing for local variations as needed. Examples of Organizational Communication studies taking a totalizing approach include studies of global teams (Gibbs, 2009; Gibson & Gibbs, 2006), global network organizations (Fulk et al., 2005; Stohl & Stohl, 2005), and cross-cultural comparative studies that draw on established cultural taxonomies (Javidan et al., 2006), as each type attempts to theorize Globalization processes that transcend particular cultures or contexts.

Scholars who take a *particularistic* view, on the other hand, tend to focus on global phenomena as embedded in particular local contexts, with an attempt to trace the contextual features and provide a deep understanding of a particular context or phenomenon rather than build to a grand narrative or theory. For instance, McAllum (2018) studied the important role of volunteers in long-term refugee resettlement, a particular aspect of the globalization process. Her qualitative study examines how volunteers' commitment was collectively structured by their relationships with other volunteer coordinators, their own significant others, and the refugees they were assisting in ways that led to organizational detachment or exit. While her study is not about globalization writ large, it helps to explain a particular aspect of national border crossing while also contributing theoretical understanding of an important Organizational Communication construct – organizational commitment.

It is important to note that particularistic research can often be framed in totalizing terms that disguise its parochial roots. Stohl (2001) outlines both theoretical and methodological parochialism that limit global research. She points out that many of our communication theories are Eurocentric yet positioned as universal; our methods are limited through different interpretations and translations of concepts and lack of equivalence in measures; and researchers are insulated in cultural and disciplinary silos, limiting international collaboration. These parochialisms result in more particularistic research perspectives (or totalizing views that are in fact less universal than claimed). As Ganesh et al. (2017) point out, these parochialisms are alive and well in contemporary communication research, even paradoxically in discussions of diversity, equity, and inclusion (DEI). They point out that much theoretical work on diversity is, in fact, based on Western models of communication, based upon North American and European research traditions – which are then unproblematically transposed onto non-Western contexts. Such parochialism could have the paradoxical effect of reifying a vocabulary of global justice and disabling attentiveness to the ways in which injustices are historically embedded in local contexts (see Chapter 4).

Scholars thus need to be deeply attentive to conceptual vocabularies and the potential impact of the imposition of terms and concepts from one sociohistorical context into another and closely account for the political problematics of translation. For instance, the term "decolonization" itself, while rooted in a Global South imaginary (Pal et al., 2022), when applied to issues such as caste, can elide the fact that caste hierarchies and inequities are in fact a precolonial, deeply historic, and defining feature of social organization in South Asia. As commentators have pointed out, right-wing Hindu activists and scholars have been deploying rhetorics of decolonization to Hinduize universities and curricula in India and the United States. Decolonization is not a metaphor (Tuck & Yang, 2012), and we thus advocate considering it in its full global and structural context rather than attaching the term to make sense of all social justice initiatives, no matter how revolutionary or reformative.

Research studies taking transformationalist vs. skeptical or totalizing vs. particularistic perspectives tend to remain largely separate in the literature. Positioning these as dialectical tensions requires scholars to put these seemingly competing views into constructive opposition with one another in order to place them in dialogue. Doing so will help to enrich larger ontological debates and conceptions of what globalization is. Each pole captures legitimate facets of contemporary globalization processes, which are multi-faceted as well as changing over time in light of the current cultural and historical context. While the convergence (transformationalist, totalizing) view tended to dominate early globalization discourse in the 1990s during the Internet dot.com boom and celebration of open markets and the information superhighway (Sturken & Thomas, 2004), post-9/11 popular discourse about globalization in the 2000s and 2010s has shifted to emphasize divergence and polarization stemming from rising political populism and economic tribalism.

Prior to 9/11, globalization discourse often emphasized the harmonious "global village" notion of one unified, borderless world. Indeed, a survey of ethnically diverse residents of Los Angeles found that the majority of participants associated globalization with utopian visions of growing interconnectedness and inclusion as new technologies made the world smaller and brought people closer together (Gibbs et al., 2004). Such optimistic views seem rather naïve in a post-9/11 world that has become increasingly ruptured by ethnic and national conflicts and divisiveness. Indeed, the skeptical viewpoint has gained traction as increasingly scholars point to the war on terrorism and other conflicts as indicative of the end of globalization (Held & McGrew, 2007). This can also be seen in the shift in political discourse and policy from economic liberalization to protectionism and from building regional alliances, such as NAFTA, the European Union, and ASEAN, to the breakdown of these international unions through Brexit and the isolationist policies of current populist leaders. Putting totalizing and particularistic perspectives and discourses into tension with one another provides flexibility to allow for changes in how globalization has been regarded and experienced over time due to the changing political landscape while helping to integrate these diverse strands into a single (yet multi-faceted) phenomenon. It also provides for a fuller understanding of the co-existence of contradictory and seemingly opposed processes and viewpoints.

Epistemological Tensions

A second set of tensions is evident in this research area around how Globalization has been studied. We examine two types of epistemological tensions: micro vs. macro and foreground vs. background.

Micro vs. Macro

Scholars of Organizational Communication have studied globalization phenomena at a variety of levels of analysis, ranging from the individual and team levels to the organizational and societal levels. At the micro level, scholars have studied individual and team interactions, processes, and outcomes in globally distributed teams and organizations (e.g., Connaughton & Shuffler, 2007; Fulk et al., 2005; Gibson & Gibbs, 2006; Yuan & Gay, 2006). For example, Gibbs (2009) conducted an ethnography of a global software team involved in offshore outsourcing work and found that global team interaction was characterized by irresolvable tensions between autonomy vs. connectedness, inclusion vs. exclusion, and empowerment vs. disempowerment. These tensions could be productive or detrimental, depending on the communicative responses to them. Those in higher status positions, such as managers, were more likely to experience communicative tensions as empowering, whereas lower-level foreign assignees were more likely to be disenfranchised by them. At the macro level, scholars have examined global discourses, networks, and social movements, taking into account the broader institutional logics represented in global organizing processes (e.g., Stohl & Stohl, 2005). For example, Ganesh and Stohl (2013) interviewed activists at the Occupy Wellington protest to capture the ubiquity of digital media and illustrate the various institutional logics operating in activist organizing practices.

Globalization crosses multiple levels of analysis and involves tensions between macro and micro phenomena. The same concepts may be studied at different levels. For example, questions of democracy and equality are at the heart of globalization. Globalization processes are fraught with power dynamics on a geo-political scale as they exacerbate divides between developed and developing countries. Zoller (2004) examined transnational corporate power by studying the discourse of the Transatlantic Business Dialogue (TABD), a formal agreement between business and governments of the European Union and the United States, finding that the discourse of dialogue can legitimize corporate hegemony and empower free markets in global trade. Power dynamics are also evident in more micro processes of global organizing such as in global team interaction and global collaboration processes. For instance, status differences have been found to arise in global work arrangements as members from the global headquarters site take on higher status than those at remote locations (Leonardi & Rodriguez-Lluesma, 2013). Another study of a global organization found that the communication visibility afforded by enterprise social media brought to light knowledge disparities among status groups and thus reinforced status hierarchies (Kim, 2018).

However, once again the literature has primarily selected one level (either micro or macro) and focused on it without explicitly examining the connections across levels. Taking a dialectical tension-based approach would require considering the ways in which micro social interactions (at the individual or team level) scale up and both shape and are shaped by more macro phenomena, such as institutional logics, discourses, and structures. For instance, studies could examine how larger institutional logics and discourses impact global team interaction and practices or how the social networks of organizational members scale up to organizational networks among institutional actors. A focus on fluid hybridity

(Ganesh & Stohl, 2020) is another way of taking both micro and macro into account by collapsing this distinction.

Foreground vs. Background

Early studies of Organizational Communication and Globalization were prone to trying to understand what globalization itself was, attempting to *assess its impact in broad terms* on Organizational Communication processes, and in this sense, globalization was very much in the *foreground* of Organizational Communication studies. For instance, Stohl (1993) posits the emergence of three major types of international organizations – international governmental organizations (IGOS), international non-governmental organizations (INGOs), and multinational corporations (MNCs) – as being a response to the increasing encounter with diversity and difference caused by the speed-up and intensification of transnational flows of information and capital. More locally, Stage (1999) assessed the impact of a global multinational corporate culture upon its subsidiary in Thailand, arguing that local employees had to explicitly negotiate the legitimacy of global culture and values in the context of local expectations about such norms as participation and workload. Dempsey et al.'s (2011) work on Transnational Feminist Networks also looked at the impact that transnationalism had upon feminist forms of organizing, arguing that transnational feminist networks emerged in order to bridge scales of organizing and create intersectional forms of solidarity across borders and social categories.

In the late 1990s and early 2000s, researchers were more prone to trying to assess the impact and significance of *particular aspects of globalization*. For instance, the word "neoliberalism," which signifies the unfettered flow of private capital across markets over the world, epitomized in the slogan "free markets," came into Organizational Communication studies around the turn of the century (see Chapter 4). Ganesh (2003), for example, looks at how neoliberalism impacted the structure of a Non-Government Organization (NGO), arguing that the overall emphasis upon a market orientation to social change significantly truncated its ability to obtain its social change goals. Ganesh and Stohl (2013) looked at how networking logics produced in one location impact activist practice in another, focusing upon the Occupy Movement and its translation from Wall Street in New York to Wellington in Aotearoa New Zealand.

Even later, scholars started to look at aspects of Organizational Communication that were "post-global," that is, were conceptualized and thought about after globalization became part of the conceptual vocabulary of Organizational Communication studies. In this sense, these studies treat globalization as part of the *background* of Organizational Communication studies, and regard it as ubiquitous, normal, and unremarkable (Stohl & Ganesh, 2014). Concepts such as entrepreneurship that emphasize agency, initiative, and freedom, as Rebecca Gill (2014) has argued, circulate as much as they do because they work to support neoliberal capitalism. Other scholars have studied similar post-global concepts such as outsourcing arrangements (Gibbs et al., 2023; Leonardi & Bailey, 2008), contingent labor (Townsley & Stohl, 2003), and cultural intelligence (Dutta & Dutta, 2013). We would argue that even the focus on cross-sectoral partnerships, exemplified well in work by Shumate and O'Connor (2010) on such notions as symbiotic sustainability between corporations and NGOs and in work by Mitra (2018) on natural resource management in the U.S. Arctic, is a product of a post-global sensibility in Organizational Communication studies.

While there has been a clear move from "foreground" to "background" thinking (Ganesh et al., 2024), we posit that a full consideration of globalization must involve holding foreground and background in dialectical tension, despite, and perhaps because of, the increasing tendency to see it as a background concept. Doing so is useful because we observe that our use of the term "globalization" in Organizational Communication studies is increasingly casual, precisely because it is a background concept. Further, the lack of explicit emphasis on globalization as a concept does not mean that the phenomenon has disappeared; rather, it has become ubiquitous. We note, for instance, that 63 entries in the 2017 *Encyclopedia of Organizational Communication* referenced the term on topics ranging from change to technology, gender, and collective action. The casualization of globalization vocabulary might encourage theoretical laziness about the term and prevent us from understanding how globalization is itself changing and impacting organizational communication anew. For example, predictions and assessments about contractions of the global economy (e.g., Sassen, 2014) upend our assumptions about the inexorable spread of globalization. What are the implications for global organizations?

Axiological Tensions

A third set of tensions deals with values, in terms of whether globalization is inherently positive or negative. We examine two types of axiological tensions. First, we examine whether globalization is understood broadly as a good or bad force, and second, we look specifically at plural vs. imperial tensions in globalization.

Force for Good vs. Evil

Some scholars have understood globalization primarily as a force for social, cultural, and political good, whereas others have considered it a corrosive or corrupt force. There are three dimensions along which scholars have tended to valorize globalization as either good or bad. First, scholars who have understood globalization in terms of cosmopolitanism have tended to see globalization as a positive force. This is particularly true of work that sees globalization in cultural terms. Taylor and Osland (2011), for example, posit that cosmopolitanism, which they understand as a cognitive and moral orientation towards the world outside the local, is a major factor in the development of cultural intelligence in organizations and promotes organizational learning. Sobre-Denton and Bardhan (2013) also developed the notion of "cosmopolitanism from below" in order to understand and explain communicative dynamics at play in an international youth hosteling chain, whose mission was to help young people gain a better appreciation and understanding of the world.

Others have valorized globalization along the lines of what one might call public and private dimensions. Some scholars understand globalization as a privatizing force, often taking an economic view of globalization in the process. Cheney and Cloud (2006), for instance, positioned globalization as a private system that privileges and promotes free markets and consequently undermines worker rights in particular and workplace democracy more broadly. Conversely, other scholars who have understood globalization in more public and democratic terms have valorized it as a force for good. Stohl and Stohl (2005), for example, examined how global networks of NGOs working on human rights issues have served to complement and strengthen not only an inter-governmental public regime that addresses human rights violations but global governance at large.

A third, and perhaps more subtle way that scholarship in Organizational Communication studies has valorized globalization has been in its use of terms such as "global" or "local" itself. Terms such as "local communities," for example, are often valorized as a force for good. Medved et al. (2001), for instance, studied how systemic exclusionary practices in healthcare could be overcome and ameliorated when providers engaged in comprehensive stakeholder dialogues with local communities. Scholars have on other occasions been aware of the need to critique and assess how local communities are valorized both in research and in practice. Dempsey (2010), for instance, used insights from transnational feminism to assess and evaluate campus-community partnerships in an American university, arguing that unreflexive understandings of local communities could perhaps undermine broader solidarities that could be formed across locations.

Notions of globalization as reflecting Western, free-market capitalism have long been critiqued, giving rise to the "anti-globalization" or global justice movement in the 1990s, which continues today. Organizational Communication scholars have long critiqued the global inequalities created by global financial institutions such as the WTO and IMF and have increasingly begun to focus on issues of global activism and transnational feminism, decolonization, and the Global South (Pal & Nieto-Fernandez, 2024; Pal et al., 2023). For instance, Iannacone (2024) presents a compelling critique of the organizational rhetoric around resettled Syrian refugees, finding that organizations whose purpose is to protect and advocate for refugees may enact harmful discursive practices that perpetuate Western, colonizing representations and erasures (see Chapter 4).

Plural vs. Imperial

Another axiological tension in our treatment of globalization can be framed in terms of plural vs. imperial. At first blush, it might appear that this tension is a subset of the large good-bad tension highlighted earlier; however, we observe that there are several instances when pluralist notions of globalization can be seen in negative terms, particularly when pluralism is understood as cultural relativism. Conversely, ostensibly imperial notions of globalization – such as global science – can actually be understood as a force for good. In Organizational Communication scholarship in particular, tension between pluralism on one hand and imperialism on the other has informed research in two senses.

First, researchers themselves have been committed to varying degrees as to whether they view globalization itself as a form of convergence or divergence (Stohl, 2001). That is, for some scholars, Globalization is seen as a communicative encounter with difference, while for others it involves the imposition of a more specific set of communicative practices, discourses, and rationalities. For instance, scholarship that has explored issues of cultural diversity in organizations has often begun from the standpoint that globalization has created those conditions (e.g., Stage, 1999). Other scholars who have understood globalization as a particular set of economic rationalities (e.g., Ganesh, 2005; Ganesh et al., 2005) see it as being a powerful converging and transformative force.

In a second sense, scholars have argued that Organizational Communication research on globalization is itself imperial. Broadfoot and Munshi (2007), for instance, argue that "much organizational communication scholarship conducted within the global context is performed and interpreted from the dominant Euro-American intellectual tradition, privileging those concepts as well as particular voices and traditions and often ignoring inequality and exploitation within the scholarly community" (p. 249). This view has been shared in varying degrees by other scholars. Stohl's (2001) work, which we have already mentioned, which identified a set of theoretical, methodological, and pragmatic parochialisms associated with Organizational Communication scholarship, is a good example of this. However, scholars diverge in the extent to which they are willing to view organizational communication as an imperial force. Zoller's (2006) and Ashcraft's (2006) responses to a provocation by Prichard (2006), who argued that much Organizational Communication scholarship was a form of American imperialism, illustrate this tension vividly (see Chapter 4).

Our own view is that axiological tensions need to be understood in complex terms. It is problematic to understand globalization as an unqualified good, but equally worrisome to treat it as a force for evil, especially at a time when, as we have discussed earlier, local and anti-democratic dynamics across the world are eroding the democratic foundations of global civil society and the global commons. Whether we are studying ethics in virtual teams, the labor implications of outsourcing, the efficacy of transnational activist organizing, or the spread of NGO networks, it is critical to pay attention to both positive and negative dynamics of globalization – including a recognition that the same dynamics may produce differing outcomes for diverse populations and groups – and to take broad synchronic (focusing on the current moment) as well as diachronic (examining changes over time) views of globalization. For instance, while the global HIV/AIDS pandemic was horrifying in its impact, historians have subsequently traced its pivotal role in the formation of LGBTQ activism in countries that had no overt track record of such mobilizations. In the final section, we will consider the different ways in which globalization research has treated communication, organization, and the C-O cycle.

Treatment of Communication and Organization

Globalization scholars come from a variety of disciplines and adopt varying conceptualizations of communication. While scholars from disciplines such as sociology, management, and political science often treat communication as a simple process of *transmission of messages*, and scholars in anthropology focus on *cultural meaning*, this chapter demonstrates that scholars in Organizational Communication tend to take *constitutive* approaches that regard global phenomena as communicatively constructed. For example, Gibbs et al. (2021) examine the discursive construction of subgroups and status differences in global teams. Another example is Kim's (2018) study of how social media use and status hierarchies are mutually constituted in global organizing processes. Indeed, the dialectical framework we draw on here is grounded in a constitutive approach (Putnam et al., 2016).

Scholarship in global Organizational Communication tends to vary in its treatment of organization, ranging from underlying assumptions of organization as process (O_1), structure (O_2), and entity (O_3). For instance, Dempsey et al.'s (2011) work on Transnational Feminist Networks takes a process (O_1) approach by examining the ways in which transnationalism leads to the emergence of feminist forms of organizing. Other research on global network organizations takes a more structural (O_2) approach (Fulk et al., 2005; Monge & Fulk, 1999), as it takes as its object of inquiry the network structures that are enabled by new communication technologies. Still other scholars regard organizations as entitative beings (O_3). This line of scholarship is exemplified by Ganesh and Stohl's (2010) research on the social justice movement in Aotearoa New Zealand, which takes on the status of a coordinated or ordered entity through collective action of various stakeholders.

The C-O cycle presented in Chapter 1 refers to the interrelationship between communication and organization. This dynamic is mirrored in Globalization theory by the relationship between agency and structure. Approaches to Globalization theory once again vary from views that emphasize structure, including both utopian (Ohmae, 1995) and dystopian globalist views (Wallerstein, 1974), to views that highlight individual agency. For instance, Wallerstein's world-system theory regards core-periphery inequalities as determining forces and thus views global capitalism as systemic and totalizing rather than influenced by individual agency.

On the other hand, anthropological and cultural approaches (e.g., Featherstone, 1990) situate globalization as a process of individual meaning-making as individuals actively appropriate global forms to (re)negotiate local cultural identity within a globalizing context. Still other scholars, such as Giddens (1991, 2003), conceptualize globalization as a structurational process (see Chapter 3) in which individual agency and interactions both shape and are shaped by global forces and structural resources, such that the local and global are mutually constitutive. Organizational scholars vary in their treatment of the C-O dynamic, but it is fair to say that theory on global Organizational Communication has been heavily influenced by Giddens' recursive view of globalization (e.g., Monge, 1998; Stohl, 2001, 2005; Stohl et al., 2007). For example, Stohl et al. (2007) conceptualize the new generation of global CSR as incorporating four key features: (1) there is no longer a distinction between "out there" and "in here," such that all organizational stakeholders must establish themselves in relation to the global system rather than outside of it; (2) "glocalization" (Robertson, 1992) involves the restructuring of social interaction across time and space such that global structures and local interactions mutually shape one another; (3) complex communication networks among societies, cultures, institutions, and individuals; and (4) permeability of public and private boundaries. This conceptualization recognizes the dynamic interplay among local communication practices and stakeholders and global social, organizational, and institutional structures.

Conclusion

In this chapter, we have framed the literature on Globalization and Organizational Communication through a theoretical framework of dialectical tensions. Our review has highlighted three overarching categories – ontological, epistemological, and axiological – that bring to light important differences in the ways that Globalization has been studied by Organizational Communication scholars in terms of (1) its very nature and how it has been defined and conceptualized, (2) how it has been studied in terms of the phenomena and types of knowledge produced, and (3) the value judgments made about it and its ethical implications. We do not seek to resolve these debates but rather to embrace them. It is important to note that discourse about globalization is changing as a reflection of our changing world – we have moved from an early focus on global connectivity and interconnectedness to our current moment of global crisis (Ganesh et al., 2024) – and these changes further underscore the complexity of the phenomena we are seeking to understand. Taken together, we hope that this framing will help to integrate the field of global Organizational Communication and provide conceptual tools to help advance scholarship in this area.

Taking a tensional approach (Putnam et al., 2016) helps to articulate differences in approaches to scholarship in this area – for instance, totalizing vs. particularistic, micro vs. macro, and plural vs. imperial – and juxtapose them in order to find connections among seemingly disparate views. In addition, framing the field through a lens of dialectical tensions provides a call for communication scholars to better conceptualize intricate nuances among interrelated phenomena that have been studied separately in the literature by placing competing views into dialogue with one another. Given the multi-faceted and historically changing nature of globalization, theorizing and studying its tensions is a way to provide for a fuller understanding of its complexities and allow for the co-existence of contradictory processes and changing views, thus enriching the field and allowing it to continue to evolve.

Recommended Supplementary Readings

Ganesh, S., & Stohl, C. (2020). Fluid hybridity: Organizational form and formlessness in the digital age. In L. Lievrouw & B. Loader (Eds.), *Routledge handbook of digital media and communication* (pp. 268–280). Routledge.

Provides an argument for the shift from network forms to fluid hybrid forms of organizing in globalization processes.

Ganesh, S., Stohl, C., & James, S. (2024). Generational shifts: The emergence of visibility in globalization research. In V. D. Miller & M. S. Poole (Eds.), *Handbook of organizational communication.* De Gruyter.

Categorizes research into four generations of globalization to show how conceptualizations and approaches have changed over time.

Ganesh, S., Zoller, H., & Cheney, G. (2005). Transforming resistance: Critical organizational communication meets globalization from below. *Communication Monographs*, 72, 169–191.

Makes the case for organizational communication research to study global social movements.

Giddens, A. (2003). *Runaway world: How globalization is reshaping our lives*. Routledge.

Primer on globalization theory from a transformationalist perspective.

Held, D., McGrew, A., Goldblatt, D., & Perraton, J. (1999). *Global transformations: Politics, economics, and culture*. Stanford University Press.

Provides a comprehensive overview of globalization theory and outlines the globalist, skeptic, and transformationalist views.

Held, D., & McGrew, A. (2007). *Globalization/anti-globalization: Beyond the great divide.* Polity Press.

Provides a comparison of the globalist and skeptic views and challenges the skeptical view that globalization is over in a post-9/11 era.

Rooney, D., & Chavan, M. (2017). Globalization/internationalization. In Scott, C. & Lewis, L. (Eds.), *International encyclopedia of organizational communication* (pp. 1005–1020). Blackwell.

Provides an overview of formal organizational dimensions of globalization.

Scholte, J. A. (2005). *Globalization: A critical introduction* (2nd ed.). Palgrave Macmillan.

Provides a comprehensive overview of the dimensions of globalization, arguing that supraterritoriality is its most defining feature.

Stohl, C. (2001). Globalizing organizational communication. In F. M. Jablin & L. L. Putnam (Eds.), *The new handbook of organizational communication* (pp. 323–375). Sage.

Provides the first comprehensive account of the state of research in globalization in organizational communication studies, drawing from a convergence/divergence dialectic.

Stohl, C., & Ganesh, S. (2014). Generating globalization. In L. L. Putnam & D. K. Mumby (Eds). *The SAGE handbook of organizational communication* (3rd ed., pp. 717–741). Sage.

Categorizes research into three generations of globalization to show how conceptualizations and approaches have changed over time.

Important Concepts: Define and Discuss

Axiological
Crisis
Eco-localism
Epistemological
Globalist
Globalization
Imperialism
Ontological
Particularistic
Pluralism
Skeptic
Totalizing
Transformationalist

Discussion Questions

1 What are the key ontological, epistemological, and axiological tensions in research on globalization?
2 How have conceptualizations of globalization and its impacts changed over time?
3 How has Organizational Communication research approached the study of Globalization at both micro and macro levels of analysis?
4 What is the value of taking a tensional approach to study Globalization, in particular, and research more broadly?
5 Think of a pressing global crisis or problem (e.g., climate change, economic inequality, social injustice, terrorism). How might an Organizational Communication scholar go about addressing this problem? What communicative phenomena, types of interaction, and stakeholders would you study?

Practitioner's Corner: Eco-Local Design

Over the last 15 years, eco-local design has become a buzzword amongst practitioners in many fields, ranging from community planning and social movement organizers on one hand to project managers and economic policy analysts on the other. The term "eco-localism" was coined to draw attention to the need for local communities to engage in cohesive communication and planning around potential global environmental and economic challenges such as climate change or global market collapse (Ganesh and Zoller, 2014). The impact of climate change, for example, is likely to be entirely local in how it manifests, and local governance mechanisms have to be developed to develop mitigating projects on a host of fronts, ranging from new stormwater drains and flood protections to robust forms of civil defense and disaster preparedness.

There are many examples of eco-local design. The transition initiatives project, which attempts to help communities be resilient in the face of environmental and economic collapse, is a fairly high-profile one (see www.transitionus.org or www.transitionnetwork.org), but so are others like Ecolocal UK (www.ecolocal.org.uk), a social enterprise that creates products and services designed to help people and communities move to a more environmentally sustainable way of life. Have a look at these websites, and pay particular attention to how the various tensions listed in this chapter might help your understanding of eco-localism. For example, you will likely find both transformationalist and skeptical understandings of globalization coexisting in eco-localism – on one hand, eco-localists believe that the global era is over, but on the other, they believe that a global localized approach is required to deal with global crises! Likewise, there are both foreground aspects to globalization as well as background aspects to globalization in eco-localism, inasmuch as eco-localists have to talk about globalization in some way to demonstrate the importance of their work but, at the same time, have to de-emphasize it in order to get people to think about and act upon these same issues in their everyday lives.

Consider how the other tensions – totalizing vs. particularistic, micro vs. macro, good vs. bad, and plural vs. imperial – are evident in eco-localism. We have said in our chapter that all these tensions need to be held *together* rather than separately to enable good practice. Whether one is a community organizer, activist, policy maker, city planner, or an elected official, designing appropriate forms of eco-local governance requires the ability to analyze the multiple and often contradictory dimensions of particular projects, and the template that we have presented here is helpful in this crucial analytical task that can enable appropriate eco-local design.

References

Albu, O. B. (2023). Managing visibilities: The shades and shadows of NGO work in repressive contexts. *Management Communication Quarterly*, *37*(3), 659–685. https://doi.org/10.1177/08933189221144991

Appadurai, A. (1990). Disjuncture and difference in the global cultural economy. In M. Featherstone (Ed.), *Global culture: Nationalism, globalism and modernity* (pp. 295–310). Sage.

Ashcraft, K. (2006). Falling from a humble perch? Rereading organizational communication studies with an attitude of alliance. *Management Communication Quarterly*, *19*, 645–652. https://doi.org/10.1177/0893318905285389

Barber, B. (1995). *Jihad vs. McWorld*. Times Books.

Broadfoot, K. J., & Munshi, D. (2007). Diverse voices and alternative rationalities: Imaging forms of postcolonial organizational communication. *Management Communication Quarterly*, *21*, 249–267. https://doi.org/10.1177/0893318907306037

Castells, M. (1996). *The rise of the network society*. Wiley-Blackwell.

Castells, M. (2012). *Networks of outrage and hope: Social movements in the internet age*. Polity Press.

Cheney, G., & Cloud, D. (2006). Doing democracy, engaging the material: Employee participation and labor activity in an age of market globalization. *Management Communication Quarterly*, *19*, 1–40. https://doi.org/10.1177/0893318905285485

Cloud, D. (2001). Laboring under the sign of the new: Cultural studies, organizational communication, and the fallacy of the new economy. *Management Communication Quarterly*, *15*, 268–278. https://doi.org/10.1177/0893318901152006
Connaughton, S. L., & Shuffler, M. (2007). Multinational multicultural distributed teams: A review and future agenda. *Small Group Research*, *38*, 387–412. https://doi.org/10.1177/1046496407301970
Dempsey, S. E. (2010). Critiquing community engagement. *Management Communication Quarterly*, *24*, 359–390. https://doi.org/10.1177/0893318909352247
Dempsey, S. E., Parker, P. S., & Krone, K. J. (2011). Navigating socio-spatial difference, constructing counter-space: Insights from transnational feminist praxis. *Journal of International and Intercultural Communication*, *4*, 201–220. https://doi.org/10.1080/17513057.2011.569973
Dutta, M. J., & Dutta, D. (2013). Multinational going cultural: A postcolonial deconstruction of cultural intelligence. *Journal of International and Intercultural Communication*, *6*, 241–258. https://doi.org/10.1080/17513057.2013.790989
Fairhurst, G. T., & Putnam, L. L. (2024). *Performing organizational paradoxes*. Routledge.
Featherstone, M. (Ed.). (1990). *Global culture: Nationalism, globalism and modernity*. Sage.
Flew, T. (2019). Digital communication, the crisis of trust, and the postglobal. *Communication Research and Practice*, *5*(1), 4–22. https://doi.org/10.1080/22041451.2019.1561394
Fulk, J., Monge, P., & Hollingshead, A. B. (2005). Knowledge resource sharing in dispersed multinational teams: Three theoretical lenses. In D. L. Shapiro, M. A. Von Glinow, & J. L. C. Cheng (Eds.), *Managing multinational teams: Global perspectives* (Vol. 18, pp. 155–188). Advances in International Management. Elsevier.
Ganesh, S. (2003). Organizational narcissism: Technology, legitimacy and identity in an Indian NGO. *Management Communication Quarterly*, *16*, 558–594. https://doi.org/10.1177/0893318903252539
Ganesh, S. (2005). The myth of the nongovernmental organization: Governmentality and transnationalism in an Indian NGO. In G. Cheney & G. A. Barnett (Eds.), *International and multicultural organizational communication* (pp. 197–223). Hampton Press.
Ganesh, S., & Stohl, C. (2010). Qualifying engagement: A study of information and communication technology and the global social justice movement in Aotearoa New Zealand. *Communication Monographs*, *77*, 51–74. https://doi.org/10.1080/03637750903514284
Ganesh, S., & Stohl, C. (2013). From Wall Street to Wellington: Protests in an era of digital ubiquity. *Communication Monographs*, *80*, 425–451. https://doi.org/10.1080/03637751.2013.828156
Ganesh, S., & Stohl, C. (2020). Fluid hybridity: Organizational form and formlessness in the digital age. In L. Lievrouw & B. Loader (Eds.), *Routledge handbook of digital media and communication* (pp. 268–280). Routledge.
Ganesh, S., Stohl, C., & James, S. (2024). Generational shifts: The emergence of visibility in globalization research. In V. D. Miller & M. S. Poole (Eds.), *Handbook of organizational communication*. De Gruyter.
Ganesh, S., Vaccarino, F., & Li, M. (2017). The bases for intercultural communication in a digital era. In S. Croucher (Ed.), *Global perspectives on intercultural communication* (pp. 355–365). Routledge.
Ganesh, S. & Zoller, H.M. (2014). Organising transition: Principles and tensions in ecolocalism. In M. Parker, G. Cheney, V. Fournier, & C. Land (Eds), *The Routledge companion to alternative organisation* (pp. 236-250). Routledge.
Ganesh, S., Zoller, H., & Cheney, G. (2005). Transforming resistance, broadening our boundaries: Critical organizational communication meets globalization from below. *Communication Monographs*, *72*, 169–191. https://doi.org/10.1080/03637750500111872
Gibbs, J. L. (2009). Dialectics in a global software team: Negotiating tensions across time, space, and culture. *Human Relations*, *62*, 905–935. https://doi.org/10.1177/0018726709104547
Gibbs, J. L., Ball-Rokeach, S. J., Jung, J., Kim, Y., & Qiu, J. (2004). The globalization of everyday life: Visions and reality. In M. Sturken, D. Thomas, & S. Ball-Rokeach (Eds.), *Technological visions: The hopes and fears that shape new technologies* (pp. 339–358). Temple University Press.
Gibbs, J. L., Boyraz, M., Sivunen, A., & Nordbäck, E. (2021). Who is this "we"? Exploring the discursive functions of subgroups in global teams. *Journal of Applied Communication Research*, *49*(1), 86–108. https://doi.org/10.1080/00909882.2020.1851745
Gibbs, J. L., Eisenberg, J., & Nekrassova, D. (2023). Second-class citizens or free agents? Social construction of equity perceptions of contractors in global offshoring arrangements. *Journal of International Management*, *29*(6), 101092. https://doi.org/10.1016/j.intman.2023.101092
Gibson, C. B., & Gibbs, J. L. (2006). Unpacking the concept of virtuality: The effects of geographic dispersion, electronic dependence, dynamic structure, and national diversity on team innovation. *Administrative Science Quarterly*, *51*, 451–495. https://doi.org/10.2189/asqu.51.3.451

Giddens, A. (1991). *Modernity and self-identity: Self and society in the late modern age*. Stanford University Press.
Giddens, A. (2003). *Runaway world: How globalization is reshaping our lives*. Routledge.
Gill, R. (2014). 'If you're struggling to survive day-to-day': Class optimism and contradiction in entrepreneurial discourse. *Organization*, *21*, 50–67. https://doi.org/10.1177/1350508412464895
González-Bailón, S., & Wang, N. (2016). Networked discontent: The anatomy of protest campaigns in social media. *Social Networks*, *44*, 95–104. https://doi.org/10.1016/j.socnet.2015.07.003
Held, D., & McGrew, A. (2003). The great globalization debate: An introduction. In D. Held & A. McGrew (Eds.), *The global transformations reader* (pp. 1–50). Blackwell Publishing Inc.
Held, D., & McGrew, A. (2007). *Globalization/anti-globalization: Beyond the great divide*. Polity Press.
Held, D., McGrew, A., Goldblatt, D., & Perraton, J. (1999). *Global transformations: Politics, economics, and culture*. Stanford University Press.
Hirst, P., & Thompson, G. (1996). *Globalization in question: The international economy and the possibilities of governance*. Polity Press.
Huntington, S. (1996). *The clash of civilizations and the remaking of world order*. Simon & Schuster.
Iannacone, J. I. (2024). Violent enactments and erasures: A Western capitalist ontology of labor in organizational rhetoric about resettled Syrian refugees. *Management Communication Quarterly*, *38*(2), 221–248. https://doi.org/10.1177/08933189231186103
Javidan, M., Dorfman, P. W., Sully de Luque, M., & House, R. J. (2006). In the eye of the beholder: Cross cultural lessons in leadership from project GLOBE. *Academy of Management Perspectives*, *20*, 67–90. https://doi.org/10.5465/amp.2006.19873410
Johnson, H. J. (1991). *Dispelling the myth of globalization: The case for regionalization*. Praeger Publishers.
Kim, H. (2018). The mutual constitution of social media use and status hierarchies in global organizing. *Management Communication Quarterly*, *32*, 471–503. https://doi.org/10.1177/0893318918779135
Kotkin, J. (1992). *Tribes*. Random House.
Leonardi, P. M., & Bailey, D. E. (2008). Transformational technologies and the creation of new work practices: Making implicit knowledge explicit in task-based offshoring. *MIS Quarterly*, *32*, 411–436. https://doi.org/10.2307/25148846
Leonardi, P. M., & Rodriguez-Lluesma, C. (2013). Occupational stereotypes, perceived status differences, and intercultural communication in global organizations. *Communication Monographs*, *80*, 478–502. https://doi.org/10.1080/03637751.2013.828155
McAllum, K. (2018). Committing to refugee resettlement volunteering: Attaching, detaching, and displacing organizational ties. *Human Relations*, *71*, 951–972. https://doi.org/10.1177/0018726717729209
McGee, M. (1990). Text, context, and the fragmentation of contemporary culture. *Western Journal of Speech Communication*, 274–289. https://doi.org/10.1080/10570319009374343
McLuhan, M., & Powers, B. R. (1989). *The global village: Transformations in world life and media in the 21st century*. Oxford University Press.
Medved, C., Morrison, K., Dearing, J., Larson, S., Cline, G., & Brummans, B. (2001). Tensions in community health improvement initiatives: Communication and collaboration in a managed care environment. *Journal of Applied Communication Research*, *29*, 137–152. https://doi.org/10.1080/00909880128107
Mitra, R. (2018). Natural resource management in the U.S. Arctic: Sustainable organizing through communicative practices. *Management Communication Quarterly*, *32*, 398–430. https://doi.org/10.1177/0893318918755971
Monge, P., & Fulk, J. (1999). Communication technology for global network organizations. In G. DeSanctis & J. Fulk (Eds.), *Shaping organization form* (pp. 71–100). Sage. http://www-rcf.usc.edu/~monge/globenet.htm
Monge, P. R. (1998). Communication structures and processes in globalization. *Journal of Communication*, *48*, 142–153. https://doi.org/10.1093/joc/48.4.142
Negroponte, N. (1995). *Being digital*. Knopf.
Ohmae, K. (1995). *The end of the nation state*. Free Press.
Pal, M., Cruz, J., & Munshi, D. (Eds.). (2023). *Organizing at the margins: Theorizing organizations of struggle in the Global South*. Palgrave Macmillan.
Pal, M., Kim, H., Harris, K. L., Long, Z., Linabary, J., Wilhoit Larson, E., Jensen, P. R., Gist-Mackey, A. N., McDonald, J., Nieto-Fernandez, B., Jiang, J., Misra, S., & Dempsey, S. E. (2022). Decolonizing organizational communication. *Management Communication Quarterly*, *36*(3), 547–577. https://doi.org/10.1177/08933189221090255

Pal, M., & Nieto-Fernandez, B. (2024). Politics of transnational feminism to decolonize feminist organizational communication: A call to action. *Management Communication Quarterly*, *38*(1), 60–85. https://doi.org/10.1177/08933189231161620

Perlmutter, H. V. (1969). The tortuous evolution of the multinational corporation. *Columbia Journal of World Business*, 9–18. https://doi.org/10.4324/9781315199689-7

Prichard, C. (2006). Global politics, academic dispositions, and the tilting of organizational communication: A provocation to a debate. *Management Communication Quarterly*, *19*, 638–644. https://doi.org/10.1177/0893318905285388

Putnam, L. L., & Boys, S. (2006). Revisiting metaphors of organizational communication. In S. Clegg, C. Hardy, & W. Nord (Eds.), *Handbook of organizational studies* (2nd ed., pp. 541–576). Sage.

Putnam, L. L., Fairhurst, G. T., & Banghart, S. (2016). Contradictions, dialectics, and paradoxes in organizations: A constitutive approach. *The Academy of Management Annals*, *10*(1), 65–171. https://doi.org/10.1080/19416520.2016.1162421

Robertson, R. (1992). *Globalization: Social theory and global culture*. Sage.

Sassen, S. (2014). *Expulsion: Brutality and complexity in the global economy*. Harvard University Press.

Scholte, J. A. (2005). *Globalization: A critical introduction* (2nd ed.). Palgrave Macmillan.

Scott, A. (Ed.). (1997). *The limits of globalization: Cases and arguments*. Routledge.

Shumate, M., & O'Connor, A. (2010). The symbiotic sustainability model: Conceptualizing NGO–corporate alliance communication. *Journal of Communication*, *60*, 577–609. https://doi.org/10.1111/j.1460-2466.2010.01498.x

Sklair, L. (1991). *Sociology of the global system: Social change in global perspective*. Johns Hopkins University Press.

Sobre-Denton, M., & Bardhan, N. (2013). *Cultivating cosmopolitanism for intercultural communication: Communicating as global citizens*. Routledge.

Stage, C. W. (1999). Negotiating organizational communication cultures in American subsidiaries doing business in Thailand. *Management Communication Quarterly*, *13*, 245–280. https://doi.org/10.1177/0893318999132003

Stephens, K. K., Jahn, J. L. S., Fox, S., Charoensap-Kelly, P., Mitra, R., Sutton, J., Waters, E. D., Xie, B., & Meisenbach, R. J. (2020). Collective sensemaking around COVID-19: Experiences, concerns, and agendas for our rapidly changing organizational lives. *Management Communication Quarterly*, *34*(3), 426–457. https://doi.org/10.1177/0893318920934890

Stohl, C. (1993). International organizing and organizational communication. *Journal of Applied Communication Research*, *21*, 377–384. https://doi.org/10.1080/00909889309365380

Stohl, C. (2001). Globalizing organizational communication. In F. M. Jablin & L. L. Putnam (Eds.), *The new handbook of organizational communication* (pp. 323–375). Sage.

Stohl, C. (2005). Globalization theory. In S. May & D. K. Mumby (Eds.), *Engaging organizational communication theory and research* (pp. 223–261). Sage.

Stohl, C., & Ganesh, S. (2014). Generating globalization. In L. L. Putnam & D. K. Mumby (Eds.), *The SAGE handbook of organizational communication* (3rd ed., pp. 717–741). Sage.

Stohl, C., & Stohl, M. (2007). Networks of terror: Theoretical assumptions and pragmatic consequences. *Communication Theory*, *17*, 93–124. https://doi.org/10.1111/j.1468-2885.2007.00289.x

Stohl, M., & Stohl, C. (2005). Human rights, nation states, and NGOs: Structural holes and the emergence of global regimes. *Communication Monographs*, *72*, 442–467. https://doi.org/10.1080/03637750500322610

Stohl, M., Stohl, C., & Townsley, N. (2007). A new generation of global corporate social responsibility. In S. May, G. Cheney, & J. Roper (Eds.), *The debate over corporate social responsibility* (pp. 30–44). Oxford University Press.

Sturken, M., & Thomas, D. (Eds.). (2004). *Technological visions: The hopes and fears that shape new technologies*. Temple University Press.

Taylor, S., & Osland, J. S. (2011). The impact of intercultural communication on global organizational learning. In M. Easterby-Smith & M. A. Lyles (Eds.), *Handbook of organizational learning and knowledge management* (pp. 581–604). John Wiley & Sons.

Tomlinson, J. (1999). *Globalization and culture*. University of Chicago Press.

Townsley, N., & Stohl, C. (2003). Contracting corporate social responsibility: Swedish expansions in global temporary agency work. *Management Communication Quarterly*, *16*, 599–605. https://doi.org/10.1177/0893318902250238

Tuck, E., & Yang, K. W. (2012). Decolonization is not a metaphor. *Decolonization: Indigeneity, Education & Society*, *1*(1), 1–40.
Wallerstein, I. (1974). *The modern world system*. Academic Press.
Wieland, S. M. B. (2011). Struggling to manage work as a part of everyday life: Complicating control, rethinking resistance, and contextualizing work/life studies. *Communication Monographs*, *78*, 162–184. https://doi.org/10.1080/03637751.2011.564642
Williamson, J. (2002). *Did the Washington Consensus fail?* Peterson Institute for International Economics. https://piie.com/commentary/speeches-papers/did-washington-consensus-fail
Yuan, Y. C., & Gay, G. (2006). Homophily of network ties and bonding and bridging social capital in computer-mediated distributed teams. *Journal of Computer-Mediated Communication*, *11*, 1062–1084. https://doi.org/10.1111/j.1083-6101.2006.00308.x
Zoller, H. (2006). Suitcases and swimsuits: On the future of organizational communication. *Management Communication Quarterly*, *19*, 661–666. https://doi.org/10.1177/0893318905285391
Zoller, H. M. (2004). Dialogue as global issue management: Legitimizing corporate influence in the transatlantic business dialogue. *Management Communication Quarterly*, *18*, 204–240. https://doi.org/10.1177/0893318904265126

21 Organizational Change

Laurie Lewis

The term *organizational change* refers to processes involved in introducing new ideas into practice. Oftentimes, in defining change, scholars will refer to a disrupted period or altered state and thereby imply that what precedes change is stability or continuity. However, in fact, organizing activity is made up of processes and thus is always in motion and always changing. As Poole (2004) argues, regarding the false separation of planned and unplanned modes of changing, "all planned change occurs in the context of the ambient change processes that occur naturally in organizations" (p. 4). Organizational life – made up of specific practices, objects, or ways of doing – can be experienced as more stable. At other times, organizational life can be punctuated by points of *change* where routine activities appear to be disrupted. At these times, we may experience our organizations as changing.

Change is a prominent process in organizational activity, whether it occurs in civic or religious organizations, governments, schools, or businesses. Engaging in change and attempts to bring change in organizations is often necessary in order to innovate, address injustices, remedy failing or poor practices, revitalize participant energy, maintain competitiveness, create variety, experiment, and adapt to environments. Scholars have examined changes of large scope, including mergers, cultural transformation, reorganizations, as well as introduction of technologies, production methodologies, employee programs, process improvements, and policies requiring, proscribing, or forbidding behaviors, among many others.

Organizations would eventually fail to adapt to their environments, stakeholders, and participants if they are unable to change. It is likely that unchanging organizations would at some point become so mismatched with the demands made on them that they would become obsolete. Organizations are embedded in multiple streams of dynamic environmental processes and thus are enmeshed in change. Organizations spend significant resources on selecting and launching change initiatives every year. Leaders of organizations are frequently expected to innovate at every level of organizational practice – bringing massive cultural changes, creating new programs, products, services, and/or rebranding old ones – perpetually changing in response to environmental demands and pressures to maintain competitive advantage. For example, corporate managers facing the widescale changes required in response to the COVID-19 pandemic had to minimize damage but could also capitalize on the resulting changes in pursuit of competitive advantages (Schmidt, 2023). Moreover, change communication during the pandemic differed in effectiveness for essential and nonessential workers, highlighting the need for messaging tailored to specific stakeholder groups (van Zoonen & ter Hoeven, 2022) and for transparency during crisis-driven change (Yue & Walden, 2023). Debates about how and what to change in organizations of every size,

DOI: 10.4324/9781003484639-24

in every sector, every industry, and along a vast array of dimensions occupy a great deal of organizational discourse. Thus, both the nature of organizations and the discourse surrounding organizations tend to demand and reinforce cycles of change.

During periods of change there is likely to be disruption of routines, rewards, expertise, status, security, familiarity, relationships, and physical surroundings, and increased demands on cognitive, physical, and emotional capacities. Individuals who participate in change programs and/or are dependent on the operation of organization (i.e., stakeholders) feel these disruptions and are active in processing and engaging in sensemaking (see Chapter 2) about the change, its causes, its consequences, and the sponsors and detractors for it.

History of Organizational Change Scholarship

There has been a rich and multidisciplinary history of scholarship about organizational change. Schlesinger and Kotter (1979) observed the prevalence of organizational change in business environments of the day:

> Today, more and more managers must deal with new government regulations, new products, growth, increased competition, technological developments, and a changing workforce. In response, most companies ... find that they must undertake moderate organizational changes at least once a year and major changes every four or five.
> (p. 106)

Twenty years later, Zorn et al. (1999) made the case that "change for change's sake" (p. 4) had become glorified to an extent that it could be considered managerial fashion for stakeholders to constantly demand change in their organizations. Zorn and colleagues also argue that the cultural and market pressures demanding constant change may lead to disastrous outcomes, including faulty decisions about what to change, poor timing of change programs, dysfunctional internal dynamics of changing organizations, and exhaustion due to repetitive cycles of change. Further, change has also long been depicted and documented as difficult and prone to failure. Failure rates have been reported to be as high as 50–75 percent (Majchrzak, 1988). Human and organizational factors have been early and often blamed for failure and difficulties during change (Bikson & Gutek, 1984). Miller et al. (1994) suggest that resistance (which they describe in terms of reduction of output, quarreling and hostility, work slowdowns, and pessimism regarding goals) plays a major role in change failure (see Hubbart, 2023 for a review of the change aversion literature).

As organizational scholars in a variety of disciplines including management, education, social work, technology transfer, and communication (among many others) have tackled the subject of organizational change, a number of approaches and foci have developed over time. Some of this work – especially some earlier work – focused on the role communication played in promoting innovativeness and the spread of innovative ideas in organizations (see Albrecht & Ropp, 1984; Fairhurst & Wendt, 1993; Rice & Rogers, 1980; Rogers, 1995; Van de Ven et al., 1989). Other scholars have focused on the formation of attitudes regarding planned changes, including resistant responses (see Ellis, 1992; Fairhurst et al., 1995; Miller & Monge, 1986; Miller et al., 1994). More recent scholarship has increasingly focused on communication during the process of implementing change and how it influences stakeholders' perspectives, behaviors, as well as individual and organizational outcomes (Lewis, 2011).

Over time there have been a number of attempts to summarize and provide overviews of trends in the research (Lewis, 2014; Lewis & Sahay, 2017; Lewis & Seibold, 1998; Poole, 2004; Poole & Van de Ven, 2004). The following sections provide an overview of the historical developments in scholarship about organizational change and highlight some key turning points and foci.

Early and Classic Models and Approaches

Early models of organizational innovation and change tend to be presented in very linear terms with steps, stages, and phases. For example, Lewin's (1951) classic model of change suggested three phases of change: unfreezing, changing, and refreezing. In his model, organizations are depicted as existing as generally stable with broken discrete periods of change activity that temporarily disrupt routines before eventually resettling into new stable periods. In another model, Rogers (1995) included the critical concepts of agenda setting, matching, redefining and restructuring (reinvention), clarifying, and routinizing. This model explores initiating stages in the first two phases. In these phases new ideas are compared against perceived problems in organizations. In the last three stages, implementation is examined. In these phases changes are brought into use and fit into existing practices.

Stages of *stability–change–restabilization* are a typical sequence in these early linear models; they imply that organizations follow a set pattern in which novel ideas are surfaced, embraced, introduced, and eventually rejected or routinized. We may critique these models by noting that they are overly linear and that they tend to assume perfectly rational consideration of benefits and disadvantages against a set of organizational needs or desires, reflecting a Western rationalistic bias. These models often presume that needs and desires are known and agreed to at the outset of a change process and that novel ideas for change are considered in terms of their fit to solve problems or increase efforts at achieving known goals. This set of assumptions is managerially biased, overlooks the existence of multiple (and often contradictory) goals, and ignores nondominant viewpoints.

In the 1980s scholars of change developed descriptive models of change implementation. Implementation has been defined as "the translation of any tool or technique, process, or method of doing, from knowledge to practice. It encompasses that range of activities which take place between 'adoption' of a tool or technique … and its stable incorporation into on-going organizational practice" (Tornatzky & Johnson, 1982, p. 193). Thus, implementation involves a set of activities – many of them communication-related – which introduce, explain, describe, or encourage usage of a change. Implementation may involve persuasive efforts to convince individuals involved in the change of its benefits. Implementers often must counter negative perceptions and concerns related to the change or the process of changing. For some implementers this will entail reaching out to those who have less enthusiastic responses to the change to influence their opinions and behaviors. Even when change is welcomed, implementers will need to instruct employees, clients, and partners on how the change will work, how problems will be resolved, and how they should engage with it. In other activity, implementers will need to monitor the installation and functioning of change programs to understand if they are meeting goals. Implementers will assess and adjust change or the ways employees and others engage with it over the course of an implementation effort.

A number of scholars have attempted to develop models that describe the approach implementers take to their tasks of bringing change into operation. Bourgeois and Brodwin

(1984) distinguished between the *commander* model and the *crescive* model. The commander model favors a highly centralized approach to implementation in which the implementer controls decision-making and adjustments during the process. However, the *crescive* model "draws on managers' natural inclinations to want to develop new opportunities as they see them in the course of their day-to-day management" (p. 242) and permits more localized control and responsiveness during implementation. These sorts of contrasting models of change implementation tended to focus on the tension between top-down control strategies and bottom-up autonomous adaptation strategies (Lewis & Seibold, 1998). As early as the 1980s, scholars making these distinctions generally favored the more bottom-up autonomous approaches that involve more local control and lower-level influence. In general, evidence has found support for their relative success in completing implementation efforts and meeting intended goals (see Baronas & Louis, 1988; Marcus, 1988). That trend has become stronger over time.

Early multidisciplinary scholarship related to organizational change tended to focus on how managers and leaders can garner support for change and be successful in terms of managerial goals. This often boiled down to overcoming resistance to change. Some early models viewed resistance as a form of organizational politics. Frost and Egri (1989, p. 243) noted that implementation is the "most vulnerable time of the innovation process ... when the dysfunctional nature of organizational politics is most often highlighted." Some scholars concentrated on identifying the most effective counterstrategies to resistance. Schein (1985) argued that power bases including expertise, information control, political access, and group support needed to be skillfully wielded in order to defeat resistance. Assessment of strategies and tactics to defeat or forestall resistance was a frequent topic of scholarship during the 1980s and early 1990s. For example, Nutt (1986, 1987) developed four models of implementation strategies (intervention, participation, persuasion, and edict) and tested their relative success in gaining traction for change programs in organizations. These models varied in the degree to which they involved a variety of stakeholders in important decision-making.

Outcomes for non-managerial stakeholders were rarely a focus in early scholarship. When non-managerial stakeholders are considered, it tends to be in terms of the degree to which they respond favorably (or not) to change and how their reactions can be made to be more favorable. The strategic goals or stakes of employees, clients, customers, members, partner organizations, or communities, among other stakeholders, were not often a point of concern or theorizing in the models of organizational change offered in this earlier scholarship.

Modern Models of Change Process

In a more encompassing theoretical effort to explain various change processes, Van de Ven and Poole (1995) described four change motors: lifecycle, teleological, dialectical, and evolutionary. Poole (2004) argues that these four theories of change are distinguishable in terms of two key dimensions: the degree to which change is premised on the actions of a single or of multiple entities, and whether the change events are *a priori* or emerging as the change process unfolds. Each of these motors accounts for different generators of organizational change. Their *lifecycle* motor depicts change processes as progressing through a necessary sequence of phases proscribed through institutional, natural, or logical causes. The *teleological* model, closest to the notion of planned change, is accomplished through intentional goal formation, implementation, and modification of behaviors. The *dialectical* motor of change emerges through the development of conflicts between entities that espouse opposing theses. This motor conceptualizes a cycle of dialectical progression of confrontation and conflict between opposing entities that generates change. Finally, the *evolutionary* model of development and change consists of repetitive sequences of variation, selection, and retention events among entities. Van de Ven and Poole argue that evolutionary change is driven by competition for scarce resources.

Lewis and Seibold (1993) developed a model of innovation modification during change processes. This initial model attempted to depict how an organizational change and the organization are both altered through a process of implementation. That model was further developed (Lewis, 2007) and elaborated (Lewis, 2011, 2019) by embracing stakeholder theory as a frame for accounting for dynamics of communication within organizational change processes. *Stakes* are those claims that individuals, groups, and organizations have in the operation of organizations and may be financial, material, social, and/or symbolic in nature. *Stakeholders* are those who have a stake in an organization's process or outputs. Figure 21.1 depicts the typical hub-and-spoke stakeholder perspective that highlights relationships between a focal organization and each of its various stakeholder groups.

Lewis' (2011, 2019) stakeholder model of change implementation communication focuses on change as a context within which organizational stakeholders assert stakes. The argument that Lewis (2011, 2019) makes depicts stakeholders in relationships with the focal organization (in all of its parts and complexity) and in relationships with one another (see Figure 21.2). This model and the accompanying argument suggests that stakeholders likely spend as much or more time negotiating stakes with one another as with the organization.

According to Lewis (2011), stakeholders play multiple roles in organizations and throughout change processes. For example, individuals and groups of stakeholders may serve in roles as opinion leaders, as bridging connectors between groups of stakeholders (see Chapter 9), as supportive counselors, and as journalists sharing information and interpretations of events. This model and argument suggests that all stakeholders participate in strategic communication during change. That is, any stakeholder may have strategic goals (e.g., to defeat the change, to garner support for the change, to use the change as a context to gain resources) and will use communication in strategic ways (e.g., to spread rumors, highlight positives, upwardly distort information, feign ignorance, provide others

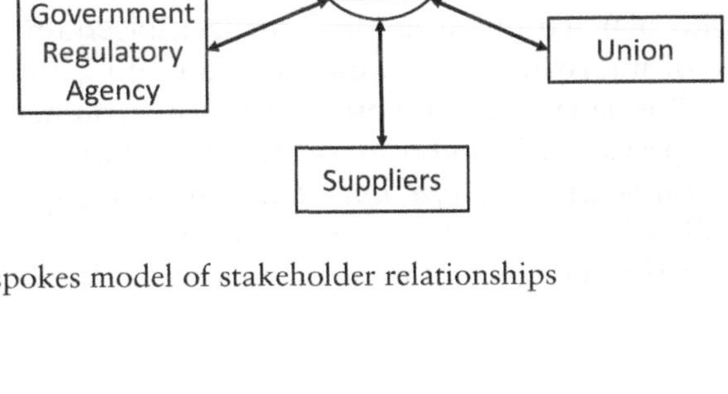

Figure 21.1 Hub and spokes model of stakeholder relationships

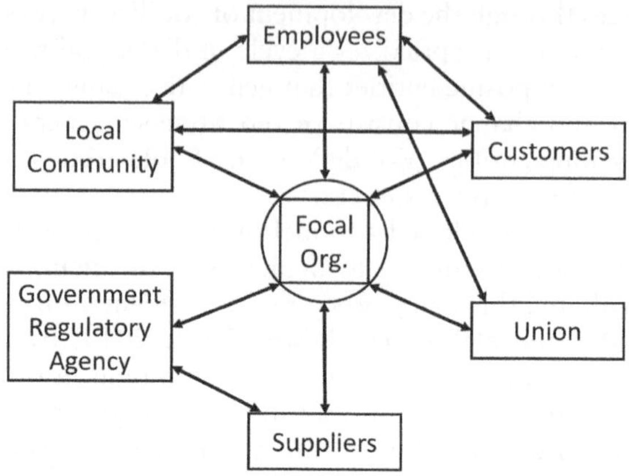

Figure 21.2 Complex stakeholder relationships

with emotional support, build alliances with powerful stakeholders) to further those goals. The heart of this model concerns the communicative strategic dimensions and modes of interaction that drive the fulfillment, denial, and negotiation of stakes during change. The model depicts a fluid and complex process that occurs in the context of the organization's total environment.

Implementers' Communication

A significant portion of change communication scholarship has focused on the choices that implementers, leaders, and change agents make to introduce change, counter resistance, and increase cooperation with changed practices, policies, and technologies. The term *change agent* and the characteristics of individuals filling this role in organizations have been a subject of significant exploration over time. Ottaway (1983) and Maidique (1980) provide historical reviews of this term and related terms (e.g., idea champion, innovator, sponsor). Kanter (1983) emphasized the importance of change agents: "Any new strategy, no matter how brilliant or responsive, no matter how much agreement the formulators have about it, will stand a good chance of not being implemented fully – or sometimes, at all – without someone with power pushing it" (p. 296). Researchers devoted attention in the 1980s to detailing the characteristics of effective change agents, including openness and responsiveness, comfort with ambiguity, comfort with oneself (Hamilton, 1988), technical qualifications, administrative ability, and leadership (Zaltman & Duncan, 1977), and risk-taking, innovativeness, and ability to articulate a compelling vision (Howell & Higgins, 1990).

Scholars' approaches to implementation communication have often tended to the central problem associated with planned organizational change: uncertainty. Uncertainty is typically defined as a lack of information or confusion related to many available possible interpretations of events. Bordia et al. (2004) propose that uncertainty during organizational change involves three types: *strategic uncertainty* (about the future of the organization and its situation in its environment); *structural uncertainty* (how the organization will operate and what its culture will be like); and *job-related uncertainty* (concerning an individual's rewards, job duties, and status). Organizations often assume that leaders' information sharing will reduce uncertainty. Scholars, leaders, and consultants often focus on the best messaging and information strategies that implementers may use to reduce uncertainty. Also leaders often focus on discovering the inaccurate information about a change process and attempt to correct it.

Announcing change is one critical part of addressing uncertainty. Often the manner, timing, message, and spokesperson of change announcements can set a tone that may have implications for the entire implementation effort (Smeltzer, 1995). Schweiger and DeNisi (1991) undertook an extensive field study to determine the impact of realistic previews of complex change (i.e., merger) on the acceptance of the change. The researchers found that providing early previews of the details of the merger and its process significantly reduced uncertainty and increased job satisfaction, commitment, and perceived trustworthiness, among other positive outcomes.

In another experimental study, Lewis et al. (2013) examined the reactions of 218 working professionals to memos announcing change. Some respondents received messages highlighting negative aspects of the change and others received messages that were more positive in presenting the change. The study sought to understand whether downplaying or highlighting negative information about the change or change process had effect on perceptions of honesty and trustworthiness of implementers, as well as to judge the impact of negative previews on initial favorability toward the change. The study's results suggest that implementers' credibility was not enhanced by the use of messages that previewed the "pain" of the upcoming change. The authors argued that complexity related to the context of the change, the expectations for implementers' communication, and the level of perceived riskiness of the change (e.g., more routine program change vs. major organizational shift) will likely drive reactions to introductory messages. Recent research has shown that employees who perceive change more positively are better able to understand their new role, which increases their resilience. Perceived supervisor support enhances this effect (Bernuzzi et al., 2023; Hubbart, 2023).

In other work related to information dissemination and announcement of change, some scholars (Leonard-Barton, 1987; Leonard-Barton & Kraus, 1985) have suggested that change implementation should be treated as an "internal marketing campaign." For example, Yue's (2022) recent study examined the use of public relations strategies for internal change communication, revealing that *bridging* strategies that focus on relationships, action, authenticity, and mutual understanding are effective at inducing employees' compliance, cooperation, and openness to change. Whereas *buffering* strategies that are organization-centric and oriented to control and manipulation had a weaker influence on compliance and cooperation and no impact on employee openness to change. However, there is little evidence that messages related to organizational change are commonly tailored to appeal to various audiences, as Leonard-Barton (Leonard-Barton, 1987; Leonard-Barton & Kraus, 1985) had recommended. Smeltzer's (1991) early study of change announcements found that in only a few rare cases in their sample did management attempt to adapt their messages to multiple audiences. Smeltzer and Zener (1992) found that organizations did not differentiate between internal and external audiences in the announcement of layoffs. The lack of attention to the unique needs, perspectives, and stakes of different audiences and stakeholders is likely to be ineffective and/or counterproductive, as illustrated by van Zoonen and ter Hoeven's (2022) study of change messaging to essential and nonessential workers during the COVID-19 crisis.

Soliciting input is another communication approach to uncertainty reduction during change. Scholars have examined and promoted the idea of input solicitation under varied terms, including participation, empowerment, positive climate, feedback, upward communication, and voice. Activities that constitute input solicitation include asking for opinions, seeking feedback, requesting opinions, and reactions to change. Such activities have long been encouraged by experts in order to manage feelings and concerns about change. Evidence suggests that soliciting input, especially in the context of a general philosophy of stakeholder participation in decision-making about change, can reap a number of benefits desired by implementers (see Bordia et al., 2004; Sagie & Koslowsky, 1994; Sagie et al., 2001), including reduction of resistance, encouraging co-operativeness, and encouraging satisfaction of stakeholders during change. For example, management scholars argue that readiness to change can be created through early solicitation because that helps employees cope with resistance (Armenakis et al., 1993). Such early conversations can promote openness, where stakeholders can discuss and understand the need for the change. According to Armenakis et al. (1993), stakeholders must believe that (a) change is necessary for the organization, (b) the particular proposed change is the correct one for them, (c) the organization is capable of implementing the change, and (d) opinion leaders are committed to the change. These beliefs can help increase the readiness or the commitment employees feel toward their organization and the change.

Research into the manner, method, and results of input solicitation during organizational change has increased over time. For example, Sahay and Lewis (2016) have made the case that input solicitation may be designed in order to provide a full voice, limited voice, or what Sahay (2017) calls "faux voice." In the case of *full voice*, stakeholders are provided meaningful opportunities to engage in discussion and assessment about a change, while implementers and decision-makers use the input that is gathered in further decision-making. Sahay discusses *limited voice* as opportunities created primarily for the purpose of "checking the box" of collecting feedback by putting on a public show that input was solicited without seriously considering the perspectives that are offered. Implementers may cherry-pick issues and concerns if there is a sense that a minimal adjustment to the change could address them. Finally, *faux voice* involves providing channels for stakeholders to vent or deposit concerns and questions without having ability to influence the change initiative in any serious way.

Zorn et al. (2000) provide examples of limited or faux voice during change in their study of a New Zealand government organization's attempt to emulate Southwest Airlines' change of culture. They reveal how employees were involved in ritual ways. These means of "involvement" of employees in the change effort were constructed in ways to ensure the predetermined outcome of acceptance of the CEO's vision. Their input was neither course-correcting nor empowering in the sense that it could alter original plans.

In an investigation of input solicitation practices of change implementers, Lewis and Russ (2012) collected interview data from implementers in 26 organizations, from a diverse set of industries, to discern both the specific methods used to solicit input as well as the criteria applied to received input to determine its value and credibility. The analyses of these data were used to construct five categories of approaches to input solicitation that refined the original Lewis (2011) categories.

- **Restricted** was the most common approach, which involved seeking input from a very select group of stakeholders and doing so in a manner that likely would confirm implementers' decisions. Input that could not easily be addressed was very unique (not widely shared) and was often discarded. Highly critical input was also often ignored and characterized as a product of general unhappiness in the organization.

- **Advisory** was the second most common approach observed in the data set. The major motivation for soliciting input was to seek affirming information or persuade providers to alter negative impressions of the change. Implementers using this approach tended to avoid "complainers." When negative input was encountered, it was typically used to identify the source of resistance.
- **Political** approach was used in only 6 of the 21. Specific "important" stakeholders were sought out for input. The "important" individuals tended to hold significant resources or other power bases.
- **Open** approach was extremely uncommon in these data (used in only three cases). In this approach, implementers solicited input from diverse groups of individuals and used a very open style of communicating. Implementers typically invited stakeholders to volunteer to offer input. If the input was viewed as "viable," it was included. If the input was considered to be "whining" or "complaining," it was discarded.
- **Widespread empowerment** approach was absent in these data. Lewis and Russ expected to find some evidence of implementers' efforts to collect widespread input from diverse stakeholders and to make use of it through rigorous evaluation and consideration but were surprised to find no examples of this model.

These categories varied in terms of commitment of implementers to maintain the change as was originally intended (fidelity) and the degree to which the implementer was genuinely interested in using collected input to direct the change (resource orientation).

In another example of a stakeholder approach to change, Barge et al. (2008) conducted a case study on a planned organizational change in a multi-stakeholder initiative. A key finding of their study identified a key tension of inclusion–exclusion. This was a key challenge specific to participation. This study elaborated on the conflict faced by implementers when including different stakeholders in different phases of the change because who got invited to the table and at which phase was critical for the organization. It raises the issue of how we resolve concerns about which stakeholders are able to voice their opinions, concerns, and viewpoints and which ones are not. Who controls those decisions, how opportunities for voice are created and the experiences of those who attempt to exercise their voice are paramount as input is invited in change initiatives. Little research has examined the inclusion of marginalized groups in organizational change processes. While there is wide agreement among scholars that change communication failures are common, scant attention has been given to employees' and other stakeholders' cultural values. Shrivastava et al. (2022) developed a conceptual framework that accounts for the diversity of cultural orientations among members of a multicultural workforce. Taking the perspective of change communication recipients, their model links four change communication functions (disrupting, envisioning, legitimizing, and co-creating) and highlights the importance of change agents' cultural sensitivity for change communication effectiveness.

Stakeholders' Communication

Lewis (2011, 2019) argues that much consequential communication during organizational change occurs among stakeholders who are not in decision-making roles. Scholars have argued that uncertainty is not only reduced through formal information dissemination, but that stakeholders also share information with each other in order to cope with uncertainty. Several types of informal communication such as grapevine communication, informal discussions, peer mentoring, socially supportive communication, among other methods, can help stakeholders to resolve uncertainties regarding tasks, roles, and relationships. Kramer (1993), in his longitudinal study on socialization during job transfers, found that requests for information from peers increased as uncertainties regarding supervisors or task roles increased. In these situations, individuals relied on more informal sources of information instead of making information requests of supervisors directly. This highlights the importance of stakeholder information sharing among stakeholders. These non-supervisory employees turned to one another to answer their questions and make sense of the change in their organization.

Although much of the earlier communication research about organizational change focused on what messages employees needed or wanted to receive, scant research has dealt with the strategic communication *among* stakeholders (including employees). For instance, stakeholders solicit input, just as implementers do. Nearly all the work on participation in implementation of change assumes that this is an activity designed by implementers who invite, to some extent or another, input from stakeholders. Those approaches ignore the important bids of stakeholders to solicit input from each other.

Ruben et al. (2008) explored this in their study of the higher education community's use of published outlets as a channel for a national conversation about the Spellings Report. The Spellings Report examined the state of higher education and laid out the need for important and significant changes. In an effort to raise alarm and provoke strategic reactions to the Spellings Report, stakeholders wrote articles for *Inside Higher Education* and *Chronicle of Higher Education*. Other stakeholders wrote online responses to these publications. In a content analysis of those posts, there is evidence of stakeholders soliciting input from one another. In the end, the Spellings Report and the interactions that followed served as a wake-up call that stirred much reaction from various stakeholders encouraging sharing of perspectives and contrasts of opinion.

Other research has examined the ways in which stakeholders tell the stories of organizational change. Although much of the scholarship about managing meaning of change has highlighted the roles implementers play in actively shaping meaning and promoting their sense of what is going on or in manipulating others' sensemaking, there is a growing body of research exploring stakeholders' influence in framing change initiatives. For example, in a study of change in two Canadian banks, Cherim (2006) describes how managerial frames are appropriated by employees. She defines appropriation as acceptance of the frame and the identities the frame implies, including internalization of the values, goals, and means to achieving them. She illustrates employees' responses to managerial frames for change in terms of their willing appropriation, reluctant appropriation, and partial appropriation. As Fairhurst and Sarr (1996) note,

> many individuals prefer to look to others to define what is real, what is fair, and what should count now and in the future. They are reluctant to manage meaning for themselves or others because there is risk involved when the stakes are high.
>
> (p. 2)

Stakeholders' stories about change initiatives have consequences for the beliefs and concerns that are held regarding change. Both hearing stories and participating in their development and elaboration can shape perceptions, emotions, and expectations (Fischer-Appelt & Dernbach, 2023). As Whittle et al. (2010) argue, "[stakeholders'] interests are not a fixed, essential entity that drives social action. Rather interests are negotiated and transformed in interaction" (p. 33). They argue that we should focus on how interests are *constructed in* discourse rather than simply *expressed in* discourse. As Lewis (2011) notes, stakeholders' storytelling about change may call attention to key concerns about change.

> Stakeholders' interactions have the ability to strategically or inadvertently give rise to these concerns for themselves and for others. The joint sensemaking about "what is really going" on during change will highlight certain aspects of the change experience and predict the future in ways that make some concerns more salient and important. Further, stakeholders may strategically highlight or de-emphasize concerns for other stakeholders with regards to key stakes those stakeholders value.
>
> (p. 248)

Leonardi's (2009) study of the implementation of a new technology in an auto manufacturing plant captured change sensemaking as it unfolded in real time. Leonardi argued that stakeholders develop interpretations of what a technology can do through both material interactions (actually using a new technology) and social interactions (talking with other stakeholders about the new technology and its use). In his study, the users of a new technology developed one interpretation of the change that so informed these stakeholders' expectations and interpretations of the change that it fundamentally shaped their material interactions with it. In this case, that shaping led to a negative assessment of what the technology could do. This study is an excellent example of empirical analysis of sensemaking as it unfolds over time and of the consequences of that sensemaking for the results of a change effort. Similarly, Malvini Redden et al. (2019) examined metaphoric framing among team members during planned change, illustrating that negative framing of change is endemic to teams regardless of how successful they perceive the change to be and, further, that the metaphors used in sensemaking both build and undermine employee resilience.

What Has Been the C–O Relationship in Organizational Change?

Throughout the body of scholarship about organizational change, organizations are generally treated as entities within which change happens (O_3). Even scholars who adopt very process-oriented (O_1) views of organizational change itself tend to treat the organization as a bounded place (physically and metaphorically). Organizations tend to be considered to be bounded by formal definitions (e.g., incorporation), membership (who is "in" and who is "out"), and activities (those occurring "within" and those interactions between the organization and external actors).

Organizational change occurs in a flow of communicative and other activity and within a context of organizational structures (e.g., authority relations, decision-making rules, physical resources, budgetary constraints, production methodologies, governing policies). In the context of change (and other organizational activity), there is an interplay between that which organizational structures encourage, delimit, forestall, and/or compel and that which communicative engagement reinforces, challenges, and manifests. In short, the change *is* what the communication *makes it be* within the context of the organization's enacted structures.

The most obvious illustration of the interplay of structure and communicative agency (the C–O cycle) in the context of organizational change concerns the very manner in which the change comes to have form in practice. As we consider a specific change – a new policy, a new production technique, a new method of service, a new procedure for decision-making – and then consider how that change looks in actual practice (e.g., the ways people really use/engage with the change), we can illustrate how what *it* is, how it is perceived, used, and regarded in interaction. That is, a hammer isn't a hammer if the way it is used and regarded is more akin to a paintbrush. If the object is used to make artwork and it is regarded by users as a means to position paint on a canvas, then it is being installed in that setting as a means to create art. This same process occurs whenever any new program, policy, technology, process, practice, or other change is introduced into an organization. The members of that organization interpret the change, discuss what it is/what it means, influence how others incorporate it into the stream of other activity, and thus socially co-construct that change.

Just as communication can create the operational lived reality of an organizational change, the structures of an organization can give rise to, forestall, encourage, or shape communication about change. As the research noted earlier makes clear, implementers often take a stance on implementation-related communication that attempts to limit the amount of negative or resistant commentary. Organizational leaders and implementers often wish to limit the forums and opportunities for those most negative to change to speak. The creation of *faux voice* opportunities where complaints, concerns, and objections may be said but are not actually heard is a means of limiting what can be contributed by disempowered stakeholders in the installation of change. Organizations use authority, rules, and practices to limit how much influence some stakeholders may have in shaping change programs. Further, implementers may highlight and privilege speakers who promote an understanding of the change that is preferred by management. They may hold up their opinions and perspectives in ways that reinforce a version of the change that is in alignment with their own vision. Using their power and authority to highlight some communication over others further reinforces their own decision-making and choices (see Chapter 12).

In organizations where full voice is enabled, leaders and implementers use the structures of organizational expression – meetings, supervisory interactions, forums – in order to provide for the full elaboration of questions, expression of concerns, and perhaps articulation of arguments opposing change. Such decisions may give rise to changing the change through the interaction, debate, and discourse of stakeholders.

Recommended Supplementary Readings

Kramer, M., Dougherty, D. S., & Pierce, T. A. (2004) Managing uncertainty during a corporate acquisition: A longitudinal study of communication during an airline acquisition. *Human Communication Research, 30*(1), 71–101.

Excellent case study of a change.

Lewis, L. K., & Russ, T. (2012). Soliciting and using input during organizational change initiatives: What are practitioners doing? *Management Communication Quarterly, 26*(2), 267–294.

Details how organizations solicit input, use input, and defensively ignore or suppress input.

Scott, C. R., Lewis, L. K., & D'Urso, S. C. (2010). Getting on the "E" list: Email list use in a community of service provider organizations for people experiencing homelessness. In L. Shedletsky & J. E. Aitken (Eds.), *Cases on online discussion and interaction: Experiences and outcomes* (pp. 334–350). IGI-Global.

Case study for a network-wide organizational change.

Scott, C. R., Lewis, L. K., Davis, J. D., & D'Urso, S. C. (2009). Finding a home for communication technologies. In J. Keyton & P. Shockley-Zalabak (Eds.), *Case studies for organizational communication: Understanding communication processes* (2nd ed., pp. 83–88). Oxford University Press.

Case study for network-wide organizational change.

Zorn, T. E., Christensen, L. T., & Cheney, G. (1999). *Do we really want constant change?* Berrett-Koehler.

Excellent argument drawing attention to the costs of the "fashion" of constant organizational change.

Important Concepts: Define and Discuss

Faux voice
Implementation
Input solicitation
Managing meaning of change
Organizational change
Stakeholder
Uncertainty

Discussion Questions

1 Is it a healthy thing to frequently make change in organizations?
2 What are the significant costs of frequently changing organizations?
3 Which matters most during organizational change; the implementers' communication or that of other stakeholders?
4 How can stories about an organizational change make a difference in how the process unfolds and the outcomes that are achieved?

Practitioners' Corner

When faced with the task of implementing an organizational change, any manager will come to a point where they will need to decide how to go about announcing the change to employees and other audiences; introducing new expectations for activity, workflow, policy, and work practice; retiring previous processes, practices, policies, and procedures; addressing questions raised about how the new change will impact personnel evaluations and alterations in goals, plans, and priorities among myriad other possible topics; and evaluating the process and outcomes of the change.

In light of the challenges involved in change implementation, managers and leaders should be thorough and thoughtful in making plans for the introduction and rollout of change. Leaders may feel that they know their own organizations, environments, and change projects well enough that they can be successful without devoting significant time to making a plan. Experienced leaders may be tempted to either "wing it" or to repeatedly use the same plan they've used before. Let's first examine each of these alternatives to engaging in specific planning for an upcoming change.

Winging It

"Winging it" involves saving time by skipping deep analysis and planning and instead approaching change through experience and gut instinct. In other words, make it up as you go along. Unfortunately, skipping the analysis and planning process in this manner can set up a scenario where the leader becomes reactionary and reliant on long-held assumptions rather than being data- or analysis-driven in their process. The "winging it" strategy can result in delay of proactive actions that might forestall problems in favor of focusing on catching problems before they become too toxic. Further, this approach may present an image to stakeholders that the implementation process is unplanned and reactionary.

Repeating an Old Plan

A second alternative to detailed analysis and planning relies on repeating what has worked in the past. Some leaders may wish to but do so in a way that mimics past change rollouts without much reflection on needs or circumstances unique to the current change initiative. These leaders work from a framework for change that serves as default strategy. If something appeared to work before, the temptation to repeat it is very strong. The flaw in the "default template" method of implementation is missing that every change initiative is unique in terms of the ways that it fits the context, the organization, the stream of work, the initial and ongoing reactions of key stakeholders, and the degree to which resources for implementation support are available.

Qualities of Effective Planning Process

Effectiveness and efficiency in strategically preparing for implementation of change involves two stages: analysis and planning. In the first phase, leaders must assemble knowledge and data about the context of the change, the change itself, the stakeholders who are relevant to the change process, and the resources and goals of the organization. In the second phase, leaders need to develop strategies and tactics to implement change in a context of existing priorities and goals for the change and the organization. Effective implementation planning should be data-driven, diversified, reflective, and recursive.

- *Data-driven.* When planning change implementation, leaders need to be able to escape their own biases and expectations. One of the best ways to do this is to draw from credible sources of data that can help leaders to escape their own preferences for viewing their organizations, stakeholders, or history.
- *Diversified.* In order to avoid groupthink and an unhealthy narrow analysis of how a change process may proceed, it is critical to have the input of participants who can represent different views and who have a good understanding of how different sets of goals, perspectives, values, experiences may come to influence the path of a change process.
- *Reflective.* Being reflective requires leaders to consider challenging information and perspectives as plausible. Holding even problematic or questionable challenges to one's own view as plausible is the best check against dismissing a critical data point that might protect the interests of the organization.
- *Recursive.* Fourth, one is never really done analyzing and planning. Leaders who are committed to a thoughtful and thorough planning process will continue to collect and analyze information – especially critical or disconfirming information – throughout an implementation process. Planning is not a "phase," it is an activity.

References

Albrecht, T. L., & Ropp, V. A. (1984). Communicating about innovation in networks of three U.S. organizations. *Journal of Communication*, *4*, 78–91. https://doi.org/10.1111/j.1460-2466.1984.tb02175.x

Armenakis, A. A., Harris, S. G., & Mossholder, K. W. (1993). Creating readiness for organizational change. *Human Relations*, *46*(6), 681–703. https://doi.org/10.1177/001872679304600601

Barge, J., Lee, M., Maddux, K., Nabring, R., & Townsend, B. (2008). Managing dualities in planned change initiatives. *Journal of Applied Communication Research*, *36*(4), 364–390. https://doi.org/10.1080/00909880802129996

Baronas, A. M. K., & Louis, M. R. (1988). Restoring a sense of control during implementation: How user involvement leads to system acceptance. *Management Information Systems Quarterly*, *12*, 111–124. https://misq.org/restoring-a-sense-of-control-during-implementation-how-user-involvement-leads-to-system-acceptance.html

Bernuzzi, C., Sommovigo, V., Maffoni, M., Setti, I., & Argetero, P. (2023). A mixed-method study on the bright side of organizational change: Role clarity and supervisor support at resources for employees' resistance. *Journal of Change Management*, *23*(2), 143–176. https://doi.org/10.1080/14697017.2023.2172057

Bikson, T., & Gutek, B. (1984). *Implementation of office automation*. RAND Corporation.

Bordia, P., Hobman, E., Jones, E., Gallois, C., & Callan, V. (2004). Uncertainty during organizational change: Types, consequences, and management strategies. *Journal of Business and Psychology*, *18*(4), 507–532. http://dx.doi.org/10.1023/B:JOBU.0000028449.99127.f7

Bourgeois, L. J., & Brodwin, D. R. (1984). Strategic implementation: Five approaches to an elusive phenomenon. *Strategic Management Journal*, *5*, 241–264. https://doi.org/10.1002/smj.4250050305

Cherim, S. (2006). Managerial frames and institutional discourses of change: Employee appropriation and resistance. *Organization Studies*, *27*(9), 1261–1287. https://doi.org/10.1177/0170840606064106

Ellis, B. H. (1992). The effects of uncertainty and source credibility on attitudes about organizational change. *Management Communication Quarterly*, *6*, 34–57. https://doi.org/10.1177/0893318992006001002

Fairhurst, G. T., Green, S., & Courtright, J. (1995). Inertial forces and the implementation of a socio-technical systems approach: A communication study. *Organization Science*, *6*, 168–185. https://doi.org/10.1287/orsc.6.2.168

Fairhurst, G. T., & Sarr, R. A. (1996). *The art of framing: Managing the language of leadership*. Jossey-Bass.

Fairhurst, G. T., & Wendt, R. F. (1993). The gap in total quality: A commentary. *Management Communication Quarterly*, *6*, 441–451. https://doi.org/10.1177/0893318993006004005

Fischer-Appelt, B., & Dernbach, R. (2023). Exploring narrative strategy: The role of narratives in the strategic positioning of organizational change. *Innovation: The European Journal of Social Science Research*, *36*(1), 85–95. https://doi.org/10.1080/13511610.2022.2062303

Frost, P. J., & Egri, C. P. (1989). The political process of innovation. In L. L. Cummings & B. M. Staw (Eds.), *Research in organizational behavior* (Vol. *13*, pp. 229–295). JAI.

Hamilton, E. E. (1988). The facilitation of organizational change: An empirical study of factors predicting change agents' effectiveness. *Journal of Applied Behavioral Science*, *24*, 37–59. https://doi.org/10.1177/0021886388241006

Howell, J. M., & Higgins, C. A. (1990). Champions of technological innovation. *Administrative Science Quarterly*, *35*, 317–341. https://doi.org/10.2307/2393393

Hubbart, J. A. (2023). Organizational change: The challenge of change aversion. *Administrative Sciences*, *13*(7), 162–170. https://doi.org/10.3390/admsci13070162

Kanter, R. M. (1983). *The change masters*. Simon & Schuster.

Kramer, M. W. (1993). Communication and uncertainty reduction during job transfers: Leaving and joining processes. *Communications Monographs*, *60*(2), 178–198. https://doi.org/10.1080/03637759309376307

Leonard-Barton, D. (1987). Implementing structured software methodologies: A case of innovation in process technology. *Interfaces*, *17*, 6–17. https://doi.org/10.1287/inte.17.3.6

Leonard-Barton, D., & Kraus, W. A. (1985). Implementing new technology. *Harvard Business Review*, *63*(6), 102–110. https://hbr.org/1985/11/implementing-new-technology

Leonardi, P. (2009). Why do people reject new technologies and stymie organizational changes of which they are in favor? Exploring misalignments between social interactions and materiality. *Human Communication Research*, *35*, 407–441. https://doi.org/10.1111/j.1468-2958.2009.01357.x
Lewin, K. (1951). *Field theory in social science*. Harper.
Lewis, L. (2019). *Organizational change: Creating change through strategic communication* (2nd ed.). Wiley-Blackwell.
Lewis, L., & Sahay, S. (2017). Organizational change. In C. R. Scott & L. Lewis (Eds.) *International encyclopedia of organizational communication* (online edition). Hoboken, NJ: Wiley-Blackwell. https://doi.org/10.1002/9781118955567.wbieoc020
Lewis, L. K. (2007). An organizational stakeholder model of change implementation communication. *Communication Theory*, *17*(2), 176–204. https://doi.org/10.1111/j.1468-2885.2007.00291.x
Lewis, L. K. (2011). *Organizational change: Creating change through strategic communication*. Wiley-Blackwell.
Lewis, L. K. (2014). Organizational change and innovation. In L. L. Putnam & D. K. Mumby (Eds.), *The new handbook of organizational communication* (pp. 503–524). Sage.
Lewis, L. K., Laster, N., & Kulkarni, V. (2013). Telling 'em how it will be: Previewing pain of risky change in initial announcements. *Journal of Business Communication*, *50*(3), 278–308. https://doi.org/10.1177/0021943613487072
Lewis, L. K., & Russ, T. (2012). Soliciting and using input during organizational change initiatives: What are practitioners doing? *Management Communication Quarterly*, *26*(2), 267–294. https://doi.org/10.1177/0893318911431804
Lewis, L. K., & Seibold, D. R. (1993). Innovation modification during intra-organizational adoption. *Academy of Management Review*, *18*, 322–354. https://doi.org/10.2307/258762
Lewis, L. K., & Seibold, D. R. (1998). Reconceptualizing organizational change implementation as a communication problem: A review of literature and research agenda. In M. Roloff (Ed.), *Communication yearbook* (Vol. 21, pp. 93–151). Sage.
Maidique, M. (1980). Entrepreneurs, champions, and technological innovation. *Sloan Management Review*, *21*(2), 59–76.
Majchrzak, A. (1988). *The human side of factory automation*. Jossey-Bass.
Malvini Redden, S., Clark, L., Tracy, S. J., & Shafer, M. S. (2019). How metaphorical framings build and undermine resilience during change: A longitudinal study of metaphors in team-driven planned organizational change. *Communication Monographs*, *86*(4), 501–525. https://doi.org/10.1080/03637751.2019.1621361
Marcus, A. A. (1988). Implementing externally induced innovations: A comparison of rule-bound and autonomous approaches. *Academy of Management Journal*, *31*, 235–256. https://doi.org/10.2307/256547
Miller, K. I., & Monge, P. R. (1986). Participation, satisfaction, and productivity: A meta-analytic review. *Academy of Management Journal*, *29*, 727–753. https://www.jstor.org/stable/255942
Miller, V. D., Johnson, J. R., & Grau, J. (1994). Antecedents to willingness to participate in a planned organizational change. *Journal of Applied Communication Research*, *22*, 59–80. https://doi.org/10.1080/00909889409365387
Nutt, P. C. (1986). Tactics of implementation. *Academy of Management Journal*, *29*, 230–261. https://www.jstor.org/stable/256187
Nutt, P. C. (1987). Identifying and appraising how managers install strategy. *Strategic Management Journal*, *8*, 1–14. https://doi.org/10.1002/smj.4250080102
Ottaway, R. N. (1983). The change agent: A taxonomy in relation to the change process. *Human Relations*, *36*, 361–392. https://doi.org/10.1177/001872678303600403
Poole, M. S. (2004). Central issues in the study of change and innovation. In M. S. Poole & A. H. Van de Ven (Eds.), *Handbook of organizational change and innovation* (pp. 3–31). Oxford University Press.
Poole, M. S., & Van de Ven, A. H. (2004). *Handbook of organizational change and innovation*. Oxford University Press.
Rice, R. E., & Rogers, E. M. (1980). Re-invention in the innovation process. *Knowledge: Creation, Diffusion, Utilization*, *1*, 499–514. https://doi.org/10.1177/107554708000100402
Rogers, E. (1995). *Diffusion of innovations* (4th ed.). Free Press.

Ruben, B. D., Lewis, L. K., Sandmeyer, L., Russ, T., Smulowitz, S., & Immordino, K. (2008). *Assessing the impact of the Spellings Commission: The message, the messenger, and the dynamics of change in higher education*. National Association of College and University Business Officers.
Sagie, A., Elizur, D., & Koslowsky, M. (2001). Effect of participation in strategic and tactical decisions on acceptance of planned change. *Journal of Social Psychology*, *130*(4), 459–465. https://doi.org/10.1080/00224545.1990.9924607
Sagie, A., & Koslowsky, M. (1994). Organizational attitudes and behaviors as a function of participation in strategic and tactical change decisions: An application of path–goal theory. *Journal of Organizational Behavior*, *15*, 37–47. https://doi.org/10.1002/job.4030150105
Sahay, S. (2017). *Communicative designs for input solicitation during organizational change: Implications for providers' communicative perceptions and decisions* [Unpublished dissertation].
Sahay, S., & Lewis, L. (2016, November). *Perspectives on soliciting and providing input during organizational change: The provider, the executive, and the consultant*. Paper presented at the annual meeting of the National Communication Association, Philadelphia, PA.
Schein, V. (1985). Organizational realities: The politics of change. In D. Warrick (Ed.), *Contemporary organizational development* (pp. 86–97). Scott Foresman.
Schlesinger, L. A., & Kotter, J. P. (1979). Choosing strategies for change. *Harvard Business Review*, *57*(2), 106–114. www.hbs.edu/faculty/Pages/item.aspx?num=45328
Schmidt, O. S. (2023). What COVID-19 has taught us about effective employee communication. *Journal of Business Continuity & Emergency Planning*, *16*(3), 210–217.
Schweiger, D. M., & DeNisi, A. S. (1991). Communication with employees following a merger: A longitudinal field experiment. *Academy of Management Journal*, *34*(1), 110–135. https://www.jstor.org/stable/256304
Shrivastava, S., Pazzaglia, F., Sonpar, K., & McLoughlin, D. (2022). Effective communication during organizational change: A cross-cultural perspective. *Cross Cultural and Strategic Management*, *29*(3), 675–697. https://doi.org/10.1108/CCSM-08-2021-0144
Smeltzer, L. R. (1991). An analysis of strategies for announcing organization-wide change. *Group and Organization Studies*, *16*, 5–24. https://doi.org/10.1177/105960119101600102
Smeltzer, L. R. (1995). Organization-wide change: Planning for an effective announcement. *Journal of General Management*, *20*, 31–43. https://doi.org/10.1177/030630709502000303
Smeltzer, L. R., & Zener, M. F. (1992). Development of a model for announcing major layoffs. *Group & Organization Management*, *17*(4), 445–472. https://doi.org/10.1177/1059601192174009
Tornatzky, L. G., & Johnson, E. C. (1982). Research on implementation: Implications for evaluation practice and evaluation policy. *Evaluation and Program Planning*, *5*, 193–198. https://doi.org/10.1016/0149-7189(82)90069-6
Van de Ven, A. H., Angle, H. L., & Poole, M. S. (1989). *Research on the management of innovations*. Ballinger.
Van de Ven, A. H., & Poole, M. S. (1995). Explaining development and change in organizations. *Academy of Management Review*, *20*(3), 510–540. https://doi.org/10.2307/258786
van Zoonen, W., & ter Hoeven, C. L. (2022). Disruptions and general distress for essential and nonessential employees during the COVID-19 pandemic. *Journal of Business and Psychology*, *37*(2), 443–458. https://doi.org/10.1007/s10869-021-09744-5
Whittle, A., Suhomlinova, O., & Mueller, F. (2010). Funnel of interests: The discursive translation of organizational change. *Journal of Applied Behavioral Science*, *46*(1), 16–37. https://doi.org/10.1177/0021886309357538
Yue, C. A. (2022). Fostering employees' positive change reactions: The role of bridging and buffering strategies. *Journal of Public Relations Research*, *34*(3–4), 152–174. https://doi.org/10.1080/1062726X.2022.2093881
Yue, C. A., & Walden, J. (2023). Guiding employees through the COVID-19 pandemic: An exploration of the impact of transparent communication and change appraisals. *Journal of Contingencies and Crisis Management*, *31*(2), 198–211. https://doi.org/10.1111/1468-5973.12430
Zaltman, G., & Duncan, R. (1977). *Strategies for planned change*. John Wiley.
Zorn, T. E., Christensen, L. T., & Cheney, G. (1999). *Do we really want constant change?* Berrett-Koehler.
Zorn, T. E., Page, D. J., & Cheney, G. (2000). Nuts about change: Multiple perspectives on change-oriented communication in a public sector organization. *Management Communication Quarterly*, *13*(4), 515–566. https://doi.org/10.1177/0893318900134001

Contributors

Dawna I. Ballard (Ph.D., University of California Santa Barbara) is Associate Professor of organizational communication and technology at the University of Texas Austin. An expert in chronemics – i.e., the study of time as it is bound to human communication – she researches what drives our pace of life and its impact on the communication practices and long-term vitality of organizations, communities, and individuals. Her forthcoming book, *Time by Design* (Fall 2025), explores how effective organizations routinely communicate slow to go fast.

Zhuo Ban (Ph.D., Purdue University) is Associate Professor in the School of Communication, Film, & Media Studies at University of Cincinnati. Her research takes a global, critical perspective to contemporary issues in Organizational Communication and Public Relations, such as globalized supply chains, offshore labor politics, and corporate social responsibility discourses. Her work has been published in international peer-reviewed journals including *Organization*, *Management Communication Quarterly*, *Journal of Applied Communication Research*, *Public Relations Inquiry*, and *Journal of International and Intercultural Communication*.

J. Kevin Barge (Ph.D., University of Kansas) is Professor of Communication at Texas A&M University and an Associate of the Taos Institute. He is also a member of the planning team for the Aspen Conference, a community of engaged organizational communication scholars focused on developing practical theory and collaborative research that bridge academic-practitioner interests. Kevin's major research interests center on developing a social constructionist approach to leadership, articulating the connections between reflexive appreciative practice and organizational change and examining ways to develop effective academic-practitioner collaborations. He has published articles on leadership, dialogue, and organizational change in *The Academy of Management Review*, *Management Communication Quarterly*, *Human Relations*, *Communication Theory*, *Journal of Applied Communication Research*, and *Communication Monographs*.

Patrice M. Buzzanell (Ph.D., Purdue University) is a Distinguished Professor of Communication at the University of South Florida and formerly at Purdue University. Fellow and Past President of the International Communication Association, she is also a Distinguished Scholar of the National Communication Association, 2024 AAAS Fellow, and has served as President of the Council of Communication Associations and the Organization for the Study of Communication, Language and Gender. Her research, teaching, engagement, and grants coalesce around organizational communication, career, work-life issues, resilience, feminist/gender analyses, ethics, and human-centered engineering design. She has been honored with Purdue and USF Mentorship Awards and ICA's B. Aubrey Fisher Mentorship Award.

Lisa V. Chewning (Ph.D, Rutgers University) is Associate Professor of Corporate Communication at Penn State University – Abington. Lisa's research interests include social networks, crisis communication, and the intersection of stakeholder communication and social media. She is co-author of the textbook *Strategic Corporate Communication: Core Concepts for Managing Your Career and Your Client's Brand*. Her research has been published in outlets such as *Management Communication Quarterly*, *Communication Monographs*, *Public Relations Review*, *Journal of Communication*, *Computers in Human Behavior*, and *Human Communication Research*.

Xavier D. Clark (Ph.D., George Mason University) is an accomplished Organizational Physician, Dignity Architect, and Critical Organizational Scholar dedicated to advancing belonging, accessibility, and wellness in workplaces and consumer environments. With expertise spanning organizational health, regulatory compliance, accessibility, DEIA strategy, and consumer behavior, Dr. Clark integrates strategic innovation with human-centered leadership to drive lasting transformation. He serves as the Executive Director of the George Mason University Pop Culture Studies Lab and CEO and Chief Compliance & Culture Officer of ACCESSory Insights, LLC, a firm committed to reimagining organizational culture through healing-centered strategy and intentional leadership. Guided by authenticity, insight, and compassion, Dr. Clark is committed to dismantling systemic barriers and empowering leaders to build cultures where people flourish – with dignity, clarity, and purpose.

Shiv Ganesh (Ph.D., Purdue University, USA) is Professor in the Department of Communication Studies at the University of Colorado at Boulder, USA. He studies collective action issues in the context of digital and global processes. Specific research projects have addressed global justice, sustainability, global south issues, and digital ubiquity and inequalities. His work is both theoretical and driven by fieldwork in multiple locations including Aotearoa New Zealand, India, Sweden, and the United States. His work has won awards from communication associations in multiple countries and he is a Fellow of the International Communication Association.

Jennifer L. Gibbs (Ph.D., University of Southern California) is a Professor of Communication at the University of California, Santa Barbara. She studies collaboration in global teams and other remote, distributed, and hybrid work arrangements and implications for the future of work. Her research also examines how new technologies such as digital media and artificial intelligence are transforming organizations and strategic communication practices. She has co-authored two books and published over 70 peer-reviewed journal articles and book chapters in a variety of disciplines. Professor Gibbs is a Fellow of the International Communication Association, as well as former Editor of *Communication Research*.

Angela Gist-Mackey, Ph.D. (she/her(s) (Ph.D., University of Missouri) is Associate Professor in the Department of Communication Studies at the University of Kansas with expertise in organizational communication. She is a scholar who researches how people use communication as they experience social mobility, adversity, stigma, and power in organizational contexts. Dr. Gist-Mackey often partners with community organizations conducting research about social class and inequity. Her scholarship explores experiences related to long-term unemployment, workforce development, blue-collar job training, and poverty among others. Dr. Gist-Mackey teaches courses in organizational communication about topics including social identity and stigma, workplace relationships, career preparation, organizational culture, and qualitative research.

Jessica Katz Jameson (Ph.D., Temple University) is Professor and Head of the Department of Communication at North Carolina State University. She studies organizational communication and conflict management, with special attention to third-party intervention, the roles of identity and emotion in conflict, and interdisciplinary collaboration. She is the author of *Communication for Constructive Workplace Conflict*, which received a 2023 Outstanding Textbook Award from the National Communication Association Organizational Communication Division. Her work appears in outlets including *Journal of Applied Communication Research*, *Negotiation and Conflict Management Research*, *Negotiation Journal*, and *Western Journal of Communication*. Jessica received a Ph.D. in Communication from Temple University in Philadelphia, Pennsylvania.

Kerk F. Kee (Ph.D., University of Texas at Austin) is Hutcheson Professor in the Department of Professional Communication at Texas Tech University. His research examines technology adoption and innovation diffusion in science organizations, health communities, and pro-environmental societies as organizational systems. His research has been funded by the National Science Foundation, among other agencies, totaling over $13M. His research has also been cited over 8,000 times, according to Google Scholar. At the time of the second edition of this book, he is serving as an Associate Editor of Management Communication Quarterly, the premier journal of the field of organizational communication.

Laurie Lewis (Ph.D., University of California at Santa Barbara) is Professor of Communication at the University of Texas at San Antonio, where she is the Director of the Center for Dialogue & Deliberation. She is the author of *Organizational Change: Creating Change through Strategic Communication* and *The Power of Strategic Listening*, co-editor of the *International Encyclopedia of Organizational Communication*, and author of numerous academic publications on topics related to organizational change, listening, and stakeholder communication. Her research investigates how organizations work most effectively through collaboration, stakeholder engagement, input solicitation, and high-quality participative processes. She has provided consulting and training for dozens of organizations from a wide range of sectors.

Shawna Malvini Redden (Ph.D., Arizona State University) is Professor of organizational communication at California State University, Sacramento. She uses qualitative, critical, and discursive methods to explore organizing processes involving emotion, identity, sensemaking, social media, and sexual harassment. Her award-winning scholarship has appeared in publications including *Management Communication Quarterly*, *Communication Monographs*, *Journal of Applied Communication Research*, and *Qualitative Health Research*. She is the author of *101 Pat-Downs: An Undercover Look at Airport Security*, a creative nonfiction book about communicating emotion and identity in airport security. To learn more about her scholarship, teaching, and writing, visit www.drmalviniredden.com.

Dron M. Mandhana (Ph.D., University of Texas at Austin) is Associate Professor in the Department of Communication at Villanova University. His research considers how effective organizing is an enacted capability constituted in everyday communication practices bound by time and space – from communication overload and media choice to messy talk in project teams. His scholarship has appeared in Annals of Family Medicine, Communication Theory, Health Communication, Communication Education, Patient Education and Counseling, and the Journal of Communication Management. He currently teaches service-based learning courses in team building and small-group communication.

Chandler Marr (Ph.D., Arizona State University) is Assistant Professor in the Department of Communication at the University of Kentucky. His research primarily explores how organizational structures enable and constrain the way employees experience and express emotions. He is particularly interested in how compassion is communicated and interpreted in occupational contexts where aggression, skepticism, and/or stoicism are prevailing emotion norms. Chandler's scholarship is often guided by theories/concepts such as compassion, emotion management, dirty work, structuration, positioning theory, and the communication theory of resilience. Overall, the goal of Chandler's research is to provide individuals and organizations with communication tools that promote flourishing and facilitate positive transformation in the face of adversity.

Jamie McDonald (Ph.D., University of Colorado Boulder) is Professor of Communication at the University of Texas at San Antonio, USA and an Associate Member of the Centre for Cross-Cultural Management at the University of Wollongong, Australia. He specializes in issues related to identity, difference, intersectionality, and organizing. His research examines topics such as queer approaches to organizing, the closeting of invisible and stigmatized identities in organizations, the experiences of immigrant scholars and students in higher education, and researcher reflexivity. He co-organizes the biennial Qualitative Research in Management and Organization (QRM) conference.

Rebecca J. Meisenbach (Ph.D., Purdue University) is Associate Professor in the Department of Communication at the University of Missouri. Her research program examines issues of organizational and individual identity in organizing processes, with a focus on nonprofit and marginalized identities. She is currently writing a book on stigma and the Miss America Organization that conceptualizes stigma as an intersectional communication process. She is a former editor of *Management Communication Quarterly* and a former associate editor of *Culture & Organization.*

Anne M. Nicotera (Ph.D., Ohio University) is Professor of Communication at George Mason University. Her research is grounded in a constitutive perspective and focuses on management/leadership communication, culture and conflict, diversity, race and gender, and aggressive communication, with a particular interest in healthcare organizations and postcolonial approaches. Her research has been published in *Management Communication Quarterly*, *Journal of Applied Communication Research*, *Health Communication*, *Nursing Administration Quarterly*, and other outlets. She has also published six books and numerous chapters. Her applied work focuses on designing and delivering organizational communication-based management and leadership training, with a special interest in antiracism.

Craig R. Scott (Ph.D., Arizona State) is the John T. Jones, Jr. Centennial Professor and Chair of the Department of Communication Studies at The University of Texas at Austin. He is also a Fellow of the International Communication Association and co-editor of the *International Encyclopedia of Organizational Communication.* Scott's research examines issues of anonymity and identity/identification in various organizational settings. His current interests focus on "hidden organizations," where a collective and/or its members communicatively conceal key aspects of their identity from various audiences.

Yejin Shin (Ph.D., The University of Arizona) is Assistant Professor in the Department of Communication, Media, and Theatre at Northeastern Illinois University. Her research focuses on organizational communication with particular emphasis on workplace relationships and socialization processes. Her current work explores communication challenges faced by minority student populations, including first-generation and international students, and how these affect their social integration and academic experiences.

Keri K. Stephens (Ph.D., University of Texas) is Professor of Organizational Communication Technology and Co-Director Technology & Information Policy Institute at the Moody College of Communication, The University of Texas at Austin. Her research program addresses communication issues around organizations, crisies/disaster, and mobile/AI technologies. She has authored over 100 peer-reviewed publications and her two most recent books, *Negotiating Control: Organizations and Mobile Communication* and *New Media in Times of Crisis* (Routledge) have won three national-level awards. She is an International

Communication Association Fellow, serves on eight journal editorial boards, and has received 12 National Science Foundation (NSF) grants and 13 state grants.

Yohanna Tesfai (M.A., University of Texas at Austin) is a doctoral candidate at the University of Texas at Austin. Her research focuses on organizational memory, workplace temporalities, and institutional logics as it pertains to cultural institutions including galleries, libraries, archives, and museums.

Sarah J. Tracy (Ph.D., University of Colorado) is Professor at The Hugh Downs School of Human Communication at Arizona State University-Tempe. Her organizational communication scholarship examines compassion, identity, emotional labor, bullying, burnout, wellbeing, qualitative research methods, and leadership. Her research has resulted in two books including *Qualitative Research Methods: Collecting Evidence, Crafting Analysis, Communicating Impact* and over 100 monographs appearing in outlets such as *Management Communication Quarterly*, *Communication Monographs*, *Qualitative Inquiry*, *Communication Theory*, and *Journal of Applied Communication Research*. To learn more about her scholarship, teaching, and public outreach, visit www.sarahjtracy.com.

Heather M. Zoller (Ph.D., Purdue University) is a Professor in the School of Communication, Film, & Media Studies at the University of Cincinnati. She is Editor-in-Chief of the *Journal of Applied Communication Research* and former Associate Editor at *Management Communication Quarterly* and *Human Relations*. Her research on organizing and health politics appears in outlets such as *Communication Monographs*, *Communication Theory*, and *Journal of Applied Communication Research*, among others. For more, see heatherzoller.com.

Author Index

Subject Index

Note: Page references in *italics* denote figures and in **bold** tables.